THE 'WAR ON TERROR' AND THE FRAMEWORK OF INTERNATIONAL LAW

The acts of lawlessness committed on September 11, 2001 were swiftly followed by a 'war on terror'. This book sets out the essential features of the international legal framework against which the 9/11 attacks and the lawfulness of measures taken in response thereto fall to be assessed. It addresses, in an accessible manner, the relevant law in relation to: 'terrorism', questions as to 'responsibility' for it, the criminal law framework, lawful constraints on the use of force, the humanitarian law that governs in armed conflict, and international human rights law. It indicates the existence of a legal framework capable of addressing events such as 9/11 and governing responses thereto. It raises questions as to the compatibility of the 'war on terror' with this legal framework, and questions the implications for states responsible for violations, for third states and for the international rule of law.

HELEN DUFFY is the Legal Director of INTERIGHTS, an international human rights law centre. She previously worked as Legal Officer in the Prosecutor's Office, International Criminal Tribunal for the Former Yugoslavia (ICTY) in The Hague, as Counsel to Human Rights Watch, New York, and as Legal Director of the Centre for Human Rights and Legal Action, Guatemala. She specialises in human rights and international criminal law. She currently lives in The Hague.

D1270643

THE 'WAR ON TERROR' AND THE FRAMEWORK OF INTERNATIONAL LAW

HELEN DUFFY

CAMBRIDGE
UNIVERSITY PRESS

CAMBRIDGE UNIVERSITY PRESS
Cambridge, New York, Melbourne, Madrid, Cape Town, Singapore, São Paulo

Cambridge University Press
The Edinburgh Building, Cambridge CB2 2RU, UK

Published in the United States of America by Cambridge University Press, New York

www.cambridge.org
Information on this title: www.cambridge.org/9780521547352

© Helen Duffy 2005

This book is in copyright. Subject to statutory exception
and to the provisions of relevant collective licensing agreements,
no reproduction of any part may take place without
the written permission of Cambridge University Press.

First published 2005

Printed in the United Kingdom at the University Press, Cambridge

A catalogue record for this book is available from the British Library

Library of Congress Cataloguing in Publication data
Duffy, Helen
The 'war on terror' and the framework of international law / Helen Duffy.
p.   cm.
Includes bibliographical references and index.
ISBN 0-521-83850-9 – ISBN 0-521-54735-0 (paperback)
1. War on Terrorism, 2001 – Law and legislation.   I. Title.
KZ6795.T47D84   2005   2004061840
345′.02 – dc22

ISBN-13   978-0-521-83850-4 hardback
ISBN-10   0-521-83850-9 hardback
ISBN-13   978-0-521-54735-2 paperback
ISBN-10   0-521-54735-0 paperback

Cambridge University Press has no responsibility for the persistence or accuracy of URLs for
external or third-party internet websites referred to in this book, and does not guarantee that any
content on such websites is, or will remain, accurate or appropriate.

For my mother Rosemary, partner Fabricio and
son Luca

CONTENTS

PREFACE AND ACKNOWLEDGEMENTS

This book grew from a paper I wrote for INTERIGHTS shortly after the September 11 attacks. The paper was motivated by the apparent marginalisation of the issue of legality in public discourse on responses to those attacks, and the surprising dearth of legal material published in their immediate aftermath. In the void where there should have been debate on which responses would serve the interests of international justice, peace, security and the rule of law, the confusion and need for clarification of legal issues grew. I was encouraged by those who used that paper in their work, including partner organisations in the many countries in which INTERIGHTS works, to publish an expanded piece that addresses additional aspects of the legal framework and considers it alongside the practice of the 'war on terror' since 11 September 2001.

Since then, international lawyers have become more vocal and there is certainly more published material. International law is no longer absent from political discourse on the 'war on terror', and indeed there may be a newfound alertness to issues of international legality in public debate that is in many respects promising. However at times it seems that there is greater confusion than ever, and with it an increased vulnerability in the international legal order. This book hopes to contribute to addressing the confusion, and the perception of legal vacuum. It is written from the perspective of a practitioner in the field of human rights and international criminal law, where international law, its legitimacy and standing, are essential tools not only to combat terrorism but to guard against future human rights abuse in other contexts.

Many people have contributed to this book, by providing ideas, research and editing assistance and experience of the 'war on terror' as a lived reality. I am grateful to all INTERIGHTS staff, past and present and to its board. Among the volunteers and associates who provided helpful research and assistance along the way are Sanchita Hosali, Debbie Sayers, Mark Pallis, Benedetta Lacey and Larissa Leiser. Particular thanks are due to Silvia Borelli for excellent research assistance in the critical months leading up to publication, and to Moni Shrestha for her spirit and her editing and production assistance. Emma Playfair lent her careful editor's eye at various stages. I would like to thank Finola O'Sullivan, Jane O'Regan, Sue Dickinson and Mary Leighton of Cambridge University Press for the diligent work on the book, and especially Finola for her support from the outset. Numerous friends and colleagues gave their time generously to reviewing, encouraging, cautioning and/or correcting, including Jeremy McBride, Federico Andreu, Jelena Pejic, Kim Prost, Elizabeth Wilmshurst, Gerry Simpson, Christine Chinkin, Claire Harris, Amelia Nice, Xavier Aguirre, Hakan Friman, Osvaldo Guariglia and Fabricio Guariglia. Immeasurable gratitude is due to Fabricio for his generous approach to partnership and unwavering belief in the project, and to Luca for giving so easily of the maternity leave that was by rights his, and for inspiring hope.

ABBREVIATIONS

ACHR/American Convention on Human Rights	American Convention on Human Rights, San Jose, 22 November 1969, OAS Treaty Series, No. 36, entered into force 18 July 1978
AI	Amnesty International
AJIL	*American Journal of International Law*
AP I/First Additional Protocol to the Geneva Conventions	Protocol Additional to the Geneva Conventions of 12 August 1949, and relating to the Protection of Victims of International Armed Conflicts, 8 June 1977, 1125 UNTS 3, entered into force 7 December 1978
AP II/Second Additional Protocol to the Geneva Conventions	Protocol Additional to the Geneva Conventions of 12 August 1949, and Relating to the Protection of Victims of Non-International Armed Conflicts, 8 June 1977, 1125 UNTS 609, entered into force 7 December 1978
BYIL	*British Yearbook of International Law*
CCPR	Covenant on Civil and Political Rights
DR	Council of Europe, *Decisions and reports of the European Commission on Human Rights*
ECHR/European Convention on Human Rights	European Convention for the Protection of Human Rights and Fundamental Freedoms, Rome,

ICCPR/International Covenant on Civil and Political Rights	International Covenant on Civil and Political Rights, New York, 16 December 1966, 999 UNTS 171, entered into force 23 March 1976
ICESCR/International Covenant on Economic, Social and Cultural Rights	International Covenant on Economic, Social and Cultural Rights, New York, 16 December 1966, 993 UNTS 3, entered into force 3 January 1976
ICJ	International Court of Justice
ICJ Reports	*Reports of the International Court of Justice*
ICLQ	*International and Comparative Law Quarterly*
ICRC	International Committee of the Red Cross
ICRC Commentary to AP I	J. Pictet *et al.* (eds.), *Commentary on the Additional Protocols of 8 June 1977 to the Geneva Conventions of 12 August 1949, Section I: Protocol Additional to the Geneva Conventions of 12 August 1949, and relating to the Protection of Victims of International Armed Conflicts (Protocol I)* (ICRC, Geneva, 1987)
ICRC Commentary to AP II	J. Pictet *et al.* (eds.), *Commentary on the Additional Protocols of 8 June 1977 to the Geneva Conventions of 12 August 1949, Section II: Protocol Additional to the Geneva Conventions of 12 August 1949, and relating to the Protection of Victims of Non-International Armed Conflicts (Protocol II)* (ICRC, Geneva, 1987)
ICRC Commentary to GC I	J. Pictet (ed.), *Geneva Convention for the Amelioration of the Condition of the Wounded and Sick in Armed Forces in the Field: Commentary* (ICRC, Geneva, 1952)

ICRC Commentary to GC II	J. Pictet (ed.), *Geneva Convention for the Amelioration of the Condition of Wounded, Sick and Shipwrecked Members of Armed Forces at Sea: Commentary* (ICRC, Geneva, 1960)
ICRC Commentary to GC III	J. de Preux (ed.), *Geneva Convention relative to the Treatment of Prisoners of War: Commentary* (ICRC, Geneva, 1960)
ICRC Commentary to GC IV	O. Uhler and H. Coursier (eds.), *Geneva Convention relative to the Protection of Civilian Persons in Time of War: Commentary* (ICRC, Geneva, 1950)
ICTR	International Criminal Tribunal for Rwanda
ICTR Statute	Statute of the International Criminal Tribunal for Rwanda, annexed to SC Res. 955 (1994), 8 November 1994
ICTY	International Criminal Tribunal for the Former Yugoslavia
ICTY Statute	Statute of the International Criminal Tribunal for the Former Yugoslavia, annexed to SC Res. 827 (1993), 23 May 1993
IHL	International humanitarian law
IHRL	International human rights law
ILC	International Law Commission
ILC Commentaries on Articles on State Responsibility	International Law Commission, Commentaries on Articles on Responsibility of States for Internationally Wrongful Acts, *Report of the ILC on the work of its 53rd session*, UN Doc. A/56/10 (2001), Chapter IV, pp. 59–365
ILC Yearbook	*Yearbook of the International Law Commission*

ILC's Articles on State Responsibility	International Law Commission, Articles on Responsibility of States for Internationally Wrongful Acts, *Report of the ILC on the work of its 53rd session*, UN Doc. A/56/10 (2001), Chapter IV, pp. 43–59
ILM	*International Legal Materials*
ILR	*International Law Reports*
IRRC	*International Review of the Red Cross*
LJIL	*Leiden Journal of International Law*
NYIL	*Netherlands Yearbook of International Law*
OAS	Organisation of American States
OAU	Organisation of African Unity
OJ	Official Journal of the European Communities
Oppenheim's International Law	R.Y. Jennings and A. Watts (eds.), *Oppenheim's International Law*, 9th ed. (London, 1992), vol. I
PCIJ	Permanent Court of International Justice
RdC	*Recueil des cours de l'Académie de droit international de L'Haye*
Reports	European Court of Human Rights, *Reports of judgments and decisions*
SAARC	South Asian Association for Regional Cooperation
SC Res.	Security Council Resolution
UDHR/Universal Declaration on Human Rights	Universal Declaration on Human Rights, GA Res. 217A (III), 10 December 1948
UN Charter	Charter of the United Nations, San Francisco, 26 June 1945, entered into force 24 October 1945
UNTS	*United Nations Treaty Series*
VCLT	Vienna Convention on the Law of Treaties between States and International Organizations or between International Organizations

TABLE OF CASES

TABLE OF CONVENTIONS

1999

1

Introduction

1.1 Preliminary remarks

The atrocities committed on 11 September 2001 ('September 11' or '9/11'), like others since then, highlight the critical importance of the international rule of law and the terrible consequences of its disregard.[1] Ultimately, however, the impact of such attacks on the international system of law depends on the responses to them and in turn on the reaction to those responses. To the extent that lawlessness is met with unlawfulness, unlawfulness with impunity, the long-term implications for the rule of law, and the peace, stability and justice it serves, will be grave. Undermining the authority of law can only lay the foundation for future violations, whether by terrorists or by states committing abuses in the name of counter-terrorism.

This book seeks to set out in an accessible fashion the parameters of the international legal framework applicable to the events of 11 September 2001 and responses thereto. It highlights questions regarding the extent to which the norms and mechanisms of the international legal system have been upheld or undermined in the so-called 'war on terror' waged since 9/11.[2] The premise is that the legitimacy of measures taken in the

---

[1] The number of people killed by the terrorist attacks against the World Trade Center on September 11 has been officially estimated by US authorities at 2,819. See 'Names of September 11 Victims Published', *Associated Press*, 20 August 2002. Shortly after the attacks, the United States and other governments identified al-Qaeda, an Islamic fundamentalist network or organisation as being responsible for the attacks, which was subsequently confirmed by members of al-Qaeda. See 'Al Qaeda Claims Responsibility for September 11', *CNN News*, 15 April 2002.

[2] The US President George W. Bush coined the 'war on terror' epithet on 20 September 2001, when he declared that '[o]ur war on terror begins with al Qaeda, but it does not end there. It will not end until every terrorist group of global reach has been found, stopped and defeated' (see Address of the US President George W. Bush to a Joint Session of Congress and the American People, 20 September 2001, available at http://www.whitehouse.gov/news/releases/2001/09/20010920-8.html. The 'war on terror' shows no sign of abating several years on.

name of the counter terrorist struggle depends on their consistency with international law. It is essentially this reference to objectively verifiable standards and processes – rather than subjective assertions as to good and evil[3] – that enable credible distinctions to be drawn between those that abide by the rules of the international community and those, like the architects of 9/11, that conspire against them.

Terror attacks such as those executed in the United States, Bali, Istanbul and Madrid in recent years render beyond doubt the challenge facing the international community to address effectively the scourge of international terrorism. They also present countless challenges for international scholars and practitioners. These include: ensuring the centrality of law, and the uncompromising governance of the principle of legality, in the highly charged debate on countering the terrorist threat; advancing an understanding of the law as sufficiently clear and accessible to provide a meaningful framework for action; demonstrating that the law enables, and indeed obliges, states to take effective measures against terrorism, and is inherently responsive to the security challenges posed by international terrorism; where the law is unsettled or unclear, or mechanisms and procedures ineffective or inadequate, promoting normative clarification or reform; monitoring, and seeking accountability in respect of, violations of international law.

This book hopes to make a modest contribution to these enormous challenges. It seeks principally to address the question whether there is an identifiable framework of international law capable of addressing the September 11 attacks and the reactions they have triggered, and to counter the notion of absolute vacuums in the international legal order. It is directed towards practitioners, students and others grappling through the fog of the 'war on terror', in which international law is often notably absent, or presented as hopelessly confused or ill equipped to address 'new challenges'. It locates the September 11 attacks, not in a normative void, but against a backdrop of international law and developing international practice, and explores the multiple internal connections between the relevant areas of international law. While reflecting that in certain areas the law may indeed be unsettled, and in others it may be in flux,[4] it suggests

---

[3] References to 'good and evil' pepper political discourse on terrorism and counter-terrorism, the most notable example being the US President's renowned speech concerning the 'axis of evil' threatening the world: see State of the Union Address, 29 January 2002, available at www.whitehouse.gov.

[4] Occasionally, it highlights areas ripe for legal development and it may contribute to the discussion on the impact of 9/11 and responses thereto on the law. An analysis of how the

that the main challenge stems not from the inadequacy of existing legal standards but from lack of respect for them.

As the UN Secretary General has noted, the 'war on terror' affects all areas of the UN agenda,[5] and this book seeks only to highlight those areas of law that are of central relevance to an understanding of the 'war on terror'. It is not an academic textbook that seeks to advance a new theory of law, nor an in depth study of the potential impact of September 11 and its responses on international law. Still less is it a comprehensive factual report on the plethora of measures taken since 9/11, or an advocacy document seeking to establish a case against any individual or government. It does not advance any agenda beyond respect for the rule of international law, as referred to above. It seeks to facilitate informed legal debate, by a broad range of participants, on specific issues of law that the 'war on terror' has thrown up, and more broadly on the role and relevance of international law in light of the global security threat that besets the start of the 21st century, in which we all have a stake.

Among the myriad questions that have arisen in the aftermath of the September 11 attacks, are the following. How should we understand the September 11 attacks: as crimes, as acts of war, as wrongs committed by a state, or as all of the above? What law governs the 'war on terror'? What is the legal significance of labelling someone a 'terrorist'? Was a state (or were states) responsible for the September 11 attacks, or for supporting or harbouring al-Qaeda, and what are the legal consequences of that? What should be, and what has been, the role of criminal law in responding to the September 11 attacks, or potentially to the responses to them? Can individuals be held to account, and if so where, and under which law? What are the obligations of states to cooperate with the criminal process, and in what circumstances should they refrain from cooperating? Was the use of force a permissible response to the September 11 attacks, and if so against whom can it lawfully be directed? What are the key legal issues arising in relation to the lawfulness of attacking Afghanistan or Iraq? Were the laws of war respected? Is the targeted assassination of individuals a lawful response? In what circumstances, and to what extent, can human rights be restricted in the name of counter terrorism? Is there really a 'legal limbo' in international law?

law may have changed since 9/11 may yet be premature, however, and is not, in any event, the objective of this study.
[5] Statement by UN Secretary-General Kofi Annan to the Security Council, 4 October 2002, Press Release SG/SM/8417, SC/7523.

1.2 Some legal basics

As this book does not assume detailed prior knowledge of international law, it is worth noting some basic legal points of relevance to the framework and application chapters that follow. These relate to the 'sources' from which the legal framework derives, the process by which that framework may change over time, and the importance of understanding it, not in an atomised way, but as an interconnected whole.[6]

1.2.1 Sources of international law

The traditional starting point of every discussion of the sources of international law is Article 38 of the Statute of the International Court of Justice,[7] which lists as 'sources' of international law: (a) international conventions; (b) customary international law; (c) general principles of law 'as recognized by civilized nations'.[8] As reflected throughout the framework, treaty and custom constitute the most important of these sources.

1.2.1.1 International treaties

Most of the rules of the international legal system derive from agreements between States.[9] Two fundamental rules govern international agreements.

---

[6] For basic questions relating to the nature of the international legal system, see *Oppenheim's International Law*, pp. 4–7 and 12–13. While the international system differs from municipal legal systems, in that there is no central legislature creating law and only a limited ability to sanction breaches of the law, it nonetheless establishes a binding, if imperfect, normative framework by which the conduct of states is regulated. For an analysis of the 'binding' nature of international law, see R. Higgins, *Problems and Process: International Law and How We Use It* (Oxford, 1994), pp. 13–16.

[7] Although Article 38 is formally only an indication to the International Court of Justice (and previously, to the Permanent Court of International Justice) as to the law applicable to cases before it, it is generally considered as 'the authoritative list of the sources of international law'. See H. Charlesworth and C. Chinkin, *The Boundaries of International Law: A Feminist Analysis* (Manchester, 2000), p. 63.

[8] While there has been extensive doctrinal debate on the meaning of 'general principles', a prevalent opinion notes that 'the phrase embraces such general principles as pervade domestic jurisprudence and can be applied to international legal questions', G. von Glahn, *Law Among Nations*, 6th ed. (New York, 1986), p. 22.

[9] The rules relating to the formation, modification, suspension and termination of international agreements are contained in two multilateral conventions, the Vienna Convention on the Law of Treaties of 1969, 1155 UNTS 331, entered into force 27 January 1980 (hereinafter VCLT 1969) and the Vienna Convention on the Law of Treaties between States and International Organizations or between International Organizations, 21 March 1986, not yet in force. Most of the provisions of the Vienna Conventions are considered to reflect customary international law.

The first is that once a State is bound by a treaty, it must fulfil the obligations deriving from it in good faith,[10] and may not for example 'invoke the provisions of its internal law as justification for its failure to perform a treaty'.[11] The second is that only States which are parties to a treaty are bound by it, and an international agreement cannot in itself produce obligations on third States.[12] For major international treaties such as those addressed in this study, states generally become bound through ratification or accession,[13] but a state that has *signed* but not ratified a treaty 'is obliged to refrain from acts which would defeat the object and purpose of the treaty'.[14]

While the vast majority of treaties normally aim at exchanging rights and obligations between the parties, some multilateral treaties lay down general rules that affect all states of the international community. This category of so-called 'law-making treaties',[15] which includes for example the multilateral conventions on the protection of human rights discussed at Chapter 7 or the Geneva Conventions and other multilateral treaties on international humanitarian law discussed at Chapter 6, may influence the development of customary international law in particular areas (see below). In particular, the fact that a large number of States have ratified a particular convention may constitute a strong indication that the rules embodied in that convention correspond to rules of customary international law.[16]

---

[10] This is commonly expressed with the Latin maxim *pacta sunt servanda*. See Article 26, VCLT 1969: 'Every treaty in force is binding on the parties and must be performed by them in good faith.'

[11] Article 27, VCLT 1969.

[12] This fundamental rule is referred to as the rule *pacta tertiis nec nocent nec prosunt*. See Section IV (Articles 34–8), VCLT 1969.

[13] See Article 11, VCLT 1969: '[T]he consent of a State to be bound by a treaty may be expressed by signature, exchange of instruments constituting a treaty, ratification, acceptance, approval or accession, or by any other means if so agreed.' Note however that signature does not generally bind the state, see Article 12, VCLT 1969.

[14] See Article 18, VCLT 1969.

[15] See I. Brownlie, *Principles of Public International Law*, 6th ed. (Oxford, 2003), pp. 12–13: 'Law-making treaties create *general* norms for the future conduct of the parties in terms of legal propositions, and the obligations are generally the same for all parties ... Such treaties are in principle binding only on parties, but the number of parties, the explicit acceptance of rules of law, and in some cases, the declaratory nature of the provisions produce a strong law-creating effect at least as great as the general practice considered necessary to support a customary rule.'

[16] See, in general, M. Akehurst, 'Custom as a Source of International Law', 47 (1974–75) BYIL 1.

1.2.1.2 Customary law

In the absence of a legislative body with the power to create rules binding on all the subjects of the international legal system,[17] the only source of 'general' rules of international law is international custom. Customary law derives from the practice of States,[18] where this practice is uniform, consistent and general and considered to be legally necessary or obligatory.[19] Generality of practice does not mean universality, and the fact that a number of States follow a certain course of conduct, and other States do not protest, may be sufficient to affirm the generality of the practice. The second prong of the test – the attitude to the practice as obligatory or 'necessary', referred to as *opinio juris* – is crucial in distinguishing State practice relevant for the purpose of identifying a customary rule from practice which denotes mere international usage.[20] While some states will be more active on the international plane, thus more influential on the evolution of customary law, once a customary rule of international law has come into being, all States are bound by it.[21]

1.2.1.3 Subsidiary sources

Article 38 further provides that, in order to determine the content of these (treaty-based or customary) rules of international law, recourse may be

---

[17] The UN Charter confers to the Security Council the power to adopt decisions which are binding on all UN Member States (and therefore on virtually every State of the international community) by virtue of Article 25 of the Charter (see Chapter 5, section A). This does not however imply that the Security Council may in any way be considered as an 'international legislative body'.

[18] 'State practice means any act or statement by a State from which views about customary law can be inferred; it includes physical acts, claims, declarations *in abstracto* (such as General Assembly resolutions), national laws, national judgments and omissions. Customary international law can also be created by the practice of international organizations and (at least in theory) by the practice of individuals', Akehurst, 'Custom as a Source', at 53.

[19] *C.d. opinio iuris sive necessitates.* As noted by the ICJ: 'Not only must the acts concerned amount to a settled practice, but they must also be such or be carried out in a certain way as to be evidence of the belief that this practice is rendered obligatory by the existence of a certain rule requiring it.' *North Sea Continental Shelf Cases (Federal Republic of Germany v. Denmark; Federal Republic of Germany v. The Netherlands), ICJ Reports 1969*, p. 3, para. 77. See Akehurst, 'Custom as a Source', at 16–18.

[20] On the distinction between custom and usage – 'a general practice which does not reflect a legal obligation' – see Brownlie, *Principles*, p. 6.

[21] States may, however, in certain circumstances, avoid obligation through persistent objection to the rule, provided that the rule is not a *jus cogens* rule (see this chapter, para. 1.2.2 below). For a discussion of custom and the role of 'bigger states', relevant to an assessment of the 'war on terror', see V. Lowe, 'The Iraq Crisis: What Now?', 52 (2003) ICLQ 859, p. 863.

had to judicial decisions and the writings of legal scholars.[22] These are referred to in the book as they may provide evidence of the content of customary or treaty law.[23] In practice, although there is no system of 'precedent' in the international system,[24] decisions of the ICJ and other international courts and tribunals are important as they are often treated as providing authoritative interpretations of the law in question, and followed as authority in later cases. As for the legal analyses of jurists, while they do not create law as such, they may 'ease or impede the passage of new doctrines into legal rules'.[25]

A 'subsidiary role' in the determination of the actual content of international law may also be attributed to the corpus of resolutions of international organisations, declarations and non-binding international instruments commonly referred to as 'soft law'. While they are not binding *per se*, they are referred to in places in this book, as they may give more detailed expression to some of the binding prescriptions and prohibitions of international law and provide evidence of customary law.

1.2.2 How international law changes

The second point to note is that the law is not static. Every legal system needs to be able to develop its rules to take into account the evolution and changing exigencies of the society it regulates.[26] The international legal system is characterised by the absence of a body entitled to create (and to modify) legal rules binding on all its subjects. But just as international law is created by States, as set out above, so is it changed by them.

While the process through which treaty-based rules of international law change is quite straightforward,[27] the process relating to the modification

---

[22] Article 38(1)(d) of the ICJ Statute specifies that the Court may have recourse to 'judicial decisions and the teachings of the most highly qualified publicists of the various nations, as subsidiary means for the determination of rules of law'. 'Judicial decisions' implies that not only the decisions of international courts, but also national jurisprudence may be relevant in the process of determining the content of rules of international law.

[23] Note that these are not themselves 'sources' of law *stricto sensu*, but provide evidence of the content of treaty or customary norms. See Brownlie, *Principles*, p. 23.

[24] See, e.g., Article 59 of the ICJ Statute.

[25] V. Lowe, 'The Iraq Crisis', p. 860.

[26] Within domestic legal systems, the task of keeping the law 'up to date' is generally carried out by the legislative power and, in varying ways, by the judiciary.

[27] A treaty, or some of its provisions, may be subsequently amended by the parties through the adoption of another international agreement. See Article 31, VCLT 1969.

or 'abrogation' of rules of customary international law is somewhat more complicated. Just as customary international law comes into existence when most States of the international community follow a certain course of action believing that it is required by a legal norm, so may customary rules lose their binding force, and change, where the consistent and general practice of states, and the *opinio juris* supporting them, ceases. In this respect, the peculiarity of the international legal system lies in the fact that 'violations of the law can lead to the formation of new law'.[28] Discussion of the practice of states in responding to 9/11, and reactions to those responses, assumes particular significance in a system where departure from existing legal standards, and responses to the same, may ultimately impact on those standards.[29]

However, several points are worthy of emphasis in this respect. The first is that, of course, not every violation of an international rule leads to a change in the law.[30] In most cases, not even consistent patterns of violations by a number of States imply that a rule has been superseded, as the 'obligatory quality' of a rule of customary law is lost only if the behaviour of those States which refuse to comply with the rule, and the reactions of other States, are supported by the belief that the rule is no longer binding.[31]

Second, some customary rules of international law are particularly difficult to modify. This is due to their status as peremptory norms of international law or *jus cogens* norms, which have been authoritatively defined as 'substantive rules of conduct that prohibit what has come to be seen as intolerable because of the threat it presents to the survival of

---

[28] Higgins, *Problems and Process*, p. 19.

[29] While not purporting to provide an in-depth analysis of potential changes in the law, which will undoubtedly engage international scholars for years to come, this book highlights areas where early indications are that the law may change, or be clarified, through recent events, and other areas where, despite disregard for the law, legal change is unlikely.

[30] The factors include the nature of the rule, the number of states 'violating' the rule and the reactions of other states to it. In respect of certain rules, such as those relating to the use of force for example, the ICJ has noted that the fact that states do not express opposition to the practice should not, generally, be taken to confirm its lawfulness. However, expressions of opposition can help to clarify the lack of *opinio juris*, and avoid the perception of acquiescence in the breach. See J. Charney, 'Universal International Law', 87 (1993) AJIL 529 at 543–5.

[31] The ICJ, determining the content of the customary rules prohibiting the use of force and intervention in the internal affairs of another State, has stated that the fact that the prohibition was frequently breached was not sufficient to deny its customary character. See *Military and Paramilitary Activities in and against Nicaragua (Nicaragua v. United States)*, *ICJ Reports 1986*, p. 14, para. 186.

States and their peoples and the most basic human values'.[32] Among the consequences of a norm having *jus cogens* status[33] is the fact that it can be modified 'only by a subsequent norm of general international law having the same character'.[34] In practice, determining that a *jus cogens* rule no longer exists, or that its content has changed, would require not only 'general' but 'universal' state practice, and strong evidence indicating that the value it protects is no longer considered a fundamental one by the international community. As will be seen, certain of the rules considered in this book, such as those relating to the fundamental prohibition on the use of force, basic human rights or core humanitarian law principles, have attained this status and are therefore extremely resistant to change. As rules which aim to protect values considered fundamental by the international community as a whole, *jus cogens* rules have the additional characteristic of creating obligations *erga omnes*, i.e. 'obligations owed by a State towards the international community as a whole'.[35]

1.2.3 The legal framework as an interconnected whole

The final point to note is that, while each of the following chapters explore a different aspect of the legal framework, they are inherently interconnected. Understanding the international system of law requires that it be seen as a whole, with each of the branches of international law understood by reference to the core principles from which they derive and to one another. These inter-connections will be highlighted throughout this book – at times requiring that the law set out in a subsequent chapter be pre-empted and at others that aspects of foregoing chapters be revisited.[36]

---

[32] See ILC Commentaries to Articles on State Responsibility, Commentary to Article 40(3). See also the definition set out in Article 53, VCLT 1969. According to the ILC's Commentaries to the 1969 Vienna Convention (*Yearbook ILC 1966*, vol. II, pp. 248 ff.) and to the Articles on State Responsibility, norms such as those prohibiting the use of force contrary to the principles of the UN Charter, genocide, torture, apartheid, slavery and other serious violations of human rights, and the rule on self-determination are generally considered peremptory norms of international law.

[33] The fact that the international community as a whole recognises a rule of general international law as a peremptory rule has important consequences for international responsibility; see Chapter 3, para. 3.1.3.

[34] Article 53, VCLT 1969. Nor can they be modified or derogated from by agreement between States: Articles 53 and 64, VCLT 1969 make clear that a treaty which conflicts with a peremptory norm is void.

[35] *Barcelona Traction, Light and Power Company, Limited, Second Phase, ICJ Reports 1970*, p. 3, at para. 33.

[36] These interconnections are drawn out further in the concluding chapter.

1.3 Structure of the book

This book consists of three parts. The first sketches out preliminary issues of law relating to 'international terrorism' and 'international responsibility' for terrorism. The second, more substantial, part explores the lawfulness of certain responses to acts such as 9/11, by reference to criminal law and the law governing peaceful settlement of disputes and resort to armed force. The third part considers constraints on how those responses may be executed, with chapters on human rights law, humanitarian law applicable in armed conflict and a case study on the application of both areas in the context of detainees held at Guantanamo Bay, Cuba.

While the focus is on the legal framework pertinent to the particular area of law, in Parts Two and Three[37] the 'framework' A section of each chapter is followed by an 'application' B section, highlighting key issues regarding the treatment of that framework in the 'war on terror'. These sections provide examples of practice post 9/11 that illustrate certain characteristics of the 'war on terror' and its relationship to international law.[38] As reflected in the emphasis on the United States, much of this practice derives from the US as the undoubted driving force behind the 'war on terror'. However, as will be illustrated, the practice of many if not most states around the globe has been affected since 9/11, directly or indirectly, whether through the adoption of new legislative or administrative measures or resort to new justifications for pre-existing practices.

While the issues highlighted in the application sections of the chapters illustrate those arising in the first few years following 9/11, the framework sections, by contrast, provide the law by which new measures may be assessed as they emerge, as they do almost daily, in the rapidly unfolding 'war on terror'.

1.4 Overview of chapters

Chapter 2, Part One addresses the question of 'terrorism' as an international legal norm. Starting from the renowned lack of a global convention defining and comprehensively prohibiting 'terrorism' as such, it sketches out international and regional developments (before and after September 11, 2001) towards a general definition of terrorism, as well as the

---

[37] Central chapters – relating to criminal justice, the use of force, humanitarian law and human rights law – follow this bifurcated structure.

[38] The book includes examples of practice from September 2001 to October 2004. Material included in the book is current as at the latter date.

proliferation of conventions addressing specific forms of terrorism. It questions to what extent, in the light of state practice, there might be said to be an accepted definition of terrorism under treaty or customary international law. It highlights other international legal norms that do, however, address the prohibition on terrorism and obligations in respect of it. The chapter concludes by inquiring as to the significance of the 'terrorism' label, and whether the 'war on terror' and analysis thereof is not more meaningfully framed around other, established, legal norms.

Chapter 3 addresses the question of responsibility for acts such as those that took place on 9/11 in the light of the rules on international responsibility. It assesses first the responsibility of states, and the basis on which acts perpetrated by private individuals, networks or organisations (such as al-Qaeda) may be attributed to a state (such as Afghanistan). It distinguishes attribution of responsibility for the attacks themselves from responsibility for other wrongs that may have been committed by the Taleban regime, and considers the consequences, under international law, of such wrongs. It enquires as to the circumstances in which other States may, and/or must, act to counter international wrongs, and the limits on such action. The final section considers the extent to which private individuals or organisations – so-called 'non state actors', such as al-Qaeda or individual members or associates thereof – may incur responsibility under international law.

In Part Two, Chapter 4 considers the issue of the September 11 attacks and responses thereto through the prism of criminal law. First, it describes the crimes that may have been committed on September 11 and outlines relevant principles of criminal law that determine who may be held responsible. Second, it considers which courts or tribunals have (or might be afforded) jurisdiction over the offences, including the relevance, present and future, of the nascent international criminal court to 'terrorist' related offences. Third, it sketches out the law and mechanisms relevant to the implementation and enforcement of international criminal law, in particular responsibilities in respect of international cooperation. While the focus is on the offences committed on September 11, it also notes, however, that the international criminal law paradigm may be relevant also to the responses to September 11, so far as they constitute crimes under international law for which individuals may be held to account.

Chapter 4, section B considers the application of the criminal law model in practice since September 2001. It questions, first, to what extent criminal law has been invoked as a key element of the counter-terrorist strategy pursued through the 'war on terror'. Secondly, it considers significant developments that have unfolded in law and practice on inter-state cooperation in criminal matters, and flags the relationship between those developments and other legal obligations, notably in the field of human rights law.

Chapter 5 considers the obligation to resolve disputes by peaceful means and the exceptional circumstances in which the use of force may be lawful, in self defence or pursuant to Security Council authorisation under Chapter VII of the UN Charter. Focusing on justifications for the use of force advanced since September 11, the chapter discusses the scope of, and limits on, the right to self defence and the role of the Security Council in authorising the use of force in the interest of international peace and security. Finally it highlights legal issues relating to other possible justifications for the use of force, most notably humanitarian intervention but also pro-democratic intervention or 'self help'.

Chapter 5, section B considers this legal framework in light of the military interventions that have been the defining feature of the 'war on terror' since 9/11. It highlights the key issues relating to the lawfulness of the use of force that arose in relation to the interventions in Afghanistan and Iraq[39] and the National Security Strategy advanced by the United States on 17 September 2001.

Part Three begins, at Chapter 6, with consideration of international humanitarian law (IHL) applicable during armed conflict. It assesses the scope of application and key norms of humanitarian law, notably those that govern legitimate targeting, permissible methods and means of warfare and humanitarian protections applicable during conflict. It highlights the responsibility of parties to the conflict for violations by those operating under their effective control, whether regular forces or irregulars, and the responsibility of all states party to the Geneva Conventions to ensure compliance with IHL standards.

In light of this legal framework, Chapter 6, section B explores to what extent the 'war on terror' really constitutes armed conflict governed by IHL at all. In this vein it asks first whether there is, or can be, a war with al-Qaeda. Second, it explores the nature of the conflicts in Afghanistan and Iraq, and which IHL obligations apply. By specific reference to the context of the Afghan conflict, it raises particular issues relating to the

---

[39] It is recognised that Iraq is not really a 'response' to 9/11 in any direct sense. Nor is it clear to what extent that attack was related to 'terrorism' at all. However, as it follows on from military action in Afghanistan, and appears to be broadly grouped as part of the 'war on terror' by the states involved, it is included within the scope of this study.

application of the legal framework on targeting, methods and means of warfare and humanitarian protections that have arisen in practice.

Chapter 7 considers the international human rights law framework of relevance to the 'war on terror'. It discusses where and when the human rights framework applies, including the applicability of human rights obligations when a state exercises its authority abroad (as many have done in the course of the 'war on terror'). The relationship between human rights law and the security challenges posed by acts of violence such as 9/11 is the focus of the chapter, including the ways in which the legal framework accommodates and is responsive to security imperatives. Specific rights implicated by terrorism and counter terrorism are then addressed. Among the issues explored is the positive duty on the state to protect against serious acts of violence and ensure that justice is done in respect of them, which requires an effective counter-terrorist strategy. Standards relating to, for example, the use of lethal force against suspected terrorists, the right to fair trial and military commissions, the requirements of legal certainty in criminal law and 'terrorism', and limits on the lawful transfer of persons from one state to another, provide parameters for the way in which that counter-terrorism strategy must unfold.

Chapter 7, section B seeks to illustrate some of the many overarching and specific questions that arise in relation to the application of this legal framework post 9/11. Questions include the applicability of human rights obligations to states acting abroad, such as in the arrest and detention of prisoners in Afghanistan, Iraq and beyond, the bombardment in Afghanistan or Iraq or the 'targeted killings' in Yemen. The chapter highlights post 9/11 practices that violate or, at a minimum raise doubts as to compliance with, the human rights framework. Among the particular issues highlighted are: anti-terrorist legislation and the principle of legality; asylum and refugee exclusion of suspected 'terrorists'; the undermining of the role of the judge post 9/11; the human rights implications of developments in international cooperation; indefinite detention practices; the erosion of the protection against torture and inhuman treatment; and the use of security laws to proscribe dissent. More general questions relate to the marginalisation of human rights law and mechanisms in the immediate aftermath of 9/11, and whether there is a discernible trend towards a more central role for human rights protection in the on-going 'war on terror'.

Chapter 8 is a case study relating to the detentions in Guantanamo Bay, Cuba as a vehicle to consider some of the issues highlighted in Chapters 6 and 7, and the interconnections between them. It considers

the status of prisoners, lawful bases for their detention and the basic procedural rights to which they are entitled under IHRL and IHL, against the
factual context of their detention in the so-called 'legal black hole'. The
chapter concludes by questioning the implications of the Guantanamo
Bay situation for the US, for other states, and for the rule of law more
generally.

PART ONE

2

'Terrorism' in international law

The events of 11 September 2001 have been ubiquitously characterised, and internationally condemned, as acts of 'international terrorism'. Their wake brought unprecedented unity of purpose on the international level as to the need to prevent, punish and otherwise combat international terrorism. A proliferation of legal measures ensued, with broad-reaching political and legal effect, including Security Council resolutions that imposed a wide range of obligations on states to prevent and suppress terrorism. These include ensuring that 'terrorist acts are established as serious criminal offences in domestic laws and regulations and that the punishment duly reflects the seriousness of such terrorist acts'.[1]

One could be forgiven for assuming that international terrorism is a readily accessible legal concept. But is the universal condemnation of terrorism matched by a universal understanding of what we mean by the term? Are the obligations to suppress and punish terrorism matched by an internationally accepted definition of what precisely it is that is to be penalised? Or to paraphrase the famous dictum of a US judge, do we simply know terrorism when we see it;[2] and is that a sufficient legal basis to give rise to obligations of states and criminal responsibility of individuals?

The search for an accepted definition of terrorism in international law has been described as 'resembl[ing] the Quest for the Holy Grail'.[3] Various diplomatic attempts – some of which are on-going – to draft a global terrorism convention have failed as consensus around a single definition of international terrorism has proved elusive. Scholars and practitioners

---

[1] SC Res. 1373 (2001), 28 September 2001, UN Doc. S/RES/1373 (2001). This resolution also established a Counter-Terrorism Committee to monitor the implementation of the resolution. SC Res. 1377 (2001), 28 November 2001, UN Doc. S/RES/1377 (2001), sets out the tasks for the Committee.

[2] *Jocabilis* v. *Ohio* US 378: 184, 197, Justice Stewart 'I know terrorism when I see it', as cited in A. Arend and R. Beck, *International Law and the Use of Force* (New York, 2001), p. 140.

[3] G. Levitt, 'Is "Terrorism" Worth Defining?', 13 (1986) *Ohio Northern University Law Review* 97.

have, over the years, put forward at least 109 possible definitions.[4] Betraying the political sensitivity underlying the issue, it is often noted that the heart of the definitional difficulty lies in the now hackneyed saying that 'one person's terrorist is another's freedom fighter'.

Legal developments relating to terrorism have not however been paralysed by the impasse in achieving a global definition. Specific conventions addressing particular types of terrorism, developments by regional organisations for their regional purposes, and advances in other areas of international law have provided legal tools to address conduct that we might commonly refer to as acts of terrorism.

This chapter will sketch out international and regional developments (before and after 11 September 2001) towards the adoption of a general definition of terrorism as part of a comprehensive convention, as well as the proliferation of specific terrorist conventions. Exploring the various definitions put forward in international practice, it will ask to what extent it can be said that there is an internationally accepted definition of terrorism under customary international law. If there is no such generic international definition, it will ask whether this leaves a gap in the international legal order. In this respect it assesses the extent to which the prohibition of terrorism and obligations in respect of it are addressed by other international legal norms. It concludes by enquiring as to the consequences of the use of the 'terrorism' label absent a definition provided in law.

'Terrorist' is a label used loosely, selectively and invariably pejoratively. In this murky area, where the defining elements of terrorism are often confused with value judgements about those accused of it, the goal of this chapter is to unravel the terminology and identify the extent to which there are objectively applicable legal standards.

2.1 Developments towards a comprehensive definition of international terrorism

2.1.1 Pre-September 11: historical developments

As early as the 1930s, serious efforts were underway to achieve consensus on a general definition of terrorism. The 1937 Convention for the

---

[4] In her Progress Report to the Sub-Commission on the Promotion and Protection of Human Rights (UN Doc. E/CN.4/Sub.2/2001/31, 27 June 2001), p. 8, Kalliopi K. Koufa, the UN Special Rapporteur on Terrorism and Human Rights, notes that 109 definitions were put forward between 1936 and 1981.

Prevention and Punishment of Terrorism defines terrorism as '[a]ll criminal acts directed against a State and intended or calculated to create state of terror in the minds of particular persons or a group of persons or the general public'.[5] Such were the difficulties in achieving consensus around this definition that the 1937 Convention was ultimately never adopted, and the search for an international consensus temporarily abandoned.

In the early seventies, the United Nations stepped into the fray and in 1972 an *ad hoc* committee of the General Assembly was mandated to consider a Draft Comprehensive Convention and produce a definition.[6] The Committee ultimately produced a report that falls short of that objective, but rather serves to underline the problems associated with the definitional quandary. Specifically, fuelled by the recent experience of wars of national liberation fought against former colonial powers, the report reveals persistent division regarding the inclusion or exclusion of 'national liberation movements' within the definition.[7] Thus attempts to derive a generic definition again fell by the wayside (in preference for the framework of conventions identifying specific forms of terrorism, on which international consensus *could* be achieved, as discussed below).[8]

By the 1990s, shifting global politics – the end of the cold war and of apartheid, the achievement of independence from colonialism for several African countries and the apparent breakthrough in the Middle East – gave those in favour of a global convention fresh hope that consensus on a generic definition of terrorism might finally be achievable.[9] In 1994 there was something of a breakthrough in the form of the 'Declaration on Measures to Eliminate International Terrorism', which although non-binding, was subsequently endorsed by the United Nations General Assembly.[10] It defined terrorism as 'criminal acts intended or calculated to provoke a

---

[5] Article 2(1), Convention for the Prevention and Punishment of Terrorism (Geneva, 1937, never entered into force), League of Nations Doc. C.546M.383 1937 V.

[6] During the 1960s the issue of international terrorism remained live, and conventions were adopted addressing specific facets of terrorism, as discussed in this chapter, para. 1.1.3 below. However, in the early seventies the killing of 28 persons by a Japanese suicide squad at Lod airport, and of 17 Israeli athletes at the Munich Olympic Games, has been described as the impetus for this renewed initiative. See J. Dugard, 'The Problem of the Definition of Terrorism in International Law', conference paper, Sussex University, 21 March 2003 (on file with author), p. 4.

[7] See A. Obote-Odora, 'Defining International Terrorism', 6.1 (1999) *E Law – Murdoch University Electronic Journal of Law*, available at http://pandora.nla.gov.au/parchive/2001/Z2001-Feb-26/www.murdoch.edu.au/elaw/issues/v6n1/obote-odora61.html.

[8] See below, this chapter, para. 1.3.   [9] Dugard, 'Definition of Terrorism', p. 6.

[10] GA Res. 50/53, 11 December 1995, UN Doc. A/RES/50/53 (1995) and GA Res. 51/210, 17 December 1996, UN Doc. A/RES/51/210 (1996).

state of terror in the general public, a group of persons or particular persons for political purposes' which, notably, it condemned as 'in any circumstances unjustifiable whatever the considerations of a political, philosophical, ideological, racial, ethnic, religious or other nature'. Thus, there was an attempt to divorce the condemnation of terrorism from the value judgements about the reasons that may underpin it.[11]

Building on this development, General Assembly Resolution 51/210 established an *ad hoc* committee in 1996, *inter alia* to streamline efforts to arrive at a Draft Comprehensive Convention. While the Committee has endeavoured (thus far unsuccessfully) to arrive at an accepted definition in the context of a comprehensive anti-terrorism convention, an indirect development came in the form of the 1999 Convention for the Suppression of Financing of Terrorism. While this Convention addresses one aspect of terrorism, it contains a generic definition of sorts by describing terrorism as

> any act intended to cause death or serious bodily injury to a civilian, or to any person not taking an active part in hostilities in a situation of armed conflict, when the purpose of such act, by its nature or context, is to intimidate a population or to compel a government or an international organisation to do or to abstain from doing an act.[12]

Since 1996, the *ad hoc* Committee has continued to debate a generally accepted definition of terrorism for the purposes of a comprehensive anti-terrorism convention, without fruition. The Committee's work was on-going when terrorism shot to the top of the international agenda on 11 September 2001, and its quest continues to the present day.

2.1.2 Post September 11: a global convention?

Following 11 September 2001, international statements demonstrated unparalleled unity in the condemnation of international terrorism. The Security Council for its part called on states not only to adopt wide-ranging measures on the domestic level, but also urged ratification of

---

[11] This definition was reiterated in subsequent General Assembly resolutions. See, e.g., GA Res. 51/210; GA Res. 52/165, 15 December 1997, UN Doc. A/RES/52/165 (1997); GA Res. 53/108, 8 December 1998, UN Doc. A/RES/53/108 (1998); GA Res. 54/110, 9 December 1999, UN Doc. A/RES/54/110 (1999) and GA Res. 55/158, 12 December 2000, UN Doc. A/RES/55/158 (2000).

[12] Alongside this formula in Article 2(1)(b), the Convention provides that 'terrorism', so far as covered by the Convention, is that conduct covered by specific terrorist conventions addressing particular forms of terrorism – see this chapter, para. 2.1.3 below.

existing conventions and support for pending conventions, in an apparent reference to the Draft Comprehensive Convention.[13]

As a working group of the *ad hoc* committee hurried to re-commence its work in this new context, all delegations were unequivocal in their condemnation of terrorism in all forms and manifestations.[14] However, beyond the rhetoric, strikingly little progress appears to have been made in achieving consensus over a generic definition of terrorism for the Draft Comprehensive Convention, and old divisions continued to characterise the negotiations, as explained below.

The current informal definition of terrorism for the purposes of the Draft Comprehensive Convention (Article 2), prepared by the Coordinator for negotiating purposes, defines terrorism as unlawfully and intentionally causing (a) death or serious bodily injury to any person; (b) serious damage to public and private property, including a State or government facility;[15] or (c) other such damage where it is likely to result in major economic loss. The definition further requires that 'the purpose of the conduct, by its nature or context, is to intimidate a population, or to compel a Government or an international organisation to do or abstain from doing any act'.[16]

While various aspects of this definition have been subject to criticism over the years on the basis of the breadth and vagueness of terms,[17] the heart of the outstanding controversy focuses on the potential authors of terrorism under the Convention's definition, in particular the 'traditional'

---

[13] In para. 3 of SC Res. 1373 (2001) (above, note 1), the Security Council called upon 'all States to . . . (e) Increase cooperation and fully implement the relevant international conventions and protocols relating to terrorism and Security Council resolutions 1269 (1999) and 1368 (2001).' SC Res. 1269 (1999), 15 October 1999, UN Doc. S/RES/1267 (1999), contains a call for 'all States to implement fully the international anti-terrorist conventions to which they are parties' and it 'encourages all States to consider as a matter of priority adhering to those to which they are not parties, and encourages also the speedy adoption of the pending conventions'.

[14] UN Doc A/C.6/56/L.6, para. 1 of Annex IV, Part A, Report of the Working Group of the Sixth Committee on 'measures to eliminate international terrorism' (29 October 2001). For an explanation of the work of the *ad hoc* committee and working groups see http://www.un.org/law/terrorism.

[15] The text further provides 'including a place of public use, a State or government facility, a public transportation system, an infrastructure facility or the environment'.

[16] Informal text of Article 2, Report of the Working Group on Measures to Eliminate International Terrorism; UN Doc. A/C.6/56/L.9, Annex I.B.

[17] See generally, F. A. Guzman, *Terrorism and Human Rights No. 1* (International Commission of Jurists, Geneva, 2002) and *Terrorism and Human Rights No. 2* (International Commission of Jurists, Geneva, 2003).

dispute regarding national liberation movements (NLMs).[18] The negotiators have sought (unsuccessfully, it would seem) to depart from the
age-old debate around the qualification or not of oppressive states versus
liberation movements as terrorists by treating the question not as part
of the definition of terrorism as such, but as a limitation on the scope of
the Convention. Thus Article 18 of the Draft Comprehensive Convention
excludes from the scope of the Article 2 definition acts carried out during
armed conflict, on the basis that another body of international legal rules,
namely international humanitarian law, already governs armed conflict,
including wars of national liberation.[19]

However, the current draft excludes only 'armed forces', thereby
exempting only state forces and not others whose conduct would also be
governed by IHL, such as non-state parties to non-international armed
conflicts, or liberation movements in the context of wars of national liberation. The proposed exclusion notes that 'the activities of armed forces
during an armed conflict, as those terms are understood under international humanitarian law, which are governed by that law, are not governed
by this Convention'. This encounters stringent resistance from delegations intent to ensure that if state forces are excluded, those they consider
'freedom fighters' or national liberation movements fighting against those
forces are likewise excluded. A counter proposal therefore seeks to exclude
both 'parties to a conflict', and to ensure that those fighting 'foreign domination' are considered within the purview of any such exclusion.[20] The
cycle of proposals and counter-proposals is likely to continue for the foreseeable future.

If any shift in negotiations can be discerned post September 11, beyond
a strengthened condemnation of acts such as those executed that day, it
may be in the expressions of support, in principle, for a global convention.
Commentators have long disagreed on the desirability of a comprehensive
Convention,[21] as much as on its content, yet reports of UN negotiations

---

[18] UN Doc A/C.6/56/L.6 (above, note 14), para. 7.
[19] Such wars are considered international conflicts under Article 1(4) of Additional Protocol I
to the Geneva Conventions. The International Convention for the Suppression of Terrorist
Bombings (New York, 15 December 1997, UN Doc. A/RES/52/164 (1997), in force 23 May
2001) took the same approach: see Preamble and Article 19.
[20] An alternative draft put forward by the Organisation of the Islamic Conference excludes
either party to a conflict, and includes situations of 'foreign occupation'. See Dugard,
'Definition of Terrorism', p. 9.
[21] See for example Dugard, 'Definition of Terrorism', pp. 12–14 and J. Murphy, 'International
Law and the War on Terrorism: The Road Ahead', 32 (2002) *Israel Yearbook on Human
Rights* 117.

post September 11 recorded that States 'reiterated the urgency of adopting a comprehensive convention on international terrorism'.[22] At least immediately following September 11, then, the quest for a global terrorism convention appeared to become accepted as a political reality, while the feasibility of achieving such a Convention, its precise content or scope, and of course the support that it might eventually muster, remain shrouded in uncertainty.

2.1.3 Specific international conventions

As attempts to arrive at a comprehensive terrorism convention floundered at various stages, the search for a generic definition was replaced by the elaboration of a framework of conventions that identify specific forms of terrorism. There are at least twelve such conventions.[23]

These conventions do not attempt to define terrorism, but address specific conduct that may fall within the purview of what is commonly referred to as terrorist activity, and set forth a framework of obligations on states parties, including measures to prevent such crimes and to cooperate in the prosecution thereof. Commonly they oblige states to either extradite or submit for prosecution persons suspected of the offences covered, subject to limited exceptions,[24] and to cooperate in, for example,

---

[22] UN Doc A/C.6/56/L.6 (above, note 14), Annex IV, para. 4, 'Informal summary of the general discussion in the working group, prepared by the Chairman', above.

[23] Convention on Offences and Certain other Acts Committed on Board Aircraft (Tokyo, 14 September 1963, 1248 UNTS 451, in force 4 December 1969); Convention for the Suppression of Unlawful Seizure of Aircraft (The Hague, 16 December 1970, 860 UNTS 12325, in force 14 October 1971); Convention for the Suppression of Unlawful Acts Against the Safety of Civil Aviation (Montreal, 23 September 1971, 974 UNTS 14118, in force 26 January 1973); Convention on the Prevention and Punishment of Crimes against Internationally Protected Persons, Including Diplomatic Agents (New York, 14 December 1973, 1035 UNTS 15410, in force 20 February 1977); International Convention against the Taking of Hostages (New York, 18 December 1979, 1316 UNTS 21931, in force 3 June 1983); Convention on the Physical Protection of Nuclear Material (Vienna, 26 October 1979, 1456 UNTS 24631, in force 8 February 1987); Convention for the Suppression of Unlawful Acts against the Safety of Maritime Navigation (Rome, 10 March 1988, IMO Doc. SUA/CONF/15/Rev.1, in force 1 March 1992); International Convention for the Suppression of Terrorist Bombings; International Convention for the Suppression of the Financing of Terrorism (New York, 9 December 1999, UN Doc. A/Res/54/109 (1999), in force 10 April 2002). M. C. Bassiouni, 'International Terrorism', in Bassiouni (ed.), International Criminal Law, vol. I, 2nd ed. (New York, 1999), pp. 765 ff, refers to 16 Conventions dealing with specific means of terror violence. See Koufa, 'Progress Report' (note 4, above) citing a total of nineteen Conventions addressing terrorism in one form or another.

[24] An explicit exception exists in certain conventions, such as the 1997 Terrorist Bombing Convention, where there are substantial grounds for believing that extradition would lead

intelligence and evidence gathering. Unlike certain other international treaties, they do not themselves purport to criminalise conduct, but to impose obligations on states to do so in domestic law.[25]

This alternative 'piecemeal' approach to terrorism was consolidated during the 1970s, with conventions addressing offences on board aircraft or at airports,[26] crimes against internationally protected persons,[27] hostage taking[28] and acts aboard ships and at sea.[29] It continued to develop in the post cold war period, alongside the frustrated quest by the 1996 *ad hoc* Committee to find a global definition. During the nineties, this resulted in two noteworthy conventions, relating to 'terrorist bombings'[30] and the financing of terrorism.[31] The Terrorist Bombings convention provides as comprehensive a terrorism convention as has been approved to date, covering the use of 'explosive or other lethal devices' in a public or state facility with intent to cause death or destruction, in particular where there is intent to cause terror in the public or particular individuals.[32] The Financing Convention prohibits provision of financial support for any of the acts covered by other *ad hoc* terrorist conventions. Notably, both these conventions apply irrespective of the political, ideological, racial or religious reasons that may underpin the acts.[33]

---

to serious human rights violations or is motivated by discrimination. The traditional exception for 'political offences' has been removed in certain treaties, such as the International Convention for the Suppression of Terrorist Bombings 1997 and the International Convention for the Suppression of the Financing of Terrorism 1999.

[25] See Convention against Torture, Convention against Genocide or the Geneva Conventions and Protocols thereto; for a discussion of 'terrorism' as a crime under international law, see below, Chapter 4, para. 4A.1.1.4. See, however, terrorism in armed conflicts, this chapter, para. 1.1.

[26] Namely, the Tokyo Convention on Offences and Certain other Acts Committed on Board Aircraft 1963; the Hague Convention for the Suppression of Unlawful Seizure of Aircraft 1970; the Montreal Convention for the Suppression of Unlawful Acts Against the Safety of Civil Aviation 1971 and its Supplementary Protocol for the Suppression of Unlawful Acts of Violence at Airports Serving International Civil Aviation 1988.

[27] Convention on the Prevention and Punishment of Crimes against Internationally Protected Persons, including Diplomatic Agents 1973.

[28] International Convention Against the Taking of Hostages 1979; Protocol for the Suppression of Unlawful Acts Against the Safety of Fixed Platforms located on the Continental Shelf 1988.

[29] Convention for the Suppression of Unlawful Acts Against the Safety of Maritime Navigation 1988.

[30] International Convention for the Suppression of Terrorist Bombings 1997.

[31] International Convention for the Suppression of the Financing of Terrorism 1999.

[32] Article 2, International Convention for the Suppression of Terrorist Bombings 1997.

[33] Article 6. Note the far-reaching provisions on cooperation, such as the exclusion of political offences, in these conventions.

Finally, the negotiation of a further convention addressing nuclear terrorism is on-going,[34] although, like the global convention, negotiations have been stymied by differences of view as to the potential authors of terrorism, and specifically whether state terrorism should fall within the Convention's scope.[35]

2.1.4 Terrorism in armed conflict

International law also provides a definition of terrorism for the specific context of armed conflict. IHL prohibits 'acts or threats of violence the primary purpose of which is to spread terror among the civilian population', in international and non-international armed conflict.[36] Serious violations of this and other IHL prohibitions may also amount to a war crime for which individuals may be held to account, as recently affirmed by the ICTY.[37] As such, terror inflicted on the civilian population in armed conflict is a special case, providing an exception to the rule that 'terrorism' as such is not defined in, and does not constitute a crime under, international treaty law.[38]

As acts of terror in armed conflict are covered by IHL, most 'Terrorism Conventions' purport not to apply in time of armed conflict, although as noted above the Draft Comprehensive Convention excludes from the scope of application only the actions of 'armed forces' of the state during conflict, leaving non state parties whose acts may respect IHL vulnerable to prosecution for terrorism.[39] By contrast, the Financing Convention

---

[34] The Draft International Convention for the Suppression of Acts of Nuclear Terrorism was proposed by the Russian Federation in 1999. It has not yet been adopted. There appear to be two outstanding issues which remain unresolved, namely the lack of agreement over the definition of terrorism and the use of nuclear weapons by military forces under Article 4.

[35] See Murphy, 'War on Terrorism', p. 24.

[36] Article 51 AP I and Article 13 AP II. See also Article 33(1) of the Fourth Geneva Convention which provides that 'terrorism is prohibited' without defining the phenomenon.

[37] States or organisations that are 'parties' to a conflict may be responsible for violations of IHL, as discussed in Chapter 6, section A on IHL. War crimes, and 'terrorism' as a crime are discussed in Chapter 4, section A. The ICTY recently adjudicated the first case concerning the offence of inflicting terror on the civilian population in armed conflict, which it found to amount to a crime under treaty law. *Prosecutor* v. *Galić*, Case No. IT-98-29-T, Judgment, 5 December 2003.

[38] For the customary status of terrorism generally, see this chapter, para. 1.2. On the customary status of the terror crime under IHL, not determined by the Court, see Prosecutor's Pre-Trial Brief, 20 February 2001, in *Prosecutor* v. *Galić*, IT-98-29, 3 October 2002. Article 22, Hague Rules on Aerial Warfare 1923, foreshadows the Additional Protocol provisions, as discussed in *Galić* brief.

[39] Article 12 of the International Convention against the Taking of Hostages 1979 contains a complete exclusion: '[T]he present Convention shall not apply to an act of

includes within its scope terrorism in the context of armed conflict, and provides a specific definition for this purpose.[40] Unfortunately, it does not reflect precisely the definition of terrorism in IHL, causing potential confusion as to the interplay of norms.[41]

2.1.5 Regional conventions

Regional organisations have, to varying degrees, assumed responsibility for addressing terrorism, giving rise to at least seven regional conventions.[42] At the regional – as at the international – level, two broad approaches emerge. On the one hand, organisations such as the Council of Europe and the League of Arab States have produced generic definitions

hostage-taking committed in the course of armed conflicts as defined in the Geneva Conventions of 1949 and the Protocols thereto, including armed conflicts mentioned in Article 1(4) of Additional Protocol I of 1977, in which peoples are fighting against colonial domination and alien occupation and against racist regimes in the exercise of their right of self-determination'; Article 19 and Preamble, International Convention for the Suppression of Terrorist Bombings 1997, excludes only 'activities of armed forces during an armed conflict', as does the current draft of the UN Draft Comprehensive Convention, Article 18. Some treaties also exclude from their scope of application military vehicles and aircraft (see Article 1(4) of the Tokyo Convention 1963, Article 3(2) of the Hague Convention 1970, Article 4(1) of the Montreal Convention 1971 and Article 2 of the Convention for the Suppression of Unlawful Acts against the Safety of Maritime Navigation 1988). By contrast, while the OAU Convention on the Prevention and Combating of Terrorism (Algiers, 14 July 1999) provides in Article 22 that '1. Nothing in this Convention shall be interpreted as derogating from the general principles of international law, in particular the principles of international humanitarian law', the specific exclusion at Article 3 appears to relate only to 'the struggle waged by peoples in accordance with the principles of international law for their liberation or self-determination, including armed struggle.

[40] Article 2(1), International Convention for the Suppression of the Financing of Terrorism 1999 refers to '[a]ny other act intended to cause death or serious bodily injury to a civilian, or to any other person not taking an active part in the hostilities in a situation of armed conflict, when the purpose of such act, by its nature or context, is to intimidate a population, or to compel a government or an international organization to do or to abstain from doing any act'.

[41] The definition differs slightly from the war crimes definition above, for example by omitting the critical 'primary purpose' to spread terror. See *Galić* judgment, note 37 above.

[42] Arab Convention on the Suppression of Terrorism ('Arab Convention'), 22 April 1998; Convention of the Organization of the Islamic Conference on Combating International Terrorism, 1 July 1999; European Convention on the Suppression of Terrorism, 27 January 1977; OAS Convention to Prevent and Punish Acts of Terrorism Taking the Form of Crimes against Persons and Related Extortion that are of International Significance, Washington, DC, 2 February 1971; OAU Convention on the Prevention and Combating of Terrorism 1999; SAARC Regional Convention on Suppression of Terrorism, 4 November 1987; Treaty on Cooperation among States Members of the Commonwealth of Independent States in Combating Terrorism, 4 June 1999.

of terrorism for their regional purposes. By contrast, others, such as the Organization of American States, do not define terrorism but refer to the existing conventions which address specific forms of terrorism.

2.1.5.1 Generic definition

Generic definitions of terrorism promulgated by regional organisations generally apply only to the member States of those organisations. To the extent that they reveal common or different understandings of the nature of international terrorism, however, they are relevant to a discussion of the definition of terrorism in customary law, as discussed below.

The Arab Convention on the Suppression of Terrorism was adopted by the League of Arab States in 1998.[43] Article 1(2) of the Convention defines terrorism as:

> Any act or threat of violence, whatever its motives or purposes, that occurs in the advancement of an individual or collective criminal agenda and seeking to sow panic among people, causing fear by harming them, or placing their lives, liberty or security in danger, or seeking to cause damage to the environment or to public or private installations or property or to occupying or seizing them, or seeking to jeopardize national resources.

This definition of terrorism has been criticised for its breadth, vagueness and consequent susceptibility to abuse.[44] In particular, the unqualified reference to 'violence' or the 'threat' of violence – irrespective of whether it achieves any actual result, or of the gravity of the violence caused or threatened[45] – allows for a potentially very broad range of conduct to be brought under the rubric of this Convention.

Pre-September 11 the European regional system had, like the international system, addressed terrorism through a piecemeal approach, rather

---

[43] Arab Convention on the Suppression of Terrorism, Cairo, 22 April 1998, in force 7 May 1999 (unofficial translation from arabic by the UN translation service available at http://edoc.mpil.de/conference-on-terrorism/related/1998CairoArabConvention.pdf).

[44] Amnesty International has outlined several concerns with this definition, including that the term violence is not defined or qualified, and that the use of the term threat may allow the labelling of those that have not committed violence but who are seen as a threat to the State – including legitimate political opponents – so as to be considered terrorists. See Amnesty International, 'The Arab Convention for the Suppression of Terrorism: a serious threat to human rights', AI Index: IOR 51/001/2002, 9 January 2002.

[45] See the International Convention for the Suppression of the Financing of Terrorism 1999 and the Draft Comprehensive Convention both of which talk of a requisite level of violence to be achieved, i.e. serious injury.

than attempting to define terrorism generically.[46] Only eight days after September 11, however, the Commission of the European Union presented a proposal to the European Council for a Framework Decision on Combating Terrorism, intended to arrive at a common European definition of terrorism.[47] The final text of that Framework Decision, adopted by the Council on 13 June 2002, states that:

> terrorist offences include the following list of intentional acts which, given their nature or their context, may seriously damage a country or international organisation where committed with the aim of:
>
> (i) seriously intimidating a population, or
> (ii) unduly compelling a Government or international organisation to perform or abstain from performing any act, or
> (iii) seriously destabilising or destroying the fundamental political, constitutional, economic or social structures of a country or international organisation.[48]

Article 1 then goes on to outline the offences to which terrorism relates, including attacks on persons, damage to property, seizure of means of transport, weapons offences and threatening to commit any of those acts,[49] while Articles 3 and 4 bring within its scope 'offences relating to a

---

[46] The only regional European convention addressing terrorism was the 1977 European Convention on the Suppression of Terrorism, adopted within the Council of Europe. This convention deals with extradition in relation to terrorist offences, defined by reference to crimes listed in other conventions. It provides a list of offences which, for the purposes of the Convention, are considered 'terrorist' offences in respect of which state parties must extradite suspects, as opposed to 'political' offences where generally the duty to extradite does not apply (Article 1). It also includes other offences involving an act of violence against the life, physical integrity or liberty of a person (Article 2(1)) and against property if the act created a collective danger for persons (Article 2(2)), where the state *may* extradite the suspect, but is not obliged to do so.

[47] See Commission Proposal for a Council Framework Decision on Combating Terrorism, 19 September 2001, COM (2001) 521 final.

[48] Article 1, Council Framework Decision on Combating Terrorism, 13 June 2002 (2002/475/JHA), OJ L164/3 of 22 June 2002 (hereinafter 'European Council Framework Decision on Combating Terrorism'). The date for transposition into domestic law was set as December 2002 but by March 2004 only eight member states had implemented. See E. Dumitriu, 'The EU's Definition of Terrorism: the Council Framework Decision on Combating Terrorism', 5 *German Law Journal* 587, at footnote 18.

[49] The European Council Framework Decision on Combating Terrorism includes at Article 1 the following acts within the definition of terrorism: 'attacks upon a person's life [or] physical integrity . . .; kidnapping or hostage taking; causing extensive destruction to a government or public facility, a transport facility, an infrastructure facility; . . . seizure of aircraft . . . or other means of public transport, places of public use, and property likely

terrorist group' and 'offences linked to terrorist offences'.[50] This Council statement was adopted as a 'common position',[51] requiring member states to take the legislative steps required to implement its terms in national law. It has been criticised for the use of 'unclear, vague and uncertain concepts.'[52]

2.1.5.2 Definitions by reference

Other regional organisations which have addressed terrorism include the Organisation of American States,[53] the African Union[54] and the South Asian Association for Regional Cooperation.[55] The terrorism conventions adopted by these organisations read very much like the European approach pre-September 11, in that terrorist activities are identified by reference to existing UN treaties which have addressed specific forms of terrorism.[56] While these regional arrangements act as a framework for extradition or prosecution of acts which have already been deemed

---

to endanger human life or result in major economic loss; manufacture, possession, acquisition, transport or supply of weapons or explosives; release of dangerous substances, or causing fires, explosions or floods, endangering people, property, animals or the environment; interfering with or disrupting the supply of water, power, or other fundamental resource the effect of which is to endanger human life; threatening to commit any of the offences listed above'.

[50] See European Council Framework Decision on Combating Terrorism, Articles 2 and 3, requiring that these forms of association be incriminated in domestic law. Article 4 addresses forms of liability that must also be reflected in national criminal law.

[51] A Council Statement is a declaration of political intent, having no legal force. For the obligations in respect of common positions, see Article 15 of the Treaty on the European Union, which provides that Member States are under an obligation to ensure that their national policies conform to the common positions adopted by the Council.

[52] See Guzman, *Terrorism and Human Rights No. 2*, p. 41. As discussed at Chapter 4, para. 4.2.2, attempts to establish a common legal definition of terrorism are coupled with broad initiatives to 'abolish extradition between member states' in favour of a streamlined surrender procedure. *Ibid.*, p. 37.

[53] OAS Convention to Prevent and Punish Acts of Terrorism Taking the Form of Crimes against Persons and Related Extortion that are of International Significance, Washington, DC, 2 February 1971, OAS Treaty Series No. 37.

[54] OAU Convention on the Prevention and Combating of Terrorism 1999, text available at http://untreaty.un.org/English/Terrorism/oau_e.pdf.

[55] SAARC Regional Convention on the Suppression of Terrorism, Kathmandu, 4 November 1987, text available at http://untreaty.un.org/English/Terrorism/Conv18.pdf.

[56] See European Convention on the Suppression of Terrorism, Strasbourg, 27 January 1977, ETS. No. 90, in force 4 August 1978. Note also that the Arab Convention, while offering a generic definition of terrorism, complements it by referring to 'terrorist offences' as those prohibited by pre-existing conventions (Article 3).

'terrorist' at international law, they do not attempt to contribute to elucidating a generic definition of terrorism.[57]

2.1.6 National measures

Many states had specific counter-terrorism legislation in place long before September 11, which, unsurprisingly, present differing definitions of terrorism reflecting diverse historical and political national contexts.[58] Not infrequently, such counter-terrorism legislation is the subject of criticism from human rights courts and bodies for its breadth and/or ambiguity.[59] Post September 11, a plethora of new anti-terrorist measures were grafted onto the canvas of existing laws, many of them enacted according to expedited national procedures.[60] The enactment of new laws is in part a

---

[57] Despite not offering a definition, some of them nevertheless note the exclusion from the concept of terrorism of struggles against self-determination.

[58] For example, in Italy, under Article 270 of the Italian criminal code, everyone who 'promotes, creates, organises or directs associations which aim at committing acts of violence in order to eliminate the democratic order' is guilty of a terrorist offence, without any requirement for religious or political motivation or spreading fear or intimidation among the population, as the law was focused on organised crime and the activities of the mafia. Post September 11, the law has been extended to cover acts with an international dimension (see K. Oellers-Frahm, 'Country Report on Italy', Conference on 'Terrorism as a Challenge for National and International Law', Max Planck Institute for Comparative Public Law and International Law, Heidelberg, 24–25 January 2003, at www.edoc.mpil.de/conference-on-terrorism/country.cfm). In Japan, Article 17(1) of the National Police Agency Organisation Act of 1954 limits terrorism to a particular political view, covering '[v]iolent or subversive activities on the basis of ultra-left ideology and other assertions with the intention of achieving their purpose by spreading fear and apprehension' (see N. Hirai-Braun, 'Country Report on Japan', Conference on 'Terrorism as a Challenge for National and International Law', at www.edoc.mpil.de/conference-on-terrorism/country.cfm).

[59] See, for example, the Human Rights Committee's criticism of the definition of 'terrorism' in Article 86 of the Egyptian Penal Code as so broad that it encompassed a wide range of acts of differing gravity (UN Doc. CCPR/C/79/Add.23 (1993), para. 8). See also the Concluding observations on the recent Israeli report (UN Doc. CCPR/CO/78/ISR (2003)), in which the Human Rights Committee stated that it was 'concerned about the vagueness of definitions in Israeli counter-terrorism legislation and regulations which, although their application is subject to judicial review, appear to run counter in several aspects to the principle of legality due to the ambiguous wording of the provisions and the use of several evidentiary presumptions to the detriment of the defendant.'

[60] Less than two months after September 11 the 342-page USA Patriot Act, which amends over fifteen statutes, passed into law. The UK government rushed through the Anti-Terrorism, Crime and Security Act 2001 within a month of submitting its draft to Parliament, thereby only allowing parliamentary debate and not the customary committee scrutiny. Both pieces of legislation afford domestic law enforcement agencies and international intelligence agencies wide-ranging powers and have been criticised for restricting human rights protections.

response to Security Council resolutions passed in response to September 11,[61] in particular Resolution 1373, passed under Chapter VII of the UN Charter (thereby imposing a legal obligation on member states of the UN), which specifically required states to ensure that 'terrorist acts' are criminalised in domestic law.[62]

None of the Security Council resolutions referring to terrorism define it, however, or refer to sources on which states should rely in formulating a definition. While the UN established a Counter-Terrorism Committee to monitor the implementation of the resolution, in practice the Security Council has left unfettered flexibility for the state to define terrorism as it sees fit.[63] Unsurprisingly then, national definitions post September 11, like those adopted hitherto, vary greatly. Equally unsurprisingly, much of the anti-terrorism legislation post September 11 has given rise to serious human rights concerns. These concerns include (but go far beyond) the broad-reaching nature of the definitions of terrorist offences.[64]

Unfolding practice on the national level should be closely observed as potentially constituting the most important developments in this field, as a matter of practical significance and as a source of state practice that could, with time, contribute to the development of customary law.

2.2 Do we know it when we see it? Defining terrorism and customary law

As has been seen, there is no global convention that can be said to establish a general definition of 'terrorism' and obligations in respect thereof, that might be binding on state parties under international treaty law. The question then is whether international state practice points to the general

---

[61] SC Res. 1368 (2001), 12 September 2001, UN Doc. S/RES/1368 (2001), called on member states to work together to stop terrorism and punish those responsible.

[62] SC Res. 1373 (2001), above, note 1.

[63] Resolution 1373 (2001) established the Committee. SC Res. 1377 (2001), above, note 1, then included among the tasks for the Committee the following: to promote best practices, including the preparation of model laws as appropriate; and to disseminate the availability of existing technical, financial, legislative and other assistance programmes to assist the implementation of Resolution 1373.

[64] See Chapter 7 on the human rights implications of broad-reaching notions of 'terrorism', exacerbated by Resolution 1373. The Counter-Terrorism Committee has, however, resisted incorporating a human rights role into its agenda, despite the human rights implications. While human rights bodies increasingly assume this role, this is impeded by excessive delays in the state provision of country reports to human rights bodies, which compare unfavourably with reports to the Council.

acceptance of an international legal definition of terrorism as a matter of *customary* international law.

A brief comparative analysis of the various generic definitions of terrorism that have emerged in international instruments thus far, as described above, may therefore be instructive in determining whether there is consensus on the essential elements of a definition of terrorism.

2.2.1 Identifying elements of a definition of terrorism from international instruments

2.2.1.1 Conduct

The conduct (or in criminal law terms the *actus reus* or material element of the offence) varies between definitions from the more restrictive approach, found for example in the Draft Comprehensive Convention and the Financing Convention which covers essentially causing death, serious injury and in some cases damage to property,[65] to the broader reaching and less precise approach, such as in the Arab Convention which covers any 'violence or threats of violence' and the 1994 Declaration which covers any 'criminal acts'. Whereas some formulations cover 'inchoate' offences, where no result occurs, others depend on certain types of injury, damage or loss having actually occurred.[66]

2.2.1.2 Purpose or motive

It is widely recognised that terrorism tends to involve two or more subjective layers. The acts are rarely an end in themselves but a vehicle to achieving particular gains, which are ideological rather than private. Beyond the normal requirement of intent in respect of the conduct (e.g., the bombing, murder, etc.), the person responsible will usually intend his or her acts to produce broader effects, namely spreading a state of terror and/or compelling a government or organisation to take certain steps towards an ultimate goal. In criminal law terms, the existence of this double subjective layer in many of the definitions appears to indicate that if there is a crime of terrorism, like certain other international offences, it is a *dolus specialis* crime, i.e. a crime that requires, in addition to the criminal intent

---

[65] The International Convention for the Suppression of the Financing of Terrorism 1999 refers only to causing 'death or serious bodily injury'.

[66] In the European Council Framework Decision on Combating Terrorism and Arab Convention 'threats' to commit specified acts suffice.

corresponding to the underlying criminal act the existence of an ultimate goal or design at which the conduct is aimed.[67]

However, despite considerable common ground on the need for such a broader design or purpose, instruments differ on its nature. Unsurprisingly, certain definitions refer to the purpose as to spread terror,[68] or 'provoke a state of terror in the general public',[69] but the 'terror' aspect is omitted from other definitions, which contemplate a broader range of possible objectives. The recent EU definition, for example, includes 'seriously destabilising or destroying the fundamental political, constitutional, economic or social structures of a country or international organisation'.[70] The Arab Convention[71] and the OAU Convention[72] are broader still in the range of possible objectives.

Commonly, definitions also refer to another subjective layer, requiring that the terror, destabilisation or other objective is in turn pursued with a view to compelling a response from another (but while this is usually from the government or state, in some definitions it may also be from an international organisation).[73]

As noted in relation to the 'authors' of terrorism, approaches also vary as to whether considerations of a political, philosophical or other nature

---

[67] Persecution and genocide, for example. For a discussion on the category of *dolus specialis* in the context of genocide, see A. Cassese, *International Criminal Law* (Oxford, 2003), pp. 103 ff.

[68] On the IHL prohibition of 'acts or threats of violence the primary purpose of which is to spread terror among the civilian population' in international or non-international armed conflict, see this chapter, para. 1.4.1.

[69] GA Res. 51/210, above, note 10.

[70] Article 1, European Council Framework Decision on Combating Terrorism.

[71] The requirement under the Arab Convention is that the individual or group involved must be 'seeking to sow panic among people, causing fear by harming them, or placing their lives, liberty or security in danger, or seeking to cause damage to the environment or to public or private installations or property or to occupying or seizing them, or seeking to jeopardize national resources' (Article 1(2)).

[72] A 'terrorist act' under Article 1(3) is one which is (i) intended to 'intimidate, put in fear, force, coerce or induce any government, body, institution, the general public or any segment thereof, to do or abstain from doing any act, or to adopt or abandon a particular standpoint, or *to act according to certain principles*; or (ii) disrupt any public service, the delivery of any essential service to the public or to create a public emergency; or (iii) create general insurrection in a State' (emphasis added).

[73] Draft Comprehensive Convention, Article 2: '[T]he purpose of the conduct, by its nature or context, is to intimidate a population, or to compel a Government or an international organisation to do or abstain from doing any act.' While the Arab Convention refers only to compelling the state, in the European common definition terrorist acts may be directed at a state *or* an international organisation.

might constitute a 'justification' for terrorism: this is explicitly ruled out in certain definitions but not in others.[74] Linked to this are different approaches to whether acts of terrorism can constitute 'political offences' and whether the political nature of an offence can constitute an exception to the duty to prosecute for terrorism.[75] Under general principles of criminal law, personal motive is irrelevant, although this is not always clear in definitions of terrorism.

2.2.1.3 Who or what is protected

A further criterion on which definitions differ is the scope of potential 'victims' of terrorist acts. The 1937 definition for example is unusual in covering only acts directed against the state. Other conventions, such as the 1999 Financing Convention, by contrast protect 'civilians' or other persons not taking a direct part in hostilities in armed conflict. More recent examples, such as the UN Draft Comprehensive Convention, include a broader range of targets, applying to injury or damage to 'any person' and to property whether 'public' or 'private'.

2.2.1.4 International element

Generally, conventions addressing 'international terrorism' explicitly restrict their application to terrorism with a cross border element. With the exception of terrorism committed in the context of non-international conflict (which as noted may be a war crime under international law), international conventions and declarations do not apply to domestic terrorism where the conduct, perpetrators and victims arise within one state. However, the regional terrorism instruments referred to express no such limitation.[76]

---

[74] E.g., Article 5, International Convention for the Suppression of Terrorist Bombings 1998 and the International Convention for the Suppression of the Financing of Terrorism 1999 contain a provision precluding any such justification, as did the 1994 Declaration. Earlier specific conventions and certain regional ones contain no such provision.

[75] The 'political offences' exception is however increasingly being eliminated, especially in relation to terrorism post September 11. See below Chapter 4, para. 4B.2.3 and this chapter, para. 2.1.4 regarding the human rights implications of this trend. Regarding specific terrorist conventions, see, e.g., Article 11, International Convention for the Suppression of Terrorist Bombings 1998 and the International Convention for the Suppression of the Financing of Terrorism 1999.

[76] See, e.g., the European Council Framework Decision on Combating Terrorism and Arab Convention.

2.2.1.5 The authors: state actors and national liberation movements

The Special Rapporteur on Terrorism and Human Rights, Ms Kalliopi K. Koufa, has found the 'degree of consensus' around the definition of terrorism not to extend to the thorny issue of 'who can be a potential author of terrorism'.[77] The questions highlighted as controversial related to whether, in turn, states and national liberation movements can be responsible for 'international terrorism'.[78]

As regards the first question whether state conduct may constitute international terrorism, existing international instruments take different approaches.[79] While the 1991 Draft Code of Crimes Against the Peace and Security of Mankind included international terrorism within the scope of crimes that can be committed by the State, terrorism was dropped from the list of offences covered by the 1996 version of the Draft Code. Most other provisions, while often not explicitly excluding the possibility of states falling within their purview, do exclude many guises of direct state terrorism by implication, either because the terror is inflicted against a state's own people (and is thus excluded by the broadly accepted 'international element' criterion referred to above), or because it takes place in armed conflict (and is explicitly excluded, as already governed by IHL).[80] While it remains sensitive – as seen for example from the fact that negotiations towards a nuclear terrorism convention have been stymied by differences of view on this critical point, which have also manifested themselves in the Draft Comprehensive Convention – the majority of 'international terrorism' provisions do not address state terrorism as such.[81]

In this respect, two points are worth clarifying. The first is that one justification for excluding 'state' terrorism from definitions of international

---

[77] Koufa, 'Progress Report', note 4, above.

[78] *Ibid.*, para. 32: '[A] descriptive (objective) definition of terrorism which focuses on certain behaviour and its effects, and does not allow consideration of the identity of the author or perpetrator, may be useful but not absolutely precise or satisfactory in containing and explaining a relativist concept, tempered by considerations of motive and politics, such as terrorism.'

[79] See Dugard, 'Definition of Terrorism', p. 5. Report of the International Law Commission 43rd session, UNGAOR, 46 Session, supp. no. 10 A/46/10 (1991), Article 24. However, many implicitly exclude state terrorism, as discussed below.

[80] See this chapter, para. 1.2.

[81] Controversial questions regarding state terrorism, and whether state action may itself constitute international terrorism – addressed here – should be distinguished from state support for international terrorism by private actors; see Chapter 3, para. 3.1.

terrorism is that the state is, or should be, accountable through other branches of law, such as human rights,[82] humanitarian law or the law on the use of force, whereas the responsibility of non-state actors is more limited.[83] Secondly, the exclusion of 'state terrorism' should be distinguished from (a) state responsibility for terrorism carried out by private actors, that are attributable to it according to the rules on state responsibility, and (b) state responsibility for sponsorship or support for terrorism.[84] Many instruments addressing international terrorism explicitly provide for state responsibility in respect of the latter. As controversial responses to September 11 continue to unfold, the debate on whether there is such a thing as 'state terrorism' is likely to be further intensified.

A yet more intractable question relates to the distinction between 'terrorism' and acts undertaken pursuant to 'the inalienable right to self determination and independence'.[85] The determination on the part of many states, particularly but not exclusively from the developing world, to exclude national liberation movements from any definition of terrorism has characterised almost all negotiations towards a definition in international practice.

As noted, the 1994 Declaration was thought to be a milestone in stating that the 'criminal acts' covered by it are 'in any circumstances unjustifiable whatever the considerations of a political, philosophical, ideological, racial, ethnic, religious or other nature', without reference to NLMs. While numerous instruments follow this approach, the subsequent Arab and African regional conventions expressly exempt from the terrorist definition peoples struggling for self-determination or national liberation in accordance with international law, 'including armed struggle against colonialism, occupation, aggression and domination by foreign forces'.[86] Under the Arab Convention, it has been noted that, while on the one hand relatively banal acts could be covered by the terrorism definition (due to the broad-reaching conduct covering by the definition), on the other, the most serious indiscriminate attacks against civilians could be excluded 'as long as [they were] perpetrated in the name of the right to

---

[82] Note that the application of human rights law as relevant to international terrorism is premised on human rights obligations extending extra-territorially.

[83] See Chapter 3, para. 3.2.   [84] *Ibid.*

[85] GA Res. 3034 (XXVII), 'Measures to Prevent International Terrorism', 18 December 1972, UN Doc. A/RES/3034 (XXVII).

[86] OAU Convention, Article 3(1); Arab Convention, Preamble and Article 2(a). See also Convention of the Organisation of the Islamic Conference on Combating International Terrorism. The OAU Convention couples this exclusion with a provision stating that 'political, philosophical . . . or other motives shall not be a justifiable defence'.

self determination'.[87] A slightly different manifestation of the same phenomenon could be seen in a European Union note accompanying the draft
European Framework decision circulated after 11 September 2001 which
in turn made some provision for justification of acts that may otherwise be
considered terrorist, by clarifying that the definition of terrorism does not
include 'those who have acted in the interests of preserving or restoring
democratic values'.[88]

This issue continues to dog the negotiation of the UN Convention,
although the debate has become somewhat more sophisticated. Article
18 of the Draft Comprehensive Convention provides that the Convention
does not apply to the conduct of armed forces in situations of armed conflict, which are governed instead by IHL. However, as noted above, dispute
remains as to whether an exception should apply to all types of conflict –
international or non-international, and including wars of national liberation and situations of 'foreign occupation' – and to all types of actors,
whether state or non-state.[89] As noted above, there is no immediately
apparent passage out of the quagmire on this most intransigent of issues.

In brief, this short survey reveals numerous commonalities but also
substantial points of divergence in the approach to the definition of terrorism to date. It is undoubtedly possible to discern, in a general way,
key features of terrorism, such as certain unlawful acts carried out for
ideological ends. It is rather more difficult to identify, from the survey of
international instruments, clear and precise elements of a definition that
can be said to have garnered international support.

2.2.2 Other international practice: General Assembly, Security Council and criminal tribunals

Various resolutions of the UN General Assembly and Security Council
have referred to the duties of states in respect of terrorism, from the duty

---

[87] E. David, *Eléments de droit pénal international – Titre* II, *le contenu des infractions internationales*, 8th ed. (Brussels, 1999), p. 539. See further Guzman, *Terrorism and Human
Rights No. 2*.

[88] The note circulated with the draft decision goes on: 'Nor can it be construed so as to
incriminate on terrorist grounds persons exercising their legitimate right to manifest
their opinions, even if in the course of the exercise of such right they commit offences.'
See Statewatch, 'Critique of the Council's Agreed Decision on the definition of terrorism', *Statewatch bulletin*, November–December 2001, available at http://www.statewatch.
org/news/2002/feb/06Aep.htm.

[89] See discussion of UN negotiations towards a global convention this chapter, para. 2.1.2
above.

to refrain from support[90] to the more proactive duty to suppress.[91] While many are non-binding,[92] these resolutions may reflect or contribute to the development of customary law regarding the obligations in question.[93] As discussed above, post September 11, the Security Council has gone further and called on states to take broad-reaching measures against 'international terrorism', including criminalising such conduct.

None of these UN initiatives provides a definition of terrorism, how-ever, and hence, one could argue, none of them gives precise content or meaning to the obligations to which they refer. The resolutions do not therefore contribute to our understanding of the meaning of interna-tional terrorism in customary international law. It could be argued that these resolutions, particularly those that refer to criminal law, presuppose sufficient understanding of the phenomenon referred to in international law.[94] But then, the current state of negotiations on a global convention, and the Security Council's call to states, in the context of resolution 1373, to advance these negotiations, belie such a view.

---

[90] GA Res. 2625 (XXV), 'Declaration on Principles of International Law concerning Friendly Relations and Co-operation among States in accordance with the Charter of the United Nations', 24 October 1970, UN Doc. A/RES/2625 (XXV), which has been cited as declara-tory of customary law with regard to the non-use of force, provides that '[e]very state has the duty to refrain from organizing, instigating, assisting or participating in acts of civil strife and terrorist acts in another State or acquiescing in organized activities within its territory directed towards the commission of such acts'. This was followed by a state-ment by the Security Council, albeit in the preambular clause of Res. 748 of 31 March 1992 imposing economic sanctions against Libya, that 'in accordance with the principle in Article 2(4) of the Charter of the United Nations, every state has the duty to refrain from organising, instigating, assisting or participating in terrorist acts in another state or acquiescing in organised activities within its territory directed toward the commission of such acts, when such acts involve the threat of use of force'.

[91] GA Res. 51/210, 'Declaration to Supplement the 1994 Declaration on Measures to Elim-inate International Terrorism', 17 December 1996, UN Doc. A/RES/51/210 (1999), states in the preamble that 'criminal acts intended or calculated to provoke a state of terror in the general public, a group of persons or particular persons for political purposes are in any circumstance unjustifiable, whatever the considerations of a political, philosophical, ideological, racial, ethnic, religious or other nature that may be invoked to justify them'.

[92] Only Security Council resolutions passed under Chapter VIII are themselves legally bind-ing. Other resolutions, including those of the GA, are not binding under the Charter but may play a significant role in the formation of customary norms. The Libya resolution (note 90 above) was a Chapter VII resolution, but the relevant clause was in the preamble, which is not legally binding.

[93] On UN declarations and resolutions and the development of custom, see the arbitration award in *Texaco Overseas Petroleum Co/California Asiatic Oil Co* v. *Libyan Arab Republic*, para. 83, reprinted in 17 ILM 1. See also *Military and Paramilitary Activities in and against Nicaragua* (*Nicaragua* v. *United States*), 1986 ICJ Reports, p. 14, paras. 188 and 198.

[94] See Cassese, *International Criminal Law*, p. 129.

The practice of international criminal tribunals may also be of relevance to the question whether there is in fact an international legal definition of terrorism. The Statutes of the ICTR and of the Special Court for Sierra Leone include terrorism as one of the crimes within their respective jurisdictions, and several detainees await trial on this count before the Special Court. It has been suggested that this creates a strong assumption that the drafters considered that there was in fact a crime of terrorism under international law at the time when the crimes within the jurisdiction of those tribunals were committed, defined with sufficient clarity to provide a basis for criminal prosecution.[95] However, it is clear from the context of these provisions, that they cover the specific prohibition on terrorism in armed conflict – which, as discussed above, is a special sub-category of terrorism which is defined in IHL, and amounts to an international crime that the ICTY has also prosecuted – rather than purporting to confer jurisdiction over a broader generic offence of terrorism in international law.[96]

Moreover, the 160 states participating in the Rome conference on the establishment of the International Criminal Court noted that no definition of the crime of terrorism could be agreed upon for inclusion in the Statute, apparently indicative of the lack of any such definition under international law at the time of the ICC Statute's adoption.[97] International criminal law practice does not therefore appear to support the existence of a definition of terrorism in customary international law (other than perhaps in respect of the war crime of inflicting terror on the civilian population).[98]

---

[95] Cassese, *International Criminal Law*, pp. 120–1, asserting that a definition of terrorism does exist and that the phenomenon also amounts to an international law crime, citing in support Article 4 of the Statute of the ICTR.

[96] The Statute of the Special Court for Sierra Leone (annex to the Agreement between the United Nations and the Government of Sierra Leone on the Establishment of a Special Court for Sierra Leone (Freetown, 16 January 2002), available at http://www.sc-sl.org/index.html) and the Statute of the ICTR, in both cases in Article 3 ('Violations of Article 3 common to the Geneva Conventions and of Additional Protocol II') at (d) cover 'acts of terrorism'. To date, there has been no judgment from the Rwandan Tribunal which interprets or further defines the word terrorism under Article 4(e). However, the Special Court has detainees awaiting trial charged with acts of terror under Article 3(e) (e.g., Brima and Kallan who are among the first seven indictees charged in March 2003).

[97] See for example Resolution E adopted by the Rome Conference on the International Criminal Court as part of its Final Act (UN Doc. A/CONF.183/10): 'Regretting that no generally acceptable definition of the crimes of terrorism and drug crimes could be agreed upon for the inclusion within the jurisdiction of the Court'.

[98] See Statutes of the ICTR and of the Special Court for Sierra Leone; *Prosecutor v. Galić*, Case No. IT-98-29-T, Judgment, 5 December 2003; see Statute of the International Criminal Court, Rome, 17 July 1998, UN Doc. A/CONF.183/9 (hereinafter 'ICC Statute').

2.2.3 Meeting the legality threshold: preliminary conclusions on customary international law?

The question whether terrorism is defined in international law is therefore controversial. While a thorough review of the practice of states in defining terrorism goes beyond the scope of this study, the differences of approach in the practice reviewed highlights the fragility of any consensus on whether there *is* an accepted definition of terrorism and if so what its content might be. The brief survey of instruments would appear to suggest that, while the heart of the definitional dispute undoubtedly relates to the potential authors of terrorism, there is divergent practice in respect of most, if not all, elements of the definition.

Commentators differ as to whether there is sufficient clarity around a definition of terrorism under customary law.[99] The heart of the issue is whether there is a sufficiently solid core of a definition to hold that there is a clear prohibition in law and, in particular, that there is an international crime carrying individual responsibility.

In making this assessment, the requirements of legality must be kept centre stage.[100] The legitimacy of the law's restriction of rights and freedoms depends on it being sufficiently clear and accessible that individuals are able to conform their behaviour to the limits of the law. As human rights courts frequently remind us, genuine uncertainty as to the content and scope of law renders that law void for vagueness, and criminal law has particularly stringent requirements of legal certainty. It is questionable whether many of the definitions advanced above, applicable in particular regional or other contexts, themselves meet the requirements of *nullum crimen sine lege*, and more doubtful yet whether the common core that might be distilled from them would meet such a test.

Responses to September 11 continue to unfold and a rule of customary law could, at least conceivably, emerge as international practice develops.

---

[99] Cassese, *International Criminal Law*, pp. 120 ff, suggests that there is consensus on the 'general notion' of terrorism and that disputes relate only to the question of National Liberation Movements, which he describes as a dispute not as to an element of the definition but as to the 'exceptions' that apply thereto. J. Paust, 'Addendum: Prosecution of Mr. bin Laden *et al.* for Violations of International Law and Civil Lawsuits by Various Victims', *ASIL Insights* No. 77, 21 September 2001, at www.asil.org, refers to international terrorism as 'recognizable international crimes under customary international law'; and the Restatement (Third) Foreign Relations Law of the United States (1987) notes that customary law 'may' confer universal jurisdiction over terrorism. See R. Higgins, 'The General International Law of Terrorism', in R. Higgins and M. Flory, *International Law and Terrorism* (London, 1997).

[100] In this respect, regard should be given to the rules of international human rights law discussed at Chapter 7 below.

National practice is being generated constantly, although, as might be expected, the definitions in domestic legislation reveal an even greater divergence of approach between them than do their international or regional counterparts. Consensus appears to be consolidating around many of the elements of a definition in the context of the negotiations around a global draft Convention, with the notable exception of the National Liberation Movement issue. However, as the Draft Comprehensive Convention has not been completed or adopted, still less signed and ratified, it would appear premature to rely on the current state of these negotiations alone as indicative of customary international law at the present time. It may be that the renewed focus on international terrorism post September 11 will lead to future changes in customary international law, to which the potential adoption and acceptance of a generic definition in a global convention would undoubtedly contribute.

For the time being, it may be tentatively concluded that international law cannot be said to prohibit or indeed penalise terrorism, according to an understood definition of the term under customary international law. So far as there remain such uncertainties and ambiguities around the existence of a definition or its scope, it must be highly doubtful whether criminal prosecution on this basis would be consistent with the cardinal principles of legality and certainty in criminal matters.

2.3 Filling the gap? Terrorism and other international legal norms

If there is no generic definition of terrorism in international law, does this leave a gap in the international legal order? Two groups of issues are worth highlighting.

First, the absence of a definition of terrorism does not mean that serious acts of violence, such as those carried out on September 11, are not criminalised under international (and of course domestic) criminal law. As noted above, acts of 'terrorism' are covered by multiple specific conventions addressing particular types or aspects of terrorism, including hijacking, hostage taking, violence against internationally protected persons, terrorist bombing and financing terrorism. Indeed, it has been described as 'difficult to imagine a form of terrorism not covered by these Conventions'.[101] As treaty law, they are however binding only on states parties to them and prosecution depends on their incorporation into

---

[101] Dugard, 'Definition of Terrorism', p. 12. On this basis, Dugard, like others, does not consider it essential or desirable to conclude a generic definition in a global convention.

domestic law. In addition, as discussed in more detail in Chapter 4, acts commonly referred to as 'terrorist' may amount to other crimes under international criminal law, including customary law of general application. Notably they may amount to war crimes (if carried out in armed conflict) and crimes against humanity (whether or not there is an armed conflict), provided the necessary elements of those crimes are met, including that they be committed against the 'civilian population'.[102]

The crimes mentioned above do not provide comprehensive coverage of the range of possible terrorist acts: for example, attacks aimed at terrorising the civilian population in time of peace, which do not meet the widespread or systematic threshold requirement of crimes against humanity, and in a state that has not ratified the specific conventions, would probably not be proscribed under international law.[103] But even in such circumstances, acts of international terrorism will be covered by ordinary domestic law. Whether or not domestic law criminalises terrorism as such, it will inevitably prohibit murder or attacks on the physical integrity of persons or on property.

The second point to note is that the lack of a definition of terrorism does not signify a lack of obligations on states to refrain from participating in or supporting acts of terrorism and to take certain proactive counterterrorist measures. Under the general rules governing relations between states, a state is obliged for example 'to not knowingly allow its territory to be used in a manner contrary to the rights of other states',[104] and to refrain from the threat or use of force, direct or indirect, against another state.[105] As regards the treatment of persons subject to a state's 'jurisdiction' or 'control', the state is also obliged under international human rights law not only to refrain from acts that jeopardise human security, but also to prevent and punish them.[106] States also have specific obligations in respect

---

[102] Terrorism against combatants would not be covered by either definition which requires that the civilian population be the object of the terror or the prohibited acts amounting to crime against humanity. See, e.g., ICC Statute definitions.

[103] Some have suggested that what is needed by way of a comprehensive definition is this definition of war crimes of terror, but applicable in time of peace, although this is, like other proposals, controversial. See website of the Terrorism Prevention Branch of the Office for Drug Control and Crime Prevention (http://undcp.org/terrorism_definitions.html) and concern expressed in Guzman, *Terrorism and Human Rights No. 1*, p. 191.

[104] *Corfu Channel (United Kingdom v. Albania), Merits, ICJ Reports 1949*, p. 22.

[105] See state responsibility in international law and obligations to refrain from force, discussed at Chapters 3 and 5.

[106] This is subject to the acts falling within the purview of human rights obligations: acts in other states generally do not, unless as a result of the exercise of the state's authority and control abroad (see controversy surrounding extra-territoriality, at Chapter 7,

of the repression of 'terrorism' as such.[107] These include, for state parties to them, the obligations arising out of the specific terrorism conventions discussed above. But obligations may also arise from, or be reflected in, UN resolutions, such as the far reaching Security Council resolutions post September 11.[108]

The importance of the existing, and proposed, terrorism conventions lies in the provision of a framework for the obligations regarding international cooperation,[109] ensuring, for example, that states are obliged to 'extradite or prosecute' persons suspected of the offences covered by them.[110] While the obligation to investigate and prosecute is not new or limited to these conventions,[111] they seek to facilitate the effective discharge of the cooperation obligation and to remove obstacles to extradition.[112] Particular 'modalities' of cooperation aimed at discharging the general obligation to cooperate, such as intelligence and evidence sharing, transfer of criminal proceedings, freezing and seizure of assets,

para. 7A.2.1. As noted above, terror within a state is not generally thought to be covered by the concept of 'international terrorism' for the purpose of the specific terrorism conventions, or the Draft Comprehensive Convention.

[107] As discussed below, the force of those obligations may be weakened or undermined by divergent interpretations of what is covered, and excluded, by the term.

[108] SC Res. 1368, above, note 61, stresses that 'those responsible for aiding, supporting or harbouring the perpetrators, organisers and sponsors of these acts will be held accountable'. Unlike SC Res. 1373 (2001), (above, note 1), this is not a binding Chapter VIII resolution, however. SC Res. 1373, at paras. 1 and 2, obliges states to adopt wide ranging measures including criminalisation, freezing of assets and denial of safe haven, as discussed at Chapter 3.1.2.

[109] Cooperation is discussed in more detail in Chapter 4, para. 4A.2 and the human rights issues raised are highlighted in Chapter 7, para. 7A.4.3.8.

[110] On the obligation to extradite or prosecute (*aut dedere aut judicare*) see also Chapter 4. The obligation as enshrined in, for example, the specific terrorism conventions is not absolute, and has been criticised for the lack of clarity as to whether a state is only obliged to extradite if it has first declined to submit the case for prosecution domestically. See 'International Terrorism: Challenges and Responses', Report from the International Bar Association's Task Force on International Terrorism, 2003, Chapter 7 (on file with author).

[111] The conventions are not unique in this sense and the duty to extradite or submit for prosecution crimes under international law, including war crimes and crimes against humanity, which would include serious cases of terrorism, and to cooperate with other states in respect of the same, is well established.

[112] The usual requirements of extradition law (such as in some cases the 'double criminality' requirement that offences must be prohibited in the requested state as well as in the state requesting extradition, or the 'political offences' exception), do not operate as a bar to extradition. Developments seeking to further remove obstacles to extradition, or to streamline the extradition process, have been initiated, or advanced with renewed impetus, post September 11, some with potentially troubling human rights implications. See Chapter 4, para. 4B.2.2 and para. 7A.8.

execution and recognition of foreign judgments, or indeed extradition provisions, such as 'conditional extradition,'[113] have been addressed selectively in particular treaties.[114] It has been suggested that if there is a gap that the potential Draft Comprehensive Convention might fill, it may not relate so much to the definition, but to the lack of a comprehensive framework for international cooperation, covering all such modalities, including clarifying the hitherto irregular, and at times confusing, rules regarding extradition.[115]

In conclusion, the focus on and overuse of the terrorism terminology may obscure the extent to which resort to terrorist tactics is already regulated by other areas of international law. As is often the case, the problem lies more with the poor enforcement of existing norms, including but going beyond specific terrorism norms, than with the lack of a generic definition. In this respect it is noted that the Security Council's call to states to ratify existing terrorism conventions appears to have borne some fruit although the crucial challenge in that respect remains implementation.[116] While a generic definition in a global convention, *if* it could be achieved and could garner near universal support, may serve the interests of legal certainty and the efficiency of inter-state cooperation, what is clear is that its absence does not mean a legal void or necessitate legal paralysis.

2.4 Conclusion

Given the outstanding differences of view on its key elements, it is difficult to sustain that international terrorism is, *per se*, a discrete and identifiable international legal norm. But, as discussed, the absence of a generic definition of terrorism leaves no gaping hole in the international legal order. Rather it would appear to be the case that what we commonly refer to as terrorism, although perhaps not defined as such, would most likely be prohibited by other international legal norms irrespective of the existence or absence of a generic definition of terrorism. In one view then, the lack of a definition of terrorism is just not that significant. As one commentator noted: 'Terrorism is a term without legal significance. It is merely a convenient way of alluding to activities, whether of states or individuals,

---

[113] Article 8(2), International Convention for the Suppression of Terrorist Bombings 1998.
[114] See IBA Task Force, 'International Terrorism', ch. 7.   [115] *Ibid.*
[116] Many of the existing specific conventions are already widely ratified, though not necessarily implemented. See Chapter 4, section B.

widely disapproved of and in which the methods used are either unlawful, or the targets protected or both.'[117]

On the other hand, there can be little doubting the political currency of the language of terrorism, particularly in the post September 11 world.[118] The stakes were raised considerably by Security Council Resolution 1373, which, in what has been described as a new 'legislative' role for the Security Council,[119] imposes binding obligations on states to take extensive counter-terrorist measures. These include criminalising 'terrorism' and support for it, imposing serious penalties, freezing assets and excluding 'terrorists' from asylum and refugee protection. Notably, however, 1373 establishes these broad-reaching obligations in respect of terrorism in general without providing a clear definition of the conduct towards which such measures should be directed, and, by contrast to earlier binding decisions taken by the Council, without limitation as to the situation or broad time frame in which it should apply.[120]

Imposing far-reaching obligations on the basis of an ambiguous concept may reap unfortunate consequences. First, it may generate uncertainty as to the precise nature of states' obligations towards the Council, and undermine those obligations. As was recently noted: 'without reaching an acceptable international definition of the term "terrorism" one can sign any declaration or agreement against terrorism without having to fulfil one's obligations as per the agreement. For every country participatory to the agreement will define the phenomenon of terrorism differently from every other country.'[121] Second, as discussed in Chapter 7, it raises fundamental concerns regarding the human rights implications of Resolution 1373, described by senior French law

---

[117] Higgins, 'General International Law'.

[118] See for example the State of the Union Speech by the United States' President, 20 September 2001: 'Either you are with us, or you are with the terrorists. From this day forward, any nation that continues to harbor or support terrorism will be regarded by the United States as a hostile Regime', available at http://www.whitehouse.gov/news/releases/2001/09/20010920-8.html.

[119] Orentlicher: see generally P. Szasz, 'Note and Comment: The Security Council starts Legislating', 96 AJIL 901, October 2002.

[120] While the September 11 attacks to which the resolution was responding would fall within any definition of terrorism, and of other crimes under international law, Resolution 1373 is not in any way limited to that situation.

[121] B. Ganor, 'Security Council Resolution 1269: What it Leaves Out', 25 October 1999, available at http://www.ict.org.il/articles/articledet.cfm?articleid=93. This reflection, made in relation to SC Res. 1269 (1999) (above, note 13), is equally applicable to subsequent Security Council resolutions addressing terrorism, particularly SC Res. 1373 (2001), above, note 1.

enforcement officials as having 'opened the universal hunting season on terrorism without defining it'.[122]

In conclusion, controversy surrounds the concept of terrorism in international law. Absent a clear and accessible meaning to be attributed to the term, and consensus around the same, its susceptibility to abuse renders it an unhelpful basis for a legal, rather than political, analysis of the September 11 events and the responses thereto. Subsequent chapters will therefore address those events and responses based on other norms of international law.

---

[122] Statement of Mr Jean-François Gayraud, Chief Commissioner of the French National Police, and of the French judge David Sénat, reported in Guzman, *Terrorism and Human Rights No. 2*, p. 26.

3

International responsibility and terrorism

The question of responsibility for the events of September 11 permeates the discussion of lawful responses to those events, and as to against whom any such response should be directed. Was a state responsible for the September 11 attacks? Can al-Qaeda, bin Laden or other individuals be considered responsible under international law? To what extent do the permissible responses to 9/11 depend on the answers to these questions?

As will be apparent from the chapters that follow, state responsibility is more relevant to some aspects of the framework of responses discussed in this book than to others. State responsibility is not generally relevant to the application of the criminal law framework, discussed in the following chapter, although as discussed there it may be relevant to whether specific crimes (notably war crimes and aggression) were committed in the course of the September 11 attacks. By contrast, as discussed in Chapter 5, it is a controversial question whether state responsibility for an armed attack is a prerequisite to justify the use of force in self defence, or at least to justify attacking that state itself.[1] Questions of 'state responsibility' are relevant, moreover, not only to the unfolding responses to 9/11 but, in turn, to the obligations of other states to react *to* those responses. In certain circumstances, the unlawful use of force, egregious violations of human rights and international humanitarian law (discussed at Chapters 5, 6 and 7 respectively), may trigger the right, or in exceptional circumstances the responsibility, of other states to take measures to end the wrong in question.

The first part of this chapter assesses the responsibility of states in the light of the rules on international responsibility. It considers the basis on

---

[1] First, as discussed at Chapter 5, on one view, self defence under Article 51 of the UN Charter only arises in response to attacks by states, although this view is increasingly controversial. Second, measures involving the use of force in self defence must be 'necessary' to avert an attack, suggesting that for such measures to be directed against the organs of a state, that state must exercise a degree of control over the attack in question.

which acts such as those that took place on September 11, perpetrated by private individuals or organisations, may be attributed to a state such that the state incurs legal responsibility for those acts. The second part considers the consequences, under international law, of such state responsibility and refers to the circumstances in which other states may, or must, react. The final section considers the extent to which so-called 'non-state actors' – private individuals, organisations or entities, such as bin Laden and al-Qaeda – may themselves incur 'responsibility' under international law.

3.1 State responsibility in international law

3.1.1 Responsibility of a state for acts of terrorism

The international responsibility of a state arises from the commission of an internationally wrongful act, consisting of conduct that (a) is attributable to a state under international law and (b) constitutes a breach of an international obligation of the state.[2] As regards acts commonly referred to as 'terrorist', committed by individuals or groups not *formally* linked to the state, it is the first part of the test that is critical.[3] The key question in assessing state responsibility for acts such as 9/11 is therefore whether the standards for attribution, which derive principally from international jurisprudence, as recently set out in the International Law Commission's Articles on State Responsibility, have been met.

The question of attribution is relatively straightforward where conduct occurs at the hand of state officials or organs of the state,[4] or persons exercising elements of 'governmental authority' in accordance with national law.[5] In respect of such persons, states are directly responsible for their conduct which amounts to an 'act of state'.[6] This is so even if the official exceeded or acted outside his or her authority.[7]

---

[2] Article 2 of the Articles on Responsibility of States for Internationally Wrongful Acts, adopted by the International Law Commission in 2001. See *Report of the ILC on the work of its 53rd session*, UN Doc. A/56/10 (2001), Chapter IV, pp. 59–365. The text of the ILC's Articles on State Responsibility and of the ILC Commentaries thereto are also reproduced in J. Crawford, *The International Law Commission's Articles on State Responsibility: Introduction, Text and Commentaries* (Cambridge, 2002).

[3] If the events of September 11 could be attributable to the state, this second prong of the test would clearly be satisfied as violence against another state would violate the rules on the use of force, set out at Chapter 5.

[4] Article 4, ILC's Articles on State Responsibility.

[5] Article 5, ILC's Articles on State Responsibility.   [6] *Ibid.*

[7] Article 7, ILC's Articles on State Responsibility.

Somewhat more controversial is the question of the standard for attribution where those directly responsible for conduct are private individuals or groups with no formal relationship with the state. As 'a transparent relationship between terrorist actors and the state is predictably uncommon',[8] this is the critical question for assessing state responsibility for acts of 'terrorism'. The law governing the standard by which states may be legally responsible although not formally linked to perpetrators is described below.[9] As explained, on the one hand, it is well established that states are not strictly responsible for wrongs orchestrated on or emanating from their territory.[10] On the other, states are responsible for conduct over which they exercised effective control.[11] Controversy and uncertainty arises (heightened post 9/11) as to whether lesser forms of involvement, such as support, 'harbouring', encouragement or even passive acquiescence in wrongs is sufficient to render the acts of criminal organisations attributable to the state.

3.1.1.1 Effective or overall control

International jurisprudence and the work of the International Law Commission support the view that the acts of private individuals may be attributed to a state which exercises sufficient control over the conduct in question. According to the International Court of Justice in the *Nicaragua* case, the test is whether the state or states in question exercised 'effective control'.[12] Although the Court found the US to have helped finance, organise, equip, and train the Nicaraguan Contras, this was not sufficient to render the Contras' activities attributable to the US. Such a level of support and assistance did not 'warrant the conclusion that these forces [were] subject to the United States to such an extent that any acts they have committed are imputable to that State'.[13] The United States was found

---

[8] See S. Schiedeman, 'Standards of Proof in Forcible Responses to Terrorism', 50 (2000) *Syracuse Law Review* 249.

[9] As responsibility turns on a complex evaluation of the facts, the sort of fact scenarios in which the test has been deemed satisfied, and when not, are also noted below.

[10] See below, para. 1.1.3. See also *Oppenheim's International Law*, pp. 502–3, noting that 'it is in practice impossible for a state to prevent all injurious acts that a person might commit against a foreign state . . . accordingly . . . state responsibility for acts of private individuals is limited'.

[11] *Oppenheim's International Law*, p. 501, refers to 'vicarious responsibility' though this has been questioned, see I. Brownlie, *Principles of Public International Law*, 6th ed. (Oxford, 2003), pp. 431ff.

[12] *Military and Paramilitary Activities in and against Nicaragua (Nicaragua v. United States of America)*, Merits, ICJ Reports 1986, p. 14 (hereinafter '*Nicaragua* case'), paras. 86–93.

[13] *Ibid.*

liable for specific activities which were proved to be the result of direct action on the part of its military or foreign nationals in its pay. Despite controversy surrounding this decision, generated by those who consider it to impose too rigorous a threshold for establishing responsibility,[14] the *Nicaragua* 'effective control' test remains authoritative. It demonstrates that attribution must be established *vis-à-vis* particular conduct (rather than over the group's actions more generally),[15] and that the threshold for attribution is high.[16]

The jurisprudence of the *Nicaragua* case has been developed by the ICTY.[17] Reflecting *Nicaragua*, the Trial Chamber in the *Tadic* case noted that the relationship between the groups and the state must be more than one of 'great dependency', amounting instead to 'a relationship of control'.[18] The Appeals Chamber, while endorsing this, found that different tests applied in respect of private individuals who are not militarily organised and paramilitary or similar groups.[19] In respect of the latter the test was whether the state exercised 'overall control' over the activities of the group,[20] rather than effective control of particular conduct. The Tribunal again reflected the *Nicaragua* judgment by emphasising that the 'mere provision of financial assistance or military equipment or training' was insufficient, requiring instead that the state have 'a role in organising, coordinating or planning the military actions'.[21]

Moreover, the ICTY noted that where the 'controlling State' is not the state where the armed clashes occur, as is the case with Afghanistan in respect of acts of al-Qaeda in the United States, 'more extensive and

---

[14] See dissenting judgments (of Judges Jennings and Schwebel) in *Nicaragua* which considered that 'substantial involvement' in the form of financial or military assistance could suffice, and the discussion of the case in G.M. Travalio, 'Terrorism, International Law and the Use of Military Force', 18 (2000) *Wisconsin International Law Journal* 145 at 265.

[15] See also ILC's Commentary to Article 8(3), confirming that state responsibility under the ILC's Articles was considered to arise in relation to particular conduct.

[16] See *Nicaragua* case, paras. 86–93. *Nicaragua* demonstrated also the evidentiary difficulty of proving state responsibility for acts of non-state actors.

[17] See *Prosecutor v. Tadic*, Case No. IT-94-1-A, Judgment (Appeals Chamber), 15 July 1999 (hereinafter '*Tadic* Appeal Judgment'). The question was whether the acts of the VRS (Bosnian Serb forces) could be imputed to the Government of the Federal Republic of Yugoslavia (Serbia and Montenegro), such that an international conflict had arisen between that state and Bosnia-Herzegovina. Note that the question arose for the purpose of determining individual responsibility for IHL violations, whereas *Nicaragua* addressed state responsibility directly.

[18] *Tadic* Appeal Judgment.

[19] For acts of individuals to be attributed to the state generally requires 'specific instructions', or they may be 'publicly endorsed or approved *ex post facto* by the State at issue'. See *Tadic* Appeal Judgment, para. 137.

[20] *Ibid.*   [21] *Ibid.*

compelling evidence is required to show that the state is genuinely in control of the units or groups, not merely by financing and equipping them, but also by generally directing or helping plan their actions'.[22]

The ILC's Articles in turn confirm the high threshold for attributing acts of private individuals to the state, providing that such acts may be attributed to the state if the person is acting on 'instructions' of the state, or under the state's 'direction or control'.[23]

In conclusion, while formulae vary slightly, it is well established that the question is ultimately one of 'control'. It is a question of degree (and an issue of fact to be established by those alleging responsibility) 'whether the individuals concerned were sufficiently closely associated with the state for their acts to be regarded as acts of the state rather than as acts of private individuals'.[24]

3.1.1.2 *Ex post facto* assumption of responsibility

Where the state does not exercise the necessary control at the time of the conduct in question, it may nonetheless assume responsibility for the wrong *ex post facto*, where it subsequently 'acknowledges or accepts' the conduct as its own.

In the *Tehran Hostages* case, the ICJ held that while the 'direct' responsibility of Iran for the original takeover of the US Embassy in Tehran in 1979 was not proved,[25] subsequent statements in the face of incidents involving hostage taking by students created liability on the part of the state.[26] To the extent that the judgment indicates that the Iranian State was considered capable of putting a stop to an on-going situation and instead chose to endorse and to 'perpetuate' it, the Court's finding against Iran is consistent with the application of the 'effective control' test. But the judgment also makes clear that even if such a test were not met, the state may become responsible through its subsequent 'approval' or 'endorsement' of wrongful acts. This approach has been followed by the ICTY[27] and, as noted above, the ILC's Articles.[28]

---

[22] *Ibid.*, para. 138.   [23] Article 8, ILC's Articles.
[24] *Oppenheim's International Law*, p. 550.
[25] See *United States Diplomatic and Consular Staff in Teheran (United States v. Iran), ICJ Reports 1980*, p. 3 (hereinafter '*Teheran Hostages*' case). Note, however that the Court held that, during the first phase of the occupation of the American Embassy, the international responsibility of Iran arose from a breach of the different primary obligations of due diligence. See *ibid.*, pp. 31–3, paras. 63–8 and discussion of due diligence below, this chapter, para. 1.2.
[26] *Ibid.*, p. 35, para. 74.   [27] *Tadic* Appeal Judgment, para. 137.
[28] Article 11, ILC's Articles on State Responsibility.

It should be noted however that what is required goes beyond mere approval of the conduct of others, to a degree of endorsement whereby the state can be said to have identified the conduct 'as its own'.[29]

3.1.1.3 Insufficiency of territorial link

The rejection of strict liability for a state on whose territory crimes are orchestrated has been long established, since before *Nicaragua*. As the ICJ noted in 1949 in the *Corfu Channel* case, it is impossible to conclude 'from the mere fact of the control exercised by a state over its territory and waters that that State necessarily knew or ought to have known of any unlawful act perpetrated therein nor that it should have known the authors'.[30] It would, moreover, be anomalous to suggest a strict liability test in the context of 9/11, potentially implicating the responsibility of the US, Germany or others in respect of those who trained and organised on their territories. Likewise, simple knowledge of suspected terrorist activities, which could potentially implicate many states, would clearly not itself be enough.

3.1.1.4 A grey area? Harbouring terrorists post 9/11

States are not then strictly responsible for international wrongs emanating from their territory but they are responsible for acts of individuals or groups over whom they exercise 'effective control', or where they subsequently endorse the conduct as their own. Before September 11 it had been suggested that there was also a difficult 'grey area',[31] wherein 'the issue becomes more difficult when a state, which has the ability to control terrorist activity, nonetheless tolerates, and even encourages it'.[32] Post September 11, this grey area has become both increasingly significant and increasingly murky.

Immediately following the events of September 11, the US President asserted that in the search for those 'responsible', no distinction would

---

[29] See the ILC's Commentary to Article 11: 'as a general matter, conduct will not be attributable to a State under Article 11 where a State merely acknowledges or expresses its verbal approval of it'.

[30] *Corfu Channel (United Kingdom* v. *Albania), Merits, ICJ Reports 1949*, p. 4.

[31] See A. Cassese, 'The International Community's "Legal" Response to Terrorism', 38 (1989) ICLQ 589 at 599. Cassese sets out six levels of involvement that a state may have in terrorist activity. The three grey areas in the middle involve the supply of financial aid or weapons, logistical or other support and acquiescence, respectively.

[32] Travalio, 'Terrorism', at 154.

be made 'between the terrorists . . . and those who harbor them'.[33] The harbouring and support language has reappeared elsewhere, including in international statements and national laws.[34] The case against Afghanistan, so far as made out by the US, amounted to the September 11 attacks having been 'made possible by the decision of the Taleban regime to allow the parts of Afghanistan that it controls to be used by this organization as a base of operation'.[35] Alternative formulations as to the link between the Taleban and al-Qaeda have included allegations that the Taleban 'protected' the al-Qaeda network,[36] while broader statements have been made as to the need for accountability of those nations 'compromised by terror'[37] or 'allies of terror'.[38]

On 7 October 2001 the US and its allies launched military operations against Afghanistan in response to the events of 9/11, triggering questions as to state responsibility. The first is whether the legal standard for

---

[33] See 'Statement by the President in his Address to the Nation', 11 September 2001, at http://www.whitehouse.gov/news/releases/2001/09/20010911-16.html: 'I've directed the full resources of our intelligence and law enforcement communities to find those responsible and to bring them to justice. We will make no distinction between the terrorists who committed these acts and those who harbor them.'

[34] For an example of this language being advanced to criminalise conduct under domestic law, on the basis of obligations under SC Res. 1373 (2001), 28 September 2001, UN Doc. S/RES/1373 (2001), see the Anti-Terrorism Act 2001 (Bill C-36), entered into force on 24 December 2001 and I. Cotler, 'Does the Anti-Terror Bill go too far?' *Globe and Mail*, 20 November 2001, A17. Section 83.23 of the bill provides: 'Every one who knowingly harbours or conceals any person whom he or she knows to be a person who has carried out or is likely to carry out a terrorist activity, for the purpose of enabling the person to facilitate or carry out any terrorist activity, is guilty of an indictable offence and liable to imprisonment for a term not exceeding ten years.'

[35] 'Letter dated 7 October 2001 from the Permanent Representative of the United States of America to the United Nations addressed to the President of the Security Council', 7 October 2001, UN Doc. S/2001/946, at http://www.un.int/usa/s-2001-946.htm.

[36] Statement by NATO Secretary-General Lord Robertson, 2 October 2001, at http://www.nato.int/docu/speech/2001/s011002a.htm: 'We know that the individuals who carried out these attacks were part of the worldwide terrorist network of Al-Quaida, headed by Osama bin Laden and his key lieutenants and *protected* by the Taleban. On the basis of this briefing, it has now been determined that the attack against the United States on 11 September was directed from *abroad* and shall therefore be regarded as an action covered by Article 5 of the Washington Treaty, which states that an armed attack on one or more of the Allies in Europe or North America shall be considered an attack against them all.'

[37] 'National Security Strategy of the United States', September 2002, at http://www.whitehouse.gov/nsc/nss.pdf (hereinafter 'US National Security Strategy').

[38] The 'allies of terror are equally guilty of murder and equally accountable to justice', Press Release, 'President Bush Speaks to UN', 10 November 2001, at www.whitehouse.gov/news, cited in D. Jinks, 'State Responsibility for Acts of Private Armed Groups', 4 (2003) *Chicago Journal of International Law* 83 at 85.

attributing the conduct of private 'terrorist' organisations to the state was met in relation to Afghanistan and the 9/11 attacks. Did the relationship between the Taleban and al-Qaeda surpass inter-dependency and reach the requisite control by the former over the latter?[39]

Whether the Taleban exercised the necessary control over al-Qaeda to be responsible for its conduct has been the subject of speculation,[40] with information emerging in the years following 9/11 – including from an official commission conducted in the United States – casting increasing doubt on the proposition.[41] The nature of the relationship is a question of fact. States involved in the military operations, while making numerous allegations of support for terrorists, did not seek to make the case, as to the exercise by the Taleban of effective or overall control of al-Qaeda.[42] Legal responsibility of Afghanistan was not asserted in terms by the states driving the Afghan prong of the 'war on terror', and was therefore not subject to the full debate and analysis that one might expect, given the severity of impending consequences for Afghanistan.

The second question that follows is whether, as some have suggested, the standard for the attribution of acts of private actors to states has changed as a result of the Afghan intervention and generally positive state responses thereto,[43] such that states that 'harbour and support' groups incur responsibility for their conduct 'independently of whether that State had overall control over the group'.[44]

---

[39] The test is effective control over specific conduct, or overall control over activities of the group, if it is militarily organised: see *Tadic* Appeal Judgment.

[40] Many commentators however deny the responsibility of Afghanistan for the September 11 attacks. See, e.g., Jinks, 'State Responsibility', 83, in particular at 93–9; M. Sassòli, 'State Responsibility for Violations of International Humanitarian Law', 84 (2002) IRRC 01.

[41] The findings of the National Commission on Terrorist Attacks Upon the United States released on 22 July 2004 (also known as the 9/11 Commission), which was created by the US Congress in November 2002 to examine and report on the facts and causes relating to the September 11 terrorist attacks, cast renewed doubt on the degree of control exercised by the Taleban over al-Qaeda, and report the opposition of senior government officials in the Taleban regime to the September 11 attacks. Less surprisingly, the reports reject any suggestion of a link between the September 11 attacks and Iraq. See 'Qaeda had targeted Congress and CIA, panel finds', *International Herald Tribune*, 17 June 2004. The reports of the Commission are available at http://www.9-11commission.gov.

[42] See C. Greenwood, 'International Law and the "War against Terrorism"', 78 (2002) *International Affairs* 301 at 311–12, noting that while the letters from the US and the UK to the Security Council accused Afghanistan of harbouring the terrorists, 'they stopped short of alleging that Afghanistan was, as a matter of international law, responsible for the attacks themselves.' See also discussion in Chapter 5, para. 5B.1.1.3.

[43] The extent of international support for the intervention is discussed in Chapter 5B.1.

[44] The consequences of such a shift would be wide-reaching, with many more states becoming legally responsible for terrorism. Particularly if the response thereto involves the use of force, this could seriously impact on international security. As has been noted, if applied,

This view appears to be based on the assumption that the decision to attack Afghanistan was premised on the attribution of al-Qaeda's actions to Afghanistan (according to a lower threshold than accepted previously, namely supporting or harbouring terrorists).[45] However, it is unclear to what extent the allegations levelled against the Taleban of harbouring and supporting terrorists amount to a legal (as opposed to political) claim at all.[46] To the extent they do, it is unclear whether the claim is that 9/11 was attributable to the state, as opposed to that providing support for terrorists itself constitutes an internationally wrongful act. It may well be that attribution was not considered a prerequisite to the lawfulness of the use of force in self-defence (or indeed that in certain quarters lawfulness was not considered an essential prerequisite for military action to proceed), rather than that the standards of attribution were considered to have been met.[47]

While the possibility that the law has shifted will fall to be considered over time, it is unclear at present whether a new standard for attribution has been proposed, still less accepted, sufficient to displace the established rules on attribution in international law.[48] Despite the post-9/11 muddying of legal waters, it appears likely that the high threshold of requiring that the state 'directs' or exercises 'effective control' over the conduct in question, and 'the traditional view . . . that state toleration or encouragement is an insufficient state connection' for attribution of responsibility, remain valid statements of the law.[49]

3.1.2 Responsibility for breach of obligations in the fight against terrorism

It should be noted that the fact that the acts of al-Qaeda may not have been attributable to Afghanistan (and the Taleban as *de facto* government

---

e.g., to United States interventions abroad, such as support for the Northern Alliance in Afghanistan and Contras in Nicaragua, this standard would also render the US liable for the actions of those groups. See Jinks, 'State Responsibility', 83 at 92.

[45] Sassòli, 'State Responsibility', at 409; Jinks, 'State Responsibility', 83 at 85–8.

[46] See, e.g., statements regarding the accountability of the 'allies of terror' and 'nations compromised by terror', reported above, notes 37 and 38 and corresponding text, alongside statements as to states that harbour or support terrorists. The supposed legal import of these phrases is often unclear.

[47] See Chapter 5, para. 5B.2.1.1 on dispute over whether state responsibility is necessary for armed attack. As discussed below, it may also be that the state is instead accused of falling foul of obligations in respect of terrorism which do not however give rise to attribution.

[48] In assessing whether new rules have emerged post 9/11 caution is warranted. As discussed elsewhere, this question should be viewed in the context of subsequent developments.

[49] R.J. Erickson, *Legitimate Use of Military Force Against State-sponsored International Terrorism* (Maxwell Air Force Base, 1989), cited in Travalio, 'Terrorism', at fn.12.

thereof) does not however mean that the latter did not breach international obligations and incur international responsibility in respect of its relationship with the al-Qaeda network.

States have obligations to take a range of measures in respect of terrorism, which existed before 9/11 but have been supplemented and strengthened since. The Security Council has obliged all states, *inter alia*, to 'refrain from providing support, active or passive', 'deny safe haven' to persons involved in terrorism,[50] 'freeze without delay terrorist assets' and cooperate fully with other states in criminal matters, stressing that 'those responsible for aiding, supporting or harbouring the perpetrators, organisers and sponsors of these acts will be held accountable'.[51]

If it can be established that a state has 'harboured or supported' terrorist groups, this may represent a breach of the obligations of the state, for example the longstanding obligation not to allow international terrorist groups to operate on its territory.[52] A critical distinction exists, however, between a state being responsible for failing to meet its obligations *vis-à-vis* terrorism on its territory, and the acts of terrorists being 'attributable' or 'imputable' to the state, such that the state itself becomes responsible for the terrorists' wrongs.[53] Not only is the latter a very different international

---

[50] See SC Res. 1373 (2001), above, note 34, para. 2. This resolution also reaffirms the 'duty to refrain from organizing, instigation, assisting, or participating in terrorist acts in any state or acquiescing in organized activities within its territory directed towards the commission of such acts'. The Preamble 'decides' that states will, *inter alia*, criminalise certain forms of assistance, 'freeze without delay funds and other financial assets (para. 1); and obliges states to 'early warning to other states and cooperation in criminal matters' (para. 2).

[51] SC Res. 1368 (2001), 12 September 2001, UN Doc. S/RES/1368 (2001). The harbouring and support language goes further than earlier UN language (see GA Res. 2625, fn 52 below).

[52] See 'Declaration on Principles of International Law concerning Friendly Relations and Cooperation among States in Accordance with the Charter of the United Nations', GA Res. 2625 (XXV), adopted by consensus on 24 October 1970, Principle 1 (indent 9): 'Every State has the duty to refrain from organizing, instigating, assisting or participating in acts of civil strife or terrorist acts in another State or acquiescing in organized activities within its territory directed towards the commission of such acts when the acts referred to in the present paragraph involve a threat or use of force.' The Declaration, adopted by consensus, may be considered an act of authentic interpretation of the Charter, restating 'basic principles of international law' (*ibid.*, para. 2). See also the *Corfu Channel Case (United Kingdom v. Albania), Merits, ICJ Reports 1949*, p. 22.

[53] Similarly, in *Nicaragua* for example, whilst the ICJ determined that the acts of Contras were not attributable to the United States this did not 'suffice to resolve the entire question of the responsibility incurred by the United States through its assistance to the contras', *Nicaragua* case, paras. 110 and 115.

wrong, it may have very different consequences in legal and political terms.[54]

As noted above, to establish state responsibility for acts of terrorism the critical issue is often not whether a wrong has occurred but whether the test for attribution has been satisfied, such that the state is responsible for the wrong. By contrast, for breach of certain other obligations incumbent on a state relating to terrorism (for instance the obligation not to allow terrorists to operate from a state's territory or to freeze funds of terrorist organisations), the problem may rather be one of proving that a breach has occurred.

In part this is because these obligations do not give rise to strict liability but rather embody a 'due diligence' test requiring reasonable measures of prevention.[55] If, for instance, the state did not know, and took the reasonable steps to ascertain whether terrorists were operating out of its territory, or whether an apparently innocent bank account held at a bank in its territory was in fact being used for money laundering by a terrorist group, there may be no breach of its obligations.

Notwithstanding the set of resolutions adopted by the Security Council after 9/11 and the extensive corpus of treaty law on the subject,[56] considerable doubt remains as to the content of customary rules defining the obligations of states in the fight against international terrorism. At present, the uncertainty around the nature and limits of certain 'obligations' – for example, those general obligations relating to 'terrorism' despite the lack of common understanding of its scope as discussed at Chapter 2 – is compounded by relative uncertainty surrounding the meaning to be attributed, for instance, to the concept of 'harbouring and supporting'

---

[54] The state becomes responsible not for supporting terrorism but for the terrorist attacks themselves. On the consequences of such responsibility, see this chapter, para. 3.1.3 below.

[55] Under a 'due diligence' standard, it is the omission on the part of the state, not the injurious act by the private actor, which constitutes the internationally wrongful act for which the state may be responsible. There is no single, agreed-upon definition of 'due diligence'. As a commentator suggests, the obligation of due diligence '. . . consists [in taking] the reasonable measures of prevention that a well-administered government could be expected to exercise under similar circumstances.' D. Shelton, 'Private Violence, Public Wrongs, and the Responsibility of States', 13 (1990) Fordham International Law Journal 1 at 21–2. See, further, R. Pisillo Mazzeschi, 'The 'Due Diligence Rule' and the Nature of International Responsibility of States', 35 (1992) GYIL, 9; P.-M. Dupuy, 'Due Diligence in the International Law of State Responsibility', in Legal Aspects of Transfrontier Pollution (Paris, 1977), p. 369.

[56] For a discussion of the regional and global conventions dealing with international terrorism, see Chapter 2, para. 2.1 above.

terrorism.[57] Such ambiguity runs the risk of creating increased vulnerability for states, while seriously undermining the force of any such obligations.

3.1.3 Consequences of international responsibility for acts of terrorism or for breach of obligations relating to the fight against terrorism

Legal consequences flow from state responsibility for an internationally wrongful act.[58] The extent to which practical consequences also ensue depends, at least in considerable degree, on the question of enforcement, the Achilles heel of the international legal system.

Upon the commission of an internationally wrongful act, certain 'secondary' obligations arise under international law.[59] If a state is responsible for an internationally wrongful act it is obliged to cease the act (if it is ongoing), offer assurances of non-repetition and make full reparation for material or moral injury suffered.[60] If the state responsible for the internationally wrongful act denies cessation of the wrongful act or refuses to comply with its secondary obligation to make full reparation, the injured state for its part may take 'countermeasures' against the responsible state to induce it to comply with these obligations.[61]

In practice, the breach of an international obligation by a state may trigger various responses. States will often resort to diplomacy to persuade states to desist from or cease internationally wrongful conducts. In addition, they may take lawful but 'unfriendly' acts, which may include, for example the breaking of diplomatic relations, limitations on trade with the wrongdoing state or the withdrawal of voluntary aid programmes. Resort to the International Court of Justice[62] or to the organs of the United

---

[57] The concept appears to import a degree of intentionality, but it is unclear, for example, whether weak states would also be deemed to harbour terrorist groups if they prove unable to control their activity within its territory.

[58] See generally, Part II, ILC's Articles on State Responsibility.

[59] The commission of an internationally wrongful act is a breach of a 'primary' obligation. The obligations that flow are 'secondary' obligations. On the distinction between 'primary' and 'secondary' rules, see J. Combacau and D. Alland, '"Primary" and "Secondary" Rules in the Law of State Responsibility: Categorizing International Obligations', 16 (1985) NYIL 81.

[60] Articles 30 and 31, ILC's Articles on State Responsibility.

[61] Article 49, ILC's Articles on State Responsibility.

[62] See generally C. Gray, *Judicial Remedies in International Law* (Oxford, 1987).

Nations to determine breaches or enforce obligations,[63] can represent a means to induce the responsible state to comply with the obligations arising from the breach.

Such measures, which are clearly permissible, are distinct from countermeasures, however, which are measures that would normally be unlawful, but for the fact that they are taken in response to an internationally wrongful act.[64] Countermeasures may consist, for example, in the suspension of the performance of trade agreements in force between the injured state and the offending state,[65] in the suspension of air services agreements or in the freezing of the assets of the offending state or its nationals by the injured state.

Countermeasures are however subject to limits: they must, as far as possible, be reversible, they can only target the responsible state,[66] they must not be disproportionate to the injury caused by the internationally wrongful act,[67] and they cannot involve the violation of fundamental human rights, humanitarian law or peremptory norms of international law.[68] Given these limits, the lawfulness of certain countermeasures commonly resorted to by states, such as economic sanctions, is controversial: while some would argue that economic sanctions constitute lawful countermeasures, others would question their compatibility with 'obligations for the protection of fundamental human rights'.[69] As the General Comment

---

[63] In practice the General Assembly or Security Council may determine a breach, although the Council has a unique role in determining the existence of acts of aggression under the Charter, and is uniquely empowered to authorise the use of force in response to a threat to international peace and security, as discussed at Chapter 5, para. 5.2.2.

[64] See ILC's Introductory Commentary to Part Three, Chapter II, para. 1, defining countermeasures as 'measures which would be contrary to the international obligations of the injured State *vis-à-vis* the responsible State if they were not taken by the former in response to an internationally wrongful act by the latter in order to procure cessation and reparation'.

[65] See, e.g., the collective measures adopted in 1982 by EC states, New Zealand, Australia and Canada against Argentina during the Falklands war. Those measures consisted, *inter alia*, in a temporary prohibition on all imports of Argentine goods (a course of conduct prohibited under Article XII(1) of the General Agreement on Tariffs and Trade).

[66] Article 49, paras. 2 and 3, ILC's Articles on State Responsibility.

[67] Article 51, ILC's Articles on State Responsibility.

[68] Article 50, ILC's Articles on State Responsibility.

[69] Article 50(1)(a). However, sanctions under Chapter VII of the UN Charter can be, and often have been, imposed by the Security Council – such as those imposed on Iraq, Libya and Sudan for refusing to cooperate or to extradite suspected terrorists. While still controversial – note that the Security Council Committee on sanctions altered the Iraqi sanctions regime to lift the sanction on civilian goods amid great controversy that they had disastrous implications for civilians while not affecting the desired target – these raise different legal questions than the right of states to do so unilaterally. See D. Cortright and

of the Committee on Economic Social and Cultural Rights, and the ILC Commentary to the Articles, reflect, sanctions should, at a minimum, be conceived and enforced so as to 'take full account of the provisions of the International Covenant on Economic Social and Cultural Rights'.[70]

The use of force is not a permissible countermeasure.[71] However, the ILC's Articles do not affect the right of every state to act in self defence, nor to take measures authorised pursuant to a Security Council resolution under Chapter VII of the Charter.[72]

In general, it is the state which is directly injured by an internationally wrongful act that may invoke the responsibility of the wrong-doing state, although it is important to note that in certain circumstances other states may, or must, respond to the wrongful act. This arises in cases where 'the obligation breached is owed to a group of States . . . and is established for the protection of a collective interest of the group' or where 'the obligation breached is owed to the international community as a whole'.[73] At a minimum, non-directly injured states can ask for cessation of the wrongful conduct, for assurances of non-repetition and for performance of the obligation of reparation (in the interest of the injured state or of the beneficiaries of the obligation breached).[74]

Moreover, the ILC Articles make clear that if the internationally wrongful act amounts to a gross or systematic breach of obligations under peremptory norms – such as serious violations of human rights or of basic rules of IHL or the unlawful use of force – states are not only entitled, but may be obliged, to act together to end the breach.[75] This was confirmed by

G.A. Lopez, *The Sanctions Decade: Assessing UN Strategies in the 1990s* (London, 2000); M. Craven, 'Humanitarianism and the Quest for Smarter Sanctions', 13 (2002) EJIL 43; M.E. O'Connell, 'Debating the Law of Sanctions', 13 (2002) EJIL 63; K. Bennoune, '"Sovereignty vs. Suffering?" Re-Examining Sovereignty and Human Rights through the Lens of Iraq', 13 (2002) EJIL 243; J. Murphy, 'International Law and the War on Terrorism: the Road Ahead', 32 (2002) *Israel Yearbook on Human Rights* 117.

[70] Committee on Economic, Social and Cultural Rights, General Comment No. 8, 5 December 1997, UN Doc. E/C.12/1997/8, para. 1. See also ILC's Commentary to Article 50, para. 7.

[71] See Chapter 5. Article 50, para. 1(a), ILC's Articles on State Responsibility specifies that countermeasures shall not affect the 'obligation to refrain from the threat or use of force as embodied in the Charter of the United Nations'.

[72] *Ibid.* Article 59 recognises that the law of the UN Charter constitutes a *lex specialis* as regards the general rules set out in the Articles. Note also that Article 21 of the ILC's Articles on State Responsibility expressly states that '[t]he wrongfulness of an act of a State is precluded if the act constitutes a lawful measure of self-defence taken in conformity with the Charter of the United Nations'.

[73] The powers of the 'non-directly injured States' are more limited than those of the states directly injured by the breach.

[74] Article 48(2)(a) and (b).

[75] ILC Articles, Articles 40 and 41. The ILC's Commentary to Article 41 recognises that Article 41(1) 'may reflect the progressive development of international law' (para. 3). The

the ICJ in *The Wall* advisory opinion of 9 July 2004.[76] States' obligations to respond in the face of a breach by another state of '*erga omnes*' obligations – such as respecting the right to self-determination and certain core aspects of international humanitarian law – was described in the following terms:

> Given the character and the importance of the rights and obligations involved, the Court is of the view that all states are under an obligation not to recognise the illegal situation resulting from the construction of the wall in the Occupied Palestinian Territory, including in and around East Jerusalem. They are also under an obligation not to render aid or assistance in maintaining the situation created by such construction. It is also for all states, while respecting the United Nations Charter and international law, to see to it that any impediment, resulting from the construction of the wall, to the exercise by the Palestinian people of its right to self-determination is brought to an end.[77]

3.2 Responsibility of non-state actors in international law

Leaving aside state responsibility, does international law recognise the responsibility of those individuals and organisations believed to have been directly responsible for 9/11 or other acts of terrorism? This raises the troublesome issue of the responsibility of 'non-state actors' in international law.

The primordial rule of international law is that it is made by states, for states. As a basic governing principle, while states are the subjects of international law, 'non-state actors' are governed instead by national law. In respect of 'terrorists' and 'terrorist organisations' – which fall within the broad non-state actor category – the principal source of applicable law is national law. International law for its part focuses on ensuring that the state meets its obligation to provide a national legal system that effectively represses acts of terrorism, within the framework of the rule of law. In general then, international obligations, emanating from various branches and sources of international law, are directed towards states.[78]

ILC Articles also specify that states must not recognise or facilitate the situation that has given rise to the wrong.

[76] *Legal Consequences of the Construction of a Wall in the Occupied Palestinian Territory*, Advisory Opinion, 9 July 2004.

[77] *Ibid.*, para. 159.

[78] See Chapter 7 on human rights law obligations enshrined in treaty and customary law. On obligations in respect of the repression of terrorism specifically, contained in Security Council resolutions for example, see above this chapter, para. 3.1 and Chapter 2.

The sharpness of this dichotomy between states and non-state actors has however been eroded to a degree through developments in international law. The following highlights ways in which international law provides for the responsibility of non-state actors and signals the prospect of future legal development in this area.

3.2.1 Criminal law

The Nuremberg judgment famously reminded us that as crimes are committed by human beings not by 'abstract entities',[79] only by holding individuals to account could crimes be prevented. Since Nuremberg, it has been well established that non-state actors may be criminally responsible not only under national law but also under international law, as discussed at Chapter 4.

The responsibility of individuals for established crimes under international law – such as genocide, crimes against humanity and war crimes – arises irrespective of whether the perpetrator was a state official or a non-state actor. This is true of all crimes within the jurisdiction of the International Criminal Court for example,[80] and is made explicit in the definition of crimes against humanity, which must be committed pursuant to a 'state or organisational plan or policy'.[81] By contrast, aggression requires state involvement, though the individual accused may or may not be a state official.[82] As discussed, specific terrorism treaties generally cover only acts committed by non-state actors.[83] However, these treaties do not themselves impose responsibility directly on individuals, but on states, and the ability to hold the individual to account under them depends on incorporation into domestic law.[84]

---

[79] Judgment of the International Military Tribunal, in *The Trial of German Major War Criminals: Proceedings of the International Military Tribunal sitting at Nuremberg, Germany*, Part 22 (London, 1950), p. 447.

[80] That the crimes within the jurisdiction of the ICC may include those committed pursuant to a terrorist campaign is clear from the definitions of those crimes. See definitions of war crimes and crimes against humanity in, e.g., ICC Statute. On terrorism as other crimes, see Chapter 4, para. 4.1.1.

[81] ICC, Finalised draft text of the Elements of Crimes, PCNICC/2000/1/Add.2. The inclusion of the requirement of a 'plan or policy' is controversial – see Chapter 4, para. 4A.1.1.3. Genocide requires no link whatsoever to a state or organisation. War crimes must be committed in association with a conflict, but may be non-international armed conflict between a state and a rebel group or groups.

[82] See Chapter 4A.1.1.3.

[83] See Chapter 2, paras. 2.1.3 and 2.1.5, for a description of treaties. State acts are generally excluded from the definitions of terrorism.

[84] See Chapter 2 on the lack of a definition of terrorism and its dubious claim to status as a crime under treaty and customary law. See also Chapter 4, para. 4A.1.1.4.

While criminal law usually focuses on the individual responsibility of natural persons, Nuremberg also provides a precedent for holding legal persons – such as corporations, political parties or government departments – criminally liable. A similar proposal contemplated in the context of the ICC Statute was rejected, albeit for practical reasons related to the functioning of that court, rather than on principled legal grounds.[85] While it is conceivable that a criminal process could be launched against legal persons such as political parties or corporations involved in terrorism, this is unlikely to be true of loose networks such as al-Qaeda which would presumably lack legal personality in any legal system, national or international. Persons forming even loose networks for a criminal purpose may, however, be individually criminally responsible under forms of liability such as 'conspiracy', 'acting in common purpose', or 'joint criminal enterprise'.[86]

As such, the law and mechanisms of national and international criminal law ensure that non-state actors – individuals and to some degree other legal persons – have duties under international law, non-compliance with which may give rise to international accountability.[87]

3.2.2 International humanitarian law

International humanitarian law, perhaps more than any other area of international law, has long been familiar with applying legal rules to non-state entities.[88] Since 1949, specific rules have been in place governing the conduct of non-international armed conflicts, binding on both the state party to the conflict and armed groups.[89]

---

[85] See United Nations Diplomatic Conference of Plenipotentiaries on the establishment of an International Criminal Court, Rome, 15 June–17 July 1998, Working Group On Procedural Matters, Consideration of Part 6 of the draft Statute (UN Doc. A/CONF.183/2/Add.1 and Corr.1). K. Ambos, 'Article 25. Individual Criminal Responsibility', in O. Triffterer (ed.), *Commentary on the Rome Statute of the International Criminal Court* (Baden-Baden, 1999), p. 475 ff, at p. 478, suggests that the exclusion reflected concerns related to the Court's particular focus and evidence, as well as operational aspects of 'complementarity', given that corporate responsibility was not recognised in the criminal law of certain legal systems.

[86] See Chapter 4, para. 4A.1.2.1.

[87] The mechanisms for implementing international criminal law – from national courts exercising various bases of jurisdiction to *ad hoc* international courts or tribunals to the ICC – are discussed at Chapter 4, in particular at para. 4A.1.3.

[88] For a detailed set of materials see http://www.coleurop.be/collegium/Collegium27.pdf.

[89] This law is enshrined in Common Article 3 of the Geneva Conventions, Additional Protocol II (provided the state against whom the conflict is being conducted is a party to the Protocol and certain thresholds have been met) and rules of customary law. Common Article 3, incontrovertibly represents customary international law and consequently binds everyone,

As discussed in Chapter 6, IHL applies only where the 'armed conflict' threshold is met, as opposed to in 'situations of internal disturbances and tensions, such as riots, isolated and sporadic acts of violence and other acts of a similar nature'.[90] Most acts commonly referred to as 'terrorist' are precisely those that delegates sought to exclude from the definition of armed conflict. Moreover, as discussed at Chapter 6, section B, it is highly doubtful whether an entity such as al-Qaeda could constitute a party to a non-international armed conflict.[91] If however the conduct of a non-state entity, properly understood, *is* conduct carried out as a party to a non-international armed conflict, that party will be bound by the body of IHL applicable to such conflicts.[92] Among the prohibitions of IHL, as noted in Chapter 6, is a specific prohibition on spreading terror among the civilian population, although numerous acts commonly referred to as terrorism will fall within other categories of IHL violation for which the armed group may be responsible as a matter of international humanitarian law.

One of the weaknesses in the current system of IHL is however the lack of effective mechanisms for enforcing responsibility. As regards the state, human rights bodies provide one mechanism for reviewing IHL compliance, albeit indirectly, and diplomatic channels may prove particularly effective. For the non-state party diplomatic avenues are less readily available or effective and there is no meaningful mechanism for holding it to account as a party, except so far as serious violations of IHL amount to war crimes and international criminal law provides such mechanisms in respect of the individuals who comprise the group.

3.2.3 Human rights law?

The development of human rights law in the aftermath of the Second World War revolutionised international law by establishing the prime exception to the rule that states are the subjects of international law. However, at least as originally conceptualised, while individuals could

---

regardless of whether they have signed or ratified the Conventions, or whether they have standing to do so. The status of aspects of AP II as customary international law is less clear although a common core of IHL rules are applicable to any type of conflicts.

[90] AP II, Article 2.

[91] On these requirements, which relate principally to the definition or identification, and level of organisation, of the entity, see Chapter 6.

[92] See Chapter 6, in particular para. 6B.1.1.4. See also J.M. Henckaerts, 'Binding Armed Opposition Groups through Humanitarian Treaty Law and Customary Law', 27 (Spring 2003) *Collegium* 123, at http://www.coleurop.be/collegium/Collegium27.pdf.

possess rights, only states bore obligations under human rights law. Several developments in human rights law have sought to ensure that the general rule against non-state actor responsibility under human rights law does not represent a legal void, whereby rights can be violated with impunity.

Human rights bodies have adopted a progressive approach to the obligations of states to 'respect and ensure' the rights within the human rights conventions, interpreting them as obliging states to take measures to prevent violations and to provide redress for them – whether committed by state entities or non-state actors.[93] Therefore the conduct of non-state actors is regulated by human rights law indirectly, in that where 'private persons [violate rights] freely and with impunity'[94] the state itself becomes responsible under human rights law.

Moreover, the lack of *direct* responsibility of non-state actors under international law is increasingly open to question, particularly as entities such as transnational corporations, armed groups or indeed arguably terrorist organisations, assume powers and exercise authority traditionally within the exclusive sphere of state control, through which they do, in practice, violate human rights.[95] Arguably, support in principle for recognising the responsibility of non-state actors in human rights law can be found even in early human rights instruments. One commentator has noted for example that the long established (but non-binding) Universal Declaration of Human Rights, covers:

> [e]very individual includ[ing] juridical persons. Every individual and every organ of society excludes no one, no company, no market, no cyberspace. The Universal Declaration applies to them all.[96]

Subsequent regional developments in Africa and the Americas, unlike the traditional Western-European approach to human rights, reflect the notion of individuals and entities as not only holders of rights but

---

[93] See, e.g., the seminal case of *Velasquez Rodriguez* v. *Honduras*, Merits, Judgment of 29 July 1988, IACtHR, *Series C*, No. 4. See also the 'due diligence' test set down by the Human Rights Committee, General Comment No. 31: 'The Nature of the General Legal Obligation Imposed on States Parties to the Covenant' (Article 2) [2004], UN Doc. CCPR/C/74/CRP.4/Rev.6, para. 8. See discussion of positive human rights obligations in Chapter 7, para. 7A.4.1 below.

[94] *Velasquez Rodriguez* v. *Honduras*, para. 176.

[95] I.e. they commit acts which, if carried out by the state, would amount to rights violations.

[96] L. Henkin, 'The Universal Declaration at 50 and the Challenge of Global Markets', 25 (1999) *Brooklyn Journal of International Law*, 25 at 25.

bearers of responsibility.[97] The intensified focus on the realisation of economic social and cultural rights in recent years has contributed to the 'softening' of the position that only states are subject to international law.[98]

In addition, a number of specific developments may suggest that there are circumstances in which a non-state actor may currently find itself directly responsible under human rights law, and/or that further developments in this field are to be expected.

First, in exceptional circumstances, a non-state entity may exercise the functions of a state, and may, arguably, thus be deemed responsible as a state under international human rights law. If an entity such as a political party, corporation, or for that matter an unlawful organisation, assumes control over part of a territory of a state, it may be considered to have assumed the obligations that correspond to this *de facto* exercise of authority or control. As the Committee against Torture noted, factions [that] exercise certain prerogatives that are normally exercised by legitimate governments may be equated to state officials for the purposes of certain human rights obligations.[99]

Second, there are important on-going developments towards a broader recognition of direct responsibility of non-state actors, that may herald further innovations in this respect.[100] Perhaps most advanced are

---

[97] For example, the Preamble of the 1981 African Charter on Human and People's Rights '[c]onsid[ers] that the enjoyment of rights and freedoms also implies the performance of duties on the part of everyone'. The equivalent instrument for the Americas is the American Declaration on the Rights and Duties of Man. In its preamble it states 'Rights and duties are interrelated in every social and political activity of man. While rights exalt individual liberty, duties express the dignity of that liberty.' Note that human rights as a corollary of human duties does not equate with respect for rights being conditional on observance of duties.

[98] Report of the International Council on Human Rights Policy, 'Beyond Voluntarism: Human Rights and the Developing International Legal Obligations of Companies', 2002, p. 64, at http://www.ichrp.org/107/1.pdf. These developments are described as having 'plac[ed] some level of responsibility on private entities such as companies'.

[99] *Sadiq Shek Elmi* v. *Australia*, Communication No. 120/1998, UN Doc. CAT/C/22/ D/120/1998 (1999), para. 6.5. In respect of warring factions in Mogadishu, the Committee against Torture found that: '*de facto*, those factions exercise certain prerogatives that are comparable to those normally exercised by legitimate governments. Accordingly, the members of those factions can fall, for the purposes of the application of the Convention, within the phrase "public officials or other persons acting in an officials capicity" contained in article 1 [of the Convention against Torture]'.

[100] For a discussion of these developments see, A. Palmer, 'Community Redress and Multinational Enterprises', at http://www.field.org.uk/PDF/redress.pdf.

developments towards recognising the responsibility of transnational corporations, as 'hav[ing] the obligation to promote, secure the fulfillment of, respect, ensure respect of and protect human rights recognized in international as well as national law, including the rights and interests of indigenous peoples and other vulnerable groups'.[101] But recent practice indicates the use of the language of 'human rights' obligations as applicable to a wider range of non-state actors. This can be seen from condemnations of violence against women, including domestic violence, as a 'violation of the rights and fundamental freedoms of women'.[102]

A similar phenomenon is increasingly apparent in the context of an international debate, particularly since September 11, in which terrorism is frequently referred to as a violation of human rights. The Security Council for example has noted that 'acts methods and practices or terrorism . . . and . . . knowingly financing, planning and inciting terrorist acts are . . . contrary to the purposes and principles of the United Nations', perhaps highlighting recognition of a degree of non-state actor responsibility under the UN Charter.[103] Another example is the proposal denouncing the 'gross violations of human rights perpetrated by terrorist groups,' adopted at the UN Human Rights Commission.[104] However, the unsettled nature of the issue is clear from the fact that the United States and the EU opposed the proposal, on the basis that:

---

[101] Many of these have occurred on the national level, but they are also apparent through the UN Global Compact on Corporations and the work of the Commission on Human Rights for example. See 'Norms on the Responsibilities of Transnational Corporations and Other Business Enterprises with Regard to Human Rights' (UN Doc. E/CN.4/Sub.2/2003/12/Rev.2 (2003)), approved by the UN Sub-Committee on the Protection and Promotion of Human Rights in August 2003. The product of a long and in-depth study of relevant standards, Article 1 of the norms provides that '[w]ithin their respective spheres of activity and influence, transnational corporations and other business enterprises have the obligation to promote, secure the fulfillment of, respect, ensure respect of and protect human rights recognized in international as well as national law, including the rights and interests of indigenous peoples and other vulnerable groups'.

[102] See M.J. Dennis, 'Current Developments: The Fifty-Seventh Session of the UN Commission on Human Rights', 96 (2002) AJIL 181. Included within the definition of violence against women were non-state actions such as 'domestic violence, crimes committed in the name of honour, crimes committed in the name of passion, [and] traditional practices harmful to women, including female genital mutilation, and forced marriages'. At the Commission the Canadian text was adopted by consensus, with seventy-five co-sponsors.

[103] SC Res. 1373 (2001), above, note 34. The UN 'purposes and principles' include the protection of human rights and the maintenance of international peace and security. See Chapter 5A.1.

[104] See Dennis, 'Current Developments', at 183.

a clear distinction must be made between acts which are attributable to States, and criminal acts which are not, so as to avoid conferring on terrorists any status under international law.[105]

Finally, it is recalled that as human rights law is closely interlinked with international criminal law and IHL – with certain violations of human rights amounting to, for example, crimes against humanity, and humanitarian law obligations being interpreted in light of human rights law (and vice versa) – responsibility may arise in respect of human rights violations indirectly, through responsibility under criminal law or IHL.[106]

In conclusion, the question of the direct responsibility of non-state actors is a troublesome one, given the theoretical underpinnings of the international legal system as essentially inter-state, but also given issues of enforcement. One commentator recently noted that this leaves international law at a 'rhetorical disadvantage' in the struggle against terrorism.[107] It may be that the use of language apparently attributing human rights responsibility to non-state actors such as terrorist groups is no more than a rhetorical attempt to redress this perceived disadvantage, as opposed to indicative of a more substantive shift towards responsibility and accountability of non-state actors.

What is clear is that international law does speak to the responsibility of 'terrorists' and 'terror networks', including for acts such as 9/11, most notably through international criminal law. Beyond that, the general rule remains that individuals and groups are responsible under national law, subject to the exceptions outlined above. Provided there are effective functioning national systems, with states determined to counter terrorism within the framework of law, there is not so much a gap in the legal order, as different spheres of regulation. As such, it may be that strengthening national systems, through focusing on the obligations of

---

[105] *Ibid.* The US and EU noted however that states' 'fight against terrorism must be carried out in accordance with international human rights law'. At the 2002 meeting of the Commission, the resolution was adopted by a vote of 33-14-6.

[106] As W. A. Schabas, 'Punishment of Non-State Actors in Non-International Armed Conflict', 26 (2003) *Fordham International Law Journal* 907 at 932–3, notes: 'If human rights law has shown itself to be somewhat limited with respect to non-state actors precisely because it is focused on the obligations of the state towards individuals within its jurisdiction, this is not the case when it comes to individual responsibility for international crimes.'

[107] J. Fitzpatrick, 'Speaking Law to Power: The War Against Terrorism and Human Rights', 14 (2003) EJIL 241.

states under international law and their effective implementation[108] is the most effective way of promoting the protection of the individual from terrorist acts, but the discussion of the importance of responsibilities of non-state actors under international law will undoubtedly continue, impelled by 9/11 and the 'war on terror'. Whether the aforementioned developments, and indications of increased openness to the idea of non-state actor responsibility, eventually crystallise into legal obligations with mechanisms for enforcement remains to be seen.

3.3 Conclusion

A state is responsible for an act of terrorism by private actors where it exercises effective control over the act, or subsequently endorses it as its own. States may also be responsible for other internationally wrongful acts related to acts of terrorism, such as failing to take reasonable measures to prevent their territories being used by terrorists. As a matter of law, state responsibility has serious implications for the wrong doing state and, potentially, for the rights and obligations of other states.

Yet there has been little clarity as regards assessments of state responsibility for 9/11 and the significance thereof.[109] Was state responsibility for 9/11 alleged, and is it thought to matter? Was Afghanistan alleged to have been responsible for 9/11 or for a different wrong? What are the lawful consequences of its wrong-doing? Was its wrong-doing an essential prerequisite for the use of force against it? Or, further afield, as a matter of law what was alleged to be the relationship, if any, between Iraq and terrorist organisations? In practice, while little clarity has attended allegations of responsibility post 9/11, vague suggestions have emerged that the attacks on Afghanistan, and perhaps to some degree Iraq,[110] were justified at least

---

[108] See obligations in relation to terrorism, such as those enshrined in the 'specific conventions', set out at Chapter 2, para. 2.1.3, and the positive obligations in respect of human security under human rights law, set out at Chapter 7, para. 7A.4.1.

[109] Uncertainties as to the law include the issues related to 'terrorism' discussed in Chapter 2, and those relating to the status and content of different formulations relating to obligations in respect of terrorism, such as those relating to 'harbouring and support' highlighted above.

[110] On 31 January 2003, President Bush, asked about proof of 'Iraq's guilt', stated: 'Secretary Powell will make a strong case about the danger of an armed Saddam Hussein . . . He will also talk about al Qaeda links, links that really do portend a danger for America and for Great Britain, and anybody else who loves freedom' (see 'President Bush Meets with Prime Minister Blair. Remarks by the President and British Prime Minister Tony Blair', White House Press Release, at http://www.whitehouse.gov/news/releases/2003/01/20030131-23.html). Although the existence of a link between al-Qaeda and Iraq has not been

in some part due to the relationship between those states and terrorism. The dramatic consequences for those states may illustrate the importance of greater clarity in the future around the nature and scope of states' obligations in respect of terrorism, the consequences of breach thereof, and permissible responses on the part of other states.

Understanding responsibility for the September 11 attacks and other acts of international terrorism is an important process in itself. If the law is to be taken seriously, responsibility must have at least potential consequences for the wrong-doing state. Confusion as to whether there is responsibility, what the standard of attribution is, and whether it matters at all, therefore has broader, serious implications for international law enforcement.

Finally, it is recalled that state responsibility may result from wrongs committed through terrorism or counter-terrorism. The challenge to injured states – and to others that, as the above framework reflects, share responsibility to act in the face of serious wrongs[111] – is to ensure that international law is upheld and enforced against states involved in 'terrorism', or in unlawful responses thereto.

---

proven, the link between Iraq and Islamist terrorism is still presented as one of the justifications for the invasion of Iraq. On 8 September 2003, US National Security Advisor, Condoleezza Rice, during an interview on NBC argued that US involvement in Iraq represents a potentially mortal blow to terrorist forces and that a transformed Iraq 'is going to be the death knell for terrorism'. See G. Miller, 'Iraq–Terrorism Link Continues to Be Problematic', Los Angeles Times, 9 September 2003. On lack of evidence of any such link, see 9/11 Congressional Report, note 41 above.

[111] As discussed above, depending on the status of the norm infringed (i.e. on whether the norm is a 'peremptory norm of international law') and on the seriousness of the breach, the commission of an internationally wrongful act may give rise to an obligation of every state of the international community to react to the wrongful conduct. As will be seen, this is relevant to various aspects of the framework of international law relevant to responses to 9/11, from the use of force to violations of international humanitarian law and human rights law.

PART TWO

4

Criminal justice

'We will direct every resource at our command . . . every instrument of law
enforcement . . . to the disruption and defeat of the global terror network.'

(President Bush, September 2001)[1]

4A The legal framework

To the extent that the events of September 11 constitute crimes under
international – or relevant national – law, those responsible, directly or
indirectly, are susceptible to international and/or domestic investigation
and prosecution.[2] This chapter focuses on highlighting certain crimes
that may have been committed on September 11, the courts or tribunals
that have (or might be afforded) jurisdiction over them and the mechanisms that exist to implement and enforce criminal law internationally.
The criminal law paradigm is, however, relevant also to the responses to
September 11, so far as they constitute crimes under international law for
which individuals may be held to account.[3] As in the other chapters that

---

[1] US President George W. Bush, Address to a Joint Session of Congress and the American
People, 20 September 2001, available at http://www.whitehouse.gov/news/releases/2001/09/
20010920-8.html.

[2] Only individual criminal responsibility is addressed here. On state responsibility for internationally wrongful acts, see Chapter 3. On state responsibility for crimes, see *Oppenheim's
International Law*, pp. 534–5, which notes the uncertain stage of development of international law on state crimes, and that the legal consequences of state action being deemed
criminal are unclear, serving primarily to record the extreme seriousness with which the
international community regards certain conduct. See also J. Dugard, 'Criminal Responsibility of States', in Bassiouni (ed.), *International Criminal Law*, vol. I, 2nd ed. (New York,
1999), p. 239–53.

[3] On allegations of such crimes having been committed in Iraq, for example, see e.g., 'UN
rights chief warns of war crimes in Iraq', *International Herald Tribune*, 5 June 2004. See also
the various allegations of serious violations during the 'war on terror' that may amount
to international crimes, discussed at Chapters 6, 7 and 8. The criminal law framework has
emerged as pertinent also to transitional justice issues in the post conflict situations that
followed 9/11, most notably in relation to the trial of Saddam Hussein and others in Iraq.

follow, Section A sets out the legal framework while Section B considers questions relating to its application post 9/11.

While individual criminal responsibility under international law is not a new phenomenon,[4] in recent years a system of international justice, with national and international components, has crystallised from the experience of addressing atrocities on the domestic and international planes. The work of the *ad hoc* international criminal tribunals for the former Yugoslavia and Rwanda ('ICTY' and 'ICTR' or 'the *ad hoc* tribunals'),[5] the Special Court for Sierra Leone,[6] the adoption of the International Criminal Court Statute and supplementary documents[7] and innovations in domestic law[8] and practice[9] have been the principal contributors. As a

---

[4] In 1945, the Nuremberg Military Tribunal observed: 'That international law imposes duties and liabilities on individuals as well as upon states has long been recognised . . . crimes against international law are committed by men, not by abstract entities, and only by punishing individuals who commit such crimes can the provisions of international law be enforced' (Judgment of the International Military Tribunal, in *The Trial of German Major War Criminals: Proceedings of the International Military Tribunal sitting at Nuremberg, Germany*, Part 22 (London, 1950), p. 447).

[5] ICTY, established by SC Res. 827 (1993), 25 May 1993, UN Doc. S/RES/827 (1993); ICTR, established by SC Res. 955 (1994), 8 November 1994, UN Doc. S/RES/955 (1994). The jurisprudence of those tribunals has made a detailed contribution to the codification and development of law in this area.

[6] The Special Court is a hybrid national–international tribunal, set up jointly by the Government of Sierra Leone and the United Nations. See Agreement between the United Nations and the Government of Sierra Leone on the Establishment of a Special Court for Sierra Leone (Freetown, 16 January 2002) and the annexed Statute of the Special Court. Both documents and the judgments of the Court are available at http://www.sc-sl.org/index. html. See A. Tejan-Cole, 'The Special Court for Sierra Leone', 14.1 (2002) *INTERIGHTS Bulletin* 37. See also the so-called hybrid courts in East Timor and Cambodia. For commentary on these tribunals, see, e.g., Human Rights Watch, *World Report 2002*, at www.hrw.org/wr2k2/internationaljustice.html and at http://www.un.org/peace/etimor/etimor.htm.

[7] The ICC Statute provides more elaboration on crimes, legal principles and procedures than ever before on the international level; see Statute of the International Court, Rome, 17 July 1998, UN Doc. A/CONF.183/9 (hereinafter 'ICC Statute'); Report of the Preparatory Commission for the International Criminal Court, Addendum, Part I, Finalized draft text of the Rules of Procedure and Evidence ('Rules of Evidence and Procedure'), 2 November 2000, UN Doc. PCNICC/2000/1/Add.1; and Part II, Finalised draft text of the Elements of Crimes ('Elements document').

[8] Recent law reform efforts in national systems, impelled in large part by ratification of the ICC Statute (which, at the time of writing, stands at 92 states) have also contributed. For an illustration of the measures adopted by individual states for the implementation of the ICC Statute, see generally C. Kreß and F. Lattanzi (eds.), *The Rome Statute and Domestic Legal Orders: Volume 1* (Baden-Baden, 2000).

[9] The increasingly active role of national courts in the prosecution of international crimes can be seen from many investigations and prosecutions, based on territoriality or other

result, the international community is now armed with a substantial body of substantive and procedural international criminal law and a range of jurisdictional options to implement it.

The experience of, among others, the *ad hoc* tribunals demonstrates the viability of prosecutions involving complex criminal networks, including against those in the highest echelons of power, and in respect of massive crimes.[10] While the investigation of crimes such as those committed on September 11 poses undoubted challenges, given their scale and complexity, and the international mobility and comparative invisibility of the alleged terrorist operators, these characteristics are not entirely unprecedented. Just as national and international justice systems have, in the past, risen to the challenge of prosecuting apparently impenetrable networks engaged in organised crime and atrocities of a genocidal scale, while respecting international standards of justice, there can be little doubt that the same is achievable in relation to 9/11 and related offences.

forms of jurisdiction. See generally 14:1 (2002) *INTERIGHTS Bulletin*, No. 1 on 'National Prosecution, International Crimes'. Among the many recent instances of judicial activism of domestic courts in the prosecution of international crimes see, e.g., the 'Dergue' trials in Ethiopia against Mengistu Haile Mariam for genocide under Article 281 of the Ethiopian Penal Code of 1957 (see Amnesty International, *Annual Report 2001*, at http://web. amnesty.org/web/ar2001.nsf/home/home?opendocument; Guatemalan investigations of former head of state Rios Montt for genocide (http://www.eyetap.org/~rguerra/caldh-announce/); Argentine cases against members of the military dictatorship and developments elsewhere in Latin America (see V. Abramovich and M.J. Guembe, 'Challenging Amnesty Law in Argentina', 14.1 (2002) *INTERIGHTS Bulletin* 7; E. Lutz and K. Sikkink, 'International Human Rights Law in Practice. The Justice Cascade: The Evolution and Impact of Foreign Human Rights Trials in Latin America', 2 (2001) *Chicago Journal of International Law* 1; Belgian prosecutions of persons responsible for the Rwandan genocide under universal jurisdiction (see L. Reydams, 'Prosecuting Crimes Under International Law on the Basis of Universal Jurisdiction: The Experience of Belgium', in H. Fischer, C. Kreß and S.R. Lüder (eds.), *International and National Prosecution of Crimes Under International Law: Current Developments* (Berlin, 2001), pp. 799 ff.). These developments have contributed to the body of international criminal law.

[10] See, e.g., the ICTY judgment in the case of a high-ranking general, Kristic, in respect of the Srebrenica massacre and genocide in the former Yugoslavia (*Prosecutor* v. *Kristic*, Case No. IT-98-33-T, Judgment, 2 August 2001); and the judgment in the case of Kordic, one of the most influential politicians in central Bosnia (*Prosecutor* v. *Kordic and Cerkez*, Case No. IT-95-14/2, Judgment, 26 February 2001). A former member of the Presidency of the Republica Srpska, Biljana Plavsic was convicted in 2003 following a guilty plea (*Prosecutor* v. *Plavsic*, Case No. IT-00-39 & 40/1, Sentencing Judgment, 27 February 2003), while the trial of former President Milosevic (*Prosecutor* v. *Milosevic*, Case No. IT-02-54) and Krajnik are on-going. See also the ICTR judgment in the case of Kambanda, former Prime Minister of Rwanda, for genocide in that country (*Prosecutor* v. *Jean Kambanda*, Case No. ICTR-97-23, Judgment, 4 September 1998).

4A.1 Crimes, principles of criminal law and jurisdiction

4A.1.1 Crimes under international and national law

Crimes under international law are particularly serious violations of norms that are not only prohibited by international law but also entail individual criminal responsibility.[11] They can be based on customary law or a binding treaty. Customary law is binding on all states and, so far as criminal responsibility is concerned, on all individuals.[12] Among the sources that can be looked to for the purposes of identifying the content of customary law in this field are the jurisprudence of international *ad hoc* tribunals, the ICC Statute and supplementary documents[13] and national court practice.

Treaties by contrast are only binding on those states party to them.[14] Although treaties bind states, they may also, as in the case of treaties governing international criminal law, affect individuals. Although international tribunals usually prosecute for crimes considered prohibited by customary law, the ICTY has indicated that individuals may be convicted on the basis of treaty law.[15] The principles of legality and non-retroactivity

---

[11] Only certain serious violations of human rights and humanitarian law carry individual criminal responsibility. See the criteria for criminal responsibility for violations of humanitarian law listed by the ICTY in *Prosecutor* v. *Tadic,* Case No. IT-94-1-AR72, Decision on the Defence Motion for Interlocutory Appeal on Jurisdiction (Appeals Chamber), 2 October 1995 (hereinafter '*Tadic* Jurisdiction Appeal Decision'), paras. 94–5.

[12] Customary law is a general and consistent practice of states accompanied by a sense of legal obligation – often referred to as 'states and *opinio juris*'. See Article 38 of the Statute of the International Court of Justice.

[13] The ICC Statute entered into force on 1 July 2002. The ICC will not have jurisdiction to prosecute crimes committed before its entry into force (Article 11) and is not binding as treaty law in respect of the September 11 attacks. It may however be relevant to the prosecution of crimes committed by nationals of states party to it in the name of responding to 9/11, or to future terrorist attacks, as discussed in Chapter 4, para. 4B.1.2.2 below. Negotiated over more than five intense years by some 160 states, the Statute may also provide guidance on customary law, although some caution is warranted in this respect as the politicised negotiating process that gave rise to the Statute resulted in an instrument that is in several respects more restrictive than customary law. With this in mind the Statute itself notes, at Article 10, that 'nothing in this part shall be interpreted as limiting or prejudicing in any way existing or developing rules of international law for purposes other than this Statute'. It is relevant therefore to look to the Statute for an assessment of customary law, but also to other interpretive sources. See ICC Elements document and ICC Rules of Procedure, note 7 above.

[14] 'Treaty crimes' include terrorism and hijacking, see note 16 below.

[15] The Appeals Chamber of the ICTY has said that 'the International Tribunal is authorised to apply, in addition to customary international law, any treaty which: (i) was unquestionably binding on the parties at the time of the alleged offence; and (ii) was not in conflict with or derogating from peremptory norms of international law, as are most customary rules of international humanitarian law' (*Tadic* Jurisdiction Appeal Decision, paras. 94–5). The

require that the accused's conduct was clearly proscribed, under international or national law, at the time of its commission.[16]

This part of the chapter will focus first on crimes against humanity, which are prohibited under customary law (and which as a matter of international law all states may exercise jurisdiction over), of direct relevance to the attacks of September 11. Whether individuals responsible for September 11 might also be held to account for war crimes or aggression is less apparent, although these crimes will be considered as potentially relevant not only to 9/11 but to determining individual responsibility for wrongs committed in the context of the use of force and the armed conflicts that followed September 11. The chapter will then return to the question of 'terrorism' and its status as a crime under international law, discussed at Chapter 2, and conclude by reference to the obvious basis for criminal responsibility – the many domestic crimes committed on September 11. The chapter does not however purport to address the full range of national and international crimes that may have been committed on 9/11, still less in response thereto.[17]

4A.1.1.1 Crimes against humanity

'Crimes against humanity' consist of certain acts – such as murder, torture or inhumane acts – directed against the civilian population on a widespread or systematic basis. Although the first legal instrument referring to 'crimes against humanity' is the Nuremberg Charter of 1945, their prohibition in international law long predates the Second

ICTY recently affirmed that international criminal conviction may be based solely on the commission of treaty crimes, although, as demonstrated by the dissenting judgment in that case, the consistency of this view with the principle of legality in criminal law remains somewhat controversial. See *Prosecutor* v. *Galić*, Case No. IT-98-29-T, Judgment, 5 December 2003, paras. 97–105, where the Trial Chamber of the ICTY found the accused criminally responsible for the crime of inflicting terror on the civilian population under Article 51 AP I, and held that it was unnecessary to establish whether the crime was customary in nature; see dissenting judgment of Judge Nieto Navia on this point. Complex questions as to how treaties become 'binding' on individuals provided one of the reasons why treaty crimes were ultimately excluded from ICC jurisdiction. For the view that treaty law may be considered applicable to individuals only so far as the individual commits crimes on the territory of a state party to the treaty, see, e.g., A. Zimmerman, 'Crimes within the Jurisdiction of the Court', in O. Triffterer (ed.), *Commentary on the Rome Statute of the International Criminal Court* (Baden-Baden, 1999), pp. 98 ff.

[16] While jurisdiction over the crime can be conferred or established after the fact (see this chapter, para. 4A.1.3 below), *ex post facto* criminalisation would amount to a violation of the basic principle of legality – *nullum crimen sine lege* – enshrined in systems of criminal law and Article 15 of the ICCPR. See this chapter, para. 4A.1.2 below.

[17] On violations committed during the 'war on terror' that may carry individual criminal responsibility, such as war crimes and torture, see Chapters 6, 7 and 8.

World War.[18] It is now well established that crimes against humanity are crimes under customary international law, hence prohibited irrespective of the suspect's nationality or of national laws.[19]

Unlike many other international crimes, such as war crimes or specific forms of terrorism, this group of crimes has never been the subject of a binding convention to which reference can be made to determine their specific content. However, regard can be had to the ICC Statute, the first treaty to set out comprehensive definitions of these crimes[20] and to earlier international instruments,[21] as well as to the ample jurisprudence emanating from prosecutions for these crimes,[22] to identify key elements of the definition of crimes against humanity.

(a) **Murder and inhumane acts**   It is uncontroversial that murder and inhumane acts are among the acts that may amount to crimes against humanity under customary law.[23] Murder is a familiar term in domestic laws,[24] and has been held in an international context to consist of killing

---

[18] M. C. Bassiouni, 'Crimes against Humanity', in Bassiouni, *International Criminal Law*, pp. 522 ff. See also R. Dixon, 'Article 7. Crimes against Humanity', in Triffterer (ed.), *Commentary on the Rome Statute*, pp. 121 ff.

[19] *Ibid.* See also S.R. Ratner and J.S. Abrams, *Accountability for Human Rights Atrocities in International Law: Beyond the Nuremberg Legacy* (Oxford, 1998), pp. 140–1.

[20] Article 10 ICC Statute notes that the definitions of all ICC crimes are for the purposes of the Statute only.

[21] See, e.g., the ILC's Draft Code of Crimes against the Peace and Security of Mankind, Report of the ILC on the work of its 48th session, 6 May–26 July 1996, GAOR, 51st session, Supp. No. 10, 30, UN Doc. A/50/10, p. 97 (hereinafter 'ILC's Draft Code of Crimes').

[22] See, e.g., the judgment and the proceedings of the Nuremberg International Military Tribunal, published in *Trials of Major War Criminals before the International Military Tribunal*, 42 vols., (Nuremberg, 1946–50). For ICTY and ICTR judgments, see, e.g., *Prosecutor v. Furundija*, Case No. IT-95-17/1-T, Judgment, 10 December 1998; *Tadic* Jurisdiction Appeal Decision, paras. 248–52; *Prosecutor v. Blaskic*, Case No. IT-95-14-T, Judgment, 3 March 2000, para. 71; *Prosecutor v. Kunarac, Kovac and Vukovic*, Cases Nos. IT-96-23 and IT-96-23/1, Judgment, 22 February 2001; *Prosecutor v. Krnojelac*, Case No. IT-97-25-A, Judgment, 17 September 2003 (Appeals Chamber); *Prosecutor v. Stakic*, Case No. IT-97-24-T, Judgment, 31 July 2003; *Prosecutor v. Akayesu*, Case No. ICTR-96-4-T, Judgment, 2 September 1998, paras. 591–2; *Prosecutor v. Kayishema and Ruzindana*, Case No. ICTR-95-1-T, Judgment, 21 May 1999, paras. 141–7; *Prosecutor v. Musema*, Case No. ICTR 96-13-T, Judgment and Sentence, 27 January 2000, paras. 942–51. See also national prosecutions, e.g., *Attorney General of Israel v. Eichmann*, 36 ILR 277, 299, 304 (Israel Supreme Court, 1962) and in *re Demjanjuk*, 612 F. Supp. 544 9N. D. Ohio 1985, aff'd, 776 F2d 571 (6th Cir. 1985).

[23] For a full range of acts that may amount to crimes against humanity, including torture, enforced disappearance, persecution, see Article 7 ICC Statute, Article 5 ICTY Statute and Article 3 ICTR Statute (which enumerate fewer acts than the ICC).

[24] See Report of the ILC on the work of its 48th session, above, note 20, p. 96: 'Murder is a crime that is clearly understood and well-defined in the national law of every State'.

with 'an intention on the part of the accused to kill or inflict serious injury in reckless disregard of human life'.[25] 'Inhumane acts', a broad term found in various international instruments and domestic laws,[26] covers the infliction of severe bodily harm[27] and serious 'cruel treatment'.[28]

(b) Widespread or systematic   One of the distinguishing features of crimes against humanity is that they are widespread or systematic. While this threshold has not always been considered necessary,[29] developments have confirmed[30] and the vast majority of commentators accept,[31] that under current international law crimes against humanity must take place in the context of a widespread and systematic attack or campaign.[32]

[25] *Prosecutor* v. *Delalic et al.*, Case IT-96-21-T, Judgment, 16 November 1998, para. 439 and *Prosecutor* v. *Akayesu* (above, note 21), paras. 589–90.

[26] Inhuman(e) acts or treatment are referred to, for instance, in the four Geneva Conventions of 1949 (Article 50, GC I; Article 51, GC II; Article 130, GC III; Article 147, GC IV); in the 'International Convention on the Suppression and Punishment of the Crime of Apartheid', 30 November 1973, GA Res. 3068 (XXVIII); in the ICCPR (Article 7); in the ECHR (Article 4); in the Convention (No. 29) Concerning Forced Labour, adopted by the ILO on 28 June 1930, in the Slavery Convention of 25 September 1926; and in the ICC Statute (Article 7).

[27] Article 18(k) of the ILC's Draft Code of Crimes mentions severe bodily harm and mutilation.

[28] The ICTY has stated that: 'the notions of cruel treatment within the meaning of Article 3 and of inhuman treatment set out in Article 5 of the Statute have the same legal meaning' (*Prosecutor* v. *Jelisic*, Case No. IT-95-10, Judgment, 11 December 1998, para. 52). The Tribunal refers to international standards on human rights, such as the Universal Declaration on Human Rights of 1948 and the United Nations Covenants of 1966, to interpret 'other inhuman acts', in order 'to identify a set of basic rights appertaining to human beings, the infringement of which may amount, depending on the accompanying circumstances, to a crime against humanity' (*Prosecutor* v. *Kupreskic et al.*, Case No. IT-95-16, Judgment, 14 January 2000, para. 566).

[29] This requirement was not included in the Nuremberg Charter, or other post Second World War legal instruments that provided the basis for prosecution of crimes against humanity.

[30] The jurisprudence of the ICTY, the ICTR Statute, the ICC Statute and national laws implementing the Statute all confirm this requirement. The matter was uncontroversial at the ICC conference as noted by D. Robinson, 'Developments in International Criminal Law: Defining 'Crimes against Humanity' at the Rome Conference', 93 (1999) AJIL 43 at 47 and in ICTY and ICTR jurisprudence: see *Prosecutor* v. *Akayesu*, para. 579; *Prosecutor* v. *Kayishema and Ruzindana*, para. 123 and *Prosecutor* v. *Blaskic* (above, note 21), para. 202.

[31] While generally accepted, at least one commentator questions whether the existence of a widespread or systematic attack is in fact a *conditio sine qua non* for the general notion of the crime against humanity: see F. Lattanzi, 'Crimes against Humanity in the Jurisprudence of the International Criminal Tribunals for the Former Yugoslavia and Rwanda', in Fischer, Kreß and Lüder (eds.), *Prosecution of Crimes*, pp. 480 ff.

[32] It has been noted that the concept of 'attack' in relation to crimes against humanity (unlike in relation to the use of force, see Chapter 5, para. 5B.2.1.1 below) has no technical meaning and it has been suggested that another term such as 'campaign' could be substituted for the word 'attack'. See S. Boelaert-Suominen, 'Repression of War Crimes through International Tribunals', International Institute of Humanitarian Law, 77th Military Course (1999) (on

It should be noted that the conduct of the particular perpetrator need not be widespread or systematic. Even a single act by a perpetrator may constitute a crime against humanity, provided it forms part of a broader (widespread or systematic) attack or campaign.[33] Conversely, the acts in question may themselves constitute the widespread or systematic attack; there is no requirement of a separate or pre-existing attack.[34] The requirement that the occurrence of crimes be widespread or systematic is disjunctive;[35] while either would suffice, 'in practice, these two criteria will often be difficult to separate, since a widespread attack targeting a large number of victims generally relies on some form of planning or organisation'.[36]

There is no one source that identifies a precise definition of these terms under customary law, and the ICC 'Elements document', although providing detailed elements of the crimes, does not include a definition of the terms.[37] However, they have been considered and applied in numerous cases, particularly by the ICTY and ICTR. As formulations vary somewhat within the jurisprudence, perhaps reflecting in part the particular factual circumstances to which they were applied, the key aspects of that jurisprudence are set out below. What is clear is that both the concepts 'widespread' and 'systematic' are intended to import a considerable element of seriousness,[38] and to 'exclude isolated or random acts'.[39]

The 'widespread' requirement may be satisfied in a range of ways.[40] Most commonly, the term is understood to refer to the *scale* of the crime. An earlier formulation of this criterion referred to 'large scale' instead of

---

file with author). See, however, the more restrictive approach taken to the interpretation of 'attack' in the ICC context, below.

[33] *Prosecutor* v. *Mrskic, Radic and Sljivancanin*, Case No. IT-95-13-R61, Review of the Indictment Pursuant to Rule 61 of the Rules of Procedure and Evidence, 3 April 1996, para. 3; *Prosecutor* v. *Tadic*, Case No. IT-94-1, Judgment (Trial Chamber), 7 May 1997.

[34] Dixon, 'Article 7. Crimes Against Humanity', p. 124.

[35] The ICC Statute (Article 7) requires attacks to be widespread *or* systematic and attempts to introduce a conjunctive test were opposed by the Rome conference that drew up the ICC Statute. See Robinson, 'Developments in International Criminal Law', at 47. The ICTY jurisprudence is unequivocal on the point: see, e.g., the *Kordic, Kupreskic*, and *Blaskic* cases (above, notes 10, 21 and 29). The latter (para. 207) states that for 'inhumane acts to be characterised as crimes against humanity, it is sufficient that one of the conditions be met'.

[36] *Prosecutor* v. *Blaskic* (above, note 21), para. 207.

[37] Statute and annex on elements of crimes.

[38] See, e.g., the Secretary-General's report, UN doc. S/25704, para. 48 (cited in *Prosecutor* v. *Tadic*, para. 646, n. 141), that crimes against humanity cover 'inhumane acts of a very serious nature'.

[39] *Prosecutor* v. *Tadic*, para. 646. See also Dixon, 'Article 7. Crimes against Humanity', p. 123.

[40] See, e.g., the *Musema* and *Akayesu* cases of the ICTR (above, note 21), which refer to widespread as covering 'massive, frequent, large-scale action, carried out collectively with considerable seriousness and directed against a multiplicity of victims'.

'widespread', defining it as 'meaning that the acts are directed against a multiplicity of victims'.[41] Following this approach, the ICTY has stated that 'widespread . . . refers to the number of victims',[42] and has defined the term as meaning acts committed on a 'large scale' and 'directed at a multiplicity of victims'.[43] Consistent with this, the term as used in the ICC Statute has been described as follows: '[t]he term widespread requires large-scale action involving a substantial number of victims'.[44]

While scale will often involve a series of acts, it need not, as 'widespread' refers also to the *magnitude* of the crime. One single egregious act of sufficient scale or magnitude may suffice. As the ICTY noted, a crime may be 'widespread' by the 'cumulative effect of a series of inhumane acts or the singular effect of an inhumane act of extraordinary magnitude'.[45] The *ad hoc* tribunals' jurisprudence therefore also indicates that 'widespread' does not necessarily imply geographic spread. This is supported by a finding in one case that crimes against humanity had been committed against part of the civilian population of just one town.[46]

With regard to the requirement of 'systematicity', several cases have held that this can be satisfied by the repeated, continuous nature of the attack or campaign,[47] a 'pattern' in its execution[48] or the existence of an underlying plan or policy.[49] Consistent with this, it has been noted that the term 'systematic' in the ICC Statute 'requires a high degree of orchestration and methodical planning'.[50]

In one recent decision, the ICTY drew these factors together, noting that any of the following may provide evidence of a systematic attack: (1) the existence of a plan or political objective; (2) very large scale or repeated and continuous inhumane acts; (3) the degree of resources employed, military or other; (4) the implication of high-level authorities in the establishment of the methodical plan.[51]

---

[41] ILC's Commentaries to the Draft Code of Crimes, Commentary to Article 18(4).

[42] *Prosecutor* v. *Tadic*, para. 648.   [43] *Prosecutor* v. *Blaskic* (above, note 21), para. 206.

[44] Robinson, 'Developments in International Criminal Law', at 47.

[45] *Prosecutor* v. *Blaskic* (above, note 21), para. 206.

[46] In *Prosecutor* v. *Jelisic*, Case No. IT-95-10-T, Judgment (Trial Chamber), 14 December 1999, the ICTY convicted the accused of crimes against humanity that were committed as part of 'the attack by the Serbian forces against the non-Serbian population in Brko' (para. 57).

[47] *Prosecutor* v. *Tadic*, para. 648, citing the ILC's Draft Code of Crimes.

[48] *Prosecutor* v. *Akayesu* (above, note 21), para. 580.

[49] Report of the ILC on the work of its 45th session, 51 UNGAOR Supp. (No.10), p. 9, UN Doc. A/61/10 (1996).

[50] Robinson, 'Developments in International Criminal Law', at 67.

[51] *Prosecutor* v. *Kordic and Cerkez*, Case No. IT-95-14/2-T, Judgment, 26 February 2001, para. 179.

(c) Attack against the civilian population   The ICC Statute imposes a higher threshold than found elsewhere in international law, by requiring that (in addition to being either widespread or systematic) there be an 'attack' against the civilian population, involving a 'course of conduct' and 'multiple acts', carried out pursuant to a 'policy'.[52] In so doing, in practice the widespread or systematic test becomes less firmly disjunctive than it otherwise would be. As an innovation,[53] it is doubtful whether this definition would be considered customary international law, and as such it may not be essential for an assessment of whether the events of September 11 amount to crimes against humanity.[54] Notably, however, even according to this quite stringent definition of crimes against humanity, there is no requirement that the acts be attributable to a state, but rather that there be a 'state or organisational' policy to commit an attack.[55] The 'policy' need not be formalised and may be inferred from all the circumstances.[56]

Finally, it is well established that crimes against humanity, unlike war crimes, must be directed against the *civilian*, as opposed to a military, population.[57] Different considerations may therefore arise as between

---

[52] Subparagraph 2(a) of Article 7 of the ICC Statute defines 'attack' as 'attack directed against any civilian population' and as 'a course of conduct involving the multiple commission of acts referred to in paragraph 1 against any civilian population, pursuant to or in furtherance of a State or organizational policy to commit such attack'. This was introduced to satisfy certain states engaged in the ICC negotiating process (that wanted to see a conjunctive not a disjunctive standard). See Robinson, 'Developments in International Criminal Law', at 67.

[53] The term 'attack' is not used either in Article 5 of the ICTY Statute, nor in Article 6(c) of the Nuremberg Charter. Although the word appears in Article 3 of the ICTR Statute, only in Article 7 of the ICC Statute is it defined so as to raise the threshold in the manner explained in this paragraph.

[54] A recent ICTY judgment to address the issue, the *Kordic* judgment, does not follow the ICC definition but expressly rejects elements of that definition. Specifically, it takes the position that there is no 'policy' requirement for crimes against humanity, despite the ICC formulation set out below. See *Kordic* judgment (above, note 50), para. 182.

[55] Article 7, ICC Statute, above.

[56] See Report of the Preparatory Commission for the International Criminal Court, Addendum, Part II, Finalised draft text of the Elements of Crimes, 2 November 2000, PCNICC/2000/1/Add.2.

[57] The population must be 'predominantly', not exclusively, civilian. See, e.g., *Naletilic and Martinovic* (Trial Chamber), 31 March 2003, para. 235, and *Prosecutor v. Kupreskic et al.*, Case No. IT-95-16 (Trial Chamber), 14 January 2000, para. 549: '[T]he presence of those actively involved in the conflict should not prevent the characterization of a population as civilian and those actively involved in a resistance movement can qualify as victims of crimes against humanity.' For standards applicable to determining the civilian nature of the population, reference can be made to IHL, see Chapter 6, para. 6A.3.1.

clearly civilian targets, such as the World Trade Center in New York, and those that may have a military role, such as the Pentagon.[58]

(d) Link to armed conflict? Crimes against humanity can be committed in times of armed conflict or in times of 'peace'. While crimes against humanity originated as an extension of war crimes,[59] the idea that such crimes can only be committed in times of war has been unequivocally rejected through developments since Nuremberg.[60]

4A.1.1.2 War crimes

Unlike crimes against humanity, war crimes must (as the name suggests) take place in war, which for legal purposes is more properly referred to as armed conflict. Once there is an armed conflict, the basic principles of international humanitarian law, including accountability, must apply.[61] Serious violations of international humanitarian law carrying individual responsibility include crimes relating to the conduct of hostilities, such as deliberate attacks on civilians or the use of weapons that cause unnecessary suffering, and crimes against protected persons, such as torture or cruel treatment carried out against persons taking no part in hostilities, as discussed more fully in Chapter 6.[62]

The classification of the September 11 attacks as war crimes depends on them constituting the initiation of, or taking place in the context of,

---

[58] Questions may arise as to whether these were components of one (predominantly civilian) attack, or were separate attacks. In either case the 'means' of attack – using civilian aircraft as bombs – itself involved targeting civilians.

[59] Bassiouni, 'Crimes against Humanity', p. 524. Note that the Nuremberg Charter (Charter of the International Military Tribunal, Annex to the London Agreement for the Prosecution and Punishment of the Major War Criminals of the European Axis of 8 August 1945 (reprinted in 39 (1945) AJIL Supplement 258)) and Charter of the Tokyo Tribunal (Charter of the International Military Tribunal for the Far East, 19 January 1946) contained such a link.

[60] Neither the ICTR nor the ICC Statute contain this element and although the ICTY Statute does, as the Appeals Chamber has noted, this is merely a jurisdictional limitation on the tribunal, rather than a requirement of crimes against humanity under international law.

[61] Long-established principles, reflected in the Martens Clause 1899 (Preamble to the Hague Convention Respecting The Laws and Customs of War on Land), provide that certain basic standards of conduct apply irrespective of the nature of the conflict ('these provisions, the wording of which has been inspired by the desire to diminish the evils of war so far as military necessities permit, are destined to serve as general rules of conduct for belligerents in their relations with each other and with populations').

[62] See also Article 8, ICC Statute, as the most comprehensive list of war crimes, and, e.g., Articles 2 and 3 ICTY Statute.

an armed conflict. If they do, the rules of international humanitarian law apply to those acts – which has consequences for rules on permissible targeting and the detention of persons in connection with an armed conflict[63] – and serious violations of those rules may be prosecuted as war crimes. As explained more fully in Chapter 6, however, it is doubtful that September 11 can properly be understood as armed conflict, which has been defined as:

> resort to armed force between States or protracted armed violence between governmental authorities and organized armed groups or between such groups within a State.[64]

While this definition was thought to be broad-reaching,[65] the events of September 11 do not fit readily into either category of conflict, absent established state responsibility[66] rendering it an international armed conflict[67] and in circumstances where al-Qaeda's structure, organisation

---

[63] If September 11 is considered an armed conflict, IHL considers legitimate the targeting of military objectives. The Pentagon attack is likely to fall into this category of legitimate target (though note it would still fall foul of the law in respect of the manner of its execution – see Chapter 6, para. 6A.3.2 below). A further consequence is that persons suspected of involvement in September 11 would automatically be detained in connection with an armed conflict and entitled to the treatment of detainees under IHL.

[64] *Tadic* Jurisdiction Appeal Decision, para. 70.

[65] This definition by the ICTY Appeals Chamber was thought innovative and sufficiently broad to cater for the full range of scenarios (given that the ICTY was addressing a conflict that had national and international components), thus ensuring the broadest application of international humanitarian law. See S. Boelaert-Suominen, 'The Yugoslavia Tribunal and the Common Core of International Humanitarian Law applicable to All Armed Conflict', (2000) 13 LJIL 619 at 630. In fact it appears to exclude conflict between organised groups and foreign states.

[66] This would have to be established according to the 'effective or overall control' test discussed at Chapter 3, para. 3.1.1.1 – then September 11 may amount to the initiation of international armed conflict between states. If so, the acts of violence may amount to grave breaches of the Geneva Conventions, which consist of certain very serious crimes, including 'wilful killing', committed in international armed conflict against protected persons such as civilians. See separate discussion on state responsibility, including *Military and Paramilitary Activities in and against Nicaragua* (*Nicaragua* v. *United States of America*), Merits, ICJ Reports 1986 (hereinafter '*Nicaragua* case'), p. 14; *Prosecutor* v. *Delalic et al.*, Case No. IT-96-21-A, Judgment (ICTY Appeals Chamber), 20 February 2001.

[67] The consequences would include that the obligations incumbent on all states in respect of grave breaches – to seek out those responsible for such breaches – would be triggered. GC I, Article 49 (duty to search for and prosecute) and Article 50 (recognition as a crime); GC II, Article 50 (duty to search for and prosecute) and Article 51 (recognition as a crime); GC III, Article 129 (duty to search for and prosecute) and Article 130 (recognition as a crime); GC IV, Article 146 (duty to search for and prosecute) and Article 147 (recognition as a crime). See M. Scharf, 'Application of Treaty Based Universal Jurisdiction to Nationals of Non-Party States', 35 (2001) *New England Law Review* 363.

and modus operandi suggest it may lack the characteristics of an 'organised armed group' capable of constituting a party to a non-international armed conflict.[68] It may be that the events of September 11 herald a new hybrid type of conflict – between organised groups and foreign states – that IHL will evolve to encompass,[69] but it is doubtful that an armed conflict arose on September 11 as a matter of law at the time of those attacks.[70]

For the purpose of accountability for September 11, navigating these relatively unchartered waters may, in any event, not be critical, to the extent that other crimes such as crimes against humanity (defined above) or crimes under domestic law (below), were committed on September 11 and an appropriate forum has jurisdiction.[71]

By contrast to the September 11 attacks, there is little dispute that armed conflict arose thereafter, notably in Afghanistan on 7 October 2001 and in Iraq on 20 March 2003;[72] the conduct of both parties to those conflicts falls to be considered against IHL and serious breaches may constitute war crimes.

4A.1.1.3 Aggression

International law provides growing authority for considering aggression to constitute a crime under international law. Aggression was defined as a 'crime against peace' under the London Agreement establishing

---

[68] See Chapter 6 on the nature of parties to a non-international armed conflict. A further issue is that armed conflict must be distinguished from a lesser level of sporadic violence.

[69] In the face of the reality that most conflicts are internal, and that distinguishing internal from international conflict is often difficult, international humanitarian law has developed from focusing almost exclusively on international conflict to addressing war crimes in internal conflict. The ICTY has been instrumental in this, by invoking a purposive rather than formalistic interpretation of law so as 'not to leave unpunished any person guilty of any such serious violation, whatever the context within which it may have been committed' (*Tadic* Jurisdiction Appeal Decision, para. 92). A similar process may need to evolve in relation to this 'other' type of conflict.

[70] It is also unclear how any such development in the law might unfold in the future, e.g., whether such armed violence would have to be 'protracted' – as set down by the ICTY to distinguish internal conflicts from civil unrest – in order to distinguish conflict from isolated attack. On the meaning of 'protracted' as opposed to 'sustained' conflict, see Boelaert-Suominen, 'Yugoslavia Tribunal', at 13.

[71] As more states have universal jurisdiction over war crimes than crimes against humanity, so the issue could become relevant for prosecution in certain states. However, as noted below, jurisdiction over other international crimes, including crimes against humanity, can be conferred *ex post facto*, provided the *nullum crimen sine lege* principle is respected.

[72] See e.g., 'Timeline Irak: A Chronology of Key Events', *BBC News*, 4 March 2004 (updated continually), at http://news.bbc.co.uk/1/hi/world/middle_east/country_profiles/737483.stm.

the Nuremberg International Military Tribunal[73] and described by that tribunal as 'the supreme international crime'.[74] The status of aggression as a crime has been reiterated by the General Assembly,[75] the International Law Commission[76] and, most recently – at least to a degree – in the ICC Statute (which allows for future ICC jurisdiction over aggression after an acceptable definition of the crime is agreed upon)[77] and subsequent ICC negotiations.[78]

For ICC purposes, the proposed definition provides that aggression is committed when a person 'being in a position effectively to exercise control over or to direct the political or military action of a State . . . intentionally and knowingly orders or participates actively in the

[73] See Article 6 of the Charter of the Nuremberg Tribunal: 'The following acts, or any of them, are crimes coming within the jurisdiction of the Tribunal for which there shall be international responsibility: (a) Crimes against Peace: namely planning, preparation, initiation or waging of a war of aggression, or a war in violation of international treaties, agreements or assurances, or participation in a Common Plan or Conspiracy for the accomplishment of any of the foregoing.'

[74] 'To initiate a war of aggression, is not only an international crime; it is the supreme international crime differing only from other war crimes in that it contains within itself the accumulated evil of the whole.' Judgment of the Nuremberg International Military Tribunal, 30 September 1946, reprinted in *The Trial of German Major War Criminals before the International Military Tribunal*, vol. 20 (Nuremberg, 1948), p. 411.

[75] The 'Declaration on Principles of International Law concerning Friendly Relations and Cooperation among States in Accordance with the Charter of the United Nations' (GA Res. 2625 (XXV), adopted by consensus on 24 October 1970) provides in Article 5(2), '[a] war of aggression is a crime against international peace. Aggression gives rise to international responsibility'. See also GA Res. 3314 (XXIX), 'Definition of Aggression', 14 December 1974, UN Doc. A/RES/3314 (XXIX). The 'principles of international law recognized by the Charter of the Nuremburg Tribunal and the judgment of the Tribunal' were also 'affirmed' by the General Assembly in Resolution 95(I), 'Affirmation of the Principles of International Law recognised by the Charter of the Nuremberg Tribunal', 11 December 1946.

[76] Article 16 of the ILC's Draft Code of Crimes, dealing with 'Crime of Aggression', provided: 'An individual who, as a leader or organizer, actively participates in, or orders the planning, preparation, initiation or waging of aggression by a State shall be responsible for the crime of aggression'. See also the ILC's Commentary to Article 16 of the Draft Code, in Report of the International Law Commission on the work of its 48th session, 6 May–26 July 1996, GAOR Supp. No. 10, UN Doc. A/51/10, at p. 83.

[77] See Article 5(2), ICC Statute: 'The Court shall exercise jurisdiction over the crime of aggression once a provision is adopted in accordance with Articles 121 and 123 defining the crime and setting out the conditions under which the Court shall exercise jurisdiction with respect to this crime. Such a provision shall be consistent with the relevant provisions of the Charter of the United Nations.'

[78] Negotiations related to the definition of aggression have proceeded on the understanding that it constitutes a crime under international law. The documents produced by state parties to the ICC Statute and by the Preparatory Commission are available at http://www.un.org/law/icc/documents/aggression/aggressiondocs.htm.

planning, preparation, initiation or execution of an act of aggression which, by its character, gravity and scale, constitutes a flagrant violation of the Charter of the United Nations'.[79] An 'act of aggression' is in turn defined as one of the non-exhaustive list of acts included in the definition of aggression presented by the General Assembly in Resolution 3314 (XXIX) of 1974, involving the unlawful use of force, for example to attack, invade, occupy militarily or blockade another state.[80]

A criminal act of aggression is therefore an unlawful use of force of a certain 'character, gravity and scale'[81] by virtue of which it 'constitutes a flagrant violation of the Charter of the United Nations'.[82] It necessarily involves force by or on behalf of a state, as opposed to non-state actors, although states may act directly, or indirectly through irregulars or others.[83]

---

[79] This basic definition of the crime of aggression has been proposed by the Preparatory Commission for the ICC in 2002. See the 'Discussion Paper on the Definition of the Crime of Aggression and Conditions for the Exercise of Jurisdiction' presented by the Coordinator of the Working Group on the Crime of Aggression, in *Report of the Preparatory Commission for the International Criminal Court – Part II*, 24 July 2002, UN Doc. PCNICC/2002/2/Add.2.

[80] See GA Res. 3314 (XXIX), above, note 73, providing that '[a]ggression is the use of armed force by a State against the sovereignty, territorial integrity or political independence of another State, or in any other manner inconsistent with the Charter of the United Nations, as set out in this Definition' (Article 1) and that '[a]ny of the following acts, regardless of a declaration of war, shall, subject to and in accordance with the provisions of Article 2, qualify as an act of aggression . . . *(a) The invasion or attack by the armed forces of a State of the territory of another State, or any military occupation, however temporary, resulting from such invasion or attack, or any annexation by the use of force of the territory of another State or part thereof;* (b) Bombardment by the armed forces of a State against the territory of another State or the use of any weapons by a State against the territory of another State . . . ; (g) The sending by or on behalf of a State of armed bands, groups, irregulars or mercenaries, which carry out acts of armed force against another State of such gravity as to amount to the acts listed above, or its substantial involvement therein' (Article 3) (emphasis added).

[81] See Article 2, GA Res. 3314 (XXIX): 'The first use of armed force by a state in contravention of the Charter shall constitute prima facie evidence of an act of aggression although the Security Council may, in conformity with the Charter, conclude that a determination that an act of aggression has been committed would not be justified in the light of other relevant circumstances, including the fact that the acts concerned or their consequences are not of a sufficient gravity'.

[82] See the proposal concerning the 'Elements of the crime of aggression (as defined in the Statute of the International Criminal Court', para. 7), contained in the 'Discussion paper' by the Coordinator of the Working Group on the Crime of Aggression. C. Gray, *International Law and the Use of Force* (Oxford, 2000), at p. 134, notes that the fact that not every unlawful use of force amounts to the crime of aggression was reflected to some degree in Article 2 of GA Res. 3314 (XXIX), the formulation of which 'reflects the general support for a distinction between frontier incidents and aggression'.

[83] GA Res. 3314 (XXIX), Article 3(g).

While its status as a crime finds strong support, as the deliberations of the ICC Working Group on the Crime of Aggression make clear, there are still areas of the definition of the crime on which there is disagreement.[84] As noted in Chapter 4, given the requirement of certainty in criminal law, one may question whether there can be a customary law crime while dispute attends its legal definition. However, by contrast to the definition of terrorism, where disagreement relates to various key elements on which criminal responsibility depends,[85] continuing dispute on the definition of aggression appears to relate principally to the mechanisms for determining an act of aggression and specifically the role of the Security Council therein.[86]

4A.1.1.4 Terrorism

The thorny issue of terrorism in international law is discussed in Chapter 2, where the lack of a global terrorism convention and absence of an accepted generic definition in customary law is noted,[87] despite the issue having been the focus of international attention since long before 9/11 and all the more since.[88] As the ICTY and other tribunals have noted on numerous occasions, individual criminal responsibility under international law can arise from certain serious violations not only of customary law but also of applicable treaty law.

As regards customary law, although some respected commentators assert that terrorism *is* a customary law crime,[89] so long as significant

---

[84] See the 'Discussion paper by the Coordinator of the Working Group on the Crime of Aggression', above, note 77. The ILC, for instance, simply asserted that aggression attracted individual criminal responsibility without seeking to define it.

[85] This distinction may be reflected by the inclusion of aggression in the ICC Statute, in contrast to the omission of terrorism, discussed in the next paragraph.

[86] Specifically, it is disputed whether the ICC should be dependent on the Council's exclusive discretion to make authoritative findings of aggression under Article 39 of the United Nations Charter, particularly given that it has been 'extremely reluctant to find that there has been an act of aggression' in the past. See Gray, *International Law*, 146, who notes that the Council 'has done so only with regard to Israel, South Africa and Rhodesia'.

[87] See, e.g., Resolution E adopted by the Rome Conference on the ICC (below, note 88): 'Regretting that no generally acceptable definition of the crimes of terrorism and drug crimes could be agreed upon for the inclusion within the jurisdiction of the Court'.

[88] See the Convention for the Prevention and Punishment of Terrorism (Geneva, 1937), League of Nations Doc. C.546M.383 1937 V. See also M.C. Bassiouni, 'International Terrorism', in Bassiouni (ed.), *International Criminal Law*, vol. I, 2nd ed. (New York, 1999), pp. 765 ff, and the discussion of recent deliberations towards a global convention in Chapter 2, para. 1.2 above.

[89] See, e.g., A. Cassese, *International Criminal Law* (Oxford, 2003), p. 139 and J. Paust, 'Addendum: Prosecution of Mr. bin Laden *et al.* for Violations of International Law

differences remain as to key elements of the definition of the crime, as sketched out in Chapter 2, many will have difficulty reconciling this view with the cardinal principles of legality and certainty in criminal matters. In this respect it may be noteworthy that the ICC negotiators ultimately drew a distinction between aggression, which was included in the Court's jurisdiction despite outstanding debate on 'operational' questions relating to the definition, and terrorism which was eventually omitted on the basis of a more fundamental absence of any accepted definition.[90] The explicit reference to the lack of such a definition in the Resolution of the ICC conference militates against its customary law status, as discussed in Chapter 2.[91] The existence of the crime of terrorism under customary law may well evolve in the future, however, perhaps impelled by on-going developments on the national and international planes.[92]

As a matter of treaty law, it was noted in Chapter 2 that particular manifestations of terrorism are defined in numerous specific terrorism conventions, from attacks on internationally protected persons to terrorist bombings to the financing of terrorism for example,[93] which contain their own definitions of the acts covered by them and oblige state parties to criminalise the conduct in domestic law and, in certain circumstances, to exercise jurisdiction.[94] However, these treaties are directed towards

---

and Civil Lawsuits by Various Victims', *ASIL Insights* No. 77, 21 September 2001, at www.asil.org, who refers to acts of international terrorism as 'recognizable international crimes under customary international law'.

[90] Resolution E adopted by the Rome Conference on the International Criminal Court as part of its Final Act (UN Doc. A/CONF.183/10) notes that the Assembly of States parties may include terrorism at some later stage once an accepted definition has been settled. See also Chapter 4, para. 4B.1.3.2(a).

[91] However, it is noted that while the reasons for exclusion related primarily to doubts as to the customary status of the crime, other factors included the perceived relative lack of gravity of the crime, the complexity in the application of treaties to individuals, fear of politicisation of the Court and a view that they are more effectively prosecuted domestically; see Chapter 4, para. 4B.1.2.2 below.

[92] Since 9/11, and SC Res. 1373 (2001), 28 September 2001, UN Doc. S/RES/1373 (2001), there has been intense activity on the national level. Since 1998 on the international level a definition of sorts was concluded in the context of the International Convention for the Suppression of the Financing of Terrorism (New York, 9 December 1999, UN Doc. A/Res/54/109 (1999), in force 10 April 2002) and negotiations towards a global convention continue, with an uncertain future that may impact on the development of custom.

[93] See also hijacking, below, which may be considered another form of terrorism.

[94] Bassiouni, 'International Terrorism', refers to 16 Conventions dealing with specific means of terror violence. The Special Rapporteur on terrorism and human rights, Ms. Kalliopi K. Koufa, in her Progress Report to the Fifty-Third Session Sub-Commission on the Promotion and Protection of Human Rights', UN Doc. E/CN.4/Sub.2/2001/31, 27 June 2001, cites 19 Conventions.

imposing obligations on states party to them, not establishing criminal responsibility of individuals. Unless the state has implemented the treaty provisions, it is subject to question whether individuals could be prosecuted on the sole basis of the treaty.

A distinction may be noted in this respect between treaties which themselves purport to criminalise, under international law, individual conduct considered to amount to 'most serious crimes of concern to the international community as a whole'[95] (the so-called *crimina juris gentium*)[96] and other treaties, dealing with the so-called crimes of international relevance, which do not establish individual criminal responsibility under international law, but merely impose an obligation on states parties to criminalise certain conducts in their national legal system.[97] The Convention against Torture, Convention against Genocide and Geneva Conventions and Protocols,[98] generally considered to fall into the former category, can be distinguished from terrorism treaties, which fall into the latter, creating state responsibility for parties to the treaty, but probably not providing sufficient basis for criminal prosecution.[99]

However, where the specific terrorism treaty has been incorporated into the domestic law of a state with jurisdiction, this issue is avoided. In practice the terrorism treaty crimes were incorporated into domestic law in several states at the time of the September 11 attacks. The United States for example had enacted legislation, e.g., in the Antiterrorism Act of 1990,[100] which provides one basis for prosecution of September 11 offences in the

---

[95] See Article 5 ICC Statute.

[96] Examples of international instruments which create individual criminal responsibility for crimes under international law are the 1948 Convention against Genocide, and the United Nations Convention against Torture and Other Cruel, Inhuman or Degrading Treatment and Punishment (New York, 10 December 1984, UN Doc. A/39/51 (1984)) (hereinafter 'Convention Against Torture').

[97] Belonging to this category of treaties, for instance, are the conventions relating to the suppression of terrorism mentioned above, and international instruments related to drug trafficking.

[98] Examples of international instruments which create individual criminal responsibility for crimes under international law are the Convention on the Prevention and Punishment of the Crime of Genocide (New York, 9 December 1948, 78 UNTS 277, in force 12 January 1951, hereinafter 'Convention against Genocide') and the United Nations Convention against Torture and Other Cruel, Inhuman or Degrading Treatment and Punishment (New York, 10 December 1984, UN Doc. A/39/51 (1984), hereinafter 'Convention Against Torture').

[99] This question is linked to the requirement of *nullum crimen sine lege*, discussed this chapter, para. 4A.1.2.2 below, as the treaties may specify the elements of crime with sufficient clarity and precision, or they may leave this to be done at the national level.

[100] 18 USC §§ 2331 ff.

US.[101] On 28 September 2001 the Security Council called on 'all States to . . . [i]ncrease cooperation and fully implement the relevant international conventions and protocols relating to terrorism'[102] and to ensure that 'terrorist acts are established as serious criminal offences in domestic laws and regulations',[103] which has led to a proliferation of domestic terrorism legislation that might provide the basis for prosecution of future offences.[104]

As noted, one sub-category of treaties that do, however, give rise to criminal responsibility for terrorism under international law, are those IHL treaties prohibiting 'acts or threats of violence the primary purpose of which is to spread terror among the civilian population', in international and non-international armed conflict.[105] Prosecuting the crime for the first time in history, the ICTY affirmed that in certain circumstances international prosecution may be possible solely on a binding treaty – in that case the Additional Protocols to the Geneva Conventions – irrespective of the customary content of the norm.[106] Although a dissenting judgment questions whether individual responsibility should be based on treaty alone, if it does not also amount to a crime under customary law, the majority view was that it was unnecessary to consider whether terror in armed conflict was also a crime under customary law.[107]

---

[101] Paust, 'Prosecution of Mr. bin Laden', notes that '[s]ection 2332(b) . . . can cover attempts and conspiracy in connection with the killing of a national of the United States (apparently anywhere) although the accused must be 'outside the United States at the time of the attempt or engagement in a conspiracy to kill'. Section 2332(c) should also be applicable, since it reaches an accused 'outside the United States' who 'engages in physical violence – (1) with intent to cause serious bodily injury to a national of the United States; or (2) with the result that serious bodily injury is caused to a national of the United States'.

[102] SC Res. 1373 (2001), above, note 90, para. 3.

[103] SC Res. 1373 (2001) also requires 'that the punishment duly reflects the seriousness of such terrorist acts'. This Resolution also established a Committee to monitor the implementation of the resolution. SC Res. 1377 (2001), 28 November 2001, UN Doc. S/RES/1377 (2001), sets out the tasks for the Committee.

[104] The non-retroactivity principle inherent in the *nullum crimen sine lege* principles precludes prosecution for offences that were not crimes at the time of commission but may permit conferral of jurisdiction *ex post facto*, see this chapter, para. 4A.1.3 below. Regarding new terror legislation, much of it is problematic from the perspective of the *nullum crimen* principle and other human rights concerns. See Chapter 7B.

[105] Article 51 AP I and Article 13 AP II. See also Article 33(1) of the Fourth Geneva Convention which provides that 'terrorism is prohibited' without defining the phenomenon.

[106] See *Galić* judgment (above, note 15). As noted above, questions have arisen as to how treaties become binding on the individual: see, e.g., Zimmerman, 'Crimes', p. 98, and the dissenting judgment of Judge Nieto Navia in *Galić*.

[107] *Ibid.*

Finally, another offence of relevance to the September 11 attacks, at times treated as a form of terrorism and at others as a separate treaty crime, is hijacking. There are a number of conventions relating to hijacking,[108] some of which oblige states parties to enact legislation criminalising the conduct and to exercise jurisdiction over suspects in specified circumstances.[109] Like the terrorism conventions, certain of those relating to hijacking have been incorporated into United States domestic law[110] and the US has in the past exercised jurisdiction in a number of cases on the basis of those treaty provisions as incorporated into domestic law.[111]

4A.1.1.5 Common crimes

Finally, it should be noted that murder and the infliction of serious physical harm are crimes in most if not all domestic jurisdictions, including the United States. The most straightforward approach in relation to these crimes is therefore prosecution in a domestic court as a common crime.[112]

The fact that acts such as those carried out on September 11 might amount to crimes under international law is however significant not only as an indicator of their egregious nature, and international character, but

---

[108] See, e.g., the Convention for the Suppression of Unlawful Seizure of Aircraft (The Hague, 16 December 1970), 860 UNTS 105, in force 14 October 1971 ('The Hague Convention'), and the Convention for the Suppression of Unlawful Acts against the Safety of Civil Aviation (Montreal, 23 September 1971), 974 UNTS 178, in force 26 January 1973 ('The Montreal Convention'). While these Conventions may be relevant to the hijacking and subsequent destruction of the four aircraft, as one commentator notes, 'extending the scope of these treaties to cover the destruction of the World Trade Center and part of the Pentagon, as well as the massive loss of life in those buildings and the causing of a state of terror in the general public, could only be done with difficulty' (A.N. Pronto, 'Terrorist Attacks on the World Trade Center and the Pentagon. Comment', *ASIL Insights* No. 77, 21 September 2001, available at www.asil.org).

[109] The states of nationality of the alleged perpetrator or the victim or the state of territory have jurisdiction under many of these treaties.

[110] Paust, 'Prosecution of Mr. bin Laden', notes: 'Prosecution in US is also possible under US legislation implementing the Montreal Convention for the Suppression of Unlawful Acts Against the Safety of Civil Aviation, (which in Article 7 thereof also requires all signatories to bring into custody those reasonably accused of international crimes covered by the treaty and either to initiate prosecution of or to extradite such persons, without any exception or limitation of such duty whatsoever)'.

[111] *United States* v. *Fawaz Yunis*, 924 F2d 1086 (DC Cir. 1991). The court upheld the US court's subject matter jurisdiction, based on the Hague Convention and the International Convention Against the Taking of Hostages (924 F2d at 7, 12–13), on the basis that the victim's state of nationality may exercise jurisdiction. The court held this to be consistent with customary international law (924 F2d at 8).

[112] Some would assert that murder is a crime that attracts universal jurisdiction, and all states should be able to exercise their jurisdiction over the events of September 11 simply on this basis. Whether or not this is the case, many states could exercise jurisdiction over mass murder based on other bases of jurisdiction set out below.

also as crimes under international law are governed by relevant principles of international law, as highlighted in the following section.

4A.1.2 Relevant principles of criminal law

4A.1.2.1 Direct and indirect individual criminal responsibility

Criminal responsibility must be individual, based on the culpability of the particular person accused. That it cannot be 'collective', or 'objective', is an essential principle of criminal law in legal systems across the globe, and reflected in international law.[113] Thus, for example, the fact of membership in – or association with – a prohibited group or organisation may raise concerns as a basis for criminal responsibility,[114] and cannot *per se* render the individual responsible for the actions of that group.[115]

---

[113] This principle of criminal law is reflected in international human rights and humanitarian law. See 'Specific Human Rights Issues: New Priorities, in Particular Terrorism', Additional Progress Report by the Special Rapporteur on Terrorism and Human Rights, Ms. Kalliopi Koufa, 8 August 2003, UN Doc. E/CN/Sub2/2003/WP.1, paras. 68 ff.; Inter-American Commission on Human Rights, *Report on Terrorism and Human Rights*, 22 October 2002, OAS/Ser.L/V/ll.116, Doc. 5 rev. 1 corr., para. 227 and Press release No. 12/03, 'Cuba: the Inter American Commission condemns the execution of three people', 16 April 2003. On the prohibition on collective punishments in IHL, see Article 33 GC IV, Article 75 AP I, Article 6(2) AP II. See also Report of the Secretary General pursuant to paragraph 2 of SC Res. 808 (1993), 3 May 1993, UN Doc. S/25704 (1993), para. 51. (See this chapter, para. 4A.1.2.1 below.)

[114] Inter-American Commission on Human Rights, *Report on Terrorism and Human Rights*, 22 October 2002, OAS/Ser. L/V/ll. 116 Doc. 5 rev. 1 corr., notes that 'no one should be convicted of an offense except on the basis of individual penal responsibility, and the corollary to this principle [is] that there can be no collective criminal responsibility . . . This requirement has received particular emphasis in the context of post-World War II criminal prosecutions, owing in large part to international public opposition to convicting persons based solely upon their membership in a group or organization.' On questions regarding the offence of 'membership of a criminal organization', see E. David, *Eléments de droit pénal international – Titre II, le contenu des infractions internationales*, 8th ed. (Brussels 1999), p. 362. As noted in Chapter 7, para. 7B.11.1, particular concerns arise in the post 9/11 context where criminal organisations are 'listed' according to procedures that lack transparency and are not subject to judicial supervision.

[115] Inter-American Commission on Human Rights, *Report on Terrorism and Human Rights* above. As the Inter-American Commission noted: 'This restriction does not, however, preclude the prosecution of persons on such established grounds of individual criminal responsibility such as complicity, incitement, or participation in a common criminal enterprise, nor does it prevent individual accountability on the basis of the well-established superior responsibility doctrine.' See also 'superior responsibility', below in this paragraph, where persons in positions of authority may in certain circumstances be indirectly responsible for the conduct of others through their own omissions. In each case, responsibility relates to the subjective culpability of the individual and not to objective facts relating to his or her position, or membership or association with a particular group.

The individual should be punished only in respect of his or her own conduct, commensurate with his or her culpability.

Under international criminal law, responsibility may be direct and indirect. Direct responsibility attaches to those who order, plan, instigate, aid and abet, or contribute by acting in 'common purpose' or joint criminal enterprise with others for the commission of a crime.[116] As regards September 11 those directly responsible are not only those who hijacked the planes but also the full networks of persons involved in various ways in planning, orchestrating and assisting their execution. While national laws vary considerably as to principles of criminal law and terminology used, they tend to encompass a similar range of forms of participation incurring criminal responsibility.[117]

Much attention has been focused on the need for a response to the September 11 events, and subsequently to allegations of criminal conduct in the context of the 'war on terror', that reaches behind the executioners to the architects, including those at the highest levels. In this respect, it is important to note that in law certain people may be responsible not only for what they do – such as ordering or instigating crimes – but also in certain circumstances for what they fail to do under the doctrine of 'superior responsibility'. While this doctrine is most readily applied in the context of clearly established military structures, it applies to military or civilian leaders. A military commander or a civilian in a position of authority may be liable if he or she knew or should have known that a crime would be committed and failed to take necessary and reasonable measures to prevent it.[118]

Moreover, this form of liability applies not only to those with formal legal authority, but also to superiors according to informal structures.[119]

---

[116] See Article 7(1) Statute of the ICTY, Article 6(1) Statute of the ICTR, Article 25 ICC Statute. Formulations vary somewhat between the tribunals' statutes and the ICC Statute.

[117] K. Ambos, 'Article 25. Individual Criminal Responsibility', in Triffterer (ed.), *Commentary on the Rome Statute*, pp. 475 ff. Domestic legal orders may also include other forms not included specifically in the international documents, such as conspiracy (covered in ICTY and ICTR practice, and the ICC Statute, only in respect of genocide, although in some circumstances forms of conspiracy will be covered by the 'common purpose doctrine' developed by the jurisprudence of the ICTY (*Tadic* Appeals Judgment), and reflected in Article 25 ICC Statute.

[118] Note that superior responsibility is not strict liability: the evidence must show that the accused had information in his or her possession on the basis of which he or she should have known the crime would be committed, was in a position to prevent it and failed to take reasonable steps to do so.

[119] See, e.g., *Prosecutor* v. *Delalic et al.*, Case No. IT-96-21-A, Judgment (ICTY Appeals Chamber), 20 February 2001 and *Prosecutor* v. *Musema*, Case No. ICTR 96-13-T, Judgment and Sentence, 27 January 2000.

The ICTR has prosecuted paramilitary leaders according to the superior responsibility doctrine.[120] Arguably, the same principle could apply to persons in positions of authority within terrorist criminal networks provided the necessary requirements, including a clear superior–subordinate relationship, could be established. As the experience of the ICTY and ICTR testifies, this can be an extremely important basis of liability, where access to evidence of high level orders sufficient to demonstrate the direct responsibility of those in the highest echelons proves elusive.

4A.1.2.2 The legality and non-retroactivity principle: *nullum crimen sine lege*

As a fundamental principle of law persons are protected from prosecution for conduct that was not criminal at the time of its occurrence. This principle, reflected in domestic and international criminal law and human rights, is enshrined in, for example, Article 15 of the ICCPR.[121] It explicitly does not, however, preclude the prosecution of conduct that was criminal under international but not domestic law at the relevant time.[122]

The *nullum crimen* rule also requires that criminal conduct must be defined according to clear, accessible and unambiguous law. The definition of crime must in turn 'be strictly construed and shall not be extended by analogy'.[123] Any ambiguity should be interpreted in favour of the person being investigated, prosecuted or convicted.[124]

Thus, for example, a person can be prosecuted for direct or indirect responsibility for crimes against humanity entailed in the September 11 attacks, even if there were no specific offence provisions in place under domestic law at the time of the commission of the offence. If domestic law requires a legislative base for the crimes or for jurisdiction, the necessary legislation can also be adopted with retrospective effect without any infringement of the *nullum crimen* rule under international

---

[120] This was the case in the prosecution of Serushago, convicted by the ICTR (*Prosecutor* v. *Omar Serushago*, ICTR 98-39-S, Sentencing Judgment, 5 February 1999).

[121] Article 15(1) of the ICCPR says: 'No one shall be held guilty of any criminal offence on account of any act or omission which did not constitute a criminal offence, under national or international law, at the time when it was committed.' For a detailed discussion of the guarantees enshrined in Article 15, see below, Chapter 7, para. 7A.4.3.4.

[122] Article 15(2) ICCPR.   [123] ICC Statute, Article 22(2).

[124] ICC Statute, Article 22(3). The subsidiary principle of *nulla poena sine lege* (no punishment without law) demands that more serious penalties should not be imposed than those applicable at the time of the commission of the offence. On compatibility with prosecution of international crimes under customary law, despite no penalty having been fixed at the time of commission, see Article 15(2), ICCPR.

law.[125] By contrast, prosecution for membership of a terrorist organisation – not itself a crime under international law – is likely to fall foul of the *nullum crimen* rule unless that crime was proscribed in clear and accessible domestic law at the relevant time.

4A.1.2.3 Bars to prosecution: amnesty and immunity

Domestic legal systems may, and often do, impose obstacles to prosecution, among them amnesty laws or immunities that preclude criminal process.[126] So far as the crimes concerned are crimes under international – as opposed to ordinary domestic – law, however, the legitimacy of national measures such as amnesties or pardons depends on their consistency with international law obligations to effectively investigate and prosecute serious crimes.[127]

Human rights bodies have consistently found amnesties or similar measures that act as a bar to investigation or criminal process to be inconsistent with the positive obligations of the state under human rights treaty law to investigate and, if appropriate, prosecute serious rights violations.[128] Such measures are increasingly rejected in practice on the international level, as reflected for example in statements of the UN Secretary General[129] and the ICTY;[130] although it is probably still too early to consider granting

---

[125] It is noted, however, that a state may still face problems in conducting such a prosecution or enacting the relevant legislation under domestic law if there are applicable constitutional or statutory limitations that do not recognise an exception for crimes recognised under customary law.

[126] Others include prescription or statutes of limitation; for the restrictions imposed on these rules by international law, see Cassese, *International Criminal Law*, pp. 316–19.

[127] These obligations are found principally in human rights law, as reflected increasingly in international criminal law. Some treaties require investigation and submission to the relevant authorities for prosecution expressly, e.g., Convention against Genocide, Convention against Torture or the grave breaches provisions of the Geneva Conventions, while general human rights treaties such as the ICCPR, ECHR and ACHR have been interpreted as doing so implicitly.

[128] See Chapter 7, below, and, in particular, para. 7A.4.1.

[129] See Seventh Report of the Secretary-General on the United Nations, Observer Mission in Sierra Leone, UN Doc. S/1999/836, 30 July 1999, para. 7: 'I instructed my Special Representative to sign the agreement with the explicit proviso that the United Nations holds the understanding that the amnesty and pardon in article IX of the [Sierra Leone Peace Agreement of 1999] shall not apply to international crimes of genocide, crimes against humanity, war crimes and other serious violations of international humanitarian law'.

[130] See *Prosecutor v. Furundzija*, Case No. IT-95-17/1-T 10 (Trial Chamber), Judgment of 10 December 1998, para. 155: 'It would be senseless to argue, on the one hand, that on account of the *jus cogens* value of the prohibition on torture, treaties or customary rules providing for torture would be null and void *ab initio*, and then be unmindful of

amnesty for serious crimes as proscribed by customary law, momentum may be gathering behind such a development.[131] Linked to the inconsistency of broad amnesty laws with particular human rights treaty obligations,[132] international criminal law authorities increasingly recognise that, whatever the effect of an amnesty in the home state as a matter of domestic law, it does not impede prosecution either before international or foreign courts.[133] As such, any attempt to confer amnesty on persons accused of crimes against humanity may well fall foul of international obligations and ultimately prove to be an ineffective bar to prosecution.

While domestic laws and constitutions may also provide immunity from criminal prosecution – for example of heads of state, government officials or parliamentarians[134] – the international legitimacy of such measures is again limited by the international obligations referred to above. The Nuremberg Charter's recognition that 'the official position of defendants, whether as heads of state or responsible officials in government departments, shall not be considered as freeing them from responsibility or mitigating punishment'[135] is reflected in the statutes of subsequent *ad hoc* tribunals and of the ICC.[136]

The situation is rendered more complex, however, by the fact that international law itself recognises certain immunities, afforded to high-ranking foreign state agents and diplomats for example. An extension of state sovereignty, these immunities developed to ensure that certain representatives of foreign states were able to discharge their functions free

a State say, taking national measures authorising or condoning torture or absolving its perpetrators through an amnesty law.'

[131] Cassese, *International Criminal Law*, pp. 314–15. Note however that the state practice of granting amnesty may be becoming more restrictive over time, and accountability norms are strengthening, indicating a possible shift in customary law in this field.

[132] See, e.g., the decision of the IACtHR in the *Barrios Altos* case (*Chumbipuma Aguirre et al.* v. *Peru*, Merits, Judgment of 14 March 2001, IACtHR, *Series C*, No. 75), reflecting earlier decisions of the UN Human Rights Committee and Inter-American Commission on Human Rights.

[133] Article 10, Statute of the Special Court for Sierra Leone and Article 40, Cambodian Law for the Establishment of Extraordinary Chambers in the Courts of Cambodia for the Prosecution of Crimes Committed during the Period of Democratic Kampuchea expressly exclude the possibility of amnesty acting as a bar to prosecution. National court cases likewise clarified that amnesty does not preclude prosecution abroad: see, e.g., references to the prosecutions of Chile's Pinochet and Argentina's Galtieri in Cassese, *International Criminal Law*, pp. 314–15.

[134] See H. Duffy, 'National Constitutional Compatibility and the International Criminal Court', 11 (2001) *Duke Journal of Comparative and International Law* 5.

[135] Article 7, London Agreement of 8 August 1945.

[136] Articles 6(2) of the ICTY and ICTR Statutes. Article 27, ICC Statute.

from political interference, and they operate for as long as the official exercises the functions to which they relate. To understand the law on immunities consistently with other developments in international law, however, it should not protect from prosecution persons charged with the most egregious crimes against the human person. However, a recent ICJ decision suggests, controversially, that sitting heads of state and foreign ministers may be considered immune from prosecution in foreign courts, even in respect of crimes under international law, for as long as they hold office.[137] It should be noted that the significance of the case is limited to prosecution before national (as opposed to international) courts and, most importantly, to sitting (as opposed to former) foreign ministers. It thereby provides at most partial, short term refuge for persons who abuse high office to commit serious crimes. The judgment does not suggest that other high-ranking officials, or other ministers such as Defence Ministers, are similarly protected.[138]

The law relating to amnesty and immunity may be of limited relevance to the prosecution of 'terrorist' networks that are unlikely to benefit from state-conferred protection from prosecution. It came briefly into the international frame in the context of purported offers of 'immunity' to Saddam Hussein in early 2003.[139] It may be of more lasting relevance in respect of other crimes committed in Iraq and the accountability of state agents, including high level officials, for crimes committed in the name of counter-terrorism.[140]

---

[137] *Case Concerning the Arrest Warrant of 11 April 2000 (Democratic Republic of the Congo v. Belgium)*, Judgment of 14 February 2002. The case – concerning a Belgian arrest warrant issued against the incumbent foreign minister of the Democratic Republic of the Congo – found that the immunity of a sitting foreign minister from prosecution in domestic courts is absolute. This decision has been criticised for its incompatibility with other developments in the areas of law highlighted above: see, e.g., A. Clapham, 'Human Rights, Sovereignty and Immunity in the Recent Work of the International Court of Justice', 14.1 (2002) *INTERIGHTS Bulletin* 29.

[138] The court refers to 'head of state, head of government and minister of foreign affairs' as enjoying immunity from jurisdiction in foreign states during office, and immunity for official functions thereafter. *Ibid.*, para. 51.

[139] The law on amnesty brings into question, e.g., the lawfulness of offers of amnesty to Saddam Hussein made by the American administration prior to the Iraq invasion. Immunity law is also relevant for example to an assessment of the criminal law enforcement options available to the international community prior to the Iraq invasion: while the prosecution by a national court of Saddam Hussein as then sitting head of state may have been problematic, an international tribunal could have proceeded, given the clarity around the non-application of immunities in that context.

[140] It may be relevant if any question arises as to protection from prosecution of high-level US representatives accused of serious crimes, particularly in Iraq or to state agents

4A.1.3 Jurisdiction to prosecute

International law and practice point to numerous possible fora for the investigation and prosecution of the September 11 offences, or to the responses thereto that amount to serious offences under international law. This section will explore these jurisdictional possibilities, and the relationship between them.

4A.1.3.1 National courts and crimes of international concern

International law recognises the right of certain states to exercise criminal jurisdiction. These are principally the state where the crime occurred, the state of nationality of suspects, the state of nationality of the victims and, for certain serious international crimes, all states, based on universal jurisdiction.[141]

Consistent with these rules, the courts of the United States may provide the natural forum for prosecution of the September 11 crimes, based on the fundamental principle that jurisdiction can be exercised by the state on whose territory a crime is committed. Nationals of several states are suspected of having been involved in the perpetration of the attacks and many other states lost nationals, in particular in the World Trade Centre attack, on the basis of which international law allows them to exercise nationality or passive personality (victim nationality) jurisdiction respectively.[142]

Under international law, any state may exercise jurisdiction over certain serious crimes, such as crimes against humanity or war crimes, on the basis that they injure not only individual victims but the international

---

responsible for 'terrorist' wrongs. For condemnation of a state affording impunity to its officials responsible for counter terrorism see, e.g., Concluding observations of the Human Rights Committee: Russian Federation, UN Doc. CCPR/CO/79/RUS (2003).

[141] As noted below, under universal jurisdiction, a state can prosecute certain serious crimes irrespective of any link between the state and the offence. The principle *aut dedere aut judicare* – the obligation to extradite or prosecute – found in numerous treaties, is a sub-species of universal jurisdiction conditioned on the presence of the suspect on the state's territory.

[142] Numerous treaties, such as those relating to hijacking and terrorism, anticipate prosecution by states beyond the territorial state, such as the state of the perpetrator's or victim's nationality: e.g., see the 1970 Hague Convention; the 1971 Montreal Convention; the Convention on the Prevention and Punishment of Crimes against Internationally Protected Persons, Including Diplomatic Agents (New York, 14 December 1973), 1035 UNTS 15410, in force 20 February 1977; the 1994 Convention on the Safety of United Nations Peacekeepers, and the International Convention for the Suppression of Terrorist Bombings, 12 January 1998. Other treaties embrace broader, universal jurisdiction.

community as a whole.[143] Customary international law has long provided for jurisdiction over such crimes[144] and certain international agreements explicitly so provide.[145] As the events of September 11 amount to crimes that carry universal jurisdiction, notably crimes against humanity and to the extent that war crimes have been committed in responding to September 11, states may exercise universal jurisdiction in respect of these serious offences.[146]

A growing number of states have universal jurisdiction laws in place,[147] to ensure that they can exercise this form of jurisdiction.[148] National courts have increasingly relied on jurisdiction to prosecute a range of

[143] See, e.g., *United States* v. *Otto*, Case no. 000-Mauthausen-5 (DJAWC, 10 July 1947): '[I]nternational law provides that certain offenses may be prosecuted by any state because the offenders are common enemies of all mankind and all nations have an equal interest in their apprehension and punishment.' For an analysis of national universal jurisdiction laws and practice, see Amnesty International, *Universal Jurisdiction: The duty of states to enact and implement legislation*, AI Index: IOR 53/002/2001. Universal jurisdiction is defined as the ability of any state to investigate and prosecute crimes committed outside its territory which are not linked to the state by the nationality of the perpetrator, nationality of the victim or the state's interests.

[144] Restatement (Third), Foreign Relations Law of the United States (1987), section 702, includes, as subject to universal jurisdiction, murder as well as causing the disappearance of individuals, prolonged arbitrary detention and systematic racial discrimination. O. Schachter, *International Law in Theory and Practice* (Dordrecht, 1991) lists 'slavery, genocide, torture and other cruel, inhuman and degrading treatment' as falling into this category. Scharf, 'Application of Treaty-Based Universal Jurisdiction', at 363, includes piracy, war crimes and crimes against humanity. The 1949 Geneva Conventions carry universal jurisdiction via their inclusion in customary international law. Amnesty International includes some serious crimes under national law such as murder: see Amnesty International, *Universal Jurisdiction*.

[145] See, e.g., the grave breaches provisions of the Geneva Conventions: 'Each High Contracting Party shall be under the obligation to search for persons alleged to have committed, or to have ordered to be committed, such grave breaches [of the present Convention], and shall bring such persons, regardless of their nationality, before its own courts.' Torture is also governed by universal jurisdiction according to customary law and treaty: see Convention Against Torture.

[146] See Section B on 9/11 as international crimes and Chapters 6, 7 and 8 on counter-terrorist responses, some of which carry individual criminal responsibility.

[147] Through the implementation of the ICC Statute, a number of states have enacted universal jurisdiction legislation which enables them to exercise such jurisdiction over genocide, crimes against humanity and war crimes, to the extent not already enshrined by law. See, e.g., International Crimes and International Criminal Court Act 2000 (New Zealand) at http://rangi.knowledge-basket.co.nz/gpacts/public/text/2000/an/026.html, and Crimes Against Humanity and War Crimes Act 2000 (Canada), at www.parl.gc.ca/36/2/parlbus/chambus/house/bills/government/C_19_C-19_4/C-19_cover-E.html.

[148] It is arguable whether they need to have such laws in place. As a matter of international law, states can and in some cases must exercise jurisdiction, but domestic law may require a legislative basis for the exercise of jurisdiction.

crimes under international law, including war crimes and crimes against humanity.[149]

Moreover, states that do not yet have such legislation in place affording them jurisdiction over the September 11 offences could enact legislation to confer universal jurisdiction and could then prosecute in respect of September 11, provided the conduct pursued was criminal at the date of commission.[150] On one view, as reflected explicitly in certain regional human rights instruments, notably in the Americas, jurisdiction over criminal matters may only be exercised by a *previously* established court.[151] On the other, the cardinal human rights principle of legality and non-retroactivity in criminal law requires that the *conduct* be criminal at the date when it was carried out, not that *jurisdiction* over the conduct be established at that time.[152] The international criminal tribunals established *ex post facto* have themselves addressed this question and found that legality did not necessarily require that the court was 'pre-established' but

---

[149] See, e.g., *re Demjanjuk*, above, note 21. *United States* v. *Otto*, above, note 142; *Attorney General of Israel* v. *Eichmann*; decision of 8 June 2001 of the *Court d'Assise* of Bruxelles in the case against Vincent Ntezimana, Alphonse Higaniro, Consolata Mukangango, Julienne Mukabutera, concerning the commission of international crimes during the Rwandan genocide (decision available in French at http://www.asf.be/AssisesRwanda2/fr/fr_VERDICT_verdict.htm); see *Regina* v. *Bow Street Metropolitan Stipendiary Magistrate, ex parte Pinochet Ugarte* [1999] 2 WLR 272 (H.L.), reprinted in 38 (1999) ILM 430 (the 1999 *Pinochet* case in which the UK House of Lords found the former President of Chile extraditable to Spain was linked to the universality principle in the Convention against Torture); on post *Pinochet* developments, see R. Brody and H. Duffy, 'Prosecuting Torture Internationally: Hissène Habré, Africa's Pinochet?', in Fischer, Kreß and Lüder (eds.), *Prosecution of Crimes*, p. 817, and C.K. Hall, 'Universal Jurisdiction: Challenges to Implementation since Pinochet I', 14.1 (2002) *INTERIGHTS Bulletin*, 3.

[150] Legislation governing jurisdiction may be necessary in order to prosecute as a matter of domestic law. On the 'retroactivity' issues, see below.

[151] The American Declaration of the Rights and Duties of Man, adopted in 1948 by the Ninth International Conference of American States, provides that every person accused of a crime be tried 'by courts previously established in accordance with pre-existing laws' (Article 26(2)); in turn, the American Convention on Human Rights requires that any accused person be afforded a hearing 'by a competent, independent and impartial tribunal, previously established by law' (Article 8(2)). For an analysis of the principle of the pre-established or 'natural' judge, including its historical development, see J.B.J. Maier, *Derecho Procesal Penal. Tomo I* (Buenos Aires, 1996), pp. 763 ff.

[152] See Article 15(2) ICCPR. See also *Streletz, Kessler and Krenz* v. *Germany* (App. Nos. 34044/96, 35532/97 and 44801/98), Judgment of 22 March 2001, ECtHR, *Reports 2001–II*. See Paust, 'Prosecution of Mr. bin Laden': 'The permissibility of such retroactive legislation was affirmed, for example, in the *Eichmann* case in Israel (also addressing similar rulings in the Netherlands and Germany), the US extradition decision in *re Demjanjuk* [note 21, above], and by the Executive officials applying the 1863 Lieber Code to acts that were already war crimes under customary international law.'

that it was established 'in keeping with the relevant procedures' and that it 'observes the requirements of procedural fairness'.[153]

The development of universal jurisdiction has not been linear, with periods of expansion and recent examples of a more restrictive approach being adopted to the circumstances in which this jurisdiction can or should be exercised by states.[154] However, universal jurisdiction remains a real international jurisdictional possibility of potential relevance in the current context, although it has not, at least as yet, emerged as a central theme in discussions around the prosecution of September 11 offences or responses thereto. This may reflect support, in principle, for the priority of the territorial state's right and responsibility to exercise jurisdiction, expressed by the OAS thus:

> [T]he principle of territoriality must prevail in the case of a jurisdictional conflict, provided that there are adequate, effective remedies in that state to prosecute such crimes and guarantee the application of rules of due process for the alleged perpetrators, and that there is an effective will to bring them to justice.[155]

The relevance and utility of universal jurisdiction, like other jurisdictional bases,[156] is most apparent in circumstances where the territorial state cannot or will not exercise jurisdiction,[157] or cannot or will not do so

---

[153] The ICTY confirmed that jurisdiction (but not criminality) can be retroactive when grappling with questions of legality in the early days of its life. See *Tadic* Jurisdiction Appeal Decision, para. 45.

[154] In the *Arrest Warrant* case, above, note 136, the Democratic Republic of Congo challenged universal jurisdiction law and although the ICJ judgment addressed only the immunity question, Belgium subsequently restricted its law to allow for investigation based on universal jurisdiction only where the suspect is present on Belgian territory.

[155] Preamble OAS Resolution 1/03 on 'Trial for International Crimes', Washington DC, 24 October 2003.

[156] The OAS Resolution 1/03 notes also 'that the principle of territoriality should prevail over that of nationality in the event that the state where the international crimes occurred wishes to bring them to justice, and that it offers due guarantees of a fair trial to the alleged perpetrators' (para. 5).

[157] Note that unlike the ICC, which will only exercise jurisdiction where no national court is willing or able to do so, there is no established rule of subsidiarity for universal jurisdiction. However, as indicated by the OAS Resolution 1/03, debate on whether there is – or should be – such a rule is live. See also the decision of the Criminal Decision of the Spanish National Court in the case concerning prosecution of acts of genocide, terrorism and torture allegedly committed in Guatemala during the 1980s, and the comment by M. Cottier, 'What Relationship Between the Exercise of Universal and Territorial Jurisdiction? The Decision of 13 December 2000 of the Spanish National Court Shelving the Proceedings Against Guatemalan Nationals Accused of Genocide', in Fischer, Kreß and Lüder (eds.),

according to standards of international justice that justify international support and cooperation.[158]

4A.1.3.2 International alternatives

Where national courts do not want or are not able to assume the investigative and prosecutorial role, recent history provides several alternative international, or quasi-international, models for the investigation or prosecution of international crimes.

(a) The ICC, terrorism and counter-terrorism The Statute establishing the International Criminal Court (ICC) was adopted in Rome on 17 July 1998, entering into force on 1 July 2002. The Court does not have retrospective jurisdiction, and cannot therefore prosecute crimes committed before the Statute's entry into force,[159] although the Security Council could, at least theoretically, confer jurisdiction on the ICC over offences before entry into force, in accordance with its Chapter VII powers.[160]

While the relevance of the ICC in the 'war on terror' is considered in the B section of this chapter,[161] certain characteristics of the ICC, pertinent to an assessment of its relevance to terrorism and counter-terrorism in the post 9/11 world, are worthy of note here. The Court has jurisdiction over genocide, crimes against humanity and war crimes committed in international or non-international armed conflict. The Statute includes aggression within the Court's jurisdiction, although this jurisdiction cannot yet be exercised until a definition is agreed upon.[162] Moreover, while

---

Prosecution of Crimes, pp. 843 ff., and the *Princeton Principles on Universal Jurisdiction* (Princeton University, 2001), available at http://www.princeton.edu/~lapa/unive_jur.pdf.

[158] Note also the obligations of states in respect of cooperation, and non-cooperation in circumstances where it would result in a serious violation of rights: see this chapter, para. 2. The duty on states to extradite or prosecute for certain serious offences, described below, can be satisfied by exercising universal jurisdiction where cooperation would be inconsistent with human rights obligations. For discussion of the limits imposed by human rights law on cooperation in criminal matters see below, Chapter 7, para. 7A.4.3.8.

[159] Article 11, ICC Statute. The ICC Statute entered into force on 1 July 2002, see J. Schense and I. Flattau, 'Implementation of the Rome Statute', 14.1 (2002) *INTERIGHTS Bulletin* 34.

[160] This would mirror the establishments of *ad hoc* criminal tribunals in the past. If the Security Council so decided, it has been questioned whether the ICC would be able to accept such jurisdiction: see, e.g., C. Greenwood, 'International Law and the "War against Terrorism"', 78 (2002) *International Affairs* 301. In relation to 9/11, this is not a realistic possibility, however, given US opposition and its veto power within the Council.

[161] See Chapter 4, para. 4B.1.2.2 below.

[162] See this chapter, para. 4A.1.1.3 for discussion of pending agreement on a definition and conditions for the exercise of jurisdiction over aggression. The first review conference,

not presently covered by the ICC Statute, it is also conceivable that 'terrorism' as such, comprising a broader ambit of conduct, may come to be included within the ICC Statute.[163]

In order for offences to be tried by the ICC, however, the Court's jurisdiction must be triggered in accordance with the Statute, which can be done in several ways.[164] The Security Council, which called for justice post September 11, could confer jurisdiction on the Court, unless the veto power prevented this.[165] Absent Council referral, the Court's jurisdiction depends on the state on whose territory the atrocities were committed, or a state whose nationals are suspected of responsibility, having ratified the Statute or accepted the Court's jurisdiction.[166] Nationals of a state party are potentially subject to the Court's jurisdiction.[167] Jurisdiction over nationals of non-state parties would depend on the state on whose territory the crime is committed being a party or accepting jurisdiction.[168]

Critically, however, ICC jurisdiction will only operate where the state itself does not take necessary and reasonable measures to investigate or prosecute allegations of serious crimes.[169]

---

in 2008, may approve this and the court could exercise jurisdiction over this crime after that date.

[163] SC Res. 1377 (2001) called for such inclusion; see 'The ICC: 9/11, Afghanistan, Iraq and Beyond', Chapter 4, para. 4B.1.2.2 below.

[164] ICC Statute, Article 13 'Exercise of Jurisdiction', which provides for referral by (a) the Security Council or (b) by a state party or (c) a *propio motu* investigation by the Prosecutor as triggering jurisdiction. In respect of the last two, however, the 'preconditions for the exercise of Jurisdiction' in Article 12 must be satisfied, namely that the state of territory or of nationality is a state party.

[165] Article 13, ICC Statute. The US is openly opposed to the Court and whether it would block this avenue for justice in such a case remains to be seen. In any event the Court does not depend on SC referral or approval (Article 13), provided there is a link via the state of territory or nationality as discussed below (Article 12: preconditions for the exercise of Jurisdiction).

[166] Article 12, ICC Statute.

[167] See P. Sands, 'Our Troops Alone Risk Prosecution', *The Guardian*, 15 January 2003.

[168] As noted above, before the ICC can act, the state of territory or nationality of the accused must be a party to the ICC treaty or accept the Court's jurisdiction (Article 12, ICC Statute).

[169] The relationship between the ICC and national tribunals is governed by the 'complementarity regime' in the ICC Statute (Statute of the International Criminal Court, Rome, 17 July 1998, UN Doc. A/CONF. 183/9 (1998), entered into force 1 July 2002). In particular, according to Article 17 of the Statute, the ICC can exercise jurisdiction only if the states with jurisdiction over conduct that forms the basis of the offences under the Statute are unwilling or unable to carry out the investigation or the prosecution. See Preamble and Articles 17–19, ICC Statute. The 'complementarity system' envisaged in the ICC Statute is distinct from the mechanisms created under the Statutes of the *ad hoc* tribunals for the Former Yugoslavia and Rwanda, which established the 'primacy' of the international tribunals over national courts. Note, however, that this prioritisation of international

(b) The role of *ad hoc* tribunals   Under Chapter VII of the UN Charter, the Security Council has broad powers to take measures for international peace and security, as discussed in Chapter 5, below. In 1994 it exercised those powers to establish two international criminal tribunals for Rwanda and the former Yugoslavia. It would be possible for the Security Council to establish a tribunal or, as has been suggested, to extend the jurisdiction of an existing tribunal, to prosecute September 11 offences or other offences of international concern.[170]

International experience also points increasingly to hybrid models of quasi-international justice that have emerged from negotiation and agreement. The approach of the Nuremberg tribunal suggests that several states can agree together to establish an international tribunal, conferring on it the power to do 'what any one of them might have done singly', namely prosecute on the basis of one of the grounds of jurisdiction mentioned above.[171] Similarly, an agreement between the UN and Sierra Leone led to the Statute of the Special Court for Sierra Leone,[172] which combines elements of national law, procedure and personnel with international components.[173] Other examples that might be described as predominantly domestic tribunals, but with an international aspect, are the human rights court established by the United Nations in East Timor[174] or the tribunal established by the Cambodian government to prosecute the crimes related to the Cambodian genocide.[175] Whether the establishment of *ad hoc* tribunals remains a feature of international practice in the future remains to

justice by the Security Council may have been premised implicitedly on the unavailability or ineffectiveness of national courts to discharge fair and effective justice in the former Yugoslavia and Rwanda at the time in question.

[170] G. Robertson, 'There is a legal way out of this . . .', *The Guardian*, 14 September 2001. Calls for an international or quasi-international tribunal abound in the context of Iraq. The ICC could also be afforded jurisdiction by the Security Council.

[171] The Nuremberg Judgment reasoned that: 'The signatory Powers created this Tribunal, defined the law it was to administer, and made regulations for the proper conduct of the Trial. *In doing so, they have done together what any one of them might have done singly*' (emphasis added), 'International Military Tribunal (Nuremberg), Judgment and Sentences', 41 (1946) AJIL 216.

[172] Report of the Secretary General on the Establishment of a Special Court for Sierra Leone, 4 October 2000, UN Doc. S/2000/915. The Court has not yet been established. See Tejan-Cole, 'Special Court', n. 7, http://www.un.org/Docs/sc/reports/2000/915e.pdf..

[173] See Draft Statute annexed to Secretary General's report, *ibid.*

[174] The United Nations Transitional Administration in East Timor (UNTAET) established such a system in the Dili district to investigate international crimes that had occurred during 1999.

[175] The Cambodian government has also, finally, agreed to create a hybrid court in which Cambodian judges would be in the majority, with international judges having a right of veto.

be seen, as the need for them should in principle be undermined by functioning national courts capable and willing of doing justice supplemented by a permanent ICC.

While perhaps an unlikely model, the *Lockerbie* court is also potentially relevant. The unusual model that emerged from the diplomatic impasse over the refusal to extradite suspects in the 1988 bombing[176] was of a national court sitting on foreign soil, applying mostly national law, with the exception that there was no jury. This arose as a compromise solution in the face of allegations as to the inability of the Scottish courts to dispense fair and impartial justice in the particular case. This scenario could similarly be relevant post September 11 if, for example, a compelling case were made out as to the potential prejudice to the fairness of trials in the US.[177]

In conclusion, international practice indicates various jurisdictional models of relevance to the prosecution of the September 11 offences and other crimes of international concern committed since then. Each have their strengths and weaknesses, their proponents, critics and sceptics. The practice relating to the application of this framework post 9/11, and the deference shown to national courts over international alternatives, is addressed in section B of this chapter.

4A.2 Implementing justice: international cooperation and enforcement

The international criminal law enforcement model depends, naturally, on international enforcement.[178] International cooperation in matters of extradition and 'mutual assistance' between states is essential for the purposes of, for example, arresting and transferring suspects, freezing assets and securing evidence.[179] As discussed below, rules governing cooperation are, in general, set out in multilateral and bilateral arrangements,

---

[176] Flight Pan Am 103 was bombed in the airspace over Lockerbie, Scotland, killing 259 people on board and 11 residents of Lockerbie.

[177] While some have suggested that prejudice could arise from the strength of national sentiment in the context of a jury trial, more likely are the human rights concerns around arbitrary detention and fair trial, discussed at Chapter 8 on Guantanamo Bay.

[178] It should be noted that the enforcement that is considered here is only enforcement for the purposes of ensuring effective criminal prosecution, as opposed to enforcement of judgments and sentences. Moreover, the events of September 11 or, potentially, wrongs committed in response to those events, may be subject to other forms of enforcement, including civil remedies, or the lodging of complaints before human rights courts.

[179] Cooperation arises also in relation to, for example, the transfer of sentenced persons, transfer of proceedings, protection of victims and witnesses and effecting compensation.

supplemented by other obligations – imposed for example by the Security Council – and are subject to other provisions of international law, notably international human rights law.

4A.2.1 Extradition

There is no general obligation to extradite in international law; the duty to extradite may arise from bilateral or multilateral extradition treaties, which also enshrine exceptions to this duty.[180] This general rule should be qualified – by reference to human rights law – in two ways. Firstly, certain offences are so serious that states are obliged to extradite persons found on their territory, or to submit them for prosecution in their own state (*aut dedere aut judicare*);[181] in addition, Security Council resolutions post September 11, asserted a duty on UN member states to deny safe haven to terrorists and to bring them to justice.[182] Secondly, as discussed further below, where there is a real risk that the fugitive would be subject to certain serious human rights violations in the state requesting extradition, human rights law imposes the obligation on states *not* to extradite.[183] A state's obligations in respect of extradition must therefore be understood not only by reference to extradition treaties, but also to other provisions of international law, including human rights law.

---

[180] States may, and increasingly do, extradite on the basis of national law without a treaty or arrangement, in accordance with the desire to improve international cooperation in respect of serious offences.

[181] This duty *aut dedere aut judicare* is a sub-species of universal jurisdiction. The duty to extradite or prosecute in respect of serious crimes is enshrined explicitly in various human rights instruments, such as the Convention against Torture, Article 5, and interpreted as implicit in the positive duty to ensure rights under more general human rights instruments: see Chapter 7. The principle is also reflected in several specific terrorism conventions: see, e.g., Article 7, Convention for the Suppression of Unlawful Seizure of Aircraft (The Hague, 16 December 1970, 860 UNTS 12325, in force 14 October 1971); Article 5(2), Convention for the Suppression of Unlawful Acts against the Safety of Civil Aviation (Montreal, 23 September 1971, 974 UNTS 14118, in force 26 January 1973); Article 7, Convention on the Prevention and Punishment of Crimes against Internationally Protected Persons (New York, 14 December 1973, 1035 UNTS 15410, in force 20 February 1977); Article 8(1) International Convention against the Taking of Hostages (New York, 18 December 1979, 1316 UNTS 21931, in force 3 June 1983).

[182] SC Res. 1373 (2001), above, note 90, does not clearly define the conduct to which it is addressed. To the extent that it covers only serious crimes under international law, such as September 11, it reflects the existing duty in international law. If it goes beyond to cover less serious acts, it is possible for the Council to impose the obligations pursuant to Articles 25, 41 and 48 of the Charter, although the lack of clarity as to the nature of those obligations undermines its force. See Chapter 5, in particular para. 2.2.

[183] See this chapter, para. 4A.2.1.2.

4A.2.1.1 Key features of extradition law

While multiple bilateral and multilateral extradition treaties exist, each with their own specific provisions, principles of extradition law can be identified from common features of extradition treaties and practice, key elements of which are sketched out below.[184]

Extradition regimes have often been criticised for their complexity, resulting in obstacles, delay in justice enforcement,[185] and potentially denial of justice, which in turn provide a disincentive to states to respect the legal process. Attempts to reform and modernise law and procedures, including the removal of domestic obstacles to extradition and streamlining procedures were underway before September 11 and were further impelled by those events, as discussed in section B.[186] Alongside these developments have been others in human rights law that seek to ensure protection for the person whose extradition is requested. Together they have significantly changed the shape of extradition law in recent years; these developments are to be welcomed so far as they enhance effectiveness, minimise arbitrariness and safeguard essential human rights protection.

• *Double criminality and 'Extraditable Offences'*: most extradition arrangements provide that an act is only extraditable if it is punishable as a crime according to the laws of both the requesting state and the requested state, or according to international law. In general, the crime need not itself be identical – if the request is for extradition for 'terrorism' offences for example the requested state need not also have an offence of terrorism in domestic law – but the conduct that forms the basis of the offence must be punishable in both states, often by a minimum specified penalty.[187]

---

[184] See also UN Model Treaty on Extradition, GA Res. 45/116, annex, UN Doc. A/45/49 (1990), 30 ILM 1407.

[185] For a discussion of some of those obstacles see Koufa, 'Progress Report', above, note 92, para. 127 (citing evidence requirements, *'forum non conveniens'* concerns, including defendants' rights issues). Generally, and on exceptions such as 'nationality' and 'political offences,' see also C. Van den Wyngaert, *The Political Offense Exception to Extradition* (Dordrecht, 1980), pp. 148–9.

[186] See in particular para. 4B.2.

[187] There will commonly be a requirement of a minimum penalty in both states of, e.g., two years' imprisonment. See, e.g., UK Extradition Act 1989. One of the developments in recent years is that States have moved from a 'list approach' to extradition to a 'penalty approach' which eliminates the need to set out all the relevant offences in a subsidiary document and replaces it with a test based on the applicable penalty.

- *Specialty and re-extradition*: it is a general rule that, once extradited, a suspect must be tried only for the crime or crimes covered in the extradition request, and only in the requesting state, unless the consent of the extraditing state is secured.
- *Ne bis in idem* (double jeopardy): as a person may not be tried twice in respect of the same offence, in certain circumstances the state need not extradite if there has been a final judgment against the suspect in respect of the conduct in question. Different manifestations of this principle appear in extradition and human rights treaties.[188]
- *The political offence exception*: to protect against extradition for politically motivated prosecution, and the potential involvement of foreign states in domestic political entanglements, an exception to obligations to extradite developed for crimes considered to be political in nature.[189] This exception has however increasingly been removed from international and national extradition provisions, in particular in respect of certain types of serious crimes such as the crimes under international law discussed above.[190] In relation to terrorism specifically, modern treaties generally exclude the political offence exception,[191] and indeed the

---

[188] Human rights treaties, however, appear to protect only against prosecution twice in the same state. This principle was expressly stated during the negotiations of the ICCPR and has been recognised by the Human Rights Committee. See M.J. Bossuyt, *Guide to the 'travaux préparatoires' of the International Covenant on Civil and Political Rights* (Dordrecht, 1987), pp. 316–18 and the decisions of the Human Rights Committee in *ARJ v. Australia* (Comm. No. 692/1996), Views of 28 July 1997 and *A.P. v. Italy* (Comm. No. 204/1986), Decision of 2 November 1987, UN Doc. CCPR/C/31/D/204/1986. However, a broader application of the *ne bis in idem* principle to extradition is contained in many extradition treaties including, e.g., Article 9 of the European Convention on Extradition, Paris, 13 December 1957, ETS No. 24, in force 18 April 1960.

[189] For background see generally Van den Wyngaert, *The Political Offense Exception to Extradition* (Dordrecht, 1980).

[190] It is commonly recognised that the political offence exception does not cover crimes under international law. International agreements expressly specify that international crimes such as torture, extra-judicial executions and forced disappearance of persons, which under certain circumstances are crimes against humanity or serious violations of humanitarian law, are extraditable offences to which the political offence exception has no relevance. See, e.g., the 1979 Additional Protocol to the 1957 European Extradition Convention, which excludes the political offences exception from extradition for war crimes and crimes against humanity; see also UN Convention against Torture and Other Cruel, Inhuman or Degrading Treatment or Punishment, Article 8; UN Principles on the Effective Prevention and Investigation of Extra-legal, Arbitrary and Summary Executions, Principle 18; Inter-American Convention on the Forced Disappearance of Persons, Article 5. See, in general, C. Van den Wyngaert, *The Political Offense Exception*, pp. 134 ff.

[191] The European Convention on the Suppression of Terrorism, Strasbourg, 27 January 1977, ETS No. 90, excludes the political offence exception from acts of hijacking or other

Security Council, in resolution 1373 (2001) insisted that states ensure 'that claims of political motivation are not recognized as grounds for refusing requests for the extradition of alleged terrorists'.[192]

- *Non-extradition of citizens*: the prohibition on the extradition of a state's own nationals is enshrined in the constitutions of numerous states, and as a result in certain extradition treaties.[193] Like certain other exceptions discussed above, it is itself increasingly subject to exception.[194]

- *Evidence sharing*: while extradition procedures vary considerably, not least between common law and civil law countries, often in extradition practice a request for extradition is accompanied by a warrant and basic evidence, sometimes referred to as '*prima facie*' evidence, or a showing of 'probable cause'.[195] Extradition proceedings are not a mini-trial and the evidence required is clearly much less than would be required to satisfy the requested state of the guilt of the suspect: thus the investigation need not be complete before the extradition is requested (nor need all available evidence be provided to the requested state). However, detention and extradition should not be requested unless or until the evidence provides reasonable grounds to suspect the individual of having committed the offence.[196] The requirement of sharing a basic degree of evidence is one way of ensuring that this is the case. However, while it remains a common feature of extradition law,[197] there are exceptions[198] and, as described in relation to developments post September 11 below,

offences against aircraft, serious attacks on internationally protected persons, kidnapping, taking of hostages, explosives and firearms offences. The United Nations Convention for the Suppression of Terrorist Bombings and the United Nations Convention for the Suppression of the Financing of Terrorism, 9 December 1999, UN Doc. A/RES/54/109 (1999) confirm that none of the offences detailed in those treaties are to be regarded as political offences for the purposes of extradition. Some but not all domestic systems have recognised a limitation on the exception: notably, US law, for example, has limited the exception to 'non violent' offences.

[192] SC Res. 1373, above, note 90, para. 3(g).
[193] Duffy, 'Constitutional Compatibility', at 20.
[194] These prohibitions are increasingly subject to exception. They do not apply to international courts and tribunals: see, e.g., Duffy, 'Constitutional Compatibility', at 20–6, and M. Plachta, '(Non-) Extradition of Nationals: A Neverending Story?', 13 (1999) *Emory International Law Review* 77 at 79.
[195] This is, traditionally, the position in common law countries. In civil law jurisdictions the requirement is often for a judicial order accompanied by sufficient information to establish dual criminality, rather than 'evidence' as such.
[196] Proceedings must be consistent with Article 9 ICCPR, which generally precludes preventive detention, but permits detention where there are reasonable grounds for suspecting the person of having committed a criminal offence, subject to procedural safeguards. See Chapter 7, in particular para. 7A.4.3.
[197] The requirement arises most often, as a well-established principle, in common law states.
[198] See, e.g., the European Convention on Extradition of 1957, discussed below.

in certain contexts the requirement has been further watered down in the name of streamlining the extradition process.[199]

- *Non-inquiry:* states will not inquire into the good faith of another state's request. This principle is long established in traditional extradition law in several states,[200] but is subject to qualification as a matter of national and international law.[201] At its strictest, such a rule might preclude the requested state from considering any evidentiary questions and require it to be blind to the circumstances of the trial and treatment of the suspect in the requesting state, neither of which reflect current international law and practice. However, while domestic courts are not obliged (nor necessarily well placed) to actively engage in a detailed assessment of another state's compliance with human rights norms, they are obliged under human rights law not to extradite where there are substantial grounds for believing that the persons' rights would be violated in the requesting state, as explained below.[202] The European Court of Human Rights has reflected these obligations, albeit in reticent terms that show at least some continuing degree of deference to the principle of 'non-inquiry':

---

[199] See Chapter 4, in particular para. 4B.2.3, in relation to the European Council Framework Decision on the European Arrest Warrant and the Surrender Procedure between Member States, 13 June 2002 (2002/584/JHA), OJ L 190/5, 18 July 2002 (hereinafter 'European Arrest Warrant'). See also the Extradition Treaty between the Government of the United Kingdom of Great Britain and Northern Ireland and the Government of the United States of America (Washington, 31 March 2003) (hereinafter 'US–UK Extradition Treaty'). A lower standard already exists for the surrender to the ICC, which is distinct from 'extradition' and states are clearly obliged to cooperate with the court by transferring suspects. As such 'a concise statement of the facts that are alleged to constitute those crimes' will be presented to the requested state. ICC Statute, Article 58(3). See also Article 91(2) on the documents to be transferred to the requested state.

[200] It is described as a rule of customary law in I. Bantekas, M. Nash and S. Mackarel, *International Criminal Law* (London, 2001), p. 149. See however J. Dugard and C. van den Wyngaert, 'Reconciling Extradition with Human Rights', 92 (1998) AJIL 188 at 190, noting that the rule traditionally applied in, e.g., US, UK and Canada, but not in continental European countries.

[201] On national restrictions, see Dugard and Van den Wyngaert, 'Reconciling Extradition', at 190–1. On international legal restrictions see Chapter 7, para. 7A.4.3.8.

[202] As human rights law obliges a state to ensure the protection of the rights of an individual on its territory and subject to its jurisdiction, and to refuse extradition if certain serious rights violations would occur on the requesting state's territory, when extradition is requested a minimal duty of inquiry may be seen to arise for the requested state to ensure that it meets its human rights obligations. This duty may arise before extradition or – where extradition is granted subject to assurances for example – thereafter (see, e.g., Concluding observations of the Human Rights Committee: Sweden, UN Doc. CCPR/CO/74/SWE (2002), para. 12). In practice, however, the onus lies on the individual to satisfy the court in the extraditing state that the necessary thresholds have been met.

To require such a review [by courts in the extraditing state] of the manner in which a court not bound by the Convention had applied the principles enshrined in Article 6 would also thwart the current trend towards strengthening international cooperation in the administration of justice, a trend which is in principle in the interests of the persons concerned. *The Contracting States are, however, obliged to refuse their cooperation if it emerges that the conviction is the result of a flagrant denial of justice.*[203]

4A.2.1.2 Extradition and human rights

In its totality, the legal framework governing extradition seeks to accommodate the essential balance between ensuring an effective system of interstate cooperation and protecting the rights of the individual.

While several key general human rights treaties such as the International Covenant on Civil and Political Rights and the European Convention on Human Rights do not address extradition explicitly, it is well established that the obligations of states to protect and ensure the human rights of individuals within their jurisdiction extend to declining to extradite (or otherwise deport or expel) persons to states where certain of their rights are at serious risk of violation.[204] As discussed more fully in Chapter 7, human rights treaties and the decisions of human rights bodies interpreting obligations on a case by case basis, indicate a prohibition on extradition where there is substantial risk of violation of certain rights in the requesting state, such as torture, inhuman and degrading treatment or punishment and, in certain contexts, the application of the death penalty or a 'flagrant denial' of fair trial rights.[205]

---

[203] *Drodz and Janousek* v. *France and Spain* (Appl. No. 12747/87), 26 June 1992, ECtHR, *Series A*, No. 240, para. 110 (emphasis added).

[204] This principle is often referred to as 'non-refoulement,' discussed in more detail in Chapter 7, para. 7A.4.3.8. While refoulement originally only applied to asylum seekers, it reflects a generally applicable obligation of a state not to return any individual within its territory to a state where he or she is at risk of being subjected to serious violations of his/her fundamental rights.

[205] It remains open whether the same principle applies to other rights violations under these conventions, as discussed in Chapter 7. Note that an express prohibition of extradition or surrender in cases where some of the rights protected would be likely to be infringed in the requesting state is also contained in certain human rights treaties or instruments. See, e.g., ACHR (Article 22(8)), UN Convention against Torture (Article 3), and European Charter of Fundamental Rights (Article 19). Similarly, the Convention Relating to the Status Refugees (Geneva, 28 July 1951, 189 UNTS 150, in force 22 April 1954) expressly sets forth a prohibition of *refoulement* of asylum seekers to a country where '[their] life or freedom would be threatened on account of [their] race, religion, nationality, membership of a particular social group or political opinion' (Article 33).

Extradition documents broadly reflect these obligations, although not consistently or systematically. The Inter-American Convention on Extradition, for example, precludes extradition 'when the offense in question is punishable in the requesting State by the death penalty, by life imprisonment, or by degrading punishment' unless sufficient assurances have been obtained previously,[206] while the European Convention on Extradition makes explicit reference only to the death penalty.[207] The UN Model Treaty on Extradition suggests that extradition be precluded where the requested State has substantial grounds to believe human rights norms on (a) discrimination, (b) torture, cruel and inhuman treatment and punishment, (c) minimum guarantees in criminal proceedings as contained in the ICCPR would not be respected, or (d) that the judgment of the requesting State has been rendered *in absentia* without the accused having the opportunity to present a defence.[208] While these provisions generally derive from – and must be interpreted by reference

---

[206] Inter-American Convention on Extradition, Caracas, 25 February 1981) *OAS Treaty Series* No. 60, in force 28 March 1992, Article 9 provides: 'The States Parties shall not grant extradition when the offense in question is punishable in the requesting State by the death penalty, by life imprisonment, or by degrading punishment, unless the requested State has previously obtained from the requesting State, through the diplomatic channel, sufficient assurances that none of the above-mentioned penalties will be imposed on the person sought or that, if such penalties are imposed, they will not be enforced.'

[207] The European Convention on Extradition of 1957 addresses extradition in the context of the death penalty. It provides (Article 11): 'If the offence for which extradition is requested is punishable by death under the law of the requesting Party, and if in respect of such offence the death-penalty is not provided for by the law of the requested Party or is not normally carried out, extradition may be refused unless the requesting party gives such assurances as the requested Party considers sufficient that the death-penalty will not be carried out.' Article 3(2) also excludes extradition where the requested state 'has substantial grounds for believing that a request for extradition for an ordinary criminal offence has been made for the purpose of prosecuting or punishing a person on account of his race, religion, nationality or political opinion, or that that person's position may be prejudiced for any of these reasons'.

[208] See UN Model Treaty on Extradition 1990, Article 3, which precludes extradition where the requested state has substantial grounds to believe human rights norms on (a) discrimination, (b) torture, cruel and inhuman treatment and punishment, (c) minimum guarantees in criminal proceedings would not be respected or (d) 'the judgment of the requesting State has been rendered *in absentia*, [and] the convicted person has not had sufficient notice of the trial or the opportunity to arrange for his or her defence and he has not had or will not have the opportunity to have the case retried in his or her presence'. Article 4 adds optional grounds for refusing extradition including: '(d) If the offence for which extradition is requested carries the death penalty under the law of the requesting State, unless that State gives such assurance as the requested State considers sufficient that the death penalty will not be imposed, or, if imposed, will not be carried out.'

to – human rights jurisprudence, they may also reflect other issues, such as life imprisonment, peculiar to particular constitutional traditions.[209]

States may seek to reconcile their commitment and obligations in respect of cooperation with human rights protection in various ways. Not uncommonly, states seek 'assurances' from the requesting state that it will act or refrain from acting in a certain way, but as human rights bodies have recently noted, this only meets their obligations so far as accompanied by genuine safeguards for the persons extradited, including effective monitoring by the sending state. It is thus emphasised that the sending state's responsibility for the rights of the person continues after extradition, by virtue of the act of expulsion.[210] States may, alternatively, be in a position to prosecute rather than extradite, in accordance with the *aut dedere aut judicare* principle applicable to certain serious offences discussed above; to this end states may take legislative measures to ensure that domestic law recognises jurisdiction over serious crimes committed outside the state's territory.[211]

4A.2.2 Mutual assistance

Mutual assistance is the process used to obtain evidence and other forms of information and legal cooperation from a foreign country. Like extradition, mutual assistance treaties are also signed on a bilateral or multilateral basis and often provide details of the procedure for the exchange of evidence and examples of the grounds on which requests can be refused.[212]

---

[209] See, e.g., life imprisonment, prohibited in several constitutions, particularly but not exclusively in Latin America. As a result, certain extradition treaties treat life imprisonment on a par with the death penalty. See, e.g., Inter-American Convention on Extradition, which unconditionally prohibits the extradition of a person when that person will be punished 'by the death penalty, by life imprisonment, or by degrading treatment in the requesting state'. While not prohibited by human rights law *per se*, life imprisonment without any possibility of early release may raise an issue of inhuman treatment, e.g., under Article 3 of the ECHR: see *Einhorn* v. *France* (Appl. No. 71555/01), Admissibility decision, 16 October 2001, para. 27.

[210] *Chahal* v. *United Kingdom* (Appl. No. 22411/93), Judgment of 15 November 1996, para. 80: 'The responsibility of the contracting state to safeguard him or her against such treatment is engaged in the event of expulsion.'

[211] See this chapter, para. 4A.1.3 above, on universal and other extra-territorial bases of jurisdiction, and advances in incorporating this into domestic systems, particularly in the context of implementing the ICC statute.

[212] Council of Europe Convention on Mutual Assistance in Criminal Matters, Strasbourg, 20 April 1959, ETS No. 30, in force 12 June 1962; Convention on Mutual Assistance in Criminal Matters between the Member States of the European Union, adopted by the European Council on 29 May 2000, OJ C 197/1 of 12 July 2000. For a comment on the EU Convention, see JUSTICE, *EU Cooperation in Criminal Matters: A Human Rights Agenda*

However, these arrangements are often less formal or rigid than in the case of extradition and states generally enjoy a larger measure of discretion to grant or decline requests for assistance.[213]

As discussed in the human rights chapter, the human rights obligations of states are less clear as regards the duty of non-cooperation in respect of mutual assistance than they are in respect of extradition of persons physically present on the extraditing state's territory, although, arguably, the same underlying principles may be held to apply.[214] While still not the norm, several mutual assistance agreements specifically exclude cooperation where, for example, the requested state has substantial grounds for believing that the request for mutual assistance has been made for the purpose of prosecuting or punishing a person on account of his race, religion, nationality or political opinion or that that person's position may be prejudiced for any of these reasons.[215] Some others suggest that other human rights concerns,[216] including the death penalty,[217] may also provide a basis for refusal to cooperate.[218]

(August 2002). See also the Scheme Relating to Mutual Assistance in Criminal Matters between Commonwealth Countries and the UN Model Treaty on Mutual Assistance in Criminal Matters, GA Res. 45/117, 14 December 1990, UN Doc. A/RES/45/117.

[213] It is increasingly common to see mutual assistance being rendered on the basis of domestic law without resort to a treaty. E.g., whereas, traditionally, extradition could only take place to a foreign state with which it enjoyed an extradition treaty, the UK has recognised that it will in principle grant assistance to any requesting state whether or not it is a treaty partner. See C. Nicholls, C. Montgomery and J. Knowles, *The Law of Extradition and Mutual Assistance in Criminal Matters: Practice and Procedure* (London, 2002), which refers to the Home Office Guidelines ('Seeking Assistance in Criminal Matters from the UK – Guidelines for judicial and prosecuting authorities', 2nd ed. (London, October 1999), ch. 2, at www.homeoffice.gov.uk/docs/guidelns.html).

[214] While extradition involves persons within the territory or jurisdiction of the extraditing state, in respect of mutual assistance the person affected may have not at any time been physically within the state's territory. However, assistance rendered in the knowledge that it may contribute to a violation of human rights in another state may violate at least 'the general spirit' of human rights conventions as 'instrument[s] designed to maintain and promote the ideals and values of a democratic society' (*Soering* v. *United Kingdom*, above, para. 87).

[215] Article 8 of the European Convention on the Suppression of Terrorism confirms that there is no obligation to afford mutual assistance in these circumstances.

[216] See also UN Model Treaty on Mutual Assistance in Criminal Matters, which envisages refusal to cooperate in case of persecution, double jeopardy (*non bis in idem*) and unfair measures to compel testimony, Articles 4(1)(c)–(e).

[217] The commentary to Article 4 of the UN Model Treaty on Mutual Assistance in Criminal Matters notes that states may wish to add other grounds for refusal, e.g., 'the nature of the applicable penalty (e.g., capital punishment)'.

[218] Some treaties and legislation have a much reduced basis for refusal in mutual assistance, limited solely to 'where execution of the request would be contrary to national security, public interest or sovereignty'.

4A.2.3 Cooperation and the Security Council

In certain circumstances, states may consider that such 'cooperative' procedures would be futile or ineffective, for example if a state whose cooperation is needed is believed to be involved in committing or concealing the crimes in question (as addressed by the ICJ in *Lockerbie*),[219] or where the urgency of the situation – due for example to well founded fear of repetition – demands swifter action than the cooperation process would provide. States may not however simply circumvent the cooperation process and unilaterally embark on coercive 'enforcement' action directly on another state's territory, without falling foul of international legal obligations owed to the other state (assuming it did not consent)[220] and to individuals under human rights law.[221]

In such circumstances, if faced with a situation in which normal cooperation procedure would be ineffective, states can call upon the Security Council to authorise criminal law enforcement action in the name of international peace and security,[222] including where necessary through the use of force.[223] Force employed must always be no more than necessary to achieve the objective, in this case the apprehension of suspects or securing vital evidence. The experience of the ICTY provides an example of Security Council authorisation for NATO enforcement of arrest warrants internationally. Although that experience concerned the transfer of

---

[219] *Questions of the Interpretation and Application of the 1971 Montreal Convention Arising from the Aerial Incident at Lockerbie* (*Libya* v. *United Kingdom*), Provisional Measures, Order of 14 April 1992, *ICJ Reports 1992*, p. 3.

[220] If a state seeks to effect law enforcement on another state's territory without its consent, it may violate the principle of non-intervention and, possibly, the prohibition on the use of force: see Chapter 5. Moreover, as the right to resort to force in self-defence depends on peaceful means being unavailable, if a state attacks a state without seeking to address the situation through enforcement of international criminal justice, where that may be possible, this may impact on the lawfulness of self-defence.

[221] If individuals are transferred for the purposes of criminal process in a way that simply circumvents the extradition process, violations of individual rights under human rights law arise, as well as breach of the obligations owed to other state parties to the extradition treaties. On human rights, see Concluding observations of the Human Rights Committee: Yemen, UN Doc. CCPR/CO/75/YEM (2002), para. 18, and generally Chapter 7. For issues relating to the unlawfulness of arrest, detention, extra-legal rendition and their impact on individual cases, see, e.g., *Oppenheim's International Law*, p. 387.

[222] The exceptions or grounds for refusal in extradition proceedings do not apply to transfer to international tribunals. See Duffy, 'Constitutional Compatibility', at 20.

[223] The Council has authorised coercive action to apprehend suspects to the ICTY. See also SC Res. 837 (1993), 6 June 1993, UN Doc. S/RES/837 (1993) in relation to Somalia. See Chapter 5, para. 5A.2.2.

persons to an international tribunal established by the Council, there is nothing to preclude the Council doing the same in respect of another national or international court seeking to ensure that justice is done and international peace and security respected.[224] In the post-September 11 context, in which the Council has called on all states to cooperate, such action would constitute a form of enforcement of its own resolutions.[225]

The enforcement of international law is never perfect, and international criminal law is no exception.[226] However, the unprecedented international consensus generated post 9/11 as regards the need to ensure accountability for serious crimes, if directed towards the apprehension of suspects and effective collective enforcement of international criminal law, could have had – or could yet have – positive repercussions far beyond the prosecution of these particular crimes.

4B Criminal justice in practice post September 11

This second part of the chapter will sketch out certain features of international practice in relation to the prosecution of crimes associated with the September 11 attacks, as it has unfolded in the first few years following those events.[227] It will highlight, and raise questions concerning, first the remarkable paucity of prosecutions, several years after the launch of what was described as the most significant investigation in history, and second the preference that has emerged through this limited practice for national over international judicial responses. It will then explore an area where there has been considerable legal industry since September 11, namely the law and practice of international cooperation.

It is worth recalling at the outset that, in light of the legal framework set out in the first section of this chapter, it is indisputable that

---

[224] Alternative provision would be made by the Council for human rights protection if extradition were to be circumvented – as was the case, e.g., to surrender before the ICTY.

[225] See, e.g., SC Res. 1373 (2001), above, note 90.

[226] See, e.g., the fact that Karadic and Mladic, indicted by the ICTY for genocide and other crimes, remain at large, despite repeated appeals by the ICTY Prosecutor for their arrest and surrender. On cooperation with the tribunals in law and practice, see A. Cassese, 'On the current trend towards Criminal Prosecution and Punishment of Breaches of International Humanitarian Law', 9 (1998) EJIL 2 and G.K. Sluiter, 'Cooperation with the International Criminal Tribunals for the Former Yugoslavia and Rwanda', in Fischer, Kreß and Lüder (eds.), *Prosecution of Crimes*, p. 681.

[227] It has been noted that the criminal justice framework as set out in the foregoing chapter applies also potentially to serious crimes committed in response to 9/11. This chapter focuses on the prosecution of 9/11 itself; see, however, this chapter, para. 4B.1.2.2, and Chapters 6, 7 and 8.

egregious crimes under international and national law were committed on September 11, 2001. Most straightforwardly, mass murder and other serious bodily offences contravened US and other domestic criminal laws. Under international law, it is relatively uncontroversial that the September 11 attacks amounted to crimes against humanity. More contentious questions arise as to the possibility of them constituting war crimes, or even aggression.[228] Specific treaty crimes, such as hijacking or terrorist bombing, may provide another source of applicable criminal law, at least so far as they are implemented into the prosecuting state's domestic law.[229] Serious doubts would surround the legitimacy of any prospective prosecution for terrorism on the basis of its status as a crime under international – as opposed to domestic – law at the time of the conduct in question.[230] The legitimacy of national terrorism prosecutions depends on the offences being clearly defined in domestic law, and the accused's individual responsibility being established.

As regards questions of jurisdiction, it is also relatively uncontroversial that many, or indeed all, states are entitled to exercise jurisdiction over the September 11 crimes.[231] Various national and international jurisdictional possibilities exist for the prosecution of these crimes. Principles of criminal law preclude certain bars to prosecution, and facilitate the accountability of the full range of perpetrators of those attacks. In short, the normative framework highlighted in Section A provided a promising starting point for addressing the September 11 atrocity through the international enforcement of criminal law.

---

[228] See Chapter 3, above, on the absence of state responsibility, relevant to these crimes. Chapter 6 below addresses in more detail the difficulty under current international law of conceptualising the relationship between states and international criminal networks as 'armed conflict'.

[229] See Chapter 2, above, for the treaty crimes relating to terrorism. For questions emerging regarding the basis on which individuals can be prosecuted for treaty crimes if there is no implementing legislation in the domestic state, see above, Chapter 4, in particular para. 4A.1.2, discussing 'treaty crimes', the *nullum crimen sine lege* and *nulla poena sine lege* principles and the ICTY decision in *Prosecutor* v. *Galić*, Case No. IT-98-29-T, Judgment, 5 December 2003. Note that there is some debate as to whether the use of an aeroplane amounts to a relevant explosive device under the Terrorist Bombing Convention.

[230] On the lack of clarity around a definition, see Chapter 2. On the legality issues arising, see '*Nullem crimen sine lege*', Chapters 4, para. 4A.1.2.2 and 7, para. 7A.4.3.5. Issues relating to respect for human rights principles in the criminal context post 9/11 are highlighted in Chapter 7, para. 7B.4.

[231] See the various theories of jurisdiction discussed above, Chapter 4, para. 1.3. Note also that in certain circumstances states may be obliged, not simply entitled, to exercise jurisdiction.

4B.1 Prosecutions in practice post 9/11

4B.1.1 Paucity of prosecutions

Of the features of international practice in the prosecution of crimes associated with 9/11, perhaps the most noteworthy is its scarcity. Despite the extraordinary degree of international attention focused on the 'war on terror', emphatic references to commitment to seeing 'justice' done,[232] and widespread detentions of 'suspicious' persons, there have been strikingly few prosecutions. In April 2004, there was finally one conviction in respect of the September 11 attacks, and that was subsequently quashed.

Germany has taken a leading role, having completed two criminal trials to date. In February 2003 the first conviction arising out of the September 11 attacks was handed down by a Hamburg court to a student for his role in supporting and organising logistics for the Hamburg branch of al-Qaeda, finding him guilty of membership in a terrorist organisation and 3,045 counts of accessory to murder in the September 11 attacks.[233] However, the conviction was quashed by the Federal Supreme Court of Germany and the case remanded for retrial, on the basis that the US had refused to share with the German courts crucial, potentially exculpatory evidence (witness testimony or transcripts of statements during interrogation by, among others, the person suspected of being the ringleader of the relevant branch of al-Qaeda).[234] The court based its finding on the basic rights of the accused to access available evidence, which it noted could not be compromised by national security concerns, and highlighted what it described as the dangers of allowing the criminal process to be manipulated by a foreign state withholding intelligence information in circumstances where its own self interest is at stake.[235]

The other German trial had ended in acquittal one month earlier for the same reason.[236] On the basis of lack of evidence that the accused had any

---

[232] See T.R. Reid, 'Blair Embraces a New Role as a Chief of War on Terror', *Washington Post*, 9 October 2001, reporting a statement of the UK Prime Minister: 'It is a fight for freedom . . . And I want to make it a fight for justice, too . . . Justice not only to punish the guilty. But justice to bring those same values of democracy and freedom to people around the world. That is what community means, founded on the equal worth of all.'

[233] Mounir Motassadeq, a 28-year-old Moroccan, was sentenced to 15 years' imprisonment in February 2003. See 'Motassadeq Convicted For Role in Sept. 11th Attacks', *Washington Post*, 20 February 2003.

[234] Decision of the Federal Supreme Court of Germany, 3 March 2004, Strafverteitiger (BGH), StV 4/2004.

[235] *Ibid.*

[236] Reportedly the evidence was made available to German authorities but permission to share with the court not granted. See P. Finn, '9/11 Suspect could face reduced charges. German judge says he understands alleged accomplice's claims of unfair trial', *Washington*

prior knowledge of the attacks, the Court acquitted, but took the unusual step of noting that it was not convinced of the defendant's innocence but unable to reach any other decision given the limited evidence available to it.[237]

There have also been some efforts to pursue criminal proceedings elsewhere. In Spain, international arrest warrants have been issued for 35 suspects, some of them at the highest levels – notably including Osama bin Laden[238] – and in respect of the September 11 attacks.[239] However, the few cases to proceed beyond the warrant stage, such as that of the al-Jazeera correspondent remanded in custody, relate not to direct involvement in the attacks but to support or membership of al-Qaeda.[240] In Italy, four cases proceeded to trial under a 'fast-track' procedure whereby a limited amount of evidence is provided and reduced sentences are handed down if convictions are secured. Once again the charges relate not to September 11 itself, but to falsifying documents, breaking immigration laws, and criminal association with the intent to obtain and transport arms.[241] In France several arrests have been made of persons allegedly linked with the Hamburg cell of al-Qaeda, but once again by September 2004, no charges had been brought.[242]

In the United States, thousands of persons are detained pursuant to the broadly framed 'war on terror', yet there have been relatively few

---

Post, 5 February 2003; 'September 11 Terror Suspect Acquitted', *Deutsche Welle*, 6 February 2004.

[237] Abdelghani Mzoudi, who was charged in a similar way to Motassadeq, was freed by a German court in December 2003 after a letter from the Federal Office of Criminal Investigation, the BKA, raised serious doubts that he had any prior knowledge of the attacks. See 'German Court Frees 9/11 Suspect', *BBC News*, 11 December 2003.

[238] See 'Spain Indicts Osama bin Laden on 9/11 Charges', *Associated Press*, 17 September 2003, reporting the indictment by investigative magistrate Baltasar Garzon of a total of 35 people for terrorist activities connected to bin Laden's al-Qaeda organisation. Notably, the Spanish indictment (based on the principle of universal jurisdiction for acts such as those of 9/11) represents the first known indictment of bin Laden for the 2001 terrorist attacks. In the United States, bin Laden is charged in an indictment returned by a grand jury in New York with multiple charges resulting from the 1998 bombings of the US embassies in Kenya and Tanzania, which killed more than 200 people, but has not yet been indicted for the acts of 9/11.

[239] There is no public indication of these international arrest warrants having been executed.

[240] R. Tremlett, 'Al-Jazeera man faces terror trial', *The Guardian*, 12 September 2003. The suspect, Tayssir Alouni, conducted exclusive interviews with Osama bin Laden during the Afghanistan war and is reportedly accused of membership of a terrorist organisation.

[241] They are charged with supplying false documents, breaking immigration laws, and criminal association with the intent to obtain and transport arms, explosives and chemicals. See 'Terror suspects go on trial in Italy', *Associated Press*, 5 February 2002.

[242] See, e.g., 'France Arrests al-Qaeda Suspects', *BBC News*, 6 June 2003, available at news.bbc.co.uk/2/hi/europe/2967202.stm; see also 'Moroccan Arrested for Sept 11

charges lodged and strikingly few trials. The convictions that have resulted involved guilty pleas that proceeded according to an expedited process, such that the normal evidentiary requirements for proving the case did not apply.[243] With the notable exception of the criminal proceedings against the so-called 'twentieth hijacker',[244] charges have not related to direct involvement in the September 11 attacks themselves.[245] Instead charges lodged in the US have related almost exclusively to support for al-Qaeda (in most cases based on evidence – of periods spent at 'training camps' in Afghanistan – which has been found insufficient by German courts).[246]

Attacks', AP, 6 June 2003 and V. Von Derschau, 'France Detains Suspected Islamic Militants', AP, 15 September 2004.

[243] See, e.g., 'Walker Lindh indicted on 10 counts', CNN.com, 6 February 2002; '"American Taleban" jailed for 20 years', *CNN.com*, 4 October 2002. Lindh was accused of being a terrorist trained by al-Qaeda, who conspired with the Taleban against Americans. He was not accused of conduct related directly to 9/11.

[244] See, e.g., *United States of America* v. *Zacarias Moussaoui*, the 'twentieth hijacker' charged with conspiracy and membership of an illegal organisation. The indictment, presented on 11 December 2001 before the District Court for the Eastern District of Virginia (Case No. 01-455-A), is the first to be issued in the US in respect of 9/11, and alleges that Moussaoui received money from the same sources in Germany and the Middle East as allegedly funded the September 11 hijackers, and that he possessed information about the application of pesticides from aeroplanes. See 'Suspected al Qaeda Operative Charged with Planning Terrorist Actions', US Department of State Press Release, 21 December 2001; J. Borger, 'First Man Charged for September 11 Attacks. Muslim Radicalised in London Faces Death Penalty', *The Guardian*, 12 December 2001. In early 2004, charges were limited and the death penalty ruled out on the basis of limited access to evidence: see D. Butler, 'German Judges Order a Retrial for 9/11 Figure', *New York Times*, 5 March 2004. HD XXX. The trial of Moussaoui is pending.

[245] Charges include that the accused did 'knowingly and unlawfully combine, conspire, confederate and agree to provide material support and resources, as that term is defined in Title 18, United States Code, Section 2339A(b), to a foreign terrorist organization, namely al Qaeda'. These cases do not address the involvement of high-level al-Qaeda operatives.

[246] See the case of Mzoudi, above, note 235 and corresponding text. See also *United States* v. *Iyman Faris*, District Court for the Eastern District of Virginia; *United States* v. *Al-Moayad*, District Court of the Eastern District of New York, Case No. M-03-0016; *United States* v. *Zayed*, District Court of the Eastern District of New York; *United States* v. *Battle, Ford, Ahmed Bilal, Muhammad Bilal, Al Saoub and Lewis*, District Court of the District of Oregon, Case No. CR 02-399 HA; *United States* v. *Mukhtar al-Bakri*, District Court of the Western District of New York, Case No. 02-M-108 and *United States* v. *Goba, Alwan, Mosed, Taher and Galab*, District Court of the Western District of New York. The legal documents supporting these US cases are available at http://news.findlaw.com/legalnews/us/terrorism/cases. As discussed at Chapter 8. Until February 2004, none had even been charged. Since then charges have been made against a tiny fraction of the detainees, none of whom has yet been prosecuted, though preliminary hearings got under way in four military commissions in August 2004. An estimated 660 persons

Strikingly few of the many persons involved in planning and executing the enormous and complex September 11 attacks, and none of the highest level architects, are among the persons accused or prosecuted to date. Several factors are likely to contribute to the remarkably scant activity emerging from the national courts. First, the evidentiary challenge that cases such as these pose is unquestionable. Among other things, illicit transnational networks are difficult to penetrate, and intelligence reports, gathered for different purposes, often lack the evidentiary credentials to prove guilt beyond reasonable doubt.

Second, to a large degree the failure of national courts post 9/11 appears to reflect a failure of international cooperation, despite the emphasis placed on enhancing cooperation in criminal matters post 9/11. In particular, US intelligence agencies have illustrated unwillingness to share information with the relevant courts in other states, impeding international justice efforts.[247] In what has been described as a 'bitter irony in the global war against terrorism',[248] the US stands accused of hampering proper convictions, but also withholding potentially exonerating information from criminal courts.[249] It was this approach by the US that provoked strong criticism, direct and indirect, from German prosecutors and courts, and that ultimately led to the quashing of the one criminal conviction that had been secured in respect of 9/11.[250]

Third, poor human rights practices may also play their role in impeding international cooperation and/or effective prosecutions. As noted below, public statements since 9/11 suggest that rights issues may thwart the ability of European states to cooperate with the US post 9/11 due to

are detained at Guantanamo Bay. Only two of them have even been charged and none prosecuted.

[247] The German efforts to prosecute in respect of 9/11 and secure US cooperation in doing so are illustrative, in particular the Mzoudi acquittal that led to open indications of frustration by German authorities and courts. See '9/11 Suspect Could Face Reduced Charges', *Washington Post*, 5 February 2003, 'Judge Frees 9/11 Suspect in Germany', *Washington Post*, 12 December 2003, 'September 11 Terror Suspect Acquitted', *Deutsche Welle*, 6 February 2004.

[248] See 'Terror Case sets Washington and Berlin at Odds', *Christian Science Monitor*, 9 February 2004.

[249] See the *Motassadeq* case, discussed at para. 4A.1.1.1 above. Lawyers alleged that '[s]tatements [the US authorities] kept secret led to a guilty verdict'. – 'Judge frees 9/11 suspects in Germany. Ruling could undo only conviction', *Washington Post*, 12 December 2003. When some of the statements by key witnesses that had been withheld during trial were eventually disclosed – following the quashing of the conviction – they included statements that the accused had not been privy to the 9/11 plot. See M. Landler, 'U.S. Report Adds Fog to 9/11 Retrial', *New York Times*, 12 August 2004.

[250] See statements in the context of the *Motassadeq* and *Mzoudi* cases, this chapter, para. 4B.1.1.1 above.

their human rights obligations (as discussed more fully below and in Chapter 7). Conversely, practices such as interrogating suspects absent safeguards against torture, have the result that much of the evidence gathered, even if shared with other states, would not in any event be admissible in a court of law.[251]

Ultimately, however, the explanation for the paucity of proceedings may lie in the simple fact that, despite the multifaceted approach to the 'war on terror' outlined post 9/11, that fight has in fact been distinctly military in nature. In late September 2001 President Bush stated that: 'We will direct every resource at our command, every means of diplomacy, every tool of intelligence, every instrument of law enforcement, every financial influence, and every necessary weapon of war to the disruption and defeat of the global terror network.'[252] Particular emphasis has been lent by other leaders to the objective of ensuring that 'justice' is done,[253] and the Security Council, for its part, underscored the justice objective in the immediate wake of 9/11 and has reiterated it since then.[254] However, a few years on, one has to ask whether the justice touted was justice in some political sense that has little to do with criminal law enforcement. While few have been prosecuted, many of those suspected of involvement in the September 11 attacks have been treated as enemy combatants and killed, or detained on uncertain legal basis, including in the 'legal black hole' at Guantanamo Bay.[255]

To the extent that the 'law enforcement' arm of the 'war on terror' has been flexed, it has been directed towards information gathering and prevention, rather than criminal prosecutions and ensuring that justice was done. Detentions, for example, appear to have focused on intelligence

---

[251] On the possibility of non-US courts relying on evidence alleged to have resulted from torture or ill-treatment see, e.g., Amnesty International's criticism of the practice of the British Special Immigration Appeals Commission (SIAC): 'Justice perverted under the Anti-terrorism, Crime and Security Act 2001', 11 December 2003, AI Index: EUR 45/029/2003. On the admissibility issue in German courts, See Landler, 'U.S. Report Adds Fog to 9/11 Retrial'.

[252] J. Harris, 'President Outlines War on Terrorism, Demands Bin Laden be Turned Over', *Washington Post*, 21 September 2001.

[253] See, e.g., the UK Prime Minister describing the UK's role as to 'construct a consensus behind a broad agenda of justice and security' (Speech in Sedgefield constituency, 5 March 2004).

[254] See, e.g., SC Res. 1368 (2001), 12 September 2001, UN Doc. S/RES/1368 (2001), para. 3, where the Security Council '[c]alls on all States to work together urgently to bring to justice the perpetrators, organizers and sponsors of these terrorist attacks'.

[255] This is the definition of the situation of the Guantanamo detainees given by the UK Court of Appeal in *R (Abbasi and another)* v. *Secretary of State for Foreign and Commonwealth Affairs* [2002] EWCA Civ. 159 (hereinafter 'Abbasi'), para. 64.

gathering, not on securing criminal trials.[256] As one German intelligence source is reported as having noted: 'we are more focused on prosecuting terrorists while the United States is mainly concerned with preventing terrorism'.[257]

In conclusion, while the lack of momentum around criminal prosecutions highlights many challenges, including those relating to evidence gathering and the need for enhanced international cooperation, it also raises general questions as to the profile and priority afforded to the pursuit of criminal justice in the post September 11 world.

4B.1.2 International v. national models of justice post 9/11

4B.1.2.1 Focus on justice at the national level

A second feature of criminal law practice pursuant to the 'war on terror' that deserves highlighting relates to the relationship between national and international jurisdictions. To the extent that there has been practice to draw on, the approach to criminal justice adopted has been national in its jurisdictional focus. But what has been, and what should be, the role of international courts, and what role might there yet be for the nascent ICC?

September 11 spawned a policy debate on the appropriate vertical and horizontal relationship between national and international courts: do (or should) national courts *per se* take priority over international ones for crimes of this nature, or vice versa?[258] Proponents of an international tribunal in the aftermath of 9/11 reflected the view, on the one hand, that justice, or indeed the perception of justice, required that September 11 offences were prosecuted by an impartial court outside the US, preferably in an international tribunal that would reflect the international nature of these egregious crimes, the international community against which the offences were committed, and that community's interest in seeing

---

[256] For those detainees who may, eventually, be tried, the willingness to detain for extended periods without normal respect for the right to trial without undue delay, has reduced the momentum that usually attends the criminal investigative and prosecutorial process in countries such as the US.

[257] See 'Terror Case sets Washington and Berlin at Odds', above, note 246.

[258] The ICC is clearly bound by 'complementarity', but it takes a different approach from the *ad hoc* tribunals, see above. In addition to the vertical relationship between international courts and national courts, questions arise as to the horizontal relationship between national bases of jurisdiction: does or should territorial jurisdiction necessary prevail over universal jurisdiction? On uncertainty surrounding these issues, see Framework, Section A above.

justice done.[259] The other (perhaps predominant) view was that, provided national courts are able and willing to do justice, which the US courts (among others) appeared in principle to be, international alternatives were unnecessary.

Similar issues arose again, albeit in a very different context, in post war Iraq, where considerably more concern was expressed as to the capacity of Iraqi courts to administer justice.[260]

The proposals for an international tribunal post 9/11 (or indeed in Iraq) never really garnered support.[261] While it remains relatively early days in a long process of investigation and prosecution of 9/11 and its aftermath, which will undoubtedly span many years and continents, early indications are that so far as criminal justice has been pursued, priority has been given to national prosecutions over international.[262] In reality, this fact is explained in very large part by the fact that the 'war on terror' is, essentially, US driven. US opposition to the ICC is as virulent as it is notorious, and its support for the *ad hoc* tribunals (which it once favoured) has waned by association.

However, while some have lamented the loss of opportunity to establish an international tribunal,[263] in principle the emphasis on national courts is consistent with the ethos of the emergent system of international justice.[264] Developing international practice – of which the ICC's deference to willing and able national courts (the 'complementarity' regime)[265] is the clearest indicator – recognises the priority of domestic

---

[259] See A.M. Slaughter, 'Terrorism and Justice', *Financial Times*, 12 October 2003, p. 23, arguing that an international tribunal comprising US and Islamic judges should be set up to try terrorists, which would not only add legitimacy to the proceedings but help overcome practical obstacles to effective prosecution.

[260] On issues relating to accountability in Iraq, see, e.g., Human Rights Watch, 'Iraq: Justice Needs International Role', Press Release, 15 July 2003, available at http://www.hrw.org/press/2003/07/iraq071503.htm, noting that: 'The Iraqi judiciary, weakened and compromised by decades of Ba'ath party rule, lacks the capacity, experience, and independence to provide fair trials for the abuses of the past'.

[261] The progress made by national courts is highlighted above: see, e.g., cases in Germany and US, above.

[262] See the limited national practice referred to above.

[263] See, e.g., M.A. Drumbl, 'Judging the September 11 Terrorist Attack', 24 (2002) HRQ 323; J. Fitzpatrick, 'Speaking Law to Power: The War Against Terrorism and Human Rights', 14 (2003) EJIL 241, in particular at 261.

[264] The relationship between the ICC and national tribunals is governed by the 'complementarity regime' in the ICC Statute (Statute of the International Criminal Court, Rome, 17 July 1998, UN Doc. A/CONF.183/9 (1998), entered into force 1 July 2002), see Section 4A.1.3.2(a) above.

[265] Articles 17–19, ICC Statute.

over international prosecution (and, arguably, also of the territorial state over others, as the most natural forum for criminal prosecution).[266] The practice post 9/11 may indeed have a contributory role in consolidating this principle of the primacy of national courts.

But this principle has two dimensions. Primacy should not be confused with exclusivity – deference lasts only as long as domestic courts are able and willing to ensure that justice is done.[267] The sovereign right of states to exercise their criminal jurisdiction is accompanied by their sovereign responsibility to do so respecting international fair trial standards as enshrined in applicable human rights law and IHL. The minimum benchmarks of a fair trial also constitute prerequisites around which international support for and cooperation with criminal prosecutions should take shape.[268] If states cannot or will not meet these international standards, other foreign, international or quasi-international tribunals should be seized of jurisdiction to ensure that justice can be done without being compromised.

It remains to be seen how unfolding practice will qualify the prioritisation of national justice,[269] and whether the conditions on which this priority depends include, as the OAS has suggested post 9/11, guaranteeing 'the application of rules of due process for the alleged perpetrators,

---

[266] See the complementarity principle in the ICC Statute, Preamble and Article 27, and the 'primacy' of ICTY and ICTR jurisdiction, at Section A above. Considerable uncertainty surrounds priorities between national courts exercising different bases of jurisdiction – see, e.g., M. Cottier, 'What Relationship Between the Exercise of Universal and Territorial Jurisdiction? The Decision of 13 December 2000 of the Spanish National Court Shelving the Proceedings Against Guatemalan Nationals Accused of Genocide', in H. Fischer, C. Kreß and S.R. Lüder (eds.), *International and National Prosecution of Crimes Under International Law* (Berlin, 2001), pp. 843 ff. See also the *Princeton Principles on Universal Jurisdiction*, 2001, available at http://www.princeton.edu/~lapa/unive_jur.pdf and the comment by S.W. Becker, 'The Princeton Principles on Universal Jurisdiction', 14. 1 (2002) *INTERIGHTS Bulletin* 15.

[267] Questions have arisen with respect to the compatibility of the proposed rules for the newly established Iraqi Special Tribunal for Crimes Against Humanity with internationally accepted fair trial standards. See, e.g., P. Ford, 'Iraqi tribunal stirs fierce debate', *Christian Science Monitor*, 1 October 2003; C. Savage, 'Tribunal for Hussein Trial Criticized', *The Boston Globe*, 17 December 2003, reporting that international law specialists warned . . . that the 7,300-word document establishing the 'Iraqi Special Tribunal for Crimes Against Humanity' contains critical holes that could undermine the integrity of what will be the most important human rights trial since Nuremberg'. On the scarcity of proceedings that have actually come to fruition in national courts re 9/11, see above.

[268] These obligations stem from law relating to extradition and mutual assistance and human rights, see Chapter 7, para. 7A.4.3.8 below.

[269] Relevant practice would include that of the US national courts and others, as well as the model of national justice advanced in Iraq at the time of writing.

and that there is an effective will to bring them to justice'.[270] In the light of controversial developments in some states, including the US, it may be that the foreign or international jurisdictional alternatives should be revived as a bulwark against ineffective or abusive national proceedings.

4B.1.2.2 The ICC: 9/11, Afghanistan, Iraq and Beyond?

The relevance of the ICC post September 11 is often dismissed by reference to the fact that the ICC Statute entered into force after September 11 and has no retroactive effect.[271] The ICC has no realistic impact on the prosecution of the September 11 attacks themselves,[272] largely due to steadfast US opposition, which has persisted in the wake of 9/11,[273] the ICC may, however, be of direct relevance to the present inquiry in two ways.

First, in the event of other offences such as those committed on September 11 arising in the *future*, the ICC may well exercise jurisdiction, forming a critical part of the international response thereto. That crimes such as those entailed in the September 11 attacks would fall within the Court's jurisdiction, for example as crimes against humanity, has been noted.[274] ICC jurisdiction will generally depend (absent Security Council referral)[275] on the state on whose territory the atrocities were committed, or a state whose nationals are suspected of responsibility, having ratified

[270] OAS Resolution 1/03 on 'Trial for International Crimes', Washington DC, 24 October 2003.

[271] The ICC Statute did not enter into force until 17 July 2002; see J. Schense and I. Flattau, 'Implementation of the Rome Statute', 14.1 (2002) *INTERIGHTS Bulletin* 34. Retroactive jurisdiction is precluded by Article 11, ICC Statute.

[272] The Security Council could, arguably, exercise its Chapter VII powers (see Chapter 5, para. 5A.2) to confer jurisdiction on the Court to go beyond Article 11, but this is not a conceivable route at least as long as the US opposes the Court and has a Security Council veto.

[273] President Clinton signed the ICC Statute shortly before leaving office on 31 December 2000 (see 'The Right Action', *New York Times*, 1 January 2001, at A6) but in May 2002, the Bush administration purported to 'undo' the signature and notified the United Nations that it did not intend to ratify (see Letter from John R. Bolton, Under Secretary of State for Arms Control and International Security, to Kofi Annan, UN Secretary-General (6 May 2002), at http://www.state.gov/r/pa/prs/ps/2002/9968.htm).

[274] SC Res. 1377 (2001), 28 November 2001, UN Doc. S/RES/1377 (2001). Note also SC Res. 1373 (2001), 28 September 2001, UN Doc. S/RES/1373 (2001), which, as noted above, categorised 'all acts of international terrorism' as threats to international peace and security. Moreover, as also noted, 'terrorism' – comprising a broader ambit of conduct – may come to be included within the ICC Statute if an acceptable definition can be agreed upon.

[275] Article 13, ICC Statute. The US is openly opposed to the Court and whether it would block this avenue for justice in such a case remains to be seen. In any event the Court does not depend on SC referral or approval (Article 13), provided there is a link via the state

the Statute or accepted the Court's jurisdiction.[276] For crimes involving international networks of individuals, it is likely that a considerable range of states would satisfy the nexus requirement.[277] Among the states already party to the ICC Statute are several whose nationals are suspected of involvement in the September 11 crimes, suggesting that should such an atrocity occur in the future, the Court would probably not have difficulty in exercising its jurisdiction.

Moreover, it may be that in the longer term the events of 9/11 and their aftermath will impact on the Court's jurisdiction over 'terrorism' in the future. This crime was excluded in 1998 primarily due to the lack of a definition, but also for other reasons, including a perception that terrorism did not rank among the most serious crimes to which the ICC should direct its attention.[278] The groundswell of 'anti-terrorist' feeling post September 11 and the willingness of states to categorise international terrorism as 'one of the most serious threats to international peace and security in the twenty-first century' may suggest that a different view would be taken after September 11.[279] Calls for the inclusion of terrorism since September 11 may impel the Assembly of States Parties to consider including terrorism, although ultimately its inclusion as a generic crime will depend on states being able to agree to an acceptable definition.[280]

---

of territory or nationality as discussed below (Article 12: preconditions for the exercise of jurisdiction).

[276] Article 12, ICC Statute.

[277] As of 3 May 2004, 94 countries are states parties to the Statute of the International Criminal Court (source: www.icc-cpi.int).

[278] While the main reason for excluding terrorism was doubt as to the customary status of the crime, other grounds included a sense that terrorism lacked the gravity of the other crimes under international law, the complexity in the application of treaties to individuals, highlighted above, and the fear of politicisation of the Court as the reasons for exclusion contained in the Statute. See Zimmerman, 'Crimes', pp. 98–9. Cassese, *International Criminal Law*, p. 125, includes politicisation, lack of seriousness and that terrorism is more effectively prosecuted at home. Cf. the condemnation of terrorism post 9/11 as 'one of the most serious threats to international peace and security in the twenty-first century'. SC Res. 1377 (2001), 12 November 2001, UN Doc. S/RES/1377 (2001). Note also SC Res. 1373 (2001), 28 September 2001, UN Doc. S/RES/1373 (2001), which categorised 'all acts of international terrorism' as threats to international peace and security, discussed in Chapter 5.

[279] On other developments since 1998, which signal not that consensus has been reached but that some progress has been made since that date, note the definition agreed upon for the purpose of the Terrorist Financing Convention (Article 2), and the narrowing of difference over the definition in the context of the comprehensive convention.

[280] SC Res. 1377 (2001), above, note 272. Note also SC Res. 1373 (2001), above, note 48, which, as noted above, categorised 'all acts of international terrorism' as threats to international peace and security.

Second, and more immediately, ICC jurisdiction may also be of real potential relevance to measures taken in *response* to September 11, which continue to unfold after the Statute's entry into force. If, as has been alleged with increasing regularity,[281] war crimes of considerable gravity have been committed in association with the armed conflicts in Afghanistan, Iraq or elsewhere, there is a potential case for the ICC, provided the preconditions for the exercise of jurisdiction are met.[282]

Afghanistan ratified the ICC statute on 10 February 2003, by virtue of which the ICC has jurisdiction over genocide, war crimes or crimes against humanity committed on Afghan territory after that date (or before that date, but after entry into force of the Statute, if the Afghan State so decided).[283] The Court's jurisdiction applies to the nationals of any state (including non-state parties such as the US) that may commit such crimes in Afghanistan. A practical impediment to the exercise of that jurisdiction arises, however, as regards US nationals as the US has negotiated special agreements with governments around the world, including the government of Afghanistan, to the effect that those governments will not transfer US personnel to the ICC.[284] (One longer term side effect of the abuses committed by the US in the course of the 'war on terror' may be an undermining of its ability to secure such agreements in the future.[285])

By contrast, Iraq has not ratified the Statute. But the UK, for example, has been a state party since 4 October 2001, satisfying the alternative

---

[281] See 'UN rights chief warns of war crimes in Iraq', above, note 227.

[282] As noted above, this requires that the state on whose territory the crime arises or the state of nationality has ratified or accepts the court's jurisdiction (Article 12) unless the Security Council refers the situation to the Court (Article 13).

[283] As noted above, before the ICC can act, the state of territory or nationality of the accused must be a party to the ICC treaty or accept the Court's jurisdiction (Article 12 of the Statute). The state can accept the Court's jurisdiction for a specific situation arising before ratification, but after entry into force of the ICC Statute.

[284] On the agreements, see, in general, Human Rights Watch, 'United States Efforts to Undermine the International Criminal Court: Impunity Agreements', 4 September 2002.

[285] These so-called 'Article 98 agreements' were controversial before (*ibid.*) but met with intensified opposition in light of evidence of US war crimes in Iraq. See, e.g., Warren Hoge, 'Annan Assails US for Seeking Peacekeeper Immunity', *International Herald Tribune*, Saturday 19 June, 2004. The US dropped its attempt to get UN backing for these agreements in light of the Iraq abuse scandals: see Warren Hoge, 'Prison Abuse Halts U.S. Bid for Troop Immunity', 24 June, 2004. On the agreements, see, in general, Human Rights Watch, 'United States Efforts to Undermine the International Criminal Court: Impunity Agreements', 4 September 2002. On questions as to their lawfulness for parties to the Statute, see J. Crawford, P. Sands and R. Wilde, 'Joint Legal Opinion on bilateral agreements sought by the United States under 98(2) of the ICC Statute'. These documents and an updated list of 'Article 98 agreements' may be consulted on the website of the Coalition for the ICC, at http://www.iccnow.org/documents/otherissuesimpunityagreem.html.

'nationality' nexus.[286] UK nationals involved in conduct that might amount to war crimes or crimes against humanity after that date are therefore potentially subject to the Court's jurisdiction.[287] Submissions calling for the investigation of such crimes by members of the UK government or military, including as a result of acting in 'common purpose' or 'joint criminal enterprise' with US nationals, have been submitted to the ICC Prosecutor.[288] One of the critical factors in the ICC Prosecutor's decision whether to proceed will, presumably, be whether or not the UK is itself taking appropriate measures to investigate thoroughly allegations on the national level.[289]

Multiple allegations have arisen as to aggression having been committed in Iraq.[290] Some of these were also submitted to the ICC Prosecutor for investigation, but were rejected as the ICC cannot (at least as yet) exercise jurisdiction over aggression.[291] The Statute and subsequent negotiations clearly anticipate that in the future acts of aggression will fall within the Court's rubric, once agreement is reached on a definition and conditions for the exercise of jurisdiction. It remains to be seen whether the events of 9/11 and those following will have a chilling, or a catalytic, effect on the ability of states to reach agreement on the exercise of jurisdiction over the crime of aggression.[292]

---

[286] The case of the United Kingdom is not however isolated, as the nationals of a number of other states party to the ICC Statute are currently taking part in the military operations in Iraq.

[287] See P. Sands, 'Our Troops Alone Risk Prosecution', *The Guardian*, 15 January 2003.

[288] 'Report of the Inquiry into the Alleged Commission of War Crimes by Coalition Forces in the Iraq War During 2003', 8–9 November 2003, pp. 14–20: the report was commissioned by Peacerights and prepared by eight academics.

[289] 'Complementarity' of the ICC to national systems, see Preamble and Articles 17–19, ICC Statute.

[290] See, e.g., 'Lawyers doubt Iraq war legality', *BBC News*, 7 March 2003, reporting a letter from UK law teachers on the unlawfulness of the prospective attack on Iraq, which described such an attack as an act of aggression. See also the interview with Saudi Arabia's Foreign Minister Prince Saud al-Faisal questioned whether '[i]ndependent action . . . would encourage people to think . . . that what they're doing is a war of aggression rather than a war for the implementation of the United Nations resolutions', Interview with BBC News Correspondent, John Simpson, http://news.bbc.co.uk/1/hi/world/middle_east/2773759.stm.

[291] 'Communications received by the Office of the Prosecutor', ICC Press Release, 16 July 2003, see www.ic-cpi.int/library.

[292] See above, para. 4A.1.1.3 for discussion of pending agreement on a definition and conditions for the exercise of jurisdiction over aggression. The first review conference of the Assembly of States Parties, in 2008, may approve this definition and preconditions, and the Court could exercise jurisdiction over this crime after that date. The US, as a non-state party, will not be directly involved in the decision of the Assembly of States Parties.

4B.2 Developments in law and practice on cooperation

Relatively few formal requests for extradition and mutual assistance appear to have been processed, or at least given public attention, post 9/11.[293] This may reflect both the lack of national prosecutions and the military (as opposed to law enforcement) focus of the 'war on terror', as suggested above. It likely also reflects the troubling fact, discussed below, that much of the rendition of persons between states post 9/11 has been 'informal', or 'extra-legal', by-passing normal extradition procedures and the safeguards entailed therein.

There have, however, been significant legal and practical developments concerning international cooperation in criminal matters since the September 11 attacks. This section sketches out some of these developments, relating in turn to the adoption of new standards and procedures for cooperation and to state practice.

4B.2.1 International standards and procedures

In numerous ways international, regional and national bodies responded to 9/11 with initiatives aimed at strengthening the obligations to cooperate in the repression of acts such as those witnessed on that date. Resolution 1373 (2001), adopted by the Security Council on 28 September 2001, provided the most significant normative landmark.[294] Going beyond earlier resolutions, it established the obligation of all states to, among other things, afford other states the greatest measure of assistance in connection with criminal investigations or proceedings in relation to terrorism.[295] The Security Council called on states to ratify existing terrorism conventions which have been identified as hitherto lacking implementation.[296] As a result, there has been a significant increase in the number of state parties to these conventions, which provide a framework for

---

[293] It is noted that it is difficult to monitor practice in respect of mutual assistance, as requests are generally confidential.

[294] SC Res. 1373 (2001), above, note 272. See also SC Res. 1368 (2001), above, note 27, which noted the importance of cooperation as part of the collective framework for countering terrorism. The significant obligations were, however, imposed in SC Res. 1373 (2001).

[295] The General Assembly has also called on states to take all necessary and effective measures to prevent, combat and eliminate terrorism. A Counter-Terrorism Sub-Committee was established by the Security Council, to which states report steps taken to comply with the resolution. See the reports to the 1373 Committee at www.un.org/Docs/SC/Committees/1373.

[296] Para. 3, Resolution 1373 (2001).

cooperation in respect of specific forms of terrorism.[297] While the Security Council also called for progress on a comprehensive terrorism convention,[298] as discussed in Chapter 2 these developments have not borne fruit, and dispute continues as to the viability and desirability of such a convention as well as key elements of the definition of terrorism.

On the regional level also, September 11 acted as the catalyst to measures to enhance cooperation. Notably, within the European Union, there have been terrorism-specific developments (such as the Framework Decision on Terrorism),[299] as well as others which, while proposed before 9/11 and going beyond cooperation on terrorism specifically, were impelled by the political imperative surrounding cooperation post 9/11. The introduction of a Pan-European Arrest Warrant in 2002, for example, streamlines and expedites the extradition procedure within Europe and removes certain traditional limits on the obligation to extradite, such as the political offence exception, rule of specialty and the double criminality requirement.[300] Other regional cooperation measures were adopted within the Council of Europe,[301] the Americas[302] and elsewhere.[303]

---

[297] On these developments, see Chapter 2, in particular para. 2.1.3. See also report of the Counter-Terrorism Sub-Committee, above.

[298] One advantage of such a Convention is that it could arguably provide a broader framework for international cooperation, though its desirability and viability remain controversial.

[299] See European Council Framework Decision on Combating Terrorism, 13 June 2002 (2002/475/JHA), OJ L 164/3 of 22 June 2002 (hereinafter 'European Council Framework Decision on Combating Terrorism'). See also the EU Action Plan on Terrorism (the 'roadmap') Commission document 10773/2/02/REV 2, 17 July 2002. This defines, shapes and provides for monitoring of the direction of joint action taken by European Governments and is frequently updated.

[300] The European Council Framework Decision on the European Arrest Warrant and the Surrender Procedures between Member States, 13 June 2002 (2002/584/JHA), OJ L 190/5, 18 July 2002 (hereinafter 'European Arrest Warrant'), will abolish dual criminality for numerous offences, the speciality principle and the political offence exception. France, Belgium, Portugal, Luxembourg and Spain have signed treaties to bring the new extradition procedures into effect by 2003. The UK intends to implement them in 2004.

[301] See, e.g., Protocol amending the European Convention on the Suppression of Terrorism (Strasbourg, 15 May 2003), ETS No. 190, not yet in force), hereinafter 'Protocol to the European Convention against Terrorism'.

[302] Inter-American Convention against Terrorism (Bridgetown, 3 June 2002, OAS Res. 1840 (XII-O/02), not yet in force).

[303] Following the introduction of the 1999 Convention on the Prevention and Combating of Terrorism which calls for increased cooperation, the African Union has produced two decisions, post 9/11: the Decision on the Elaboration of a Code of Conduct on Terrorism (OAU Doc. Assembly/AU/8(II) Add. 11) and the Decision on Terrorism in Africa (OAU Doc. Assembly/AU/Dec.15 (II)). In addition, the South Asian Association for Regional

Cooperation between other states and the United States has been the focus of particular attention post 9/11. For example, trans-Atlantic cooperation between European Union member states and US law enforcement and intelligence agencies has led to several – at times controversial – new measures.[304] New extradition and mutual legal assistance treaties have been concluded between the US and EU, with further negotiations underway.[305] These treaties expedite the extradition process, facilitate access to information and the exchange of personal data and strengthen operational links between investigative and law enforcement agencies.[306] These are supplemented by bilateral agreements, including for example a controversial treaty between the UK and US which in numerous respects goes further than the US–EU treaty in facilitating extradition, and undermining rights protection.[307]

Enhanced cooperation for bringing persons to justice and securing reliable evidence is essential if states are to meet their obligations to prevent and punish serious crimes such as those committed on 9/11. For the most part then the industry in this field – aimed at establishing clear obligations and efficient procedures for giving effect to them – is, or at least should be, a positive development. However, as highlighted below, questions arise as to some of these developments, in particular their compatibility with other international obligations, notably in the field of human rights.[308]

Co-operation (SAARC) recently adopted an Additional Protocol to the SAARC Regional Convention on Combating Terrorism, on 6 January 2004.

[304] At the EU summit in Copenhagen in September 2002, agreement was reached between the US and the EU on how to swiftly and effectively exchange information between their respective forces. See 'EU–US co-operation in fighting terrorism', EU Presidency Press release, 14 September 2002. See also 'Informal EU Justice and Home Affairs Council, 13–14 September 2002', *Statewatch News online*, September 2002. In general, compatibility with human rights obligations has been a common source of controversy in deliberations on cooperation between certain states and the US post 9/11, as discussed further in this chapter.

[305] See Council Decision of 6 June 2003 concerning signature of the Agreements between the European Union and the United States of America on extradition and mutual legal assistance in criminal matters; Agreement on extradition between the European Union and the United States of America, 7 July 2003; Agreement on mutual legal assistance between the European Union and the United States of America, 7 July 2003, published in OJ L 181, 19 July 2003, 25 ff.

[306] Eurojust (the provisional public prosecution agency of EU) and the US are to consider cooperation agreements. Joint Investigation Teams may be established where appropriate.

[307] See this chapter, para. 4B.2.2.2. below.

[308] More detail on their compatibility with obligations in the field of human rights is discussed at Chapter 7, para. 7B.8.

4B.2.2 Streamlining the extradition process? Developments in extradition procedure

The adoption of measures such as the Pan-European arrest warrant ('European Arrest Warrant')[309] and new procedures for US–UK extradition[310] significantly change extradition practice and procedures between the states affected by them. While aimed at modernising and expediting notoriously tardy extradition procedures, some criticise the curtailment of the role of the judge in extradition proceedings as dismantling essential human rights protection.[311] Among the controversial measures adopted are those highlighted below.[312]

4B.2.2.1 Lowering evidentiary requirements in extradition proceedings

Among the steps taken in the name of expediting the extradition process are those that seek to remove the requirement that the requesting state provide a basic degree of evidence to the requested state.[313] The European Arrest Warrant for example – initiated before the September 11 attacks but which advanced more rapidly thereafter – lowers the threshold, requiring only the provision of basic 'information' (as opposed to evidence) regarding the alleged offence, where it was committed and the involvement of the suspected perpetrator.[314] While controversial, concerns about the adoption of the European Arrest Warrant were to some degree assuaged by the fact that it removes this requirement only as between EU countries, and

---

[309] European Arrest Warrant, above, note 298.

[310] Extradition Treaty between the Government of the United Kingdom of Great Britain and Northern Ireland and the Government of the United States of America, Washington, 31 March 2003 (hereinafter 'US–UK Extradition Treaty').

[311] See 'Mutual Recognition of final decisions in criminal matters', *Statewatch*, at http://www.statewatch.org/news/sept00/16ftamut.htm; and JUSTICE at www.justice.org.uk/publications/listofpublications/index.html. The European Arrest Warrant requires a judicial (as opposed to executive) decision in the issuing state (Article 1). The Warrant must not, however, be applied so as to 'have the effect of modifying the obligation to respect fundamental rights and fundamental legal principles as enshrined in Article 6 of the Treaty of the European Union'. See also the Preamble setting out the possibility of refusing extradition if the prosecution is for discriminatory purposes. The question however is how these rights will be safeguarded in practice given the streamlined procedure.

[312] Also controversial are the restriction of the rule of specialty in the European Arrest Warrant and of the *ne bis in idem* principle (as regards third states) in the US–UK treaty.

[313] As noted above, there are broad differences between civil and common law traditions, with the evidentiary requirements being most relevant, at least principally, to the latter. This change is more significant for common law than civil law countries.

[314] Article 8, European Arrest Warrant.

proposals to do the same for other countries was rejected by the EU and opposed explicitly in the UK parliament at the time.[315]

Despite this, the subsequent UK–US Extradition treaty also removes the requirement that a basic level of evidence[316] be provided in requests from the US to the UK (but not vice versa).[317] While similar to the European Arrest Warrant procedure, greater controversy arises from the context of extradition requests emanating from the US. Specifically, numerous cases have arisen post 9/11 that raise the question whether extradition requests are being made by the United States as a precautionary measure – a method of achieving preventative detention abroad – prior to the establishment of sufficient evidence to justify submitting the suspect to criminal process.[318]

For example, in the UK, the case of Lofti Raissi – an Algerian national detained at the request of the US on suspicion of involvement in training the September 11 pilots – resulted in his release from high security detention after five months, after the US authorities consistently failed to provide evidence to justify his extradition. This case, like others that have arisen elsewhere,[319] highlights concerns as to how it would have unfolded had extradition been requested after the entry into force of the new US–UK extradition treaty removing the evidentiary requirement, and the potential impact on similar cases in the future. The prospect of Raissi having been extradited despite the lack of evidence against him, and ranking among the many detained without trial by the US, underscores the importance of safeguarding judicial protections at the extradition stage.

---

[315] At the time of the European Arrest Warrant, the EU refused to accept the lowering of this standard to non-EU countries. The UK parliament Home Affairs Committee at that time also 'express[ed] concerns at proposals to relax the requirement that extradition requests from non-European countries must demonstrate that there is a prima facie case to answer'. See Home Affairs Committee, House of Commons Press Release 2002–03, 5 December 2002, No. 5 'Home Affairs Committee savages EU arrest warrant proposals'. Despite this, this was done in the UK–US bilateral treaty.

[316] Previously, under the prior treaty, evidence sufficient for the committal of the individual in the UK was required.

[317] Article 8(3)(c), US–UK Extradition Treaty. Whereas the US would provide basic statements of 'information' the UK would still have to demonstrate 'a reasonable basis to believe that the person sought committed the offense'. The differential is purportedly justified by reference to the US constitutional guarantee not to be extradited without judicial oversight of the evidence against him or her.

[318] On the human rights standards applicable to arrest and the general prohibition on preventive detention, see Chapter 7, para. 7A.4.3.3.

[319] See for example the case dismissed by the Bosnian Supreme Court due to lack of evidence, below, despite which the authorities transferred the suspect.

4B.2.2.2 Removal of double criminality and political offence exceptions

The European Arrest Warrant has drawn particular criticism for the removal of the double (or 'dual') criminality principle, by virtue of which a state does not extradite for conduct not punishable in its own law. This rule, which serves both to protect the state from embarrassing diplomatic difficulties and the individual from abusive prosecution,[320] has often been described as a principle of customary law.[321] Particular concern arose from the 'ill-defined nature of the 32 categories of offence which will be exempt from the dual criminality requirement',[322] which include 'terrorism', 'participation in a criminal organisation' and 'racism and xenophobia'.[323] Given the inherent susceptibility to abuse of broadly defined laws (including – as the work of human rights courts and bodies demonstrates – laws of 'terrorism'),[324] the double criminality safeguard guaranteed an essential element of judicial oversight in the extraditing state.

Both the US–UK treaty and the European Arrest Warrant remove the 'political offence' exception. Unlike the double criminality principle, this exception has grown increasingly controversial (in particular as it came to be seen as providing a 'legal loophole for terrorists')[325] and has been excluded by various extradition arrangements as regards serious

---

[320] The principle remains relevant within the European context (particularly perhaps in an expanded Europe) so far as fundamental differences remain, e.g., in laws relating to abortion and homosexuality, which some states criminalise yet the prosecution of which would be considered by other states unjustified and amounting to a human rights violation. On the rationale as, in part, protecting the *nullum crimen sine lege* principle, see J. Dugard and C. Van den Wyngaert, 'Reconciling Extradition with Human Rights', 92 (1998) AJIL 188.

[321] See I. Brownlie, *Principles of Public International Law*, 6th ed. (Oxford, 2003), p. 313 and I. Stanbrook and C. Stanbrook, *Extradition: Law and Practice* (Oxford, 2000), p. 20.

[322] See Home Affairs Committee report on Extradition Bill, above. The Committee expressed concern at the erosion of the dual criminality principle, 'in particular . . .' given the ill-defined nature of the offences. It also noted with concern the process by which these proposals were processed, with no debate on the issue in the House of Commons.

[323] Article 2.2, European Arrest Warrant.

[324] This is evident in lamentable international practice regarding 'terrorism' offences, detailed by the reports of human rights bodies: see Chapters 2 and 7. Such broadly defined offences may cover not only the sort of serious offences entailed in 9/11 but also much less serious offences.

[325] For an increasingly rare defence of this principle, see C.H. Pyle, *Extradition Politics and Human Rights* (Philadelphia, 2001), in particular ch. 15, 'Gutting the Political Offense Exception', pp. 197–206.

crimes.[326] So far as its removal applies to serious crimes under international law,[327] clarifying that they are neither 'political' nor justifiable, whatever their underlying ideology, it is to be welcomed as consistent with shifts in international law and practice in favour of accountability. However, the removal of this exception in the context of broadly defined offences of terrorism and association therewith, which often cover more and less serious crimes and are susceptible to politicisation, underscores the importance of a broad and operational rule of non-refoulement, discussed below,[328] to ensure that extradition is not sought as a vehicle for political repression or other human rights abuse.[329]

4B.2.2.3 Cooperation standards and human rights

Section A above records the obligations of states – by virtue of bilateral extradition and mutual assistance treaties as well as positive obligations in international human rights law – to cooperate with one another in the repression of serious crime and, in certain circumstances, to *refrain* from providing such cooperation on human rights grounds.[330] Particular issues arise concerning the compatibility of international standards on cooperation advanced since September 11, referred to above, and the obligation to refuse to extradite where there is a substantial risk of torture or certain other serious violations of human rights in the requesting state – often referred to as the obligation of 'non-refoulement'.

These issues are discussed in the context of international human rights law at Chapter 7 below. Suffice to note here that certain developments in relation to cooperation standards since 9/11 emphasise the duty of

---

[326] See Chapter 2 on terrorism conventions, and Chapter 4, para. 4A.2, as regards crimes under international law.

[327] Note however that the breadth of definitions means that conduct of far less gravity would also be covered.

[328] Note that the non-discrimination rule (which is included in the Preamble of the European Arrest Warrant) reduces the dangers of political abuse inherent in the application of the terrorism label and the European Arrest Warrant confirms that it does not affect the duties of states in respect of human rights. The challenge, however, will be to ensure that the protections that human rights law does afford are operational within the streamlined procedure envisaged.

[329] The historical roots of the political offence exception relate principally in sovereignty and political expediency, to avoid one regime becoming embroiled in the political affairs of another, though it has since been used by individuals to challenge extradition. See Dugard and Van den Wyngaert, 'Reconciling Extradition' at 188, noting that this exception allows states to refuse extradition where the individual 'is engaged in the struggle for human rights in the requesting state'.

[330] See also Chapter 7, para. 7A.4.1.1.

cooperation but neglect to take a holistic approach and reflect the obligation to do so consistently with human rights law. At times this law has apparently been ignored (as in Security Council Resolution 1373, which imposed broad-reaching obligations without any reference to human rights)[331] and at others it has been reflected only selectively or restrictively (as in the Protocol amending the European Convention on Terrorism, which referred to some of the rights that require to be protected through the obligation of non-refoulement, but not to others).[332] This may have generated confusion as to applicable legal standards and rendered the rights vulnerable, although it must be noted that, ultimately, both the Security Council and the Council of Europe, have clarified that the obligations in respect of cooperation against terrorism must be interpreted consistently with international human rights.[333]

4B.2.3 Inter-state cooperation in practice post 9/11

Questions arise as to how states are responding – or will respond – in practice to requests to cooperate in relation to alleged terrorist cases post 9/11. The sensitivity relating to evidence and intelligence sharing *by* the US authorities with courts in other states and the resulting difficulty in relation to US cooperation was illustrated above. An additional feature of international cooperation, including by other states *with* the US post 9/11, is concern as human rights violations committed during the 'war on terror', including the use of torture or ill treatment, reliance on overbroad concepts of terrorism or support thereof as an instrument of arbitrariness, fair trial violations, arbitrary detention and the imposition of the death penalty.

---

[331] SC Res. 1373 (2001), above, note 272.

[332] Protocol amending the European Convention on the Suppression of Terrorism, Strasbourg, 15 May 2003, ETS, No. 190 (not yet in force). The Protocol precludes extradition where there is a risk of torture but not inhuman or degrading treatment or denial of justice and fails therefore to reflect fully relevant human rights law. For discussion of the Protocol, see Chapter 7, para. 7B.8 below.

[333] See, e.g., SC Res. 1456 (2003), 20 January 2003, UN Doc. S/RES/1456 (2003), where the Security Council declared that 'States must ensure that any measure taken to combat terrorism comply with all their obligations under international law, and should adopt such measures in accordance with international law, in particular international human rights, refugee, and humanitarian law'. See also the Draft Explanatory Report on the European Convention on Terrorism as it will be revised by the Protocol amending the Convention upon its entry into force, adopted on 13 February 2003 (text available at http://conventions.coe.int/Treaty/en/Reports/Html/090-rev.htm).

4B.2.3.1 Extradition and human rights concerns

As regards the question of the impact on cooperation practice of human rights obligations, the landscape is mixed. The work of the human rights bodies post 9/11 demonstrates numerous occasions on which states have shown little, or only selective, respect for these obligations by transferring suspected terrorists despite a substantial risk to their basic rights.[334] At the same time other examples of state practice post 9/11 suggest that several states have indicated their inability to cooperate given human rights concerns, notably in relation to the trials in or by the United States.[335]

In relation to the death penalty, where the practice of European states to require 'assurances' that the death penalty will not be applied as a precondition to extradition is well established, the EU states have made clear that 'no EU country will extradite suspects to the US if the death penalty might apply'[336] and the Council of Europe has likewise confirmed that all Member States should refuse to extradite in such cases.[337] Consistent with this, cases such as that of Mamdouh Mahmud Salim – who faces charges of terrorist conspiracy in the US – have proceeded on the basis of undertakings given by the United States to German officials that prosecutors would not seek the death penalty if the suspect were extradited to the US.[338]

It remains uncertain how a request to extradite a suspect who faces other violations, such as being held unlawfully in Guantanamo Bay, or (once they are operational) standing trial before a US established military commission, for example, might be handled in the future.[339] However,

---

[334] The case work of the Human Rights Committee, for example, illustrates the piecemeal approach in state practice offering protection from certain rights and not others, at odds with the human rights obligations of the state. See, e.g., Concluding observations of the Human Rights Committee: Portugal, UN Doc. CCPR/CO/78/PRT (2003), para. 12.

[335] The use of military commissions, and the criticism of them for their due process deficit, are addressed at Chapter 6. The military commissions proposed by the US are discussed in Chapter 8 on Guantanamo Bay.

[336] Statement by Danish Justice Minister Lene Espersen delivered during the Danish Presidency of the EU. See I. Black, 'Extradition of terror suspects ruled out. EU will not expose prisoners to US death penalty', *The Guardian*, 14 September 2002.

[337] Council of Europe, Resolution 1271 (2002), 'Combating Terrorism and Respect for Human Rights'. This accords with the ECtHR's decision in *Soering* v. *United Kingdom* (Appl. No. 10438/88), Judgment of 7 July 1989, *Series A*, No. 161 (discussed above, Section A).

[338] See 'Death Penalty Phase of Bombings Trial Begins', *CNN.com*, 30 May 2001, at http://cnnstudentnews.cnn.com/2001/LAW/05/30/embassy.bombings.01.

[339] As the majority of Guantanamo detainees were not formally extradited, there is surprisingly little practice in this respect.

in one potential case concerning eight alleged Islamic terrorists, Spain confirmed it would not agree to a request to extradite the men unless the United States agrees that they would be tried by a civilian court and not by the military commissions.[340] It is reported as having insisted that persons extradited would 'not be subject to military or special tribunals, or to summary justice' and they must be tried in public with the opportunity to confront one's accuser.[341]

While this issue has not been tested fully post 9/11, the Spanish incident may indicate the practice of seeking assurances of respect for human rights in the criminal process as a condition of cooperation as a possible approach.[342] It remains to be seen, however, first whether states would be willing to adopt such an approach systematically, and secondly whether they would do so in a manner that ensures that assurances are meaningful, including through the effective monitoring of their implementation.[343]

4B.2.3.2 Mutual assistance cooperation and human rights

Practice is more difficult to assess in the field of mutual assistance cooperation, due to the confidentiality and relative informality of mutual assistance requests. It would appear, however, that in several cases since September 11 European states have indicated their unwillingness to provide mutual assistance if the evidence would be used towards the application of the death penalty. Examples of states having publicly informed the US that they would withhold evidence absent assurances that it would

---

[340] S. Dillon, 'A Nation Challenged: The Legal Front; Spain Sets Hurdle for Extraditions', *New York Times*, 24 November 2001, reporting that a spokesman for Spain's Foreign Ministry confirmed that Spain would only extradite detainees to countries that offer defendants the legal guarantees provided by Spanish courts. The Foreign Ministry spokesman said, 'if we're talking about a tribunal in the United States with summary procedures and military judges, then these are not the same conditions that would characterise a trial in Spain or France or England or anywhere else in Europe'.

[341] J. Yoldi, 'España advierte a EEUU de que no extraditará a miembros de AlQaeda', *el País*, 23 November 2001.

[342] This approach is established between Europe and the US in relation to the death penalty, and envisaged expressly in certain extradition treaties. See, e.g., Article 11, European Convention on Extradition and Article 9, Inter-American Convention on Extradition.

[343] On the requirement of human rights law regarding monitoring, the Human Rights Committee charged with the implementation of the ICCPR has noted that in order to legitimately rely on assurances, states must make 'serious efforts to monitor the implementation of those guarantees' and 'institute credible mechanisms for ensuring compliance of the receiving State with these assurances from the moment of expulsion'. Concluding observations of the Human Rights Committee: Sweden, UN Doc. CCPR/CO/74/SWE (2002), para. 12. See also Concluding observations of the Human Rights Committee: New Zealand, UN Doc. CCPR/CO/75/NZL (2002), para. 11.

not be used to secure the death penalty, include statements from Germany and France in relation to the provision of documentary evidence against the alleged September 11 conspirator, Zacarias Moussaoui in 2002.[344] The German statement emphasised that it was necessary to distinguish between sharing information with the United States that is necessary to help prevent another attack and handing over evidence that could help sentence a person to death.[345] As the recently commenced military commissions become fully operational, it may be that human rights concerns will impede mutual assistance cooperation. It is noted that this principle of non-cooperation in light of human rights concerns has been reflected, to a limited degree, in mutual assistance arrangements entered into since September 11, as well as in earlier such arrangements.[346]

4B.2.3.3 'Irregular rendition' and the rule of law

Alongside these developments in law and practice are others that highlight questions of a more disturbing nature regarding the application of the criminal law framework post 9/11. Reports abound of the established legal process for cooperation – through extradition and mutual legal assistance – being distorted, or indeed entirely circumvented. Reports from several states detail interference by the executive in pending judicial matters (beyond that permitted by extradition law),[347] thereby disregarding the judicial function, and jeopardising the independence of the judiciary and the protection of rights. Cases falling into this group include the

---

[344] Germany's former Justice Minister, Herta Daeubler-Gmelin, said that Germany would provide documents only on condition that they 'may not be used for a death sentence or an execution' (*Associated Press*, 1 September 2002). Marylise Lebranchu, the then French Minister of Justice, stated that, under Article 6 of the treaty governing judicial cooperation between France and the United States, France could either refuse assistance, or make it conditional on certain demands. She confirmed that 'any document should only be passed on to the Americans to help them with their enquiries on condition that such document [is] not used to get a conviction carrying a death penalty' (statement reported at www.ahram.org.eg/weekly/2002/597/in4.htm).

[345] See the statement of the German Justice Minister, above, note 129.

[346] See, e.g., the Inter-American Convention against Terrorism which specifically notes that the obligation of mutual assistance does not apply where there is a substantial basis for believing that the request has been made for the purpose of prosecuting on discriminatory grounds: Article 14 (Non-discrimination), Inter-American Convention against Terrorism. The Convention also reflects more generally the duty to interpret the convention in accord with, among other areas of international law, international human rights law. This reflects other pre-existing standards; see, e.g., Article 8, European Convention on Terrorism.

[347] Domestic laws vary as to the role of the executive and the judiciary in the decision to extradite. See, generally, G. Gilbert, *Aspects of Extradition Law* (Dordrecht, 1991).

decision by Malawian authorities to hand over to the CIA persons suspected of financing terrorists despite pending judicial proceedings,[348] or
the Bosnian government's seizure of Algerian individuals suspected by
the US of terrorism, despite them having been released by the Bosnian
Supreme Court on the basis that there was insufficient evidence against
them.[349]

In some cases, states have reportedly adopted a practice of entirely
bypassing the extradition process for transfer of persons from one state
to another, thereby avoiding judicial scrutiny, the requirement of *prima
facie* evidence against the individual and the human rights safeguards
inherent in that process. This is illustrated by media reports of hundreds
of individuals having been arrested since September 11, handed over to
the United States informally and transferred to third countries.[350]

4B.3 Conclusion

The September 11 attacks constituted atrocious crimes of genuine international concern. Their immediate wake saw unprecedented international
solidarity with the United States and a shared global commitment to
justice. Remarkable unity of purpose attended international dialogue on
combating terrorism post 9/11, such that an opportunity undoubtedly
existed to strengthen the system of international cooperation generally,
and to successfully investigate and prosecute the international crimes in
question and the transnational networks responsible for them. Questions

---

[348] See International Commission of Jurists, Center on the Independence of Judges and
Lawyers, 'US and Malawi: Rule of Law Compromised in Fight against Terrorism', 1 July
2003, available at http://www.icj.org/IMG/pdf/Rule_of_Law_Compromised_270603_pdf.
[349] Human Rights Watch, *World Report 2003*, Introduction, p. 7, at http://www.hrw.org/
wr2k3/.
[350] R. Chandrasekaran and P. Finn, 'US behind Secret Transfer of Terror Suspects', *Washington
Post*, 11 March 2002: 'Since September 11 the US government has secretly transported
dozens of people suspected of links to terrorists to countries other than the United States,
bypassing extradition procedures and legal formalities . . . suspects have been taken to
countries including Egypt and Jordan, whose intelligence services have close ties to the
CIA and where they can be subjected to interrogation tactics – including torture and
threats to families – that are illegal in the United States, the sources said. In some cases,
US intelligence agents remain closely involved in the interrogation'. See also K. Khan and S.
Schmidt, 'Key 9/11 Suspect Leaves Pakistan in US Custody', *Washington Post*, 17 September
2002, which reports five al-Qaeda suspects having been arrested in Pakistan, handed to
the US authorities and flown out on unmarked CIA flights to unknown destinations. The
source quoted a senior Pakistani Interior Ministry official stating that, as with all other
al-Qaeda suspect cases in Pakistan, no formal extradition process was completed and that
Pakistan has handed over about 200 non-Pakistani terrorist suspects this way.

arise as to whether the opportunity to improve the system of international cooperation in the enforcement of law has been seized or squandered.

Since then, there have been massive arrests and detentions, yet little role for criminal courts. The use of the machinery of criminal process (whether detention or investigative steps) has been directed towards prevention – 'arresting and detaining *potential* terrorist threats'[351] – rather than seeing criminal justice done against those responsible for serious crimes.[352] Justice is a long process and time is one of the many resources that have to be invested in thorough investigations that can provide the basis for a respectable criminal process. It remains to be seen whether the apparently low priority afforded to criminal justice will shift as the fight against terrorism unfolds.

In relation to both domestic criminal process and international cooperation, practice reveals striking disregard for the normal process of law. As discussed in Chapter 7, persons detained on suspicion of criminal activity are not infrequently denied access to courts, still less is their right to trial within reasonable time respected (which might, had it been respected, have created greater impetus and momentum behind the criminal process). The established legal process for cooperation appears to be systematically dispensed with, replaced by informal rendition that raises fundamental questions as to whether 'cooperation' since September 11 is about strengthening, or undermining, the rule of law and international law enforcement. This selective lack of regard for the legal process of cooperation raises doubts as to the value of the effort dedicated to enhancing that legal framework. Finally, as regards standards and procedures advanced in the name of enhancing cooperation and the international justice it serves, careful attention must be given to assessing whether they have on occasion themselves undercut important safeguards that are all the more critical post 9/11.

---

[351] Testimony of Attorney-General John Ashcroft before the US House of Representatives, Committee on the Judiciary, 5 June 2003, at http://www.usdoj.gov/ag/testimony/2003/060503aghouseremarks.htm.

[352] See, e.g., statement by German official noting the US focus on prevention not prosecution, above, note 255.

Peaceful resolution of disputes and use of force

We the Peoples of the United Nations determined to save succeeding generations from the scourge of war . . . to reaffirm faith in fundamental human
rights . . . to establish conditions under which justice and respect for the
obligations arising from treaties and other sources of international law can
be maintained . . . to unite our strength to maintain international peace
and security, and to ensure, by the acceptance of principles and the institution of methods, that armed force shall not be used, save in the common
interest . . . have resolved to combine our effort to accomplish these aims.

(Preamble, UN Charter, 26 June 1945)

5A The legal framework

5A.1 The obligation to resolve international disputes by peaceful means

Any enquiry into the lawfulness of responses to the events of September
11 must begin from the obligation to resolve disputes by peaceful means.[1]
This obligation is enshrined in Article 2(3) of the Charter of the United
Nations, which states: 'All Members shall settle their international disputes
by peaceful means in such a manner that international peace and security,
and justice, shall not be compromised.'[2]

---

[1] 'The expression "international disputes" covers not only disputes between states as such,
but also other cases that come within the ambit of international regulation, being certain
categories of disputes between states on the one hand and individuals, bodies corporate, and
non-state entities on the other', I.A. Shearer, *Starke's International Law*, 11th ed. (Sydney,
1994), at p. 441.

[2] Note that a similar obligation was already enshrined in the so-called Briand–Kellog Pact
of 1928, in which the contracting parties agreed, *inter alia*, 'that the settlement or solution
of all disputes or conflicts of whatever nature or of whatever origin they may be, which
may arise among them, shall never be sought except by pacific means' (Article 2, Treaty
Providing for the Renunciation of War as an Instrument of National Policy, Paris, 27 August
1928, in force 24 July 1929).

Within the category of peaceful means of dispute resolution fall traditional methods directed towards addressing state responsibility,[3] which are not addressed in detail here. Suffice to note that these include arbitration, judicial settlement, non-adjudicatory methods such as negotiation, good offices, mediation, conciliation or inquiry, and settlement under the auspices of the United Nations or regional organisations.[4] The International Court of Justice, as the principal judicial organ of the United Nations,[5] is empowered to determine infringements by one state of the rights of another, order provisional measures to prevent or discontinue such violations,[6] and advise states on the correct interpretation of the law in the event of uncertainty.[7] While its reputation for slow proceedings and lack of independent enforcement authority have undermined the Court's standing and perceived relevance, particularly in situations of urgency, the Court has become more active in recent years.[8] In addition to these traditional methods, where the wrong amounts to criminal conduct individuals may be brought to justice. As discussed in Chapter 4, persons who are directly responsible for a crime or, in certain circumstances, indirectly responsible for failing to prevent it, can be brought to justice before national courts or international tribunals for their part in the commission of national and/or international crimes.

The question of the lawfulness of the use of force, discussed below, should only arise in circumstances where none of these peaceful means are

---

[3] The avenues for peaceful dispute settlement discussed here pre-suppose a level of state responsibility, discussed at Chapter 3. Note, however, that one of the issues the ICJ could be called on to determine is state responsibility itself. Individual responsibility is discussed separately at Chapter 4.

[4] See *Starke's International Law*, pp. 442–71. Note that settlement under the auspices of the UN would include General Assembly and Security Council involvement. The broad powers of the Council to decide what measures shall be taken to resolve disputes, which can cover peaceful and, if necessary, coercive measures, are discussed below.

[5] Article 92, UN Charter.

[6] The Court can order provisional measures to prevent or discontinue violations, which are binding. See, e.g., *LaGrand (Germany v. United States)*, 27 June 2001, *ICJ Reports 2001*, p. 3, paras. 98–109.

[7] The law governing the contentious and advisory jurisdiction of the Court is not addressed here. For the conditions that apply before the Court's jurisdiction can be seized, see, e.g., *Starke's International Law*, pp. 450–65.

[8] ICJ judgments rely ultimately for enforcement on the Security Council or others. In considering the reputation for delay it should be noted that this applies less to requests for provisional measures, which by their nature are brought as urgent measures that the applicant state claims are necessary to prevent irreparable harm. See, e.g., *LaGrand* case, above, note 6.

at the aggrieved states' disposal, or where such means have been exhausted or found to be ineffective.[9]

5A.2 The use of force in international law: general rule and exceptions

This section sets out relevant law on the question whether, and if so in what circumstances, states are entitled to resort to the use of force under international law. The legality of the use of force under international law is referred to as the '*jus ad bellum*'.[10]

The current rules governing the lawfulness of the use of force are contained in the UN Charter and customary international law. The advent of the UN Charter represented a moment of legal metamorphosis, when traditional legal concepts such as the 'just war' and lawful reprisals were radically altered by the new law of the United Nations, which greatly restricted the circumstances in which the use of force can be lawfully deployed.[11]

The underlying 'purposes' of the UN Charter are set out in Article 1, the first of which is:

> To maintain international peace and security, and to that end: to take effective collective measures for the prevention and removal of threats to the peace, and for the suppression of acts of aggression or other breaches of the peace, and to bring about by peaceful means, and in conformity with

---

[9] This requirement manifests itself throughout the law on the use of force, as will be seen below, for example in the 'necessity' condition on the exercise of self defence and in the Security Council's power to take 'necessary measures'. On questions relating to the interplay between necessity of force and criminal sanctions see below, and section B.

[10] The *jus ad bellum* is the body of rules governing when force can lawfully be used. It must be distinguished from the *jus in bello* that encompasses the rules that apply once force has been used and a conflict is underway, and which applies irrespective of whether the resort to force (*jus ad bellum*) was lawful. The *jus in bello*, which regulates the conduct of hostilities and treatment of persons, and requires, *inter alia*, that civilians must not be the object of attack, is addressed in Chapter 6.

[11] See L. Henkin, 'Use of Force: Law and US Policy', in Henkin *et al.*, *Right* v. *Might: International Law and the Use of Force* (New York, 1991), pp. 37 ff.: 'The [UN] Charter remains the authoritative statement of the law on the use of force . . . In the future, the only "just war" would be war against an aggressor – in self defence.' The prohibition of the use of force in international relations contained in Article 2(4) of the Charter was foreshadowed, albeit in narrower terms, in the Briand–Kellog Pact (above, note 2) concluded in 1928, in which the United States, Germany, Belgium, France, Italy, Poland, Japan and Czechoslovakia 'condemn[ed] recourse to war for the solution of international controversies, and renounce[d] it as an instrument of national policy in their relations with one another', Article 1.

the principles of justice and international law, adjustment or settlement of international disputes or situations which might lead to a breach of the peace.

The primacy of this objective is reflected throughout the Charter's preamble, which opens with the famous expression of determination 'to save succeeding generations from the scourge of war'.[12] Article 2 then sets out certain fundamental 'principles', one of which is the general rule prohibiting the use of force.[13] Article 2(4) obliges all Members of the United Nations to

> refrain in their international relations from the threat or use of force against the territorial integrity or political independence of any State or in any other manner inconsistent with the Purposes of the United Nations.[14]

The overwhelming majority of commentators recognise that the obligation enshrined in Article 2(4) of the Charter reflects customary international law.[15] The International Court of Justice in the *Nicaragua* case[16] noted that Article 2(4) reflects custom,[17] despite the fact that state practice is 'not perfect', in the sense that States have not 'refrained with complete consistency from the use of force'.[18] The prohibition of the use of force against another State is one of the very few rules of international law which are recognised as having attained the status of *jus cogens*.[19] As a 'peremptory norm' of international law, no derogation from it is allowed, and only another peremptory norm can change or override this rule.

---

[12] Preamble, UN Charter.

[13] Article 2(4) enshrines one of the fundamental principles of the UN Charter, alongside sovereignty and human rights.

[14] The references to territorial integrity and political independence were not intended to qualify the prohibition, but on the contrary to emphasise (and thus to strengthen) the protection of the nation state from aggressive interference by other states. For reference to the process whereby this language came to be included, see, e.g., T. M. Franck, *Recourse to Force. State Action Against Threats and Armed Attacks* (Cambridge, 2002), p. 12; C. Gray, *International Law and the Use of Force* (Oxford, 2000), pp. 25–6.

[15] See, generally, A. Randelzhofer, 'Article 2(4)', in B. Simma *et al.* (eds.), *The Charter of the United Nations. A Commentary*, 2nd ed. (Oxford, 2002), pp. 133–5, citing authoritative writings in support of this position.

[16] *Military and Paramilitary Activities in and against Nicaragua (Nicaragua v. United States), Merits, ICJ Reports 1986*, p. 14 (hereinafter '*Nicaragua* case').

[17] *Ibid.*, para. 190.

[18] *Ibid.*, para. 186: 'It is not to be expected that in the practice of States the application of the rules in question should have been perfect, in the sense that States should have refrained, with complete consistency, from the use of force.'

[19] See ICJ, *Nicaragua* case, para. 190 and ILC Commentaries to Articles on State Responsibility, Commentary to Article 40(4). See Chapter 1, para. 1.2.1.

Moreover, the resort to force by states in contravention of this rule may amount to an act of aggression for which states, but also individuals, may be responsible.[20] As discussed below, it may also amount to an 'armed attack' against another state, a prerequisite for the use of force in self defence.[21]

Like any other treaty,[22] the UN Charter must be interpreted according to its ordinary meaning, as understood in context, and in accordance with its object and purpose.[23] As Articles 1 and 2 set out the Charter's underlying purposes and governing principles, respectively, all other provisions of the Charter must be interpreted in accordance with these provisions. Moreover, by virtue of the 'general rule of interpretation' set forth in Article 31 of the Vienna Convention on the Law of Treaties, in interpreting the Charter, it is necessary to take into account the subsequent practice of Member States of the United Nations (and of the organs of the United Nations), in so far as it 'establishes the agreement of the parties regarding its interpretation'.[24] In addition, some commentators point out

---

[20] The UN Charter designates the Security Council as the organ competent to determine, *in concreto*, if a breach of the prohibition of the use of force amounts to an act of aggression. For the definition of aggression see GA Res. 3314 (XXIX) of 14 December 1974, UN Doc. A/RES/3314 (XXIX), Article 1 of which provides: 'Aggression is the use of armed force by a State against the sovereignty, territorial integrity or political independence of another State, or in any other manner inconsistent with the Charter of the United Nations, as set out in this Definition.' Article 3 lists acts which 'regardless of a declaration of war, shall . . . qualify as an act of aggression' which includes '(g) The sending by or on behalf of a State of armed bands, groups, irregulars or mercenaries, which carry out acts of armed force against another State of such gravity as to amount to the acts listed above, or its substantial involvement therein.' For a discussion of the definition of aggression see Chapter 4, para. 4A.1.1.3.

[21] However, not every act of unlawful use of force will be sufficiently serious to amount to an act of aggression or an armed attack. See *Nicaragua* case, 195.

[22] Article 5, VCLT 1969 specifies that 'The . . . Convention applies to any treaty which is the constituent instrument of an international organization.'

[23] See Article 31, VCLT 1969: 'A treaty shall be interpreted in good faith in accordance with the ordinary meaning to be given to the terms of the treaty in their context and in the light of its object and purpose', para. 1.

[24] Article 31(3)(a) and (b), VCLT 1969: 'There shall be taken into account . . . any subsequent agreement between the parties regarding the interpretation of the treaty or the application of its provisions [and] any subsequent practice in the application of the treaty which establishes the agreement of the parties regarding its interpretation.' The ICJ has emphasised the relevance of subsequent practice of member states to the interpretation of the Charter. See, e.g., *Reparation for Injuries suffered in the Service of the United Nations, Advisory Opinion, ICJ Reports 1949*, p. 174, in particular at p. 180. See also, on the relevance of the subsequent practice of the organs of the United Nations, *Certain Expenses of the United Nations (Article 17, paragraph 2, of the Charter), Advisory Opinion, ICJ Reports 1962*, pp. 157 and 159 ff.

that the Charter, as a document with quasi-constitutional status, must be interpreted as a living instrument, responsive to changing circumstances and the new challenges of the contemporary world.[25]

Certain exceptions to the general prohibition on the use of force are contemplated in the Charter itself. Leaving aside the question of intervention by invitation, which has less apparent significance in the post September 11 context,[26] the exceptions involve:

(a) the use of force in self defence, and
(b) Security Council authorisation of force, on the basis that the Council determines it necessary for the maintenance or restoration of international peace and security.

While other possible justifications for the use of force are at times advanced, such as 'humanitarian intervention', 'pro-democratic intervention' or 'self help', they provide doubtful legitimacy for the use of force, as discussed further below. Instead, to rest on a secure legal foundation, any resort to armed force should either constitute self defence or be authorised by the Security Council. It is these legal justifications that have been invoked explicitly by states post September 11, in particular in relation to Afghanistan and Iraq, as discussed in Chapter 5B below. An understanding of their scope is therefore essential to an assessment of the lawfulness of states' responses to the events of 11 September 2001.

5A.2.1 Self defence

Article 51 of the UN Charter provides that:

> Nothing in the present Charter shall impair the inherent right of individual or collective self defence if an armed attack occurs against a Member of the United Nations, until the Security Council has taken measures necessary to maintain international peace and security.

---

[25] See Franck, *Recourse to Force*, pp. 5–9. On the question of the dynamic, evolutive interpretation of the Charter, see also G. Ress, 'Interpretation', in B. Simma *et al.*, *Commentary*, p. 13, at p. 27, stating that: 'a dynamic-objective understanding, free from historical perceptions, of treaties such as the Charter and other statutes of international organizations is necessary'.

[26] For another view, see M. Byers, 'Terrorism, the Use of Force and International Law after September 11', 51 (2002) ICLQ 401, pp. 403–4 who describes it as a 'possible legal justification' in relation to Afghanistan. However, invitation does have potential relevance to the right to use force in the relevant states after regime change introduced a government friendly to those executing the 'war on terror'.

As the Charter's reference to the 'inherent' right of self defence reflects, Article 51 was intended to encompass customary international law. Where Article 51 lacks specificity, an understanding of its content can therefore be informed by customary law.[27] However, customary law continues to exist alongside the Charter and, as noted below, in limited respects its content may not be identical.

Self defence is an exception to the 'general duty of all states to respect the territorial integrity of other states',[28] and the only exception to the prohibition on the use of non-UN authorised force.[29] As *Oppenheim's International Law* notes, '[l]ike all exceptions, it is to be strictly applied'.[30] The strict approach is particularly important given that self defence operates, at least initially, in the absence of a mechanism to ascertain the validity of a state's claim to exercise the right. In practice, states resorting to force very often invoke self defence as a basis for the legality of action, even where no such tenable justification exists.[31]

The essence of self defence, as the term suggests, lies in its defensive objective: it is neither retaliation or punishment for past attacks, nor deterrence against possible future attacks.[32] The former distinguishes permissible self defence – which consists of necessary and proportionate measures to protect oneself against a future threat – from prohibited reprisals – which are responsive and largely punitive.[33] While earlier law

---

[27] See, e.g., the tests of necessity and proportionality, which are not explicit in the Charter but are principles of customary law held by the ICJ to be relevant to the interpretation of the 'inherent' right of self defence under Article 51, see *Nicaragua*, para. 194. By contrast, the rules on reporting to the Security Council *are* explicit in the Charter but are not rules of customary law. They are binding as conventional law on the UN member states as parties to the Charter, *Nicaragua*, para. 194.

[28] *Oppenheim's International Law*, p. 421.

[29] On other possible legal justifications for unilateral resort to force advanced by certain authors but of doubtful legal standing in current international law, see this chapter, para. 5A.3

[30] *Oppenheim's International Law*, p. 421.

[31] Gray, *International Law*, p. 85. A. Cassese, *International Law* (Oxford, 2001), p. 306, points out that self defence has been abused in practice, especially by great powers.

[32] See discussion of anticipatory or pre-emptive self defence, this chapter, para. 5A.2.1.1(a). Prevention of future attacks that fall outside the scope of permissible self defence may however amount to threats to international peace and security for which the Security Council (alone) is empowered to authorise force.

[33] Note that the permissibility of reprisals as a justification for resort to otherwise unlawful force (within the *jus ad bellum*) is distinguishable from the more complex rules (according to humanitarian law, *jus in bello*) governing the permissibility of reprisals during armed conflict. In the latter, reprisals may in limited circumstances be permissible where it is decided at a senior level that a reprisal is necessary to prevent a greater violation of humanitarian law.

allowed reprisals in limited circumstances,[34] the law changed with the advent of the UN Charter, which is on its face inconsistent with retaliatory or punitive measures of force.[35] In 1970, the Friendly Relations Declaration, considered to constitute customary law on the point, confirmed that 'states have a duty to refrain from acts of reprisal involving the use of force'.[36] Central to an assessment of justifiable self defence is an assessment of the actual threat to a state, and an identification of the measures necessary to avert that threat, to which defensive action must be directed and limited. The conditions which are generally considered to require satisfaction before resort to force can be justified as self defence are set out below.

5A.2.1.1 Conditions for the exercise of self defence

(a) **Armed attack** Article 51 contemplates self defence only 'if an armed attack occurs against a Member of the United Nations'. As affirmed by the International Court of Justice, '[s]tates do not have a right of . . . armed response to acts which do not constitute an "armed attack" '.[37] However, as noted below, the 'armed attack' requirement is the most controversial of the self defence conditions, and highlights a number of areas where international law is unsettled.

While there is no accepted definition of armed attack for these purposes, it involves resort to force against another state's territorial integrity or political independence[38] signifying the use of force of considerable

---

[34] Prior to the UN Charter, the definitive statement of the permissible use of reprisals is found in the 1928 *Naulilaa* case, which held that reprisal must be preceded by a violation of international law and an unsuccessful demand for redress, and be reasonably proportionate. See C. Waldock, 'The Regulation of the Use of Force by Individual States in International Law', 81 (1952) RdC 455, pp. 458–60.

[35] See Article 2(4), Article 42 and Article 51, above.

[36] GA Res. 2625 (XXV), 'Declaration on Principles of International Law Concerning Friendly Relations and Co-operation among States in Accordance with the Charter of the United Nations', 24 October 1970, UN Doc. A/RES/2625 (XXV), para. 6. While not a binding instrument, the Friendly Relations Declaration, adopted by consensus by the General Assembly, may be considered an authentic interpretation of the Charter, and provides insight into the understanding of states as to the law in 1970. The Declaration is generally considered to reflect customary international law, binding on all states. See the *Nicaragua* case, para.188. See also D.W. Bowett, 'Reprisals Involving Recourse to Armed Force', 66 (1972) AJIL 1 at 6–8; for a contrary view see R.J. Beck and A.C. Arend, 'Don't Tread on Us: International Law and Forcible State Responses to Terrorism', 12 (1994) *Wisconsin International Law Journal* 153.

[37] *Nicaragua*, para. 110.

[38] See the language of Article 2(4). While the majority view appears to be that the attack needs to be against the territorial integrity or political independence of states, others state that attacks against nationals suffice, as discussed below.

seriousness in terms of its scale and effects. The ICJ, setting out certain parameters for when interference in a state might amount to an attack against it, found for example that the supply of arms or logistical support was not *per se* sufficient to constitute an armed attack, while sending armed bands or mercenaries into the territory of another states was.[39] An armed attack for the purposes of Article 51 has been said to exclude 'isolated or sporadic attacks'.[40]

The attack need not be immediate, or occur all at once, but may arise over time. (However, if an attack were to continue over a prolonged period it may bring into question the *need* to resort to measures of self defence, discussed below, as collective action under the Charter may then be possible.)

One matter in dispute is whether an attack against a state's nationals, or its interests, could suffice to constitute an armed attack. Support in state practice and academic writing for 'self defence' to cover defence of nationals abroad is limited,[41] although such a right may exist in certain exceptional circumstances.[42] By contrast, the protection of broader 'interests' beyond the integrity and independence of the state, and, arguably, nationals abroad, finds no justification within the law of self defence. While the problems of nationals or state 'interests' have been critical to the lawfulness of the use of force by the US in other contexts,[43] they appear of less relevance to its response to the events of September 11, which

---

[39] *Nicaragua*, para. 195.

[40] A. Cassese, 'The International Community's "Legal" Response to Terrorism', 38 (1989) ICLQ 589 at 596, states that self defence 'requires a pattern of violent terrorist action rather than just being isolated or sporadic acts'.

[41] Gray, *International Law*, pp. 108–9, notes that 'few states have accepted a legal right to protect nationals abroad', and she cites only the United States, the United Kingdom, Belgium and Israel as having relied upon this argument.

[42] D.W. Bowett, *Self Defence in International Law* (New York, 1958), p. 93 notes that it is unreasonable to characterise *every* threat to nationals located abroad as a threat to the security of the state. Byers, 'Terrorism, International Law and the Use of Force', at 406 refers to the tacit approval by most states of the Entebbe incident wherein Israel stormed a hijacked plane in Uganda carrying Israeli nationals. In addition to questions as to whether self defence arises at all are those relating to the proportionality of force to the objective of rescuing nationals or protecting particular interests.

[43] See the assessments of the lawfulness of the use of force by the US in Sudan and Afghanistan, purportedly in self defence as a result of the bombing of the US embassies, in, e.g., L.M. Campbell, 'Defending Against Terrorism: A Legal Analysis of the Decision to Strike Sudan and Afghanistan', 74 (2000) *Tulane Law Review* 1067. See also S. Schiedeman, 'Standards of Proof in Forcible Responses to Terrorism', 50 (2000) *Syracuse Law Review* at 249.

clearly met the 'scale and effects'[44] threshold, and which took place on US territory.[45]

Two particular issues have given rise to the greatest controversy as regards the scope of an Article 51 'armed attack', both of which are of central relevance in the post September 11 context explored in the second part of this chapter. The first is the thorny issue of whether 'anticipatory' or 'pre-emptive' self defence is permissible and, if so, the parameters of such a right. The second is whether the use of force by non-state actors may constitute an 'armed attack' for the purposes of triggering self defence, or whether a state must be responsible to justify the use of force against that state. These are discussed in turn below.

(i) A right of anticipatory self defence? The existence of a right to 'anticipatory' or 'pre-emptive' self defence – in other words a right to resort to force in self defence before an armed attack has occurred or to prevent or avert a future attack – is the subject of considerable controversy.[46]

Article 51 of the UN Charter permits resort to force in self defence 'if an armed attack occurs against a member of the United Nations'. The 'ordinary meaning' of the Article 51 language appears to require that an attack has actually happened or 'occurred', as opposed to being simply threatened,[47] as does a 'contextual' reading of the provision which, unlike other provisions of the Charter, omits any reference to the 'threat' of attack.[48]

---

[44] See *Nicaragua*, para. 195, where the Court notes that an armed attack is judged by its 'scale and effects'.

[45] Schiedeman, 'Standards of Proof', notes, in relation to the US bombing attacks of 1998, that 'with regard to the embassy bombings, neither the territorial integrity nor the political independence of the United States was at risk'. Different considerations pertain to the attacks of September 11. Note that these could be of some potential relevance to other States, should they seek to rely on having lost nationals during those events as a basis for self defence (rather than collective self defence at the US request), though there is little evidence of states having done so. The issue may be of broader relevance should the use of force be invoked in response to other attacks in the future. See, e.g., US National Security Strategy, discussed at Chapter 5.B.3.

[46] The extent of the significance of this issue was not immediately apparent in the wake of the September 11 attacks, but has been brought into sharp focus by the subsequent debate on legal justifications for the invasion of Iraq, and by the US National Security Strategy of 17 September 2002, which promotes a broad-reaching right to resort to preemptive force in the future. US President George W. Bush, 'The National Security Strategy of the United States of America', 17 September 2002, available at http://whitehouse.gov/nsc/nss.pdf (hereinafter 'US National Security Strategy'). See discussion in para. 5B.3.

[47] See generally M. Bothe, 'Terrorism and the Legality of Preemptive Force', 14 (2003) EJIL 227, specifically at 228.

[48] See Article 2(4) and Article 39, belying any suggestion that the omission of the threats from Article 51 was inadvertent. See Bothe, 'Preemptive Force', at 228–9.

Opinion may be more divided in relation to a 'purposive' interpretation of the provision – whether permitting anticipatory self defence furthers or undermines the Charter's objectives. On the one hand, opponents of the right can highlight the dangers of permitting pre-emptive strikes based on a state's own assessment of risk, as a slippery slope that may ultimately lead to the abolition of the prohibition on the use of force altogether, inconsistent with the Charter's fundamental purposes and principles. On the other, a compelling argument advanced in support of a right to 'anticipatory self defence' is that it is illogical or unreasonable to require a state to wait until it has been attacked to 'defend' itself.[49] A ready analogy is provided by criminal law, where the absurdity of needing to wait to be fatally shot to invoke self defence is apparent.[50] The nature of contemporary weapons systems – and the possibility of an initial potentially devastating attack – are cited as bolstering the argument in favour of a more flexible interpretation of Article 51.[51] As one commentator recently noted, 'no law . . . should be interpreted to compel the *reductio ad absurdum* that

---

[49] See O. Schachter, 'The Right of States to Use Armed Force', 82 (1984) *Michigan Law Review* 1620 at 1634, where Professor Schachter justifies 'anticipatory self defence' by stating: 'It is important that the right of self defence should not freely allow the use of force in anticipation of an attack or in response to the threat. At the same time, we must recognize that there may well be situations in which the imminence of an attack is so clear and the danger so great that defensive action is essential.' See also W.F. Warriner, 'The Unilateral Use of Coercion under International Law: A Legal Analysis of the United States Raid on Libya on April 14, 1986', 37 (1988) *Naval Law Review* 49 at 56 where the author describes the prerequisite for self defence as 'an actual or threatened violation of substantive rights of the claimant state'. See also T.M. Franck, 'When, If Ever, May States Deploy Military Force without Prior Security Council Authorization?' 5 (2001) *Washington University Journal of Law and Policy* 51 at 59–60, who notes in this respect that it may be necessary to respond to 'challenging transformations' such as increased weapons capability.

[50] Like its international counterpart, criminal law does however recognise strict limits on the circumstances in which preemptive action may be taken. See A. Ashworth, *Principles of Criminal Law*, 3rd ed. (Oxford, 1999), pp. 147–8: 'The use of force in self defence may be lawful where a preemptive strike is imminent. This is a desirable rule . . . and it would be a nonsense if the citizen was obliged to wait until the first blow was struck. The liberty to make a preemptive strike . . . should be read as subject to that duty [to avoid conflict] . . . A law which allows pre-emptive strikes without any general duty to avoid conflict runs the risk, as Dicey put it, of over stimulation.' For similar principles of self defence in different legal systems, see G.P. Fletcher, *Rethinking Criminal Law* (Oxford, 2000), pp. 85 ff.

[51] At times these arguments suggest that the law has, therefore, changed whereas at others they suggest it ought to change to accommodate these changing circumstances. The crucial distinction between the law as it stands (*de lege lata*) and the law as it ought to develop (*de lege ferenda*) is not always clear in discussions on this area of law. On changing circumstances post the Charter's inception and the argument in favour of flexible interpretation, see Franck, *Recourse to Force*, pp. 5–9.

states invariably must await a first, perhaps decisive, military strike before using force to protect themselves'.[52]

The opposing camps may be reconciled to some degree to the extent that there is room for debate as to when an attack actually 'begins'.[53] Thus the rejection of a right of anticipatory self defence does not oblige states to act as sitting ducks until harm is suffered to the extent that preparatory acts, coupled with a clear intent to attack, might be considered to constitute the effective commencement of the attack.[54] The intent element will, however, be most readily demonstrated, in the context of a series of attacks, where there has been a prior attack.

It should be noted that, in addition to those that argue a right to anticipatory self defence based on an expansive interpretation of the Charter, are others that assert a right of anticipatory self defence under customary law that goes beyond the Charter.[55] While there was a customary right to self

---

[52] *Ibid.*, p. 98. However the same commentator went on to acknowledge that 'a general relaxation of Article 51's prohibitions on unilateral war-making to permit unilateral recourse to force whenever a state feels potentially threatened could lead to another *reductio ad absurdum*'.

[53] Note that the clause 'if an armed attack occurs' was inserted in Article 51 at the initiative of the US delegation at the San Francisco Conference. During the debate on Article 51, the US representative made clear that the insertion of such caveat 'was intentional and sound. We did not want exercised the right of self defence before an armed attack has occurred', and that preparatory acts (such as the fact that a State sends its fleet to attack another State) do not justify use of force in self defence but only the preparatory acts necessary to 'be ready in the case an armed attack came'.

[54] M.E. O'Connell, 'Debating the Law of Sanctions', 13 (2002) EJIL 63; Bothe, 'Preemptive Force', at 229–30 suggests that the requirement of armed attack is uncontroversial and that it is on the meaning of such attack that there is controversy. He suggests that certain imminent attacks may be seen as 'equivalent to an armed attack', arguing that such an expansive approach is very common in practice. Note however the argument that self defence, as an exception, should be strictly construed, above.

[55] The Article 51 reference to the 'inherent' right of self defence is often cited as supporting the continued existence of customary rules alongside the Charter. Schachter, 'The Right of States', at 1633, states that: 'On one reading [of Article 51] this means that self defence is limited to cases of armed attack. An alternative reading holds that since the Article is silent as to the right of self defence under customary law (which goes beyond cases of armed attack) it should not be construed by implication to eliminate that right . . . It is therefore not implausible to interpret Article 51 as leaving unimpaired the right of self defence as it existed prior to the Charter.' See also G.M. Travalio, 'Terrorism, International Law and the Use of Military Force', 18 (2000) *Wisconsin International Law Journal* 145 at 149, stating, similarly, that 'the presence of an armed attack is *one* of the bases for the exercise of the right of self defence under Article 51, but not the *exclusive* basis' (emphasis in original). While the reference to the inherent right clearly reflects customary right, it may be odd if the framers intended a parallel inconsistent body of law to run alongside the Charter, which in many ways operates as an international constitution.

defence pre-Charter (as acknowledged by the reference to the 'inherent' right in Article 51 itself), which appears to have included a limited right to anticipatory self defence,[56] the question is whether the right survived the introduction of Article 51, clearly worded to the contrary. It is difficult to imagine that the Charter's framers intended a parallel inconsistent body of law to run alongside the Charter, particularly given that the Charter operates in many ways as an international constitution.

It is also doubtful whether there is sufficient state practice since 1945 to support the existence of such a customary norm at variance with the Charter, as recourse to anticipatory self defence as a legal justification for using force remains limited.[57] On one of the few occasions on which it was expressly invoked, in relation to Israel's attack on the Iraqi nuclear reactor in 1981, states generally shied away from debating the lawfulness of anticipatory self defence as such, but the underlying action met with condemnation as a violation of the law on use of force.[58]

At a minimum, it could be said that the majority of states have been reluctant to accept such a right, while doctrinal debate among academic commentators, before and after September 11, reveals little consensus.[59]

---

[56] See the *Caroline* case, discussed below.

[57] For discussion of state practice post Charter, see Gray, *International Law*, p. 112, stating that 'the majority of states reject anticipatory self defence'. The author notes states have however avoided authoritative pronouncements on anticipatory self defence and refers to the 'clear trend' to justify actions by bringing them within Article 51 language rather than resort to anticipatory self defence as a justification (*ibid.*, pp. 113–15). See also Franck, *Recourse to Force*, pp. 99–108. On international condemnation of pre-emptive action in the past, see, e.g., Cassese, *International Law*, pp. 309 ff.; J. Paust, 'Legal Responses to International Terrorism', 22 (1999) *Houston Journal of International Law* 17.

[58] On 19 June 1981 the Security Council unanimously condemned Israel for the air strike in Iraq, calling on Israel to refrain from such acts or threats in the future and stating that Iraq was entitled to compensation. See SC Res. 487 (1981), 19 June 1981, UN Doc. S/RES/487 (1981). See the comment by Franck, *Recourse to Force*, who suggests that on other occasions where there appeared to be anticipatory self defence, despite state's reluctance to refer to it as such, state reactions have been more equivocal.

[59] Many writers hold that there is no right of self defence until an armed attack has actually commenced. See, *inter alia*, I. Brownlie, *International Law and the Use of Force by States* (Oxford, 1981), pp. 256–7, Gray, *International Law*, p. 112. And it was recently noted that 'the overwhelming majority of legal doctrine . . . clearly holds anticipatory self defence to be unlawful' (Bothe, 'Preemptive Force', at 230). However, this is debatable to the extent that a number of authoritative commentators recognise a right to act in self defence against an *imminent* armed attack. See, e.g., Bowett, *Self-Defence*, pp. 187–92; *Oppenheim's International Law*, p. 421; C. Greenwood, 'International Law and the Pre-emptive Use of Force: Afghanistan, Al-Qaida, and Iraq', 4 (2003) *San Diego International Law Journal* 7. See also E.P.J. Myjer and N. D. White, 'The Twin Towers Attack: An Unlimited Right to Self-Defence?', 7 (2002) *Journal of Conflict and Security Law* 5 and O'Connell, 'Law of Sanctions'.

Oppenheim's International Law suggests that the position is that 'while anticipatory action in self defence is normally unlawful, it is not necessarily unlawful in all circumstances'.[60]

What *is* clear, and on which there is broader consensus, is that *if* a right to anticipatory self defence exists, it is limited. The circumstances in which anticipatory self defence might be permitted can be found in the seminal *Caroline* case of 1837,[61] the language of which has been widely cited as establishing, and at the same time strictly limiting, the circumstances in which the use of self defence in anticipation of an attack might be permissible. The *Caroline* test has been endorsed in subsequent judicial decisions, and is broadly cited as enshrining the appropriate customary law standard.[62] It may be that the *Caroline* formula represents the law pre-Charter and that a more restrictive view should be taken in light of Article 51. It is difficult to see, by contrast, how a broader right of anticipatory self defence could have developed since the advent of the Charter's Article 51. As such, as recently described, the *Caroline* test may be considered 'as far as pre-emptive self defence possibly goes under current international law'.[63]

The test proposed by US Secretary of State and agreed by the opposing party, the British, was that there had to be a necessity that was 'instant, overwhelming, and leaving no choice of means, and no moment for

---

[60] *Oppenheim's International Law*, p. 421.

[61] The correspondence between the US and the British Government relating to the case is reproduced in 29 (1841) *British and Foreign State Papers* 1137–1130 and 30 (1842) *British and Foreign State Papers* 195–196.

[62] See, e.g., the judgment of the Military Tribunal at Nuremberg in the trial of Goering, where the Tribunal recalled that preventive action in foreign territory is justified only in the circumstances described by Webster in the *Caroline* case. See also D.J. Harris, *Cases and Materials on International Law*, 5th ed. (London, 1998), p. 896: 'It is generally accepted that, as the *Nicaragua (Merits)* case confirms, in customary international law action taken as self defence remains subject to the *Caroline* requirements of necessity and proportionality'; R. Higgins, *Problems and Process: International Law and How We Use It* (Oxford, 1994), p. 242, stating that 'Under customary international law, self defence fell to be tested against the criteria enunciated by US Secretary of State Webster in the *Caroline* Case'; and Campbell, 'Defending Against Terrorism', at 1076.

[63] Bothe, 'Preemptive Force'. The more expansive view of pre-emptive self defence put forward since September 11, notably in the US National Security Strategy, to the effect that force may be deployed, not to respond to an attack or imminent threat of attack, but to prevent threats from materialising and deter potential attacks, is discussed at Chapter 5, para. 5A.3 below. As noted there, it is unlikely that the doctrine indicates any shift in the law, at least in the short term. See US National Security Strategy, above, note 46: 'To forestall or prevent such hostile acts by our adversaries, the United States will, if necessary, act preemptively.' Similar arguments were invoked by the US in Iraq. See Bothe, 'Preemptive Force', at 237 referring to, for example, SC Res. 487, above, note 58, relating to the Israeli attack against the Baghdad nuclear reactor.

deliberation'.[64] It makes clear that a distinction must be drawn between a real and immediate threat of armed attack, and a potential or speculative risk thereof. While some may question whether the need for 'no moment for deliberation' goes too far, it emphasises the immediacy of the threat, which is accepted as a critical criterion. While a threat, like an attack itself, may arise over a period of time, and it is a question of degree at what point it becomes real and immediate, the passage of considerable time between a threat arising and its response may raise doubts concerning the requirement of immediacy (and with it the necessity of the use of force as a response, discussed below).

Finally, it follows from the above test that the *capacity* to inflict harm, however grave, is insufficient, unless the circumstances indicate a real and imminent threat to carry out an armed attack. As such, there is little to suggest that the existence of weapons, even those of mass destruction, is considered *per se* sufficient to justify a claim to self defence. The rationale is reflected in domestic criminal law, where the fact that someone intends harm, or indeed possesses a weapon with the potential to do harm, or both, plainly would not justify the use of force in self defence, whereas brandishing a weapon where the context indicates an immediate and unavoidable threat, would do so.[65]

(ii) State responsibility for the attack: a sine qua non?   A second controversial question relating to the scope of an 'armed attack' under Article 51 is whether a state must be responsible for the attack for the right to self defence to be triggered, or whether the right to self defence arises even where a non-state actor is responsible for the attack (without its acts being attributable to any state). The significance of this question in determining the scope of the law of self defence in the contemporary world was put beyond doubt by the September 11 attacks.[66]

---

[64] Letter dated 24 April 1841 from the US Secretary of State Webster to the Government of the United Kingdom, Fox, reprinted in Harris, *Cases and Materials*, p. 895. As noted below, the *Caroline* 'necessity and proportionality' test applies to any action of self defence, but it is 'even more pressing in relation to anticipatory self defence than [it is] in other circumstances'. *Ibid.*, at 421.

[65] See Ashworth, above, on the imminence and duty to prevent conflict and Fletcher, *Criminal Law*.

[66] 9/11 was widely attributed to the al-Qaeda network in circumstances where state responsibility for the attacks remained uncertain and was not directly asserted. See, e.g., document published by the UK Government, 'Responsibility for the Terrorist Atrocities in the US, 11 September 2001', 4 October 2001. For a discussion of the responsibility of al-Qaeda, see S.D. Murphy (ed.), 'Contemporary Practice of the United States Relating to International

The international law of *jus ad bellum*, including self defence, developed premised on the assumption that disputes and resolutions would occur between states and those that act on their behalf. Yet this assumption has been subject to increasing doubt in recent years. On the one hand, the language of Article 51 of the Charter does not explicitly require state involvement in the attack to trigger self defence.[67] Nor does the logic of self defence (as permitting a state to take whatever action might be necessary to defend itself against an actual or imminent attack) require proof of state involvement in that attack. Indeed, the seminal *Caroline* case of 1837 involved non-state actors, operating without any apparent state support, indicating that – at least pre-Charter – the law had no difficulty with self defence against force employed by non-state actors.[68]

On the other hand, while the proposition that self defence might arise in response to non-state actor terrorist attacks might not be problematic in principle, concerns do arise from the reality that non-state actors do not operate out of the high seas but are based in other states' territories. Doubts arise as to whether an interpretation of Article 51 that allows those states to be attacked absent a substantial link to the offending non-state actor is consistent with the purposes and principles of the UN Charter, and the protection of the territorial integrity and political independence of states.[69] This is particularly so where terrorist cells operate globally,

---

Law Contemporary Practice', 96 (2002) AJIL 237. Responsibility of the state for acts of al-Qaeda would depend on satisfaction of the test whereby acts of private actors become attributable to the state – discussed at Chapter 3.

[67] Note, however, that as the Charter was drafted on an assumption that all force was inter-state and that it governed inter-state relations, too much reliance on the omission of express wording from the Charter would be misplaced.

[68] The *Caroline* case of 1837, which, as noted above, sets down the customary law of self defence, involved the destruction by the British of an American ship, the *Caroline*, which was assisting forces rebelling against the Crown in Canada. It was common ground that the US government had tried to restrain the private initiatives supporting the insurrection and arguably there was not therefore any state involvement. See M. Reisman, 'International Legal Responses to Terrorism', 22 (1999) *Houston Journal of International Law* 3 at 46.

[69] The question of the (potentially wrongful) use of force being committed against the state would most obviously arise where state institutions are the object of attack, but it arises also whenever force is used in the territory of another state without the consent of the government. See Travalio, 'Terrorism', at footnote 29: 'Even if it is true that Article 51 justifies the use of force in self defence against non-state actors (a proposition that is by no means clear), an attack against the non-state actors that violates the territory of the state in which they are located must itself be justified under international law. In other words, unless an 'armed attack' by terrorists can be imputed to the state from which the terrorists originate, it is hard to see how the application of Article 51 to terrorist attacks advances the argument for the permissibility of military force in response.' See also O. Schachter, 'The Lawful Use of Force by a State Against Terrorists in Another Country', reprinted in

potentially rendering many states susceptible to attack if, for example, mere presence on the state's territory would suffice to justify force in self defence. A rule that would lead to such widespread vulnerability can readily be questioned as inconsistent with the purposes of the UN.[70]

The predominant view before September 11 appeared to be that for self defence to be justified, acts of individuals or groups must be attributed to the state,[71] with controversy centring instead on the standard for attributing responsibility.[72] While some commentators said so explicitly, other writers, and indeed the ICJ judgment in *Nicaragua*, appeared to *assume* that a state must be involved in the armed attack.[73] It appeared at least arguable that the response to the events of September 11 – notably the widespread reference to the Afghanistan intervention being justified despite state responsibility not having being made out against Afghanistan – indicated a different view of the law, or at least that the law may shift influenced by the events of 9/11 and responses thereto.[74]

H.H. Han (ed.), *Terrorism and Political Violence: Limits and Possibilities of Legal Control* (New York, 1993).

[70] See principles governing Charter interpretation, set out above. Arguably, this vulnerability is addressed to some degree by a strict application of the necessity and proportionality test, discussed below, which would strictly limit the use of force against states and their representatives in respect of threats over which they have no control. See also Chapter 5, para. 5B.2.1.5 on the application of this to Afghanistan.

[71] See, for example, Cassese, 'Legal Response to Terrorism', at 596, who notes that unless the attack is imputable to the State and becomes a 'state act' then 'there can be no question of a forcible response to it'. At 597, the author notes that 'If . . . we want to find out whether the use of force is permitted, we must first ascertain whether there has been an armed attack on the State using force by the State against which force is used.' See also Travalio, 'Terrorism', noting that a lack of state involvement means that the use of force cannot rely on Article 51. A minority view was that non-state actors could be responsible for armed attacks before September 11 – see, e.g., R. Wedgwood, 'Responding to Terrorism: The Strikes against Bin Laden', 24 (1999) *Yale Journal of International Law* 559 at 564.

[72] See Chapter 3.1. As one writer noted: 'States do not today challenge the view that action by irregulars can constitute an armed attack; the controversy centers on the degree of state involvement that is necessary to make the actions attributable to the state and to justify action in self defence in particular cases', Gray, *International Law*, p. 97.

[73] The ICJ appeared to assume state involvement in the armed attack when it found there to be broad agreement that the 'nature of the acts which can be treated as constituting armed attacks' covers both action by regular military armed forces but also 'the sending by or on behalf of a state of armed bands, groups . . .', *Nicaragua*, para. 195. The ICJ noted that rendering assistance to armed groups, while it may amount to unlawful intervention, did not itself constitute an armed attack; instead, it was essential to demonstrate that the acts of the irregulars were attributable to the state, according to an 'effective control' test.

[74] Widespread reference to the right to 'self defence' post 9/11, including by the Security Council on 12 September 2001, has been cited as indicating that non-state actors may be responsible for an Article 51 attack (given that the acts were attributed to al-Qaeda but not necessarily the Afghan state). See, e.g., Greenwood, 'International Law and the "War against Terrorism"', 78 (2002) *International Affairs*, 301. While persuasive, another view holds that

However, the ICJ has since reiterated its view that 'Article 51 of the Charter . . . recognizes the existence of an inherent right of self-defence in the case of armed attack by one State against another State.'[75] Despite strong dissenting judgments on this point,[76] this statement of the Court must, in the words of one of those dissenting judges, 'be regarded as a statement of the law as it now stands'.[77]

If a state link is required, the key question becomes the standard by which action of non-state actors becomes attributable to the state. As already discussed in more detail in Chapter 3, the level of support which may render the state responsible for the attack is a question of degree, dependent ultimately on the exercise of sufficient control over those directly responsible for the attack.[78] While support for terrorists falling short of effective control may be prohibited in international law, it does not necessarily render the state constructively responsible for an armed attack, or entitle other states to use force against it. As the global practice of terrorism and counter-terrorism continues to unfold, the law on self defence, and on state responsibility, and the relationship between the two, is likely to develop.

(b) Necessity and proportionality As noted, necessity and proportionality are universally recognised as requirements of the law of self defence, under customary law and the UN Charter.[79]

---

states implicitly recognised that there was a degree of state involvement underlying those attacks. See, e.g., L. Sadat, 'Terrorism and the Rule of Law', 3 (2004) *Washington University Global Studies Law Review* 135 at 150; M. Sassòli, 'State Responsibility for Violations of International Humanitarian Law', 84 (2002) IRRC 401 and D. Jinks, 'State Responsibility for the Acts of Private Armed Groups', 4 (2003) *Chicago Journal of International Law* 83. Note that if this view is correct, it may suggest a lowering of the applicable test for attribution of responsibility, and the evidentiary requirements for establishing such responsibility, as discussed at Chapter 3. However, others offer alternative explanations. See Chapter 5, para. 5B.1.1.1, below.

[75] *Legal Consequences of the Construction of a Wall in the Occupied Palestinian Territory*, Advisory Opinion, 9 July 2004, para. 139.

[76] Opinion of Judges Higgins, para. 33, and Opinion of Judge Kooijmans, para. 35. Kooijmans describes the ICJ as having by-passed the approach of the Security Council in Resolution 1373.

[77] Higgins, *ibid.*

[78] See ICJ in the *Nicaragua* case, discussed in Chapter 3. Other formulae for support have been put forward. See, e.g., Cassese, *International Law*, p. 312, who describes the degree of support required as 'major and demonstrable'. As noted in Chapter 3, some suggest the standard may be falling post 9/11.

[79] *Nicaragua*, para. 176. The necessity and proportionality rules are 'well established in customary international law'. See also *Legality of the Threat or Use of Nuclear Weapons*, Advisory Opinion of 8 July 1996, *ICJ Reports 1996*, p. 226 (hereinafter 'Nuclear Weapons Advisory Opinion'), para. 141. Gray, *International Law*, p. 105.

For self defence to be justified, there must be an imminent *threat* of force or a continuing attack, as discussed above, and any response must be *necessary* to avert that threat.[80] These factors, which (unlike the armed attack requirement) are prospective as opposed to retrospective, are critical in distinguishing self defence from reprisals.

As noted above, the requirement reflected in the *Caroline* case of 1837, is of a 'necessity . . . that . . . is instant, overwhelming, and leaving no choice of means, and no moment for deliberation'.[81] The necessity of force presupposes that all alternative, peaceful means have been exhausted, are lacking or would be ineffective as against the anticipated threat.[82] The necessity principle is therefore linked to the 'general principle . . . whereby States can only have recourse to military force as a last resort'.[83]

As the *Caroline* case shows, necessity may imply a degree of *immediacy*. While an immediate response may not be an effective response, the longer the time lapse, the more tenuous the argument becomes as to the urgent necessity of unilateral action, as opposed to collective action under the UN umbrella.

Logically, for measures to be necessary to avert a threat, they must be capable of doing so. A relevant question in determining the right to self defence is therefore the *effectiveness* of any proposed measure. If measures against those responsible for an attack will increase the threat then they can hardly be said to be necessary to avert it. To this extent questions relating to the impact of the use of force as a counter terrorist strategy, and the likelihood of encouraging or impeding future acts of terrorism, are questions of potential relevance not only to the political expediency but also to the lawfulness of the use of force.

Proportionality and necessity are intertwined, with proportionality requiring that the force used be *no more* than necessary to meet the threat presented. Consistent with the underlying purpose of self defence, to defend the state from on-going or imminent harm, the proportionality test should be applied *vis-à-vis* the requirements of averting the threat, as opposed to in respect of the scale of that threat or of any prior armed

---

[80] *Nicaragua*, para. 176. The requirements that must be met any time self defence is invoked are often stated as the interrelated concepts of necessity, proportionality and immediacy. The *Caroline* case of 1837 set down what has been described as the customary law standard on necessity and proportionality. Campbell, 'Defending Against Terrorism', at 1067 and Y. Dinstein, *War, Aggression and Self Defence* (Oxford, 2000), p. 205.

[81] See note 63, above.

[82] See Schiedeman, 'Standards of Proof', at 270. For questions as to the exhaustion of such means post 9/11 see section B, below.

[83] Cassese, 'Legal Response to Terrorism', at 596.

attack.[84] Arguments as to numbers of persons killed in the original attack outweighing numbers killed in subsequent counter-measures are of political relevance only.

One commentator has noted, as an example of the limits imposed by the necessity and proportionality test, that 'the victim of aggression must not occupy the aggressor's territory, unless strictly required by the need to hold the aggressor in check and prevent him from continuing the aggression by other means'.[85]

The question of whether (and which) States are responsible for an armed attack (whether or not, as discussed above, a *sine qua non* of self defence) is relevant to the question whether particular measures are justified as necessary and proportionate. Logically, necessity and proportionality require a link between the target of 'defensive action' and the threat being defended against. Targeting state institutions, for example, absent evidence of their connection to the threat or their ability to control that threat, is difficult to justify as a necessary and proportionate measure of self defence.

In summary, the use of force in self defence is not automatically justified, even where there has been an armed attack and there is evidence of an imminent second attack or continuing attack that needs to be repelled. An appraisal must then be made, in the light of the facts, of the necessity and effectiveness of the measures proposed to counter that threat, and whether the measures proposed are proportionate to it. It follows from the necessity (and proportionality) test, that self defence can only be justified where the targets of defensive action have been clearly identified, such that their contribution to the threat in question has been properly assessed.

(c) Self defence and the Security Council Two particular issues arise regarding the relationship between the right to self defence and the role of the Security Council. The first is the immediate requirement that any individual or collective self defence measure be reported to the Council. The second, though somewhat more controversial, is the limitation on the right to self defence as only justifying the use of force under the Charter *until* the Council is engaged.

---

[84] Necessity and proportionality are thus closely interrelated. See, for example, Schiedeman, 'Standard of Proof', who notes that the requirement of proportionality 'demands that the action be necessary to repulse and to end the attack'. See, however, *Nicaragua*, para. 176, which states that self defence should be proportionate to the 'attack'.

[85] Cassese, *International Law*, p. 305.

On the reporting obligation, Article 51 of the UN Charter provides that:

> Measures taken by Members in the exercise of this right of self defence shall be immediately reported to the Security Council and shall not in any way affect the authority and responsibility of the Security Council under the present Charter to take at any time such action as it deems necessary in order to maintain or restore international peace and security.

Reflecting this, Article 5 of the NATO treaty, which provides for the organisation to act 'in exercise of the right of individual or collective self defence recognised by Article 51 of the Charter of the United Nations', specifically provides that 'Any such armed attack and all measures taken as a result thereof shall immediately be reported to the Security Council.'

While the ICJ found there to be no requirement under customary law to report to the Security Council, the requirement is explicit in the Charter itself and that it is binding on all UN members is uncontroversial.[86] Failure to report may, moreover, constitute evidence that the state did not consider itself to be acting in self defence.[87]

As regards the second issue of the relationship between the right to unilateral self defence and collective action, the Charter (reflected again in the NATO treaty), certainly appears to envisage self defence by member states as a temporary right, pending Council engagement. Article 51 provides for:

> the inherent right of individual or collective self defence if an armed attack occurs . . . , *until* the Security Council has taken measures necessary to maintain international peace and security.

The NATO Treaty records at Article 5 that '[s]uch measures [of collective self defence] shall be terminated when the Security Council has taken the measures necessary to restore and maintain international peace and security'.

The Charter clearly assumes that once states can, they will seek Council engagement. No provision is made for state preference to continue to exercise the unilateral right of self defence. It is generally recognised, however, that if the Council is not engaged, for whatever reason, self defence continues for as long as the other conditions for the exercise of self defence

---

[86] *Nicaragua*, para. 200.   [87] *Ibid.*

are met. But when the Council *does* engage to take those measures the Council (as opposed to the state) deems necessary, the Charter envisages that the right to use force in self defence is superseded.

The opposing view, that the right to self defence permits the continued use of unilateral force alongside Security Council engagement, and unaffected by it, depends on the view that the customary law of self defence continues alongside the Charter, providing for contradictory rights and obligations.[88] Whatever the state of customary law on deference to the Council, and its relationship to the Charter,[89] it is noted that one of the other criteria for self defence, accepted as customary law, is the 'necessity' requirement. As discussed above, unilateral resort to force would be of doubtful necessity if measures were being taken under the collective security umbrella.

Questions may arise as to what constitutes 'engagement' by the Council, which is not defined. At one end of the spectrum, passing a resolution noting a situation or expressing concern (such as perhaps resolution 1368 of 12 September 2001) is not likely to be considered sufficient for 'engagement'. At the other end, it is not of course necessary that the Council step in to authorise force for it to become engaged, as this would pre-empt the decision, vested in the Council alone, as to whether force was the best course of action.[90]

5A.2.1.2 Individual or collective self defence

The UN Charter enshrines the notion that self defence can be individual or collective, but the precise meaning of 'collective self defence' has generated

---

[88] The doubtful legitimacy of this view is highlighted above. While some commentators argue that the right of self defence under customary law continues alongside the role of an engaged Security Council, the clear use of the 'until' language in the Charter appears to indicate otherwise as a matter of Charter law binding on UN member states.

[89] As there is limited practice in exercise of the right of self defence, which is an exceptional measure, it may be difficult to assess whether there is, post Charter, a customary rule on this particular aspect of it.

[90] SC Res. 1368 (2001), 12 September 2001, UN Doc. S/RES/1363 (2001). Measures such as those imposed in SC Res. 1373 (2001), 28 September 2001, UN Doc. S/RES/1373 (2001), given the breadth of their reach, could be argued to constitute Council 'engagement' to take the measures necessary for international peace and security. The Council may, however (as it did in the case of SC Res. 1373), engage to take particular steps while making clear that they do so consistent with the continuing relevance of the right of self defence: '*Reaffirming further* that such acts, like any act of international terrorism, constitute a threat to international peace and security', and the 'inherent right of individual or collective self defence as recognized by the Charter of the United Nations as reiterated in Res. 1368 (2001).'

some debate. Specifically, it is disputed whether Article 51 permits only the collective exercise of individual self defence (by states all of whom are subject to the attack or threat thereof), or whether it empowers other states, whose interests are not affected, to support a victim state in the exercise of that state's right of self defence.

The majority of the ICJ in the *Nicaragua* case took the latter view: that a state's interests need not be directly affected in order to exercise collective self defence, provided the injured state requests assistance.[91] One commentator notes that this corresponds to state practice since 1945.[92] However, another view is seen from the strong dissenting judgment of Judge Jennings in *Nicaragua*, who distinguishes self defence from 'vicarious defence' and notes that 'there should, even in 'collective self defence', be some real element of self'. This approach is followed by a number of other commentators.[93]

The scope of 'collective' self defence is potentially relevant to the legitimacy of the use of force by states which were not the victims of the 'armed attack'.[94] However, it is noteworthy that the entitlement of other states to act on the invitation of the US has not been a feature of the debate post September 11, perhaps indicating that the right to act in collective self defence in these circumstances is no longer controversial.[95]

---

[91] *Nicaragua*, paras. 104–5. See also A. Cassese, 'Legal Response to Terrorism', at 597: 'Collective self defence requires that the State has been requested or authorised to intervene by the [injured] State.'

[92] See Gray, *International Law*, p. 139, describing the insistence on third state interest as 'far fetched'.

[93] See Sir Robert Jennings' dissenting opinion in *Nicaragua*, 545. Gray, *International Law*, p. 139 notes that 'many others follow the Jennings approach' (while herself describing the position as 'far fetched in the light of state practice since 1945'). See also Dinstein, *War*.

[94] As discussed, an attack against the state is generally thought to involve an attack against the territorial integrity or political independence of a state, while a minority view holds that attacks against nationals (but not other state interests), would suffice. Accepting defence of nationals as a basis for self defence does not necessarily open up the possibility that any of the states whose nationals were killed on September 11 could use force in self-defence unless the attack against them was an ongoing or imminent attack.

[95] States' reasons for taking military action are not often, or rarely, set out in clear legal terms. It may be that other justifications could be invoked by the states intervening militarily alongside the US, e.g., at least some could have been based on protection of their own territory or (although less likely) defence of their nationals. Note, however, that while nationals of many countries died in the September 11 attacks on the World Trade Center, as self defence must be against an ongoing or imminent attack, it is questionable whether attacks on other states' nationals would meet that test.

The recognition of the collective nature of the right to self defence is reflected in various treaties, including the NATO treaty.[96] Article 5 provides:

> The Parties agree that an armed attack against one or more of them in Europe or North America shall be considered an attack against them all and consequently they agree that, if such an armed attack occurs, each of them, in exercise of the right of individual or collective self defence recognised by Article 51 of the Charter of the United Nations, will assist the Party or Parties so attacked by taking forthwith, individually and in concert with the other Parties, such action as it deems necessary, including the use of armed force, to restore and maintain the security of the North Atlantic area.

No autonomous right to use force is, or could be, contained in the NATO treaty or any other agreement.[97] Indeed the Charter would prevail over any other agreement inconsistent with its terms.[98] As the NATO treaty clause itself indicates, the lawful use of collective force is limited by the UN Charter. Neither NATO nor any other organisation can take forceful measures, whether or not in the interest of common security, unless the conditions for the exercise of self defence, set out above, are satisfied.[99] In this sense, the right enjoyed by the regional or other collective security organisation is the same as that of any individual state.

The significance of the NATO treaty in this respect is, however, twofold. First, to the extent that the right of other states to use force in collective self defence requires a request from the state immediately affected by the attack, the NATO treaty is seen to operate as a standing request to other members to assist in its defence. Secondly, while action in collective self defence under the UN Charter (unlike a decision by the Security Council) is permissive, not obligatory,[100] the NATO treaty goes further, by *obliging* states parties to it to act. But, as noted above, these arrangements can only

---

[96] North Atlantic Treaty, Washington, 4 April 1949, 34 UNTS 243. For another regional security treaty, see, e.g., Inter-American Treaty of Reciprocal Assistance, Rio de Janeiro, 2 September 1947, 21 UNTS 324, in force 3 December 1948, Article 3(1). Like the NATO treaty, this regional security treaty was also activated post 9/11: see K. De Young, 'OAS Nations Activate Mutual Defense Treaty', *Washington Post*, 20 September 2001.

[97] The treaty expressly derives its authority from the UN Charter and is subject to its constraints.

[98] Article 103, UN Charter.

[99] Unlike the Security Council, NATO has no independent powers to authorise the use of force. Unless it is mandated to act on behalf of the Security Council, NATO power is predicated on the principle of self defence.

[100] Proposals to oblige other member states to assist victims of aggression were rejected during the negotiation of the Charter. See Franck, *Recourse to Force*, p. 46.

oblige states to take measures that they are *entitled* to take consistent with the UN Charter provisions on self defence.

As set out in the following section, only the Security Council[101] can authorise measures in the interest of peace and security that are not justified in the self defence of any state. However, the Council may, and in practice does, mandate collective or regional organisations to take those measures on its behalf.

5A.2.2 Security Council: maintenance of international peace and security

In situations where self defence cannot be justified, the only legitimate use of force is that authorised by the Security Council.[102] The Security Council has broad powers, under Chapter VII of the UN Charter,[103] to determine the existence of any threat to the peace, breach of the peace, or act of aggression[104] and to take (or to authorise) those measures – including ultimately the use of force – that it deems necessary to address the situation.

Article 39 of the Charter empowers the Security Council to 'make recommendations, or decide what measures shall be taken . . . to maintain or restore international peace and security'. The 'measures' referred to in Article 39 are further specified in the Articles that follow. In particular, Article 41 concerns 'measures not involving the use of armed force' that the Security Council may adopt to give effect to its decisions and establishes an obligation on Member States to apply such measures. Supplementing those powers, Article 42 confers on the Security Council unique powers to mandate enforcement action, where the non-coercive measures are deemed, or proved to be, inadequate.

---

[101] Arguably, the General Assembly may assume the powers that fall primarily to the Security Council, as it did when the latter was unable to discharge its mandate during the Cold War due to paralysis of the decision making process. The General Assembly passed the 'Uniting for Peace' Resolution (GA Res. 377 (V), 3 November 1950, UN Doc. A/RES/377 (V)) to address the situation in Korea, pursuant to which it established a temporary UN presence in Korea.

[102] As noted above, under the Charter, even where self defence can initially be justified, the lawfulness of the use of force ultimately turns on subsequent UN Security Council authorisation.

[103] Chapter VII is entitled 'Action with Respect to Threats to the Peace, Breaches of the Peace and Acts of Aggression'.

[104] Article 39 authorises the Security Council 'to determine the existence of any threat to the peace, breach of the peace, or act of aggression'. This categorisation of the situation by the Security Council is a pre-requisite to forceful action under Chapter VII (but does not *per se* indicate authorisation of the use of force).

The language of Security Council resolutions under Chapter VII may be recommendatory – 'calling on' all states, or particular states, to take action – or it may be mandatory, 'deciding' that specific measures should be adopted. It is these 'decisions' that are binding on member states which, under Article 25, are required 'to accept and carry out' the Council's decisions. If questions arise as to non-compliance with these obligations, it is for the Council to decide whether there has been a breach and what measures are appropriate in response.[105]

The UN Charter originally envisaged a form of international police force at the beckoning of the Council. Article 43 commits all members 'to make available to the Security Council, on its call and in accordance with a special agreement or agreements, armed forces, assistance, and facilities, including rights of passage, necessary for the purpose of maintaining international peace and security'. This UN force has however never come into being and, in practice, the Council has instead discharged its enforcement mandate by delegation,[106] nominating member states generally, or specific states, to take measures involving the use of force.[107] Numerous situations have arisen where states, regional organisations or 'coalitions of the willing' have been authorised to take 'all necessary measures' (which in Council speak clearly includes forceful measures) to give effect to the Council's decisions.[108]

5A.2.2.1 The Security Council and international peace and security: powers and limitations

The Security Council's power to decide measures involving the use of force is ample but not limitless. The Council enjoys a broad discretion to determine the existence of a threat to or a breach of international peace

---

[105] These measures may of course involve the use of force. See automaticity debate, below.

[106] Franck, *Recourse to Force*, p. 43, refers to the Security Council authorisation of action by states and others, as opposed to the Security Council itself taking action, as the 'adapted power' of the Council. C. Gray, 'From Unity to Polarisation: International Law and the Use of Force against Iraq', 13 (2001) EJIL 1 at 2–3 notes increasing concern, since the 1991 Iraq invasion, to ensure that the Council retains control over UN authorised, but state executed, operations.

[107] The use of force may be authorised or – at least theoretically – mandated by the Council.

[108] The following such situations have arisen since the Cold War era: Kuwait (1990–91), Somalia (1992–93), Rwanda (1994), Haiti (1993), Bosnia-Herzegovina (1995–), Great Lakes (1996), Central African Republic (1997), Albania (1997), Kosovo (1999–), and East Timor (1999). See S. Chesterman, *Just War or Just Peace. Humanitarian Intervention and International Law* (Oxford, 2001), p. 123 and Gray, 'From Unity to Polarisation', at 2–3. The latter notes that 1991 was a watershed in terms of Council activism under Chapter VII.

or security, or whether particular conduct constitutes an act of aggression.[109] The text of Article 42 poses some limits on the power of the Security Council to adopt coercive measures, however, by specifying that measures implying the use of armed force should constitute the *extrema ratio*, to be taken only where 'the Security Council considers that measures [provided for in Article 41] would be inadequate or have proven to be inadequate' and that the measures adopted must be '*necessary* to maintain or restore international peace or security'. Moreover, the course of action decided by the Security Council must be consistent with the purposes and principles of the United Nations as defined in Articles 1 and 2 of the Charter.

(a) 'Threat to or breach of international peace and security' and terrorism

The first condition for the application of measures under Chapter VII of the Charter is, as noted above, that the situation must amount to a threat to, or breach of, 'international peace and security'. The concept of 'threat to, or breach of, international peace and security' has been given an increasingly broad interpretation by the Security Council. Through practice, the phrase has come to include matters that would originally – when the Charter was framed – have been thought internal questions for the state. For example the deposing of a democratically elected government,[110] the commission of extremely serious violations of human rights,[111] or non-international conflicts[112] have all been deemed to constitute threats to 'international peace and security'.[113] In practice the standard to be applied by the Council has come to be viewed as fairly flexible, with security against overuse residing in the collective mechanism that applies it rather than in the confines of its terms, by contrast to the stricter standards governing unilateral use of force.[114]

---

[109] For discussion of the definition of aggression, see Chapter 4, para. 4A.1.1.3.

[110] See SC Res. 841 (1993), 16 June 1993, UN Doc. S/RES/841 (1993), concerning Haiti.

[111] See SC Res. 418 (1977), 4 November 1977, UN Doc. S/RES/418 (1977) concerning apartheid in South Africa and SC Res. 232 (1966), 16 December 1966, UN Doc. S/RES/232 (1966) concerning white minority rule in Rhodesia.

[112] See SC Res. 713 (1991), 25 September 1991, UN Doc. S/RES/713 (1991), concerning Somalia and SC Res. 794 (1992), 3 December 1992, UN Doc. S/RES/794 (1992) concerning Bosnia-Herzegovina.

[113] See discussion on humanitarian intervention and pro-democratic intervention, paras. 3.3.1 and 3.3.2 in this chapter.

[114] It falls to the state invoking self defence, in the initial stage, to apply and determine the legitimacy of its recourse to force. Susceptibility to abuse in the absence of any external oversight is great and therefore the exception to the prohibition on the use of force must be narrowly construed.

Security Council Resolution 748 (1992), addressing Libya's refusal to extradite the Lockerbie bombing suspects,[115] was the first in a series of resolutions in which the Council articulated a relationship between terrorism and international peace and security. Like subsequent resolutions on the attempted assassination of Egypt's President Mubarak[116] and the bombings of the US embassies in Tanzania and Kenya,[117] the Lockerbie resolution noted that 'the suppression of acts of international terrorism, including those in which States are directly or indirectly involved, is essential for the maintenance of international peace and security'. Likewise, Security Council resolutions adopted in response to September 11 and subsequently have unequivocally determined the events of that day to be a threat to international peace and security.[118]

While the terms of Security Council resolutions 1368 and 1373 of September 2001, and the resolution that followed the Madrid bombing of March 2003, suggest that 'any act of international terrorism' amounts to a threat to international peace and security,[119] this is to be doubted, particularly given the absence of international accord around the substance and scope of the definition of terrorism. Moreover, the Council's own earlier Resolution 1269 of 1999 '[u]nequivocally condemns all acts, methods and practices of terrorism . . . *in particular those which could threaten international peace and security*'.[120] What is clear is that the concept of a threat to international peace and security *may* encompass acts of 'terrorism', to which Chapter VII action could be directed.

(b) Measures to maintain and restore international peace and security

As noted above, the fact that there is a threat to international peace and security itself is not sufficient to trigger the legitimate use of force.

---

[115] SC Res. 748 (1992), 31 March 1992, UN Doc. S/RES/748 (1992).

[116] SC Res. 1044 (1996), 16 August 1996, UN Doc. S/RES/1044 (1996).

[117] SC Res. 1189 (1998), 13 August 1998, UN Doc. S/RES/1189 (1998) and SC Res. 1267 (1999), 15 October 1999, UN Doc. S/RES/1267 (1999).

[118] See SC Res. 1368 (2001), above, note 90. On 28 September 2001 the SC adopted SC Res. 1373 (2001), above, note 90, described as a 'wide-ranging, comprehensive resolution with steps and strategies to combat international terrorism'.

[119] SC Res. 1368 (2001), above, note 90, condemns 9/11 as, 'like any act of international terrorism', 'a threat to international peace and security'. The Preamble of resolution 1373 (2001), above, note 90, likewise notes that 'such acts, like any act of international terrorism, constitute a threat to international peace and security'. See also SC Res. 1530 (2004), 11 March 2004, UN Doc. S/RES/1530 (2004), where the Council, condemning the bomb attacks in Madrid on 11 March 2004, stated that it 'regard[ed] such act, like any act of terrorism, as a threat to peace and security'.

[120] SC Res. 1269 (1999), 19 October 1999, UN Doc. S/RES/1269 (1999) (emphasis added).

Consistent with the principles of the UN as enshrined in Articles 1 and 2 of the Charter,[121] and reflected in the language of Article 42, for military action to be possible, the Security Council must consider non-military measures under Article 41 of the Charter to be (or have been) inadequate. This does not imply that non-military measures have to have been ordered and implemented in practice, but only that the Security Council has to determine that those measures would be ineffective for the purpose of restoring international peace and security.

Logically, necessity encapsulates an element of proportionality – the particular measures taken should be capable of furthering international peace and security and the force used should be no more than necessary to achieve this purpose. These are essentially factual questions for the Council's assessment.

The Council has broad discretion to decide which measures are appropriate to maintain and restore international peace and security. Measures that the Council may decide to authorise or mandate under the Chapter VII rubric of maintaining international peace and security cover a wide array, some involving armed force and others not, as history attests. In the post-Cold War period, non-forceful measures have included establishment of *ad hoc* criminal tribunals,[122] the imposition of a war reparations procedure,[123] and attempts to force the extradition of alleged terrorists.[124]

The Council has authorised 'enforcement action' through coercive measures, for example, to restore a democratically elected government in Haiti[125] and to end apartheid in South Africa,[126] white minority rule in Rhodesia[127] and armed conflicts in Bosnia-Herzegovina[128] and Somalia.[129] The use of force for the purpose of cross-border criminal law enforcement – which may be impermissible if unilateral[130] – also forms

---

[121] See Article 2(3) on resolution of disputes through peaceful means and Article 2(4) on the non-use of force.

[122] On the establishment of the *ad hoc* tribunals for the former Yugoslavia and Rwanda, see Chapter 4.

[123] Reparation procedure for Iraq, described by Chesterman, *Just War or Just Peace*, pp. 121– 2. Chesterman also refers to the demarcation of a territorial boundary between Iraq and Kuwait, *ibid.*, p. 122.

[124] Extradition measures involved suspects from Libya and Sudan, Chesterman, *ibid.*

[125] SC Res. 841 (1993), above, note 110.   [126] SC Res. 418 (1977), above, note 111.

[127] SC Res. 232 (1966), above, note 111.   [128] SC Res. 713 (1991), above, note 112.

[129] SC Res. 794 (1992), above, note 112.

[130] History indicates several examples of unilateral enforcement action in the territory of other states having been condemned. See for example *United States* v. *Alvarez-Machain* 504 US 655 (1992) and *Attorney General of Israel* v. *Eichmann* (Israel Supreme Court 1962), reprinted in 36 ILR 277 at 299, 304. *Oppenheim's International Law*, p. 387, distinguishes

part of the Council's enforcement arsenal, and has been invoked in several situations in recent years.[131]

As regards measures that may overstep the constitutional limits highlighted above, it has recently been questioned to what extent the Council is empowered, for example, to authorise 'regime change', given the Charter's protection of states' 'political independence' as a fundamental principle.[132] The Security Council has in fact intervened only once to effect a change of government – where a *de facto* government had usurped power, causing serious unrest, and the Security Council authorised force to restore the democratically elected government – and it did so emphasising the exceptional nature of the measure.[133] While removal of an unpopular government by the Council, as an end in itself, would not find support in the Charter, the Council would appear to be empowered to authorise force against a regime which it found to pose a threat to peace and security, which could not be averted other than through the regime's demise.

While it is clear that the Security Council's powers are limited to action taken in accordance with the Charter, less clear are the consequences of overreach, and whether any other body is entitled to review the Council's decisions.[134] While this issue may become relevant to decisions of the Security Council to authorise measures of force in the future, it is not central in the absence of such Council authorisation in the first years of the 'war on terror'.[135]

such unlawful incursions into territory in pursuit of criminals from 'hot pursuit' in maritime matters, which 'involves no violation of territorial sovereignty'.

[131] See, e.g., SC Res. 837 (1993), 6 June 1993, UN Doc. S/RES/837 (1993), in relation to Somalia. The possibility of invoking Security Council powers for the enforcement of criminal law is addressed at Chapter 4.

[132] R. Singh and A. MacDonald, 'Legality of use of force against Iraq', Opinion for Peacerights, 10 September 2002, available at http://www.lcnp.org/global/IraqOpinion10.9.02.pdf (hereinafter 'Singh and MacDonald, Opinion on Iraq'), note at para. 79: '[W]hile the Security Council can demand that Iraq achieve certain results, it cannot dictate its choice of government. The Security Council resolutions require Iraq to meet a long list of requirements. These *could* be met by Saddam Hussein's government. While the Security Council, or certain members of it, may not like that government, a change of regime cannot be considered absolutely necessary to achieving the Security Council's legitimate aims.'

[133] See SC Res. 841 (1993) on Haiti, above, note 110, which was justified in part by reference to broader implications for the region.

[134] For a discussion of the limits on Council action and the role of the ICJ and ICTY in reviewing the powers of the Council, see S. Lamb, 'Legal Limits to UN Security Council Powers', in G. Goodwin-Gill and S. Talmon (eds.), *The Reality of International Law: Essays in Honour of Ian Brownlie* (Oxford, 1999), pp. 361 ff. and J. E. Alvarez, 'Judging the Security Council', 90 (1996) AJIL 1.

[135] It is uncontroversial that force was not explicitly authorised. Regarding implied authorisation and Iraq, see this chapter, para. 5 B.2.1.1 below.

5A.2.2.2 Express and implied authorisation to use force: interpreting resolutions

Consistent with general principles of legal interpretation, a Security Council resolution must be interpreted according to the ordinary meaning of the language used, understood in its context and in light of the resolution's purpose. This analysis can be informed by debates that lead to the resolution's adoption and, to a more limited degree, by statements made thereupon.[136]

Given the justifications invoked by states for the use of force post September 11 (particularly in Iraq), discussed in section B of this chapter, two issues relating to the interpretation of Resolutions and the manner in which the Security Council authorises states to use force are worthy of mention. The first is whether authorisation can be inferred from earlier Security Council resolutions; the second is whether states can unilaterally 'enforce' obligations imposed by the Council, absent a decision of the Council to that effect.

'Implied authorisation' is, *per se*, a controversial notion. Its legitimacy has been questioned as stretching too far 'legal flexibility'.[137] In practice, reliance by states on implied authorisation as a legal justification in the past has been limited and, where invoked, subject to criticism.[138]

---

[136] See *Legal Consequences for States of the Continued Presence of South Africa in Namibia (South West Africa) Notwithstanding Security Council Resolution 276*, Advisory Opinion, ICJ Reports 1971, p. 15 at p. 53: 'The language of a resolution of the Security Council should be carefully analysed before a conclusion can be made as to its binding effect. In view of the nature of the powers under Article 25, the question whether they have been in fact exercised is to be determined in each case, having regard to the terms of the resolution to be interpreted, the discussions leading to it, the Charter provisions invoked and, in general, all circumstances that might assist in determining the legal consequences of the resolution of the Security Council.' As an authoritative commentator notes: 'The passage [of the Advisory Opinion of the ICJ] suggests an approach to interpretation similar to that set out in Article 31(1) of the VCLT 1969', i.e., 'A treaty shall be interpreted in good faith in accordance with the ordinary meaning to be given to the terms of the treaty in their context and in the light of its object and purpose', M. Byers, 'The Shifting Foundations of International Law: A Decade of Forceful Measures Against Iraq', 13 (2002) EJIL 21.

[137] R. Higgins, 'International Law in a Changing International System', 58 (1999) *Cambridge Law Journal* 78 at 94: 'In our unipolar world, does now the *very adoption* of a resolution under Chapter VII of the Charter trigger a legal authorisation to act by NATO when *it* determines it necessary? If that is so, then we may expect that in the future Russia will again start exercising its veto in the Security Council, to make sure resolutions are not adopted, thus undercutting the possibility of useful political consensus being expressed in those instruments.'

[138] See generally Gray, 'From Unity to Polarisation', which addresses the use of force in Iraq up to and including 2001; see also Higgins, 'Changing International System'.

Characteristically, it has been asserted not as a primary justification for resort to force but one coupled with the breach by the target state of its international obligations and/or humanitarian intervention,[139] an approach which has been described as a 'combination of a series of weak arguments in the hope that cumulatively they will be persuasive'.[140]

Moreover, practice attests to the fact that where the Council authorises force it will generally do so in clear terms. For example, Resolution 678 of 19 November 1990, one of many Security Council Resolutions handed down during the Gulf Conflict and universally understood to authorise the use of force, stated that: 'the Security Council authorises member states cooperating with the government of Kuwait to use all necessary means to uphold and implement Resolution 660'.[141] The *all necessary means* language, while a euphemism, is universally understood in the diplomatic context as synonymous with the authorisation of necessary force.[142]

Given the fundamental principle prohibiting resort to force, and the exceptional nature of the right to do so, there must be a strong presumption against implied (as opposed to clearly expressed) authorisation[143] or open-ended authorisation to use force, and in favour of a strict interpretation that limits the right to use force to the particular situation and purpose to which the authorisation was directed.[144]

Moreover, given the unique power vested in the Council to determine breaches of peace and security and to authorise force, if necessary,

---

[139] Implied authorisation appeared to be relied upon in relation to the use of force in the no-fly zones of Northern Iraq, although the UK later specified its legal justification as humanitarian intervention which, it noted, 'supported' SC Resolution 688. See SC Res. 688 (1990), 5 April 1991, UN Doc. S/RES/688 (1991), requiring humanitarian relief to the Kurds in Northern Iraq. For UK justification see Hansard debate, 26 February 2001, in Gray, 'From Unity to Polarisation', at 9. It was also invoked by at least some states involved in the Kosovo NATO action, although again alongside other justifications, notably humanitarian intervention.

[140] Gray, 'From Unity to Polarisation', at 16 notes that this cumulative 'weak argument' approach is 'typical legal reasoning, and common in the area of the use of force'.

[141] SC Res. 660, 2 August 1990, UN Doc. S/RES/660 (1990) called for the withdrawal of Iraq from Kuwait.

[142] By contrast, as discussed in Chapter 5, para. 5B.1.1.4, below, the absence of such language in the post-September 11 resolutions was critical to their being broadly considered not to authorise the use of force in Afghanistan.

[143] This is sometimes referred to as the 'automaticity' question.

[144] The fact that SC Res. 1368, above, note 90, is framed as against 'terrorism' in general, rather than any particular situation, and could thus be invoked by any state as justifying the use of force in a broad range of situations, provides an additional reason why the resolution could not be interpreted as authorising force consistently with the UN Charter.

resolutions must not be interpreted in a manner that would ultimately divest the Council of this role.[145] The Council will often threaten to authorise force in the event of non-compliance, by referring to the 'severest consequences' that a material breach of a resolution will attract. But it remains within the exclusive power of the Council to decide whether there has been a breach, whether at that point in time the breach amounts to a threat to international peace and security and whether, in turn, the threat necessitates and justifies coercive measures. While it can and does delegate the carrying out of measures of enforcement, the Council does not, and could not (without abrogating its constitutional responsibilities), delegate the power to decide whether the particular situation, in the light of all prevailing circumstances, justifies the use of force. Often resolutions expressly indicate the Council's intention to decide what measures should be taken in the event of a breach but even where they do not this may be inferred from the Council's exclusive remit under the Charter.

It follows that where a state does not meet its obligations under Council resolutions, there is no automatic right of other states to 'enforce' these obligations. The power to authorise enforcement resides in the Council itself, in accordance with its powers and responsibilities under the Charter, and not with member states.[146] An attempt to justify force on this basis would fall foul of the international law it purports to uphold.

5A.2.2.3 Veto power and the 'failure' of the Council to act

A Security Council resolution is passed by a majority of states sitting on the Council voting in its favour, absent the use of the veto by one of the Council's five permanent members.[147] This system was intended to ensure that the crucial decisions vested in the Council – prime among them the exceptional power to authorise force (in a world pledged 'to save succeeding generations from the scourge of war') – would be subject to political balance, with the safeguards against overuse implicit in such a system. In other words, it was never meant to be easy to get Council approval to use force under the Charter system.

This system, and the veto power in particular, has been subject to criticism since its inception.[148] During the Cold War criticism was harshest

---

[145] See the discussion of attempts to rely on authorisation given in the context of the invasion of Kuwait to justify force against Iraq in a quite different context, section B below.

[146] Article 39, Article 42.

[147] The five permanent members of the Security Council are China, France, Russia, the UK and the US.

[148] Certain non-permanent members have long challenged the legitimacy of the veto power. Some commentators contend that the Council, as envisaged at its inception, has essentially

and most justified, as an abuse of the veto power by major powers in a bipolar world resulted in a period of Security Council inertia.[149] International practice developed to accommodate the situation, and the General Assembly assumed certain of the powers that vested 'primarily' in the Council in order to address situations such as the Chinese intervention in Korea.[150]

Whatever the constitutional legitimacy of the General Assembly assuming such a role (which is not uncontroversial),[151] two distinctions are merited. The first is between collective action under the UN umbrella in the form of General Assembly authorised force[152] and unilateral action by states: while the former may be lawful the latter is precisely what the Charter sought to curb. Second, while concerns around the functioning of the Council have certainly not disappeared,[153] they take on a very different complexion in a post-Cold War era of relative Security Council activism. Despite the veto, which the US now invokes more than any other permanent member, numerous resolutions have been passed in recent years, including authorising the use of force. The stagnation of the Cold War era, where the Council could be described as virtually dysfunctional, is distinct from a scenario where diplomacy fails and a functioning Council cannot agree. The secondary General Assembly 'powers' have not however been invoked for decades, consistent with the Security Council again assuming its role (however imperfectly) as overseer of the legitimate use of force.

---

failed. Franck, *Recourse to Force*, p. 52 notes: 'The noble plan for replacing state self-help with collective security failed because it was based on two wrong assumptions: first, that the Security Council could be expected to make speedy and objective decisions as to when collective measures were necessary; and second, that states would enter into the arrangements necessary to give the Council an effective policing capability.' Many others, while acknowledging its imperfections, support it as the only available system of collective security. See generally Cassese, *International Law*, Chapters 13 and 14, and Bothe, 'Preemptive Force'.

[149] See Gray, *International Law*, p. 145.

[150] See 'Uniting for Peace' Resolution, above, note 101, and the establishment of UN forces in Korea, above. It was also invoked on numerous other occasions: see Chesterman, *Just War or Just Peace*, pp. 118–19, 121.

[151] See *Certain Expenses* case, *ICJ Reports 1962*, p. 151, at pp. 164–5 and 168. A presumption was that action taken by the UN for the fulfilment of one of the UN Charter's purposes was not *ultra vires*.

[152] The rationale is that while the Council has primary responsibility for international peace and security under the Charter, the General Assembly can assume 'secondary' responsibility where the Council is paralysed.

[153] See A. Clapham, 'Peace, the Security Council and Human Rights', in Danieli, Stamatopolou and Dias (eds.), *The Universal Declaration of Human Rights: Fifty Years and Beyond* (New York, 1998), p. 375, at pp. 375–6.

It is worthy of emphasis, in conclusion, that the obligation on states is not to give the Council a first opportunity to authorise force, before themselves proceeding unilaterally, but to refrain from the use of force unless or until such authorisation is achieved. In other words, Council authorisation is a *sine qua non* for the legitimate resort to force other than in self defence.

5A.3 Other justifications for the use of force?

As noted above, the UN Charter contains a prohibition on the use of force by states, and one explicit exception thereto in the case of self defence. The starting point for assessing each of the purported legal justifications highlighted below, which are of potential relevance to the use of force post September 11, is their incompatibility with the plain wording of the Charter. Their validity depends essentially on the establishment of a compelling argument that a pre-existing customary rule continues to exist post Charter, or that a new customary rule has developed alongside the Charter.[154]

The reluctance on the part of the majority of states as regards the development of custom that would extend or dilute exceptions to the prohibition on the use force might be explained as follows:

> The charter does not authorise any exception to this [Article 2(4)] rule except for the right of self defence. This is no coincidence or oversight. Any formal exceptions permitting the use of force or military interventions in order to achieve other aims, however laudable, would be bound to be abused, especially by the big and strong, and to pose a threat, especially to the small and weak.[155]

Unlike self defence or Security Council authorisation, the justifications referred to below were not invoked directly by states resorting to force post September 11 and as such cannot constitute legal justifications for action taken. However, as they have been alluded to, tangentially but repeatedly, they are included as relevant to whether, as a matter of law, they *could* have been invoked convincingly as legal justifications for military action.

---

[154] As noted below, attempts to interpret Article 2(4) as itself consistent with other justifications for resort to force have been broadly discredited. It is noted that there is however only limited scope for the development of customary law rules that are inconsistent on their face with the provisions of the Charter, as these have themselves become established customary law. See Gray, *International Law*, pp. 4–5.

[155] Swedish representative to the Security Council, debate on Entebbe incident involving use of force by Israel against hijackers in Uganda, SC 1940th meeting, in Chesterman, *Just War or Just Peace*, p. 26.

5A.3.1 Humanitarian intervention

Proponents of the doctrine of humanitarian intervention assert that international law allows states, in exceptional circumstances, to intervene militarily to avert 'grave humanitarian crisis'[156] or 'humanitarian catastrophe'.[157]

First, a crucial distinction must be drawn between the controversial assertion of the right of humanitarian intervention by states, acting individually or in coalitions, and the power of the Security Council to authorise military force on humanitarian grounds. As noted above, the Security Council has the power to take enforcement measures it deems necessary pursuant to international peace and security, which has been interpreted by the Council as encompassing prevention of humanitarian crisis.[158] While some states still seek to rely (at least selectively) on outdated 'domestic affairs' objections, it is generally recognised – consistent with the current understanding that human rights are not purely 'internal' matters for the state but matters of international concern – that the Council has the power to authorise military intervention to avert humanitarian disaster even where the crisis arises solely within the confines of one nation state.[159]

Different questions arise in respect of the right of states however. That the prohibition on the use of force by states in Article 2(4) is inconsistent on its face with such a right is generally accepted, even by many

---

[156] UK justification in Iraq no-fly zones, 26 February 2001, House of Commons Hansard Debates, in Gray, 'From Unity to Polarisation', at 9.

[157] See for example W.M. Reisman, 'Coercion and Self Determination: Construing Charter Article 2(4)', 78 (1984) AJIL 64; F. Teson, *Humanitarian Intervention: An Inquiry into Law and Morality*, 2nd ed. (New York, 1997). For a detailed critique of these theories, and others, see, in general, Chesterman, *Just War or Just Peace*.

[158] As already noted, the Security Council authorised coercive measures under Chapter 7 against apartheid in South Africa and white minority rule in Rhodesia (see above, note 111). More recently, the Security Council has decided the adoption of coercive measures to end non-international armed conflicts in Bosnia-Herzegovina (SC Res. 713 (1991), above, note 112) and Somalia (SC Res. 794 (1992), above, note 112). See Franck, *Recourse to Force*, pp. 44 and 137.

[159] In practice, however, such crises have usually been accompanied by a plainly 'international' element, such as refugee influx into neighbouring countries or the prospect of other states becoming drawn into an armed conflict. See discussion of the approach of the Security Council in Franck, *Recourse to Force*, p. 43. The author refers to the 'gradual attrition of distinctions between what is "domestic" and "international"', as the international community responds to new facts and threats that are redefining the threshold of what is seen to constitute a threat to the peace, requiring a powerful collective response', *ibid.*, p. 44.

proponents of humanitarian intervention.[160] As such, there is, at a minimum, a 'heavy burden of proof – an obligation to rebut a solid negative
presumption'[161] on those who seek to justify recourse to force on these
grounds. Proponents seek to do so, for example, by reference to shifting
attitudes to human rights having led to the emergence of a customary law
right to use force to secure their protection within the framework of – or
alongside – the UN Charter.

State practice in support of the emergence of such a customary
right remains limited. While numerous interventions have involved a
humanitarian element, such as interventions by India in East Pakistan
in 1971, Vietnam in Cambodia in 1978 and Tanzania in Uganda in
1979, the states involved relied primarily on other, more traditional,
forms of justification, such as self defence. A right to intervene to avert
humanitarian catastrophe was asserted by the United Kingdom in context
of the Gulf War in 1991,[162] and again, most forcefully, by some (but not
all) of the states involved in the NATO intervention in Kosovo in 1999.[163]
As the Kosovo intervention is often cited by proponents of humanitarian
intervention, it is noteworthy that many of the states involved relied
principally on other justifications, such as Security Council support, as

---

[160] See Fourth Report of the Forth Foreign Affairs Committee, 1999–2000, at www.
parliament.the-stationery-office.co.uk/pa/cm1999/28/2802.htm, inquiring into, *inter
alia*, the lawfulness of the Kosovo intervention, which noted that the 'sternest critic'
as well as the 'firmest supporter' of humanitarian intervention in Kosovo (referring to
Professors Brownlie and Greenwood, respectively) agreed that 'the provisions of the UN
Charter were not complied with'. A minority view attempts to square the circle by holding
that Article 2(4) only prohibits use of force against the 'territorial integrity or political
independence' of states, and not the use of force which fell short of government over-
throw or territorial gains, or which pursued Charter objectives such as protection of
human rights. However, the *travaux préparatoires* of the Charter demonstrate that the
quoted language intended to strengthen the prohibition, not create an exception to it, and
the argument was decisively rejected in the *Corfu Channel* case before the International
Court of Justice (*Corfu Channel (United Kingdom* v. *Albania), Merits, ICJ Reports 1949*,
p. 4); see Chesterman, *Just War or Just Peace*, p. 49.

[161] Franck, *Recourse to Force*, p. 151, notes that Articles 2(4) and 51 'establish a heavy burden
of proof – an obligation to rebut a solid negative presumption – on those who, on their
own initiative, would deploy force in the absence of, or disproportionate to, an armed
attack'.

[162] Statement of the United Kingdom Foreign and Commonwealth Office, reported in Gray,
International Law, p. 30.

[163] Statement of United Kingdom to the Security Council, justifying 'an exceptional measure
to prevent an overwhelming humanitarian catastrophe,' SCOR 3988th meeting, 24 March
1999 at 12. Gray, *International Law*, p. 33 notes that only the Netherlands and the UK
asserted that the action was a legal (as opposed to moral) response to a humanitarian
catastrophe.

the legal basis of the campaign.[164] The same was true of the interventions in Afghanistan and Iraq, discussed below.[165]

However, just as humanitarian intervention has not been invoked frequently by states as a legal justification for action, nor has intervention in circumstances where the motivation was – at least in part – humanitarian met with consistent condemnation from states or the Security Council.[166] While this may indicate that the interventions were considered lawful, it may simply be that benevolent motivation or ultimately favourable humanitarian results are mitigating factors leading states to turn a blind eye, or to be lenient, in the face of what remains unlawful behaviour. It has also been pointed out that lack of response may evidence the common inadequacy of enforcement of international law, rather than an endorsement of the legality of humanitarian intervention.[167]

As so few states have asserted a legal right to intervene on humanitarian grounds, it follows that the parameters of the concept remain undeveloped. The UK – seen to be an advocate of a right to humanitarian intervention in the Iraq and Kosovo contexts[168] – has justified as lawful intervention occurring only in the following certain exceptional circumstances:

> Every means short of force has been tried to avert this situation. In these circumstances and as an exceptional measure on grounds of overwhelming humanitarian necessity, military intervention is legally justifiable. The force now proposed is directed exclusively to averting a humanitarian catastrophe, and is the minimum judged necessary for that purpose.[169]

---

[164] Numerous states relied on the fact that the action supported the Security Council's objectives for Kosovo, despite the absence of authorisation for military action due to the use of the veto power and the intense controversy the NATO attacks generated within the Council. See for example the apparent US reliance on Security Council authorisation, as a White House spokesman noted that Resolutions affirmed 'that the deterioration of the situation in Kosovo constitutes a threat to international peace and security', in S. Murphy, 'Legal Regulation of the Use of Force', 93 (1999) AJIL 628 at 631. On the arguments of states before the ICJ, noting that only Belgium argued humanitarian intervention, see Chesterman, *Just War or Just Peace*, p. 46.

[165] See Section B.2.1.6.

[166] Absence of condemnation may be a principal measure of state practice and *opinio juris*, but not necessarily so: see Gray, *International Law*, pp. 18–19.

[167] Chesterman, *Just War or Just Peace*.

[168] This was a reversal of its previous view that such intervention was 'at best not unambiguously illegal' (see the internal document of the UK Foreign and Commonwealth Office cited in Chesterman, *ibid.*, p. 2).

[169] Statement by the UK representative to the Security Council, S/PV 3988 (1999) 12, in Chesterman, *Just War or Just Peace*, p. 212. On the grounds put forward in relation to Iraq, see Gray, *International Law*, p. 30. The UK does not advocate a general right of humanitarian intervention but one arising in exceptional circumstances.

Academic proponents of the development of the law on humanitarian intervention have suggested different prospective formulae, including for example the addition of a requirement that execution be by a 'multinational force'.[170]

The issue of humanitarian intervention is extremely sensitive, lying as it does at the heart of the twin objectives of the UN Charter to prohibit the use of force and to protect humanity.[171] While States can and should take measures to ensure respect for human rights,[172] the question is whether unilateral resort to military force is one such permissible measure. In the context of the *Nicaragua* case the ICJ answered this question in the negative:

> while the USA might form its own appraisal of the situation as to respect for human rights in Nicaragua, the use of force could not be the appropriate method to monitor or ensure such respect.[173]

Likewise, as discussed at Chapter 3, the International Law Commission Articles on State Responsibility preclude the use of force as a counter measure against international wrongs.[174] Rather, it would appear to remain the exclusive remit of the UN Security Council to legitimise coercive measures, other than in self defence, 'whatever be the present defects in international organisation'.[175]

In summary, although the issue remains controversial, it is doubtful that the heavy burden of establishing a customary right of humanitarian

---

[170] Recommendations of Professor Vaughan Lowe, in Foreign Affairs Committee Kosovo Report, p. 369. See also recommendations of Professor Christine Chinkin. For other academics' proposed guidelines see R.B. Lillich, *Humanitarian Intervention and the United Nations* (Charlottesville, 1973); Teson, *Humanitarian Intervention*.

[171] See Article 2(3) (on human rights) and Article 2(4), UN Charter. Note however that the statement of Russia before the Security Council in the context of the Kosovo debate questioned whether 'the unilateral use of force will lead precisely to a situation with truly devastating humanitarian consequences', SCOR (LIV) 3988th meeting, at 2–3 in Franck, *Recourse to Force*, pp. 167–8.

[172] See Articles 40 and 41 of the ILC's Articles on States Responsibility regarding the collective responsibility for serious breaches of international obligations, including human rights, discussed in Chapters 3 and 7.

[173] See Gray, *International Law*, p. 28.   [174] ILC's Articles, Article 50.

[175] *Corfu Channel* case, above, note 160, p. 29. Some have asserted that where the Council cannot or will not act, states 'cannot simply stand by and let a humanitarian catastrophe unfold'. See statement by the Netherlands in the context of the Security Council Kosovo debate in Franck, *Recourse to Force*, p. 167. However, as discussed above, this argument has less force in the post Cold War context where the Council, while remaining reticent to invoke force and undoubtedly politically motivated is no longer paralysed by the veto power.

intervention has been satisfied at the present time, particularly given the scarcity with which such a right has been invoked by states.[176] Two independent enquiries in the wake of the Kosovo intervention found it to have been illegal but morally justifiable, and called for the elaboration of new legal guidelines in this area.[177] As practice develops the law may well shift to accommodate an exception permitting coercive response to an imminent humanitarian crisis.[178] It remains to be seen whether coherent principles permitting intervention can be elaborated and accepted, and if so how they can be implemented with procedural and evidentiary safeguards against abuse; this issue is likely, once again, to revert to questions regarding the role of a collective security mechanism in implementing any exception to the cardinal principle prohibiting the use of force.

5A.3.2 Pro-democratic intervention

Some writers also assert a right to pro-democratic intervention. In some ways this is a subspecies of humanitarian intervention, with the rationale for the lawfulness of the use of force in this context being, not that it averts humanitarian crisis, but that it promotes democratic governance.[179] As democracy is asserted to be itself a human right, and as such one of the values protected by the UN Charter, the principal argument is that the prohibition on use of force does not prevent coercive measures in pursuit of the other values enshrined in the UN Charter.[180] The assertion of this exception to the use of force suffers from all of the difficulties of

---

[176] This militates strongly against its legality as discussed in Gray, *International Law*, p. 18 referring to the ICJ in the *Nicaragua* case: '[F]or the Court the fact that states did not claim new right of intervention was a decisive factor in the rejection of the emergence of any customary law right.'

[177] See Independent International Commission on Kosovo, *The Kosovo Report: Conflict, International Response, Lessons Learned* 164 (2000). See also Foreign Affairs Committee Kosovo Report, para. 138, 'we conclude that NATO'S military action, if of dubious legality in the current state of international law, was justified on moral grounds'.

[178] It is noted that states resorting to use of force post September 11, including the erstwhile foremost proponent of the humanitarian justification, the UK, while emphasising the humanitarian element to the military approach, have not sought to rely on humanitarian intervention as a legal justification. This may have a chilling impact on the development of law permitting humanitarian intervention.

[179] See Reisman, 'Coercion and Self Determination'.

[180] On democracy as a human right, see, in general, J. Crawford, 'Democracy and International Law', 93 44 (1993), BYIL 113. Other proponents suggest, even more controversially, that an undemocratic government loses its claim to sovereignty, and the protection of international law.

humanitarian intervention, discussed above, aggravated by the assertion of a lower threshold for intervention. As such this purported justification is hotly contested and finds little support in legal doctrine.

State reliance on the right to intervene in the interests of democracy as a legal justification, as opposed to a positive political side effect, is scarce.[181] This may reflect the fact that, as one commentator notes, 'if taken literally such a rule would render up to a third of the world's states susceptible to intervention on this basis. More realistically, it opens the way to selective application of a principle that is prone to abuse.'[182] While the United States is cited as relying on it in Grenada, it expressly distanced itself from such a claim in its 1989 invasion of Panama, noting that 'we are not claiming a right to intervene in favour of democracy where we are not welcomed. We are supporters of democracy but not the gendarmes of democracy.'[183]

As noted above, unilateral state action must again be distinguished from that of the Security Council. Yet it is noteworthy that even the Council has been reticent to authorise forceful measures to remove one government (whatever its political complexion or indeed human rights record) and replace it with another in the name of international peace and security. The sole example of it having done so was Haiti, where the Security Council, emphasising the 'unique character of the present situation in Haiti' authorised the use of force to remove the military junta that had overthrown the first democratically elected government, and to return the ousted President Aristide.[184]

5A.3.3 Self help: breakdown in international enforcement?

A further theory that purports to justify the use of force, advanced by a few commentators, holds that a state is entitled to resort to force where another state unlawfully violates its essential interests, and the international enforcement machinery contemplated in the UN Charter fails. One scholar has recently described it as an argument of 'some moral force' that an aggrieved state should be able to enforce its own rights where the 'source

---

[181] Gray, *International Law*, pp. 42–3.

[182] Chesterman, *Just War or Just Peace*, p. 90. Gray, *International Law*, pp. 42–4 asserts that 'state practice cannot support such a new right' and denies the right of a state to use force unilaterally, even to restore an ousted democratic government.

[183] Statement of the United States to the Security Council, S/PV 2902, reported in Gray, *International Law*, p. 43.

[184] See *ibid.*, pp. 43–4.

of the right' does not do so.[185] Flying, as it does, in the face of the clear prohibition in Article 2(4) and the foundations of the collective security system established in the UN Charter, a particularly heavy onus would lie on the proponent of such a view.

However, state practice in support of self help as a legal justification (as opposed to a factor mitigating the culpability of illegal resort to force) is again limited.[186] Moreover, the ICJ in the *Corfu Channel* case noted that Albania had violated its international obligations but found that, while this was an extenuating circumstance, it did not justify recourse to force.[187] Likewise, the International Law Commission's Draft Articles on State responsibility, while recognising that counter measures against another state that has violated its obligations are permitted, make clear that such measures 'shall not affect . . . the obligation to refrain from the threat or use of force contained in the UN Charter'.[188] While a state may, in the face of violations, take measures of 'self help', it appears highly doubtful under the current system of international law that these would include resort to force.

A form of coercive self help is contemplated in the Charter in extreme circumstances, namely those justifying self defence. But beyond these limits, ambiguity surrounds the scope of the potential justification – which interests might be protected beyond those within the purview of the right of self defence – and of course, how might it operate in practice. As has been noted, the assertion of this right 'bears no relation to the text of Article 2(4) and establishes no limits on which rights may be vindicated or by whom'.[189] Enforcement of international law has always been and remains a predominant Achilles heel in the international legal system. If its inadequacies, and those of the Security Council veto system in particular, are to be relied upon in any particular scenario to justify unilateral action it may represent the unravelling of the collective fabric of the UN Charter and a danger few would readily endorse.

---

[185] See Franck, *Recourse to Force*, p. 109, where he opines that the protracted failure of the UN to redress an egregious wrong may give rise to a limited right of self help.

[186] *Ibid.*, at 112 ff. The practice surveyed may highlight that, at times, states were willing to demonstrate a lenient approach in the face of resort to force to enforce the state's rights, as opposed to indicating endorsement of the lawfulness of the action. Gray, *International Law*, p. 25, notes that an attempt by Israel to rely on, among others, an argument of the ineffectiveness of the UN machinery was not supported by other states.

[187] *Corfu Channel* case, above, note 160, p. 35. See also *Nicaragua*, para. 202, on general principle of non-intervention. See also Chesterman, *Just War or Just Peace*, p. 54.

[188] Article 50, ILC's Articles.

[189] Chesterman, *Just War or Just Peace*, p. 56, referring to the theory of 'self help', in support of humanitarian intervention, put forward by Reisman, 'Coercion and Self Determination'.

5B The use of force post September 11

In the immediate wake of the attacks of 11 September 2001, the United States committed itself to a sustained 'war on terror',[190] a significant component of which has involved the use of military force by the United States and its allies in several countries, notably Afghanistan[191] and Iraq.[192] Further military action in other states has been foreshadowed, alongside a broader policy of pre-emptive force which has been advanced, most notably, in the United States National Security Strategy of 17 September 2002.[193]

Multiple questions arise regarding the application of the legal framework set out in the preceding section of this chapter. This section seeks to highlight some of those questions considered to be of particular significance to an assessment of the lawfulness of the use of force employed since September 11 and the potential development of the law in this field.

5B.1 Afghanistan

The military intervention in Afghanistan began on 7 October 2001 and continues to the present day. The legal justification for military action, advanced by both the United States and its principal ally, the United Kingdom, was self defence in anticipation of a future attack. Both states reported to the Security Council under Article 51. The US noted that measures were taken as a response to the armed attacks of 9/11 and to 'prevent and deter' further attacks.[194] The United Kingdom took a narrower view,

---

[190] See Address of the US President George W. Bush to a Joint Session of Congress and the American People, 20 September 2001, available at http://www.whitehouse.gov/news/releases/2001/09/20010920-8.html. The categorisation of this as a 'war' is discussed in section B, chapter 6.

[191] The so-called 'Operation Enduring Freedom' began in the immediate aftermath of September 11, on 7 October 2001.

[192] The US military campaign against Iraq ('Operation Iraqi Freedom') and the parallel British military operation ('Operation Telic') began on 19 March 2003.

[193] See US President George W. Bush, 'The National Security Strategy of the United States of America', 17 September 2002, available at http://whitehouse.gov/nsc/nss.pdf (hereinafter 'US National Security Strategy'), discussed below, this chapter, para. 5B.3. See also US President George W. Bush, 'State of the Union Address', 29 January 2002 (available at http://www.whitehouse.gov/news/releases/2002/01/20020129-11.html): 'We must prevent the terrorists and regimes who seek chemical, biological or nuclear weapons from threatening the United States and the world . . . States like [Iraq] and their terrorist allies, constitute an axis of evil, arming to threaten the peace of the world.'

[194] See 'Letter dated 7 October 2001 from the Permanent Representative of the United States of America to the United Nations addressed to the President of the Security Council',

justifying the use of force in self defence 'to avert the continuing threat of attacks from the same source' as the September 11 attacks.[195] However, when it came to the objectives of military action, these were presented, at various points and in various guises, as attacking al-Qaeda training camps and personnel, compelling the Taleban to hand over al-Qaeda suspects, and, ultimately, toppling the Taleban regime.[196]

The unprecedented unity following the September 11 attacks translated into either open or tacit support for military action in Afghanistan.[197] Many states indicated their support for the campaign overtly, for example by allowing their airspace to be used,[198] or offering logistical support.[199] There was little state opposition expressed in respect of the military action, and the validity of the legal justifications proferred appeared to almost go unquestioned behind expressions of condolence and sympathy with the US.[200] At first, critical appraisal of the lawfulness of the Afghan

available at http://www.un.int/usa/s-2001-946.htm: 'In response to these attacks, and in accordance with the inherent right of individual and collective self-defense, United States armed forces have initiated actions designed to prevent and deter further attacks on the United States . . . We may find that our self-defence requires further actions with respect to other organizations and other States.'

[195] See 'Letter dated 7 October 2001 from the Chargé d'affaires of the Permanent Mission of the United Kingdom of Great Britain and Northern Ireland to the United Nations addressed to the President of the Security Council', available at http://www.ukun.org/xq/asp/SarticleType.17/Article_ID.328/qx/articles_show.htm: 'These forces have now been employed in exercise of the inherent right of individual and collective self defence, recognized in Article 51, following the terrorist outrage of 11th September, to avert the continuing threat of attacks from the same source.'

[196] On the objectives of the campaign, see the statement made on 7 October 2001 by the UK Prime Minister, explaining the reasons for the military operations in Afghanistan ('Attack on Afghanistan: Tony Blair statement', *CNN*.com, 7 October 2001, at http://edition.cnn.com/2001/WORLD/europe/10/07/gen.blair.speech). See also the report on the military objectives of the campaign released by the British Ministry of Defence (Ministry of Defence, 'Defeating International Terrorism: Campaign Objectives', available at http://www.operations.mod.uk/veritas/faq/objectives.htm). Noting apparent inconsistencies between descriptions of campaign objectives advanced at different times, see, e.g., V. Lowe, 'The Iraq Crisis: What Now?', 52 (2003) ICLQ 859 at 860.

[197] C. Gray, 'The US National Security Strategy and the New "Bush Doctrine" on Preemptive Self Defense', 2 (2002) *Chinese Journal of International Law* 440 at 441, cites China, Russia, Japan and Pakistan as having supported the intervention.

[198] E.g., Greece and Turkey. See House of Commons Research Paper 01/72, 'September 11: The Response', 31 October 2001, available at http://www.parliament.uk/commons/lib/research/rp2001/rp01-072.pdf (hereinafter 'House of Commons Research Paper 01/72'), p. 28.

[199] Japan pledged logistical support. See House of Commons Research Paper 01/72, p. 29–30.

[200] Even the Islamic conference communiqué of 11 October 2001 was notably silent on the US bombardment, while stating that 'We have endorsed a global consensus and condemnation of terrorist acts, condolence and sympathy with the United States and a commitment to eradication of international terrorism.' See 'Islamic Leaders

intervention from academics and civil society was also extremely cautious and hesitant; considerably more such criticism has emerged as some distance is gained from the autumn of 2001.[201]

State reactions to the use of force in Afghanistan, as elsewhere, are relevant to an assessment of the lawfulness of the use of force in that context and may, potentially, impact on the development of the law and influence responses to other situations in the future. However, one incident itself rarely changes the law, particularly if it conflicts with an established rule of law, and the events in question must be seen in the context of how similar situations were addressed in the past and in particular whether they are replicated in the future.

5B.1.1 Key questions arising

The questions arising as relevant to the lawfulness of the use of force in Afghanistan, addressed below, relate principally to whether the right of self defence was triggered and the requirements of necessity and proportionality met. Specific questions include the following: could the use of force in self defence be justified where al-Qaeda, as opposed to the state of Afghanistan, was considered responsible for the September 11 attacks; could regime change be justified in these circumstances; was Afghanistan a case of anticipatory self defence;[202] was the use of force a last resort and did the states involved discharge the burden of so demonstrating; what relevance should be attached to the failure to engage the Security Council to take the necessary measures, in preference for prolonged reliance on self defence?

5B.1.1.1 Self defence against terrorism?

Among the key legal issues of relevance to the lawfulness of the intervention is whether self defence could justify the use of force in Afghanistan

condemn terrorism', CNN.com, 11 October 2001, at http://edition.cnn.com/2001/WORLD/meast/10/11/gen.qatar.oic/. Iran was among the few states opposed to the intervention, expressed by the Foreign Minister Kamal Kharazi thus: 'It should be proved this military attack should be useful. I don't find it useful. That is why our position is that this war is not acceptable.' ('Islamic Leaders Condemn Terrorism', *ibid.*)

[201] See, e.g., E. P. Myjer and N. D. White, 'The Twin Towers Attack: An Unlimited Right to Self-Defence?', 7 (2002) *Journal of Conflict and Security Law* 5; J. Paust, 'Use of Armed Force against Terrorists in Afghanistan, Iraq and Beyond', 35 (2002) *Cornell International Law Journal* 533, who criticise the lawfulness of the intervention as it unfolded against the Taleban as well as al-Qaeda. See also S. Kapferer, 'Ends and Means in Politics: International Law as Framework for Political Decision Making', 15 (2002) *Revue québéquoise de droit international* 101.

[202] As this issue was not controversial in relation to Afghanistan but came into sharp focus in relation to Iraq, anticipatory self-defence in Afghanistan is considered at Section 5.B.2 below.

in response to 'terrorist' attacks by a non-state actor such as al-Qaeda. In other words, where individuals, networks or organisations are responsible for an attack, can self defence be used against them on the territory of another state, even where their actions cannot be attributed to that state? Do the Afghan intervention and responses thereto suggest that non-state actors can be responsible for an 'armed attack' and that state responsibility is not (or is no longer) a prerequisite for the use of force in self defence?[203]

Notably, while multiple allegations were lodged against the Taleban,[204] the case for its legal responsibility for the September 11 attacks was never made out in terms by the states seeking to engage in military action in Afghanistan.[205] From information publicly available, it is open to question whether the Taleban regime had the power and authority in respect of al-Qaeda to satisfy the degree of control required for the acts of private entities to be legally attributed to it. This is a question of fact, the onus of proof in respect of which would normally rest with those seeking to establish responsibility, but intervening states in Afghanistan declined to do so. No evidence of the regime's 'control' over al-Qaeda, nor clarity as to the other allegations against the regime (and legal consequences thereof), was therefore advanced.

---

[203] There can be little doubt that the events of 9/11 met other 'armed attack' criteria relating to scale and intensity threshold; the focus here is on authorship and the status of actors as the controversial issue.

[204] There were various references to the Taleban having 'harboured', 'supported' or 'protected' al-Qaeda (UK letter to the Security Council, statements by US President and NATO Secretary General, discussed at Chapter 2) but not to the regime having been legally responsible for the attacks. See, e.g., the statement made on 7 October 2001 by the UK Prime Minister (above, note 195): 'We made clear following the attacks upon the US on September 11 that we would take action once it was clear who was responsible. There is no doubt in my mind, nor in the mind of anyone who has been through all the available evidence, including intelligence material, that these attacks were carried out by the al Qaeda network headed by Osama bin Laden. Equally it is clear that they are harboured and supported by the Taliban regime inside Afghanistan. It is now almost a month since the atrocity occurred. It is more than two weeks since an ultimatum was delivered to the Taliban to yield up the terrorists or face the consequences. It is clear beyond doubt that the Taliban will not do this. They were given the choice of siding with justice, or siding with terror. They chose terror . . . We have set the objective to pursue those responsible for the attacks, to eradicate bin Laden's network of terrorism and to take action against the Taliban regime that is sponsoring him.'

[205] The Taleban would need to be directly or indirectly responsible for the attacks: acts of private individuals become attributable to the state where the latter exercises 'effective control' over the former; the Taleban may also be responsible for 'indirect aggression' where it has 'substantial involvement' in the activities of al-Qaeda. For more detail on applicable standards, see this chapter, section A and Chapter 3.

The September 11 attacks were nonetheless broadly characterised – including, in their immediate aftermath, by the Security Council,[206] NATO[207] and other bodies[208] – as amounting to 'armed attacks' for the purposes of self defence. On one view these statements, and the conduct of at least some intervening states, may have been based on *assumptions* as to the responsibility of Afghanistan, consistent with state responsibility being a prerequisite of the law of self defence.[209] But on another view the acceptance of the right to self defence as arising in response to the September 11 attacks, absent assertions of state responsibility, strengthens the case that such responsibility was not (or is no longer) a prerequisite for self defence under Article 51.[210] It has been suggested then that these widespread references to the right to 'self defence' post 9/11, including by the Security Council on 12 September 2001, represent a shift in the law, and dispose of the hitherto unsettled question.[211] While perhaps not dispositive, the Afghan intervention and reactions thereto do appear to tilt the balance away from the necessity of a state responsibility nexus.[212] However, this apparent shift was swiftly countered by a subsequent ICJ opinion reasserting the traditional view that self defence arises in response to an attack by or on behalf of a state.[213]

---

[206] The fact that, in Resolution 1368 (2001), albeit in a preambular paragraph, the Security Council, whilst reaffirming the determination 'to combat by all means threats to international peace and security caused by terrorist acts' (preambular paragraph 2), recognised the 'inherent right of individual or collective self-defence in accordance with the Charter' (preambular paragraph 3) seems to imply that the Security Council accepts that terrorist attacks carried out by private organisations can constitute 'armed attacks' under Article 51 of the Charter.

[207] NATO press release (2001) 124.

[208] NATO, OAS, EU and others organisations also affirmed the right of self defence. See Gray, 'Bush Doctrine', p. 441.

[209] By noting that force would be used against 'the same source' as the September 11 attacks, while identifying the Taleban as one of the objectives of the military intervention, the UK's position could be interpreted as having been premised on an assumption that the test had been satisfied. (See however C. Greenwood, 'International Law and the "War against Terrorism"', 78 (2002) *International Affairs* 301 at 303, noting that no such allegations of responsibility were made). See L. Sadat, 'Terrorism and the Rule of Law', 3 (2004) *Washington University Global Studies Law Review* 135 at 150.

[210] See Greenwood, 'War against Terrorism'.

[211] See, e.g., Greenwood, 'War against Terrorism'. Like the Security Council, NATO, the OAS, the EU and other international organisations also referred to the right of 'self defence' shortly after 9/11.

[212] As noted in this chapter, para. 5B.4 this development will have to be assessed in context, in light of subsequent approaches to other similar situations.

[213] Wall Opinion, para. 139, discussed at Section 5.A.2.1.1.(ii).

If a state nexus was required, the question is whether states simply disregarded this in Afghanistan, or whether they might have been endorsing a lower standard than the traditional 'effective control' test for attributing conduct to the state.[214]

Certainly, it is noteworthy that the reactions of states and commentators supportive of the use of force in Afghanistan do appear to rest on assumptions of some degree of 'culpability' on the part of the Afghanistan *de facto* government. It is not however always apparent whether this is a legal prerequisite (or factor rendering the operation more politically palatable), and what precisely is the *legal relevance* of the various formulae put forward to the effect that the Taleban had supported, harboured, protected, or provided safe haven for terrorists[215] or that it had 'violated international law' in its relationship with al-Qaeda,[216] or otherwise.[217] While certain of the wrongs committed by the Taleban regime may well create rights and obligations on the part of the international community, so far as they fall short of amounting to state involvement in an armed attack against another state, their relevance for the purposes of the law of self defence remains unclear.[218]

If a state need *not* be responsible for an attack, must it have otherwise failed in its duties to prevent terrorists operating out of its territory in order to be vulnerable to attack pursuant to the right of self defence? What of a weak, failed or other state that did take all reasonable steps to prevent terrorism but was unable to do so? If a mere territorial link between a state and a responsible organisation were to be sufficient to justify use of force against that state, might the states of 'North America,

---

[214] The assertion has been made that the recognition of 'self defence' represents not a rejection of the state responsibility requirement, but a lowering of the standard by which the conduct of individuals becomes attributable to the state – see for example Jinks and Sassòli in Chapter 3 on responsibility in international law.

[215] For instances where these formulae were used, see Chapter 3 on responsibility. Note also that the US National Security Strategy commits the US to holding to account 'nations that are compromised by terror'.

[216] Greenwood, 'War against Terrorism', at 313. See the rule against the use of force being invoked as a remedy for violation of obligations, discussed above.

[217] Allegations range from various forms of tolerance, support or harbouring of terrorists, to failing to hand over bin Laden and other suspects to a notoriously atrocious human rights record. But these wrongs, which do provoke a right and duty to take steps against a regime, either do not provide a legal justification for using force, or (in the case of humanitarian intervention) were not invoked as doing so.

[218] On state responsibility and permissible action against wrongdoer states, see Chapter 3 above. As noted in section A above, the use of force is not justified as a counter measure against wrong-doing states, unless justified in self defence.

South America, Europe, Africa, the Middle East and across Asia' which, according to reports, have terrorist cells operating in their territories, be susceptible to attack?[219] The direct planning of the September 11 attacks took place in several countries, including the US and Germany, so might those states be vulnerable to attack from others defending against the global terrorist threat?

The use of force against terrorists in a state's territory absent responsibility for their action raises questions as to the respect for the territorial integrity and political independence of the state, reflected in Article 2(4). Such questions are all the more pressing, however, where force is used not only against private actors on the state's territory but against the institutions of the state itself, with a view to bringing about a change in regime. It can be accepted as compelling that the rationale of self defence requires a state to be able to take necessary measures to defend itself against those responsible for an imminent or on-going attack, whatever their status and wherever their location. It may remain doubtful, however, on what basis force can then be directed against the institutions of a state, with a view to regime change, where that state has not been found, or indeed alleged, to be responsible for the attack, as discussed below.[220]

Given the implications for national and international security, any suggestion that force can be used against states, including to remove their representatives, based on their links with terrorists, should be accompanied by clarity as to legal standards (and evidentiary and procedural requirements) concerning such links. The treatment of this issue since September 11 may indicate that this is an area where greater clarity is required if the Afghan situation is not to provide a pretext for the use of force in the future on the basis of uncertain links between states and private 'terrorist' groups operating out of their territory.

5B.1.1.2 Regime change as necessary and proportionate?

A related question is whether regime change (which arose in Afghanistan and shortly thereafter in Iraq) was a legitimate objective under the law of self defence, and specifically how it measures up against the necessity and proportionality test? This question is particularly pertinent where a state

---

[219] US National Security Strategy, p. 5.
[220] For example brief incursions onto foreign territory to take particular measures of defence, such as the removal of a base from which an attack is being launched, followed by immediate withdrawal, can be distinguished from removal of a government of the state on whose territory that base is located. These questions are closely linked to fulfilling the requirements of necessity and proportionality and regime change, discussed in this paragraph.

does not exercise sufficient 'control' over the organisation's conduct to be legally responsible for it, as set out in Chapter 3: in what circumstances, then, is the government's removal nonetheless strictly necessary and proportionate to avert the threat? A particularly heavy onus must lie on states seeking to rely on their own right of self defence to remove another government, given the Charter's fundamental principle of sovereign equality and respect for the political independence of states, to demonstrate the strict necessity of such measures.[221]

Despite statements by the UK that force would be directed against the 'same source' as the September 11 attacks, the military intervention in Afghanistan went beyond the targeting of al-Qaeda operations, to the removal of the Taleban regime.[222] However, the UK government was evidently uncomfortable with the concept of regime change and sought carefully to restrict its justification for the removal of the Taleban as necessary to destroy the al-Qaeda network (even if, as noted above, it did not then clarify the factual basis on which its assessment of this relationship between the Taleban and al-Qaeda was based).[223]

Concerns about 'regime change' were even more apparent in relation to Iraq. In that context, while the US placed considerable emphasis on 'regime change' and the removal of Saddam Hussein, going so far as to place a bounty on his head, it is noteworthy that European states supportive of the United States again sought to distance themselves from these objectives, emphasising that 'Our goal is to safeguard world peace

---

[221] Article 2(4) and 2(7) UN Charter.

[222] On the objectives of the Afghan intervention against al-Qaeda and the Taleban, see, e.g., Blair speech of 7 October 2001, above. The document on the objectives of the military campaign in Afghanistan released by the British Ministry of Defence (above, note 195) expressly states that one of the immediate objectives of the so-called Operation Veritas was to bring about '[a] sufficient change in the leadership to ensure that Afghanistan's links to international terrorism are broken . . . where necessary taking political and military action to fragment the present Taliban regime, including through support for Pushtoon groups opposed to the regime as well as forces in the Northern Alliance'.

[223] See, e.g., statement of the UK Prime Minister: 'Our target the whole time is to close down the terrorist network in Afghanistan. Since the Taliban regime stand between us and that objective, then we have to remove them. If they choose – as they have done so far at least – to side with bin Laden . . .' ('Blair: We have no choice but war', *The Mirror*, 31 October 2003). See also 'Radio Interview with Tony Blair', on ABC Local Radio, Australia, 1 October 2001: 'If [the Taleban] are not prepared to give up bin Laden, which they could do if they wanted to, then they become an obstacle that we have to disable or remove in order to get to bin Laden. So that's their choice. So it's not as if we set out with the aim of changing the Taliban regime, but if they remain in the way of achieving our objective, namely that bin Laden's associates are yielded up, and the terror camps are closed. Then the Taliban themselves become our enemy' (transcript available at http://www.abc.net.au/am/s379311.htm).

and security by ensuring that this regime gives up its weapons of mass destruction.'[224] As such, it may be doubtful then whether the Afghan situation, particularly when seen in context of the Iraqi one that followed it, provides any basis for asserting a new legal doctrine of regime change. The lawfulness of targeting the Taleban depends on whether doing so was genuinely necessary to protect the intervening states – a question of fact that appears never to have been clearly established.[225]

More generally, the apparent escalation in terrorist activity since the Afghan intervention and launch of the global 'war on terror' has contributed to broader questions concerning the *effectiveness* of focusing on force as a counter-terrorist strategy, which as noted above are relevant also to the necessity of that force.[226] Where the weapon of terrorists is fear, and some have suggested this is intensified by government reactions in the 'war on terror',[227] the effectiveness of those reactions must be called into question.

5B.1.1.3 Last resort?

A question much discussed in relation to Iraq but relevant also to the use of force in Afghanistan and elsewhere is whether the military intervention was, as it must be, a last resort, having exhausted all peaceful means in accordance with Article 2(3). According to statements by the US President and UK Prime Minister, the bombardment of Afghanistan and the Taleban was justified, in part, by reference to the fact that attempts to secure the extradition of bin Laden and others had been unsuccessful. Before 9/11, extradition of bin Laden had certainly been sought through the Security Council,[228] although post 9/11 it took the form of a demand, outwith the

---

[224] Open letter of the Prime Ministers or Presidents of the Czech Republic, Denmark, Hungary, Italy, Poland, Portugal, Spain and the United Kingdom, 30 January 2003, available at http://www.useu.be/Categories/GlobalAffairs/Iraq/Jan3003EuropeLetterIraq.html.

[225] Public doubts as to the relationship between the Taleban and al-Qaeda, and whether the former really controlled the actions of the latter, have grown since the beginning of the intervention: see, e.g., the reports of the 9/11 Commission (National Commission on Terrorist Attacks Upon the United States, created by the US Congress in November 2002 to examine and report on the facts and causes relating to the 9/11 terrorist attacks) noting that members of the Taleban leadership opposed the attacks for strategic reasons.

[226] See Gray, 'Bush Doctrine', at 440.

[227] The US National Security Strategy has been described as 'alarm[ist]' about the threat of terrorism', Gray, 'Bush Doctrine'.

[228] See, e.g., SC Res. 1333 (2000), 19 December 2000, UN Doc. S/RES/1333 (2000). Post 9/11, the Council again urged compliance with earlier resolutions. 'Security Council Urges Taliban to Comply with Texts Ordering Bin Laden Handover', United Nations Information Centre, 18 September 2001, available at http://www.un.org.pk/latest-dev/hq-pre-010918.htm.

extradition process, that he and others be 'turned over' for extradition from the United States.[229]

Did this suggest that military action (at least against the Taleban) may not have been necessary if the Taleban had cooperated and been 'prepared to give up bin Laden'?[230] If so, were all efforts to handle this matter as a criminal law route exhausted? Was the extradition route seriously engaged by the US administration, according to the law and practice discussed at Chapter 4? Or did the 'no negotiation' approach to the demand that the Taleban hand over suspects, and the refusal to recognise normal requirements of the extradition process such as the provision of even a basic showing of evidence, suggest that the 'extradition' ultimatum was essentially of presentational significance? Could requests for extradition have been made more effective if bolstered by Security Council authorisation to use coercive measures, as strictly necessary, pursuant to criminal law enforcement?

While it would be far-fetched to suggest that the existence of the complex system of national and international criminal justice automatically renders the right to use force in self defence redundant, is it not at least one of the alternatives that states are obliged to explore in assessing the necessity of resorting to force?[231] Yet the criminal law paradigm and its relationship to the necessity of the use of force was virtually absent from post September 11 discourse by those that were responsible, ultimately, for the Afghan intervention. While people can reasonably disagree on whether law enforcement measures alone would have been effective to meet the threat posed,[232] might they have minimised the need for

---

[229] According to reports, the US demanded extradition and the Taleban responded by asking for proof of bin Laden's involvement before extradition would be considered, and later (with the prospect of air strikes looming) said it would consider turning him over to a third country. The US administration indicated that it would not negotiate. After strikes began, the Taleban reiterated this offer. See, e.g., *Toronto Star*, 6 October 2001, p. A4). One report (*Associated Press*, 7 October 2001) quoted the ambassador as saying that legal proceedings could begin even before the United States offered any evidence: 'Under Islamic law, we can put him on trial according to allegations raised against him and then the evidence would be provided to the court.' It may be that cooperation was not feasible and would not have weakened al-Qaeda sufficiently, but, as has been noted, 'that case was never really made in public'. See R. Falk, 'Appraising the War against Afghanistan', available at http://www.ssrc.org/sept11/essays/falk.htm, p. 2.

[230] See Radio Interview with Tony Blair: 'If they are not prepared to give up bin Laden, which they could do if they want, they become an obstacle. That is their choice', ABC Radio, note 32 above.

[231] It could for example debilitate the target organisation and undermine the threat, leaving less scope for military action even if it failed to avert the threat altogether.

[232] Prior efforts to secure suspects and process suspected terrorists are a factor in such a determination. However, the possibility of unprecedented post 9/11 unity providing the

military action? The question remains whether, in these circumstances, the case for the necessity of force (of the nature and scale employed in Afghanistan) was adequately made out.

5B.1.1.4 The relationship between self defence and the Security Council

Indications are that in the wake of 9/11 the Security Council was poised to assume its responsibility in respect of a situation that it condemned, the day after the attacks, as a 'threat to international peace and security',[233] in clear reference to its unique powers to determine and take measures (including if necessary the use of force) to address such threats. It also '[e]xpresse[d] its readiness to take all necessary steps to respond to the terrorist attacks of 11 September 2001, and to combat all forms of terrorism, in accordance with its responsibilities under the Charter of the United Nations'.[234] However, this dimension of the Council's role was never invoked by states, which proceeded instead to act unilaterally and through US-led 'coalitions of the willing'.[235]

Military action in Afghanistan therefore prompts questions as to the correct relationship between permissible self defence and collective action under the Charter. Is there not a preference for collective action underpinning the purpose and principles of the UN Charter, the mechanisms established thereunder and the language of Article 51? While the US and its allies may have fulfilled the obligation under Article 51 to 'report' measures taken in self defence to the Council, should they not have attempted to secure a mandate from the Council instead of relying on self defence one month after the attack?[236] Does the Article 51 reference to self defence 'until the Security Council has taken measures necessary to maintain international peace and security' not so suggest, and does the refusal to engage the Council undermine the collective security mechanism?[237]

---

basis for an enhanced cooperation initiative, if necessary supported by the use of force as a law enforcement tool, should also be considered. See Chapter 4.

[233] SC Res. 1368 (2001), 12 September 2001, UN Doc. S/RES/1369 (2001), para. 1.

[234] *Ibid.*, para. 5.

[235] It has been pointed out that not only was no authorisation sought, nor was the coalition ever brought under the umbrella of the UN, in contrast to the Gulf Coalition that used force against Iraq in 1990. See Myjer and White, 'The Twin Towers Attack', at 7.

[236] Note also that questions have been raised as to whether the requirement of 'immediacy' was met by action taken outside the Security Council framework one month on: see generally Myjer and White, 'The Twin Towers Attack'.

[237] Article 51 itself provides for self defence 'until the Security Council has taken measures necessary to maintain international peace and security' and imposes an obligation to report.

So far as the use of force is unilateral (permissibly so in the case of self defence) the underlying assessments – such as whether alternative means exist, whether a threat is imminent, or whether it is necessary in the wake of an attack to remove governments perceived to be sympathetic to terrorist causes – are in turn unilateral. In part this highlights the importance of having strict and clearly defined criteria for self defence, but it also underlines the importance of a collective mechanism assuming its role at the earliest opportunity. Growing lack of confidence in the reliability of intelligence on the basis of which decisions are made, generated through the 'war on terror', underscores the importance of checks on individual states' discretion to act. By refusing to engage – rather than only report to – the Security Council, states avoided accountability and oversight of the resort to armed force internationally.

5B.2 Iraq

In relation to Iraq, the justifications for the use of force differed from those invoked in relation to Afghanistan, and they differed as between states involved in the intervention. Unlike in Afghanistan, there was no suggestion that the targets of intervention were responsible for the events of 9/11, and in that sense Iraq was not a 'response' to September 11 at all. Though tangential links between Iraq and terrorism were floated sporadically, the Iraq intervention represented an extension of the 'war on terror' beyond terrorists to the longstanding question of the threat posed by the alleged existence of weapons of mass destruction and by Saddam Hussein's regime.

While many arguments were raised before and after intervention, separately and cumulatively, the US appears to have relied both on self defence and on the 'enforcement' of UN resolutions as legal bases for intervention.[238] The UK's legal justification was Security Council authorisation: that even without securing the desired further UN resolution authorising

---

[238] After the adoption of SC Res. 1441/(2002) (8 November 2002, UN Doc. S/RES/1441 (2002)), the US Permanent Representative to the UN noted that the resolution 'does not constrain any state from acting to defend . . . or to enforce relevant UN resolutions' (US Permanent Representative to the UN Ambassador John Negroponte, statement to the UN Security Council, US Mission to the UN Press Release, 8 November 2002, available at www.un.int/usa/02_187.htm). See generally, also W.H. Taft IV and T. Buchenwald, 'Agora: Future Implications of the Iraq Conflict: Preemption, Iraq, and International Law', 97 (2003) AJIL 557.

the use of force in Iraq, authorisation could be implied from earlier resolutions of the Council.[239]

The degree of support or, at least, passive acquiescence in the use of force in Afghanistan stands in sharp distinction to the subsequent global divisions over the lawfulness of the resort to force in Iraq. While proponents of military action can be found among states and legal commentators, the Iraq intervention has provoked unprecedented opposition, based in significant part on widespread concerns as to its lawfulness. Unusually outspoken statements on the unlawfulness of the Iraq intervention were heard before and after the intervention, including from many states, individually[240] and collectively,[241] the UN Secretary-General,[242] legal scholars and international civil society.[243] Reports suggest that

---

[239] See 'Legal Basis for Use of Force against Iraq', opinion published by the UK Attorney General, Lord Goldsmith, on 17 March 2003, available at http://www.number-10.gov.uk/output/Page3287.asp.

[240] See, e.g., the responses of France, Russia, China, Syria, Egypt, Saudi Arabia, Kuwait, Bahrain, Iran discussed in House of Commons Research Paper 02/64, 'Iraq and Security Council Resolution 1441', 21 November 2002, available at http://www.parliament.uk/commons/lib/research/rp2002/rp02-064.pdf., pp. 33–6. The French President Chirac, on 23 September 2003 stated that 'The war launched without Security Council authorisation shook the multilateral system . . . No one should assign themselves the right to use force unilaterally and pre-emptively. No one may act alone' (see 'Bush urges UN unity on Iraq', BBC News, 23 September 2002, at http://news.bbc.co.uk/1/hi/world/americas/3130880.stm). The Vatican's UN observer, Archbishop Renato Martino, criticised the attack as 'unilateralism, pure and simple' (see 'Vatican reasserts opposition to war in Iraq', Catholic News, 4 October 2002, at http://www.cathnews.com/news/210/27.php) while Saudi Arabia's Foreign Minister Prince Saud al-Faisal questioned whether 'Independent action . . . would encourage people to think . . . that what they're doing is a war of aggression rather than a war for the implementation of the United Nations resolutions' (see Interview with BBC News Correspondent John Simpson, at http://news.bbc.co.uk/1/hi/world/middle_east/2773759.stm). Subsequently, following the Madrid attacks of March 2004, newly elected Spanish president Jose Luis Rodriguez Zapatero noted that 'You cannot combat terrorism with war. What war does, as has happened in Iraq, is to proliferate hate, violence and terror', El Pais, 16 March 2004.

[241] Communiqué of the Arab Summit held in Sharm El-Sheikh, 1 March 2003, available at http://www.arabicnews.com/ansub/Daily/Day/030303/2003030324.html. In an interview about the Summit, Arab League Secretary-General Amr Moussa said: 'We shall definitely oppose the war. We cannot be a part of it or contribute to it or sympathize with it . . . What's the hurry to conduct a war that is extremely unpopular in the region, in the world, and unjustified?' (at http://www-cgi.cnn.com/2003/WORLD/meast/03/01/sprj.irq.arab.ministers/).

[242] 'Annan says US will violate Charter if it acts without approval', New York Times, 11 March 2003.

[243] Widespread opposition to the Iraq action was evident from demonstrations around the world, of unparalleled proportions. Objections to the lawfulness of the intervention

unlawfulness had, at one point, been acknowledged from within the US administration itself.[244]

The onus lay on states seeking to justify the use of force to demonstrate its lawfulness, and international reactions raise serious doubts as to whether this onus was discharged.[245]

5B.2.1 Key questions arising

Among the questions arising regarding the lawfulness of the use of force in Iraq are the following: whether the Security Council 'authorised' the use of force, implicitly; whether states can act to 'enforce' earlier resolutions against Iraq, where the Council itself fails to do so; whether a broad right of anticipatory self defence might be invoked to justify the use of force in this context; and whether the intervention that unfolded was strictly necessary and proportionate, pursuant to its objectives.

---

which came, in addition to more predictable sources, from usually reticent quarters, was unusually concerted and coordinated, and led to unprecedented internal divisions and resignations in several countries. See e.g.: 'Letter to *The Times*', Sir Franklin Berman, UK legal adviser from 1991 to 1999, and Sir Arthur Watts, UK legal adviser from 1987 to 1991, expressing 'regret' that the search for a second resolution had been abandoned, stating that the onus was on the government to account 'for their actions to the international community in whose name they claim to act' (see *The Times*, Letters, 20 March 2003). See also the open letter to the UK Prime Minister from a group of sixteen academic lawyers arguing that military action without a new, clear United Nations mandate 'will seriously undermine the international rule of law' (see 'War Would Be Illegal', *The Guardian*, 7 March 2003); 'Coalition of the Willing – A Pre-emptive Strike on Iraq Would Constitute a Crime against Humanity, Write 43 Experts on International Law and Human Rights', *Sydney Morning Herald*, 26 February 2003; J. Sallot, 'Attack Illegal, Experts Say', *Globe and Mail*, 20 March 2003, reporting an open letter signed by 31 of Canada's professors of international law holding that a US attack on Iraq 'would be a fundamental breach of international law and would seriously threaten the integrity of the international legal order that has been in place since the end of the Second World War'; E. MacAskill, 'Adviser Quits Foreign Office over Legality of War', *The Guardian*, 22 March 2003; T. Happold 'Short Quits Blair's Government', *The Guardian*, 12 May 2003; M. Tempest, 'Cook Resigns from Cabinet over Iraq', *The Guardian*, 17 March 2003; US Department of State, Daily Press Briefing by Richard Boucher, 11 March 2003, at http://www.state.gov/r/pa/prs/dpb/2003/18621.htm, reporting the resignation of two senior officers of the US Department of State 'in relation to the situation with Iraq'.

[244] O. Burkeman and J. Borger, 'War Critics Astonished as US Hawk Admits Invasion Was Illegal', *The Guardian*, 20 November 2003, noting comments by the Pentagon's Richard Perle: 'I think in this case international law stood in the way of doing the right thing.'

[245] Article 2(4) puts the onus on states seeking to justify the use of force. See also Watts and Berman, 'Letter to *The Times*', above.

5B.2.1.1   Security Council authorisation?

Questions relating to the role of the Security Council come into sharpest focus in relation to the use of force in Iraq. The first question, critical to the lawfulness of the action in Iraq, is whether the Security Council had in fact implicitly authorised use of force in Iraq. This is essentially a question of the correct interpretation of the resolutions in questions, though it raises broader questions regarding the proper approach to the interpretation of Chapter VII resolutions.

The background facts to the assertion of implied authorisation are, in brief, as follows. In 1991, in the context of the Iraqi invasion of Kuwait, Resolution 678 authorised states to 'use all necessary means' to effect Iraqi withdrawal from Kuwait and 'to restore international peace and security in the region'. Resolution 686 marked a provisional cessation of hostilities, while expressly preserving the right to use force under Resolution 678, and Resolution 687 imposed a permanent ceasefire, without reference to the right to use force. The Resolution 687 cease-fire was conditional on Iraqi destruction of existing weapons of mass destruction and non-acquisition of others, and to this end cooperation with the UN weapons inspectors. Subsequent resolutions, including Resolution 1154, found Iraq in 'material breach' of these conditions, ordered that immediate access be given to the inspectors and warned of 'the severest consequences' of failure to do so, while explicitly noting that the Council would 'remain actively seized of the matter'.[246]

Post September 11, and post Afghanistan, the US and UK sought a further resolution on Iraq.[247] After negotiation, Resolution 1441 (2002) was passed.[248] It found Iraq in 'material breach' of earlier resolutions and gave it 'a final opportunity to comply with its disarmament obligations' by setting up an 'enhanced inspection team'. It warned that non-cooperation would constitute a 'further material breach' which would 'be reported to the Council for assessment' and that the Council would 'convene immediately . . . in order to consider the situation and the need for full compliance with all of the relevant Council resolutions in order to secure international peace and security'. The Council 'Recall[ed], in that context, that the Council has repeatedly warned Iraq that it will face

---

[246]   SC Res. 1154 (1998), 2 March 1998, UN Doc. S/RES/1154 (1998) and SC Res. 1205 (1998), 5 November 1998, UN Doc. S/RES/1205 (1998).

[247]   See C. Lynch, 'US Presses UN to Back Tough New Iraq Resolution', *Washington Post*, 7 November 2002.

[248]   SC Res. 1441 (2002), above, note 235.

serious consequences as a result of its continued violations of its obligations'. Subsequent attempts (driven by the UK and US) to negotiate a
further resolution authorising the use of force failed; while many states
opposed the use of force, it was the French expression of intention to
veto any resolution seeking to authorise force that led the US and UK to
abandon 'the UN route'.[249]

One of the legal justifications invoked for resorting to force was
nonetheless Council authorisation, on the basis of what might be
described as a mixture of cumulative, implied, and revived authorisation.
In the UK, in accordance with advice of the Attorney General published in
summary form on March 2003,[250] the argument simply put was that the
authorisation to use force in resolution 678 was suspended conditionally
(not revoked) by Resolution 687 and that once the Council had found
Iraq in breach of those conditions (Resolution 1441) the original right to
use force was revived.

This argument has given rise to intense controversy on various grounds,
stemming from the ordinary meaning of UN resolutions, their context
and purpose.[251] The first is that while resolution 678 uncontroversially
authorised force, it did so for a particular purpose, namely to address
the situation occasioned by the Iraqi invasion of Kuwait, in the context
of circumstances prevalent in 1990. Absent express Council indication
to the contrary, such authorisation cannot be interpreted as supportive
of the use of force in a very different conflict, to address a very different
threat, in 2003, in the context of circumstances necessarily quite distinct
from those prevalent over a decade earlier.

Second, the plain wording of Resolutions 1154 and 1441, passed since
the 1990 resolution, make clear the Council's intention to remain 'seized'
of the matter at each stage and to itself 'consider' how to address the situation as it unfolds.[252] The context of the debate in the Council leading
to the adoption of other Iraq resolutions, and statements made thereupon, reveal no agreement that states should have a right to use force as a
result of those resolutions or an automatic right to do so in the event of a

---

[249] See the speech given by the UK Prime Minister on 5 March 2003, justifying military
action in Iraq and warning of the continued threat of global terrorism (available at
http://politics.guardian.co.uk/iraq/story/0%2C12956%2C1162991%2C00.html).
[250] See above.   [251] See Chapter 5.
[252] See the *travaux préparatoires* to Resolutions 1154 and 1441, referred to in R. Singh and A.
MacDonald, 'Legality of Use of Force against Iraq', Opinion for Peacerights, 10 September
2002, available at http://www.lcnp.org/global/IraqOpinion10.9.02.pdf (hereinafter 'Singh
and MacDonald, Opinion on Iraq'), para. 58.

further breach. Indeed such 'automaticity' was expressly rejected by certain participating states in the context of Resolution 1441.[253] In addition, the fact that renewed attempts were made to achieve a further resolution expressly authorising force was thought to undermine the argument ultimately advanced that no such resolution was necessary anyway.

This spawns general questions regarding Security Council resolutions and their interpretation. These include whether the authorisation to use force can ever be implied or, given the exceptional nature of the use of force, and the stakes involved, it must be clear and explicit, and understood as limited to the context and purpose for which it was given.[254] As regards the 'shelf life' of any authorisation to use force, can the assessment of the requirements of international peace and security at one point have continued relevance many months and years later, or does it require clear revival by the Council? Could an overly flexible interpretation of resolutions have a chilling impact on the willingness of states to reach decisions within the Council in the future?[255] Can – as the notion of 'automaticity' suggests – the Council delegate to member states determinations as to what action, including the use of force, might be necessary in the event of breach of its resolutions? Or, as has been suggested, in accordance with the constitutional role of the Council is it to be doubted not only whether the Council *did* delegate, but also whether it *could have* delegated, such an assessment to individual states?[256]

5B.2.1.2 Force to enforce?

Explaining the US vote in favour of Security Council Resolution 1441 (2002), the US Permanent Representative to the UN, Ambassador John Negroponte, stated that '[i]f the Security Council fails to act decisively in the event of a further Iraqi violation, this resolution does not constrain any member state from acting to defend itself against the threat posed by Iraq, or *to enforce relevant UN resolutions and protect world peace and security*'.[257] In the absence of Council authorisation, can states rely on a breach of international obligations, including Security Council resolutions, to justify the use of force?

---

[253] *Ibid.*   [254] See Framework, Section A above.

[255] See R. Higgins, 'International Law in a Changing International System', 58 (1999) *Cambridge Law Journal* 78.

[256] As noted in the Framework, under the Charter it is for the Council to decide not only if there is a breach and if it amounts, at the relevant time, to a threat to international peace and security, but also what measures would be appropriate to address such a threat.

[257] Statement of the US Permanent Representative to the UN, Ambassador John Negroponte, following adoption of Resolution 1441, cited above, note 235.

There is no apparent legal basis for the unilateral use of force pursuant to law enforcement within the framework of international law. Statements such as that cited appear to conflate and confuse the 'inherent' right to self defence under the Charter and the right to use force to enforce law or otherwise protect international peace and security, which is not inherent and exists only if conferred by the Security Council. As noted, the measures of self help that a state may take to enforce its own rights against an offending state cannot amount to the use of force. Moreover, while certain circumstances, such as serious violations of human rights, may give rise to the responsibility of a broader range of states to act to stop the breach, there is no unilateral use of force other than in self defence.[258]

5B.2.1.3 Veto abuse and failure to act?

In advancing this role for states, or specifically the United States, as enforcers of obligations (and thereby protectors of the 'relevance of the UN'), emphasis was placed on Security Council failure to act. In the context of the Iraq invasion, it was justified by reference to the fact that no explicit authorisation could be obtained because the veto power had been 'abused', in particular by France which had threatened its use 'unreasonably'.

This implies a doctrine of 'reasonableness' surrounding the use of the veto that international law does not recognise and which would, in practice, eviscerate the Council's authority.[259] When the Charter was adopted, the veto power for the five permanent members was inserted for political reasons, to maintain a degree of political 'balance' in the decisions of the Security Council, an inherently political body, albeit one with unique legal powers. States' reasons for voting and vetoing, which are in turn often political and controversial in nature, cannot affect the legal effect of the veto power.[260] Permitting a state to use force based on its assessment of what the Council *would* have done had all members acted 'reasonably' would clearly be a nonsense.

As noted, history does provide the precedent of the General Assembly's assumption of the Council's responsibilities where the latter was deemed

---

[258] See Chapter 3, para. 3.1.3. On the disputed right to intervention to prevent humanitarian catastrophe, see this chapter, paras. 5A.3.1 and 5B.2.1.6.

[259] As highlighted by legal scholars in the UK context: see 'Lawyers Doubt Iraq War Legality', 7 March 2003, at http://news.bbc.co.uk/1/hi/uk_politics/2829717.stm. It has also been pointed out that the position may not serve the interests of the US and UK as beneficiaries of the veto power, and in the case of the former the state having resort to that power most frequently.

[260] Article 27 of the Charter provides that non-procedural matters require nine out of fifteen votes, including the concurring votes of the permanent members.

unable to discharge its mandate, though a broad-reaching difference of view (as over the issue of Iraq) is of course distinct from the paralysis of the Cold War era. In any event, in the Iraq context assertions of Council failure did not give rise to assertions of an alternative role for the General Assembly or other established collective mechanism, but rather resort to the unilateral, US-led, use of force.[261]

Both the US and UK expressed a preference for Council authorisation while reserving their right to use force unilaterally or multilaterally outside the UN framework if UN consensus could not be achieved and the Security Council 'fails to act decisively'.[262] This would appear to imply that Council authorisation is optional rather than mandatory and that, at most, resort to the Council is a remedy to be exhausted before invoking force unilaterally. Despite the rhetoric of ensuring the 'relevance' of the UN and the enforcement of its decisions, an approach whereby a State gives the Council time within which to act, threatening do so itself if the Council does not, raises broader questions relating to the ultimate impact on the legitimacy of the Charter's collective security mechanism.

Do events post September 11 therefore indicate a marginalisation of role of the Security Council in favour of unilateral or selective collective approaches, and if so what might be the impact of such a shift in other situations? Or, assessed with the benefit of a longer lens, will the harsh criticism of the use of force in Iraq indicate a backlash away from unilateralism accepted in relation to Afghanistan towards endorsement of 'the UN route'? The Iraq experience may provide a catalyst for a serious assessment of whether and how the Security Council system might

---

[261] Neither the GA nor for that matter NATO (though, as noted above, the latter has no independent authority unless self defence) were involved in resort to force in Iraq.

[262] See, e.g., 'Powell Says No Quid-Pro-Quos Exchanged for U.N. Vote', US Department of State Press Release, 10 November 2002, at http://usinfo.state.gov/topical/pol/arms/02111003.htm: 'I can assure you if [Saddam Hussein] doesn't comply this time, we are going to ask the U.N. to give authorization for all necessary means. If the U.N. isn't willing to do that, the United States, with like-minded nations, will go and disarm him forcefully . . . the president has made it clear that he believes it is the obligation of the international community, in the face of new non-compliance, to take whatever actions the president feels necessary to remove those weapons of mass destruction. And if the U.N. does not act, then the president is prepared to act.' See also speech of the UK Prime Minister in the House of Commons, 25 February 2003: 'If the UN cannot be the way of resolving this issue, that is a dangerous moment for our world. That is why over the coming weeks we will work every last minute that we can to reunite the international community and disarm Iraq through the UN. It is our desire, and it is still our hope, that this can be done . . . If disarmament cannot happen by means of the UN route because Saddam Hussein is not co-operating properly, then what? We shall be left with a choice between leaving him there, with his weapons of mass destruction, in charge of Iraq – the will of the UN having therefore been set at nothing – and using force.'

be strengthened, reformed and made more effective[263] and ultimately to renewed support for the collective security system enshrined in the UN Charter.[264]

5B.2.1.4 Anticipatory self defence?

Post 9/11 the issue of anticipatory self defence first arose in relation to Afghanistan as any armed attack committed on 9/11 was apparently over by the time the military response was launched on 7 October, although the threat of future attacks remained.[265] Hitherto controversial questions regarding anticipatory self defence were hardly raised in that context, leading to assertions shortly after the Afghan invasion that 'in the changed post-September 11 environment, the concept of anticipatory self defence requires no explanation or justification'.[266] To the extent that the apparent acceptance of anticipatory self defence in Afghanistan may strengthen the case for such a right, it would, however, do so only in very limited circumstances. In Afghanistan those circumstances included (a) a prior attack, (b) an expressed intention to carry out future attacks, and, arguably, (c) an indication by the Security Council that the requirements of self defence have been satisfied.[267] Any analysis of the impact of the law in this field must therefore take account of these limitations[268] and be assessed in context, in particular in light of the controversy generated over the subsequent assertions of anticipatory self defence in Iraq and elsewhere.

In relation to Iraq, the US made several references to the need to act 'to defend itself against the threat posed by Iraq'.[269] Unlike Afghanistan,

---

[263] This is likely to be among the issues addressed by the high-level panel appointed by the Secretary General to consider 'Threats, Challenges and Change', see UN Doc. SG/A/857, 4 November 2003.

[264] See state responses, highlighted in this chapter, para. 5B.4, that may indicate movement in this direction.

[265] See US letter to the Security Council which emphasised the preventive and deterrent effect of the use of force.

[266] W.K. Lietzau, 'Combating Terrorism: Law Enforcement or War?', in M.N. Schmitt and G.L. Beruto (eds.), *Terrorism and International Law, Challenges and Responses* (Sanremo, 2003), p. 75 at p. 77.

[267] Preamble, SC Res. 1368 (2001), above, note 230, and SC Res. 1373 (2001), 28 September 2001, UN Doc. S/RES/1373 (2001).

[268] Account should also be taken of the peculiarities of the Afghan situation; see this chapter, para. 5B.4.

[269] Statement of the US Representative to the UN, above, note 235. Similar justifications for the military action in Iraq have been put forward by the US President. See, e.g., George W. Bush, UN General Assembly in New York City Address, 12 September 2002, available at http://www.whitehouse.gov/news/releases/2002/09/20020912-1.html. See also Taft IV and Buchenwald, 'Agora: Future Implications'; J. Yoo, 'Agora: Future Implications of the Iraq Conflict: International Law and the War in Iraq', 97 (2003) AJIL 563.

there was no meaningful attempt to link Iraq to the attack of September 11 or other attacks, or indeed to al-Qaeda, and as such the justification was clearly anticipatory self defence, without any prior attack.

The heart of the controversy on Iraq relates to the nature of the 'threat' posed by Iraq and the alleged weapons of mass destruction. Lawful self defence depends on a real and immediate threat arising as against the intervening nations themselves.[270] The key question is what threat, if any, Iraq represented to the US and its allies and whether it met the established criteria for invoking self defence.[271] In the UK, it was, with time, made clear that Iraq was not considered by the government to pose an imminent threat to the UK, but then no reliance had been placed by the UK on self defence.[272]

The US focused on much publicised concerns regarding the possession of weapons of mass destruction by Saddam Hussein's regime, in apparent support of the right to use force to prevent 'dangerous nations' threatening the US and the world with 'destructive weapons'.[273] While the possession and development of weapons of mass destruction certainly raise legal issues,[274] including the fact that Iraq specifically had obligations in this respect imposed by the Security Council,[275] unlawfulness in this respect does not *per se* justify the use of force in self

[270] See Chapter 5A.2.1. There was no evidence of other nations in the Middle Eastern region having requested that the intervening forces act in 'collective self defence, so the threat must have been to the intervening states'. See M. Bothe, 'Terrorism and the Legality of Preemptive Force', 14 (2003) EJIL 227 at 234. Where the threat is against one of those states, others can however act in collective self defence if requested to do so by the 'victim' state.

[271] Recall that the *Caroline* case requires a necessity that is 'instant, overwhelming, and leaving no choice of means, and no moment for deliberation,' see Framework, section A above.

[272] In the context of the extended debate on the '45 minute claim' published by the UK Government in a dossier of evidence against Iraq, the UK Government clarified that there was not thought to be any such imminent threat to the UK from Iraq. See R. Norton-Taylor and N. Watt, 'No. 10 Knew: Iraq No Threat', *The Guardian*, 19 August 2003.

[273] President Bush's State of the Union Address: 'I will not wait on events, while dangers gather. I will not stand by, as peril draws closer and closer. The United States of America will not permit the world's most dangerous regimes to threaten us with the world's most destructive weapons.' On US reliance on self defence in Iraq, see Ambassador Negroponte's intervention before the Security Council, cited above, note 235.

[274] In the Advisory Opinion on *Nuclear Weapons* the ICJ noted that, under the terms of the Non-Proliferation Treaty, all states had an obligation in good faith to seek nuclear disarmament via international negotiations. See in this respect R. Falk, 'Appraising the War against Afghanistan'.

[275] Note Security Council resolutions directed against specific states detailing their obligations to disarm, see, e.g., SC Res. 687 (1991), 3 April 1991, UN Doc. S/RES/687 (1991), concerning the conditions for the ceasefire in Iraq, including disarmament, discussed in section A.

defence.[276] The critical question, whether any such weapons represented a real and immediate threat to the US, was not addressed by the US, which preferred to advance an expanded conception of anticipatory self defence as enabling states to act pre-emptively before such threats are formed. If Iraq did not pose an immediate threat, it did, it was suggested, pose a potential threat. This view was expounded in the context of its controversial US National Security Strategy published in the months preceding Iraq: the extent to which that criterion accords with existing law or alters that law is discussed below. Suffice to recall that the claims to lawfulness in the context of Iraq met with little support from other states; the apparent attempt, at least at the early stages, to rely on self defence arguments found particularly few defenders outside the US, and appears with time to have been deemphasised by the United States itself.[277]

The fact that, as is now known, evidence did not emerge of weapons of mass destruction in Iraq following the invasion underscore the questions, highlighted above, as to the degree of evidence that should be required for the use of force against another state, and the lack of any procedure for safeguarding the application of the law of self defence, when states adopt a unilateralist approach outwith the UN framework.

5B.2.1.5 Necessity and proportionality?

Two further groups of issues arising in Iraq deserve brief mention. The first is once again the fundamental concern as to whether, in accordance with the Charter, the force employed was entirely necessary, there being no alternative, from the weapons inspectorate to criminal law enforcement, supported by coordinated international cooperation. The heavy onus on those states seeking to resort to force to demonstrate the legitimacy thereof has already been noted.

The second group of issues relate to proportionality, notably of the continued occupation of Iraq.[278] These issues are relevant to the lawfulness of action relying on self defence, as discussed above, but also to those taken pursuant to Security Council authorisation. If force is justified by reference to previous resolutions which are considered – as in the UK

---

[276] It may, however, be a breach of international peace and security, but, as already noted, this must be determined by the Security Council.

[277] See Taft IV and Buchenwald, 'Agora: Future Implications', writing in 2003, who place less emphasis on self defence than Negroponte and Bush did in the autumn of 2002; this may be explained by an evolution in the US position, or internal differences of view, or both; see note 266, above.

[278] Note that questions also concern the proportionality of the force used to the objectives pursued.

Attorney General's opinion – to authorise force to effect disarmament, the coercive measures taken must be those directed exclusively towards that objective, and be proportionate thereto. Questions may be raised as to whether regime change,[279] continued occupation,[280] and the assumption of powers and governmental responsibility can be said to meet that test.

So long as Council authorisation or self defence continue to be the purported bases on which the lawfulness of intervention, or occupation, of Iraq or Afghanistan rest,[281] there is a continuing obligation to demonstrate the necessity and proportionality of force used. The longer operations continue and the more powers are assumed, the more the case for necessity diminishes and concerns regarding proportionality grow.

5B.2.1.6 Humanitarian intervention?

Finally, both the US and UK peppered their discourse on Iraq, and Afghanistan, with references to the humanitarian situations in those countries, but without purporting to rely on humanitarian intervention as a legal justification as such.[282] Some have questioned whether

---

[279] As noted above, the UK's discomfort with regime change as an objective under international law was apparent from the emphasis on such a change as a necessary consequence (but not an aim) of military action.

[280] It seems that concerns as to the legality of US–UK occupation of Iraq in the absence of a Security Council resolution have been raised by the UK Attorney General in a subsequent opinion. See C. Dyer, 'Occupation of Iraq Illegal, Blair Told', *The Guardian*, 22 May 2003, reporting on a memo from the UK Attorney General to the Prime Minister, dated 26 March 2003, in which the former reportedly 'made clear that all activity beyond essential maintenance of security would be unlawful without a further Security Council resolution'.

[281] The legal basis for the continued 'intervention' of foreign troops may at a certain point shift to being at the invitation of the new government, in which case it acts under and subject to that mandate; clarity as to the legal basis is necessary to ensure that the intervention is governed by law.

[282] See e.g., US President's Message to the Iraqi People, 10 April 2003, at http://www.whitehouse.gov/news/releases/2003/04/20030410-2.html: 'In the new era that is coming to Iraq, your country will no longer be held captive to the will of a cruel dictator.' And 'A Vision for Iraq and the Iraqi People', paper published by the UK Government on 17 March 2003, available at http://www.pmo.gov.uk/output/Page3280.asp: 'The Iraqi people deserve to be lifted from tyranny and allowed to determine the future of their country for themselves. We pledge to work with the international community to ensure that the Iraqi people can exploit their country's resources for their own benefit, and contribute to their own reconstruction, with international support where needed. We wish to help the Iraqi people restore their country to its proper dignity and place in the community of nations, abiding by its international obligations and free from UN sanctions.' See also the remarks made by the US President on Operation Iraqi Freedom and Operation Enduring Freedom ('President Bush Reaffirms Resolve to War on Terror, Iraq and Afghanistan', White House Press Release, 19 March 2004, available at http://www.whitehouse.gov/news/releases/2004/03/20040319-3.html): 'Citizens

humanitarian intervention might not have provided a more plausible basis for legality than other arguments advanced.[283] The reluctance of states to advance the argument, particularly on the part of the UK as the erstwhile proponent of a doctrine of humanitarian intervention in exceptional circumstances, may be seen to reflect the controversial nature of the right and undermine the case for its establishment in international law. Or, more compellingly, it may reflect acknowledgement that the formulae of pre-requisites advanced in other contexts for such intervention – notably the requirement of imminent humanitarian catastrophe or crisis – were not satisfied, despite the undoubted brutality of the regimes in question. In addition, it may be that the timing of the interventions, following 9/11, belied the notion that the true objective (as opposed to desirable side effect) was humanitarian in nature.

5B.3 United States National Security Strategy

The President of the United States presented his National Security Strategy on September 2002. Three aspects thereof are highlighted with a view to questioning their relevance to the application of the legal framework post September 11 and in the future.

5B.3.1 Expanding self defence?

First, the US National Security Strategy appears to depart radically from the standard for self defence established in international law, set out in the legal framework in Chapter 5, section A above. It premises self defence not on an existing attack, nor indeed (expressly rejecting the *Caroline* criteria) an imminent attack. The focus is on the threat represented by 'terrorists and tyrants', but that threat need not necessarily exist, as the US National Security Strategy envisages military action 'against such emerging threats before they are fully formed' with an emphasis on the language of prevention, pre-emption and deterrence.[284] Such a policy of pre-emptive

---

of Afghanistan have adopted a new constitution, guaranteeing free elections and full participation by women . . . Today, as Iraqis join the free peoples of the world, we mark a turning point for the Middle East, and a crucial advance for human liberty.' Cf. K. Roth, 'War in Iraq: Not a Humanitarian Intervention', Human Rights Watch, *World Report 2004*.

[283] See, e.g., R. Falk, 'Appraising the War against Afghanistan', 31 January 2002, at http://www. ssrc.org/sept11/essays/falk.htm.

[284] The US National Security Strategy refers to 'prevent[ing] our enemies from threatening us . . . with WMDs' (p. 7) and to 'dissuad[ing] future military competition; deter[ing] threats against the US and against US' interests, allies and friends' (p. 29). It states that the US will 'exercise our right of self defence by acting preemptively against such terrorists,

force does not apparently require clear and specific evidence of impending attack, but covers situations where 'uncertainty remains as to the time and place of the enemy's attack'.[285] It is unclear how speculative the threat, or potential threat, might be to purport to justify the pre-emptive use of force in self defence.

The threat is embodied in 'terrorists' on the one hand, and 'tyrants' and 'rogue states . . . determined to acquire WMDs' on the other. While the link between the two is referred to throughout the US National Security Strategy – by reference to the 'crossroads of radicalism and technology' and the 'overlap between states that sponsor terrorism and those that pursue weapons of mass destruction' – the basis for the assertion of this link has been the subject of controversy in relation to Iraq and beyond.[286] As intent to possess or indeed mere possession of weapons must be itself insufficient to justify the use of force, what evidence might be required, if any, as to the plans or immediate intentions of the state for it to amount to a threat that could plausibly give rise to the legitimate exercise of self defence?

In the absence of an actual attack, questions arise not only relating to the evidence of a threat giving rise to self defence, but also as to how proportionality might be measured.[287] In particular, where the potential threat from rogue states is thought to be nuclear attack, it has been questioned what would be the proportionate response.[288]

The expansive approach to the threat in question is coupled with a broad view of against whom or what such a threat might be directed – including 'the United States, the American people and our interests at home and abroad'.[289] As noted, while defence of territory and (more controversially) of nationals has long been the US position, the ambiguity and

---

to prevent them from doing harm against our people and our country . . . by identifying and destroying the threat before it reaches our borders'.

[285] 'The greater the threat, the greater is the risk of inaction – and the more compelling the case for taking anticipatory action to defend ourselves, even if uncertainty remains as to the time and place of the enemy's attack. To forestall or prevent such hostile acts by our adversaries, the United States will, if necessary, act preemptively', National Security Strategy, section V.

[286] See G. Miller, 'Iraq – Terrorism Link Continues to Be Problematic', Los Angeles Times, 9 September 2003.

[287] Note that proportionality is measured against the threat rather than the armed attack, but the latter provides an indication of the former.

[288] The US National Security Strategy has been described as 'alarm[ist] about the threat of terrorism': see Gray, 'Bush Doctrine'.

[289] See also reference to the protection of US friends and allies in US National Security Strategy, p. 29.

potentially extremely wide-reaching scope of the reference to other 'interests' begs questions as to the nature of such interests and limits thereon. The protection of interests beyond the integrity and independence of the state, and, arguably, nationals abroad, finds no justification within the law of self defence.

If the 'revolutionary'[290] view of self defence advanced in the US National Security Strategy were to be accepted, the implications for the law on the use of force, and its application in other situations, would be serious. Particularly so where the expansive view of anticipatory self defence combines with the apparent loosening or abolition of the state responsibility link: the net impact is that an unclear threat from an unclear entity with unclear links to states may render those states and their representatives vulnerable to attack.

But there is cause to doubt that the US National Security Strategy marks such a shift in international law. First, it is doubtful whether the document was intended to present a legal argument as to the state of the law. As one commentator noted, '[t]he Security Strategy provisions on pre-emptive action may yet prove more a rhetorical device designed to put pressure on Iraq than a serious attempt to rewrite international law on self defense'.[291] Second, the approach to anticipatory self defence advanced in this document and in relation to Iraq has met with a chilly response internationally. On the one occasion when it appears to have been relied upon, by the US in relation to Iraq, it was not endorsed by any other state involved in that intervention and met with firm rebuke from many other states and commentators. The perceived excess of such a claim may indeed have impelled a reassertion of the collective security system.[292]

5B.3.2 Internationalism, unilateralism or exceptionalism?

The US National Security Strategy describes itself as 'based on a distinctly American internationalism'.[293] While there are several references to allies, coalitions and international institutions (in that order), it clearly presents

---

[290] Gray, 'Bush Doctrine'.   [291] Gray, 'Bush Doctrine', at 447.

[292] See Chirac statement, below, note 298. The Russian President has similarly stated that, while Russia agreed with the United States that it was important to 'make sure that Iraq has no weapons of mass destruction in its possession', the Russian Government 'do believe that we have to stay within the framework of the work being carried out within the United Nations' (see 'Chirac, Putin: No Need for War', CNN.com, 10 February 2003, at http://www.cnn.com/2003/WORLD/meast/02/10/sprj.irq.france.putin.

[293] US National Security Strategy, p. 1.

a multilateral approach to the use of force as optional rather than mandatory and places emphasis on the readiness of the US to use pre-emptive force unilaterally. It notes that: '[w]hile the US will constantly strive to enlist the support of the international community, we will not hesitate to act alone, if necessary, to exercise our right of self defence by acting preemptively'.[294] A second feature of the US National Security Strategy of particular note is therefore its unilateralism.

Finally, questions may also be asked regarding the prominence and relevance of international law in the US National Security Strategy. As noted above, there is no apparent attempt, direct or indirect, to justify the policy by reference to international law. International law is referred to explicitly only once, with regard not to US policy but in the characterisation of 'rogue states' which, *inter alia*, 'display no regard for international law, threaten their neighbours, and callously violate international treaties to which they are party'.[295] Does the US National Security Strategy envisage that those rules applicable to others are applicable also to the US? And conversely, does it envisage that the same standards regarding pre-emptive self defence that it advances for the US should be available to others? If the answer to either or both is negative, it may be that the questions arising relate not so much to a doctrine of unilateralism as one of US exceptionalism, with the consequent challenges for the universality of international law inherent in such an approach.

5B.4 Conclusion

The interventions in Afghanistan and Iraq that followed 9/11 are in many ways very different. Not least among the differences are states' reactions to them. The use of force in Afghanistan, like the September 11 attacks that preceded it, met with international unity. The use of force in Iraq caused international division rarely seen in the post-Cold War era.

But to varying degrees and in different ways, both raise issues regarding an expansive approach to 'self defence' and a failure to engage the collective security system, in preference for a unilateralist approach, whether exercised individually or through informal coalitions of the willing. The

---

[294] US National Security Strategy, p. 7. It also notes that 'wherever possible, the US will rely on regional organisations and states . . . where they meet their obligations to fight terrorism' (*ibid.*, p. 8).

[295] Rogue states are also described as violating human rights, being determined to acquire weapons of mass destruction, sponsoring terrorism, rejecting basic human values and 'hat[ing]' the United States and everything for which it stands'. US National Security Strategy, p. 14.

more exorbitant claims that arose in the context of Iraq and beyond relate to the purported right to use force to topple governments in the name of defending one's state, friends and allies from potential danger, and to do so without Security Council approval, where the Council does not respond to the request by states to take the required action. The lack of indication of acceptance of such an approach by the broader international community of states means that it is highly unlikely, however, at least for the time being, to impact on international law.[296] In this respect the very different response to the Afghan intervention, by contrast, raises more difficult questions.

The unity around Afghanistan is on one level surprising, given that the Afghan intervention raises a number of questions (highlighted above). Among them is the fact that Afghan territory and the institutions of the Afghan government were attacked without clarity as to whether the state was considered responsible for the original attack (or for an imminent threat) or only for other wrongs in respect of terrorists on its territory, and what relevance, if any, such responsibility had to the justification of the use of force against it. Whatever the lawfulness or not of the use force in the particular circumstances of Afghanistan, the danger of its legacy may stir so far as legal principles of broader application are discerned and relied upon to justify the use of force in other contexts in the future, for example against any of the many other states with terrorist cells operating out of their territory on the basis of unclear standards of responsibility.

The reaction to Afghanistan, or lack thereof, is perhaps less surprising than at first appears, given the global political context into which plans for the Afghan military campaign emerged and states' reactions were rendered. Shock and revulsion at the September 11 attacks, followed by apprehension as to the response that might ensue, particularly in light of the threatening rhetoric that those not 'for' the campaign would be considered 'against' it, and held to account accordingly.[297] Afghanistan was not only a pariah state with an exceptionally notorious human rights record, for which it had been widely condemned, its de facto government was also uniquely unpopular in the region and beyond. At least in the short term there was much to be lost and little to be gained geopolitically from

---

[296] See the discussion on 'how international law changes' above, Chapter 1, para. 1.2.2.

[297] See, for example, the State of the Union Speech by the United States' President, 20 September 2001: 'Either you are with us, or you are with the terrorists. From this day forward, any nation that continues to harbor or support terrorism will be regarded by the United States as a hostile regime' (at http://www.whitehouse.gov/news/releases/2001/09/20010920-8.html).

opposition to this conflict. It is easy to speculate that certain reactions, or the absence thereof, may have been based less on a view as to the lawfulness of military action and more on flexibility borne of a reluctance to defend the Taliban or take the intervening forces to task.

In assessing the impact that state reactions may nonetheless have had on the law,[298] reference should be had to Afghanistan intervention not in isolation but in context, by reference for example to events that followed immediately thereafter, such as the intervention in Iraq and Israeli attacks on Syria,[299] and the more critical reactions thereto. States have continued to express the same reservations with self defence being invoked against terrorist groups on another state's territory as were heard before 9/11. With time, and in the wake of the Iraq intervention they have come to place renewed stress on the collective security system as opposed to unilateral force – that 'the role of the United Nations should be brought into full play'.[300] In particular, assertions of the unilateral right to use force pre-emptively have been openly rejected.[301] When it is assessed, as it must be, by reference to subsequent statements and responses to events, it has been suggested that the impact on the law of actions and reactions post 9/11 will be less striking than it may at first have appeared.

---

[298] Political motivation does not change the actions and reactions, what states say and what they do not, which are what counts for the purposes of assessing the necessary *opinio juris* and whether the Afghan conflict contributes to a change in customary law. But where there is ambiguity, regard can legitimately be had to the context in which state reactions unfold. Such political factors may be directly relevant to assessing the precedential value, if any, of action, and the likelihood that similar 'flexibility' would be shown in the future. As such they may be relevant to an assessment of whether a rule of customary law is consolidating.

[299] During the Security Council debate following the Israeli bombardment of Syria in October 2003, many states expressed their deep concern about the attack. See, e.g., the statement of the Spanish representative denouncing the 'extreme gravity of the attack perpetrated against Syria today, which was a patent violation of international law and worthy of condemnation'. See 'Security Council Meets in Emergency Session Following Israeli Air Strike against Syria – Syria Asks Council to Condemn Attack; Israel Says Attack Response for Islamic Jihad's Bombing in Haifa', UN Press Release, 5 October 2003, UN Doc. SC/7887.

[300] Remarks by President Bush and President Jiang Zemin in Press Availability Western Suburb Guest House (Shanghai, 9 October 2001. http://www.whitehouse.gov/news/releases/2001/10/20011019-4.html).

[301] See, e.g., the statement of the French President, Jacques Chirac, on 23 September 2003: 'The war launched without Security Council authorisation shook the multilateral system . . . No one should assign themselves the right to use force unilaterally and pre-emptively. No one may act alone' ('Chirac Says Iraq War Caused UN Crisis', BBC.com, 23 September 2003, at http:news.bbc.co.uk/1/hi/world/americas/3130880.stm).

PART THREE

6

International humanitarian law

I observed that men rushed to war for slight causes or no causes at all, and that arms have once been taken up there is no longer any respect for law, divine or human.

Hugo Grotius, 1625[1]

6A The legal framework

Earlier parts of this book have focused on the characterisation of the September 11 attacks and explored which responses may be lawful within the international legal framework, including the criminal law response and the circumstances in which it is lawful for states to resort to armed force. This part, by contrast, addresses the rules that limit *how* these responses may be executed.

The focus is on the law applicable once there has been a resort to force, and an armed conflict has arisen.[2] This law (the *jus in bello*) applies irrespective of whether the use of force is itself lawful (according to the *jus ad bellum*, addressed at Chapter 5). The rules that govern armed conflict derive from a branch of international law, known as international humanitarian law (IHL), that comes into play in armed conflict, addressed in this chapter, and a core of international human rights law that applies in all situations, addressed in the next.

IHL applies in 'armed conflict' and imposes constraints on how that conflict may be waged. Its objective is to protect certain persons who do

---

[1] H. Grotius, *On Laws of War and Peace* (Paris, 1625), para. 28.
[2] There is some controversy about precisely when armed conflict began post September 11, and whether the events of September 11 might themselves constitute the initiation of such conflict. As noted later in this chapter, it may also be controversial whether the conflict has ended, or when it might end. It is, however, uncontroversial that for a period an armed conflict existed, having arisen, if not before, then with the military action that commenced on 7 October in Afghanistan, with IHL applicable thereto. On each of these, see Chapter 6, section B below.

not (or no longer) take part in hostilities and to limit the methods and means of warfare for the benefit of all.[3] Its precise content varies, to a limited degree, depending on the international or non-international nature of the conflict, although a common core of principles applies to both.

This chapter will consider the law that defines whether there is an armed conflict, if so what sort of conflict, and when it begins and ends. It will then consider particular aspects of the law against which the legitimacy of measures taken in armed conflict must be assessed. Examples of questions concerning the application of this legal framework post September 11 in the context of the so-called 'war on terror' will be flagged in the chapter that follows. IHL issues also arise, however, in Chapter 7, which explores human rights law (IHRL) including the relationship between IHL and IHRL and in Chapter 8, a case study on the application of the legal framework of IHL and IHRL to the detainees held by the United States in Guantanamo Bay, Cuba.

6A.1 When and where IHL applies

6A.1.1 Armed conflict: international or non-international

IHL applies in time of armed conflict. While the terminology of 'war' is often invoked, it should be noted that 'such references may prove to be more of emotional and political significance than legal'.[4] This is all the more true of emotive references in the post-September 11 world to the

---

[3] The principal international instruments dealing with international humanitarian law are the four Geneva Conventions of 1949 and the two Additional Protocols to the Geneva Conventions adopted in 1977. As noted by the ICJ, however, other rules are equally relevant. See *Legality of the Threat or Use of Nuclear Weapons, Advisory Opinion, 8 July 1996, ICJ Reports 1996*, p. 226 (hereafter '*Nuclear Weapons* Advisory Opinion'), para. 75: 'The "laws and customs of war" as they were traditionally called were the subject of efforts at codification undertaken in The Hague (including the Conventions of 1899 and 1907), and were based partly upon the St Petersburg Declaration of 1868 as well as the results of the Brussels Conference of 1874. This "Hague Law" and, more particularly, the Regulations Respecting the Laws and Customs of War on Land, fixed the rights and duties of belligerents in their conduct of operations and limited the choice of methods and means of injuring the enemy in an international armed conflict. One should add to this the "Geneva Law" (the Conventions of 1864, 1906, 1929 and 1949), which protects the victims of war and aims to provide safeguards for disabled armed forces personnel and persons not taking part in the hostilities. These two branches of the law applicable in armed conflict have become so closely interrelated that they are considered to have gradually formed one single complex system, known today as international humanitarian law. The provisions of the Protocols of 1977 give expression and attest to the unity and complexity of that law.'

[4] C. Greenwood, 'Scope of Application of Humanitarian Law', in D. Fleck (ed.), *The Handbook of Humanitarian Law in Armed Conflict* (Oxford, 1995), p. 39, at p. 44.

'war on terror'. For legal purposes the question is whether there is an 'armed conflict', and if so which rules of IHL apply to assess measures taken in the context of it.

'Armed conflict' is not defined in IHL treaties.[5] However, the ICTY provided the following definition:

> [A]n armed conflict exists whenever there is a resort to armed force between States or protracted armed violence between governmental authorities and organized armed groups or between such groups within a State.[6]

The question whether an armed conflict exists involves an essentially factual assessment,[7] rather than one 'laden with legal technicalities'.[8] No relevance should be attached, for example, to the existence or otherwise of a 'declaration of war', or to acknowledgement by the parties that they are in a state of war.[9] Likewise, it is irrelevant that an opposing party (or other states) recognise the status of the other party, for example as the recognised government representative of the state, in determining whether there is, in fact, an 'armed conflict' or its nature.[10] Instead, the essential characteristic of any armed conflict, international or non-international (considered in turn below), is the resort to force between two or more identifiable parties.

An international armed conflict exists where force is directed by one state against another irrespective of duration or intensity.[11] Such a conflict

---

[5] See ICRC Commentary GC I, pp. 49–51.

[6] *Prosecutor v. Dusko Tadic*, Case No. IT-94-1-AR72, Decision on the Defence Motion for Interlocutory Appeal on Jurisdiction (Appeals Chamber), 2 October 1995 (hereinafter '*Tadic* Jurisdiction Decision'), para. 70. See also ICC Statute.

[7] While indisputably a question of fact, disputes arise not infrequently as to whether particular facts satisfy the threshold, particularly of non-international armed conflicts. As explained below, this is no less true as regards the disputed war on al-Qaeda post September 11.

[8] Greenwood, 'Scope of Application', at p. 42.

[9] *Ibid.*, p. 45. Common Article 2(1) of the Geneva Convention makes clear their applicability 'to all cases of declared war or of any other armed conflict which may arise between two or more of the High Contracting Parties, even if the state of war is not recognised by one of them'.

[10] This may arise, as it did in Afghanistan, where a state or government is not recognised. The fact that a state party to a treaty is not represented by a recognised government does not affect either the international nature of the conflict or applicable IHL (Article 4 (A)(3), GC III). See, in general, D. Schindler, 'The Different Types of Armed Conflicts according to the Geneva Conventions and Protocols', (1979–II) 163 RdC 117.

[11] See the ICRC Commentary to Common Article 2 of the Geneva Conventions: 'Any difference . . . leading to the intervention of members of the armed forces is an armed conflict . . . It makes no difference how long the conflict lasts or how much slaughter takes place' (see, e.g., ICRC Commentary to GC VI, p. 19). See, however, the view that a 'very small and insignificant incident' between states may not meet the conflict threshold: V. Muntarbhorn, 'Legal Qualification and International Humanitarian Law as Lex Specialis:

may also arise where a state or states intervene in a non-international conflict. They may become parties by intervening with their own troops, having other participants act on their behalf,[12] or by rendering direct support to the military operations of one of the parties.[13]

Commentators differ as to whether a non-international conflict is 'internationalised' in this way simply by the fact of intervention of an outside state, irrespective of whether it intervenes on the side of rebels or of state forces. One commentator notes: 'whenever a state chooses to send its armed forces into combat in a previously non-international armed conflict in another state – whether at the invitation of that state's government or a rebel party – the conflict must then be considered an international armed conflict'.[14] Another view is that international conflict only arises where the outside state intervention is on the side of the rebels, such that there are state forces engaged in the conflict on both sides, as otherwise the 'asymmetric' nature of the conflict between states and non-state actors qualifies it in principle as non-international.[15]

10 Basic Questions Concerning International Armed Conflicts . . . and Answers?', paper presented at the 27th Round Table on Current Problems of International Humanitarian Law, 'International Humanitarian and other Legal Regimes: Interplay in Situations of Violence', Sanremo, 4–6 September 2003 (hereinafter '2003 Sanremo Round Table on IHL'). The proceedings of the Round Table will be published in G. L. Beruto and G. Ravasi (eds.), *27th Round Table on Current Problems of International Humanitarian Law; Sanremo, 4–6 September 2003; 'International Humanitarian and other legal regimes: interplay in situations of violence'* (Milan, forthcoming). Not every use of force on another state's territory amounts to armed conflict: for example, force used in the course of carrying out an arrest may not be force directed 'against the state' and an armed conflict would not necessarily arise.

[12] See ICTY, *Tadic* Jurisdiction Decision: '[I]n addition, in case of an internal armed conflict breaking out on the territory of a State, it may become international (or depending upon the circumstances, be international in character alongside an internal armed conflict) if (i) another State intervenes in that conflict through its troops, or alternatively if (ii) some of the participants in the internal armed conflict act on behalf of that other State.' If the state does not intervene directly but only through one of the warring factions, the Appeals Chamber found, according to the doctrine of state responsibility, that state must have 'overall control' over the faction to render the conflict international (*ibid.*, paras. 137–40).

[13] Greenwood, 'Scope of Application', p. 50. The author states that this applies to military support as distinct from financial, political and intelligence support, which will not suffice.

[14] G. Aldrich, 'The Laws of War on Land' 94 (2000) AJIL 42 at 62. The author goes on to note that in such a situation, two armed conflicts – one international and the other non-international – may co-exist within one territory, or the entire conflict may become international (depending, *inter alia*, on facts such as the degree of control exercised by states over entities within the territory).

[15] D. Fleck, 'Non-International Armed Conflict: Legal Qualifications and Parties to the Conflict', paper presented at the 2003 Sanremo Round Table on IHL.

In accordance with the definition of armed conflict set out above, generally the parties to international armed conflict are two or more states.[16] However, cases of total or partial military occupation, even where it is met with no armed resistance, and even where there is no longer any opposing party, are also international conflicts for the purposes of IHL.[17] Finally, since the 1970s, wars of self-determination against colonial domination have likewise been included within the rubric of international conflicts for the purposes of IHL.[18]

The classification of *non-international* armed conflict creates somewhat greater scope for dispute as to whether a particular situation amounts to an armed conflict, as opposed to 'internal disturbances and tensions [or] isolated and sporadic acts of violence'[19] which are explicitly excluded by IHL from the scope of armed conflict. Factors relevant to such a factual determination include the nature, intensity and duration of the violence,[20] and the nature and organisation of the parties.[21]

The parties to non-international armed conflict may be 'governmental authorities and armed groups', or two (or more) armed groups.[22] Critically, the non-state (or 'insurgent') groups that may constitute parties

---

[16] Note by way of exception that 'armed conflicts in which peoples are fighting against colonial domination or racist regimes in the exercise of their right of self determination' are also included as international armed conflicts for the purposes of IHL. See Article 1(4), AP I.

[17] Greenwood, 'Scope of Application', p. 41. On special rules governing occupation see this chapter, para. 6A.3.4.

[18] Liberation movements may also be covered: see Article 1 AP I: '3. This Protocol, which supplements the Geneva Conventions of 12 August 1949 for the protection of war victims, shall apply in the situations referred to in Article 2 common to those Conventions. 4. The situations referred to in the preceding paragraph include armed conflicts in which peoples are fighting against colonial domination and alien occupation and against racist regimes in the exercise of their right of self-determination, as enshrined in the Charter of the United Nations and the Declaration on Principles of International Law concerning Friendly Relations and Co-operation among States in accordance with the Charter of the United Nations.'

[19] Article 1(2) AP I: 'This Protocol shall not apply to situations of internal disturbances and tensions, such as riots, isolated and sporadic acts of violence and other acts of a similar nature, as not being armed conflicts.'

[20] M. Sassòli, 'Non-International Armed Conflict: Qualification of the Conflict and Its Parties', paper presented at the 2003 Sanremo Round Table on IHL, and Fleck, 'Non-International Armed Conflict'. The nature of the violence includes whether it is a military or police operation, or collective or coordinated hostilities.

[21] See, in general, ICRC, Report on 'International Humanitarian Law and the Challenges of Contemporary Armed Conflict' (Geneva, 2003), (hereinafter 'ICRC Report on IHL and Contemporary Armed Conflicts'); Sassòli, 'Non-International Armed Conflict'; Fleck, 'Non-International Armed Conflict'.

[22] See ICC Statute, Article 8(2)(f).

must be capable of identification as a party to the conflict and have attained a certain degree of internal organisation.[23] While they must be *capable* of observing the rules of IHL,[24] compliance with IHL is not itself a criterion.[25] Nor is control of territory a requirement to constitute a party to a non-international armed conflict (although it is a jurisdictional threshold for the application of one of the applicable treaties, Additional Protocol II).[26] Non-international armed conflict generally arises, as the ICTY noted, 'within a state', although the conflict need not unfold, at least entirely, within one state's geographic borders.[27]

6A.1.2 Temporal scope of IHL

When, in accordance with the criteria set out above, an armed conflict begins, involving the use of force between identifiable parties, the application of IHL is automatically triggered. IHL applies from the initiation of an armed conflict until the general close of military operations.[28]

While historically it has not been uncommon for conflict to end with a declaration or treaty, legally a formal declaration is as unnecessary to bring about an end of military operations as it was to initiate 'armed conflict'. As explained in relation to the existence of armed conflict, above,

---

[23] The ICRC emphasises the 'identifiable nature of the parties, and those associated with them': see 'ICRC Report on IHL and Contemporary Armed Conflicts', p. 19. On discipline as a criterion, see Sassòli, 'Non-International Armed Conflict'.

[24] See 'ICRC Report on IHL and Contemporary Armed Conflicts', pp. 18–19.

[25] Sassòli, 'Non-International Armed Conflict'.

[26] On applicable treaty law, see this chapter, para. 6A.2, which discusses whether or not AP II applies as treaty law, and core customary norms applicable in non-international conflict. Some of AP II may itself apply as customary law. The territorial requirement is however a jurisdictional threshold for the application of AP II. See Fleck, 'Non-International Armed Conflict' and Sassòli, 'Non-International Armed Conflict'.

[27] Conflicts certainly may spill over beyond a state's national borders and the geographic limits are probably not an essential characteristic of non-international armed conflict. Note however that the fact that military operations connected to a non-international armed conflict spill over into the territory of other states does not necessarily change the non-international character of the conflict.

[28] The precise formulae used vary between IHL instruments. Article 6 GC IV provides, for example, that it applies on the territory of the parties until 'the general close of military operations', and on occupied territory until the end of occupation. Article 118 GC III refers to the duty to repatriate at the 'cessation of active hostilities'. The *Tadic* Jurisdiction Appeal Decision invokes the perhaps looser phrase 'until a general conclusion of peace is reached'. See also H.-P. Gasser, 'Protection of the Civilian Population', in Fleck (ed.), *Handbook of Humanitarian Law*, p. 209 at p. 221. This does not limit obligations that states may have beyond the end of hostilities, for example to identify weapons that may continue to cause injury beyond the cessation of hostilities.

the questions are primarily factual ones: has there been a definitive cessation of active hostilities, bringing the conflict to an end? In case of non-international armed conflict, are any on-going hostilities of insufficient scale or intensity to constitute an armed conflict, having reverted to sporadic violence? A temporary or tentative cessation of hostilities is clearly insufficient to bring about a general conclusion of peace.[29] Where the other party to the conflict capitulates, or indeed no longer exists, in such a way that there is no realistic prospect of renewed hostilities of significant intensity between two identifiable parties, then it should follow that the cessation of hostilities is definitive and the conflict terminated. In relation to situations of occupation, discussed below, the IHL obligations of the occupying state continue for a longer period, until one year after the occupation comes to an end.

6A.1.3 Territorial scope of IHL

In the event of an armed conflict, 'international humanitarian law continues to apply in the whole territory of the warring States (or, in the case of non-international conflicts, the whole territory under the control of a party, whether or not actual combat takes place there)'.[30] The reach of IHL therefore extends far beyond the immediate 'area of operations' or zone of battle.

The territory of state parties (together with the high seas and exclusive economic zones) is known as the 'area of war'.[31] While the area of war is extensive, it is not unlimited and does not in general extend for example to the territory of other states not party to the conflict, unless those states allow their territory to be used by one of the belligerents.[32]

6A.2 Applicable law

IHL can be found in treaties and customary law, considered in turn below. The rules that govern any armed conflict depend, to some extent, on the international or non-international nature of the conflict, and the applicability of particular treaties depends also on whether they have been ratified by all parties to the conflict. However, certain core rules

---

[29] Greenwood, 'Scope of Application', p. 62.
[30] *Tadic* Jurisdiction Appeal Decision, para. 70. Territory includes land, rivers and air space.
[31] Greenwood, 'Scope of Application of IHL', p. 51.
[32] *Ibid.*, p. 51. If neutral territory is drawn into the area of war, and hostilities are conducted there, rival belligerents may also be entitled to take measures on that territory.

of customary law are applicable irrespective of treaty ratification or the nature of the conflict.

Historically, the focus of IHL was on governing international armed conflict, to which a more comprehensive body of treaty law therefore applies.[33] Developments in practice and legal thinking, however, have 'blurred' the distinction between international and non-international conflict and the rules applicable to each,[34] such that a 'common core' of customary IHL applies whatever the nature of the conflict.[35] In any event, the international or non-international distinction is further diminished where a state undertakes, as the United States has, to apply the same law of war to all conflicts in which it conducts military operations, however classified.[36]

Beyond treaties and customary law, reference must also be made to how IHL has been interpreted and applied by judicial bodies, national and international. While such jurisprudence was historically quite scarce, a noteworthy shift came with the work of the UN ad hoc tribunals for the former Yugoslavia and Rwanda.[37] By applying IHL in the context of concrete criminal cases, this jurisprudence has often led to a more rigorous analysis of the precise content and meaning of IHL.[38]

---

[33] The fact that some divergence in rules of conduct and levels of protection remain can be seen from the ICC Statute (which includes more crimes for international than non-international conflict). Moreover certain detailed rules, such as those governing the treatment of prisoners of war (described below, para. 6A.3.3.2, this chapter), could not be considered applicable in non-international conflict.

[34] As noted above, the jurisprudence of the *ad hoc* tribunals builds on the basic principles of humanity to find that prohibitions that derive from instruments addressed only to international conflict may in certain circumstances be deemed to apply to both types of conflict. See *Tadic* Jurisdiction Decision (paras. 119–24).

[35] The ICTY has developed this approach to a common core of war crimes. See S. Boelaert-Suominen, 'The Yugoslavia Tribunal and the Common Core of International Humanitarian Law applicable to All Armed Conflict', 13 (2000) LJIL 619 at 630.

[36] See for example, the instruction issued by the chairman of the US Joint Chiefs of Staff stating that the 'Armed Forces of the United States will comply with the law of war during the conduct of all military operations and related activities in armed conflict, however such conflicts are characterized' (statement reported in T. Meron, 'The Humanization of Humanitarian Law', 94 (2000) AJIL 239 at 262); see also the 'Declaration on the Rules of International Humanitarian Law Governing the Conduct of Hostilities in Non-International Armed Conflict', IRRC, Sep–Oct, 1990, 404–8, referred to by Gasser, 'Protection of the Civilian Population', at pp. 209 and 212: 'German soldiers . . . are required to comply with the rules of international humanitarian law in the conduct of military operations in all armed conflicts however such conflicts are characterised.'

[37] International Tribunal for the former Yugoslavia, established by SC Res. 827 (1993), 25 May 1993, UN Doc. S/RES/827 (1993); ICTR, established by SC Res. 955 (1994), adopted on 8 November 1994, UN Doc. S/RES/955 (1994).

[38] Grave breaches and other serious violations of IHL may carry individual responsibility, but note that not *all* violations of IHL are criminal: see Chapter 4, para. 4A.1.1.2.

A long-established and intricate body of treaty law regulates the conduct of international conflicts and the protection of persons and property therein, such as the Hague Regulations of 1907,[39] the four Geneva Conventions of 1949, the First Additional Protocol thereto of 1977 and the Hague Convention on Cultural Property of 1954.[40] To bind states parties to the conflict as treaty law,[41] the particular treaties must have been ratified or acceded to by those parties.[42] The US, UK and Afghanistan are all party to the four Geneva Conventions, which were therefore binding on those states in the international armed conflict in Afghanistan as treaty law, though few other relevant treaties have been accepted by all parties.[43] While historically certain IHL treaty provisions only applied as treaty law if all parties to the conflict were parties to the treaty,[44] contemporary IHL rejects such a principle. The Geneva Conventions for example are binding

[39] Hague Regulations Respecting the Laws and Customs of War on Land, annex to the Convention (IV) Respecting the Laws and Customs of War on Land (The Hague, 18 October 1907), 3 *Martens Nouveau Recueil* (Series 3) 461, in force 26 January 1910 (hereinafter 'Hague Regulations 1907').

[40] IHL instruments relating to conduct of hostilities and to the protection of persons caught up in armed conflict, are often broadly referred to as 'Hague' and 'Geneva' law respectively. By contrast, non-international armed conflicts are regulated by a fairly skeletal body of treaty law. Historically, little attention was focused on non-international conflict. Prior to 1949, IHL treaties basically regulated international, not civil, wars. The normative gap was narrowed by common Article 3 to the Geneva Conventions and AP II.

[41] The nature and number of parties to a conflict is a question of fact that may change over time. For the purposes of the conflict in Afghanistan, the position of Afghanistan, the US and UK is considered.

[42] See the Vienna Convention on the Law of Treaties, 23 May 1969, 1155 UNTS 33, in force 27 January 1980. According to Article 18, VCLT, States are also required not to defeat the object and purpose of a treaty that they have signed but not yet ratified.

[43] The following have been ratified by Afghanistan, the US and UK: Protocol for the Prohibition of the Use of Asphyxiating, Poisonous or Other Gases, and of Bacteriological Methods of Warfare, Geneva, 17 June 1925, 94 LNTS 65, in force 8 February 1928 (ratified by Afghanistan 9 December 1986, UK 9 April 1930 and US 10 April 1975); Procès-verbal relating to the Rules of Submarine Warfare set forth in Part IV of the Treaty of London of 22 April 1930, London, 6 November 1936, 173 LNTS 353, in force 6 November 1936 (ratified by Afghanistan 25 May 1937, UK and US 6 November 1936); Geneva Conventions of 12 August 1949 (ratified by Afghanistan 26 September 1956, UK 23 September 1957 and US 2 August 1955); Convention on the Prohibition of the Development, Production and Stockpiling of Bacteriological (Biological) and Toxin Weapons and on their Destruction, Convention on the Prohibition of the Development, Production and, Stockpiling of Bacteriological (Biological) and Toxin Weapons and on Their Destruction, Washington, London, Moscow, 10 April 1972, 1015 UNTS 163, in force 26 March 1975 (hereinafter 'Biological Weapons Convention'), (ratified by Afghanistan 26 March 1975, UK and US 26 March 1975).

[44] This is true of 'Hague law' treaties governing 'conduct of hostilities' but not of the Geneva Conventions or Additional Protocols for example and is, at this stage, essentially of historical interest only.

on states parties engaged in armed conflicts, irrespective of whether other parties to the conflict are party to the Conventions. This reflects the fact that the core of IHL treaty provisions, by their nature, enshrine obligations *erga omnes* (i.e. obligations owed to all states, not merely the other parties to the treaty)[45] and that the content of many key provisions of treaties such as the Geneva Conventions is also customary law, discussed below.

Moreover, where a treaty *is* applicable, its binding nature on parties to the conflict is not affected by the fact that an adversary may violate the obligations contained therein.[46] Non-observance of particular binding rules by one party does not justify violations by another.[47] In this vein, the ICTY has emphasised that crimes committed by an adversary can never justify the perpetration of serious violations of IHL.[48]

As regards non-international armed conflicts, a far more limited body of treaty law applies, the core provisions of which are Common Article 3 of the Geneva Conventions and Additional Protocol II of 1977, which applies when certain conditions are met.[49] Given the relative dearth of treaty rules, the scope of customary law is of particular significance.[50]

---

[45] See Article 1 of the Geneva Conventions imposing obligations on *all* high contracting parties. See also ICRC Commentary to GC I: 'A State does not proclaim the principle of the protection due to wounded and sick combatants in the hope of saving a certain number of its own nationals. It does so out of respect for the human person as such.' See also *Barcelona Traction, Light and Power Company, Limited (Belgium* v. *Spain), Second Phase, ICJ Reports 1970*, p. 3 at p. 32. Meron, 'Humanization', at 249 and T. Meron, 'The Geneva Conventions as Customary Law', 81 (1987) AJIL 348 at 349.

[46] 'Reciprocity' in the observance of IHL was a traditional principle that has been rejected in modern IHL. See Meron, 'Humanization', at 247–8 and 251.

[47] See Article 51(8) AP I: 'Any violation of these prohibitions shall not release the Parties to the conflict from their legal obligations with respect to the civilian population.' See also Article 60(5) Vienna Convention on the Law of Treaties enshrining the principle that, as regards treaties of a 'humanitarian character', the breach of treaty obligations is no excuse for material breach by other parties.

[48] See the discussion of this principle – *'tu quoque'* – in *Prosecutor* v. *Kupreskic et al.*, Case No. IT-95-16-T, Judgment, 14 January 2000, paras. 765, 515–36 and *Prosecutor* v. *Martic*, Rule 61 Decision, Case No. IT-95-11-I, 8 March 1996, paras. 15–17.

[49] Article 1 AP II sets out the jurisdictional threshold for the application of that treaty, requiring that the organised groups are under responsible command and exercise control over part of the state's territory.

[50] Note also that one of the applicable treaties contains a restrictive 'territorial control' threshold that would not apply in customary law. See Article 1(1) AP II: 'This Protocol . . . shall apply to all armed conflicts . . . which take place in the territory of a High Contracting Party between its armed forces and dissident armed forces or other organized armed groups which, under responsible command, exercise such control over a part of its territory as to enable them to carry out sustained and concerted military operations and to implement this Protocol.'

Among the fundamental principles of IHL that apply, irrespective of the application of treaty law,[51] are the competing considerations of *humanity*[52] and *military necessity*, reflected throughout IHL,[53] from which the particular principles of *distinction, proportionality* and the prohibition on causing *superfluous injury or unnecessary suffering* derive.[54] These principles can be considered customary international law, applicable to all conflicts.[55] The treaties mentioned above remain relevant so far as they reflect or provide evidence of customary law, and the rules contained therein may therefore be binding on states whether or not they are parties to particular treaties. Among the critical treaties that are recognised to fall into this category are the Geneva Conventions of 1949 and the Hague Convention Respecting the Laws and Customs of War on Land of 1907.[56]

---

[51] For a detailed analysis of the content of the customary rules of IHL, see the comprehensive Study on Customary International Humanitarian Law Applicable in Armed Conflicts (forthcoming) prepared by the ICRC Legal Division and over 50 national research teams (hereinafter 'ICRC Study on Customary IHL').

[52] T. Meron, *Human Rights and Humanitarian Norms as Customary Law* (Oxford, 1991), p. 74, notes that 'no self respecting state' would deny the application of the principle of humanity to internal as well as international conflicts. On the 'elementary considerations of humanity' having the force of *jus cogens*, see *Prosecutor v. Delalic et al.*, Case No. IT-96-21-A, Judgment (ICTY Appeals Chamber), 20 February 2001, para. 143.

[53] See S. Oeter, 'Methods and Means of Combat', in Fleck, *Handbook of Humanitarian Law*, at pp. 131 ff.

[54] See Meron, *Human Rights and Humanitarian Norms*, p. 74. See for example Article 35(2), AP I.

[55] As early as 1899, the Martens Clause (Preamble to the Hague Convention Respecting the Laws and Customs on Land) provided that certain basic standards of conduct apply irrespective of the nature of the conflict: ('these provisions, the wording of which has been inspired by the desire to diminish the evils of war so far as military necessities permit, are destined to serve as general rules of conduct for belligerents in their relations with each other and with populations'). Later common Article 3 of the Geneva Conventions enshrined the same 'principles of humanity' are considered customary law applicable to all conflicts. The ICJ in the *Nicaragua* case (*Military and Paramilitary Activities in and against Nicaragua (Nicaragua v. United States of America), Merits, ICJ Reports 1986*, p. 14, para. 218) and the ICTY in the *Tadic* Jurisdiction Decision (para. 102) have found that 'at least with respect to the minimum rules in common Article 3, the character of the conflict is irrelevant'.

[56] The 1993 Report of the UN Secretary General introducing the Statute of the ICTY (Report of the Secretary General pursuant to paragraph 2 of Security Council Resolution 808 (1993), 3 May 1993, UN Doc. S25704), stated: 'The part of conventional international humanitarian law which has beyond doubt become part of international customary law is the law applicable in armed conflict as embodied in: the Geneva Conventions of 12 August 1949 for the Protection of War Victims; the Hague Convention (IV) Respecting the Laws and Customs of War on Land and the Regulations annexed thereto of 18 October 1907; the Convention on the Prevention and Punishment of the Crime of Genocide of 9 December

The bulk of the provisions of the First Additional Protocol to the Geneva Conventions are recognised as forming part of customary law.[57]

As noted above, as a matter of customary law, there are now few outstanding areas in which the content of legal protection in international and non-international conflict is different.[58]

6A.3 Specific aspects of IHL

The following section sketches out certain IHL rules concerning selection of legitimate targets, lawful methods and means of warfare and the humanitarian protection due to persons affected by an armed conflict, which derive from principles of general application. Reference will be made where appropriate to particular treaty provisions, which may either be directly applicable to the conflict as such, or reflect customary law. As discussed in Section B of this chapter, the rules are directly relevant to an assessment of the lawfulness of military action taken in response to the September 11 attacks.

6A.3.1 Targeting: the principle of distinction and proportionality

IHL regulates who and what may be the legitimate target of military action during armed conflict. At the heart of these rules is the principle of distinction, which counters the notion of total war. It requires that civilians and civilian objects must be distinguished from military targets, and operations directed only against the latter. Distinction is the single most important principle for the protection of the victims of armed

---

1948; and the Charter of the International Military Tribunal of 8 August 1945.' The report was unanimously approved by SC Res. 827 (1993), above, note 38.

[57] The UK is party to AP I, but Afghanistan and the US are not, although the US signed it on 12 December 1977. However, as the ICRC notes, 'it is not disputed that most of [AP I's] norms on the conduct of hostilities also reflect customary international law.' The ICTY has noted that: 'While both Protocols have not yet achieved the near universal participation enjoyed by the Geneva Conventions, it is not controversial that major parts of both Protocols reflect customary law' (*Prosecutor* v. *Kordic and Cerkez*, IT-95-14/2-PT, Decision on the Joint Defence Motion to Dismiss the Amended Indictment, 2 March 1999, para. 30).

[58] See Fleck, 'Non-International Armed Conflict'. The rules on POW status, e.g., do not apply in non-international armed conflict. Therefore insurgents, if captured, can be prosecuted for fighting against the state whereas POWs cannot. Other protections are, however, due to both, including humane treatment, safeguards against arbitrary detention and fair trial guarantees. See also Chapter 8. For a description of the general approach of the ICTY to the issue, see Boelaert-Suominen, 'Yugoslavia Tribunal'.

conflict, and is a principle of customary law applicable to all types of armed conflict.[59]

As explained below, attacks are unlawful if they are: (a) directed specifically against civilians or civilian objects; (b) launched indiscriminately without distinction between civilians and military targets or (c) directed at military objectives, but anticipated to cause damage to civilians or civilian objects that is disproportionate to the military advantage anticipated at the time of launching the attack.[60] The law imposes certain positive obligations on those responsible for attacks to ensure that these rules are given meaningful effect.

6A.3.1.1 Directing attacks against protected persons or property

Only 'military objectives' may be the legitimate object of attack. As discussed below, military objectives consist of, among others, 'combatants,' generally understood as members of the armed forces that take part in hostilities, and objects which make a contribution to the adversary's military capability, the destruction of which would give rise to definite military advantage.[61]

(a) Combatants In international armed conflict, members of the armed forces of an adversary are the most obvious military objective.[62] 'Combatants' include not only regular troops but may also comprise, under certain conditions, irregular groups that fight alongside them. The lethal targeting of those who fight with the adversary's forces, which may amount to murder if there is no armed conflict, is considered lawful in time of conflict under IHL. If a party could incapacitate and capture, instead of killing, a combatant, with no added military cost, the question may arise as to whether this should be done, consistent with the principles of humanity and military necessity. While this may be an area for legal development, at present there is no clear prescription to this effect in IHL.

However, as soon as combatants are *hors de combat* (not engaged in military action), voluntarily or involuntarily, for example through injury,

---

[59] The 'ICRC Study on Customary IHL' confirms that the law set out below on military objectives, indiscriminate attacks, proportionality and precautions in attack are customary law for all types of armed conflict: see 'ICRC Report on IHL and Contemporary Armed Conflicts', p. 16. See also, in general, Oeter, 'Methods and Means', p. 105.

[60] See Article 51(2) and (4) AP I and Article 13 AP II.

[61] See Article 52(2) of Protocol I and Article 13 of Protocol II.

[62] Article 4A(1), (2), (3) and (6) of the Third (Prisoners of War) Geneva Convention and Article 43 of AP I list persons who are members of armed forces or who are otherwise entitled to combatant status and thus have the right to engage in hostilities.

illness, surrender or capture, they are no longer military objectives but become entitled to the protection of the law. Hence it is unlawful to kill a person who has been wounded, has surrendered or been captured, or otherwise no longer participating in the conflict.[63] In these circumstances killing and taking prisoner are not lawful interchangeable alternatives.

While members of the armed forces are generally lawful targets, certain persons accompanying the armed forces, such as medical and religious personnel, are not. Also, it is generally not legitimate to attack members of government: politicians, and even armed personnel such as the police, may only be legitimately targeted under IHL where they are part of the armed forces of the state. This is a question of fact, dependent on the political–military role of individuals in position of authority within the particular regime.

(b) Civilian immunity   The cardinal rule of humanitarian law is that civilians must not be the object of attack. While this follows logically from the afore-mentioned rule that only military objectives may be targeted, explicit provision for civilians appears throughout humanitarian law.[64] Civilian immunity from attack is lost only where the person takes an active and direct part in hostilities.[65] Direct participation should be narrowly construed, and does not include for example support for, or affiliation to, the adversary.[66]

All persons who are neither combatants nor take a direct part in hostilities should be protected from attack as civilians. Critically, if any doubt arises as to whether someone is a combatant or a civilian, he or she must be presumed a civilian.[67] The fact that combatants are among the civilian population does not necessarily deprive the population of its civilian character, and the legitimacy of targeting a 'mixed' group would depend on the question of proportionality, discussed later in this

---

[63] Note that for civilians the test is whether they are taking a 'direct part in hostilities', a stricter test than for combatants.

[64] See for example, Article 51(2) AP I and Article 13(2) AP II: '[T]he civilian population as such, as well as individual civilians, shall not be the object of attack.'

[65] Article 51(3) of AP I refers to persons who 'take a direct part in hostilities'. Civilians and the civilian population are defined in Article 50 AP I as: '1. A civilian is any person who does not belong to one of the categories of persons referred to in Article 4(A)(1)(2)(3) and (6) of the Third Convention and in Article 43 of this Protocol.' The civilian population may become a legitimate objective where they take up arms and fight alongside armed forces.

[66] ICRC, 'Developments', notes that the precise content of the term may be ripe for clarification.

[67] As noted in Article 50 AP I: 'In case of doubt whether a person is a civilian, that person shall be considered a civilian.'

section.[68] IHL also contains rules specifically prohibiting 'inflicting terror on the civilian population'.[69]

As discussed below, attacks against the civilian population are prohibited not only where they are deliberately directed against the civilian population as such, but also where they are 'indiscriminate' or 'disproportionate'.[70] There is no exception to this prohibition, and the notion that it is limited by the principle of military necessity has been rejected.[71]

(c) Objects   As regards objects that may be targeted, the most widely accepted definition is that in Article 52 of Additional Protocol I, which states:

> In so far as objects are concerned, military objectives are limited to those objects which by their nature, location, purpose or use make *an effective contribution to military action* and whose total or partial destruction, capture or neutralisation, in the circumstances ruling at the time, *offers a definite military advantage.*[72]

This definition has been described as almost certainly embodying customary law.[73]

The basic rule is that attacks against civilian objects are prohibited.[74]

The ICTY considers the prohibition on attacking 'civilian objects' or

---

[68] 'The presence within the civilian population of individuals who do not come within the definition of civilians does not deprive the population of its civilian character.' AP I, Article 50(3).

[69] Article 51 AP I prohibits '[a]cts or threats of violence the primary purpose of which is to spread terror among the civilian population'. See also *Prosecutor* v. *Galić*, Case No. IT-98-29-T, Judgment, 5 December 2003.

[70] While this section focuses on only military attacks directed against civilians as such, many other acts against civilians are prohibited by IHL, expressly or implicitly: see 'Humanitarian Protections'. Note that other forms of attack against the civilian population may also be violations, and indeed war crimes, such as inflicting terror on the civilian population (Articles 51(2) AP I and 13(2) AP II), which is being prosecuted for the first time before the ICTY in the *Galić* case, note 71 above, or crimes of sexual violence (Article 8, ICC Statute, prosecuted in, *inter alia*, *Prosecutor* v. *Kunarac, Kovac and Vukovic*, Cases No. IT-96-23 and IT-96-23/1, 22 February 2001).

[71] The Trial Chamber of the ICTY in *Galić*, above, expressly rejected the suggestion that the rule can be derogated from by invoking military necessity.

[72] Article 51(2) AP I (emphasis added).

[73] See Meron, *Human Rights and Humanitarian Norms*, pp. 64–5. The author notes that the Article 52 definition has been incorporated into the US military manual and the Convention on Prohibitions or Restrictions on the Use of Certain Conventional Weapons (Convention on Prohibitions or Restrictions on the Use of Certain Conventional Weapons which may be deemed to be Excessively Injurious or to have Indiscriminate Effects, Geneva, 10 October 1980, 1342 UNTS 7, in force 2 December 1983).

[74] Article 52 AP I: 'General protection of civilian objects: Civilian objects shall not be the object of attack or of reprisals. Civilian objects are all objects which are not military

'dwellings and other installations that are used only by civilian populations' part of customary law, applicable to all conflicts.[75] In addition to this general rule, attacks against certain specific categories of objects, such as buildings dedicated to religion, charity, education, the arts and sciences, historic monuments[76] and cultural property[77] are specifically prohibited by particular international instruments.

Some of the most difficult issues of targeting arise in relation to objects with dual military and civilian uses, such as bridges, roads, electric-power installations or communications networks. The lawfulness of targeting television networks, for example, which arose during the NATO bombing of the former Yugoslavia (and again in Afghanistan),[78] has been questioned by several commentators,[79] and was subject to a legal challenge before the European Court of Human Rights.[80] The question of fact is whether the target makes an effective contribution to military action and its destruction offers direct military advantage. International humanitarian law provides that 'in case of doubt whether an object which is normally dedicated to civilian purposes, such as a place of worship, a house or other

objectives as defined in paragraph 2.' On AP I rules governing conduct of hostilities as custom, see 'ICRC Report on IHL and Contemporary Armed Conflicts', p. 8.

[75] *Tadić* Jurisdiction Decision, paras. 110–11 and the Trial Chamber's decision of 2 March 1999 on the joint defence motion to dismiss the amended indictment in *Prosecutor* v. *Kordić and Cerkez*, above, note 59, para. 31: 'It is indisputable that the general prohibition of attacks against the civilian population and the prohibition of indiscriminate attacks or *attacks on civilian objects* are generally accepted obligations. As a consequence, there is no possible doubt as to the customary status of these specific provisions as they reflect core principles of humanitarian law that can be considered as applying to all armed conflicts, whether intended to apply to international or internal armed conflicts.'

[76] Article 56, 1907 Hague Regulations: 'The property . . . of institutions dedicated to religion, charity and education, the arts and sciences, even when State property, shall be treated as private property. All seizure of, destruction or willful damage done to institutions of this character, historic monuments, works of art and science, is forbidden, and should be made the subject of legal proceedings.'

[77] Hague Convention for the Protection of Cultural Property in the Event of Armed Conflict 1954, Articles 53 and 85. See Article 1 (definition) and Article 4. See also Article 53, AP I and Article 16, AP II. The obligation to respect cultural property 'may be waived only in cases where military necessity imperatively requires such a waiver' (Article 4(2)).

[78] See para. 6B.2.1, below.

[79] Meron, 'Humanization', at 276; see also M. Cottier, 'Did NATO Forces Commit War Crimes during the Kosovo Conflict? Reflections on the Prosecutor's Report of 13 June 2000', in H. Fischer, C. Kreß and S. R. Lüder (eds.), *International and National Prosecution of Crimes under International Law: Current Developments* (Berlin, 2001), p. 505.

[80] In *Banković* v. *Belgium*, before the European Court of Human Rights, the applicants relied on invoking violations of IHL arguments within a human rights framework. The question of targeting was not addressed by the Court, as it found that it lacked jurisdiction in such a case (see *Banković and others* v. *Belgium and 16 other contracting States* (Appl. No. 52207/99), Admissibility Decision, 12 December 2001, *Reports 2001-XII* (hereinafter '*Banković*')). This issue is discussed in the following chapter.

dwelling or a school, is being used to make an effective contribution to military action, it shall be presumed not to be so used'.[81]

Finally, while it is a serious violation of humanitarian law to deliberately put military objectives in the vicinity of civilians, doing so does not necessarily justify an attack from the adversary. If destruction of a target offers direct military advantage, that advantage must outweigh any incidental loss to civilians, all feasible steps having been taken to minimise civilian losses.[82] The lawfulness of an attack in an area where there is both a legitimate target and persons or objects that are immune from attack depends on questions of proportionality, as discussed below.

6A.3.1.2 Indiscriminate attacks and those causing disproportionate civilian loss

In addition to the rule that attacks must not be specifically directed against civilians and civilian objects is the rule that attacks must not be indiscriminate, that is, directed against military and civilian objectives without distinction.[83] The prohibition on indiscriminate attacks is a fundamental aspect of the customary principle of distinction, applicable in all conflicts.[84]

Closely linked to the principle of distinction is the 'proportionality' rule, which requires that those directing attacks against military objectives must ensure that civilian losses are not disproportionate to the direct and concrete military advantage anticipated to result from the attack.[85] Proportionality is generally accepted as a norm of customary international law.[86]

---

[81] Article 52(3), AP I.

[82] See the discussion of proportionality and precautionary measures that must be taken by commanders, including the duty to minimise civilian loss and warn civilians of impending attacks, in this part, below.

[83] Article 51 AP I refers to five forms of indiscriminate attacks, all of which are prohibited: those which *are not* directed at a specific military objective (para. 4(a)), those which employ a method or means of combat which *cannot be directed* at a specific military objective (para. 4(b)), those which employ a method or means of combat the *effects of which cannot be limited* (para. 4(c)), an *area attack* treating separate and distinct military objectives in an area containing a concentration of civilians as a single military objective (para. 5(a)), and an attack which may be expected to cause incidental civilian casualties or civilian property damage *disproportionate* to the expected military advantage. Different classifications of the same principles appear in different contexts.

[84] *Tadić* Jurisdiction Decision, para. 127; *Prosecutor* v. *Kordić and Cerkez*, Decision on the Joint Defence Motion to Dismiss the Amended Indictment, 2 March 1999, above, para. 31.

[85] Article 51(5) AP I.

[86] See J. Gardam, 'Proportionality and Force in International Law', 87 (1993) AJIL 391; W.J. Fenrick, 'Attacking the Enemy Civilian as a Punishable Offence', 7 (1997) *Duke Journal of*

There is no precise formula for this proportionality calculus, and the relative weight to be attached to civilian and military losses will depend on all the circumstances.[87] However, a few specific points deserve emphasis. First, the military advantage anticipated must be 'direct and concrete'.[88] It cannot be long-term or speculative. The assessment of military advantage against potential loss must be made in relation to a *particular* military operation, not in relation to a battle, still less to a conflict as a whole.[89] Such an evaluation cannot be made after the fact, when the number of civilian and military casualties can be compared, but based on the information available at the relevant time and in the context of all the prevailing circumstances.

Finally, a mistaken evaluation of proportionality, just like a mistaken identification of a target, is not necessarily unlawful. However, nor is ignorance as to the nature of the target, its military contribution or the extent of civilian losses *per se* an excuse. IHL lays down certain duties on those responsible for attacks that safeguard the principles of distinction and proportionality; if civilian losses result from a situation where these duties have not been observed, then a violation of IHL has occurred (and a crime may also have been committed by the person responsible for ordering the attack as discussed at Chapter 4, Section B).

6A.3.1.3 Necessary precautions in attack

Complicated issues of targeting may arise, for example in respect of defended cities with 'dual use' facilities and close intermingling of civilian and military elements. Likewise, rural terrain and guerrilla tactics may

---

Comparative and International Law 539 at 545. The author notes that, while there is debate on the customary nature of the proportionality rule, 'it is a logically necessary part of any decision making process which attempts to reconcile humanitarian imperatives and military requirements during armed conflict'. See also W.H. Parks, 'Air War and the Law of War', 32 (1990) *Air Force Law Review* 1.

[87] There has been relatively little experience in the prosecution of 'conduct of hostilities' crimes. See, generally, the decision of the ICTY in *Prosecutor* v. *Blaskic*, Case No. IT 95-14-T, Judgment, 3 March 2000, and the comment by W. J. Fenrick, 'A First Attempt to Adjudicate Conduct of Hostilities Offences: Comments on Aspects of the ICTY Trial Decision in *Prosecutor* v. *Tihomir Blaskic*', 13 (2000) LJIL 931.

[88] Article 57(2) AP I.

[89] See L. Doswald-Beck, 'The Value of the 1977 Geneva Protocols for the Protection of Civilians', in M.A. Meyer (ed.), *Armed Conflict and the New Law. Aspects of the 1977 Geneva Protocols and the 1981 Weapons Convention* (London, 1989), pp. 137 ff. Note, however, that some states take a broader view of the proportionality calculus, as reflected in the ICC Statute's reference to proportionality as involving an assessment of the 'overall military advantage anticipated' (Article 8(2)(b)(iv)).

make target identification difficult. However, core principles of international humanitarian law require that every responsible military commander must take certain feasible precautions to ensure the lawfulness of a military attack.[90]

These include the commander's duty to verify the nature of the target. It is no excuse that a commander or other person who plans or decides upon an attack does not have the information available as to the true nature of a target, as IHL imposes a duty to inquire. If a commander cannot, upon inquiry, obtain the necessary information, he or she cannot attack assuming the target to be legitimate. On the contrary, if in doubt, the assumption must be that the target is protected.[91]

While an attacking side will understandably want to protect its forces, this does not take priority over precautions to protect civilians in the planning and execution of an attack, whose protection IHL clearly emphasises.[92]

Moreover, even if a target is identified and is legitimate (being a military objective that satisfies the proportionality rule), commanders must take all feasible steps to *minimise* the damage to civilian life and objects resulting from the military action. These include giving warnings of attacks that may affect the civilian population[93] and, where there is a choice of targets, choosing those least injurious to civilian life or objects.[94]

---

[90] Article 57 AP I.

[91] This principle is reflected in Article 50(1) AP I, which states that 'in case of doubt whether a person is a civilian, that person shall be considered to be a civilian'. See also the ICTY decision in *Blaskić* (above, note 87). As noted above, a similar principle is reflected in Article 50 in respect of objects.

[92] See ICRC Report on IHL and Contemporary Armed Conflicts, p. 13.

[93] Article 57(2)(c) AP I. See Meron, *Human Rights and Humanitarian Norms*, p. 65, noting that an expert study on behalf of the Joint Chiefs of Staff described this duty as customary law. Note, however that the failure to give a warning during the NATO Kosovo campaign is the subject of the ECHR claim in the *Banković* case.

[94] See Article 57(2) AP I: '(a) Those who plan or decide upon an attack shall: (i) Do everything feasible to verify that the objectives to be attacked are neither civilians nor civilian objects and are not subject to special protection but are military objectives within the meaning of paragraph 2 of Article 52 and that it is not prohibited by the provisions of this Protocol to attack them; (ii) Take all feasible precautions in the choice of means and methods of attack with a view to avoiding, and in any event to minimizing, incidental loss of civilian life, injury to civilians and damage to civilian objects; (iii) Refrain from deciding to launch any attack which may be expected to cause incidental loss of civilian life, injury to civilians, damage to civilian objects, or a combination thereof, which would be excessive in relation to the concrete and direct military advantage anticipated; (b) An attack shall be cancelled or suspended if it becomes apparent that the objective is not a military one or is subject to special protection or that the attack may be expected to cause incidental loss of civilian life, injury to civilians, damage to civilian objects, or a combination thereof, which would

6A.3.2 Methods and means of warfare: unnecessary suffering

The prohibition on waging war in a manner that causes unnecessary suffering and superfluous injury is generally accepted as part of customary international law. The expression 'unnecessary suffering and superfluous injury' is used in a number of legal instruments, yet nowhere is it defined.[95] The concept is, however, clearly linked to the customary principle that all suffering caused in conflict should be pursuant, and proportionate, to military necessity. As such, the ICJ has described causing 'unnecessary suffering to combatants' as causing 'harm greater than that unavoidable to achieve legitimate military objectives'.[96]

While an evaluation of what amounts to unnecessary suffering is likely to be case and context specific, certain methods and means of warfare are considered by definition to cause unnecessary suffering. For example, attacks directed against civilians are *per se* unnecessary and prohibited. Moreover, in addition to the specific treaty provisions that regulate the use of particular weapons,[97] certain weapons are deemed by their nature to cause 'unnecessary suffering' and therefore to be prohibited under customary law.

The customary law prohibition on weapons causing unnecessary suffering covers those that are either (a) cruel or excessive in the nature and degree of suffering they cause or (b) incapable of distinguishing combatant from civilian.[98] Among the first group are weapons considered so *inherently abhorrent* that they are banned absolutely, even when directed against combatants or other lawful targets, such as blinding laser weapons

---

be excessive in relation to the concrete and direct military advantage anticipated; (c) Effective advance warning shall be given of attacks which may affect the civilian population, unless circumstances do not permit.' See also Article 50(7) AP I.

[95] See Article 23(e) 1907 Hague Regulations; Article 35 AP I and the CCW Convention 1980.

[96] *Nuclear Weapons* Advisory Opinion, para. 78. On the status of the principle as 'established custom', see Oeter, 'Methods and Means' at p. 401.

[97] See Convention on the Prohibition of the Use, Stockpiling, Production and Transfer of Anti-Personnel Mines and on their Destruction, Oslo, 18 September 1997, 2056 UNTS 577, in force 1 March 1999 (hereinafter 'Landmines Convention'); Article 23(e) 1907 Hague Regulations; Article 35 AP I; Convention on the Prohibition of the Development, Production and Stockpiling of Bacteriological (Biological) and Toxin Weapons (note 44, above), and Convention on the Prohibition of the Development, Production, Stockpiling and Use of Chemical Weapons and on Their Destruction, Paris, 13 January 1993, in force 29 April 1997 (hereinafter 'Chemical Weapons Convention').

[98] In its *Nuclear Weapons* Advisory Opinion, the ICJ held: 'States must never make civilians the object of attack and consequently never use weapons that are incapable of distinguishing between civilian and military targets . . . States do not have unlimited freedom of choice of means in the weapons they use' (para. 78).

or poisons.[99] The second group covers weapons that are banned due to their inability to distinguish between civilian and soldier and hence *inherently indiscriminate* by nature, which arguably includes anti-personnel landmines.[100]

Considerable controversy has centred around whether particular weapons systems fall within this definition and are prohibited by general international law. For example, while the issues remain unsettled as a matter of law, serious questions have been raised as to the lawfulness of the use of cluster bombs.[101] This is for two main reasons. First, because they are designed to disperse submunitions over a wide area and cannot be confined within the parameters of a military target.[102] Second, due to a high reported initial failure rate – estimated at 7 per cent on cluster bombs employed by the US – a significant amount of bomblets do not detonate

[99] On this basis, the use of certain conventional weapons is limited by the CCW Convention, which has four Protocols prohibiting the use of specific conventional weapons. See Protocol I to the CCW Convention, on Non-Detectable Fragments, Geneva, 10 October 1980, in force 2 December 1983 (prohibiting the use of weapons the primary effect of which is to injure by fragments not detectable in the human body by X-rays); Protocol II to the CCW Convention, on Prohibitions or Restrictions on the Use of Mines, Booby Traps and Other Devices, Geneva, 10 October 1980, amended on 3 May 1996, in force 3 December 1998; Protocol III to the CCW Convention, on Prohibitions or Restrictions on the Use of Incendiary Weapons, Geneva, 10 October 1980, in force 2 December 1983; Protocol IV to the CCW Convention, on Blinding Laser Weapons, Geneva, 13 October 1995, in force 30 July 1998. Other international instruments prohibit the use of 'projectiles the object of which is the diffusion of asphyxiating or deleterious gases' (see Second Hague Declaration 1899 (Declaration (IV, 2) concerning asphyxiating gases, The Hague, 29 July 1899, 26 *Marten Nouveau Recueil* (Series 2) 1002, in force 4 September 1900) and asphyxiating, poisonous or other gases (see Article 23(a) of the 1907 Hague Regulations and the Geneva Protocol of 1925 (Protocol for the Prohibition of the Use of Asphyxiating, Poisonous or Other Gases, and of Bacteriological Methods of Warfare, Geneva, 17 June 1925, 94 LNTS 65, in force 8 February 1928)). See ICJ, *Nuclear Weapons* Advisory Opinion, para. 54.

[100] Anti-personnel landmines have often been cited as violative of these principles, due to their inability to distinguish civilian from military limbs. In addition this prohibition is now the subject of the 1997 Landmines Convention. Landmines, booby-traps, and other devices were also included in the 1980 Convention on the Use of Certain Conventional Weapons Which May be Deemed to be Excessively Injurious or to Have Indiscriminate Effects (Protocol II).

[101] The inherent lawfulness of cluster bombs has not been adjudicated. See ICTY decision in the preliminary hearing in the case of *Prosecutor v. Martić*, Case No. IT-95-11-R61, Review of the Indictment, 8 March 1996, discussed below, note 107. See also 'Ticking Time Bombs: NATO's Use of Cluster Munitions in Yugoslavia', Human Rights Watch Report, June 1999 and 'Cluster Bomblets Litter Afghanistan', Human Rights Watch Press Release, 16 November 2001 (both available at http://www.hrw.org).

[102] See Section 6B.2.2 and, e.g., 'Strange Victory: A Critical Appraisal of Operation Enduring Freedom and the Afghanistan War', n. 3, Project on Defense Alternatives, Research Monograph No. 6, 30 January 2002, available at http://www.comw.org/pda.

immediately, lying dormant until disturbed at some future point.[103] The unpredictability of the person or object that will ultimately detonate the bomblets is such that the impact of these bomblets may be considered indiscriminate. In these circumstances, they effectively act as landmines, which have been subject to a widely ratified comprehensive treaty prohibition[104] and which are considered a violation of the prohibition on the use of indiscriminate weapons.[105]

The legal status of cluster bombs has not been adjudicated upon and it remains doubtful that as a matter of law they could be characterised as inherently indiscriminate, and thus prohibited *per se*. However, the compatibility of using such weapons with the principles of IHL has been brought into question increasingly, by human rights groups,[106] the ICTY[107] and earlier US practice in other contexts.[108] It is likely that, at a minimum, the decision to use such bombs in certain contexts, such as within the vicinity of populated areas, would amount to an

---

[103] See 'Long After the Air Raids, Bomblets Bring More Death', *The Guardian*, 28 January 2002.

[104] Convention on the Prohibition of the Use, Stockpiling, Production and Transfer of Anti-Personnel Mines and on their Destruction, Oslo, 18 September 1997, 2056 UNTS, in force 1 March 1999. As of 23 October 2003, 141 States are party to the Landmines Convention (source: http://www.icbl.org/ratification).

[105] See also Human Rights Watch, 'International Humanitarian Law Issues'.

[106] See reports in the context of Afghanistan, above. For earlier reports, see, e.g., Human Rights Watch, 'Ticking Time Bombs: NATO's Use of Cluster Munitions in Yugoslavia', June 1999 at http://www.hrw.org/reports/1999/nato2/; Human Rights Watch, 'Cluster Bomblets'.

[107] The ICTY in the preliminary hearing in the case of *Prosecutor* v. *Martić*, IT-95-11-R61, Review of the Indictment, 8 March 1996, indicated that the use of cluster bombs in the circumstances of that case may provide the basis for an indiscriminate attack charge. In its report on the NATO bombing, the Prosecutor's office of the ICTY did not find that the use of cluster bombs *per se* provided sufficient basis for prosecution of individuals, while acknowledging the controversy around the lawfulness of these weapons and 'clear trend' towards their prohibition. See 'Final Report by the Committee Established to Review the NATO Bombing Campaign Against the Federal Republic of Yugoslavia', above, note 12 and Prosecutor's Report on the NATO Bombing Campaign (*ibid.*).

[108] Reportedly during the 1995 Operation Deliberate Force in Bosnia, air combat commander Major-General Michael Ryan prohibited the use of cluster bombs, in recognition of the inherent danger to civilians. A US Air-Force-sponsored study concluded at the time noted that the 'problem was that the fragmentation pattern was too large to sufficiently limit collateral damage and there was also the further problem of potential unexploded ordnance'. See Human Rights Watch, 'International Humanitarian Law Issues' and 'Cluster Bomblets'. This may point to increased acknowledgement in state practice that the lawfulness of these weapons is at least questionable. It certainly reflects a pragmatic policy of limiting, if not avoiding, the use of what are increasingly controversial weapons.

indiscriminate attack, or one that fails to take all feasible measures to limit civilian casualties, in violation of the rules governing targeting in IHL.

Other weapons systems may also be deemed to be inherently indiscriminate. In one case, the ICTY appears to have regarded home-made mortars as indiscriminate weapons.[109] While nuclear weapons have been found not to be *per se* unlawful, the International Court of Justice has found that their use would be 'scarcely reconcilable' with the principles of IHL. It ruled that:

> It follows from the above-mentioned requirements that the threat or use of nuclear weapons would generally be contrary to the rules of international law applicable in armed conflict, and in particular the principles and rules of humanitarian law. However, in view of the current state of international law, and of the elements of fact at its disposal, the Court cannot conclude definitively whether the threat or use of nuclear weapons would be lawful or unlawful in an extreme circumstance of self-defence, in which the very survival of a State would be at stake.[110]

6A.3.3 Humanitarian protections

IHL governs not only the conduct of hostilities on the battlefield, addressed above, but also affords protection to persons in the hands of 'the enemy', namely prisoners of war, the sick and wounded, and civilians who find themselves in territory controlled by opposing forces. The key provisions of the Geneva Conventions provide that such persons are considered 'protected' from the moment when they fall into the hands of the adverse party.

---

[109] In the *Blaskić* case (above, note 89, paras. 501 and 512), the use of homemade mortars provided the basis for a conviction for an indiscriminate attack charge. The judgment (para. 512) states: 'The Trial Chamber inferred from the arms used that the perpetrators of the attack had wanted to affect Muslim civilians. The "baby-bombs" are indeed "home-made mortars" which are difficult to guide accurately. Since their trajectory is "irregular" and non-linear, they are likely to hit non-military targets.'

[110] *Nuclear Weapons* Advisory Opinion, para. 95, suggesting that weapons may not be *per se* unlawful, but their *use* may be: 'Thus, methods and means of warfare, which preclude any distinction between civilian and military targets, or which would result in unnecessary suffering to combatants, are prohibited. In view of the unique characteristics of nuclear weapons . . . the use of such weapons in fact seems scarcely reconcilable with respect for such requirements. Nevertheless, the Court considers that it does not have sufficient elements to enable it to conclude with certainty that the use of nuclear weapons would necessarily be at variance with the principles and rules of law applicable in armed conflict in any circumstance.'

All persons taking no active part, or no longer taking part, in hostilities are entitled to protection under IHL; protections are due both to those who have never taken part in hostilities and to those who once did but are now *hors de combat*. Common Article 3 to the Geneva Conventions, which is customary international law applicable in all situations, provides that such persons must be treated humanely, without discrimination, and specifically prohibits violence to life and person, including cruel treatment, hostage-taking, outrages upon personal dignity and carrying out of sentencing and executions without certain judicial guarantees.[111] Beyond Article 3, more detailed provisions are contained elsewhere in the Geneva Conventions and Protocols. Many of these provisions may be considered to reflect and give expression to fundamental principles of IHL, in particular the principle of humanity, and as such reflect customary law.

6A.3.3.1 Civilians

The duty to protect the civilian population is at the heart of IHL. Rules regarding targeting of civilians are described above. As noted, for as long as civilians take up arms and participate directly in hostilities they may lose their immunity from attack. They may also be prosecuted under domestic laws for engaging in conflict.[112] However all civilians, whether or not they took up arms, are entitled to the humanitarian protections set out in Common Article 3,[113] the Fourth Geneva Convention (which applies to civilians that 'find themselves . . . in the hands of a Party to the Conflict or Occupying Power[114] of which they are not nationals')[115] and Additional Protocol I.

---

[111] Common Article 3 provides: 'To this end the following acts are and shall remain prohibited at any time and in any place whatsoever, with respect to the above-mentioned person: violence to life and person, in particular murder of all kinds, mutilation, cruel treatment and torture; taking of hostages; outrages upon personal dignity, in particular humiliating and degrading treatment; the passing of sentences and the carrying out of executions without previous judgment pronounced by a regularly constituted court affording all the judicial guarantees which are recognized as indispensable by civilized peoples.'

[112] It is not a violation of IHL or a war crime to engage in conflict but nor does IHL offer protection from prosecution under domestic law, other than for POWs.

[113] Common Article 3 provides humanitarian protection to all persons who do not, or no longer, take active part in hostilities.

[114] Specific obligations relating to Occupying Powers are addressed at 'Occupiers' Obligations' below.

[115] See Article 4 GC IV and *Tadic* Jurisdiction Decision, below.

The power into whose hands protected persons fall is obliged to refrain from violating their rights, but also to take necessary proactive steps to ensure their protection.[116] IHL makes explicit reference to a range of human rights protections,[117] for example 'respect for persons, honour, family rights, their religious convictions and their manners and customs',[118] procedural rights relating to detention and fair trial,[119] and property rights,[120] and particular groups, such as children, requiring of particular protection.[121] The duty of humanitarian protection extends also to ensuring that relief operations are conducted for the benefit of civilians, in territory under the control of a party to the conflict.[122]

6A.3.3.2 Prisoners of war and the wounded or sick

Although combatants and other persons taking a direct part in hostilities are military objectives and may be attacked, the moment such persons surrender or are rendered *hors de combat*, they become entitled to protection.[123] That protection is provided for in common Article 3 and the First and Third Geneva Conventions relating to the treatment of the 'wounded, sick and shipwrecked' and 'prisoners of war', respectively,[124] supplemented (for international conflicts) by Additional Protocol I. As

---

[116] Gasser, 'Protection of the Civilian Population', p. 212: 'This means taking all measures required to ensure the safety of civilians, e.g., the establishment of safety zones or evacuation . . . To leave the civilian population to its fate when danger arises from fighting would be a breach of this general duty to protect.' See particular rules applicable in this chapter, para. 6A.3.4.

[117] Article 38 GC IV (medical care, religion, freedom to leave territory, as discussed by Gasser, 'Protection of the Civilian Population', p. 283), and Article 39 GC IV (right to work).

[118] Article 27(1) GC IV.

[119] The provisions of GC IV and AP I in this respect are discussed in relation to the prisoners at Guantanamo Bay in the case study at Chapter 8.

[120] The guarantee of property rights is found principally in Article 46(2) of the 1907 Hague Regulations rather than the Geneva Conventions, although see also Article 53 GC IV.

[121] Article 24 GC IV; see also Article 77 AP I. These rights under IHL are supplemented by those enshrined in human rights law, which applies to all persons within a state's territory and subject to its jurisdiction, irrespective of nationality, as described in the following chapter.

[122] See Article 59 GC IV on the duties of occupying powers to 'allow and facilitate rapid and unimpeded passage' of relief operations and Article 23 GC IV which imposes an obligation on all high contracting parties. Article 70 AP I extended the obligation to accept humanitarian relief to civilians in any territory of a party to the conflict.

[123] This section deals with POWs and Sick and Wounded. The rights of detainees not entitled to any greater protection are discussed in Chapter 8 in relation to the Guantanamo detainees.

[124] GC I and III.

noted above, these Conventions are binding as treaty law, but the key provisions are in any event customary in nature.[125]

As regards 'prisoner of war' status, which arises in international armed conflict, the Third Geneva Convention imposes limits on those who are entitled to such status. These include: (a) members of the armed forces of the opposing party, whether they belong to a recognised government or not, (b) members of militia or volunteer corps, provided they satisfy certain conditions, namely 'being commanded by a person responsible for his subordinates; having a fixed distinctive sign recognisable at a distance; carrying arms openly; conducting their operations in accordance with the laws and customs of war'[126] and (c) *levées en masse*.[127] AP I recognises some loosening of these criteria,[128] and commentators have noted the need for flexibility in order 'to avoid paralysing the legal process as much as possible and, in the case of humanitarian conventions, to enable them to serve their protective goals'.[129]

Among the most basic protections owed to POWs under the Convention is the duty to treat them humanely and protect them from danger,[130] to supply them with food, clothing and medical care[131] and to protect them from public curiosity.[132] The procedural guarantees due to POWs are discussed in detail in relation to the detainees held at Guantanamo Bay at Chapter 8. In brief, they are also entitled to elaborate due process guarantees, including trial by courts that respect the same standards of justice as those respected by the courts that would try the military of the detaining state.[133] They may not be subject to any coercion in order

---

[125] See, e.g., Report of the UN Secretary General introducing the Statute of the ICTY, above, note 59. Note that POW status does not however apply in non-international armed conflict, although, as noted below, the principles may be applied in that context, too.

[126] Article 4(A) GC III.   [127] Article 4(6) GC III.

[128] See Article 44(3) AP I: 'In order to promote the protection of the civilian population from the effects of hostilities, combatants are obliged to distinguish themselves from the civilian population while they are engaged in an attack or in a military operation preparatory to an attack. Recognizing, however, that there are situations in armed conflicts where, owing to the nature of the hostilities an armed combatant cannot so distinguish himself, he shall retain his status as a combatant, provided that, in such situations, he carries his arms openly: (a) During each military engagement, and (b) During such time as he is visible to the adversary while he is engaged in a military deployment preceding the launching of an attack in which he is to participate. Acts which comply with the requirements of this paragraph shall not be considered as perfidious within the meaning of Article 37, paragraph 1 (c).'

[129] T. Meron, 'Classification of Armed Conflict in the Former Yugoslavia: Nicaragua's Fallout', 92 (1998) AJIL 236.

[130] Article 19 GC III.   [131] Article 20 GC III.   [132] Article 13 GC III.

[133] See Article 84 and Articles 99–108 GC III.

to extract information from them and are entitled to disclose only their names and date of birth and rank or position within the armed forces.[134] POWs may not be subject to any punishment or reprisal for action taken by the forces on whose side they fought. A POW should not then be prosecuted by the capturing power for participation in hostilities or for any lawful acts of war, although, consistent with the duty to prosecute war crimes,[135] serious violations of IHL are subject to prosecution. When hostilities have ceased POWs must be repatriated.[136] Other detailed rules regarding, *inter alia*, personal possessions, camps, structure, complaints and correspondence are set out in the Convention.[137]

If any doubt arises as to entitlement to POW status, the matter must be determined by a competent tribunal.[138] Pending such determination, the captured individual shall in any case enjoy the protection guaranteed to prisoners of war by the Third Geneva Convention.[139]

On numerous occasions, states have, as a matter of practice, extended POW status to cover persons not strictly entitled to such status under IHL, as was for example the practice of the United States in Vietnam.[140] This may reflect in part the core humanitarian principles reflected in IHL manifest in the specific provisions of GC III, but also the desire to ensure similar treatment of their own forces if captured.

In any event, if the prisoners in question do not qualify for POW protection under the Geneva Convention itself, to the extent that certain of the provisions of that Convention are derived from the principles of humanity (and military necessity), they may apply as customary law.

---

[134] Article 17 GC III.

[135] The Geneva Conventions expressly oblige states to prosecute grave breaches, applicable in international conflict, while other sources, including the preamble to the ICC Statute, suggest an obligation to prosecute war crimes in all conflicts.

[136] Article 118 GC III provides that 'POWs shall be released and repatriated without delay after the cessation of active hostilities.'

[137] See for example, H. Fischer, 'Protection of Prisoners of War', in Fleck, *Handbook of Humanitarian Law*, pp. 321 ff. and H. McCoubrey, *The Regulation of Armed Conflict* (Dartmouth, 1990), pp. 89–108. These provisions would appear not to fall within the rubric of common Article 3 and would depend on an assessment of the customary status of the particular provisions of GC III.

[138] GC III, Article 5. While the tribunal must be 'independent' it need not necessarily be international, according to existing rules. The inclusion of an international element in that tribunal has been proposed to safeguard its independence. See H.P. Gasser, 'International Humanitarian Law: An Introduction' in H. Haug (ed.), *Humanity for all: the International Red Cross and Red Crescent Movement* (ICRC, Geneva, 1993), p. 22.

[139] Article 5 GC III.

[140] See the description of US practice in Vietnam, in Gasser, 'International Humanitarian Law'.

Moreover, as discussed in more detail in Chapter 8, they are, in any event, entitled to other protections under IHL, under GC IV or, at a minimum, under common Article 3 and Article 75 AP I.[141]

With regard to the sick or wounded, as noted above they may not be subject to attack and, as with all persons *hors de combat*, they are entitled to humane treatment. In addition, there is a positive obligation under the First Geneva Convention to search for and collect the sick and wounded.[142] They must be protected, cared for and their medical needs attended to.[143] To this end, protection must also be afforded to medical personnel and equipment.[144]

The First Geneva Convention concerned only the injured or sick among the armed forces. However, AP I deems it to cover also civilians and others in medical need. Even when AP I is not binding as treaty law,[145] the principle of caring for sick and wounded civilians is consistent with the basic principle of humanity and the general duty to protect civilians, under customary law.[146]

6A.3.4 Occupiers' obligations

IHL enshrines obligations specifically directed towards territory 'placed under the control of the hostile army', or 'occupied', during armed conflict.[147] Where a power is present on the territory in question and exercises *de facto* control of it, it is in occupation. The key criterion is whether the state exercised effective control, which may transcend the formal assumption of responsibility by a new authority. The obligations set out in IHL apply whether or not the occupying power meets with armed resistance.[148]

---

[141] *Tadić* Jurisdiction Decision, para. 102, citing the ICJ in the *Nicaragua case*, para. 218. Once again, human rights provisions, outlined below, apply to persons detained on a state's territory or under its jurisdiction and supplement the specific provisions of IHL. In general, IHL protects persons associated with one party to a conflict who find themselves in the hands of an opposing party. Human rights law by contrast applies to all persons on a state's territory or under its jurisdiction, irrespective of nationality.

[142] Article 15 GC I.

[143] *Ibid.*, and Article 12 GC I; see also Article 10 AP I and Article 7 AP III.

[144] Articles 24 and 25 GC I.   [145] The US and Afghanistan are not parties to AP I.

[146] See W. Rabus, 'Protection of the Wounded, Sick and Shipwrecked', in Fleck, *Handbook of Humanitarian Law*, p. 293 at p. 294, noting that AP I, Articles 6 and 8, extend the definition of the sick to cover those civilians who need medical assistance.

[147] Article 42 1907 Hague Regulations. The ICJ has recently analysed in depth the sources and the extent of the obligation of the occupying powers both under IHL and IHRL in its Advisory Opinion on the *Legal Consequences of the Construction of a Wall in the Occupied Palestinian Territory*, 9 July 2004 (see, in particular, paras. 123–31).

[148] 'ICRC Report on IHL and Contemporary Armed Conflicts', p. 14.

The obligations incumbent on the occupying power are found in the Fourth Geneva Convention, the Hague law that preceded it[149] and the subsequent provisions of AP I; the bulk of these provisions reflect customary law.[150] As with other areas, these obligations supplement those of IHRL, which apply wherever the state exercises its authority or control.[151]

On the one hand, IHL establishes positive obligations on the occupying power to administer the territory, including establishing or maintaining law and order and a functioning legal system,[152] protecting the population from attacks from their troops and private parties.[153] The human rights of the occupied population must be respected[154] and they must not be detained other than where 'imperative reasons of security' so justify, and then subject to procedural safeguards.[155] The power must ensure that the population have adequate food, medical supplies and facilities and, where necessary, that relief operations can be carried out.[156]

On the other hand, IHL limits the authority of the occupying power, reflecting the transitional nature of occupation, to prevent it from benefiting from the occupation at the expense of the local population, or from making far-reaching or unnecessary changes in the political structure or legal system during its occupation.[157]

6A.3.5 Responsibility and ensuring compliance under IHL

Parties to an armed conflict are bound to respect the applicable rules of IHL. They will be responsible for violations of those rules by their own armed forces. They will also be responsible for violations by other irregular

---

[149] In particular, the 1907 Hague Regulations, above, note 57.

[150] See 'ICRC Report on IHL and Contemporary Armed Conflicts', p. 8.

[151] See Chapter 7 Section A, the IHRL Framework for controversy as to extra-territorial application of IHRL in certain circumstances; note however that the application to occupied territories, where the state controls the territory in question, is not, however, controversial and would meet any of the tests advanced.

[152] Article 43, 1907 Hague Regulations.

[153] Article 47, 1907 Hague Regulations. For the IHRL obligations in this respect, see Chapter 7, para. 7A.4.1.

[154] Article 27 GC IV enshrines the general obligation: specific rights are provided for elsewhere, e.g., rights to fair trial (Article 75(1) GC IV).

[155] These include appeal and six-monthly review.   [156] See Articles 55–60 GC IV.

[157] See, e.g., Articles 43 and 64 GC IV. The fact that this limitation is subject to exception in the interests of the population may provide a basis for the non-application of laws that would violate human rights law, in accordance with the obligations of the occupying power under that body of law, as some human rights groups have noted.

forces that fight alongside their own forces, where these could be said to fall under their 'overall control'; such control arises where the Party 'has a role in organising, co-ordinating or planning the military actions of the military group'.[158]

Moreover, all states party to the Geneva Conventions have obligations to 'ensure respect' for the Conventions by all states.[159] Article 1 common to the Geneva Conventions imposes the duty on all High Contracting Parties to *respect* and to *ensure respect* for the Conventions, meaning that they should 'do everything in their power to ensure that it is respected universally'.[160] In 1968 and 1977 this positive obligation was reaffirmed without controversy by a broad representation of states, as a result of which the First Additional Protocol makes similar provision.[161] Whether or not party to a conflict, states parties to the Geneva Conventions are therefore obliged to take reasonable and appropriate measures to ensure

---

[158] *Tadic* Jurisdiction Decision, para. 137: 'control by a State over subordinate *armed forces or militias or paramilitary units* may be of an overall character (and must comprise more than the mere provision of financial assistance or military equipment or training). This requirement, however, does not go so far as to include the issuing of specific orders by the State, or its direction of each individual operation. Under international law it is by no means necessary that the controlling authorities should plan all the operations of the units dependent on them, choose their targets, or give specific instructions concerning the conduct of military operations and any alleged violations of international humanitarian law. The control required by international law may be deemed to exist when a State (or, in the context of an armed conflict, the Party to the conflict) *has a role in organising, coordinating or planning the military actions* of the military group, in addition to financing, training and equipping or providing operational support to that group. Acts performed by the group or members thereof may be regarded as acts of *de facto* State organs regardless of any specific instruction by the controlling State concerning the commission of each of those acts (emphasis added).' See Chapter 3, above. Note that this test of responsibility of a party to the conflict under IHL is distinct from the individual criminal responsibility that may attach to a commander or other superior in respect of the acts or omissions of his or her subordinates (see Chapter 4, para. 4A.1.2.1).

[159] Common Article 1 of the Geneva Conventions. See the ICRC Commentary on GC IV, p. 16: 'The proper working of the system of protection provided by the Convention demands in fact that the Contracting Parties should not be content merely to apply its provisions themselves, but should do everything in their power to ensure that the humanitarian principles underlying the Conventions are applied universally.'

[160] Common Article 1. This positive obligation was reaffirmed without controversy during the negotiation of AP I. See W.T. Mallison and S.V. Mallison, 'The Juridical Status of Privileged Combatants under the Geneva Protocol of 1977 concerning International Conflicts', 42 (1978) *Law and Contemporary Problems* 4 at 12.

[161] Mallison and Mallison, 'Juridical Status'; note that Article 1(1) of AP I paraphrases the obligations set forth in Article 1 of the 1949 Conventions.

that other parties observe the Conventions.[162] This obligation applies in respect of international and non-international armed conflicts.[163]

It follows from this obligation on all states parties that they should not directly facilitate or encourage violations, for example by cooperating with an offending state in criminal or military matters,[164] where it is believed that IHL is being violated.[165] Moreover, beyond desisting from committing, encouraging or assisting such violations, the positive obligation to ensure respect requires positive measures to prevent violations by other states parties. As the ICJ noted in *The Wall*:

> In addition, all the States parties to the Geneva Convention relative to the Protection of Civilian Persons in Time of War of 12 August 1949 are under an obligation, while respecting the United Nations Charter and international law, to ensure compliance by Israel with international humanitarian law as embodied in that Convention.[166]

States parties would enjoy discretion to decide what measures they deem necessary or effective, which may entail invoking the under-utilised inter-state judicial mechanisms,[167] or, at a minimum, making diplomatic representations regarding violations. As observance of humanitarian law transcends the sphere of interest of any individual state, action should not be taken only by states parties to the conflict, nor should it be limited to representations or other measures be limited to the protection of a state's own nationals.

Finally, while not all violations of IHL carry individual criminal responsibility, serious violations may also amount to war crimes for which individuals can be held to account before national or international

---

[162] ICRC Commentary to AP I, p. 18. This reflects the fundamental nature of IHL obligations as obligations *erga omnes*, see Introduction.

[163] See 'ICRC Report on IHL and Contemporary Armed Conflicts', p. 21.

[164] Criminal cooperation may include transferring individuals through extradition or other process, while military assistance may include provisions of weapons or other logistical assistance or certain types of training.

[165] See Meron, 'Geneva Conventions', at 349. The ICJ in the *Nicaragua* case (above, note 56), para. 220, asserted the customary nature of such an obligation: 'that general principles of humanitarian law include a particular prohibition [to refrain from encouraging persons or groups to commit violations of Article 3], accepted by States, and extending to activities which occur in the context of armed conflicts, whether international in character or not'.

[166] ICJ, *Legal Consequences of the Construction of a Wall in the Occupied Palestinian Territory*, Advisory Opinion, 9 July 2004, para. 159

[167] Recourse to the ICJ is available between states, and human rights bodies such as the Human Rights Committee under the ICCPR could be invoked by one state against another.

courts.[168] As discussed at Chapter 4, responsibility may be direct – for committing, ordering or aiding and abetting the commission of violations – or indirect, for superiors who fail to take necessary and reasonable measures to prevent violations by formal or informal subordinates. A specific additional positive obligation on states parties to the Geneva Conventions is the duty, in the event of grave breaches of the Conventions, such as mistreatment of POWs or depriving them of the rights of a fair trial, to seek out and prosecute those individuals responsible.[169]

Despite these obligations, it is often noted that the challenge to IHL lies in ensuring effective compliance. Beyond the responsibility of states, outlined above, the ICRC has a crucial, but limited, role as monitor of compliance with IHL and protector of persons caught up in armed conflict.[170] Other mechanisms exist in principle,[171] but in practice are not utilised, or grossly under-utilised, with the result that it is doubtful whether

---

[168] All violations involve the responsibility of the party to the conflict, but only some serious violations of humanitarian law entail individual criminal responsibility under customary or conventional law, as discussed at Chapter 4. See, e.g., Article 3 Statute of the ICTY or Article 8 ICC Statute. Where violations do amount to war crimes they may be subject to prosecution on the national or international level. Certain war crimes carry universal jurisdiction, under treaty or customary law. See W. J. Fenrick, 'Article 8. War Crimes', in O. Triffterer (ed.), *Commentary on the Rome Statute of the International Criminal Court* (Baden-Baden, 1999), pp. 173 ff.

[169] 'Grave breaches' provisions appear in all four Geneva Conventions and AP I. See, e.g., Articles 147 and 148 of GC IV and Article 85 AP I. For direct and indirect criminal responsibility, see Chapter 4, para. 4A.1.2.1.

[170] For a detailed analysis of the role of the ICRC, and in particular of what the author defines as the 'watchdog function' of the ICRC, see, in general, Y. Sandoz, *The International Committee of the Red Cross as Guardian of International Humanitarian Law* (Geneva, 1998). However, the ICRC's strength is also its limitation, in that it generally works confidentially and without publicly condemning any party. Its effectiveness as a mechanism of accountability is accordingly limited. See, however, statements in relation to Guantanamo Bay and Iraq, in the context of which the ICRC appears to have adopted an unusually visible and vocal approach. See, e.g., the recent report on Guantanamo Bay, in which the ICRC publicly expresses its concerns about the impact the seemingly open-ended detention is having on the internees: ICRC, 'Guantanamo Bay: Overview of the ICRC's work for internees', 30 January 2004, available at www.icrc.org.

[171] The Geneva Conventions set up the institution of Protecting Powers, i.e., neutral states or some other entity that, following designation by the parties to the conflict, will act to protect the interests of wounded or sick personnel, prisoners of war, internees, or other persons controlled by a hostile power. As noted by the ICRC (see ICRC Commentary to AP I, p. 77), such institution has, in practice, rarely been used and is now generally considered to lack credibility. For a discussion of these, see, e.g., Y. Sandoz, 'Mechanisms of Implementation under IHL, International Human Rights Law and Refugee Law', paper presented at the 2003 Sanremo Round Table on IHL, and 'ICRC Report on IHL and Contemporary Armed Conflicts'.

currently any meaningful IHL mechanism exists for rendering account-able parties that violate IHL, still less to provide individual or collective redress for victims of violations. Human rights mechanisms may, in certain circumstances, fulfil this role.[172] The need and/or desirability of an additional mechanism specifically directed towards IHL is currently under discussion but remains contentious.[173]

6B International humanitarian law and the 'war on terror'

Since September 11 the world has been constantly reminded that it is at war, albeit 'a different kind of war' than we have ever experienced before.[174] A correct understanding of whether IHL applies in any given situation depends on an understanding of whether that situation in fact amounts to an armed conflict. If so, the question that follows is the nature of that conflict and applicable IHL rules.

The first part of this chapter therefore considers three basic questions relating to the scope and nature of armed conflicts that have arisen post 9/11. Is there, or can there be, an armed conflict of global reach against al-Qaeda or other terrorist network? As regards the conflict in Afghanistan, was it (or is it) international or non-international, and when did it, or will it, end? Regarding the conflict in Iraq, what law applies and when will the occupier's obligations cease? The second part of the chapter highlights specific questions to have arisen regarding compliance

---

[172] The 'ICRC Report on IHL and Contemporary Armed Conflicts' notes (p. 23) that the role of human rights mechanisms in this respect was encouraged; these bodies should, however, ensure they have the capacity to apply IHL effectively within the framework of IHRL. Note, however, that human rights bodies are not universally available: see IHRL Framework (no regional mechanism in Asia and the Optional Protocol to the ICCPR has not been universally ratified).

[173] See proposals to establish a mechanism for individual complaint under IHL, advanced at the Hague centennial conference 1999, in 'ICRC Report on IHL and Contemporary Armed Conflicts', above. Experience to date may suggest, however, that ultimately the challenge is not so much to generate new mechanisms, as to ensure the political commitment to support whichever mechanisms – existing or new – are charged with IHL implementation.

[174] 'The President has made very plain to the American people that the war on terrorism is not a traditional war . . . in the sense that there is one known battlefield or one known nation or one known region. The President has made clear that we will fight the war on terrorism wherever we need to fight the war on terrorism . . . this is a different kind of war, with a different kind of battlefield, where known political boundaries, which previously existed in traditional wars do not exist in the war on terrorism.' (Press Gaggle by Ari Fleischer, White House Press Secretary, 5 November 2002, available at http://www.whitehouse.gov/news/releases/2002/11/20021105-2.html#3).

with the IHL framework, by reference to the example of the Afghanistan conflict.

6B.1 Armed conflicts since 9/11

6B.1.1 Armed conflict and 'terrorist groups of global reach'

It is at times tempting to dismiss post 9/11 references to the 'war on terror' as simply a rhetorical device with no more meaning than the wars on drugs or on crime oft-invoked in political circles. While there clearly cannot be an armed conflict with an abstract phenomenon, too much sleight of hand would overlook the seriousness with which the view is advanced by governments and at least some commentators, that there is an armed conflict with al-Qaeda, and other (unidentified) terrorist networks or organisations.[175]

It is a question that has demanded much international attention – and reaped considerable division and uncertainty – since 9/11. Should al-Qaeda and other networks be considered parties to an armed conflict, to be defeated militarily in accordance with IHL, or should they properly be understood as criminal organisations, requiring effective law enforcement? Many policy arguments, emphasising the merits and demerits of considering al-Qaeda a party to a conflict have been advanced since September 11, of particular relevance to on-going discussions as to whether IHL should develop in response to new challenges posed by 9/11 and the response thereto.[176] The focus of this section, however, is on

---

[175] 'The war on terror begins with al-Qaeda, but it does not end there. It will not end until every terrorist group of global reach has been found, stopped, and defeated', Address of the US President George W. Bush to a Joint Session of Congress and the American People, 20 September 2001, available at http://www.whitehouse.gov/news/releases/2001/09/20010920-8.html. On 13 November 2001 President Bush stated that there was 'a state of armed conflict' resulting from the 'acts of war' carried out by international terrorists on September 11. For a comment on this position see, e.g., J. Paust, 'There is No Need to Revise the Laws of War in Light of September 11th', November 2001, available at http://www.asil.org/taskforce/paust.pdf. See also Memorandum from the President of the United States. 'Humane Treatment of al Qaeda and Taliban detainees', 7 February 2002, on file with author, which concludes that the US is engaged in 'armed conflicts' with al Qaeda and the Taliban. The armed conflicts are deemed to be 'international' in nature, but IHL is then found inapplicable to the former (as it involves non-state actors) and as offering no protection to the Taliban as 'enemy combatants' (as discussed at Chapter 8).

[176] Policy arguments as to the desirability of such development include: on the one hand, the need to reflect contemporary reality as to the capacity of non-state entities to engage in large scale armed violence and the need for appropriate regulation. On the other, the suggestion that applying IHL language to the conduct of organisations such as

whether, under current international law, the relationship between states engaged in the so-called 'war on terror' and al-Qaeda can meet the criteria for the contemporary definition of armed conflict. As set out in the previous chapter, these criteria require firstly, the use of force, and secondly, the existence of identifiable parties to the conflict with particular characteristics. These are considered below, in relation to the questions whether there might be an international or a non-international armed conflict with al-Qaeda.

6B.1.1.1 International armed conflict with al-Qaeda?

September 11 leaves no room for doubt that entities such as al-Qaeda can and do resort to the 'use of force' across international frontiers, satisfying the first criterion for international armed conflict. The key doubt that arises, however, relates the nature of the 'parties' to an international conflict which, according to current IHL, must be states. The sole exception to this relates to 'liberation movements' engaged in a struggle against colonial domination, within the meaning of IHL.[177] Armed groups such as al-Qaeda, or armed individuals, may of course act under the authority of a state or states.[178] But they cannot themselves constitute a party to an international conflict absent such state involvement.

Shortly after the September 11 attacks, one commentator suggested that: 'until now, the law of armed conflict has always been considered to be a matter between states (unless a civil war), but the law has been moving slowly towards recognizing as quasi-states dissident armed factions and authorities representing liberation movements. It might be

al-Qaeda confers inappropriate legitimacy on what are essentially international criminal organisations, and justifies certain of their violent actions as lawful acts of war; that IHL is not essential (or appropriate) to regulate and prohibit terrorist violence, which is adequately regulated by criminal law, national and international, whereas reference to IHL in areas traditionally governed by IHRL may be simply a guise to justify lower standards of protection (e.g., on the use of lethal force). In general, this view holds that unravelling the rationale of IHL (as applicable to two identifiable parties, distinguishable from the civilian population, and capable of respecting IHL) may ultimately undermine IHL protection for all. The legal and policy debate, still in embryonic form, is undoubtedly set to continue. For an outline of positions, see, e.g., ICRC, Report on 'International Humanitarian Law and the Challenges of Contemporary Armed Conflict' (Geneva, 2003) (hereinafter 'ICRC Report on IHL and Contemporary Armed Conflicts'), pp. 5–6.

[177] Article 1(4) AP I includes 'armed conflicts in which peoples are fighting against colonial domination and alien occupation and against racist regimes in their exercise of the right of self-determination' within the definition of international armed conflict within the meaning of Common Article 2 of the 1949 Geneva Conventions.

[178] On legal standards for attributing the conduct of private actors to states, see Chapter 3, para. 3.1.1.

possible to argue that a state can be involved in an armed conflict against an organization.'[179] This perspective, while not perhaps reflecting current law, signals a possible direction for future legal development.

6B.1.1.2 Non-international armed conflict with al-Qaeda?

As regards non-international armed conflict, the use of force employed must reach a certain threshold of intensity and be distinguishable from sporadic or isolated acts of violence. Arguably, the resort to violence witnessed on September 11 and since then comfortably reaches this threshold. It is, again, the second aspect of the test that is the critical one: can an entity such as al-Qaeda possess the characteristics of an armed group as understood by IHL, such that it can be a party to a non-international armed conflict?[180] The key questions are whether they have: sufficiently identifiable scope and membership, sufficient organisation and structure, and a capability of abiding by the rules of IHL.[181] A particular problem, at least in the light of current understandings of the nature of al-Qaeda, relates to the difficulty in defining what is variously described as an organisation, a movement or 'a series of loosely connected operational and support cells'[182] as an identifiable and distinct party to a conflict. Related issues include how one can define and identify with sufficient clarity the relationship between disparate individuals and their membership, support or sympathy for al-Qaeda. Yet the very logic, structure and effective

---

[179] See comment of A.P.V. Rogers, 'Terrorism and the Laws of War: September 11 and its Aftermath', 21 September 2001, available at http://www.crimesofwar.org/expert/attack-apv.html.

[180] See the range of factors set out in the Framework, section A.

[181] In addition to the foregoing, insurgents often control territory although this is not necessarily a requirement. See D. Fleck, 'Non-International Armed Conflict: Legal Qualifications and Parties to the Conflict' and M. Sassòli, 'Non-International Armed Conflict: Qualification of the Conflict and Its Parties', background papers presented at the 27th Round Table on Current Problems of International Humanitarian Law, 'International Humanitarian Law and Other Legal Regimes: Interplay in Situations of Violence', Sanremo, 4–6 September 2003 (hereinafter '2003 Sanremo Round Table on IHL'). The proceedings of the Round Table will be published in G.L. Beruto and G. Ravasi (eds.), *27th Round Table on Current Problems of International Humanitarian Law; Sanremo, 4-6 September 2003; 'International Humanitarian and other legal regimes: interplay in situations of violence'* (Milan, forthcoming); Paust, 'No Need to Revise the Laws of War'.

[182] The UK Government relies on this definition, first provided in the letter of 19 September 2002 from the Chairman of the Security Council Committee established pursuant to Resolution 1267 of 1999: see 'SIAC "Generic Determination" of 29 October 2003 [Cases SC/1/2002; SC/6/2002; SC/7/2002; SC/9/2002; SC/10/2002 para. 130: *Ajouaou and others* v. *Secretary of State for the Home Department*, available at http://www.courtservice.gov.uk/judgments/siac/outcomes/GenericDetermination.htm.

operation of IHL depends precisely on the ability to identify and distinguish the opposing party, with critical implications for targeting and humanitarian protection.[183] Although some commentators suggest otherwise,[184] it is widely considered, even post 9/11, that these organisations lack the characteristics of armed groups and that IHL is not the most appropriate legal framework to govern the relationship between persons associated with al-Qaeda and those states executing the 'war on terror'.

6B.1.1.3 9/11 as armed conflict?

The previous sections foreshadow the question whether an armed conflict might be said to have been initiated on 9/11, or only thereafter.[185] If it emerges that a state was involved in the September 11 attacks,[186] then an international conflict may have begun (and war crimes been committed) on 11 September 2001.[187] However, as noted in previous chapters, there has been no serious suggestion by states involved in the Afghanistan intervention that that state was legally responsible for the September 11 attacks, and it is doubtful that the criteria whereby acts are attributable to states

---

[183] See 'ICRC Report on IHL and Contemporary Armed Conflicts', p. 19; Paust, 'No Need to Revise the Laws of War'.

[184] See, e.g., D. Jinks, 'September 11 and the Laws of War', 28 (2003) *Yale Journal of International Law* 1. Numerous commentators have expressed the view that *if* there can be an armed conflict with an international network of this nature, it must be non-international in nature. It has been suggested that given the characteristic of the parties to a conflict to understanding the nature of the conflict, it should be considered a non-international one despite the transnational and international nature of membership and of attacks. See Beruto and Ravasi (eds.), *27th Round Table on Current Problems*. It may also be that the situation flags the prospect of the law developing to encompass a new, hybrid, sort of armed conflict that does not readily fit within either of the two existing paradigms.

[185] For armed conflict post the international intervention in Afghanistan of 7 October 2001, see below. Note that these *in bello* issues are distinct from the *jus ad bellum*, governing the legitimacy of resort to force (see section A, Chapter 5 above). Hence, the question whether an attack by a terrorist group triggers self defence, itself a controversial issue, addressed in that chapter, is distinct from the question whether an attack gives rise to an armed conflict, addressed here.

[186] Unless, of course, the minority view is taken that no state involvement is necessary for an international conflict.

[187] If so, one repercussion is that at least the greater part of those attacks would amount to violations of IHL and may indeed constitute 'war crimes' (as well as other crimes under international law). While the attack on the World Trade Center was undoubtedly an unlawful attack against a civilian target, in the context of an armed conflict the targeting of the Pentagon may be militarily justifiable (although the method of attack may remain open to question). See Chapter 4, para. 4A.1.1.2. See also Paust, 'No Need to Revise the Laws of War', at 3. The 'other crimes' include crimes against humanity which require no armed conflict.

would have been satisfied.[188] As regards the possibility of 9/11 amounting to non-international armed conflict with al-Qaeda, while the first prong of the test – requiring that the violence is more than an 'isolated' or 'sporadic' act of violence – can, at least arguably, be met by the September 11 violence itself, or by seeing it as part of a campaign over time,[189] as explained above doubts arise as to the second prong. Under current law it is unlikely that an international entity of uncertain nature, scope or membership may be a party to a non-international armed conflict. September 11 does not therefore appear to represent the initiation of a non-international armed conflict either. References to it as an 'act of war' are therefore misleading.[190]

6B.1.1.4 Conclusion: IHL and 'terrorist' groups

The view that armed conflict may arise between states and organisations such as al-Qaeda has relatively little support, even in the post September 11 era. As noted, however, there can be little doubt that traditional concepts of armed conflict are increasingly subject to question post 11 September 2001. The seeds of debate have been sown as to whether it may be, or should be, possible for an armed conflict to arise between states and entities such as al-Qaeda. While asserting that an armed conflict can be waged with an entity such as al-Qaeda may not be an accurate assessment of the law as it stood at the time of the September 11 attacks, or indeed as it stands in the first few years thereafter, the current debate highlights this as an area deserving of further analysis, and where legal development could, conceivably, unfold.

Several concluding distinctions may be worthy of emphasis as regards the unravelling of the relationship between IHL and terrorism. First, the terrorist label, always of doubtful relevance in international law given the ambiguity surrounding its meaning and scope, is not legally significant, still less decisive, to the application of IHL.[191] To assess the existence of an

---

[188] See Chapter 3, para. 3.1.1. See also C. Greenwood, 'International Law and the "War against Terrorism"', 78 (2002) *International Affairs* 301.

[189] The intensity of the attack is beyond dispute, but even large scale attacks, if isolated, may not satisfy this criterion. The more critical question of fact is whether, for example, it forms part of a pattern of attacks over a period of time. In light of the history of al-Qaeda attacks pre- and post-9/11, it is likely that this prong could be satisfied.

[190] 'On September the 11th, enemies of freedom committed an act of war against our country', Address of the US President George W. Bush to a Joint Session of Congress and the American People, 20 September 2001, available at http://www.whitehouse. gov/news/releases/2001/09/20010920-8.html.

[191] In conflict situations one party may not infrequently refer to another as a terrorist or resorting to terror tactics. In particular, many states do, in practice, deny the existence of

armed conflict and application of IHL, the question is not whether there can be an armed conflict with a 'terrorist' organisation but whether, on the facts, the requirements regarding the use of force and the nature of the parties have been satisfied.[192]

Second, networks like al-Qaeda, like any other groups of individuals, may however become *involved* in an armed conflict by fighting alongside, or in connection with, a party that meets the criteria set out above,[193] as would appear to be the situation in Afghanistan for example. This situation must be distinguished, however, from the ability of the entity to itself constitute a party to an armed conflict, considered above.

Third, as noted, IHL is not silent on 'terrorism' to the extent that parties to a conflict, whether state or non-state, may be responsible for 'terrorism' or related offences occurring in the context of international or non-international armed conflict, as defined by IHL for these purposes.[194] Moreover, in armed conflict conduct that may be considered to exploit 'terrorist' tactics may of course also amount to other violations of IHL, the most obvious being attacks against civilians or civilian objects[195] or perfidy, also explicitly prohibited in international law.[196] However, the commission of 'terrorism' in this context should not be confused as bearing upon the key question whether particular groups meet the necessary criteria to constitute parties to a conflict.

6B.1.2 The Afghan conflict, its nature, beginning and end

6B.1.2.1 Nature of the conflict post October 2001?

By contrast to the uncertainty surrounding ambiguous notions as to the 'war on terror' or being at war with terrorists, relative clarity attends

---

non-international armed conflicts within their state, preferring to refer to the violence as terrorism, in an attempt to preclude the application of IHL.

[192] The question, as sometimes posed, whether there can be an armed conflict with a 'terrorist' organisation is not therefore the most helpful and cannot be answered in the abstract.

[193] See, e.g., the Afghan conflict in which components of al-Qaeda appear to have fought with the Taleban.

[194] Article 33(1) GC IV relates to imposing collective penalties and prohibits 'all measures . . . of terrorism' against civilians, while the Additional Protocols I and II prohibit '[a]cts or threats of violence the primary purpose of which is to spread terror among the civilian population', Article 51(2) AP I; Article 13(2) AP II. *Prosecutor* v. *Galic*, Case No. IT-98-29-T, Judgment, 5 December 2003.

[195] AP I, Article 85.

[196] Article 37 AP I. The ICRC Report on IHL and Contemporary Armed Conflicts, p. 7, notes that 'suicide actions' against civilians are prohibited. Attacks in which individuals engaging in hostilities pose as civilians, of which numerous examples emerge post 9/11, amount to perfidy, and the use of human shields, for example, is also prohibited.

the fact that an international armed conflict arose in Afghanistan, if not before, then with the military action that commenced on 7 October 2001. The parties to the conflict in Afghanistan on and following 7 October 2001 were the armed forces of the US and its allies on the one hand, and Afghanistan represented by the Taleban and its supporters (including elements of al-Qaeda), on the other.

There was also an armed conflict in Afghanistan before the 2001 intervention, though it was probably non-international in nature.[197] The intervention of several allied states on that date, on behalf of rebel armed groups, resulted in an international conflict, albeit one that appears to have been waged alongside, and in connection with, the continuing non-international conflict between the Northern Alliance and the Taleban.[198]

6B.1.2.2 Nature of the conflict post June 2002?

Somewhat more difficult questions relate to the nature of the conflict post 19 June 2002, once the Taleban government had been definitively removed from power and the *Loya Jirga* constituted.[199] At that point the state of Afghanistan came to be represented by a government and forces friendly to the US and allied states, Afghanistan's erstwhile enemy, and rebel forces on the one hand (presumably a mixture of al-Qaeda and remnants of the Taleban) fought against the state of Afghanistan and other states on the other.

As such, the net result is a conflict between states and armed groups, apparently therefore of the non-international variety.[200] The situation in Afghanistan where a non-international armed conflict existed before the military intervention of 7 October 2001, may then have reverted to a situation of non-international armed conflict post June 2002, albeit with the rebels and government forces having changed face. It should be noted however that a certain degree of controversy arises concerning the impact

---

[197] Contentions that Pakistan fought alongside the Taleban pre-7 October 2001, if true, suggest the conflict may already have been internationalised. Paust, 'No Need to Revise the Laws of War', at 3. Note however difference of view on international vs. non-international nature of a conflict where an intervening state fights alongside government as opposed to insurgents. See Chapter 5, para. 5A.1.1.

[198] The two conflicts occur simultaneously, and overlap, although it may be argued that, at least in some respects, the international armed conflict encompasses the non-international one under way previously.

[199] See 'Karzai sworn in as president', *BBC News*, 19 June 2002, at http://news.bbc.co.uk/1/hi/world/south_asia/2052680.stm.

[200] It is a question of fact whether the remnants of the Taleban meet the requirements of a 'party' to a conflict, set out above, though it seems very likely that they would.

of the engagement of outside states, with one (although perhaps minority) view holding that the continuing involvement of the US beyond June 2002 means that the conflict remains international.[201]

6B.1.2.3 War without end?

A further question relating to the Afghan conflict is whether it continues to the present day, and, if so, when it might end.[202] As noted, the international armed conflict in Afghanistan appears to have ended on 19 June 2002. If so, what impact does this have on applicable IHL? For example, if the international conflict is over, is there another legal basis for detaining persons originally held pursuant to IHL applicable in international conflicts? POWs, for example, should be released at the end of the international conflict, unless prosecuted, or some other legal basis exists to justify their continued detention.[203]

As regards the non-international armed conflict post June 2002, the question whether the relevant criteria for armed conflict continue to be satisfied must be assessed on an on-going basis. At a certain point the intensity of hostilities will wane, and the requirement of on-going violence of significant intensity (as opposed to isolated or sporadic acts of violence) will no longer be satisfied.[204] At a certain point the Taleban may also be

---

[201] Whereas where a state intervenes on behalf of rebels (as arguably occurred on 7 October 2001) there is uncontroversially an international armed conflict, dispute remains over whether the support of outside states on the side of state forces automatically renders a conflict international. See Chapter 5, para. 5A.1.1.

[202] The official position of the US Government is that the war *against* Afghanistan is over, though its role in Afghanistan continues: see 'In coordination with the government of Afghanistan, the coalition here continues to train the Afghan National Army, provide civil affairs support, and disrupt, deny, and destroy terrorist and anti-government forces in order to establish a stable and secure Afghanistan' (Press release of the US Department of Defense, 10 January 2004, at http://www.defendamerica. mil/afghanistan/update/feb2004/au022804.html). It is clear, however, that military operations conducted by coalition forces are still ongoing: 'Operation Avalanche continues with four Infantry battalions conducting security and interdiction operations. Yesterday, 2nd Battalion, 87th Infantry regiment air assaulted into an objective in the eastern part of the country' (Press release of the US Department of Defense, 17 December 2003, *ibid.*).

[203] On lawful bases for detention see Chapter 8, para. 8B.4.1. Once international armed conflict ends, and becomes non-international, prisoners can no longer be held as POWs. They should then be released or put on trial, unless there is another basis for their detention (in accordance with IHRL).

[204] It appears that, at the time of writing, over two years on from the Afghanistan intervention, there remains fighting of such intensity. See, e.g., S. Saleem Shahzad, 'Afghanistan: Now it's all-out war', *Asia Times*, 24 February 2004, reporting that 'a massive land and air military operation on either side of the border between Afghanistan and Pakistan is . . . under way, with the main goals of catching leading commanders of the Afghan resistance, as

definitively defeated in such a way that the party to the conflict may cease to exist and (as there can be no conflict with al-Qaeda, as discussed above) what was an armed conflict will revert to acts of violence regulated not by IHL but by other areas of law, notably criminal law and human rights law.

Post 9/11, uncertainty and obfuscation as to the existence and scope of the 'war(s)', has spilled over, inevitably, into confusion as to when, if ever, armed conflicts will end.[205] Understanding the parameters of the conflict, as arising between identifiable parties in the particular context of Afghanistan (or Iraq), rather than against terrorism more broadly in the world at large, is the first step towards meaningful implementation of, and monitoring of respect for, IHL (and human rights law that assume greater prominence after the conflict ceases).[206]

6B.1.3 The conflict in Iraq and obligations of occupying forces

International forces intervened militarily in Iraq on 19 March 2003 giving rise to an international armed conflict.[207] Shortly thereafter there ensued a situation of occupation, also governed by the law of IHL applicable to international armed conflict.[208] While the existence and nature of the Iraqi conflict is relatively straightforward,[209] among the important questions that arise in relation to the scope of conflict and application of IHL is when the coalition forces' 'occupier's obligations' cease. The institution

well as Osama bin Laden and Taliban leader Mullah Omar'. See also M. Townsend *et al.*, 'The secret war', *The Observer*, 21 March 2004, reporting ongoing battles between US and Pakistani troops and al-Qaeda and Taleban militants in the eastern part of Afghanistan.

[205] As noted above, persons detained in the context of an international conflict in Afghanistan and entitled to POW status are entitled to release upon the cessation of the international conflict, so implications for the rights of prisoners are serious.

[206] See Chapter 7, para. 7A.3.4 on the relationship between IHL and IHRL during armed conflict.

[207] See SC Res. 1483 (2003), 22 May 2003, UN Doc. S/RES/1483 (2003), recognising the Iraq situation as an international armed conflict.

[208] Applicable IHL includes specific obligations incumbent on occupying forces, described at Chapter 6, para. 6A.3.4.

[209] Many questions arise as to the satisfaction of those obligations by coalition forces, which are not explored here. Certain issues, such as torture and ill-treatment, are discussed at Chapter 7 (see 7.B.5), and others, relating to procedural rights of detainees, at Chapter 8. See C. Gray, 'From Unity to Polarisation: International Law and Use of Force against Iraq', 13 (2001) EJIL 1. For an ongoing analysis of the many IHL issues arising in Iraq, see also http://www.ihlresearch.org/iraq and http://electroniciraq. net/news/660.shtml. Issues arising in the Afghan conflict are highlighted below, by way of illustration, although similar issues arose in relation to Iraq.

of a new government in Iraq took effect in June 2004, but as Chapter 6 notes, the transfer of formal authority does not necessarily end the occupier's responsibilities, unless an alternative functioning government has assumed *de facto* control over its population and territory.[210] It will be a question of fact, for on-going assessment, whether effective control is retained by the erstwhile occupiers or assumed by the new Iraqi government. The law of occupation applies, moreover, until one year after there is a general close of military operations or the occupying power ceases to exercise such effective control.[211]

6B.2 The Afghan conflict and particular issues of IHL compliance

Many issues of compliance with IHL have arisen in the course of the 'war on terror', in relation to measures taken in Afghanistan, Iraq and beyond. This section highlights three groups of IHL issues to have arisen by reference to examples from the military action in Afghanistan that commenced on 7 October 2001. The first group emerges from the aerial bombardment campaign executed by the United States and its allies ('Operation Anaconda' and 'Operation Infinite Justice')[212] and raises questions of targeting and the principle of distinction. The second relates to the methods and means of warfare employed. The third concerns the humanitarian protection afforded to those who have fallen into the power of the Coalition and its Northern Alliance allies.

6B.2.1 Targeting

6B.2.1.1 Civilian casualties and targeting in Afghanistan

Reports appear to indicate that several thousand civilians were killed (and many civilian objects destroyed) during the early stages of the military campaign.[213] However, numbers of civilian deaths do not themselves add

---

[210] The test for occupation is a factual one based on the effective control of territory or persons. However, IHL provides that the rules continue to apply to occupation one year after withdrawal: see Article 6 GC IV.

[211] As noted above, it continues for longer where the occupying power continues to exercise control in the territory. See Article 6(3) GC IV and Article 3(b) AP I.

[212] Following protests, principally by the Muslim community in the US, 'Operation Infinite Justice' was renamed 'Operation Enduring Freedom' on 25 September 2001.

[213] Professor M. Herold's independent study on civilian casualties in Afghanistan, for example, which was widely cited by the media, states that at least 3,767 civilians were killed by US bombs between 7 October and 10 December, a figure which has recently been revised to nearing 4,000. See 'A Dossier on Civilian Victims of United States' Aerial Bombing

up to violations of IHL. The key question to be addressed in relation to any particular incident is whether the underlying conduct of hostility rules were fully respected.

In respect of some incidents, the question is whether the selected target was a legitimate military target. An example is the bombardment on 11 October 2001 of the Afghan radio station,[214] reminiscent of the attack on the television station during the Kosovo conflict, which provoked considerable controversy as to the legitimacy of target selection.[215] US Defense Secretary Rumsfeld sought to justify the attack on the basis that the radio station was 'the propaganda machine of the opposing forces', while others question the legitimacy of targeting civilian radio and television stations, even where they are used for propaganda purposes.[216]

In relation to the majority of controversial aerial bombardment incidents, however, where persons or property attacked were clearly not *per se* legitimate targets, the question is not target selection as such, but whether there is an IHL justification for hitting what is, on its face, an unlawful target. Such justification may be based, for example, on mistaken identity or proportionality.[217] Among the reported incidents of aerial bombardment that raise such questions are attacks on: a wedding party at Uruzgan on 1 July 2002, resulting in 30 civilian fatalities,[218] Chaskar village, resulting

---

of Afghanistan: A Comprehensive Accounting', most recent edition of study available at http://pubpages.unh.edu/%7Emwherold. A more conservative report places the number of civilian deaths due to aerial bombardment between 1,000 and 1,300. See Conetta, 'Strange Victory'.

[214] See Amnesty International, 'Afghanistan: Accountability for Civilian Deaths', News Release, 26 October 2001, AI Index: ASA/11/022/2001.

[215] Final Report by the Committee Established to Review the NATO Bombing Campaign Against the Federal Republic of Yugoslavia, 12 June 2000, available at http://www.un.org/icty/pressreal/nato061300.htm; Report of the Prosecutor on the NATO Bombing Campaign, 39 (2000) ILM 1257. See M. Cottier, 'Did NATO Forces Commit War Crimes during the Kosovo Conflict? Reflections on the Prosecutor's Report of 13 June 2000' in H. Fischer, C. Kreß and S.R. Lüder (eds.), *International and National Prosecution of Crimes under International Law: Current Developments* (Berlin, 2001), pp. 505 ff., especially at pp. 516–30.

[216] See Amnesty International, 'Afghanistan: Accountability for Civilian Deaths', note 217 above.

[217] At no time has it been the official policy of the Coalition to target civilians, and few commentators would contend that attacks on civilians were intentional; the emphasis in the following is thus on the more pertinent questions regarding the obligations in place to safeguard the principle of distinction.

[218] See Amnesty International, 'Afghanistan: Accountability for Civilian Death Toll', 2 July 2002, AI Index: ASA 11/013/2002.

in 25 civilian deaths,[219] Thori village, resulting in 23 civilian deaths,[220] and Chowkar-Karez village, resulting in 25–35 civilian deaths,[221] but there are many others.[222]

In a number of cases, such as Thori village (located near a military base), there reportedly was a legitimate military target in the vicinity. Where military objectives are hit alongside protected persons or property,[223] the question is whether there were sufficient attempts to distinguish the two, whether the proportionality of foreseeable civilian losses as against the military advantage anticipated, and whether all feasible steps were taken to minimise such losses,[224] including the use of methods and means of warfare which are not inherently unreliable or indiscriminate but as precise as possible, and which limit as much as possible collateral losses.[225] The proportionality assessment is not a numbers game, involving simple balancing of military casualties against numbers of civilians.[226] In the

---

[219] Human Rights Watch, 'Afghanistan: New Civilian Deaths Due to U.S. Bombing', 30 October 2001, at http://www.hrw.org/press/2001/10/afghan1030.htm.

[220] Human Rights Watch, 'Afghanistan: U.S. Bombs Kill Twenty-three Civilians: Rights Group Urges Immediate Investigation', 26 October 2001, at http://www.hrw.org/press/2001/10/afghan1026.htm.

[221] Human Rights Watch, 'Afghanistan: New Civilian Deaths Due to U.S. Bombing' (above, note 222).

[222] For a list of similar 'incidents', see S. Kapferer, 'Ends and Means in Politics: International Law as Framework for Political Decision Making', 15 (2002) *Revue québéquoise de droit international* 101. In addition to the human rights reports cited, see the following press reports: on claims of civilian deaths caused by US air strikes on hospital near Kandahar, see 'Afghan hospital strike "kills 15"', *The Guardian*, 31 October 2001. On US bombing of village in eastern Afghanistan and claims of hundreds of civilian deaths (30 December 2001), see 'US bombers "Kill 100 Afghan Civilians"', *The Guardian*, 31 December 2001. On 3,500 civilians estimated dead in conflict, see 'Out of the Ruins', *The Guardian*, 13 November 2002.

[223] Where the military target was not hit, the question becomes accuracy and the considerations are those in relation to error, set out below.

[224] As noted above, the situation must be appraised from the point of view of the reasonable commander at the time of the attack, taking into account conditions of conflict.

[225] See this chapter, para. 6A.3.2. This may involve choosing to employ precision guided weapons. See Human Rights Watch, 'International Humanitarian Law Issues and the Afghan Conflict: Open Letter to North Atlantic Treaty Organization (NATO) Defense Ministers', 17 October 2001, at http://www.hrw.org/press/2001/10/nato1017-ltr.htm.

[226] See, e.g., the judgment of the ICTY in the *Galić* case (note 197, above), in particular at paras. 51–61. See also, in general, S. Oeter, 'Methods and Means of Combat', in D. Fleck (ed.), *The Handbook of Humanitarian Law in Armed Conflicts* (Oxford, 1995), at pp. 178–80. On standards of proportionality as applied by human rights law, see also the decision of the IACtHR in *Neira Alegria et al. v. Peru*, Judgment of 19 January 1995, IACtHR, *Series C*, No. 21, concerning arbitrary deprivation of life as a consequence of the disproportionate use of force by prison guards trying to crush a riot.

presence of heavy civilian casualties, however, sufficient doubt arises as to respect for IHL that the onus lies with the party responsible for ensuring compliance with IHL and in possession of the relevant information, to account for the lawfulness of the action.

In other cases, such as the wedding party, reportedly there were no military targets in the vicinity.[227] The purported justification in such cases may be mistaken identity as to the nature of targets. Like the proportionality of any anticipated civilian losses, the assessment of targets must be made in light of information available at the time, taking into account the conditions of the conflict.

However, just as IHL contains no 'strict responsibility' for civilian losses incurred, neither does it provide an automatic escape clause based on simple mistake or lack of knowledge. Rather, IHL requires positive measures of commanders to ensure (within reason) that information is available to them to make the necessary assessments as to the accuracy of target assessment as well as the collateral impact of attack. Again, in such circumstances, the onus lies with the state to demonstrate that the necessary information was achieved and precautions taken to justify the lawfulness of its action.

6B.2.1.2 Targeting prisoners: Mazar-I-Sharif

Another example of controversial targeting issues of a different nature lies in the case of the Qala-i-Jhangi fortress near Mazar-I-Sharif, to which surrendered Taleban combatants were taken by the Northern Alliance in November 2001.[228] Accounts of events thereafter vary: certain press reports indicate that fighting started after a Taleban prisoner blew up himself and one of two American CIA operatives,[229] while US officials referred to the ensuing exchanges of fire between the prisoners and Northern

---

[227] The US described the attack on the wedding party as 'anti-aircraft fire on a coalition reconnaisance patrol flight'. It has been suggested that confusion may have arisen from the traditional gunfire salute at Afghan weddings. See Amnesty International, 'Afghanistan: Accountability for Civilian Death Toll', above, note 221. According to human rights groups reports, the attack on Chowkar-Karez may fall into the same category, as the village was forty miles away from the Taleban stronghold of Kandahar and none of the witnesses interviewed by Human Rights Watch knew of Taleban or al-Qaeda positions in the area of the attack.

[228] The fortress was reportedly under the control of the infamous Northern Alliance General Dostam, although the US also had a presence. See the discussion of issues of responsibility in this chapter, para. 6A.3.5 above.

[229] 'Fatal errors that led to massacre', *The Guardian*, 1 December 2001.

Alliance as a 'pitched battle'.[230] Days of surface and aerial bombardment followed, resulting in the death of the majority of prisoners. A photographer witnessed the aftermath, and claimed to have seen among the corpses approximately fifty persons whose hands had been bound.[231]

How does the US/Northern Alliance response to the reported Taleban uprising measure up against the framework of IHL? The legal starting point is that, as prisoners in the hands of enemy forces, the captives were entitled to the protection of IHL, including immunity from attack as well as 'humanitarian protections'.[232] This immunity is premised, however, upon the persons not being engaged in hostilities. It is a question of fact whether prisoners resumed, or took up, active hostilities and were therefore no longer immunised from attack but became legitimate military targets. The incident gives rise to several questions for the relevant authorities.

The first is whether only legitimate military objectives were targeted. What was the military objective targeted at Mazar-I-Sharif: was it individuals all of whom had indeed taken up arms (in which case targeting them would appear legitimate)? Or was the attack launched, not against individuals but against the fortress? Did the taking up of arms reach a sufficient level to transform the fort into a military target[233] on the basis that, as the ICRC noted, '[i]f 700 prisoners were heavily armed then it may be argued that the fortress became a legitimate combat target'?[234]

---

[230] Kenton Keith, the chief US spokesman in Islamabad: 'What happened in Mazar-i-Sharif Was a Pitched Battle', reported *ibid.*

[231] See R. Fisk, 'We Are the War Criminals Now', *The Independent*, 29 November 2001, reporting the statement of an Associated Press photographer who saw Northern Alliance soldiers removing the bindings from the hands of the dead Taleban fighters.

[232] While, as discussed in more detail in Chapter 8 on Guantanamo Bay, the precise protections which prisoners are due depends on their status under IHL – as prisoners of war (covered by GC III) or civilians (covered by GC IV) – all persons *hors de combat* in the hands of the adversary are entitled to the basic protection against, *inter alia*, attack or inhumane treatment (see, e.g., Common Article 3 of the Geneva Conventions, Article 75 AP I). If, as reported, the prisoners were Taleban fighters, they were most likely entitled to POW status; the US, reversing its initial position, has recognised that POW status applies to captured Taleban. The execution of prisoners, or reprisals against prisoners for acts against the adversary, is a violation of IHL and may indeed amount to a grave breach of the Geneva Conventions. See para. 6A.3.3, 'Humanitarian Protections' in the Framework section, and below.

[233] The number of armed prisoners remains unknown. The *Guardian* reports indicate that a significant number of prisoners were armed with their own weapons (retained due to the lack of search) as well as military stockpiles in the fortress itself.

[234] ICRC statement reported in 'Allies Justify Mass Killing of Taliban Prisoners in Fort', *The Guardian*, 29 November 2001.

The second related question is proportionality. If, consistent with press reports, the occupants of the fortress were both armed persons (who had lost their immunity from attack) and prisoners, including bound prisoners (who are therefore *hors de combat*), the proportionality of the attack may be questionable.

The third related question is whether suitable precautions were taken to minimise casualties. This obligation clearly applies in respect of 'collateral damage' to prisoners who had not themselves taken up arms. However, while it has been noted that there is generally no obligation in IHL to seek to arrest rather than kill combatants in a battlefield scenario, different considerations may attend conflict in a prison that was under the control of one party, when that control is then lost. It may be that the legitimate objective in such case is to regain control of the prison and prisoners, with the least injury and loss of life possible.

If the objective of the use of force was to enable persons detaining prisoners to regain control of an uprising (which IHL and indeed IHRL would allow), was an all-out assault on the fort and its occupants proportionate to the aim of regaining such control? Or were there alternative ways to achieve this, short of the two days of aerial and surface bombardment that resulted, predictably, in the loss of lives of all prisoners? These questions remain unanswered. Calls for an inquiry into this event have apparently not borne fruit.[235]

6B.2.2 Methods and means: cluster bombs in Afghanistan

As noted in the relevant part of the previous chapter, the use of weapons that are indiscriminate, or which cause cruel and unnecessary suffering or superfluous injury, is a violation of IHL. In the Afghanistan conflict, as in the Iraqi conflict that followed, particular controversy surrounds the use of cluster bombs.

It has been reported that between October and the end of 2001, 1,210 cluster bombs were employed by allied forces in Afghanistan.[236] Each

---

[235] See Amnesty International, 'Afghanistan: Amnesty International Calls for Urgent Inquiry into Violence in Qala-I-Jangi', 27 November 2001, AI Index: ASA 11/036/2001, and Amnesty International, 'Afghanistan: Inquiry into Qala-I-Jangi Fort Killings Must Not Be Swept under the Carpet', AI Index: ASA 11/042/2001, noting that such calls have been ignored.

[236] See Human Rights Watch Report, 'Fatally Flawed: Cluster Bombs and Their Use by the United States in Afghanistan', December 2002, http://hrw.org/reports/2002/us-afghanistan/ and Human Rights Watch, 'Cluster Bomblets Litter Afghanistan', 16 November 2001 at http://www.hrw.org/press/2001/11/CBAfgh1116.htm. The former notes that

aerial cluster bomb contains a significant amount of smaller 'bomblets' which, when deployed, cover an extensive area.[237] As the framework section of this chapter indicates, cluster bombs are controversial as they disperse submunitions over a wide area and cannot therefore be directed with precision or confined within the parameters of a military target.[238] In Afghanistan UN reports state that US cluster bombs targeting a military compound near the city of Herat, struck not only a mosque used by the military but also a village some 500 to 1,000 metres away.[239] They also give rise to controversy based on their initial failure rate.[240] Unsurprisingly then, reports also record bomblets lying dormant in Afghanistan long after military attacks, until disturbed at some future point causing random civilian deaths.[241]

Indications of shifting policy towards cluster bombs by the US in other contexts[242] did not lead to the avoidance of the use of these controversial weapons in Afghanistan. As noted above, cluster bombs are of increasingly doubtful legality.[243] It is likely that the decision to use such bombs in certain contexts, such as within the vicinity of populated areas, would amount to an unlawful attack. In respect of incidents where these controversial weapons have been employed and heavy civilian casualties have resulted, the party should bear the burden of justifying their use and that the duty of care to protect civilians from the effects of these weapons was satisfied.

1,228 cluster bombs containing 248,056 bomblets were dropped during the aerial bombardment campaign and the latter notes that in the first few weeks of November 2001, the US had deployed 350 cluster bombs. Human Rights Watch notes that the use of such weapons was more restricted than in the past, and that their accuracy was improved by new technology, but to an insufficient degree to alleviate concerns. See, however, Conetta, 'Strange Victory'.

[237] For the controversy around the use of cluster bombs by the US military, see also 'US Deploys Controversial Weapon', *The Guardian*, 12 October 2001. The 1,210 cluster bomb units reportedly deployed between October to December 2001 gave rise to the dispersal of a total of 244,420 bomblets. See further Conetta, 'Strange Victory'.

[238] Para. 6A.3.2.

[239] See 'US Cluster Bombing Provokes Anger', *The Guardian*, 25 October 2001.

[240] Chapter 6.

[241] See 'Long After the Air Raids, Bomblets Bring More Death', *The Guardian*, 28 January 2002. Concerns have been expressed by, *inter alia*, Amnesty International and Human Rights Watch: see Amnesty International, 'Accountability for Civilian Deaths', above, note 217.

[242] See statement regarding US policy in Bosnia, mentioned in Chapter 6, section A; note 110, above.

[243] See reports of human rights groups, the ICTY and US practice in other contexts, referred to in para. 6A.3.2.

Finally, other dubious circumstances attend the use of such weapons that compound concerns as to unlawfulness. These are given dramatic illustration by the statement issued by US 'Psychological Operations' to the people of Afghanistan:

> Noble Afghan people: as you know, the coalition countries have been air-dropping daily humanitarian rations for you. The food ration is enclosed in yellow plastic bags. They come in the shape of rectangular or long squares. The food inside the bags is Halal and very nutritional . . . In areas away from where food has been dropped, cluster bombs will also be dropped. The color of these bombs is also yellow . . . Do not confuse the cylinder-shaped bomb with the rectangular food bag.[244]

It is doubtful that the duty of care owed to the civilian population has been discharged in respect of the facts and circumstances surrounding resort to the use of cluster bombs in Afghanistan.

6B.2.3 Humanitarian protection of prisoners: executions, torture and inhumane treatment

It is perhaps surprising that many of the most controversial aspects of the application of the IHL framework post 9/11 have arisen in relation to humanitarian protections, designed to protect the human dignity of persons who do not (or no longer) take active part in hostilities – a principle with which few would take open exception. These issues have arisen in several contexts post 9/11 including in relation to the detentions in Guantanamo Bay, Cuba, addressed separately in the case study at Chapter 8. Many of the specific questions to arise regarding the application of the IHL framework post 9/11 are therefore addressed in that chapter, despite many of them having also arisen elsewhere. These include: the entitlement to POW status,[245] or to be treated as civilians caught up in conflict; what are so-called 'unlawful combatants' and what is the legal significance of the epithet; is there a 'protection gap' in the Geneva Conventions, such that certain persons are without protection of the law?

---

[244] US Psychological Operations Radio, 28 October 2001, quoted in *BBC News*, 'Radio Warns Afghans over Food Parcels', 28 October 2001, at http://news.bbc.co.uk/hi/english/world/monitoring/media_reports/newsid_1624000/1624787.stm

[245] The question of denial of POW status of prisoners was particularly strking in Iraq. See, e.g., D. Jehl and N.A. Lewis, 'U.S. Disputed Protected Status of Iraq Inmates', *New York Times*, 23 May 2004.

However, beyond Guantanamo Bay (where the issues raised relate principally to the denial of essential procedural rights to detainees),[246] there are many other examples of the treatment of prisoners disregarding international law. Allegations relate to, *inter alia*, summary executions, torture and ill-treatment.[247] These issues have captured international attention most sharply in relation to the widely reported torture and mistreatment of prisoners at Abu Ghraib prison in Iraq.[248] However, evidence has emerged recurrently of serious violations elsewhere in Iraq – committed by other foreign forces[249] – as well as beyond.

In Afghanistan concerns about mistreatment by the US relate to interrogation techniques[250] ranging from the issuance of death threats against prisoners[251] to the imposition of other forms of gross physical and psychological duress.[252] One such case involves the widely reported allegations of ill treatment of detainees in United States custody at the Bagram Air Base north of Kabul.[253] In December 2002 two men being held for questioning at the base died in circumstances where official autopsies concluded that the deceased had suffered 'blunt force injuries' and that their deaths were

---

[246] Note however the allegations of physical and psychological abuse in that context also: see, e.g., 'Guantanamo abuse same as Abu Ghraib, say Britons', *The Guardian*, 14 May 2004.

[247] While the focus is on treatment of prisoners, it is recognised that numerous other humanitarian issues arise, such as the obligations to allow humanitarian relief to affected civilians which has been criticised by UN agencies and others. See Kapferer, 'Ends and Means in Politics', at 117, who describes the decision to continue bombing despite repeated warnings about impact on humanitarian aid efforts as perhaps the single most serious issue of IHL compliance in relation to Afghanistan.

[248] See, e.g., 'America's shame', *The Guardian*, 1 May 2004; S. Chan and M. Amon, 'Prisoner Abuse Probe Widened. Military Intelligence at Center of Investigation', *Washington Post*, 2 May 2004.

[249] Allegations of abuse by UK troops – including beatings, 'sharp, jabbing movements into the area beneath the ribs', hooding and pouring freezing water on detainees – emerged in the context of a challenge in UK courts to the UK Government's decision not to institute investigations. See 'High Court Challenge over Iraqi Civilian Deaths', *The Guardian*, 28 July 2004, available at http://www.guardian.co.uk/Iraq/Story/0,2763,1270930,00.html

[250] To the extent that persons interrogated were entitled to POW status (or a doubt existed as to this entitlement which had not yet been adjudicated), certain forms of persistent interrogation may itself raise questions as to lawfulness. See Chapter 8.

[251] Video footage demonstrating such threats by the CIA agents of prisoners held at the Mazar-I-Sharif fortress was released. See, e.g., Amnesty International reports, above, note 238.

[252] See, e.g., allegations concerning the Bagram Air Base, below.

[253] T. Wagner, 'Amnesty Criticizes U.S. for Afghan Deaths', *Associated Press*, 30 November 2003. Amnesty research revealed 'ill treatment that may amount to torture'.

homicides;[254] despite an official undertaking to investigate the matter, no information has been made public.

Other examples of mistreatment relate, for example, to abysmal conditions of detention resulting in death and serious injuries at the hand of the Northern Alliance.[255] Numerous allegations have also emerged of the extra-judicial execution of prisoners by Northern Alliance fighters.[256]

Executions, torture and ill-treatment do not raise complex legal questions regarding the application of the IHL framework. If established, they are straightforwardly violations of IHL. In light of parallel allegations arising from Guantanamo Bay, Iraq, Afghanistan and elsewhere, others have emerged as to these practices revealing a systematic policy of either encouraging, purporting to justify or turning a blind eye to, such abuse.[257] More complex questions of fact, and to a lesser degree law, relate to the criminal responsibility of those that ordered or, under the doctrine of superior responsibility, failed to prevent such practices.[258] At an absolute minimum, questions have been raised as to whether those in positions of

---

[254] D. Campbell, 'Afghan Prisoners Beaten to Death at US Military Interrogation Base. "Blunt Force Injuries" Cited In Murder Ruling', *The Guardian*, 7 March 2003. See also J. Turley, 'Rights on the Rack. Alleged Torture in Terror War Imperils U.S. Standards of Humanity', *Los Angeles Times*, 6 March 2003 and C. Gall, 'U.S. Military Investigating Death of Afghan in Custody', *New York Times*, 4 March 2003.

[255] See 'Slow Death on the Jail Convoy of Misery', *Daily Telegraph*, 19 March 2002, which reports on transporting Taleban prisoners for days in crammed freight containers, without sufficient air, resulting in the death of hundreds of prisoners. Dire prison conditions in Afghanistan are also reported.

[256] On reports of wounded prisoners shot dead by victorious Northern Alliance troops in Kunduz (26 November 2001), see 'Alliance accused of brutality in capture of Kunduz', *The Guardian*, 27 November 2001. On the alleged massacre of hundreds of pro-Taleban Pakistani fighters by the Northern Alliance in Mazar-I-Sharif, of whom it is not clear whether they died in battle or were executed after surrender, see 'Hundreds of Pakistanis Believed Massacred', *The Guardian*, 13 November 2001.

[257] See, e.g., R. Brody, 'What about the Other Secret U.S. Prisons?', *International Herald Tribune*, 4 May 2004. See also S. Goldenberg, 'CIA Accused of Torture at Bagram Base', *The Guardian*, 27 December 2002 and S. Goldenburg, 'Guantanamo Record Contradicts Claims that Prisoner Abuse Was Isolated', *The Guardian*, 19 May 2004, reporting that 'the abuse at Abu Ghraib was systematic, part of a policy instituted at US military detention centres from Guantanamo and Afghanistan to Iraq'. On allegations of 'justifying' torture see Chapter 7, para. 7B.5.

[258] Persons in positions of authority, at various levels in the chain of command from direct superior to the head of the armed forces, may, depending on the facts established, be responsible for ordering, aiding and abeting or for failing to take reasonable measures to prevent serious violations of IHL. See Chapter 4, para. 4A.1.2.1, 'Individual Responsibility'.

responsibility are doing sufficient to discharge their duty to ensure that their troops respect IHL, and the extent of 'institutional and personal responsibility' at 'high levels'.[259]

These allegations highlight the challenge of ensuring compliance with IHL standards by a party's own troops, and the particular issues that arise in respect of irregular forces, such as the Northern Alliance. One question to be addressed in relation to the multiple allegations of serious and systematic mistreatment by the Northern Alliance in Afghanistan is the legal relationship between those acts and the US and its allies in Afghanistan. The US Defense Secretary Donald Rumsfeld has stated that US policy has been to 'have the forces on the ground that have been opposing the Taliban and Al-Qaida take prisoners themselves and then allow us to do whatever interrogating might be appropriate'.[260] Is the interdependent relationship highlighted above one whereby local forces were, as a matter of fact, under the effective or overall control of the United States and its allies, such that US responsibility arises in respect of wrongs committed by those irregular forces?[261]

In addition to the responsibility incumbent on parties to the conflict in respect of violations by their troops or irregulars under their control, broader duties arise for those parties, and other states party to the Geneva Conventions, as a result of the positive duties to ensure respect for IHL.[262] This implies a duty to refrain from collaborating and cooperating with those that flout IHL standards, and includes a duty to make reasonable inquiries into the activities of potential allies before forging alliances; the duty plainly cannot be reconciled with the formation

---

[259] See, e.g., the Final Report of the Independent Panel to Review DoD Detention Operations, the 'Shlessinger report' (available at http://www.defenselink.mil/news/Aug2004/d20040824finalreport.pdf) finding, in relation to the Abu Ghraib scandal, that 'there is both institutional and personal responsibility at higher levels'.

[260] Department of Defence, News Briefing, Secretary Rumsfeld and General Myers, 26 November 2001, available at http://www.defenselink.mil/news/Nov2001/g011126-D-6570C.html.

[261] See this Chapter, para. 6A.3.5 and Chapter 3, above, *Prosecutor* v. *Dusko Tadic*, Case No. IT-94-1-AR72, Decision on the Defence Motion for Interlocutory Appeal on Jurisdiction, 2 October 1995 (ICTY Appeals Chamber), para. 137. If the US was not responsible for the actions of the Northern Alliance in general, it may nonetheless have been responsible for particular operations carried out at the behest of, or in concert with, the US.

[262] Common Article 1 of the Geneva Conventions, see Chapter 3, para. 3.2.2, above. On the implications for states involved in the war on terror, see Chapter 7, para. 7A.2. in para. 6A.3.5, 'Responsibility and Ensuring Compliance under IHL', Framework, above. These questions also have to be considered by reference to Chapter 3, above.

of alliances with notorious leaders, renowned for past violations, as in Afghanistan.[263]

Questions also arise as to the compatibility of these duties with the 'message' sent to troops on the ground and local 'partners'. Since the Abu Ghraib scandal, questions have focused on the message being sent to US troops regarding the importance of respect for international law and the Geneva Conventions, in light of the notorious disregard for those Conventions in certain situations. Similar questions arise with renewed intensity in relation to those one step removed, who may lack much of the training and preparation enjoyed by regular troops, but who nonetheless are invited to act in consort with coalition forces in Afghanistan.[264] These concerns may be exemplified by comments such as the Secretary of Defense's statement reportedly indicating a preference to see bin Laden dead than brought to trial alive.[265] While there is no suggestion that the US directly sanctioned the execution of prisoners, one may reasonably question whether the importance of compliance with IHL, including the duty to protect persons from the minute they are rendered *hors de combat*, translated into the message conveyed by the US authorities. Questions regarding the partnership between the coalition and the Northern Alliance, whether it impeded – or facilitated – the commission of violations and related questions of legal responsibility, are deserving of further analysis.

6B.2.4 Transparency, inquiry and onus of proof?

Assessing the lawfulness of many of these controversial measures highlighted above depends on information, including of an intelligence nature, to which the public does not, generally, have access. This was particularly so during a military campaign that was characterised by a relative lack of transparency, both in terms of information briefings from the states involved and the absence of media on the territory of the conflict.[266] In

---

[263] See for example, 'Slow Death on the Jail Convoy of Misery', *Daily Telegraph*, 19 March 2002, reporting that 'the captors owe allegiance to Gen Abdul Rashid Dostum, the northern warlord whose men committed similar atrocities in 1997'.

[264] Assuming that he could be lawfully targeted while engaging in hostilities, once he had laid down arms, including through injury, he is protected and his execution would be a serious violation of IHL.

[265] See E. Vulliamy, 'US marines set for mission to hunt out and kill bin Laden', *The Observer*, 25 November 2001. Similar ambiguity surrounded 'encouragement to US troops and others to rein in Saddam Hussein, "dead or alive"'.

[266] The Afghan conflict contrasts unfavourably in this respect with the Kosovo campaign of 1999, wherein NATO held daily briefings and the Iraq conflict where media presence

such circumstances, and in the face of widespread casualties, the onus shifts to the responsible armed forces to demonstrate that the prerequisites of IHL were satisfied in the particular case.

However, repeated calls for explanations and, as appropriate, independent inquiries into apparent violations – including in relation to the controversial Mazar-I-Sharif incident referred to above – have gone unheeded. As an exceptional case, following the deaths of prisoners in US custody at the Bagram Air Base in Afghanistan displaying 'blunt force injuries', the US authorities stated that an inquiry would be conducted,[267] but the progress or findings of the investigation were then never made public, despite repeated requests for a full and public criminal investigation and explanation.[268]

6B.3 Conclusion

By suggesting that the 'war on terror' is an armed conflict of global reach, of which Afghanistan was but a part, the implication is that the rules of IHL applicable in armed conflict govern all aspects of the counter-terrorist measures taken post September 11. But while the multi-faceted 'war on terror' may include the military action taken in Afghanistan, it certainly goes far beyond armed conflict in any legal sense.[269] The Afghan and Iraq interventions led to armed conflicts between identifiable parties, which have or will come to an end as described above. But neither the September 11 attacks nor the subsequent fight against terrorism appear to meet the legal criteria of armed conflict.

---

was considerable. See Amnesty International, 'Afghanistan: Accountability for Civilian Deaths', note 217 above, which describes as 'disturbing' the lack of public information, and notes the lack of access given to impartial observers.

[267] Campbell, 'Afghan Prisoners Beaten to Death', above, note 254. Note that the US government declared itself unable to comment on the matter on the basis of a pending inquiry.

[268] On 12 November 2003, the Lawyers Committee for Human Rights sent a letter (see www.lchr.org) to General John R. Vines, Commander of the US forces in Afghanistan, asking for information on the investigations to be made public, to no apparent avail. See also Wagner, 'Amnesty Criticizes U.S.'. On the positive duties of the state in respect of persons in detention, the duty to investigate and prosecute incidents such as this after the event, and the 'onus of proof' see Chapter 7, section A.

[269] See R. Goldman: 'In reality, while using the term "war", the US is essentially talking about a comprehensive global strategy to confront and defeat terrorism. In that campaign, military force is only one, and not the dominant, tool.' He notes that '[t]he use of the term "war" in connection with the global campaign against terrorism is thus something of a rhetorical flourish'. 21 September 2001, http://www.crimesofwar.org/expert/paradigm-goldman.html.

While the 'war on terror' nomenclature may simply be a rhetorical flourish, it fuels troubling confusion as to applicable legal rules. The 'war' rhetoric may seek to emphasise the security imperative, and perhaps, erroneously, to suggest that that imperative trumps observance of the law.[270] It may seek to justify the application of IHL (in preference to international human rights law, discussed in the following chapter) and correspondingly different, and lower, standards of protection.[271] Critically, as a war whose objective is destroying 'terror' or 'terrorist networks of global reach' may never end, the terminology of war provides a pretext, for example, to detain persons by reference to provisions of IHL that permit detention of combatants during armed conflict, but on an indefinite basis. Fundamentally, clarity as to whether war is war, and IHL is applicable, is important as it is an essential aspect of legality.[272] Ambiguity provides the scope for manipulation of the law and the selective application of standards when it suits the protagonists' agenda of the moment. Where confusion exists, or is generated, around applicable law, the rule of law and respect for it cannot but suffer.

In respect of those aspects of the war that are indeed armed conflicts governed by IHL, allegations have emerged of violations and, as yet, of a failure to conduct thorough investigations and, subject to genuine and compelling security concerns, to make the findings of such investigations public. Critical questions moving forward will be the commitment of states parties – those directly responsible and others – to ensure that effective measures are taken to avoid repetition, in these conflicts or others, including holding to account those individuals directly and indirectly responsible for IHL violations amounting to war crimes.

---

[270] This is misguided and misleading, given the regulation of conflict through IHL and a core of human rights law: on the relationship between human rights law and IHL, see the following chapter.

[271] While certain legal standards – such as the absolute prohibition on ill-treatment or torture – are enshrined in both IHL and IHRL, in respect of questions such as targeting and the lawfulness of detention, standards differ dramatically. Understanding whether conduct is carried out pursuant to an armed conflict may make the difference between an act being characterised as a legitimate act of targeting or an extra-judicial execution, as lawful administrative detention under IHL or arbitrary detention. See Chapter 7, para. 7B.2, below. It may also impact on individual criminal responsibility for war crimes, but note that in armed conflict an individual may be responsible for 'war crimes' where similar conduct in time of peace may not carry individual accountability in international law (though it will most likely be covered by domestic law).

[272] On the principle of legality underpinning any system of law and applicable at all times, including in time of emergency, see also Chapter 7, below.

Great emphasis has been placed by some on the novel features of the international landscape post 9/11 with particular emphasis on the new kind of war raising new kinds of challenges. Implicitly and explicitly, the relevance of IHL and its capacity to meet the challenges of contemporary conflict has been attacked following 9/11. Debate around the need, or not, to revise IHL has consumed considerable attention. To the extent that it might lead to strengthening respect for IHL and its protection, this effort may well be of long term benefit. However, considered reflection by international experts has tended to reject the idea that 9/11 or its aftermath reveal the need for radical revision of IHL. Behind the smoke-screen of this debate the real challenges continue to lurk, only reinforced by 9/11 and its aftermath. As a meeting of experts recently concluded, they relate not to the normative content of IHL but to 'the need to focus on judicial and non-judicial techniques to convince both state and non-state actors to respect the law, and on the strengthening of the effectiveness of the implementation mechanisms'.[273]

This chapter has highlighted some of the IHL issues arising post 9/11 specifically in relation to Afghanistan; further issues relating to IHL and its relationship with other branches of law are addressed in other chapters – on criminal law, above, and in the chapters that follow on human rights law and the case study on detentions at Guantanamo Bay, Cuba.

---

[273] See *VII Round Table on Current Problems of International Humanitarian Law*, 'International Humanitarian Law and Other Legal Regimes: Interplay in Situations of Violence,' Summary Report prepared by the International Committee of the Red Cross, November 2003. The report noted also the attack on the 'inalienable nature of the values' which underlie IHL.

7

International human rights law

The epithet 'subversive' had such a vast and unpredictable reach, the struggle against the 'subversive' had turned into a demential generalized repression with the drift that characterizes the hunting of witches and the possessed.

(National Commission on the Disappeared, Argentina, 1984)[1]

[I]t is not only possible, but also necessary, to fight terrorism while respecting human rights.

(Council of Ministers, Council of Europe, 2002)[2]

7A The legal framework

The basic rules of international human rights law (IHRL) are, for the most part, straightforward. While IHRL protects and promotes a broad range of rights,[3] at its core it is intended to ensure a basic standard of protection for all human beings at all times in all places.

Human rights obligations, which are essentially incumbent upon states,[4] entail 'negative' obligations not to violate protected rights

---

[1] Argentine National Commission on the Disappeared (CONADEP), *Nunca Mas: The Report of the Argentine National Commission on the Disappeared* (1984).

[2] Preamble, *Guidelines on Human Rights and the Fight against Terrorism*, adopted by the Committee of Ministers of the Council of Europe on 11 July 2002.

[3] These include the right to life, liberty and security, freedom of expression or religion, discussed here, but also economic, social and cultural rights such as the rights to food and education. The systematic denial of economic, social and cultural rights is often cited as one of the root causes of international terrorism: on the relationship between respect for these rights and terrorism, see, e.g., A. Lieven, 'The Roots of Terrorism, and a Strategy Against It', 68 (2001) *Prospect Magazine* 13. An analysis of this relationship is not within the scope of this study.

[4] State responsibility and the position of non-state actors is discussed at Chapter 3, para. 3.2. See also para. 7A.4.2 in this chapter.

and 'positive' obligations to take necessary measures to 'ensure' their protection.[5] Establishing an effective counter-terrorism strategy to guard against the commission of serious violations of human security such as those committed on September 11 is not only consistent with the human rights framework, it is required by it. But to be lawful – and indeed, as has been noted in recent months, to be effective – that strategy must in turn respect and be informed by the limits of IHRL.[6] The content of human rights law is not blind to, but accommodates, the real security issues to which the events of September 11 gave dramatic illustration. Human rights law continues to apply, however, albeit in potentially more restrictive form, even in times of national emergency or armed conflict.[7]

As with previous chapters this one is in two parts. Section A sets out the framework of IHRL in relation to the following: first, the sources of human rights law that can be drawn on to assess the rights applicable in any particular situation; second, where, to whom and in what circumstances human rights law is applicable, including the role of IHRL when the state acts beyond its own territory; third, the IHRL framework, and its adaptability, in times of crisis or emergency; fourth, the content of certain specific rights commonly implicated by the 'war on terror'. Section B highlights issues concerning the application of this framework in responses to September 11. An analysis of the application of the framework of IHRL (and IHL) in a concrete case is found in Chapter 8.

7A.1 Sources and mechanisms of international human rights law[8]

International human rights law is found first in international and regional treaties that bind those states that have become parties to the treaties through ratification. Ratification of human rights treaties is widespread; for example, at the time of writing, 152 states have ratified the International Covenant on Civil and Political Rights, including the US, UK,

---

[5] See para. 7A.4.1. in this chapter.

[6] The importance of making human rights concerns integral to counter-terrorism efforts has been emphasised by the UN Secretary-General Kofi Annan in an address to the Security Council's session on counter-terrorism: 'in the long term, we shall find that human rights, along with democracy and social justice, are one of the best prophylactics against terrorism. [W]hile we certainly need vigilance to prevent acts of terrorism, and firmness in condemning and punishing them, it would be self-defeating if we sacrifice other key priorities – as human rights – in the process' (Security Council, Summary Record of the 4453rd meeting, 18 January 2002, UN Doc. S/PV.4453).

[7] On the relationship between IHRL and the more specific rules of international humanitarian law also in armed conflict see para. 7A.3.4 in this chapter.

[8] See Chapter 1, para. 1.2.1.

Afghanistan and Iraq.[9] The European Convention on Human Rights and Fundamental Freedoms has been ratified by a total of 45 states of the Council of Europe[10] the American Convention on Human Rights by 25 states of the Americas[11] and the African Charter on Human and People's Rights by 53 African states.[12] For those states that have signed but not ratified a convention (for example the US with the ACHR), while they are not legally bound by it, they undertake to act in good faith, and not inconsistently with its spirit.[13] In addition to these general human rights treaties, are others that address specific violations or protect specific groups of persons, such as the Convention on the Elimination of All Forms of Discrimination against Women[14] and the Convention on the Rights of the Child.[15] In addition, the UN Charter, binding on all 191 UN member states,[16] might itself be seen (albeit not exclusively) as 'a human rights instrument imposing human rights obligations on the 191

---

[9] For the status of ratification of the ICCPR, and of the main UN human rights conventions, see Office of the UN High Commissioner for Human Rights, at www.unhchr.ch.

[10] Source: Council of Europe Treaty Office, at http://conventions.coe.int.

[11] Source: OAS Secretariat for Legal Affairs, at http://www.oas.org/juridico/english/Sigs/ b-32.html. In addition to the American Convention on Human Rights, a particularly relevant instrument for the protection of human rights in the OAS system is represented by the American Declaration of the Rights and Duties of Man, OAS Res. XXX. Although the American Declaration, approved by the Ninth International Conference of American States in 1948, was initially intended to be a non-binding instrument, the human rights bodies of the Inter-American system have constantly applied the Declaration as an 'indirectly binding' legal text. See Inter-American Commission on Human Rights, *James Terry Roach and Jay Pinkerton* v. *United States*, Case 9647, Res. 3/87, 22 September 1987, *Annual Report 1986–87*, p. 147, at p. 165. See also *Certain Attributes of the Inter-American Commission on Human Rights (Arts. 41, 42, 44, 46, 47, 50 and 51 of the American Convention on Human Rights)*, Advisory Opinion OC-13/93, 16 July 1993, IACtHR, *Series A*, No. 13, paras. 42–5, where the Court refers to the Declaration as a source of 'international obligations'.

[12] African Charter on Human and People's Rights, Banjul, 27 June 1981, OAU Doc. CAB/LEG/67/3 rev. 5, reprinted in 21 ILM 58, entered into force 21 October 1986.

[13] See Article 18, VCLT 1969.

[14] Convention on the Elimination of All Forms of Discrimination Against Women, New York, 18 December 1979, 1249 UNTS 13 (hereinafter 'CEDAW'). As of November 2003, CEDAW has been ratified by 174 states (source: Office of the UN High Commissioner for Human Rights, at www.unhchr.ch) including the UK (7 April 1986), and has been signed by Afghanistan (14 August 1980) and the US (17 July 1980).

[15] Convention on the Rights of the Child, 20 November 1989, 1577 UNTS 44 (hereinafter 'CRC') As of November 2003, the CRC has been ratified by 192 states, including Afghanistan (28 March 1994), the United Kingdom (16 December 1991) and signed by the United States on 16 February 1995 (source: Office of the UN High Commissioner for Human Rights, at www.unhchr.ch).

[16] See www.un.org/Overview/unmember.html.

Member States of the United Nations'[17] in that it stipulates 'promoting and encouraging respect for human rights and for fundamental freedom for all without distinction as to race, sex, language or religion' as one of the underlying purposes of the United Nations.[18] Binding treaty provisions are supplemented by the many so-called 'soft law' standards of relevance to human rights, contained in, for example, resolutions of the UN General Assembly or other international or regional bodies.[19]

Alongside treaty provision is customary international law which obliges all states, regardless of whether they have ratified a relevant international or regional treaty, to respect certain rights and freedoms.[20] As noted, the existence of a norm of customary international law generally depends on both practice that is 'extensive and virtually uniform' and *opinio juris*, in other words 'general recognition that a rule of law or legal obligation is

---

[17] See B. Simma (ed.), *The Charter of the United Nations, A Commentary*, 2nd ed. (Oxford, 2002), pp. 92–3; I. Brownlie, *Principles of Public International Law*, 6th ed. (Oxford, 2003), p. 532.

[18] Article 1(3). See also Article 1(2) which refers to developing friendly relations between nations 'based on respect for the principle of equal rights and self determination of peoples', and Articles 55 and 56. See Chapter 5, in particular the discussion of 'humanitarian intervention', as regards the relationship with the Article 1(1) purpose 'to maintain international peace and security' and the prohibition on the use of force in Article 2(4).

[19] While not binding *per se*, they give more detailed expression to some of the binding prescriptions and prohibitions of international law and may reflect customary law, see Chapter 1, para. 1.2.1.3. The Universal Declaration on Human Rights is foremost among the non-treaty instruments. Other instruments of relevance to human rights and the 'war on terror' include: UN 'Code of Conduct For Law Enforcement Officials', GA Res. 34/169, 17 December 1979, UN Doc. A/RES/34/169 (1979); Turku Declaration on Minimum Humanitarian Standards, Helsinki, 2 December 1990; Paris Minimum Standards of Human Rights Norms in a State of Emergency, approved by consensus during the 61st Conference of the International Law Association, Paris, 26 August – 1 September 1984 (reprinted in 79 (1985) AJIL 1072); UN 'Body of Principles for the Protection of All Persons under Any Form of Detention or Imprisonment', GA Res. 43/173, 9 December 1988, UN Doc. A/RES/43/173 (1988); UN Standard Minimum Rules for the Treatment of Prisoners, adopted 30 August 1955 by the First United Nations Congress on the Prevention of Crime and the Treatment of Offenders, UN Doc. A/CONF/611, Annex I; Basic Principles on the Independence of the Judiciary, UN Doc. A/CONF.121/22/Rev. 1 at 59, adopted at the 1985 Milan conference and approved by the UN General Assembly (GA Res. 40/32, 29 November 1985 and GA Res. 40/146, 13 December 1985); UN Basic Principles on the Role of Lawyers, adopted at the 8th UN Congress on Crime Prevention 1990; the Declaration of Basic Principles of Justice for Victims of Crime and Abuse of Power 1985, the Proclamation of Teheran, proclaimed by the International Conference on Human Rights at Teheran on 13 May 1968 and the Johannesburg Principles on National Security, Freedom of Expression and Access to Information, UN Doc. E/CN.4/1996/39.

[20] Treaties that are not binding on a state may be relevant to assessing the state's obligations insofar as they reflect customary law.

involved'.[21] However, in the case of international human rights law and humanitarian law, it has been suggested by some commentators that the existence of a consistent, 'extensive and virtually uniform' practice is not as important, and that *opinio juris*, as expressed in international organisations, or by ratifying a treaty, plays a much greater role.[22] The fact that in some countries there may be daily occurrences of torture, arbitrary detention and extra-judicial killings does not preclude the existence of customary international human rights norms as these acts, while practiced, are universally regarded as unlawful.[23]

The question whether particular rights are sufficiently supported by state practice and *opinio juris* to have passed into customary law is the subject of much debate. Some commentators suggest that a substantial number of the rights contained in the 1948 Universal Declaration on Human Rights reflect customary law[24] while others would cite more restrictive lists.[25] The Restatement (Third) of the Foreign Relations Law of the US, for example, adds prolonged arbitrary detention, systematic racial discrimination, extra-judicial executions and causing the disappearance of individuals as prohibited in customary law.[26]

The significance of the debate on the content of customary law is diminished by the fact that so many states have assumed human rights obligations through treaties; custom is therefore often referred to simply to underscore the universality of those obligations. But in certain instances it may arise that a state is not bound by the relevant treaty law or, as discussed below, seeks to 'derogate' from its terms, and customary status must be assessed to determine which norms are binding nonetheless.[27]

---

[21] *North Sea Continental Shelf, ICJ Reports 1969*, p. 43. See the Statute of the International Court of Justice, Article 38(1)(b) which refers to international custom as 'evidence of a general practice accepted as law'. See Chapter 1.

[22] See, in general, T. Meron, *Human Rights and Humanitarian Law as International Customary Norms* (Oxford, 1989).

[23] See the approach of the ICJ in *Military and Paramilitary Activities in and against Nicaragua, Merits, ICJ Reports 1986*, p. 14. See also R. Higgins, *Problems and Process: International Law and How We Use It* (Oxford, 1994), pp. 19–22.

[24] The Universal Declaration was adopted in 1948 without dissent. See R. B. Lillich, 'Civil Rights', in T. Meron (ed.), *Human Rights in International Law* (Oxford, 1988), pp. 116 ff. The Proclamation of Teheran underlines that 'The Universal Declaration of Human Rights states a common understanding of the peoples of the world concerning the inalienable and inviolable rights of all members of the human family and constitutes an obligation for the members of the international community' (para. 2).

[25] O. Schachter, *International Law in Theory and Practice* (Dordrecht, 1991), cites, *inter alia*, 'slavery, genocide, torture and other cruel, inhuman and degrading treatment'.

[26] Restatement (Third) of the Foreign Relations Law of the United States (1987), section 702.

[27] As noted below, para. 7A.3.3 in this chapter, derogations from treaty provisions are allowed in situations of emergency, but states would remain bound by custom. On 'conditions for

It may also be of particular significance in states where customary – as opposed to treaty law – forms part of domestic law.

Some of these customary norms are additionally accepted and recognised as having attained the status of *jus cogens*. As such, the obligation cannot be deviated from in any circumstances, and cannot be changed through shifting state practice as other customary norms can; instead it can only be overridden by the establishment of another *jus cogens* norm.[28] Any assessment of the impact of practice post September 11 on changing law must therefore be mindful of the peremptory status of certain human rights. Commentators differ on which rights have attained this status, with some suggesting that it largely reflects the core non-derogable rights in the ICCPR (discussed below),[29] and others the shorter list of non-derogable rights common to the 'three major human rights treaties'.[30] International bodies have advanced various illustrative 'lists': most significantly the list of the Human Rights Committee includes 'collective punishments, through arbitrary deprivations of liberty or by deviating from fundamental principles of fair trial',[31] while the International Law Commission, in its Commentary to the 2001 Articles on Responsibility

derogation', see para. 7A.3.2.1 in this chapter. Custom is also significant in interpreting treaty law as no valid derogation from treaty law can depart from other international obligations, including customary international law.

[28] Article 53, VCLT 1969, defines *jus cogens* as 'a peremptory norm of general international law . . . a norm accepted and recognized by the international community of States as a whole as a norm from which no derogation is permitted and which can be modified only by a subsequent norm of general international law having the same character'.

[29] See Lillich, 'Civil Rights', p. 118, fn. 17: 'In seeking to determine what human rights protected by the Political Covenant have achieved *jus cogens* status, a good starting point is the list of rights which art. 4(2) makes nonderogable.' But note that the Human Rights Committee has noted that 'the enumeration of non-derogable provisions in Article 4 is related to, but not identical with, the question of whether certain human rights obligations bear the nature of peremptory norms of international law'. See Human Rights Committee, General Comment No. 29: Derogations during a state of emergency (Article 4) [2001], UN Doc. HRI/GEN/1/Rev.6 (2003) at 186, para. 11. It continues by noting that '[t]he proclamation of certain provisions of the Covenant as being of a non-derogable nature . . . is to be seen partly as recognition of the peremptory nature of some fundamental rights ensured in treaty form in the Covenant (e.g., Articles 6 and 7). However, it is apparent that some other provisions of the Covenant were included in the list of non-derogable provisions because it can never become necessary to derogate from these rights during a state of emergency (e.g., Articles 11 and 18).'

[30] J. Fitzpatrick, *Human Rights in Crisis. The International System for Protecting Rights During States of Emergency* (Washington, 1994), p. 67. The author suggests the minimal standard of non-derogable rights common to the specified conventions covers life, freedom from torture and inhuman and degrading treatment or punishment, slavery and the prohibition of retrospective legislation.

[31] General Comment No. 29 (above, note 28), para. 11.

of States for Internationally Wrongful Acts, lists the prohibitions of aggression, genocide, slavery and racial discrimination, crimes against humanity, torture, apartheid, the basic rules of humanitarian law in armed conflict and the right to self determination, as being generally accepted as norms from which no derogation is permitted.[32]

These international norms are accompanied by mechanisms for the enforcement of human rights. The first group of mechanisms are the 'treaty bodies' charged with overseeing the application of their particular constituent treaty. For example, the Human Rights Committee is the body charged with the authoritative interpretation and application of the ICCPR. The European Court of Human Rights fulfils this function in respect of the ECHR, as do the Inter-American Commission on Human Rights and the Inter-American Court on Human Rights in relation to the ACHR and the American Declaration of the Rights and Duties of Man and the African Commission on Human and People's Rights in relation to the African Charter.[33] The functions of these bodies vary, but commonly they provide a forum (in respect of states that have accepted their jurisdiction) for individual cases to be brought alleging violations of human rights,[34] as well as often having a broader function in promoting legal standards and monitoring specific situations.[35] Some of them have the power to issue decisions that states are legally obliged to follow: the

---

[32] See ILC Commentaries to Articles on State Responsibility, Introductory Commentary to Part Two, ch. III; A. Clapham, 'Human Rights Sovereignty and Immunity in the Recent Work of the International Court of Justice', in 14.1 (2002) *INTERIGHTS Bulletin* 29.

[33] For the functions of the Human Rights Committee in relation to the ICCPR, see Articles 28 ff. ICCPR; for the ECtHR in respect to the ECHR, see Article 19 ECHR; for the Inter-American Commission and Court on Human Rights in relation to the ACHR see Article 33 ACHR; the Committee on the Elimination of Discrimination against Women in relation to CEDAW, see Article 17 CEDAW; the Optional Protocol to CEDAW; and the Committee on the Rights of the Child regarding CRC, see Article 43 CRC.

[34] In the Inter-American system individuals petition the Inter-American Commission on Human Rights, which may take the case before the Court, although a recent rule change provides for a degree of direct victim intervention before the Court. See A. Bovino, 'The Victim before the Inter-American Court of Human Rights', 14.1 (2002) *INTERIGHTS Bulletin* 40. Article 5(3) of the Protocol to the African Charter on Human and Peoples' Rights on the Establishment of an African Court on Human and Peoples' Rights (Burkina Faso, 8–10 June 1998), provides that 'the Court may entitle ... individuals to institute cases directly before it, in accordance with article 34(6) of this Protocol' where the State against which the complaint is lodged has made a declaration accepting the competence of the Court to hear individual claims. Before the ECtHR, individuals can, since the introduction of Protocol 11, institute cases directly, though previously applications were presented to the European Commission.

[35] See, e.g., the General Comments of the Human Rights Committee, or its observations on country reports, referred to later in this chapter. For examples of the role of various human

decisions of the European Court of Human Rights and Inter-American Court of Human Rights are binding on the parties to the ECHR or states which have accepted the jurisdiction of the Inter-American Court, respectively. By contrast, the decisions of the Human Rights Committee, the Inter-American Commission on Human Rights, and the African Commission on Human and People's Rights have traditionally been considered not legally binding, although the approach to this question may be evolving through jurisprudence.[36] However, the critical importance of the determinations of each of the above mechanisms lies in the fact that they provide authoritative interpretations of the treaties in question, which clearly are binding on state parties to them.

A second group of mechanisms are those set up by the UN Commission on Human Rights or regional bodies to investigate human rights issues which are not linked to ratification of particular treaties. These include the Working Group on Arbitrary Detention or the Special Rapporteurs established to explore, monitor and report on respect for particular human rights.[37]

International provisions are paralleled by the human rights guarantees manifest in the national laws and constitutions of most, if not all,

---

rights bodies in clarifying legal standards and monitoring compliance post September 11, see section B following.

[36] The Human Rights Committee has indicated that respect of the interim measures is obligatory, by finding that non-respect for those decisions constitutes a breach of the ICCPR and its Optional Protocol and the duty of the State to cooperate with the Committee in individual communications: see, e.g., *M. Dante Piandiong, M. Jesus Morallos and M. Archie Bulan* v. *Philippines* (Comm. No. 869/1999), decision of 19 October 2000, UN Doc. CCPR/C/70/D/869/1999, paras. 5.1, 5.2 and 5.4; *Denzil Roberts* v. *Barbados* (Comm. No. 504/992), decision of 19 July 1994, UN Doc. CCPR/C/51/D/504/1992, para. 6.3; *Gilbert Samuth Kandu-Bo, Khemalai Idrissa, Tamba Gborie, Alfred Abu Sankoh, Hassan Karim Conteh, Daniel Kobina Anderson, John Amadu Sonica Conteh, Abu Bakarr Kamara, Abdul Karim Sesay, Kula Samba, Victor L. King and Jim Kelly Jalloh* v. *Sierra Leone* (Comm. Nos. 839, 840 and 841/1998), decision of 4 November 1998, UN Doc. CCPR/C/64/D/839, 840 & 841/1998. As an indication of evolution as regards the position of the Inter American Commission, see the comments of the Inter-American Court of Human Rights in *Loayza Tamayo* v. *Peru*, Judgment of 17 September 1997, para. 80.

[37] E.g., Special Rapporteurs on Torture, Inhuman and Degrading Treatment (see, e.g., http://www.oneworld.org/scf/mcr/srt.htm), the Independence of Lawyers and Judges (see http://www.frontlinedefenders.org/manual/en/rij_m.htm), the Freedom of Expression (see, e.g., http://www.cidh.oas.org/Relatoria/default.htm); there are UN and regional special rapporteurs. Procedures for dealing with communications relating to violations of human rights and fundamental freedoms (the so-called 1503 and 1235 procedures, established by Resolution 1235 (XLII) of 6 June 1967 and Resolution 1503 (XLVIII) of 27 May 1970 of the Economic and Social Council, respectively) are also available before the UN Human Rights Commission.

domestic legal systems.[38] By applying national and at times international human rights norms to address challenges to the lawfulness of domestic counter-terrorist measures (as legal challenges post September 11 demonstrate)[39] national courts exercise primary responsibility to provide a mechanism for the redress of violations. IHRL is subsidiary to national systems and provides norms and mechanisms that protect the individual where national legal regimes fail to do so.[40]

7A.2 Scope of application of human rights obligations

7A.2.1 Territorial scope of human rights obligations – 'the jurisdiction question'

Generally, a state is not considered responsible for human rights violations arising on another state's territory. This is subject to certain increasingly important qualifications, of relevance to an appraisal of the 'war on terror'.[41]

First, it is generally accepted that where a State acts towards an individual subject to its jurisdiction in a manner that leads to a violation of that individual's rights, the State is responsible, even if the violations arise outside its territory (provided that the risk of violation had been foreseeable at the relevant time). Typical examples of this kind of 'extraterritorial reach' of human rights obligations, as seen from the case law of the human rights bodies, is the transfer of persons, through expulsion or extradition, to another state where there is a substantial risk of their rights being violated.[42] These obligations are explained in relation to 'non-refoulement' later in this chapter.[43]

Moreover, by way of second qualification, certain breaches of obligations which occur entirely at the hand of other states, on other territories,

---

[38] See H. Duffy, 'National Constitutional Compatibility and the International Criminal Court', 11 (2001) *Duke Journal of Comparative and International Law* 5 at 15.

[39] E.g., the challenge in UK courts re Guantanamo Bay detainees invoked the Human Rights Act and through it European and international jurisprudence (*R (Abbasi and another)* v. *Secretary of State for Foreign and Commonwealth Affairs* [2002] EWCA Civ. 159 (hereinafter '*Abbasi*')); similarly the cases of *Rasul, Odah* and *Hamdi* in US courts invoked the US constitution and international human rights law (see para. 7B.6 below).

[40] Hence the 'exhaustion of domestic remedies' rule applied by most (but not all) human rights mechanisms.

[41] On specific issues raised post September 11, see para. 7B.1 below.

[42] See, e.g., cases referred to in para. 7A.4.3.8, this chapter.

[43] The sending state will itself be responsible for violations of the rights of the individual in the other state by virtue of having expelled the person, despite the risk involved. See para. 7A.4.3.8 in this chapter.

may nonetheless be of such a nature that all states collectively have an interest, or indeed a duty, to cooperate to end the violation, even where no other link exists between the state and the violation in question. These developments are also discussed elsewhere.[44]

The third and principal qualification relates to situations where the state itself acts outside its own territory. Human rights law obliges the state to protect the rights of all persons over whom the state exercises authority or control. The precise language delineating the scope of human rights obligations varies between treaty provisions: for example, the ECHR and ACHR provide that states must secure the rights to 'everyone within their jurisdiction',[45] while the ICCPR refers to the state party's obligations to 'respect and ensure to all individuals within its territory and subject to its jurisdiction the rights recognised in the present convention'.[46] Both for the ICCPR, where 'territory' and 'jurisdiction' present a disjunctive test, and for regional treaties, which do not mention 'territory' at all, it has become well established that a state has obligations both towards persons within its borders and beyond, where that state exercises sufficient authority and control abroad.[47]

Human rights courts and bodies, international and regional, have long recognised that where a state exercises such authority and control it assumes the obligation to respect the human rights of persons affected thereby. Thus, for example, the Human Rights Committee found Uruguay responsible for kidnapping and mistreatment by Uruguayan security forces on Argentinian soil[48] and Israel responsible for violations

---

[44] See para. 7B.3.4.2 in this chapter and Chapter 3, para. 3.1.3.

[45] Article 1 ECHR refers to 'secur[ing] to everyone within their jurisdiction' the rights protected therein, and Article 1 ACHR, similarly, refers to 'ensur[ing] to all persons subject to their jurisdiction' the ACHR rights. The African Charter on Human and Peoples Rights makes no reference to jurisdiction or territory, simply emphasising the duty to protect the rights in the Charter.

[46] Article 2, ICCPR. The test is well established as a disjunctive one, according to jurisprudence interpreting the provision, see below.

[47] On the disjunctive nature of the territory or control test, see T. Meron, *Human Rights in Internal Strife: Their Protection* (Cambridge, 1987), p. 40.

[48] See *Lopez Burgos v. Uruguay* (Comm. No. 52/1979), Views of 29 July 1981, UN Doc. CCPR/C/13/D/52/1979 and *Celiberti de Casariego v. Uruguay* (Comm. No. 56/1979), Views of 29 July 1981, UN Doc. CCPR/C/13/D/56/1979, in particular the individual opinion of Tomuschat (attached to both decisions); *Montero v. Uruguay* (Comm. No. 106/1981), Views of 31 March 1983, UN Doc. CCPR/C/18/D/106/1981, para. 5. See also Concluding Observations of the Human Rights Committee: United States of America, UN Doc. CCPR/C/79/Add.50 (1995); para. 19, and generally Human Rights Committee, General Comment No. 31: The Nature of the General Legal Obligation Imposed on States Parties to the Covenant (Article 2) [2004], UN Doc. CCPR/C/74/CRP.4/Rev.6. Likewise, the extra-territorial application of the International Covenant on Economic Social and

in occupied territory,[49] the European Court of Human Rights found Turkey responsible for violations by its military in Cyprus,[50] and the Inter-American Commission on Human Rights has acknowledged that the human rights obligations of the United States continued to apply during the US invasion of Grenada[51] and, most recently, in respect of the detainees in Guantanamo Bay.[52]

The principle underlying the extra-territorial application of a state's human rights obligations has been clearly expressed in the decisions of these bodies. The Human Rights Committee has described it as 'unconscionable' to 'interpret the responsibility under the . . . Covenant as to permit a state party to perpetrate violations of the Covenant on the territory of another state, which violations it could not perpetrate on its own territory'.[53]

The extra-territorial reach of the obligations created by human rights treaties has been recently restated by the Human Rights Committee in the following terms:

> States parties are required by article 2, paragraph 1, to respect and ensure the Covenants rights to all persons who may be within their territory and to all persons subject to their jurisdiction. This means that a State party

Cultural Rights extends to areas not necessarily within the state's sovereign territory and jurisdiction. See Concluding Observations of the Committee on Economic, Social and Cultural Rights: Israel, UN Doc. E/C.12/1/Add.90 (2003), (para. 15) and Concluding observations of the Committee on Economic, Social and Cultural Rights: Israel, UN Doc. E/C.12/1/Add.69 (2001), paras. 11–12.

[49] Concluding observations of the Human Rights Committee: Israel, UN Doc. CCPR/C/79/Add.93 (1998); Concluding observations of the Human Rights Committee: Israel, CCPR/CO/78/ISR (2003).

[50] *Loizidou* v. *Turkey* (Appl. No. 15318/89), Merits, 18 December 1996, 23 (1996) EHRR 513. See also *Cyprus* v. *Turkey* (Appl. No. 25781/94), Merits, Judgment of 10 May 2001, ECtHR, *Reports 2001-IV*. The European Court of Human Rights has considered numerous other cases where extra-territorial application of the Convention has been explicitly endorsed, or not raised as an issue in dispute. See note 56, below. Note, however, the apparently more restrictive approach in *Banković and others* v. *Belgium and 16 other Contracting States*, (Appl. No. 52207/99), Admissibility decision of 19 December 1999, *Reports 2001-XII* (hereinafter '*Banković*'), discussed below, concerning the bombardment of Belgrade by NATO forces.

[51] See *Coard et al.* v. *the United States*, Inter-American Commission on Human Rights (Case 10.951), Report No. 109/99, 29 September 1999, Annual Report of the IACHR (1999). The Inter-American Commission referred to similar previous cases involving the assassination of a Chilean diplomat in the US and attacks by Surinamese officials in the Netherlands (see in particular, *ibid.*, note 7).

[52] On 13 March 2002 the Commission authorised precautionary measures in favour of detainees being held by the United States at Guantanamo Bay, Cuba. See Inter-American Commission on Human Rights, *Precautionary Measures in Guantanamo Bay*, Cuba, 13 March 2002.

[53] *Lopez Burgos* v. *Uruguay* (above, note 47), para. 12.

must respect and ensure the rights laid down in the Covenant to anyone within the *power or effective control* of that State Party, even if not situated within the territory of the State Party . . . This principle also applies to those within the power or effective control of the forces of a State Party acting outside its territory, regardless of the circumstances in which such power or effective control was obtained.[54]

The Inter-American Commission has similarly noted that:

Given that individual rights inhere simply by virtue of a person's humanity, each American state is obliged to uphold the protected rights of any person subject to its jurisdiction. While this most commonly refers to persons within a state's territory, it may under given circumstances, refer to conduct with an extraterritorial locus where the person concerned is present in the territory of one state, but subject to the control of another state – usually through the acts of the latter's agents abroad.[55]

More recently, this approach was confirmed in the decision of the Inter-American Commission to adopt precautionary measures in relation to persons detained at Guantanamo Bay,[56] in which the Commission stated that the key question was not nationality or geographical locus but 'whether, under the specific circumstances, that person fell within the state's authority and control'.

In turn, the judgments of the European Court of Human Rights and decisions of the European Commission of Human Rights have often taken a similar tack, recognising for example that

[t]he High Contracting Parties are bound to secure the said rights and freedoms to all persons under their actual responsibility, whether that authority is exercised within their own territory or abroad.[57]

---

[54] Human Rights Committee, General Comment No. 31, above, note 48 (emphasis added).
[55] *Coard et al.* v. *the United States*, para. 37.
[56] See Inter-American Commission on Human Rights, *Precautionary Measures in Guantanamo Bay*, citing *Coard* v. *the United States*, para. 37.
[57] *Cyprus* v. *Turkey*, Commission Admissibility decision, 26 May 1975, 2 DR 125. See also *Drodz and Janousek* v. *France and Spain* (Appl. No. 12747/87), Judgment of 26 June 1992, ECtHR, *Series A*, No. 240; *Hess* v. *United Kingdom* (Appl. No. 6231/73), Commission Decision on Admissibility, 28 May 1975, 2 DR 72 (on UK responsibility for the administration of the Allied Military Prison in Berlin); *Reinette* v. *France* (Appl. No. 14009/88), Commission Decision on Admissibility, 2 October 1989, 63 DR 189 (on French responsibility for detaining persons on St Vincent); *Stocké* v. *Federal Republic of Germany* (App. 11755/85), Judgment of 19 March 1991, *Series A*, No. 199 (concerning the abduction of a person for the purposes of bringing them within German territory), see para. 166. See also *Xhavara and others* v. *Italy and Albania* (App. 39473/98), admissibility decision of 11 January 2001, unreported, concerning damage done to Albanian refugees by an Italian war vessel off the coast of Italy; *Issa and others* v. *Turkey* (Appl. No. 31821/96), Admissibility decision of 20 May

The Commission indicated in one case that the critical question was whether the state's acts or omissions 'affect' individuals abroad.[58]

In a recent case, however, the European Court of Human Rights adopted a restrictive approach, emphasising that while human rights obligations may extend beyond a state's own territory, such extra-territorial application of obligations should be considered exceptional. In *Banković* v. *Belgium* (the admissibility decision concerning allegations of human rights violations resulting from the bombardment of the Belgrade television station *Radio Televizije Srbije* by NATO forces on 26 April 1999), the Court found that the aerial bombardment by NATO forces (including states parties to the ECHR) failed to fall within any such exception. There is no suggestion in the judgment that military action is *per se* excluded from the scope of the Convention,[59] but rather the key issue appears to be the lack of control by NATO states over Belgrade, the territory on which the alleged violations took place.[60] The European Court rejected the arguments that it is sufficient that a state has control over the *individuals* directly affected by its military action, as opposed to control of the territory itself, and that the distinction between control of the ground and air space was, in modern warfare, untenable.

As a judgment focused quite restrictively on the facts of the case, it is difficult to discern from it the contours of the sort of extra-territorial exercise of authority that *would*, in the Court's view, fall within the scope of the Convention. What is clear is that the Court accepted that where the state exercised 'effective control of the relevant territory and its inhabitants abroad' it remains bound by the Convention to respect the rights of persons on that foreign territory. It also appears to suggest, perhaps somewhat doubtfully, that where the 'consent' of the territorial state has

---

2000, concerning Iraqi shepherds killed by Turkish forces during a military operation in Iraq; *Ilascu and others* v. *Moldova and the Russian Federation* (Appl. No. 48797/99), Judgement of 8 July 2004 [Grand Chamber] (concerning Russian actions in Moldova) and *Öcalan* v. *Turkey* (Appl. No. 46221/99), ECtHR, Admissibility Decision of 14 December 2000.

[58] *Cyprus* v. *Turkey*, Commission Admissibility decision, 26 May 1975, 2 DR 125 at 282: '[T]he authorized agents of the state, including diplomatic or consular agents and armed forces, not only remain under its jurisdiction when abroad but bring any other person or property within that jurisdiction . . . to the extent that they exercise authority over such persons or property. Insofar as, by their acts or omissions, they affect such persons or property, the responsibility of the state is engaged.'

[59] This is borne out by the later case of *Djavit An* v. *Turkey* (Appl. No. 20652/92), Judgment of 20 February 2003.

[60] Military action was capable of satisfying the jurisdictional threshold where the state exercised control of the territory. See *Banković*, above, para. 70, referring to *Loizidou* v. *Turkey*.

been obtained before acting, such that the state exercises all or some of the public powers normally exercised by the government, the Convention is more readily applicable.[61] It was not in dispute in the case that the Convention covers the 'classic' exercise of legal authority in the form of arrest, detention or exercise of judicial authority abroad by state agents.[62]

Questions arise as to the potential implications of the *Banković* judgment. In the European context questions include the compatibility of the Court's strict constructionist approach in this case[63] with its general approach to the Convention as a 'living instrument'.[64] The decision sits incongruously with the changing nature of state practice and evolving concepts of responsibility in international law generally.[65] Its application

---

[61] *Banković*, para. 71. However, the logic of the Convention which ascribes rights directly to individuals (rather than creating purely inter-state obligations) renders doubtful that consent of the territorial state itself should be relevant to the intervening state's obligations. (The fact of consent may, however, be relevant to the responsibility of the territorial state for potentially facilitating human rights violations against persons within its jurisdiction – a question that may be relevant to the Yemen attack by the US, discussed below, where popular speculation held it that the US acted with the consent or authorisation, and indeed cooperation, of the Yemen authorities.) By contrast the Human Rights Committee noted explicitly in *Lopez Burgos* v. *Uruguay* (above, note 47), para. 12.3, that the state is accountable for violations which its agents commit upon the territory of another state 'whether with the acquiescence of the government of the state or in opposition to it'.

[62] See the submission by the UK Government in *Banković*, paras. 45 ff. The Court did not expressly address these points in the judgment, but neither does it contradict or question the earlier jurisprudence on the extra-territorial application of the Convention in such cases.

[63] See the discussion of the drafting history of Article 1 of the ECHR and of similar Articles of other instruments for the protection of human rights (*Banković*, paras. 19 ff.) The heavy reliance on the *travaux préparatoires* in interpreting the concept of 'jurisdiction' (see *ibid.*, para. 65: '[T]he extracts from the *travaux préparatoires* detailed above constitute a clear indication of the intended meaning of Article 1 of the Convention which cannot be ignored') led the Court to conclude that 'The Convention was not designed to be applied throughout the world, even in respect of the conduct of Contracting States' (*ibid.*, para. 80).

[64] See, e.g., *Tyrer* v. *United Kingdom* (Appl. No. 5856/72), Judgment of 25 April 1978, ECtHR, Series A, No. 26, para. 3: 'the Convention is a living instrument which . . . must be interpreted in the light of present-day conditions'. See also *Soering* v. *United Kingdom* (Appl. No. 10438/88), Judgment of 7 July 1989, Series A, No. 161, para. 120; *Dudgeon* v. *United Kingdom* (Appl. No. 7525/76), Judgment of 22 October 1981, ECtHR, Series A, No. 45. The European Court's fairly expansive approach to substantive rights may contrast with a restrictive approach to procedural matters.

[65] In an increasingly interconnected world a strict territorial approach becomes more difficult to justify and sits uncomfortably with other developments, such as in relation to universal jurisdiction, discussed in Chapter 4; para. 4A.1.3.1, collective responsibility, discussed in para. 7A.4.2.2, this chapter, and Chapter 3, and the movement towards recognising a right of humanitarian intervention, discussed in Chapter 5, para. 5A.3.

in future cases remains speculative, although it should be noted that in a subsequent case concerning the Turkish Cypriot authorities, the European Court reiterated earlier jurisprudence set down in the *Loizidou* and *Cyprus* cases, apparently unaffected by the *Banković* judgment. The Court held that responsibility for human rights violations arises where:

> as a consequence of military action – whether lawful or unlawful – [the state] exercises effective control of an area outside its national territory.[66]

Other questions relate to its impact, if any, beyond the region.[67] In light of the approach previously endorsed by other bodies, such as the Human Rights Committee or the Inter-American Commission on Human Rights, it is perhaps doubtful that such bodies would adopt the restrictive *Banković* requirement of effective control of territory.[68] In this context, it is worth noting that the Human Rights Committee's General Comment No. 31, which, as already noted, adopted a different approach on the issue of extraterritorial application of human rights instruments from that of *Banković*, was adopted *after* the European Court's decision.[69] This accords with the August 2004 advisory opinion of the ICJ, noting that 'the International Covenant on Civil and Political Rights is applicable in respect of acts done by a State in the exercise of its jurisdiction outside its own territory'.[70] The following month, the Human Rights Committee emphasised the Covenant's applicability abroad, including specifically military-led operations, noting that 'The State party should respect the safeguards established by the Covenant, not only in its territory but also when it exercises its jurisdiction abroad, as for example in the case of peacekeeping missions or NATO military missions.'[71] Moreover, in justifying

---

[66] *Djavit An* v. *Turkey*, note 59 above.

[67] See Inter-American Commission on Human Rights, *Precautionary Measures in Guantanamo Bay*, discussed in section B.

[68] The 'control of territory' requirement does not sit easily with extra-territorial arrests being covered, which does not involve control of the country in which such an arrest is made. The effective control test in international law of responsibility, is set out at Chapter 3; however in *Banković* the Applicants noted that the requirement of effective control of territory arises only where 'indirect' responsibility is in question. See applicants' arguments, para. 99.

[69] See Human Rights Committee, General Comment No. 31 (note 48, above and corresponding text).

[70] *Legal Consequences of the Construction of a Wall in the Occupied Palestinian Territory*, Advisory Opinion, 9 July 2004, para. 111. The Court describes this extra-territorial reach of the ICCPR as 'natural', 'considering the object and purpose of the [ICCPR]', para. 109.

[71] Concluding Observations of the Human Rights Committee: Belgium, UN Doc. CPR/CO/81/BEL, 12 August 2004, para. 6.

its reasoning, the *Banković* judgment emphasised the regional scope of the Convention, which was intended to apply to the 'legal space of the contracting parties', of which the former Yugoslavia was not part, rather than throughout the world.[72] Such considerations would not apply to the application of a treaty such as the ICCPR, which is indeed intended to enshrine global standards.

The impact of the *Banković* case on legal standards in respect of extra-territoriality may thus be less striking than it at first appears.[73]

7A.2.2 Personal scope of human rights obligations: irrelevance of nationality

Human rights obligations apply to nationals and aliens alike.[74] Provided the person comes within the 'jurisdiction' of the state, it matters not to the application of the human rights framework whether that person is a national of the state. As noted by the Inter-American Commission, '[t]he determination of a state's responsibility for violations of the international human rights of a particular individual turns not on the individual's nationality'.[75] Human rights law thus protects nationals and non-nationals alike, although in limited circumstances certain rights – notably relating to political life – are enjoyed only by a state's own citizens.[76]

Conversely, persons are not generally considered subject to a state's jurisdiction, for the purposes of invoking the application of human rights treaties, on the sole basis of nationality.[77]

---

[72] *Banković*, para. 80.

[73] Its significance for the 'war on terror' is highlighted in section B. As noted below, some of the measures taken post September 11, such as detentions outside sovereign territory, are covered by the human rights framework irrespective of whether the *Banković* test or a more flexible standard is applied. It is more relevant, however, to certain other questions relating to the conduct of the conflict itself.

[74] See Human Rights Committee, General Comment No. 31 (note 47, above), para. 10: 'the enjoyment of Covenant rights is not limited to citizens of States Parties but must also be available to all individuals, regardless of nationality or statelessness, such as asylum seekers, refugees, migrant workers and other persons, who may find themselves in the territory or subject to the jurisdiction of the State Party'. See also H.-P. Gasser, 'Protection of the Civilian Population', in D. Fleck (ed.), *The Handbook of Humanitarian Law in Armed Conflict* (Oxford, 1995), p. 209, at p. 280.

[75] Inter-American Commission on Human Rights, *Precautionary Measures in Guantanamo Bay*. It turns instead on whether 'that person fell within the state's authority and control'.

[76] General Comment No. 15: The position of aliens under the Covenant [1986], in UN Doc. HRI/GEN/1/Rev.6 (2003), at 140.

[77] See, e.g., the *Abbasi* judgment, above, para. 49 (for the argument that the requirement that a plaintiff was within the jurisdiction of the United Kingdom for ECHR purposes

Distinctions in the application of human rights law based on a person's nationality, far from justifying differential treatment, may bring the state into conflict with one of the human rights obligations – the duty not to discriminate on grounds such as race, sex, religion, sexual orientation or *national origin*.[78]

7A.3 Human rights in crisis or emergency: accommodating security imperatives

No circumstances, however extreme, render the framework of human rights law redundant: on the contrary, human rights protections are most important in times of national and international strain. The framework of human rights law thus applies at all times, including in time of emergency or indeed armed conflict (at which point this body of law intersects with the body of IHL, as discussed below).

However, while the law is omnipresent, it is also responsive to exceptional situations, including terrorist threats and the existence of armed conflict. It accommodates exceptional circumstances in several ways as discussed below.[79] First, certain specified rights may be restricted where this is necessary, for example to protect public order or the fundamental rights of others, subject to certain limits. Second, in times of 'public emergency' a broader range of rights may be suspended (or 'derogated' from), such that a more restrictive body of 'core' human rights law applies, though this is again subject to conditions and limitations. Third, the synergy between IHRL and IHL, such that in armed conflict many of the provisions of one branch of law must be interpreted in light of the other means that human rights law can respond as necessary to the special exigencies of armed conflict, which IHL is specifically designed to address. Finally, there is an inherent flexibility in the law, by virtue of which the question whether rights have been violated will generally depend on the totality of the circumstances of the particular situation or case: what is reasonable in one situation, in light of other safeguards, may not be reasonable in another, as seen for example in the jurisprudence

---

'was satisfied because, as Mr. Abbasi was a British national, the United Kingdom government had jurisdiction to take measures in relation to him') and para. 70 (where these arguments are rejected: 'These principles come nowhere near rendering Mr. Abbasi within the jurisdiction of the United Kingdom for the purposes of Article 1 on the simple ground that every state enjoys a degree of authority over its own nationals').

[78] See Article 26 ICCPR, Article 14 ECHR, Article 18 ACHPR and Article 24 ACHR.

[79] See generally General Comment No. 29, above, note 29.

on the interpretation of the rights to liberty and fair trial, discussed at Chapter 8.[80]

7A.3.1 Lawful limitations: treaty 'claw back' clauses

Some treaty provisions expressly recognise that certain rights are not absolute and may be restricted in certain circumstances, for example where 'necessary to protect public safety, order, health or morals or the fundamental rights and freedoms of others'.[81] This is one of the ways in which the human rights framework accommodates security concerns falling short of a situation of 'emergency'.[82]

However, these restrictions – or 'claw back' clauses[83] – attach only to a limited number of rights.[84] Under the ICCPR for example these clauses relate to freedom of movement (Article 12), freedom of conscience and religion (Article 18) and freedom of expression (Article 19). They do not therefore permit restrictions on rights relating to liberty and security (Article 9) or the right to a fair trial (Article 14).[85]

Moreover, lawful restrictions on these rights under claw back clauses must satisfy certain conditions. They must (a) be subject to the principle of legality, that is be provided for in clear and accessible law; (b) serve one of the legitimate aims set out in the particular convention (for example national security, public order); (c) be no more than strictly necessary to meet that aim and the measures must be proportionate to it. As exceptions, these clauses must be strictly construed.[86]

---

[80] See, e.g., discussion on the European Court of Human Rights' jurisprudence in relation to detention, also discussed in Chapter 8.

[81] See Article 18 ICCPR, 'freedom to manifest one's religion or beliefs'. The specific reasons justifying restrictions vary between Articles and between conventions, but common criteria are national security, public order, health and morals and/or rights and freedoms of others. Unlike 'derogation' clauses, these provisions do not require a general 'state of emergency' in the country in question.

[82] Certain (but not all) aspects of the rights affected by claw back clauses may also be limited through derogation in the event of emergency and the 'inherent limits' approach, discussed below.

[83] R. Higgins, 'Derogations under Human Rights Treaties', 48 (1976–77), BYIL 281.

[84] These restrictions apply to a smaller group of rights and do not affect, e.g., the rights to life, humane treatment, liberty or the majority of judicial guarantees. With the exception of religious freedom (see Article 18 ICCPR), they tend not to apply to non-derogable rights, discussed below.

[85] As regards fair trial rights under Article 14, the claw back clause applies only as an exception to the general rule that the press and public should be allowed access to criminal trials.

[86] Commentators warn of the dangers entailed in a broad interpretation of these clauses. See Lillich, 'Civil Rights', p. 119.

7A.3.2 *Temporary suspension: derogation clauses*

Generally, international and regional human rights treaties, notably the ICCPR, ECHR and ACHR,[87] allow states in certain situations, and subject to specific safeguards, to renounce parts of their obligations in respect of certain rights.[88] The six conditions that must be satisfied for states parties to human rights treaties to lawfully derogate from their human rights obligations are set out below.[89]

7A.3.2.1 Conditions for derogation

(a) Public emergency threatening the life of the nation   Not every national disturbance or catastrophe justifies derogation. Both the ICCPR and ECHR require the existence of a 'public emergency threatening the life of a nation,' while the ACHR refers to an 'emergency that threatens the independence or security of a State Party'.[90] While the emergency need not affect the whole population,[91] it does need to be serious enough that 'the organised life of the community of which the state is composed'[92] is

---

[87] Article 4 ICCPR, Article 27 ACHR and Article 15 ECHR.

[88] In contrast to other international human rights instruments, the African Charter does not contain a derogation clause. The African Commission concludes: 'Therefore limitations on the rights and freedoms enshrined in the Charter cannot be justified by emergencies or special circumstances. The only legitimate reasons for limitations to the rights and freedoms of the African Charter are found in Article 27(2), that is that the rights of the Charter "shall be exercised with due regard to the rights of others, collective security, morality and common interest".' There must be a legitimate state interest, limitations must be strictly proportionate and absolutely necessary and 'a limitation may never have as a consequence that the right itself becomes illusory'. See *Media Rights Agenda and Constitutional Rights Project* case (Comm. Nos. 105/93, 128/94, 130/94, 152/96), 12th Annual Activity Report 1998–99, paras. 67–70.

[89] The derogation clauses in the particular treaties govern the conditions and procedure that states are bound to comply with in order to derogate, and the 'core' of human rights that is non-derogable. See, e.g., General Comment No. 29, Council of Europe, 'Study on human rights protection during situations of armed conflict, internal disturbances and tensions', document prepared by Francoise Hampson, Strasbourg, 31 October 2001, Doc. CDDH (2001)021 rev., pp. 6 ff. and 'Study on the Principles Governing the Application of the European Convention on Human Rights during Armed Conflict and Internal Disturbances and Tensions', prepared by Jeremy McBride, consultant to the Steering Committee for the Development of Human Rights of the Council of Europe, Doc. DH-DEV(2003)001, 19 September 2003.

[90] See Article 4 ICCPR, Article 15 ECHR and Article 27(1) ACHR.

[91] See *Ireland* v. *United Kingdom* (Appl. No. 5310/71), Judgment, 18 January 1978, ECtHR, *Series A*, No. 25, para. 207.

[92] See *Lawless* v. *Ireland* (Appl. No. 332/57), Judgment of 1 July 1961, ECtHR, *Series A*, No. 3, para. 28.

threatened. The threat that justifies derogation must of course relate to the state seeking to derogate, as opposed to any other state.[93]

As with any exception, derogation must be strictly construed and the legal measures that allow for derogation must therefore be precise.[94] The need to derogate must be based on an accurate examination of the actual situation in the country, not mere predictions of future attack.[95] A situation of 'armed conflict' on the territory of a state would most likely amount to such an emergency,[96] as would other situations that might threaten the life or security of the nation in question.[97]

Derogation must be 'strictly required by the exigencies of the situation'[98] – a standard which is intentionally high, given the important implications of derogation, namely suspending certain human rights protections. It follows that measures of derogation should be no more, and for no longer, than strictly necessary. The importance of this is highlighted by the fact that, in practice, states have not infrequently invoked 'quasi-permanent' states of emergency under national law to justify otherwise impermissible restrictions on human rights.[99]

---

[93] In cases involving derogation due to 'terrorist threats', the threat must have arisen in the state itself. See, e.g., *Aksoy* v. *Turkey* (App. 21987/93), Judgment 18 December 1996, ECtHR, *Reports 1996-VI*, para. 68; see also para. 7B.3 of the application section of this chapter, in respect of the debate regarding the justifiability of derogation post 9/11.

[94] The Human Rights Committee has deplored 'the lack of clarity of the legal provisions governing the introduction and administration of the state of emergency' (Comment of the Human Rights Committee: Nepal (10/11/1994), UN Doc. CCPR/C/79/Add.42, para. 9).

[95] See Human Rights Committee, *Landinelli Silva et al.* v. *Uruguay* (Comm. No. 34/1978), Views of 8 April 1981, UN Doc. CCPR/C/12/D/34/1978 and the decision of the European Commission of Human Rights in the *Greek case*, 12 (1969) *Yearbook of the European Convention on Human Rights* 170. On the role of the human rights overseeing body in reaching these determinations, see para. 7A.3.2.1(b), 'Procedural Requirements', below.

[96] Only the regional instruments expressly refer to 'war' as a ground for derogation. However, as one commentator asserts, this does not mean derogations are not permitted under the ICCPR but instead that 'express reference to war was struck out in 1952 in order to prevent giving the impression that the United Nations accepted war' (M. Nowak, *UN Covenant on Civil and Political Rights: CCPR Commentary* (Kehl am Rheim, 1993), p. 79).

[97] See M. Nowak, *CCPR Commentary*, p. 79, where he states that 'in addition to armed conflict and internal unrest, serious natural or environmental catastrophes may also lead to an emergency'.

[98] See, e.g., Article 4 ICCPR.

[99] See, e.g., Concluding observations of the Human Rights Committee: Syrian Arab Republic, UN Doc. CCPR/CO/71/SYR (2001), para. 6, where the Committee expresses concern about the 'quasi permanent emergency' declared in Syria since 1963. See also 'semi-permanent emergency' in Egypt, discussed in Concluding observations of the Human Rights Committee: Egypt, UN Doc. CCPR/CO/76/EGY (2002), para. 6.

(b) Procedural requirements for derogation and supervision   Derogation clauses contain procedural safeguards. Commonly, they require a state availing itself of derogation to proclaim the emergency in the state, inform other states party to the particular instrument of the provisions which it intends to suspend and provide notification to the relevant overseeing treaty body.[100] The notification must clearly detail the rights from which the state is seeking to derogate (as it cannot be a blanket derogation), the reasons and the nature of the measures taken.[101] The decision whether such an emergency has arisen is not a unilateral decision of a state, but ultimately rests with the treaty bodies that supervise the implementation of the treaty in question.[102]

In addition to international procedural requirements, intended to ensure appropriate international oversight, the Human Rights Committee has noted the need for domestic judicial oversight of derogation. It has noted that 'constitutional and legal provisions should ensure that compliance with Article 4 of the Covenant can be monitored by the Courts'.[103]

(c) Inalienable 'non-derogable' rights applicable in all situations   The universal and inalienable nature of certain human rights is well established, as reflected in the derogation clauses themselves. As such, there

---

[100] Notification is completed through an intermediary, namely the depository of the given treaty, e.g., the ICCPR requires the Secretary-General of the UN to fill this role, while for the ACHR it is the Secretary General of the Organization of American States. A second notification must be completed via the same procedure as soon as the state of emergency has ended and the measures are no longer necessary. The Human Rights Committee has stated that it deplores the failure to observe the duties under Article 4(3), of the Covenant 'to notify the Secretary-General of the United Nations and through him other States parties to the Covenant of the proclamation of a state of emergency'. Concluding observations of the Human Rights Committee: Lebanon, CCPR/C/79/Add.78 (1997), para. 10. The procedural requirements of each treaty to which a state is party must be met.

[101] N. Questiaux, UN Special Rapporteur on states of emergency, 'Study of the Implications for Human Rights of Recent Developments Concerning Situations Known as States of Siege or Emergency', UN Doc. E/CN.4/Sub.2/1982/15.

[102] These bodies ensure the observance of the requirements for lawful derogation. See e.g., *Aksoy* v. *Turkey*, para. 68: 'Contracting Parties do not enjoy an unlimited discretion. It is for the Court to rule whether, *inter alia*, the states have gone beyond the "extent strictly required by the exigencies" of the crisis. The domestic margin of appreciation is thus accompanied by a European supervision. In exercising this supervision, the Court must give appropriate weight to such relevant factors as the nature of the rights affected by the derogation and the circumstances leading to, and the duration of, the emergency situation.'

[103] Concluding observations of the Human Rights Committee: Colombia, UN Doc. CCPR/C/79/Add 76 (1997), para. 38.

is a core of rights that must be protected at all times. As this includes situations of armed conflict, the core of IHRL complements the more specific applicable rules of IHL,[104] which together provide the standard for treatment of persons in conflict.[105]

The list of 'non-derogable' rights varies between treaties. However, common to all these provisions are the rights not to be arbitrarily deprived of life, freedom from torture or inhuman or degrading treatment or punishment, freedom from slavery, rights relating to legality and non-retroactivity in criminal matters.[106]

However, reference to these lists is somewhat misleading, as international courts and bodies interpreting human rights treaties have consistently noted that, in addition, certain aspects of other rights (which are not non-derogable *per se*), are also applicable in all situations. Notably, the right to *habeas corpus*, core fair trial guarantees or access to a remedy[107] constitute core procedural guarantees which have been deemed to be non-derogable, and to provide safeguards essential for the protection of other non-derogable rights, such as freedom from torture and inhuman treatment.[108] In addition, discrimination in respect of these rights is also non-derogable.

(d) Consistency with other obligations   Any derogation from human rights treaties must not affect other international obligations, whether treaty or customary. Derogation from one human rights treaty does

---

[104] See Chapter 6.

[105] As noted at para 7A.2.1, the state is responsible for human rights violations so far as it enjoys 'effective control' of the situation.

[106] The ICCPR, as an international convention ratified by Afghanistan, the US and UK, deserves specific attention. Among the rights that Article 4 of the ICCPR explicitly provides as non-derogable are the right to life (Article 6), the prohibition on torture or cruel treatment (Article 7), slavery (Article 8(1) and (2)), imprisonment due to contractual obligations (Article 11), legality in the field of criminal law, including the requirement of 'clear and precise provisions' and prohibition on retroactive penalties (Article 15), recognition before the law (Article 16) and freedom of thought, conscience and religion (Article 18). The ACHR (Article 27) has a longer list than the ICCPR, while Article 15 of the ECHR lists specifically as non-derogable norms only Article 2 (right to life), 3 (prohibition of torture and inhuman/degrading treatment), 4(1) (prohibition of slavery) and 7 (non-retroactivity in criminal law), but note below on key aspects of liberty and fair trial and the right to a remedy.

[107] The right to a remedy (Article 2(3)) has been described by the Human Rights Committee as a right that remains effective in time of emergency. See General Comment No. 29 (above, note 29), para. 14.

[108] These and other specific rights are discussed below (see para. 8B.4.3, in this chapter, and Chapter 8, para. 8B.4, in relation to the detainees held at Guantanamo Bay).

not signify derogation from another.[109] As such, although a European state may derogate from the ECHR for example, it remains bound by the ICCPR, unless it similarly derogates from that treaty. Even if it does derogate from both, as the list of non-derogable rights in the ICCPR is longer, covering religious freedom and discrimination for example, derogation can never entitle states parties to the ICCPR to infringe those rights.

Likewise, derogation from treaty responsibilities does not affect customary law obligations (discussed below). In practice, customary law is not likely to be broader in scope than the non-derogable core of treaty rights, so an issue is unlikely to arise. However, if a dispute arose as to, for example, the right to impose prolonged arbitrary detention in the event of a derogation,[110] as such detention is prohibited by international custom it becomes relevant that no derogation purporting to justify arbitrary detention could be justified.

Critically, derogation from human rights treaties cannot justify violations of the obligations enshrined in IHL, which do not permit of any derogation.[111] As such, the provisions of IHL relating to fair trial rights, or the rights of detainees, will remain applicable, irrespective of derogation from certain fair trial or liberty provisions of human rights treaties.[112]

(e) **Measures strictly necessary and proportionate**   Where circumstances do justify derogation in principle, and where the rights in question are not non-derogable, the question is whether each measure taken pursuant to the emergency situation is 'strictly required by the exigencies of the situation'.[113] Measures taken pursuant to derogation must be both

---

[109] This is relevant to a state such as the UK that is party to both the ECHR and the ICCPR. Although it has not recognised the right of individual petition to the Human Rights Committee, it is bound by the ICCPR. Thus when the UK first derogated from the ECHR, and it had not done so from the ICCPR, it remained bound by the full extent of the obligations under that treaty. On the UK derogations, see the Human Rights Act 1998 (Designated Derogation) Order 2001 (SI 2001/3644), available at www.hmso.gov.uk/si/si2001/20013644.htm.

[110] As noted above, the prohibition is not explicitly rendered non-derogable by human rights treaties, but by the interpretation of those treaties by human rights bodies.

[111] See Human Rights Committee, General Comment No. 29 (above, note 29), para. 3.

[112] See Chapter 8 and section B below.

[113] Article 4 ICCPR and Article 15 ECHR. In *Aksoy* v. *Turkey*, the European Court held that 'although the Court is of the view – which it has expressed on several occasions in the past – that the investigation of terrorist offences undoubtedly presents the authorities with special problems, it cannot accept that it is necessary to hold a suspect for fourteen days without judicial intervention'.

strictly necessary and proportionate to the emergency in question.[114] As the Inter-American Commission has noted, this requirement covers 'the prohibition on the unnecessary suspension of certain rights, imposing restrictions more severe than necessary, and unnecessarily extending the suspension to areas not affected by the emergency'.[115]

The European Court of Human Rights has stressed the importance of taking into account all circumstances in making an assessment of necessity and proportionality. The nature of the right in question is a critical factor; the European Court has noted for example that while liberty is a derogable right, the fact that it is a 'fundamental human right [involving] the protection of the individual against arbitrary interference by the State' is relevant to assessing the lawfulness of measures taken.[116] Where, for example, liberty is restricted in a way not normally permitted, the question whether other safeguards are in place, including *habeas corpus* and legal representation, will also be relevant to an assessment of the lawfulness of measures taken.[117]

(f) Non-discrimination in application of derogation   Moreover, any derogation must not be applied discriminatorily.[118] As reflected in the wording of the ICCPR derogation clause, measures that would otherwise be justifiable will be impermissible where they are applied solely on the ground of race, colour, sex, language, religion or social origin.

7A.3.3 Customary law and emergency

This chapter has focused on human rights treaty law obligations, given the widespread nature of ratification of human rights treaties. Customary international law[119] also provides for exceptional rules to accommodate emergency situations, with doctrines of 'state of necessity' and '*force majeure*' providing that, in very exceptional circumstances, a state's failure

---

[114] See Human Rights Committee, General Comment No. 29 (above, note 29), para. 4.

[115] *The Civilian Jurisdiction: The Anti-Terrorist Legislation*, OEA/Ser.L/V/II.106, Doc. 59 rev., 2 June 2000; see para. 70 ff.

[116] *Aksoy* v. *Turkey*, para. 76.

[117] *Ibid.*, para. 81 and *Brannigan and McBride* v. *the United Kingdom* (App. Nos. 1453/89 and 1454/89), Judgment of 26 May 1993, ECtHR, *Series A*, No. 258-B, paras. 49–50.

[118] See, e.g., Article 4 ICCPR. See also Human Rights Committee, General Comment No. 29 (above, note 29), para. 8 and *Civilian Jurisdiction*, para. 70. Note also that the anti-discrimination provisions of CEDAW and CERD are non-derogable.

[119] Customary international law is not usually critical given treaty obligations, as discussed in para. 7A.1, this chapter.

to comply with its obligations is not unlawful.[120] A 'state of necessity' may arise where an act is 'the only means of safeguarding an essential interest of the State against a grave and imminent peril',[121] and *'force majeure'* is 'the occurrence of an irresistible force or of an unforeseen external event beyond the control of the State, making it materially impossible in the circumstances to perform the obligation'.[122] However, the relevance of these doctrines in the human rights context are limited. As discussed above, certain rights have *jus cogens* status and must be respected at all times, without exception.[123]

7A.3.4 Harmony in conflict? The relationship between IHL and human rights law

IHL and international human rights law intertwine and together form the body of law governing situations of armed conflict.[124] The following is a brief summary of the interrelationship between these strands of international law.

International humanitarian law comes into operation in times of armed conflict and applies beyond the termination of hostilities to a general close of military operations. It is designed specifically to regulate the conduct of armed conflict, and to address the particular issues that arise therefrom. By contrast, international human rights law applies at all times; although it is not directed specifically at the peculiarities of war, it enshrines minimum standards relevant to all situations, including armed conflict. Temporally, the two strands of law therefore overlap and apply simultaneously during armed conflict.

---

[120] Note that these 'circumstances precluding wrongfulness' apply also with respect to obligations deriving from treaty law, but may not be invoked in respect of *jus cogens* norms, which always apply and which probably include non-derogable human rights norms. See ILC's Articles on State Responsibility, Article 25(2)(b).

[121] See Article 25, ILC's Articles on State Responsibility. Note, however, that necessity may not be invoked as a circumstance precluding wrongfulness where the act of the state 'seriously impair[s] an essential interest of the State or States towards which the obligations exists, or of the international community as a whole' (Article 25(1)(b)).

[122] Article 23, ILC's Articles on State Responsibility. These customary rules do not, however, affect the treaty obligations discussed above.

[123] On the definition of *jus cogens*, see Chapter 1, para. 1.2 and differences between commentators and bodies on which rights have attained such status (Lillich, 'Civil Rights', pp. 117 ff., Fitzpatrick, *Human Rights in Crisis*, p. 67 and Human Rights Committee, General Comment No. 29 (above, note 29), para. 11).

[124] On whether or which of the situations post 9/11 are properly understood as 'armed conflict', see Chapter 6, section B.

As discussed above, the geographic scope of a state's obligations under treaty or customary international human rights law extends throughout its territory and may extend beyond, to wherever the state has *de facto* control of territory or where it exercises its 'authority', 'power' or 'control' abroad. IHL generally applies throughout the territory of warring parties but may spill over, with the conflict, into other states. As such, the territorial purview of both bodies of law may cover measures taken within a state and on foreign soil.

In time of armed conflict or other emergency, at a minimum states are obliged to protect a 'core' of rights under treaty and customary human rights law, and they may be obliged, under treaties to which states are party, to protect a fuller range of rights unless they have been properly derogated from. These human rights are guaranteed to all persons, without distinction, and nationality, affiliation to adversaries to a conflict or criminal conduct are not bases for denying the application of human rights.

By contrast, in general IHL protects persons associated with one party to a conflict who find themselves in the hands of an opposing party and defines rules applicable to the conduct of hostilities. Moreover, certain aspects of the protections contained in IHL depend upon the status of the individual. For example, the rules of targeting are based on the cornerstone principle of distinction that protects civilians but not combatants, and certain detailed rights are afforded only to certain categories of prisoner, such as prisoners of war. The IHL rights afforded to particular categories of persons may go beyond those in IHRL. Persons falling outside such categories are, however, at all times entitled, by virtue of their humanity, to the core rights protected in IHRL (as well as minimal level of protection reflected in IHL itself).

The position was summarised by the ICJ in the following terms:

> the protection offered by human rights conventions does not cease in case of armed conflict, save through the effect of provisions for derogation of the kind to be found in Article 4 of the International Covenant on Civil and Political Rights. As regards the relationship between international humanitarian law and human rights law, there are thus three possible situations: some rights may be exclusively matters of international humanitarian law; others may be exclusively matters of human rights law; yet others may be matters of both these branches of international law.[125]

---

[125] *Legal Consequences of the Construction of a Wall in the Occupied Palestinian Territory*, Advisory Opinion, 9 July 2004, para. 106 and fn. 123.

Critically, in the event of apparent inconsistency in the content of the two strands of law, the more specific provisions will prevail: in relation to targeting in the conduct of hostilities, for example, human rights law will refer to more specific provisions (the *lex specialis*) of humanitarian law.[126] In such circumstances it is not that human rights law ceases to apply, but that it must be interpreted in light of the detailed rules of IHL. As such, the protection from arbitrary deprivation of life and arbitrary detention are non-derogable human rights[127] that continue to apply in armed conflict; but targeting or detention is not arbitrary, and the rights are not violated, where permitted under IHL.[128] Similarly, just as human rights law in armed conflict is informed by the standards of IHL,[129] many provisions of IHL are in turn interpreted in the light of the fuller jurisprudence available from human rights law.[130] Each strand therefore provides a tool in the interpretation of the other.[131]

As discussed at Chapter 6, while IHL principally binds parties to armed conflict (whether state or, for non-international armed conflicts, non-state), international human rights law essentially imposes obligations on states and confers rights on individuals. However, as discussed at Chapter 4, serious violations of human rights and IHL may amount to crimes under international law for which individuals may be held to account, such as genocide, crimes against humanity – whether committed in time of peace or war – or war crimes.

---

[126] See *Advisory Opinion on the Legality of the Threat or Use of Nuclear Weapons, ICJ Reports 1996*, p. 226, para. 25, in which the ICJ observes that 'the protection of the International Covenant on Civil and Political Rights does not cease in time of war, except by operation of Article 4 of the Covenant'.

[127] Derogation clauses in human rights treaties may explicitly reflect this, but where this is not specified it may be implied. Article 15(2) of the ECHR notes that the right to life is not violated where the deprivation is 'a lawful act of war', whereas, e.g., Article 4 of the ICCPR does not.

[128] The killing of a civilian, by contrast, would violate both IHL and human rights law.

[129] See Human Rights Committee, General Comment No. 29, paras. 9 and 11; Inter-American Commission on Human Rights, *Abella* v. *Argentina* (Case 11.137), Report No. 55/97, Annual Report of the IACHR 1997, paras. 158–61; Inter-American Commission on Human Rights, *Precautionary Measures in Guantanamo Bay*; ECtHR, *Banković* v. *Belgium*, above.

[130] The due process guarantees in common Article 3 are an example of IHL provisions interpreted in the light of human rights provisions and jurisprudence.

[131] E.g., the IHL rules regarding 'aliens in the territory of a party' provide rules on specific issues arising in time of conflict which complement the human rights law that would also apply to such persons. See H.-P. Gasser, Protection of the Civilian Population', in Fleck, *Handbook of Humanitarian Law*, p. 280. See also T. Meron, 'The Humanization of Humanitarian Law', 94 (2000) AJIL 239.

Finally, while specific mechanisms exist under human rights treaties, enabling individuals or states parties to bring petitions alleging violations by states which have accepted the authority of those mechanisms, no such judicial mechanisms exist under IHL treaties.[132] For states, there remains the option of bringing an inter-state action to the International Court of Justice, but they rarely do so, and individuals cannot presently invoke IHL treaties directly. In a number of cases human rights bodies have, however, invoked and effectively applied IHL in the context of a human rights case, providing a remedy for IHL violations that would otherwise not exist and highlighting the importance of the synergy between these two areas for the protection of persons during armed conflict.[133]

7A.4 Human rights obligations and terrorism

7A.4.1 Protecting human security: positive human rights obligations

General human rights conventions like the International Covenant on Civil and Political Rights, American Convention on Human Rights and European Convention on Human Rights and Fundamental Freedoms enshrine the duty of states bound by the conventions to 'respect' and 'ensure' the rights protected.[134] This duty comprises both the negative obligation not to infringe the rights and the positive duty to 'ensure' their protection. The latter has consistently been interpreted by human rights courts and bodies as involving the duty to prevent violations and, in the wake of serious violations, to investigate them and, where evidence supports prosecution, to bring to justice those responsible.[135] These duties

---

[132] While human rights are often enforceable by victims through national and international fora, IHL lacks comparable complaint mechanisms. On enforcement through criminal law, see Chapter 4. Implementing mechanisms anticipated in IHL treaties, such as the (effectively redundant) role of the 'protecting power,' and that of the ICRC, are non-judicial in nature.

[133] See, e.g., *Abella* v. *Argentina*, paras. 157–71; Inter American Commission on Human Rights, *Precautionary Measures in Guantanamo Bay*; see also ECtHR, *Banković*, para. 25.

[134] See Article 1 ACHR and Article 2 ICCPR 1966. Article 1 of the ECHR refers similarly to the obligation to 'secure' the rights under the Convention.

[135] See, e.g., *Velásquez Rodríguez* v. *Honduras, Merits*, Judgment of 29 July 1988, IACtHR, *Series C*, No. 4, which describes the obligation as comprising the duty 'to use the means at its disposal to carry out a serious investigation of violations committed within its jurisdiction, to identify those responsible, to impose the appropriate punishment and to ensure to the victim adequate compensation'. This decision has been endorsed in several subsequent cases before the Inter-American Court: see *Blake* v. *Guatemala*, Preliminary Objections, Judgment of 2 July 1996, *Series C*, No. 27, para. 39, and *Castillo Paez* case, Judgment of 3 November 1997, *Series C*, No. 34, para. 90. See the similar approach adopted by the

apply whether state agents or private individuals are directly responsible for the original violations, as the state incurs responsibility for acts of private individuals if it fails to exercise 'due diligence', involving reasonable measures, to prevent violations or investigate them effectively.[136]

The 'prevention and accountability' obligations of the state correspond to the 'justice' rights of victims and their families in respect of certain serious human rights violations. Most directly, the rights implicated are the right to due process of law – comprising the right of any suspect to a fair trial but also the victims' right to access justice[137] – and the right to a remedy in respect of violations, requiring that action is taken in the face of serious violations.[138] Less directly, other rights, including life, liberty, security and physical integrity, that can only be adequately protected in the context of a state of law and accountability, are implicated where a state fails to take measures towards accountability in the face of such

Committee against Torture (Annual Report to the General Assembly, 9 September 1996, UN Doc. A/51/44, para. 117) and the Human Rights Committee (e.g., General Comment No. 20: Prohibition of torture or cruel, inhuman and degrading treatment or punishment (Article 7) [1992], UN Doc. HRI/GEN/1/Rev.6 (2003) at 151, General Comment No. 31, note 47, above, Concluding observations: Senegal, UN Doc. CCPR/C/79/Add.10 (1992), and the decision of 25 July 1996 regarding Peru's amnesty law Decree 26,479). For the approach of the European Court of Human Rights see *MC* v. *Bulgaria*, judgment of 4 December 2003, [2003] ECHR 646, p. 28: 'the Court considers that States have a positive obligation inherent in Articles 3 and 8 of the Convention to enact criminal law provisions effectively punishing rape and to apply them in practice through effective investigation and prosecution', para. 154; also para.150. See also e.g., *Assenov* v. *Bulgaria*, Judgment of 28 October 1998, ECtHR, *Reports 1998-VIII*, noting the State's 'general duty under Article 1 [to conduct] an effective investigation' as otherwise the rights protected under the Convention would be 'ineffective in practice' (para. 102) and *X and Y* v. *Netherlands*, Judgment of 26 March 1985, ECtHR, *Series A*, No. 91.

[136] See Human Rights Committee, General Comment No. 31 (note 48 above), para. 8: 'the positive obligations on States Parties to ensure Covenant rights will only be fully discharged if individuals are protected by the State, not just against violations of Covenant rights by its agents, but also against acts committed by private persons or entities that would impair the enjoyment of Covenant rights in so far as they are amenable to application between private persons or entities. There may be circumstances in which a failure to ensure Covenant rights as required by Article 2 would give rise to violations by States Parties of those rights, as a result of States Parties' permitting or failing to take appropriate measures or to exercise due diligence to prevent, punish, investigate or redress the harm caused by such acts by private persons or entities'.

[137] See the decisions of the Inter-American Commission to this effect in the cases involving amnesty laws. The government of Uruguay argued unsuccessfully that the right to a 'fair trial' in Article 8 was limited to a defendant (*Mendoza et al.* v. *Uruguay* (Cases 10.029, 10.036, 10.145, 10.305, 10.372, 10.373, 10.374 and 10.375), Report No. 29/92, OEA/Ser.L/V/II.83 Doc. 14 at 154 (1993)).

[138] See Article 2(3)(a) ICCPR; Article 13 ECHR; Article 25(2)(a) ACHR; Article 7 ACHPR.

violations.[139] So far as it serves to protect and ensure the protection of non-derogable rights under treaty law, the obligation to hold to account perpetrators of serious violations may itself be seen as a non-derogable obligation.[140]

In addition to the general human rights treaties' obligations to respect and ensure, certain other treaties and instruments addressing specific human rights (and, as noted above, humanitarian law)[141] explicitly enshrine the duty to investigate and prosecute.[142] While the extent of 'accountability' obligations under *customary* law remains controversial, there is considerable support for the view that there is also such a duty, at least in respect of the most atrocious crimes, such as crimes against humanity.[143]

---

[139] This rationale underpins the human rights cases concerning the positive obligations referred to above.

[140] See below for the non-derogability of 'judicial guarantees' for the protection of human rights. See *Barrios Altos* case (*Chumbipuma Aguirre et al. v. Peru*), Merits, Judgment of 14 March 2001, IACtHR, *Series C*, No. 75, paras. 41–4; see also D. Orentlicher, 'Settling Accounts: The Duty to Prosecute Human Rights Violations of a Prior Regime', 100 (1991) *Yale Law Journal* 2537, para. 2562 and 2568 ff.

[141] Within humanitarian law, the four Geneva Conventions of 12 August 1949 contain quite clear obligations on states parties to seek out, prosecute and punish those who commit 'grave breaches' of the Conventions, which cover crimes such as unlawful killing, torture and inhumane acts. 'Grave breaches' provisions appear in all four Geneva Conventions and Additional Protocol I of 1977: see, e.g., Articles 147, 148 of GC IV and Article 85 AP I.

[142] See the United Nations Convention against Torture and Other Cruel, Inhuman or Degrading Treatment and Punishment, New York, 10 December 1984, UN Doc. A/39/51 (1984). Other examples include: Convention Concerning Forced or Compulsory Labour, adopted on 28 June 1930 (ILO No. 29), 39 UNTS 55; Convention on the Prevention and Punishment of the Crime of Genocide, New York, 9 December 1948, 78 UNTS 277; Supplementary Convention on the Abolition of Slavery, the Slave Trade, and Institutions and Practices Similar to Slavery, Geneva, 7 September 1956, 226 UNTS 3; International Convention on the Suppression and Punishment of the Crime of *Apartheid*, New York, 30 December 1973. As for non-binding instruments that reflect acceptance of this duty, see Principles on the Effective Prevention and Investigation of Extra-legal, Arbitrary and Summary Executions, ESC Res. 1989/65, Annex, 1989, UN ESCOR supp. (No. 1) at 52, UN Doc. E/1989/89 (1989).

[143] See, e.g., the 'Principles of International Cooperation in the Detection, Arrest, Extradition, and Punishment of Persons Guilty of War Crimes and Crimes against Humanity', adopted by UN GA Res. 3074 (XXVIII) of 3 December 1973, UN Doc. A/RES/3074 (XXVIII), which provides that '1. War crimes and crimes against humanity, wherever they are committed, shall be subject to investigation and the persons against whom there is evidence that they have committed such crimes shall be subject to tracing, arrest, trial and, if found guilty, to punishment.' See, generally, Orentlicher, 'Settling Accounts', in particular at 2592–3 and 2600 for customary international law. According to Orentlicher, by 1991 the Restatement of Foreign Relations Law of the United States considered customary

7A.4.1.1 Positive obligations and the implications for counter-terrorism

These obligations clearly have implications for states in the wake of atrocities such as those committed on September 11. Where 'terrorism' results in serious violations of human rights,[144] the state has a responsibility to establish an effective counter terrorism strategy that couples 'preventive' measures with thorough investigation and accountability after the event. The duty to protect encompasses the obligation to provide timely information concerning dangers to human security arising from terrorist threats.[145] Seen through the prism of human rights law, then, invoking the criminal law paradigm is not simply an option for a state, it is a matter of legal obligation, not satisfied by or interchangeable with other measures that may be taken, such as the use of military force.[146] The same obligations of investigation and accountability apply whether violations arise from acts of terrorism or in the name of a counter-terrorism strategy.[147]

Justice rights and accountability obligations also have implications for the *way* in which the criminal law framework is applied to persons suspected of serious violations. Among the measures likely to be inconsistent with the obligations summarised above are the application of amnesty laws which preclude any criminal process, prescription which bars prosecution after a limited amount of time or immunities or defences which provide impunity for serious violations.[148]

---

law violated by impunity for 'torture, extra-legal executions and disappearances' (*ibid.*, pp. 2582–3). On the definition of crimes against humanity and the characterisation of the September 11 attacks as such, see Chapter 4, para. 4A.1.1.1.

[144] Note that some broad definitions of terrorism (discussed below, para. 7B.4) would encompass less serious acts, that would not constitute serious rights violations. Many acts of terrorism, however, and certainly those of the nature and scale of September 11, clearly would.

[145] *Oneryildiz* v. *Turkey*, Judgment of 18 June 2002; see also *Osman* v. *United Kingdom* (App. 23452/94), Judgment of 28 October 1998, ECtHR, *Reports 1998-VIII*.

[146] Those criminal law measures will themselves be subject to the constraints of the human rights framework, whether or not arising in the context of armed conflict. On the relationship between the criminal law framework and use of force, see question raised at Chapter 5.

[147] See, e.g., *Asencios Lindo et al.* (Case 11.182), Report No. 49/00, Annual Report of the IACHR 1999, para. 58 and *Kiliç* v. *Turkey*, (Appl. No. 22492/93) Judgment of 28 March 2000, ECtHR, *Reports 2000-III*; Concluding observations of the Human Rights Committee: Russian Federation, UN Doc. CCPR/CO/79/RUS (2003).

[148] See, e.g., *Barrios Altos* case (above, note 140) on the compatibility of amnesty laws with the state's duties in respect of justice and accountability. See generally Chapter 4, para. 4A.1.2.3.

7A.4.1.2 Inquiry and onus of proof

Linked to the foregoing positive obligations is the onus that lies with the state, in certain circumstances, to demonstrate that it has met those obligations, as opposed to the onus resting with the individual to prove the violation. This is particularly so where – as is not infrequently the situation in human rights cases, and all the more so in the shrouded world of counter-terrorism – the facts lie wholly, or in large part, within the exclusive knowledge of the authorities.

Moreover, in the event that death or injury occurs in situations that might reasonably be thought to fall within the control of the state, the state must demonstrate that it was *not* the result of a violation of its human rights obligations. This may arise for example where a law enforcement operation results in death, particularly where the plans, orders and training are known only to the state,[149] or where prisoners suffer death or sustain injuries in a state's custody.[150] In such circumstances, as the European Court of Human Rights has noted, 'strong presumptions of fact will arise in respect of injuries and death which occur. Indeed, the burden of proof may be regarded as resting on the authorities to provide a satisfactory and convincing explanation.'[151]

7A.4.2 State responsibility and human rights violations

7A.4.2.1 Agents and private actors

Generally speaking, as already noted, a state will be responsible for the acts of its agents, whether or not they act within their authority, and for private actors, where the state fails to exercise due diligence to prevent the violations or repress them after the event.[152] The state may, particularly where it is operating extra-territorially, act in consort with local groups or with other states and may assume responsibility for their acts, whether or not carried out at its behest.[153] For example, as the European Court of

---

[149] See the decision of the ECtHR in *McCann, Farrell and Savage* v. *United Kingdom*, Judgment of 27 September 1995, *Series A*, No. 324.

[150] See *McKerr* v. *United Kingdom*, Judgment of 4 May 2001, ECtHR, *Reports 2001-III*.

[151] *Ibid.*, para. 109.

[152] The law governing attribution to the state of responsibility for the conduct of private actors is summarised at Chapter 3, as is the position regarding the responsibility of non-state actors. Particular rules of human rights law governing the responsibility of the state for violations, whether by state agents or private actors, are set out in relation to 'positive obligations' in para. 7A.4.1, this chapter.

[153] For comment on the responsibility of the UK for acts of the US in the conduct of the Iraq war, see 'Report of the Inquiry into the Alleged Commission of War Crimes by Coalition

Human Rights has noted, the obligations to secure Convention rights and freedoms derive from the fact of 'control whether it was exercised directly, through the respondent State's armed forces, or through a subordinate local administration'.[154]

7A.4.2.2 Collective responsibility and violations by others?

Finally, human rights violations by *other* states, while potentially matters of concern in policy terms, have not traditionally been thought to be matters of legal interest to the state, still less to create legal obligations on the state to act.[155] However, there are indications of a growing sense of community interest in the prevention of serious rights violations, and accountability in respect thereof, that may be eroding this position.[156] Notably, the International Law Commission's Articles on Responsibility of States for Internationally Wrongful Acts indicate, firstly, that all states may have an interest in raising a complaint against another regarding human rights abuses, on the basis that the duty to respect human rights is owed to the international community as a whole, i.e. they are obligations *erga omnes*.[157] But the ILC Articles go further, indicating that where the

---

Forces in the Iraq War During 2003', 8–9 November 2003, commissioned by Peacerights, pp. 14 and 15.

[154] *Banković*, para. 70, referring to *Loizidou* judgment (preliminary objections) and to the subsequent *Cyprus* v. *Turkey* judgment where 'the Court added that since Turkey had such "effective control", its responsibility could not be confined to the acts of its own agents therein but was engaged by the acts of the local administration which survived by virtue of Turkish support'.

[155] This does not address a state's responsibility for supporting another in the commission of violations, but the situation where it has no involvement in those violations.

[156] Note also another related trend in international law to seeing human rights, in particular serious violations thereof, as matters of concern not for the state alone but for the international community. See, e.g., the changing concept of matters within the 'domestic jurisdiction' of a state (see Article 2(7) UN Charter), and universal jurisdiction (see Chapter 4, para. 4A.1.3).

[157] See Article 48, ILC's Articles on State Responsibility, on 'Invocation of responsibility by a State other than the injured State'. See *Barcelona Traction, Light and Power Company, Limited, Second Phase, ICJ Reports 1970*, p. 3, at p. 32, paras. 33–4: 'In particular, an essential distinction should be drawn between the obligations of a State towards the international community as a whole, and those arising vis-a-vis another State in the field of diplomatic protection. By their very nature the former are the concern of all States. In view of the importance of the rights involved, all States can be held to have a legal interest in their protection; they are obligations *erga omnes*. Such obligations derive, for example, in contemporary international law, from the outlawing of acts of aggression, and of genocide, as also from the principles and rules concerning the basic rights of the human person including protection from slavery and racial discrimination. Some of the corresponding rights of protection have entered into the body of general international law, others are conferred by international instruments of a universal or quasi-universal

obligation breached derives from a peremptory norm of general international law, and the breach is 'serious'[158] all states have a *duty* to cooperate to end the wrong.[159] The Commentaries to the ILC Articles specify that the obligations under peremptory norms of general international law:

> arise from those substantive rules of conduct that prohibit what has come to be seen as intolerable because of the threat it presents to the survival of States and to their people and *the most basic human values*.[160]

This development may be seen as part of a trend towards collective responsibility, of which the shift from viewing human rights as internal matters of state sovereignty to matters of international concern, universal jurisdiction[161] and, arguably, the movement towards recognising a limited right of humanitarian intervention,[162] also form part.

7A.4.3 *Specific rights protected and counter-terrorism*

The following are some of the rights protected in human rights law, which may be implicated by acts carried out in the name of counter-terrorism. Their application post September 11 is considered in Section B below.

---

character.' See also J. Crawford, *Third Report on State Responsibility* (52nd session of the ILC (2000)), UN Doc. A/CN.4/507 and Add. 1–4, p. 44, para. 92, stating that an obligation *erga omnes partes* of a treaty (in our case a human rights treaty) 'has been expressly stipulated in that treaty for the protection of the collective interests of the States parties' and 'concern[s] obligations in the performance of which all the States parties are recognized as having a common interest, over and above any individual interest that may exist in a given case'.

[158] See, in general, ILC's Articles on State Responsibility, Part II, Chapter III 'Serious breach of obligations under peremptory norms of general international law'. Article 40 defines the scope of application of the chapter, stating that it applies 'to the international responsibility which is entailed by a serious breach by a State of an obligation arising under a peremptory norm of international law' (para. 1) and that a breach is 'serious' if 'it involves a gross systematic failure by the responsible State to fulfil the obligation' (para. 2).

[159] See Article 41, ILC Articles on State Responsibility, 'Particular consequences of a serious breach of an obligation under this chapter', stating that: '(1) States shall cooperate to bring to an end through lawful means any serious breach within the meaning of Article 40. (2) No State shall recognize as lawful a situation created by a serious breach within the meaning of Article 40, nor render aid or assistance in maintaining that situation.'

[160] ILC Commentaries to Articles on State Responsibility, Commentary to Article 40(3) (emphasis added). The Commentary lists among the examples of peremptory norms the prohibition of genocide, of slavery and slave trade, of apartheid and racial discrimination, of torture and cruel and inhuman treatment (*ibid.*, paras. 4 and 5).

[161] See Chapter 4 A.1.3 on universal jurisdiction. Where the violations are grave breaches, the *duty* to seek out criminals and ensure their accountability is explicit in IHL. In respect of other war crimes the duty to hold to account is more controversial, but referred to e.g., in the Preamble of the ICC Statute.

[162] See Chapter 5, under 'Humanitarian Intervention'.

7A.4.3.1 Life: arbitrary deprivation, lethal use of force and the death penalty

The duty to protect human life is at the heart of a state's obligations in relation to terrorism: the duty to take measures to protect from terrorist attacks, as well as the duty to protect the life of persons associated with terrorism are of paramount importance.[163]

It was noted above in relation to positive obligations that the state may be responsible not only for unlawful killing by its own agents, but also by private parties where it failed to take effective action to prevent the deaths. The fact that a state possessed information as to terrorist threats and failed to act on it could conceivably be sufficient to render the state responsible if the threats are realised, although this would depend on there being clear information indicating a 'real and immediate risk' in circumstances where the state was in a position reasonably to prevent deaths and failed to do so.[164]

More commonly, the issue that terrorism gives rise to is the nature of – and limits on – the duty of the state to protect the lives of suspected 'terrorists'. This may arise in the context of criminal law enforcement operations, or indeed in the context of armed conflict. The right to life belongs to the category of non-derogable rights that must be respected at all times, including in conflict.[165] As stated by the Inter-American Commission:

> [t]he American Convention, as well as other universal and regional human rights instruments, and the 1949 Geneva Conventions share a common nucleus of non-derogable rights and a common purpose of protecting

---

[163] Human Rights Committee, General Comment No. 6: Right to Life (Article 6) [1994], UN Doc. HRI/GEN/1/Rev.6 (2003) at 127, para. 3: 'The protection against arbitrary deprivation of life which is explicitly required by the third sentence of Article 6(1) is of paramount importance. The Committee considers that States parties should take measures not only to prevent and punish deprivation of life by criminal acts, but also to prevent arbitrary killing by their own security forces. The deprivation of life by the authorities of the State is a matter of the utmost gravity. Therefore, the law must strictly control and limit the circumstances in which a person may be deprived of his life by such authorities.'

[164] See, e.g., the case of *Osman* v. *United Kingdom* (above, note 145), before the ECtHR. In that case, the police did not have such information and hence the failure to act on death threats was deemed insufficient to render the UK responsible when the threats were carried out (para. 121).

[165] The paramount importance of the right to life is constantly stressed by the monitoring bodies of human rights treaties. See, e.g., Human Rights Committee, General Comment No. 6 (above, note 163).

human life and dignity. These human rights treaties apply both in peacetime, and during situations of armed conflict . . . Both Common Article 3 and Article 4 of the American Convention protect the right to life and, thus, prohibit, *inter alia*, summary executions in all circumstances.[166]

Under IHRL, persons can never be arbitrarily deprived of their life. Within the context of armed conflict, IHL applies alongside human rights law, as discussed above. What constitutes 'arbitrary deprivation of life' must be interpreted in the light of all applicable law including IHL. As IHL permits the killing of a combatant – a legitimate military target – this deprivation of life in the context of armed conflict is not arbitrary.[167] The killing of persons in armed conflict in circumstances where there is no IHL justification, such as killing of civilians, or the extra-judicial killing of persons outside the context of armed conflict, including persons suspected of a criminal offence, would however amount to arbitrary deprivations of the right to life.

Absent an armed conflict, the lethal use of force by law enforcement agents must be absolutely necessary to achieve a legitimate aim, such as protecting life or, possibly, effecting a lawful arrest or detention.[168] Certain human rights treaty provisions specifically so provide[169] while others simply express the prohibition on 'arbitrary' (as opposed to lawful) deprivation of life and have been interpreted by the authoritative bodies as

---

[166] Inter-American Commission on Human Rights, *Abella* v. *Argentina* (Case 11.137), Report No. 5/97, Annual Report of the IACHR 1997, para. 161.

[167] See *Advisory Opinion on the Legality of the Threat or Use of Nuclear Weapons, ICJ Reports 1996*, p. 226, para. 25, in which the ICJ held, with regard to the application of the right to life during hostilities, 'the test of what is an arbitrary deprivation of life, however, then falls to be determined by the applicable *lex specialis*, namely, the law applicable in armed conflict which is designed to regulate the conduct of hostilities'.

[168] Article 2(2) ECHR notes that where employed in defence against unlawful violence, to effect lawful arrest or detention or quell a riot or insurrection, lethal force will not constitute an unlawful deprivation of life, provided action taken is no more than 'absolutely necessary', but see also interpretation in, e.g., *Ogur* v. *Turkey* case, below, note 175. The UN Basic Principles on the Use of Force and Firearms by Law Enforcement Officials, adopted at the Eighth United Nations Congress on the Prevention of Crime and the Treatment of Offenders (Havana, 27 August – 7 September 1990), UN Doc. A/CONF.144/28/Rev.1 at 112 (1990)) provides that 'intentional' lethal use of firearms may only be made when 'strictly unavoidable in order to protect life'. See also Principles on the Effective Prevention and Investigation of Extra-legal, Arbitrary and Summary Executions, recommended by ECOSOC Res. 1989/65 of 24 May 1989, and Inter-American Commission on Human Rights, *Report on Terrorism and Human Rights*, 22 October 2002, OAS Doc. OEA/Ser.L/V/II.116, para. 87.

[169] Article 2(2) ECHR, *ibid*. No similar provision appears in the ICCPR or ACHR.

comprising a necessity and proportionality test.[170] As recently underlined by the Inter-American Commission of Human Rights, for example, IHRL tolerates the use of lethal force by law enforcement officials only 'where strictly unavoidable to protect themselves or other persons from imminent threat of death or serious injury, or to otherwise maintain law and order where strictly necessary and proportionate'.[171]

The defence of the state from the threat of terrorism does not *per se* provide a justification for resort to lethal force. Indeed the Human Rights Committee has condemned the use of lethal force, even where the State faces 'terrorist violence, which shows no consideration for the most basic human rights'.[172] Instead, to meet the 'necessity' test, a law enforcement operation must be planned as well as carried out in a manner that strictly limits the danger of recourse to the use of force.[173] As the European Court of Human Rights has noted, if lethal force is used absent 'all feasible precautions in the choice of means and methods of a security operation mounted against an opposing group with a view to avoiding and, in any event, minimising incidental loss of civil life', it will be deemed unnecessary, and amount to the arbitrary deprivation of life.[174] As noted, again, by the European Court of Human Rights, the person should generally be given an opportunity to surrender, unless doing so would itself present an imminent danger to life.[175] As noted above, where death does result from the lethal use of force, the obligation arises to ensure that 'a thorough effective and independent investigation is automatically carried out'.[176]

---

[170] The ICCPR and the ACHR refer to the prohibition on the 'arbitrary' deprivation of life (Articles 6 and 4, respectively). Article 1 of the American Declaration of the Rights and Duties of Man also provides for the right to life without any explicit qualification.

[171] Inter-American Commission on Human Rights, *Report on Terrorism and Human Rights*, para. 87. See also Principle 9 of the UN Basic Principles on the Use of Force and Firearms by Law Enforcement Officials, note 168 above.

[172] See Concluding Observations of the Human Rights Committee: Peru, UN Doc. CCPR/C/79/Add.8 (1992), para. 8. See also E. Gross, 'Thwarting Terrorist Attacks by Attacking the Perpetrators or Their Commanders as an Act of Self Defence: Human Rights Versus the State's Duty to Protect its Citizens', 15 (2001) *Temple International and Comparative Law Journal* 195.

[173] See *McCann, Farrell and Savage* v. *United Kingdom*, Judgment of 27 September 1995, ECtHR, *Series A*, No. 324, where the use of lethal force against suspected members of the IRA amounted to a violation of Article 2(2). This finding was based largely on what was found to be defective planning of the operation: see C. Warbrick, 'The Principles of the European Convention on Human Rights and the Responses of States to Terrorism', (2002) EHRLR 287 at 292.

[174] *Ergi* v. *Turkey* (App. 23818/94), Judgment of 28 July 1998, 32 (2001) EHRR 388, para. 79.

[175] *Ogur* v. *Turkey* (App. 21594/93), Judgment of 20 May 1999, ECtHR, *Reports 1999-III*.

[176] McBride, 'Study on Principles', above, note 88, para. 18. See *Semsi Onen* v. *Turkey* (Appl. No. 22876/93), Judgment of 15 May 2002, ECtHR, para. 87.

At least as regards situations other than armed conflict, it is clear that lethal force may not be used as an alternative to arrest and detention.[177] The use of lethal force in the course of a lawful law enforcement operation must be distinguished from the specific targeting and killing of an individual. Other than lawful targeting in the context of armed conflict or death inflicted pursuant to the appropriate legal process resulting in the death penalty, targeted killings are impermissible, amounting to an extra-judicial execution; the practice of extra-judicial killings by Israeli state agents has recently been condemned, *inter alia*, by the Human Rights Committee.[178] The UN Special Rapporteur on extra-judicial, summary, or arbitrary executions, likewise defined the policy of 'targeted pre-emptive killings' of suspected terrorists as a 'grave human rights violation'.[179] The prohibition of extra-judicial executions is prohibited in customary law[180] and has attained the status of a fundamental norm of *jus cogens*.[181]

The death penalty is not *per se* prohibited by international law, although particular instruments abolish or restrict the application of the penalty. For example, Protocol No. 6 and Protocol No. 13 to the ECHR,[182] the

---

[177] As noted in Chapter 6, while the letter of IHL would not appear to require efforts to arrest rather than kill a lawful combatant militarily engaged, it may be argued that such a preference (at least so far as causes no military disadvantage) is implicit. See, e.g., discussion in 'International Humanitarian and other Legal Regimes: Interplay in Situations of Violence', 27th Round Table on Current Problems of International Humanitarian Law; Sanremo, 4–6 September 2003 (hereinafter '2003 Sanremo Round Table on IHL'), on file with author. The proceedings of the Round Table will be published in G. L. Beruto and G. Ravasi (eds.), *27th Round Table on Current Problems of International Humanitarian Law; Sanremo, 4–6 September 2003; 'International Humanitarian and other Legal Regimes: Interplay in Situations of Violence'* (Milan, forthcoming). See also F. Martin, 'Using International Human Rights Law for Establishing a Unified Use of Force Rule in the Law of Armed Conflict', 64 (2001) *Saskatchewan Law Review* 347 at 373.

[178] See Concluding Observations of the Human Rights Committee: Peru, above, and Gross, 'Thwarting Terrorist Attacks'.

[179] See 'Civil and Political Rights, Including questions of: Disappearing, and Summary Executions', 9 January 2002, UN Doc. E/CN.4/2002/74. For a detailed discussion of the legality of the Israeli practice of extra-judicial executions of terrorists under IHRL and IHL, see O. Ben-Naftali and K. R. Michaeli, ' "We Must Not Make a Scarecrow of the Law": A Legal Analysis of the Israeli Policy of Targeted Killings', 36 (2003) *Cornell International Law Journal* 233.

[180] See, e.g., Inter-American Commission on Human Rights, *Armando Alejandre, Jr. et al.* (Case 11.589), Report No. 86/99 (1999): 'The forbidding of extrajudicial executions thus raises to the level of imperative law a provision of international law that is so basic that it is binding on all members of the international community.'

[181] See, e.g., Restatement (Third) of the Foreign Relations Law of the United States (1987), para. 102(2).

[182] Protocol No. 6 to the European Convention for the Protection of Human Rights and Fundamental Freedoms, Concerning the Abolition of the Death Penalty, Strasbourg, 28 April 1983, ETS No. 114, in force 1 March 1985 (hereinafter 'Protocol No. 6'); Protocol

Second Protocol to the ICCPR[183] and the Protocol to the American Convention on Human Rights to Abolish the Death Penalty[184] impose an obligation on States parties to abolish the death penalty.[185] In addition, general instruments such as the ICCPR and American Convention on Human Rights restrict the circumstances in which the penalty may be applied.[186]

Notably, however, the imposition of capital punishment following a judicial process that does not accord with the highest standards of justice will itself amount to an arbitrary deprivation of life. As the Inter-American Court noted: 'Because execution of the death penalty is irreversible, the strictest and most rigorous enforcement of judicial guarantees is required of the State so that those guarantees are not violated and a human life not arbitrarily taken as a result.'[187]

7A.4.3.2 Torture, cruel, inhuman and degrading treatment

Torture, cruel, inhuman and degrading treatment are prohibited both under conventional and customary international law.[188] In addition to the prohibition in general international and regional human rights

---

No. 13 to the European Convention for the Protection of Human Rights and Fundamental Freedoms, Concerning the Abolition of the Death Penalty, Vilnius, 3 May 2002, ETS No. 187, in force 1 July 2003 (hereinafter 'Protocol No. 13').

[183] Second Optional Protocol to the International Covenant on Civil and Political Rights, aiming at the Abolition of the Death Penalty (GA Res. 44/128, UN Doc. A/44/49 (1989), entered into force 11 July 1991).

[184] Protocol to the American Convention on Human Rights to Abolish the Death Penalty, Asuncion, 8 June 1990, OAS Treaty Series No. 73.

[185] Note, however, that only Protocol No. 13 to the ECHR provides for absolute abolition, whilst the other instruments allow for the retention of the death penalty as a criminal sanction in times of war.

[186] The Concluding Observations of the Human Rights Committee: Egypt (above, note 98), para. 16 noted that an expansion of the penalty 'runs counter to the sense of Article 6, paragraph 2, of the Covenant'. Article 4(2) ACHR specifically prohibits the reintroduction of the death penalty where abolished and its expansion to cover new crimes.

[187] The Right to Information on Consular Assistance, in the Framework of the Guarantees of the Due Process of Law, Advisory Opinion OC-16/99, 1 October 1999, IACtHR, *Series A*, No. 16, para. 136. See also Restrictions to the Death Penalty (Article 4.2 and 4.4 of the American Convention of Human Rights), Advisory Opinion OC-3/83, 8 September 1983, IACtHR, *Series A*, No. 3 and the decision of the ECtHR in *Öcalan* v. *Turkey* (Appl. No. 46221/99), Merits, Judgment of 12 March 2003. In these circumstances, the death penalty may also amount to cruel or inhuman treatment.

[188] The Trial Chamber in *Prosecutor* v. *Delalic et al.*, Case IT-96-21-T, Judgment of 16 November 1998 examined the 'almost universal condemnation of the practice of inhuman treatment' and concluded that 'there can be no doubt that inhuman treatment is prohibited under conventional and customary international law' (para. 517). The prohibition of torture has attained *jus cogens* status.

instruments,[189] other conventions specifically address torture, inhuman and degrading treatment, including the widely ratified Convention against Torture.[190] International humanitarian law also contains this prohibition, which is applicable to all categories of persons under IHL.[191] The prohibition on torture constitutes a norm of *jus cogens*.[192] There can be no justification for torture, nor for inhuman or degrading treatment or punishment. As the Human Rights Committee recently recalled:

> The Committee is aware of the difficulties that the State Party faces in its prolonged fight against terrorism, but recalls that *no exceptional* circumstances *whatsoever can be invoked as a justification for torture*, and expresses concern at the possible restrictions of human rights which may result from measures taken for that purpose.[193]

The conduct of the person mistreated is entirely irrelevant to the prohibition, as is the purported reason for the mistreatment, whether serving the 'greater good', 'protecting communities from terrorist violence' or extracting information concerning future terrorist threats for example.[194] As one

---

[189] Article 5 Universal Declaration of Human Rights, Article 7 ICCPR, Article 3 ECHR, Article 5(2) ACHR and Article 5 African Charter on Human and Peoples' Rights.

[190] See also the Inter-American Convention to Prevent and Punish Torture. On specific international instruments that prohibit torture, see Professor P. Kooijmans, Special Rapporteur for Torture, 'Torture and other Cruel, Inhuman or Degrading Treatment or Punishment', Report of the Special Rapporteur, UN Doc. E/CN.4/1986/15, 19 February 1986, para. 26.

[191] The prohibition against torture in humanitarian law is expressly found in Common Article 3, as well as the four Geneva Conventions including the grave breaches provisions, and the First and Second Additional Protocols of 1977. See also Articles 12 and 50 GC I; Articles 12 and 51 GC II; Articles 13, 14, 87 and 130 GC III; Articles 27, 32 and 147 GC IV; Article 75 of AP I and Article 4 of AP II.

[192] *Prosecutor v. Kunarac, Kovac and Vukovic*, Case No. IT-96–23-T, Judgment, 22 February 2001, para. 466, quoting the judgment of 16 November 1998 in *Prosecutor v. Delalic et al.*, para. 454. See also *R v. Bow Street Metropolitan Stipendiary Magistrate and others ex parte Pinochet Ugarte* 2 WLR 827 (House of Lords 1999). The Lords unanimously found that the prohibition on torture had evolved into a prohibition 'with the character of *jus cogens* or a peremptory norm.'

[193] Concluding Observations of the Human Rights Committee: Egypt, above, note 98, para. 4 (emphasis added). See also, e.g., Human Rights Committee, General Comment No. 20 (above, note 135). See also Committee against Torture, Summary account of the results of the proceedings concerning the inquiry on Egypt, UN Doc. A/51/44, paras. 180 ff., in particular para. 222, and the decision of the ECtHR in *Chahal* v. *United Kingdom* (Appl. No. 22414/93), Judgment of 15 November 1996, *Reports 1996-V*.

[194] *Ibid.*, para. 79. See also paras. 73–4: 'Article 3 prohibits in absolute terms torture or inhuman or degrading treatment or punishment and . . . its guarantees apply irrespective of the reprehensible nature of the conduct of the person in question'. The Human Rights Committee, in its Concluding observations on Israel, UN Doc. CCPR/C/79/Add. 93 (1998), para. 19, condemns guidelines authorising ' "moderate physical pressure" to obtain information considered crucial to the protection of life'.

of the most basic human rights protections, its application at all times, to all human beings, is as a matter of law uncontroversial.

Human rights treaties, as well as ample jurisprudence of human rights bodies (and increasingly domestic and international criminal tribunals), illustrate what may constitute torture and inhuman and degrading treatment or punishment.[195] The abuse may be physical or mental in nature.[196] While both torture and inhuman and degrading treatment involve the infliction of serious physical or mental pain or suffering, torture is characterised by a particular level of severity[197] and by the additional requirements that it be imposed for a particular purpose[198] and, generally speaking, that it involve a state official, directly or indirectly.[199] Torture, inhuman and degrading treatment have as their distinguishing feature conduct that 'violate[s] the basic principle of humane treatment, particularly the respect for human dignity'.[200]

---

[195] Article 1 of the Convention against Torture states that 'the term "torture" means any act by which severe pain or suffering, whether physical or mental, is intentionally inflicted on a person for such purposes as obtaining from him or a third person information or a confession, punishing him for an act he or a third person has committed or is suspected of having committed, or intimidating or coercing him or a third person, or for any reason based on discrimination of any kind, when such pain or suffering is inflicted by or at the instigation of or with the consent or acquiescence of a public official or other person acting in an official capacity'. On jurisprudence, see, e.g., the decisions of the ECtHR in *Aydin* v. *Turkey* (Appl. No. 23178/94), Judgment of 25 September 1997, 25 (1998) EHRR 251, paras 73, 80–7; *Aksoy* v. *Turkey*, paras. 39–40, 61–4; *Selmouni* v. *France* (Appl. No. 25803/94), Judgment of 28 July 1990, 29 (2000) EHRR 403 and those of the IACtHR in *Castillo Petruzzi and others* v. *Peru*, Merits, Judgment of 30 May 1999, IACtHR, *Series C*, No. 52, paras. 192–9. See also *Prosecutor* v. *Kunarac* and IT-96-23/1 'Foca', Trial Judgment, 22 February 2001 and Appeal Judgment, 12 June 2002; and *Prosecutor* v. *Furundzija*, Case No. IT-95-17/1-T (Trial Judgment), 10 December 1998 and Appeal Judgment, 21 July 2000, in front of the ICTY.

[196] *Loayza Tamayo Case*, IACtHR, Judgment of 17 September 1997. On death penalty absent rigorous standards of justice as cruel or inhuman treatment, see *Öcalan* v. *Turkey*, Merits (note 187 above).

[197] See the ECHR torture case *Selmouni* v. *France* (above, note 195).

[198] Article 1 of the Convention against Torture, for instance, defines 'torture' as 'any act by which severe pain or suffering, whether physical or mental, is intentionally inflicted on a person *for such purposes as obtaining from him or a third person information or a confession, punishing him for an act he or a third person has committed or is suspected of having committed, or intimidating or coercing him or a third person, or for any reason based on discrimination of any kind*' (emphasis added).

[199] Differences between torture as a human rights norm and as a norm of humanitarian law, which does not contain such a requirement, were referred to in the *Kunarac* judgment before the ICTY, paras. 468 ff.

[200] *Celibici Judgment*, para. 544; *Prosecutor* v. *Blaskic*, Case No. IT 95-14-T, Judgment, 3 March 2000, paras. 154–5.

Certain forms of humiliation, coercive interrogation, sensory deprivation or other extreme conditions of detention, for example, are likely to fall foul of these obligations. Other strict conditions of detention, such as isolation and solitary confinement are unlikely *per se* to amount to a violation, unless for a prolonged period of time.[201] The application of certain penalties may, in certain circumstances, also give rise to a violation.[202]

7A.4.3.3 Liberty and security

The rights of persons related to arrest and detention[203] are discussed fully in the context of the case study at Chapter 8. In respect of the detention of persons suspected of involvement in terrorism, human rights bodies have shown themselves willing to afford states certain flexibility, for example to detain persons for longer than would normally be permitted, in response to the challenges of combating terrorism, provided certain safeguards are met.[204] Particular flexibility arises in the event of national emergency leading to derogation: the right to liberty is not a non-derogable right as such, and certain states have derogated from human rights obligations in order to detain persons perceived as posing a terrorist threat, other than pursuant to normal criminal procedure. In particular, derogation may foreshadow 'preventive' or 'administrative' detention, which would otherwise be inconsistent with the lawful bases for detention anticipated in human rights treaties. The measures have, however, often been the source of challenges regarding compatibility with human rights law.[205]

---

[201] See Warbrick, 'Principles', referring to *McCallum* v. *United Kingdom* (Appl. No. 9511/81), Judgment of 30 August 1990, *Series A*, No. 183, and noting that isolation will not violate Article 3 ECHR. In the case of *Castillo Petruzzi et al.*, however, the Inter-American Court of Human Rights found that 'prolonged isolation and forced lack of communication are in themselves cruel and inhuman treatment'. The case involved complete exclusion from the outside world for over a month and solitary confinement for one year.

[202] See, e.g., *Soering* v. *United Kingdom*, note 63 above; and *Öcalan* v. *Turkey*, note 187 above. On life imprisonment without any possibility of early release raising an issue under Article 3 of the ECHR, see the Court's final decision as to admissibility in *Einhorn* v. *France* (Appl. No. 71555/01), Admissibility decision, 16 October 2001.

[203] See, e.g., Article 9 ICCPR, Article 5 ECHR and Article 7 ACHR.

[204] These safeguards are discussed in more detail in Chapter 8, para. 8B.4.

[205] In the UK various challenges arose from the procedure adopted for detaining persons in relation to the terrorist threat in Northern Ireland, which found their way to the European Court of Human Rights. *McVeigh, O'Neill and Evans* v. *United Kingdom* (App. Nos. 8022/77, 8025/77, 8027/77), Report of the Commission, 18 March 1981, 25 DR 15; *Murray* v. *United Kingdom*, Judgment of 28 October 1994, *Series A*, No. 300. Controversial measures post 9/11 are highlighted in section B.

As discussed in the following chapter, certain core aspects of the right to liberty remain protected at all times; notably, detention must not be arbitrary but must be subject to legal regulation and judicial review. The Human Rights Committee has noted that, given the need to ensure continued procedural guarantees, including judicial guarantees,[206] to protect other non-derogable rights, the prohibition on 'unacknowledged detention' is itself non-derogable.[207] Indeed the prohibition on prolonged arbitrary deprivation of liberty has been classified as a *jus cogens* norm.[208]

7A.4.3.4 Fair trial guarantees

Article 14 of the ICCPR, like its regional counterparts, sets out extensive fair trial guarantees that are often under strain in the context of alleged terrorist offences.[209] The right guarantees a fair and public hearing before an independent and impartial tribunal.[210] The Human Rights Committee has noted that the right to an independent and impartial tribunal is 'an absolute right that is not subject to any exception'[211] and that, even in emergency, 'only a court of law may try and convict a person for a criminal offence'.[212]

Special tribunals, such as military tribunals, have on numerous occasions been found by human rights bodies not to meet the 'independent and impartial tribunal' threshold.[213] In particular, they have often been

---

[206] General Comment No. 29 (above, note 28), para. 15.

[207] *Ibid.* para. 13. See also *Judicial Guarantees in States of Emergency*, Inter-American Court of Human Rights Advisory Opinion (OC-9/87) and *Habeas Corpus in Emergency Situations, (Arts. 27(2) and 7(6) of the American Convention on Human Rights)*, Advisory Opinion OC-8/87 of 30 January 1987, IACtHR, *Series A*, No. 8 (1987).

[208] General Comment No. 29, para. 11.

[209] On the scope and application of these rights, like those relating to detention, see also Chapter 8.

[210] See, e.g., Article 14(1) ICCPR.

[211] *Miguel González del Río* v. *Peru* (Comm. No. 263/1987), Decision of 28 October 1992, UN Doc CCPR/C/46/263/1987.

[212] General Comment No. 29 (para. 16).

[213] See *Incal* v. *Turkey* (App. 22678/93), Judgment of 9 June 1998 (2000) 29 EHRR 449. *Polay Campos* v. *Peru* (Comm. No. 577/1994), Views of 9 January 1998, UN Doc. CCPR/C/61/D/577/1994, where the Committee criticised the use of 'faceless judges' to judge persons accused of terrorism, in part on the basis that '[i]n a system of trial by "faceless judges", neither the independence nor the impartiality of the judges is guaranteed, since the tribunal, being established *ad hoc*, may comprise serving members of the armed forces. [S]uch a system also fails to safeguard the presumption of innocence'. See also UN Commission of Human Rights Resolution 1989/32, which recommends against 'ad hoc tribunals . . . to displace jurisdiction properly vested in the courts'. Report of the

criticised as inappropriate for the trial of criminal offences involving civilian suspects, and in certain circumstances for exercising jurisdiction over certain types of serious human rights violations, whether the suspects are military or civilian.[214]

Commonly, resort to special courts also raises questions as to compatibility with specific fair trial guarantees, such as access to counsel of

Special Rapporteur on Independence of judges and lawyers, para. 78. See F.A. Guzman, *Terrorism and Human Rights No. 1* (International Commission of Jurists, Geneva, 2002), pp. 231–5.

[214] For the Human Rights Committee approach see, e.g., Concluding observations: Slovakia, UN Doc. CCPR/C/79/Add.79 (1997), para. 20, recommending that law be changed to 'prohibit the trial of civilians by military tribunals in any circumstances'; Concluding observations: Lebanon, UN Doc. CCPR/C/79/Add.78 (1997), para. 14, recommending transfer of 'cases concerning civilians and all cases concerning the violation of human rights by members of the military, to the ordinary courts'. From the Inter-American system, see, e.g., the strong criticism of military courts and tribunals by the Inter-American Commission on Human Rights in its reports on Chile (e.g., *First Report on the Situation of Human Rights in Chile*, OAS Doc. OEA/Ser.L/V/II.34, doc. 21 (1974)); Colombia (e.g., *Report on the Situation of Human Rights in the Republic of Colombia*, OAS Doc. OEA/Ser.L/V/II.53, doc. 22 (1981)); Argentina (e.g., *Report on the Situation of Human Rights in Argentina*, OAS Doc. OEA/Ser.L/V/II.49, doc. 19 (1980)). In a decision concerning Paraguay, it has added that the fact that crimes were committed by military persons is not *per se* sufficient to justify military jurisdiction, stating that 'military justice may be applied only to military personnel who have committed crimes in the line of duty, and that military courts do not possess the independence and impartiality required to try civilians' (*Lino César Oviedo* v. *Paraguay* (Case No. 12.013), Report No. 88/99, 27 September 1999, para. 30). See also Inter-American Convention on Forced Disappearance of Persons, Article 9, which provides that persons accused of forced disappearance shall be tried by ordinary courts. The African Commission on Human and Peoples' Rights has similarly condemned the setting up of military tribunals and has taken the view that the military court system should be confined to military offences committed by military personnel: see, e.g., African Commission on Human and Peoples' Rights, Decision of 6 November 2000 (Comm. No. 223/98) (Sierra Leone), and, in general, the 'Resolution on the Right to Fair Trial and Legal Aid in Africa', adopted by the Commission on 15 November 1999. From the European system, see *Findlay* v. *United Kingdom* (Appl. No. 22107/93), Judgment of 25 February 1997, ECtHR, *Reports* 1997-I, in particular paras. 74–7. See also *Coyne* v. *United Kingdom* (Appl. No. 25942/94), Judgment of 24 September 1997, ECtHR, *Reports* 1997-V, paras. 56–8; *Demirel* v. *Turkey* (Appl. No. 39324/98), Judgment of 28 January 2003, paras. 68–71 and *Cyprus* v. *Turkey* (Appl. No. 25781/94), Merits, Judgment of 10 May 2001, ECtHR, *Reports* 2001-IV. The UN Working Group on Arbitrary Detention considered that military courts should not be used, *inter alia*, to try civilians, if the 'victims included civilians' or the crimes 'involved risk of jeopardising a democratic regime', UN Doc. E.CN/4/1999/63, 18 December 1998, para. 80. See also the 2002 Report on 'Administration of justice through military tribunals and other exceptional jurisdictions', prepared by the Special Rapporteur, Louis Joinet (UN Doc. E/CN.4/Sub.2/2002/4). For an analysis of military commissions in international law, see generally F.A. Guzman, *Fuero Militar y Derecho Internacional* (International Commission of Jurists, Bogotá, 2003).

choice and to evidence;[215] indeed the Human Rights Committee recognised that often 'the reason for the establishment of such courts is to enable exceptional procedures to be applied which do not comply with normal standards of justice'.[216] Moreover, it has been suggested that even where 'military justice' *is* appropriate, it should not impose the death penalty in any circumstances.[217]

The fair trial right involves a trial in 'public', although this is not absolute and may be limited in exceptional circumstances[218] where there is pressing need to do so, for example due to witness and victim protection.[219] As restrictions on public trials are an exception, and 'the publicity of hearings is an important safeguard in the interest of the individual and of society at large',[220] the need to hold criminal trials completely *in camera* would be difficult to justify.[221]

The accused has the absolute right to be presumed innocent until proven guilty,[222] and public statements by state officials relating to suspected terrorists may jeopardise this aspect of a fair trial.[223] International fair trial provisions also specifically provide for certain 'minimum' procedural guarantees that are detailed in, for example, Article 14(3) of the

---

[215] See generally, D.A. Mundis, 'Agora: Military Commissions: The Use of Military Commissions to Prosecute Individuals Accused of Terrorist Acts', 96 (2002) AJIL 320. See specific guarantees referred to below.

[216] Human Rights Committee, General Comment No. 13: Equality before the Law (Article 14) [1984], UN Doc. HRI/GEN/1/Rev.6 (2003) at 135, para. 4.

[217] Working Group on Arbitrary Detention, UN Doc. E/CN.4/1999/63, 18 December 1998, para. 80.

[218] That trials in public should be restricted only in 'exceptional circumstances' is specified in General Comment No. 13 (above, note 216), para. 6. Article 14 ICCPR anticipates that exclusion of the press or public may be permissible 'for reason of morals, public order or national security in a democratic society, or when the interest of the private lives of parties so requires, or to the extent strictly necessary in the opinion of the court in special circumstances where publicity would prejudice the interests of justice'.

[219] Article 14(1) specifies certain exceptional circumstances where the press and public may be excluded. On permissible restrictions under the ECHR, see *P.G. and J.H. v. United Kingdom* (Appl. No. 44787/98), Judgment of 25 September 2001, ECtHR, *Reports 2001-IX*, para. 29; *Lamanna v. Austria* (Appl. No. 28923/95), Judgment of 10 July 2001; *B. and P. v. United Kingdom* (App. Nos. 36337/97 and 35974/97), Judgment of 24 April 2001; *Fejde v. Sweden*, (App. 12631/87), Judgment of 29 October 1991, ECtHR, *Series A*, No. 212 and, at the Human Rights Committee, *Kavanagh v. Ireland* (Comm. No. 819/98), Views of 4 April 2001, UN Doc. CCPR/C/71/D/819/1998.

[220] General Comment No. 13 (above, note 216), para. 6.

[221] See Warbrick, 'Principles', 302.   [222] Article 14(2) ICCPR.

[223] *Allenet de Ribemont v. France* (Appl. No. 15175/89), Judgment of 7 August 1996, ECtHR, *Series A*, No. 308.

ICCPR. The right to be informed in detail of the nature and cause of the charges, and the rights to prepare one's defence and to cross-examine witnesses, make the use of, for example, secret evidence and anonymous witnesses (where witness identity is withheld from the accused), highly controversial.[224] The rights to consult counsel of choice on a confidential basis, to have time and facilities for the preparation of a defence, to an interpreter, not to be compelled to testify against oneself, and to lodge an appeal, are all further specifically provided for in these fair trial human rights provisions.[225] There is, however, no international human right to trial by jury, although this may be provided for in national law, depending on the nature of the legal system.

The provisions relating to fair trial, like those rights relating to liberty and detention, permit derogation. However, the Human Rights Committee has noted that no circumstances justify 'deviating from fundamental principles of fair trial, including the presumption of innocence'.[226] Certain fundamental aspects of the guarantees contained in the fair trial provisions are likely to be considered a *sine qua non* of fair trial that thus remain applicable at all times, such as the presumption of innocence or right of a person accused of serious offences to know the charges against him or her and to independent legal advice. In many cases however the appropriate assessment will not be the presence of particular safeguards in isolation but rather whether the totality of the proceedings amount, in the circumstances, to a fair trial.[227]

Finally, it should be noted that in determining international standards relating to the rights of suspects and accused persons, regard may also be had to the developing area of international criminal law, which

---

[224] In the context of the ICC Statute and Rules, Article 68(5) of the Statute and Rule 81(4) suggest that complete anonymity has been ruled out from ICC proceedings, while other measures to protect the safety and well-being of witnesses can and should be taken, and do not raise doubts as to incompatibility with the rights of the accused. See F. Guariglia, 'The Rules of Procedure and Evidence for the International Criminal Court: A New Development in International Adjudication of Individual Criminal Responsibility', in A. Cassese, P. Gaeta and J. Jones (eds.), *The Rome Statute of the International Criminal Court: A Commentary* (Oxford, 2002), pp. 1111 ff., at pp. 1125–6. For a different view see C. Kreß, 'Witnesses in Proceedings Before the International Criminal Court', in H. Fischer, C. Kreß and S.R. Lüder (eds.), *International and National Prosecution of Crimes under International Law* (Berlin, 2001), pp. 375 ff.

[225] See Chapter 8.

[226] General Comment No. 29, para. 11. Core fair trial issues are discussed more fully at Chapter 8, in particular at para. 8B.4.5.

[227] See *McCallum* v. *United Kingdom* (Appl. No. 9511/81), Judgment of 30 August 1990, *Series A*, No. 183.

generally reflects, and may at times exceed, the minimum guarantees in human rights treaties. For example the right to remain silent without any adverse inference being drawn from the same, and the prohibition on the admissibility of evidence illegally obtained, are both provided for unequivocally in the ICC Statute, Articles 55(1)(a), (2)(b), 67(1)(g) and 69(7). The European Court of Human Rights by contrast has taken a more flexible approach, finding that there is no rule prohibiting the admissibility of, for example, interceptions in violation of Convention rules, and that inferences may be drawn from the decision of the accused to remain silent, provided the overall fairness of proceedings is maintained.[228] While it would go too far to assert that states are legally bound to meet ICC standards in domestic proceedings, the standards that were ultimately approved by 120 states for ICC purposes[229] must lay some claim to being relevant to informing the interpretation of human rights treaties, and to themselves embodying emerging fair trial standards.

7A.4.3.5 Certainty and non-retroactivity in criminal law

The requirement of legality and certainty in criminal law enshrined in Article 15 of the ICCPR[230] and other instruments[231] is often referred to as the fundamental principle *nullum crimen sine lege*. It is one of the rights which human rights treaties explicitly proscribe derogation.[232] The European Court of Human Rights has noted that the relevant provision 'occupies a prominent place in the Convention system of protection, as

---

[228] On the right to remain silent see *Murray (John)* v. *United Kingdom* (Appl. No. 14310/88), Judgment of 7 April 1993, ECtHR, *Series A*, No. 300-A. On the admissibility of evidence, see *Austria* v. *Italy* (Appl. No. 788/604), 11 January 1961, 4 *Yearbook of the European Convention of Human Rights* 116 at 140.

[229] In total, 120 states voted in favour of the Statute, with only seven against. See www.un.org/icc/index.htm.

[230] ICCPR, Article 15(1) states: 'No one shall be held guilty of any criminal offence on account of any act or omission, which did not constitute a criminal offence, under national or international law, at the time when it was committed. Nor shall a heavier penalty be imposed than one that was applicable at the time when the criminal offense was committed. If, subsequent to the commission of the offence, provision is made by law for the imposition of the lighter penalty, the offender shall benefit thereby.'

[231] See Universal Declaration of Human Rights, Article 11(2): Article 7(1) ECHR, Article 7(2) African Charter and Article 9 ACHR; see also Articles 22 (*Nullum crimen sine lege*) and 23 (*Nulla poena sine lege*) of the ICC Statute.

[232] Article 4, ICCPR, Article 15, ECHR and Article 27, ACHR all expressly proscribe derogation from the rights.

is underlined by the fact that no derogation from it is permissible under Article 15 in time of war or other public emergency'.[233]

These provisions prohibit prosecution for conduct that was not criminal at the time carried out. Hence the Human Rights Committee has found violations of, *inter alia*, Article 15 in respect of convictions for terrorist offences under legislation which did not exist at the time of the alleged offences, even where the law in force at that time criminalised other relevant offences to which similar penalties applied.[234] The related provisions addressing the principle *nulla poene sine lege* seek to ensure also that, where the conduct was criminal, a heavier penalty cannot be imposed than the one in force at the time of the commission of the offence. The temptation to increase penalties retrospectively as policy imperatives shift, for example in the wake of a terrorist attack, must therefore be resisted.[235]

The provisions of Article 15 and comparable regional provisions are not however confined to prohibiting the retrospective application of the criminal law, but enshrine more generally the requirements of legal certainty in respect of criminal law. Specifically, offences must be clearly defined in law in a way that is both accessible and foreseeable; it follows that, as only the law can define a crime and prescribe a penalty, criminal law must not be extensively construed to an accused's detriment, for instance by analogy.[236] Terrorist legislation has not infrequently been subject to criticism as falling foul of the requirements of legality, enshrined in Article 15, as a result of ill-defined, over-broad definitions of terrorist offences in domestic law.[237]

Notably, however, Article 15 expressly does not apply to preclude the prosecution of conduct that was an offence under international (but not national) law at the time committed.[238] Thus this rule does not

---

[233] See *S.W.* v. *United Kingdom* and *C.R.* v. *United Kingdom*, Judgments of 22 November 1995, Series A, No 335-B and 335-C, cited in *Streletz, Kessler and Krenz* v. *Germany*, Judgment of 22 March 2001, 33 EHRR 31, para. 50. The passage continues: 'It should be construed and applied, as follows from its object and purpose, in such a way as to provide effective safeguards against arbitrary prosecution, conviction and punishment.'

[234] *Gómez Casafranca* v. *Peru* (Comm. No. 981/2001), Views of 19 September 2003, UN Doc. CCPR/C/78/D/981/2001.

[235] See ECtHR, *Welch* v. *United Kingdom*, Judgment of 9 February 1995, cited in McBride, 'Study on Principles', para. 49.

[236] For a reasoned discussion of these requirements, which have been set down in jurisprudence for some time, see *Kokkinanis* v. *Greece* (Appl. No. 14307/88), Judgment of 25 May 1993, ECtHR, Series A, No 260-A.

[237] See, e.g., Concluding Observations of the Human Rights Committee: Egypt, UN Doc. CCPR/C/79/Add.23 (1993), para. 8; Concluding observations on the recent Israeli report (UN Doc. CCPR/CO/78/ISR (2003)) and para. 7B.4 of this chapter.

[238] Article 15(2) ICCPR provides that: 'Nothing in this article shall prejudice the trial and punishment of any person for any act or omission which, at the time when it was committed,

prohibit the prosecution of, for example serious terrorist attacks such as September 11 so far as they amount to crimes against humanity, which are prohibited in international law.[239] As terrorism is not clearly defined in international law, the ability to prosecute for terrorism as such would depend on sufficient specificity and clarity in domestic law to meet the requirements of *nullum crimen sine lege*.

7A.4.3.6 Freedom of expression, association and assembly

The human rights to free expression, association and assembly are often called into question in the presence of a perceived terrorist threat, whether by prohibiting expression of dissent, or proscribing certain organisations or forms of collective activity. Human rights law emphasises the importance of these rights, not only in themselves, but because they are essential to a functioning democratic system of government, which may itself be put under strain by terrorist and counter-terrorist measures.

These rights fall within the 'claw back clauses' referred to above, which explicitly allow for their restriction, provided the three-fold criteria are met: the restriction is provided for in clear and accessible law, pursues a specified legitimate aim[240] and is strictly necessary and proportionate.[241] These criteria must be strictly applied. As the European Court has noted in relation to free speech, the choice the Court must make is not 'between two conflicting principles but with a principle of freedom of expression that is subject to a number of exceptions which must be narrowly interpreted'.[242]

As regards 'the freedoms of information and expression', described as 'cornerstones in any free and democratic society', the Human Rights

was criminal according to the general principles of law recognized by the community of nations'; Article 7(2) of the ECHR provides in similar terms: 'This Article shall not prejudice the trial and punishment of any person for any act or omission which, at the time when it was committed, was criminal according to the general principles of law recognized by civilized nations.' Prosecution on the basis of offences enshrined in international criminal law has been found by the ICTY, e.g., not to breach the *nullum crimen* rules.

239 See Chapter 4 regarding crimes in international law committed on September 11.
240 According to Article 19 ICCPR these are national security, public order, public health or morals.
241 The first requirement of being 'provided for in clear and accessible law' meets with the difficulty of ill-defined concepts of terrorism. The second – the legitimacy of the aim of combating terrorism – is less likely *per se* to give rise to controversy. The third – the necessity of the measures, covering the ability of the measures adopted to meet that aim and the reasonableness and proportionality of the measures taken in response – provides the most common basis of successful challenge to a state's justification for restrictions.
242 *Sunday Times* v. *United Kingdom (No. 1)*, 29 March 1979, ECtHR, *Series A*, No. 30, para. 65.

Committee has noted that '[i]t is in the essence of such societies that its citizens must be allowed to inform themselves about alternatives to the political system/parties in power, and that they may criticise or openly and publicly evaluate their Governments without fear of interference or punishment, within the limits set by Article 19, paragraph 3'.[243] Political speech is broadly considered deserving of particular protection, no less so in a context of violence and civil unrest.[244]

However, where 'remarks incite people to violence, the State enjoys a wider margin of appreciation when examining the need for an interference with freedom of expression'.[245] The line between virulent or even offensive criticism and incitement must not, however, be confused.[246] Nor should 'a message . . . of intransigence and a refusal to compromise with the authorities as long as the objectives of [a proscribed organisation have] not been secured', which has been found to be permissible, be confused with 'texts [which] taken as a whole . . . incite to violence or hatred'.[247]

---

[243] See also *Aduayom et al.* v. *Togo* (Comm. No. 422-24/1990), para. 7.4. See also, e.g., *Media Rights Agenda et al.* v. *Nigeria*, African Commission on Human and People's Rights, Communication Nos. 105/93, 128/94, 130/94, 152/96, para. 52 and *Lingens* v. *Austria* (Appl. No. 9815/82), Judgment of 8 July 1986, ECtHR, *Series A*, No. 103, para. 41: 'freedom of expression . . . constitutes one of the essential foundations of a democratic society and one of the basic conditions for its progress and for each individual's self-fulfilment'.

[244] See the decision of the ECtHR in *Castells* v. *Spain* (Appl. No. 11798/85), Judgment of 23 April 1992, *Series A*, No. 236. On political speech, see also: ECtHR, *Sener* v. *Turkey* (Appl. No. 26680/95), Judgment of 18 July 2000; Human Rights Committee, *Keun-Tae Kim* v. *Korea* (Comm. No. 574/1994), Views of 4 January 1999, UN Doc. CCPR/C/64/D/574/1994, para. 12.2; *Lingens* v. *Austria*, above, and African Commission on Human and People's Rights, *Amnesty International, Comité Loosli Bachelard, Lawyers Committee for Human Rights, Association of Members of the Episcopal Conference of East Africa* case, Comm. No. 48/90, 50/91, 52/91, 89/93, 13th Annual Activity Report 1999–2000.

[245] *Sener* v. *Turkey*, above, para. 40; see also *Ozgur Gundem* v. *Turkey* (Appl. No. 23144/93), Judgment of 16 March 2000, ECtHR, *Reports 2000-III* and *Surek* v. *Turkey* (No. 2) (Appl. No. 24), Judgment of 8 July 1999, where there was no violation given direct incitement to violence.

[246] See *Incal* v. *Turkey* (Appl. No. 22658/93), Judgment of 9 June 1998, ECtHR, Reports *1998-IV; Aksoy* v. *Turkey* (Appl. No. 21987/93), Judgment of 10 October 2000, ECtHR, *Reports 1996-VI; Thorgeirson* v. *Iceland* (Appl. No. 13778/88), Judgment of 25 June 1992, ECtHR, *Series A*, No. 239, para. 63: '[F]reedom of expression . . . is applicable not only to "information" or "ideas" that are favourably received or regarded as inoffensive or as matter of indifference, but also to those that offend, shock or disturb'. See also McBride, 'Study on Principles', para. 59.

[247] *Surek and Ozdemir* v. *Turkey* (App. Nos. 23927/94 and 24277/94), Judgment of 8 July 1999, para. 61. Turkish courts found the interviews given by a leading member of a proscribed organisation, accusing the authorities of fascism and calling on 'all revolutionaries and democrats' to 'unite forces', to constitute praise for Kurdish terrorist activities. The ECtHR took the view that, in that case, these were not sufficient reasons for interfering with the

The international expert report, the Johannesburg Principles on National Security, Freedom of Expression and Access to Information, suggests that expression may be punished as a threat to national security only where intended to incite imminent violence, likely to incite such violence and where there is a direct and immediate connection between the expression and the likelihood or occurrence of such violence.[248]

The right to association is closely linked with free expression, and plays an important role in the democratic, cultural and social life of a state, but is often under threat where the fear of terrorism prevails. This right does not prevent organisations that promote violence from being dissolved, provided there is clear evidence[249] and judicial control.[250] Restrictions on assembly, in turn, are clearly contemplated where there are genuine risks to life, health or safety, but efforts should be made to accommodate alternative arrangements that meet those concerns while respecting the essence of the right.[251]

In time of emergency, as these rights are derogable, the state may rely on a valid derogation, provided again it meets the conditions and constraints already discussed above, including, again, the requirement that the particular measures restricting rights be necessary in response to the emergency and proportionate to it.

7A.4.3.7 Property rights

Certain human rights provisions also enshrine the right to property.[252] Undoubtedly, the state may limit the enjoyment of property, and ultimately may confiscate it, provided certain safeguards are in place.

---

applicants' right to freedom of expression, absent clear incitement to violence or hatred. The same principle applied despite the 'one-sided view of the origin of and responsibility for the disturbances in south-east Turkey'. See also *Erdogdu* v. *Turkey* (Appl. No. 25723/94), Judgment of 15 June 2000, ECtHR, *Reports 2000-VI* and *Ceylan* v. *Turkey* (Appl. No. 23556/94), Judgment of 8 July 1999, *Reports 1999-IV*.

[248] See Johannesburg Principles on National Security, Freedom of Expression and Access to Information ('Johannesburg Principles'), UN Doc E/CN.4/1996/39. These 'soft laws' elaborate international treaty standards in the field of free expression. See also Siracusa Principles on the Limitation and Derogation Provisions in the International Covenant on Civil and Political Rights ('Siracusa Principles'), 7 (1985) HRQ 3.

[249] *United Communist Party and Others* v. *Turkey* (Appl. No. 19392/92), Judgment of 30 January 1998, ECtHR, *Reports 1998-I*, where dissolution was based on assumptions not facts, in violation of the right to association.

[250] See, e.g., *Refah Partisi (Welfare Party) and Others* v. *Turkey* (App. Nos. 41340/98; 41342/98; 41343/98; 41344/98), Judgment of 13 February 2003.

[251] See, e.g., *Cisse* v. *France* (Appl. No. 51346/99), Judgment of 9 April 2002, ECtHR, *Reports 2002–III*.

[252] Article 1, Protocol No. 1 to the ECHR, Article 14 African Charter and Article 21, ACHR. There is no such right in the ICCPR.

Substantively, there should be conditions on which property may be confiscated which should be provided for in law, and there should be a fair process for determining whether those conditions have been met in any particular case. The right to a fair hearing in determining one's civil rights and obligations applies to the confiscation of property.[253] Appropriate provision should be made for property used, damaged or confiscated in the public interest.[254]

Where there has been a criminal conviction involving a finding that property was obtained through unlawful means involving links with terrorism, the legitimacy of confiscation is unlikely to be controversial.[255] However, where the state acts based on intelligence information, or assumptions, as to the source of property, absent a fair procedure wherein the persons affected are given an opportunity to be heard, confiscation may well fall foul of the obligations of the state in respect of property rights (as well as other violations).[256] Again, this right may be derogated from in the event of a national emergency, provided the derogation and the measures taken meet the tests, notably relating to necessity and proportionality, set out above.

7A.4.3.8 Non-refoulement, state cooperation (extradition and mutual assistance) and human rights

As discussed previously, the decision to surrender or expel someone to another state where there is a real risk of that person's rights being violated may itself constitute a human rights violation.[257] The duties of the state in this respect – referred to as the principle of 'non-refoulement' – arise commonly in relation to extradition, discussed here, but apply equally in the context of other procedures for the removal of persons from a state,

---

[253] Article 6(1) ECHR e.g., provides for the right to a fair hearing in the determination of civil rights, which applies to applicable property rights.

[254] *Stran Greek Refineries and Statis Andreadis* v. *Greece* (Appl. No. 13427/87), Judgment of 9 December 1994, ECtHR, *Series A*, No. 301-B, para. 72.

[255] It is noted that the SC Res. 1373 (2001), 28 September 2001, UN Doc. S/RES/1373 (2001) calls on states to taking wide-ranging measures to seize property, without specifying procedures. The legitimacy of measures taken may depend on the steps taken by the state itself. See *Phillips* v. *United Kingdom* (Appl. No. 41087/98), Judgment of 5 July 2001, *Reports 2001-VII*, paras. 35 and 53.

[256] E.g., it may potentially infringe rights relating to the right to be heard and the presumption of innocence: See *Phillips* v. *United Kingdom*, above, where the presumption of innocence was not violated as there had been a criminal conviction.

[257] The principles and features of the law relating to extradition, and human rights implications, are discussed at Chapter 4, para. 4A.2.1. See generally J. Dugard and C. Van den Wyngaert, 'Reconciling Extradition with Human Rights', 92 (1998) AJIL 187.

such as under refugee or asylum law.[258] Consistent with general principles of human rights law, the obligation of non-refoulement applies to all persons, irrespective of the crime of which he or she may be accused. While persons may be denied 'refugee status' because they are suspected of certain serious crimes – covering war crimes, crimes against humanity and, according to the Security Council's controversial Resolution 1373, acts of 'terrorism'[259] – the principle of non-refoulement protects all persons, including terrorist suspects.[260] Indeed, the fact that a person is suspected of terrorism, in circumstances where a state is known to violate the rights of such persons, may be a factor precluding extradition on grounds of non-refoulement.[261]

The duties of states in respect of 'non-refoulement' are reflected, directly and indirectly, in extradition and human rights treaties.[262] The multi-lateral and bilateral extradition treaties contain provisions either prohibiting extradition, or permitting states parties to refuse it (where they would otherwise be obliged to extradite), where specific human rights issues arise, including the death penalty, torture or inhuman treatment, fair trial and discrimination. Among such treaties are the Inter-American Convention on Extradition[263] and European Convention on Extradition,[264] with the UN Model Treaty on Extradition making similar

---

[258] See Human Rights Committee, *T.* v. *Australia* (Comm. No. 706/1996), Views of 7 November 1997, UN Doc. CCPR/C/61/D/706/1996. See also the ECtHR in *Ahmed* v. *Austria* (Appl. No. 25964), Judgment of 17 December 1996, 24 (1997) EHRR 278 where the applicant's life was endangered by his suspected membership of an opposition group; see also *Chahal* v. *United Kingdom* (above, note 193). Note that the obligations apply also in the context of 'informal rendition' of persons that by-pass normal legal process.

[259] Article 1F of the Convention on the Status of Refugees.

[260] See, e.g., *MBB* v. *Sweden*, 104/98, Decision of the Committee against Torture, 5 May 1999.

[261] *Chahal* v. *United Kingdom* (Appl. No. 22411/93), Judgment of 15 November 1996, para. 81, concerning deportation of a terror suspect from the UK to India.

[262] On extradition treaties, see Chapter 4, para. 4A.2.1.

[263] Inter-American Convention on Extradition, Caracas, 25 February 1981, reprinted in 20 ILM 723, which unconditionally prohibits the extradition of a person when that person will be punished 'by the death penalty, by life imprisonment, or by degrading treatment in the requesting state'. Specifically, Article 9 of the Convention provides: 'The States Parties shall not grant extradition when the offense in question is punishable in the requesting State by the death penalty, by life imprisonment, or by degrading punishment, unless the requested State has previously obtained from the requesting State, through the diplomatic channel, sufficient assurances that none of the above-mentioned penalties will be imposed on the person sought or that, if such penalties are imposed, they will not be enforced.'

[264] European Convention on Extradition, Paris, 13 December 1957, ETS No. 24. Article 11 addresses extradition in the context of the death penalty. It provides: 'If the offence for which extradition is requested is punishable by death under the law of the requesting Party, and if in respect of such offence the death-penalty is not provided for by the law of the requested Party or is not normally carried out, extradition may be refused unless the

provision.[265] The extradition provisions are of course binding only on states parties to the particular extradition treaties – a far smaller number of states than are party to the major human rights treaties.

Unlike the extradition treaties, general human rights treaties do not themselves spell out the circumstances in which states are obliged to extradite or to refrain from doing so, although certain more recent human rights treaties or instruments, such as the United Nations Convention against Torture[266] and the European Charter of Fundamental Rights,[267] contain specific provisions precluding extradition in certain circumstances.[268] The jurisprudence of overseeing bodies of general human rights treaties, specifically the European Court of Human Rights and the Human Rights Committee, have however recognised in the context of particular cases, and in relation to particular rights, that the obligations in the ECHR and ICCPR apply to the decision to extradite.[269] As the law

requesting party gives such assurances as the requested Party considers sufficient that the death-penalty will not be carried out.' Article 3(2) also excludes extradition where the requested state 'has substantial grounds for believing that a request for extradition for an ordinary criminal offence has been made for the purpose of prosecuting or punishing a person on account of his race, religion, nationality or political opinion, or that that person's position may be prejudiced for any of these reasons'.

[265] UN Model Treaty on Extradition, UN Doc. A/RES/45/116, 14 December 1990. Article 3 of the Model Treaty precludes extradition where the requested state has substantial grounds to believe human rights norms on (a) discrimination, (b) torture, cruel and inhuman treatment and punishment, (c) minimum guarantees in criminal proceedings would not be respected or (d) 'the judgment of the requesting State has been rendered *in absentia*, [and] the convicted person has not had sufficient notice of the trial or the opportunity to arrange for his or her defence and he has not had or will not have the opportunity to have the case retried in his or her presence'. Article 4 adds optional grounds for refusing extradition including: '(d) If the offence for which extradition is requested carries the death penalty under the law of the requesting State, unless that State gives such assurance as the requested State considers sufficient that the death penalty will not be imposed, or, if imposed, will not be carried out.'

[266] Article 3, Convention against Torture requires that 'no state party shall expel, return or extradite a person to another state where there are substantial grounds for believing that he would be in danger of being subjected to torture'.

[267] Adopted in 2001, Article 19 of the Charter states that '(n)o one may be removed, expelled or extradited to a State where there is a serious risk that he or she would be subjected to the death penalty, torture or other inhuman or degrading treatment or punishment'.

[268] See also Article 13 of the Inter-American Convention to Prevent and Punish Torture which prevents extradition on the grounds of torture or inhuman/degrading treatment. In the context of IHL, the Geneva Conventions also prohibit transfer of persons in particular circumstances. See Article 12, GC III and Article 45 GC IV.

[269] The obligation not to extradite where there is risk of violations has been held in the European context to derive from 'the obligations of states under the European Convention for the Protection of Human Rights and Fundamental Freedoms, as interpreted consistently with the general spirit of the Convention, an instrument designed to maintain and promote the ideals and values of a democratic society'. *Soering* v. *United Kingdom* (above,

has developed on a piecemeal, largely case-by-case, basis, it is difficult to elaborate clear parameters of the duty of non-cooperation, or to say categorically to which rights the obligation of non-cooperation applies. As regards the rights protected, extradition is undoubtedly proscribed by human rights law where there are substantial grounds for believing that the person extradited will be subject to torture, inhuman or degrading treatment or punishment in the other state.[270] While difficult questions can of course arise as to whether a particular situation in a foreign country, as applied to a particular individual, would amount to torture or ill-treatment,[271] the obligation not to extradite if there are substantial grounds for believing that such violations will arise is, at this stage, well established in law.[272]

As the death penalty is not *per se* prohibited in general international law,[273] nor therefore is extradition where the penalty may be applied. However, parties to specific treaties prohibiting the penalty may be prohibited from extraditing where the penalty may be imposed as a result, and, as noted above, the imposition of capital punishment may also amount to cruel treatment and extradition be prohibited on that basis. In addition, the European Court of Human Rights has taken the lead in clarifying that a substantial risk of violation of fair trial rights, amounting to a 'flagrant denial of justice', would also preclude extradition,[274] although some

---

note 63), para. 87. Before the Human Rights Committee, see, e.g., *Cox* v. *Canada* (Comm. No. 539/1993), Views of 9 December 1994, UN Doc. CCPR/C/52/D/539/1993.

[270] On the scope of such treatment which may arise from, e.g., the application of the death penalty or life imprisonment with no possibility of early release, extreme prison conditions or harsh interrogation techniques, see para. 7A.4.3.2, above. See Dugard and Van den Wyngaert, 'Reconciling Extradition', at 200.

[271] See, e.g., Human Rights Committee, *Kindler* v. *Canada* (Comm. No. 470/1991), Views of 11 November 1993, UN Doc. CCPR/C/45/D/470/1991 and *Ng* v. *Canada* (Comm. No. 469/1991), Views of 7 January 1994, UN Doc. CCPR/C/49/D/469/1991. See also ECtHR, *Öcalan* v. *Turkey*, Merits (above, note 187). The Committee against Torture noted that, in deciding whether such danger exists, the relevant authorities should consider 'the existence in the State concerned of a consistent pattern of gross, flagrant, or mass violations of human rights' (*Ayas* v. *Sweden* (Comm. No. 97/1997), Views of 12 November 1998). Personal circumstances of the accused are also relevant: see, e.g., the decision of the Human Rights Committee in *Kindler* v. *Canada*, above.

[272] E.g., the Inter-American Commission has described the obligation of 'non-refoulement' in situations where there is a risk of torture as itself a peremptory norm of international law. Annual Report of the Inter-American Commission on Human Rights 1985, OEA/Ser.L/V/II.66, Doc. 10, rev.1 1985 in F.A. Guzman, *Terrorism and Human Rights No. 2* (International Commission of Jurists, Geneva, 2003), p. 246.

[273] See above, Chapter 7, para. 7A.4.3.1.

[274] See *Drozd and Janusek* v. *France and Spain*, para. 110, discussed above, Chapter 4, para. 7A.4.2.1 on the nature and limits of the duty of an extraditing state to make

hesitation as to the extent to which non-refoulement covers violations of fair trial rights remains.[275] At least for state parties to the Inter-American Torture Convention, extradition to face trial 'by special or *ad hoc* courts' may also fall foul of human rights obligations.[276] In principle, discrimination in criminal proceedings has also been recognised as potentially giving rise to such a duty not to extradite.[277] By contrast, the right to private and family life has in one case been considered insufficient to prevent extradition to face criminal charges.[278]

The consistent application of the reasoning in existing case law may indicate that the non-refoulement principle should be applied more broadly to other rights. It may be that in respect of those rights that can be restricted in the public interest – such as the rights to free expression, association or privacy – the extraditing authority must balance the risk of violation in the other state against the public interest in justice and crime prevention.[279] While jeopardy to these rights may justify non-extradition, it does not necessarily do so. By contrast, where there is substantial reason to believe that a violation of a right that does not permit of restriction would ensue – such as torture or ill-treatment, violations of *nullum crimen sine lege* or violations of core aspects of the rights to liberty

---

assessments as to another state's judicial system. See also *Soering* v. *United Kingdom* (above, note 64), which envisaged non-extradition in cases of 'flagrant denial of a fair trial' and *Einhorn* v. *France* (Appl. No. 71555/01), Admissibility decision, 16 October 2001, where the ECtHR considered extradition pursuant to trial *in absentia* absent the possibility of obtaining a retrial as a potential violation. The Court rejected the idea that an extremely hostile media campaign in the requesting state had itself amounted to a 'flagrant denial of justice' in that case. See also Article 3 of the 1990 UN Model Treaty on Extradition which refers explicitly to the fair trial guarantees of Article 14, ICCPR. Note that, e.g., arbitrary detention may amount to violation of fair trial rights.

[275] The Human Rights Committee declined to decide on the question in *ARJ* v. *Australia*. See also Dugard and Van den Wyngaert, 'Reconciling Extradition', at 204, noting that the reluctance may reflect diverse visions of fairness.

[276] Article 13, Inter-American Convention to Prevent and Punish Torture states that 'extradition shall not be granted nor shall the person sought be returned when there are grounds to believe that his life is in danger, that he will be subjected to torture or to cruel, inhuman or degrading treatment, or that he will be tried by special or ad hoc courts in the requesting State'.

[277] Extradition treaties reflect this obligation more clearly than human rights law, and to the author's knowledge human rights bodies have not yet determined any case concerning allegations of discrimination in relation to extradition.

[278] E.g., *Aylor Davis* v. *France* (Appl. No. 22742/93), European Commission on Human Rights, Admissibility Decision, 20 January 1994, DR 76-B, 164, and Swiss Federal Tribunal judgment, *X.* v. *Bundesamt für Polizeiwesen* (1991) ATF 117 Ib 210, cited in Dugard and Van den Wyngaert, 'Reconciling Extradition', at 204.

[279] See Dugard and Wyngaert, 'Reconciling Extradition', at 187.

and trial – extradition should be denied, without any such 'balancing' of interests.[280] Human rights bodies have not yet addressed the obligations of non-refoulement in relation to freedom from arbitrary deprivation of liberty and it remains to be seen whether the principle of non-refoulement will be held to apply. (The impact of practice post 9/11 is discussed in the section B of this chapter.)

Nor has human rights case law, at least as yet, provided any clear indication as to whether there can be said to be a more general obligation of non-cooperation beyond the duties in respect of extradition. In other words, do such obligations arise in relation to the sharing of intelligence, or gathering of evidence, where it is known that the net result will be violations of human rights in another state?

One the one hand, as a matter of strict treaty construction, a person subject to trial in another state is not within the requested state's 'territory', and only arguably subject to its 'jurisdiction'.[281] On the other, while the link is more remote than in extradition cases, it may be none the less real in terms of impact if on the basis of that state's cooperation the person's rights are violated. As the European Court of Human Rights has pointed out, any interpretation of the scope of a human rights convention should be consistent with 'the general spirit of the Convention, an instrument designed to maintain and promote the ideals and values of a democratic society'.[282] The obligation to implement a treaty in good faith[283] would presumably preclude facilitating or encouraging other states to commit violations;[284] likewise, if the breach in the other state would be a gross or systematic breach of a peremptory norm, further positive duties to cooperate to end the wrong may take effect, inconsistent with cooperating with the wrongdoers.[285] Interpreting the underlying principles of non-refoulement as applicable to other forms of cooperation also finds support in those mutual assistance treaties that reflect exceptional circumstances

---

[280] See *Chahal* v. *United Kingdom* (above, note 193).

[281] On 'the Jurisdiction Question', see above, para. 7A.2.1, this chapter.

[282] *Soering* v. *United Kingdom* (above, note 64), para. 87.

[283] Article 31 of the Vienna Convention on the Law of treaties states that '[a] treaty shall be interpreted in good faith in accordance with the ordinary meaning to be given to the terms of the treaty in their context and in the light of its object and purpose'.

[284] See aspects of state practice post September 11 discussed below, which may reflect the desire of states not to cooperate with the US in circumstances likely to lead to human rights violations, Chapter 4 on 'Criminal Justice' and state cooperation.

[285] Chapter 3, and Article 41, ILC's Articles on State Responsibility, above. As for the specific obligations to ensure respect for the Geneva Conventions, see Chapter 6, para. 6A.3.5.

where human rights considerations may constitute an exception to the duty to provide such assistance.[286]

7A.5 Conclusion

The foregoing are only some of the specific rights implicated in times of terrorism and counter-terrorism. Others, not explored here but often restricted in times of counter-terrorism, include private and family life,[287] thought, conscience and religion[288] and the right to seek asylum.[289] What should be clear from the foregoing is that while IHRL is contained in numerous different treaties, covering a broad range of rights which accommodate security concerns in several different ways, it enshrines certain cross-cutting principles applicable to all rights and in all circumstances. Among them are the principle of legality, including independent judicial oversight, the prohibition on arbitrariness or discrimination, and the requirement of necessity and proportionality.[290]

---

[286] The European Convention on the Suppression of Terrorism e.g., confirms in Article 8, that there is no obligation to afford mutual assistance if the requested State has substantial grounds for believing that the request for mutual assistance has been made for the purpose of prosecuting or punishing a person on account of his race, religion, nationality or political opinion or that that person's position may be prejudiced for any of these reasons. See also UN Mutual Assistance Treaty which envisages refusal to cooperate in case of persecution, double jeopardy (*non bis in idem*) and unfair measures to compel testimony, Article 4(1)(c)–(e). As noted in Chapter 4, section B, the principle may also be reflected to a degree in preliminary state practice post 9/11.

[287] Many rights issues surround increased resort to surveillance and interceptions, which may be justified only where there are objective criteria, and some form of supervision to forestall abuse. See ECtHR, *Peck* v. *United Kingdom*, Judgment of 28 January 2003.

[288] Interference with religious freedom depends on demonstrating a clear link between the threat in question and the exercise of religious freedom, which may be difficult to do in the context of terrorism. See ECtHR, *Agga* v. *Greece*, Judgment of 17 October 2002. Moreover, necessary interference with religious practice must not be prolonged or make religious observance impossible – see *Cháre Shalom ve Tsedek* v. *France*, Judgment of 27 June 2002.

[289] Article 40, Universal Declaration of Human Rights and Refugee Convention, 1951. The right to asylum is subject to limits, notably where the individual has committed a serious non-political offence. One troubling effect of declaring that 'terrorist offences' are inherently non-political is that the individuals deemed, without due process of law, to fall under this broad rubric are then denied asylum. However, this right should be distinguished from the right to non-refoulement, above, applicable to asylum seekers and all other persons facing expulsion for whatever reason, and no matter what offences they may be suspected of having committed. The specific issues relating to refugee law are not developed here, though mentioned briefly in the application section. See brief study in the original INTERIGHTS paper, by Guglielmo Verdirame, available at www.interights. org.

[290] See generally McBride, 'Study on Principles', above, note 89.

The following section of this chapter asks questions relating specifically to the application of this legal framework in practice since 11 September 2001.

7B Human rights and security post September 11

The prosecution of the so-called 'war on terror', on the international, regional and national levels, gives rise to a plethora of questions regarding the application of the above framework of human rights law since September 11. Tension between counter-terrorism and human rights is nothing new and many questionable practices adopted in the name of counter-terrorism existed, like terrorism itself, long before September 11. One of the most insidious long-term effects of the events of that day and the responses thereto may be to clothe old practices in the new legitimacy of the 'global war on terror'. In addition, new legislative and other 'counter-terrorist' measures, national and international, have proliferated in the wake of September 11 giving rise to additional challenges.

While an in-depth analysis of the wide-reaching human rights implications of September 11 falls outside the scope of this study, this section seeks to illustrate some of the key questions as to the application of the foregoing legal framework that have arisen recurrently, or are of particular significance. While the focus is on whether and how the law has been applied (or disregarded), it touches on areas where the law may be clarified, or develop, as a result of state responses to terror, and, in turn, the reactions to those responses.

7B.1 Executing the 'war on terror' extra-territorially

'Human rights' discourse post September 11 is often couched in terms of counter-terrorist measures adopted by states within their own borders. Yet the global 'war on terror' has been executed in large part on the international stage, characterised by an increased exercise in military and/or law enforcement powers by states beyond their national boundaries. Advocacy of the view that 'known political boundaries . . . do not exist in the war on terrorism' suggests that this may be a continuing trend.[291]

---

[291] According to the White House Press Secretary 'the President has made very plain to the American people that the war on terrorism is not a traditional war . . . in the sense that there is one known battlefield or one known nation or one known region. The President has made clear that we will fight the war on terrorism wherever we need to fight the war on terrorism . . . this is a different kind of war, with a different kind of battlefield,

In this context, critical questions arise in relation to the application of international human rights law extra-territorially,[292] rendered more pressing by repeated reports of states violating human rights abroad, jettisoning standards by which they would consider themselves bound at home.[293] Do the IHRL obligations of states apply, for example, to the activities of ground troops, or bombardment by air forces, in Afghanistan or Iraq, or to the killing of suspected al-Qaeda operatives in Yemen, or to the 'off shore' detention of prisoners?

7B.1.1 Detention of prisoners abroad?

The arrest and detention of prisoners since 9/11 have led to widespread allegations – and considerable evidence – of torture and other mistreatment.[294] Does the human rights framework apply to these arrests and detentions, despite them having been carried out in Afghanistan, Iraq, in Guantanamo Bay Cuba, the Indian Ocean island of Diego Garcia[295] or on international waters?[296]

---

where known political boundaries, which previously existed in traditional wars do not exist in the war on terrorism.' (Press Gaggle by Ari Fleischer, 5 November 2002, available at http://www.whitehouse.gov/news/releases/2002/11/20021105-2.html#3).

[292] See legal framework section in this chapter, para. 7A.2.1; it is relatively uncontroversial that states may be responsible for their actions abroad provided they exercise a sufficient degree of authority and control over the situation, but more controversial is the nature of authority or control required, e.g., must the state exercise control over all or part of the 'territory' in which military action takes place, as opposed to over the particular people or situation in respect of which the state's authority is exercised?

[293] J. Fitzpatrick, 'Speaking Law to Power: The War Against Terrorism and Human Rights', 14 (2003) EJIL 241 at 246 suggests that one of the first consequences of the global 'war on terrorism' may consist in the increase of the commission of extra-territorial human rights violations.

[294] See Chapter 6 on IHL which discusses the multiple reports of mistreatment of prisoners in Afghanistan and elsewhere.

[295] As the situation of detainees in Guantanamo Bay is discussed in the following chapter, it is not further addressed here. A report published by the Washington Post at the end of 2002 reports that 'according to U.S. officials, nearly 3,000 suspected al Qaeda members and their supporters have been detained worldwide since September 11, 2001. In contrast to the detention centre at Guantanamo Bay, where military lawyers, news reporters and the Red Cross received occasional access to monitor prisoner conditions and treatment, the CIA's overseas interrogation facilities are off-limits to outsiders, and often even to other government agencies. In addition to Bagram and Diego Garcia, the CIA has other secret detention centres overseas, and often uses the facilities of foreign intelligence services.' See D. Priest and B. Gellman, 'U.S. Decries Abuse but Defends Interrogations. "Stress and Duress" Tactics Used on Terrorism Suspects Held in Secret Overseas Facilities', *Washington Post*, 26 December 2002.

[296] Reports note that a number of individuals apprehended during the military operations in Afghanistan have been detained in detention facilities in off-shore US Navy

In this respect questions regarding the applicability of the human rights framework should be straightforward, with previous decisions from, for example, the Human Rights Committee, Inter-American Commission on Human Rights and the monitoring organs of the ECHR having specifically decided that the human rights obligations of the state under whose authority persons are detained are to apply irrespective of where, geographically, that authority is exercised.[297] Indeed, in the context of the *Banković* case, the UK government itself accepted that the ECHR would apply to arrests and detentions abroad.[298] As the essential question is a *de facto* one relating to whether the state exercises sufficient power, authority or control,[299] it appears then that human rights obligations apply towards individuals arrested and detained by the power of the state, irrespective of whether that power is exercised within the state, in another state or between states. The real issue to be addressed regarding arrest and detention is not, or should not be, whether human rights law is applicable, but whether the arrests or detentions are lawful according to the applicable legal framework.[300]

7B.1.2 Aerial bombardment in Afghanistan or Iraq?

More controversial is the extra-territorial application of the IHRL framework in other contexts: does the aerial bombardment in Afghanistan or

---

ships. See, e.g., Human Rights Watch, 'Background Paper on Geneva Conventions and Persons Held by US Forces', 29 January 2002; M. Chinoy, 'Marines setting up detention center', *CNN.com*, 15 December 2001. See also P. Wolfowitz and Gen. Pace, *DoD News Briefing*, 18 December 2001, where the US Deputy Secretary of Defense acknowledged the presence of five detainees ('one Australian, one American, and three Taliban/al Qaeda') aboard the USS Peleliu (transcript available at http://www.dod.gov/transcripts/2001/t12182001_t1218dsd.html).

[297] Cases such as *Ilascu* v. *Russia*, *Lopez Burgos* v. *Uruguay*, *Coard* v. *US* and the recent decision of the Inter-American Commission on Human Rights regarding *Precautionary Measures in Guantanamo Bay*, cited at Chapter 7A.2.1 above, all concerned arrest and detention abroad and reiterated the principle of extraterritorial application of human rights obligations in this context.

[298] See, e.g., pages 13 and 24 of the UK Government's pleadings in *Banković*, below, note 303, on file with author, wherein governments opposing the application of the ECHR in the context of aerial bombardment themselves draw a clear distinction between those facts and the 'classic' authority of the state to arrest and apprehend.

[299] See, e.g., Human Rights Committee, General Comment No. 31: The Nature of the General Legal Obligation Imposed on States Parties to the Covenant (Article 2) [2004], UN Doc. CCPR/C/74/CRP.4/Rev.6.

[300] This is discussed in Chapter 8, in relation to Guantanamo Bay. In the context of armed conflict, the lawfulness of detention under IHRL must be understood by reference to IHL and the lawful bases for detention provided for therein.

Iraq, for example, fall to be assessed against the intervening states' human rights obligations? Two approaches may be distinguished. According to the first, the intervening state exercised 'power', 'authority' and 'control' over the operations, and the individuals who suffered the effects of those operations, hence human rights law is applicable. Thus, on this view, while undoubtedly IHL provides the principal legal norms for assessing, for example, the legitimacy of targeting and lawfulness of killings in armed conflict, the human rights framework and the institutions charged with its implementation[301] are of continued relevance alongside IHL. The same logic by which human rights bodies have in the past deemed IHRL applicable to military operations by ground troops applies to operations conducted aerially.[302]

However, a more restrictive view may be identified from the approach of the European Court of Human Rights in *Banković*.[303] The rationale of that case may indicate either that aerial bombardment is somehow *per se* excluded from the human rights framework, or (somewhat more plausibly given the terms of the judgment) that it is effective control of the *territory* in question that is key for the military campaign – including its aerial dimension – to be governed by human rights treaty obligations.[304] Such an approach would limit (but not exclude) oversight by the European Court of Human Rights of bombardment by states such as the UK in Afghanistan or Iraq and, if applied more broadly, it could conceivably limit the application of the ICCPR obligations in respect of action by the US or others.[305]

---

[301] As noted above, where the human rights framework applies, it carries with it available mechanisms for individual redress; where IHL applies those bodies may have reference to, and effectively apply, IHL to the situations before them.

[302] Aerial bombardment or ground troops should not be the distinguishing factor. See discussion above and the Applicants' submissions in *Banković*, below, note 303, on file with author.

[303] See discussion, para. 7A.2.1 Section A of this chapter.

[304] The Court acknowledged that military operations by ground troops in territory over which the state exercises effective control are covered by the ECHR. It did not make explicit whether, e.g., the action of ground troops in territory not so controlled would be covered by the ECHR, nor whether conduct by air forces in controlled territory would be covered by it, i.e., whether the aerial or control factor was the critical one, although it is suggested that the tenor of the judgment suggests that territorial control is, in the Court's view, key. See *Banković and others* v. *Belgium and 16 other Contracting States* (Appl. No. 52207/99), ECtHR, Admissibility decision of 19 December 1999, *Reports 2001-XII* (hereinafter '*Banković*'), paras. 71 ff.

[305] As discussed in the Framework section A above, it is unclear whether this rationale would be applied by other bodies, which have historically made statements (see, e.g., the statement that it is 'unconscionable' to apply different human rights standards at home and abroad made by the Human Rights Committee in *Lopez Burgos* v.

As discussed above, *Banković* is however of questionable relevance beyond the regional, or indeed the European, context.[306] Moreover, the apparent relief from extra-territorial human rights obligations that it implies is limited. If control of territory *is*, as *Banković* suggests, the critical factor in engaging human rights responsibilities, then at least from the point when the US and its allies became occupying forces of parts of Afghanistan or Iraq – as evidenced for example by the presence of considerable ground troops and ultimately the absence of an alternative functioning government – the human rights framework may then be relevant (alongside IHL) to an assessment of military operations, however executed.

7B.1.3 Targeted Killings?

On 3 November 2003, the US authorities carried out an aerial attack on Yemen soil (reportedly with the consent of the Yemen authorities) resulting in the death of Qaed Senyan al-Harithi – a suspected high-level member of al-Qaeda and five other suspected al-Qaeda associates.[307] Is the human rights framework applicable to this incident?

It may be that this operation, directed against persons suspected of involvement in the attack on the USS Cole in Aden, should be subject to the same logic as that governing the application of IHRL to arrest and detention abroad. The Yemen attack compares peculiarly with law enforcement operations: it was aimed at and resulted in death rather than arrest, involved not a traditional ground police operation but an aerial one, and it took place under uncertain legal authority.[308] But it would

Uruguay (Comm. No. 52/1979), Views of 29 July 1981, UN Doc. CCPR/C/13/D/52/1979, para. 12.3) apparently inconsistent with this approach. As regards the US it is bound by the ICCPR, but has not accepted the jurisdiction of the Human Rights Committee under the First Optional Protocol.

[306] The approach has been thus far supported by other bodies interpreting other instruments. Its impact may be limited to bombardment by European states (outside the regional zone of the ECHR), as the judgment emphasises the ECHR's objective of rights protection 'in an essentially regional context and . . . in the legal space of the Contracting Parties' (*Banković*, para. 80). See by contrast, the approach of the Inter-American Commission on Human Rights in *Precautionary Measures in Guantanamo Bay* (Cuba, 13 March 2002).

[307] See D. Johnston and D.E. Sanger, 'Yemen Killing Based on Rules Set Out by Bush', *New York Times*, 5 November 2002.

[308] See the statement of the US National Security Advisor: 'The president has given broad authority to U.S. officials in a variety of circumstances to do what they need to do to protect the country. We're in a new kind of war, and we've made very clear that it is important that this new kind of war be fought on different battlefields.' (Condoleezza Rice, Interview on *Fox News*, 10 November 2002, above).

be anomalous if these peculiarities were distinguishing factors precluding the application of human rights law: if the framework that would have applied had the suspects been arrested were not to apply because they were killed or if the aerial (as opposed to ground) method of execution were to make a difference, or, particularly ironically, if the lack of judicial authorisation of the operation were itself to render the situation beyond the oversight of human rights law.

If on the other hand there is a principled basis to distinguish this case from extra territorial arrest or detention, and it were to be treated instead as a military operation conducted through aerial bombardment, the situation may reflect the scenario discussed in the previous section. However, even assuming that the European Court of Human Rights' restrictive approach in the form of the *Banković* case were to be followed, this particular operation may still fall within IHRL on the basis that the consent of the territorial state was (reportedly) obtained in advance.[309]

The real issue in relation to the Yemen attack is not whether IHRL is applicable or excluded, but, as discussed in the next section, whether IHL also applies and whether the attack in question is justified according to applicable law.[310]

7B.1.4 Clarifying and enforcing extra-territorial human rights law?

In conclusion, it is clear that many operations carried out beyond a state's borders in the context of the 'war on terror' 'of global reach'[311] undoubtedly fall within the purview of the IHRL framework. At a strict minimum, these include the exercise of law enforcement authority such as arrest and detentions abroad, wherever carried out, and other operations conducted on territory effectively controlled by the state, or possibly where the state acts on the invitation of the authority exercising such control.

If the global 'war on terror', and its myopic approach to national boundaries, continues to gain ground, it may with time lead to clarification of

---

[309] On the questionable relevance of the consent of the territorial state, as suggested by the *Banković* judgment (para. 71), see para. 7A.2.1.

[310] This question is addressed in this chapter, para. 7A.2.

[311] The 'global' character of the war against terror has been underlined by the US administration ever since 9/11: 'The war on terror begins with al-Qaida, but it does not end there. It will not end until every terrorist group of global reach has been found, stopped, and defeated', G.W. Bush, Address to a Joint Session of Congress and the American People, 20 September 2001, available at http://www.whitehouse.gov/news/releases/2001/09/20010920-8.html.

those areas of greater uncertainty as to the applicability of human rights norms beyond the state's territory.[312] Fundamentally, it may also serve to underscore, or to undermine, the thesis presented years ago, but more relevant now than ever, that the key factor is not where, but whether, the state exercises its power and responsibility. A purposive approach, focused on ensuring rights protection rather than strict territorial limits certainly finds support in the spirit of the human rights instruments, particularly those with universal aims.

It remains to be seen to what extent human rights bodies and mechanisms will rise to the challenge of addressing these issues. Early indications are of a reticence by certain human rights bodies to incorporate proactively such an approach into their everyday work.[313] Those bodies charged with addressing individual petitions alleging violations of human rights are, however, likely to be called on to do so in the context of individual cases arising from state action abroad; their role in so doing is all the more important where the reach of national laws or national courts is treated as territorially limited.[314]

Individuals alleging violations by states that have ratified the ICCPR and Optional Protocol will have recourse to the UN Human Rights Committee, which therefore provides a potential mechanism to challenge the actions of some but not all members of the US-led coalitions in

---

[312] While the importance of the extra-territoriality issue is highlighted by the 'war on terror', it is by no means limited to it. The issue is increasingly relevant given the reality of the globalisation of the exercise of power and responsibility.

[313] Note that the reports of human rights bodies and specialists post 9/11, while often thorough in other respects, not infrequently entirely fail to address the question of extra-territoriality (with the exception of the principle of non-refoulement/extradition). See, e.g., Inter-American Commission on Human Rights, *Report on Terrorism and Human Rights*, 22 October 2002, OAS Doc. OEA/Ser.L/V/II.116; Council of Europe, Guidelines on Human Rights and the Fight against Terrorism, adopted by the Committee of Ministers on 11 July 2002 at the 804th meeting of the Ministers' Deputies (hereinafter 'Council of Europe, Guidelines on Human Rights and Terrorism'); OSCE Charter on Preventing and Combating Terrorism, adopted by the Ministerial Council of the Organization for Security and Co-operation in Europe on 7 December 2002 (hereinafter 'OSCE Charter on Terrorism'). The work of the thematic special rapporteurs tends likewise to assume a focus on violations within the states' own boundaries. However, the fact that UN High Commissioner for Human Rights has underlined the obligations of states in Iraq and Afghanistan (albeit with a focus on respect for IHL) may presuppose the applicability of the framework of IHRL.

[314] See, e.g., discussion of the approach of US courts in Guantanamo Bay and arguments concerning non-application of the US Torture Protection Act extra-territorially, discussed at Chapter 8. Human rights courts step in once domestic remedies fail or have been exhausted.

Afghanistan and Iraq for example.[315] Regional mechanisms such as the European Court of Human Rights[316] and the Inter-American Commission on Human Rights[317] may provide a remedy for violations by states parties to the relevant regional instruments, although the willingness of at least the European Court to address some aspects of military operations abroad remains doubtful.[318] On the other hand, a promising indication is found in the fact that in the one case where an individual petition has been brought in relation to these issues – in this case before the Inter-American Commission addressing the off shore detention on Guantanamo Bay – the Commission did not hesitate to reaffirm that:

> [t]he determination of a state's responsibility for violations of the international human rights of a particular individual turns not on the individual's nationality or presence within a particular geographic area, but rather whether under specific circumstances, that person fell within the state's authority and control.[319]

7B.2 The 'war' and human rights

The misleading overuse of the language of 'war', and the consequent jeopardy to the integrity of international humanitarian law, was noted in the previous chapter. In several respects, however, the conceptualisation of counter terrorism as a 'war on terror' may also have an impact on the perception and application of the human rights framework.

---

[315] For example, the Coalition taking part in operation 'Anaconda' in Afghanistan included the US, UK, Canada, Denmark, France, Germany and Norway. All are parties to the ICCPR and all, bar the US and UK, are parties to the Optional Protocol by virtue of which the Human Rights Committee has authority to receive individual petitions.

[316] In respect of obligations incumbent on European states party to the ECHR, individuals automatically have the right to petition to ECtHR, although in light of *Banković* it is doubtful that the Court would consider itself to have jurisdiction at least as regards violations arising out of aerial bombardment.

[317] Recourse to the Inter-American Commission on Human Rights exists for states bound by the American Convention on Human Rights or the American Declaration on the Rights and Duties of Man, including (as regards the latter) the United States. An example of an application brought against the US, under the American Declaration of Human Rights to the Inter-American Commission is the above mentioned request for precautionary measures in Guantanamo Bay. For those states that accept the Court's jurisdiction, cases can also be brought before the IACtHR.

[318] The Court's decision not to accept jurisdiction in *Banković* was based in part on a reluctance to extend jurisdiction beyond the 'regional' sphere of application of the Convention. Other bodies have not addressed the *Banković* scenario directly and their approach to it, if or when they do, remains uncertain.

[319] Inter-American Commission on Human Rights, *Precautionary Measures in Guantanamo Bay*, citing *Coard et al.* v. *the United States*, para. 37.

At times, the 'war' is invoked in an apparent attempt to suggest human rights are simply inapplicable. While politically insidious, from a legal point of view this can be straightforwardly dismissed as a clear misunderstanding of the human rights framework and its continued relevance in situations of emergency.[320] However, even on a correct understanding of IHRL (as not displaced by IHL but complementary to it), the existence of conflict and application of IHL as the *lex specialis* undoubtedly has a dramatic transformative effect on the nature of particular rights. Notably, killings and detentions may be permissible in conflict while they would otherwise amount to arbitrary deprivations of life and liberty. A precise appreciation of when 'war' is really war as opposed to a rhetorical device, is therefore critical to the shape of human rights protection.[321]

At the same time, recourse to the legal standards applicable in 'war' has been selective post 9/11, invoked to justify what would be impermissible under IHRL, yet without acknowledging that corresponding rights under IHL take effect. It is this attempt to suspend one set of legal protections, without acknowledging the application of another, that leaves rights particularly vulnerable.[322] The following may serve as an example.

7B.2.1 The Yemen attack: armed conflict or assassination?

The US authorities justified the aerial attack on an allegedly high-level member of al-Qaeda and five others as a military operation[323] related to an armed conflict, governed by the laws of IHL, with this particular attack purportedly justified as the killing of persons perceived to be

---

[320] Undoubtedly the most relevant body of law in assessing the lawfulness of certain action in armed conflict is IHL. One specific advantage that the application of the human rights framework enjoys over the application of IHL, however, lies in the availability of mechanisms for individual redress.

[321] While the focus here is on applicable international law, it is noted that the existence of war may also change applicable domestic law. One example is the domestic law of the United States relating to the 'assassination' of foreign nationals prohibited during peacetime since 1975, while during wartime a different (and more permissive) body of law is used to define assassination. See M.N. Schmitt, 'State Sponsored Assassination in International and Domestic Law', 17 (1992) *Yale Journal of International Law* 609.

[322] Note that IHL itself enshrines protections of the human person that in some cases go beyond those of IHRL – see, e.g., Prisoners of War discussion in Chapter 8, Guantanamo Bay.

[323] The strike in Yemen was apparently carried out by the CIA, and not by the US armed forces. See 'Deputy Secretary Wolfowitz Interview With CNN International', 5 November 2002, at http://www.defenselink.mil/transcripts/2002/t11052002_t1105cnn.html.

enemy combatants.[324] As recalled below, the rules on targeting in IHL stand in stark contrast to those governing law enforcement operations under IHRL, such that the legitimacy of US claims that this was a military operation carried out in the context of armed conflict are critical to the lawfulness of this lethal attack.[325]

Although the US authorities appeared to suggest that the attack was part of a global war against terror, in which al-Qaeda members are enemy fighters and the world is a battlefield, as discussed in Chapter 6 it is doubtful that there can be an armed conflict against al-Qaeda in any legal sense.[326] Could then the attack on Yemen soil be seen to have taken place in the context of, or in association with,[327] the conflict in Afghanistan?[328] The key issue is likely to be the relationship of the individuals targeted to that conflict: were they 'combatants' engaged in the Afghan conflict, in which case they were entitled to fight but could legitimately be attacked by the adversary?[329] Or were they 'unprivileged combatants', essentially

[324] S.M. Hersh, 'Manhunt – The Bush Administration's new strategy in the war against terrorism', *The New Yorker*, 23–30 December 2002, 66–73; 'Washington Changes its Tune on Targeted Killing', *The Guardian*, 6 November 2002, 13. It has also been suggested that the Yemen attack may be understood as an exercise in self defence. This question, which relates to the right to use force (*jus ad bellum*), discussed at Chapter 5, is independent of the question whether the force is employed lawfully (*jus in bello*) which must be assessed by reference to the framework of IHL or IHRL discussed here.

[325] The US argument as to the legitimacy of this action may be premised on one of two views: (a) that the human rights framework is simply inapplicable to military operations in time of war (see extra-territoriality above); or (b) that it is superseded to the extent that the rules governing the right to life in this context are those of IHL which applies as *lex specialis*. It should be noted that even if one accepts the qualification of the operation as a military operation in the context of the global 'war on terror', the legality of the conduct of the US agents would still have to be questionable in line with IHL principles governing distinction and proportionality. See Chapter 6, para. 6A.3.1.

[326] The law as it stands suggests that there can be no international armed conflict with an international organisation as one of the parties.

[327] The criterion for determining whether an act is governed by IHL is whether or not the act is committed in the context of or in association with an armed conflict. See, however, 'Introduction to Article 8 – War Crimes', *International Criminal Court, Elements of Crimes*, UN Doc. PCNICC/2000/1/Add.2 (2000), which sets a higher threshold for the qualification of an act as a war crime within the jurisdiction of the ICC, requiring that, for an act to constitute a war crime or a serious breach of IHL, it must take place in the context of *and* be associated with an armed conflict.

[328] As noted in this chapter, para. 7B.1.2, the Afghan conflict commenced, if not before, on 7 October 2001. While one instance of the use of armed force may, in certain circumstances, give rise to the existence of an armed conflict, there is nothing to suggest that any such conflict arose in Yemen, particularly given purported consent by the Yemen state.

[329] See the IHL rules governing the definition of 'armed conflict' and its territorial scope, Chapter 6, para. 6A.1. Doubts arise from the occurrence of the attack outside the territory

civilians who took up arms in the context of the conflict, in which case they lose their immunity and can be killed, but only for as long as they are directly participating in hostilities?[330] Or, as seems more likely, do the crimes of which they are suspected have nothing to do with the Afghan conflict at all, in which case the Yemen action should properly be understood as an exercise in extra-territorial law enforcement against al-Qaeda and the legality of the action assessed in the light of the standards of IHRL?[331]

Although under IHRL the use of force by law enforcement officials may be tolerated, it is subject to extremely strict limits.[332] The question is whether the use of lethal force was 'strictly unavoidable to protect themselves or other persons from imminent threat of death or serious injury'[333] and whether the obligation to plan and execute operations with a view to ensuring that lethal force is not employed was met. While difficult issues of necessity and proportionality may arise in law enforcement cases gone-wrong, this is distinct from planned execution, where no imminent threat is envisaged and where no attempt is made to apprehend the suspected criminal, which is manifestly inconsistent with legal standards. Indeed discussion of the lawfulness of the Yemen scenario was to some degree foreshadowed in a recent decision of the Human Rights Committee, in which it condemned the practices of targeted killings by Israel, irrespective of the threat of terrorism that the state may seek to confront.[334]

Viewed through the prism of human rights law, then, the action of US agents in Yemen territory appears to constitute a violation of the internationally recognised right to life, amounting to an extra-judicial execution,

---

of any of the states involved in any such conflict, although the issue of the parties to the conflict is more likely to be the definitive one. See G.L. Neuman, 'Humanitarian Law and Counterterrorist Force', 14 (2003) EJIL 283, in particular at 296–8.

[330] See Article 50 GC IV and Chapter 6 above.

[331] Other issues may arise regarding possible breach of the territorial sovereignty of another State under international law, although in the present case, since the action was reportedly conducted with the consent of Yemen authorities, these are unlikely to pose particular problems.

[332] See para. 7A.4.3.1.

[333] Inter-American Commission on Human Rights, *Report on Terrorism and Human Rights*, para. 87; see also para. 107.

[334] See Concluding observations of the Human Rights Committee: Peru, UN Doc. CCPR/C/79/Add.8 (1992), para. 8. E. Gross, 'Thwarting Terrorist Attacks by Attacking the Perpetrators or Their Commanders as an Act of Self Defence: Human Rights Versus the State's Duty to Protect its Citizens', 15 (2001) *Temple International and Comparative Law Journal* 195.

an international legal norm that has attained *jus cogens* status.[335] The onus lies on the state carrying out the attack to demonstrate its legitimacy,[336] which it may do by showing that the requirements of human rights law were in fact met or that, in accordance with IHL, it reasonably believed upon proper inquiry that the targeted individuals were combatants in the Afghan conflict or other persons directly participating in active hostilities in relation to that conflict, as they drove through Yemen territory. However, reports suggest that the US has refused to present any such justification for its action.[337]

Finally, if a state seeks to rely on 'wartime' standards, the consequences of the application of the IHL framework must be taken on board in their entirety. Thus, if the suspected al-Qaeda operatives are to be treated as combatants for targeting purposes, they (and other al-Qaeda operatives) are also entitled to be treated as POWs if captured. On the other hand, if they are instead considered to be unprivileged combatants, they are for IHL purposes 'civilians' entitled to the protections of the Fourth Geneva Convention upon capture.[338] However, as discussed in Chapter 8, the authorities apparently reject both of these, denying the entitlement of similarly placed persons to POW status or to protection as civilians under the Geneva Conventions.[339]

The Yemen incident is therefore an example of how resort to the ambiguous language of war may be invoked to avoid responsibility under IHRL, without either a) demonstrating the justification for reliance on IHL standards or b) accepting the consequences that flow therefrom in terms of the application of IHL protections. In this way a policy of

---

[335] Restatement (Third) of the Foreign Relations Law of the United States, para. 102(2). As there can be no derogation from the right to life under human rights treaties, and as 'necessity' cannot justify violations of *jus cogens* norms, the human rights framework does not appear to provide any justification for this action. As discussed in Chapter 4, such executions are among the violations in respect of which all states may exercise jurisdiction and individuals may be held to account.

[336] See para. 7A.4.1.2.

[337] Ari Fleischer, White House Press Secretary, responding to a question on the 'transparence of the operation' and reliability of intelligence: '[T]he President has said very plainly to the American people that this is a war in which there will sometimes be visible moments and sometimes there are going to be long lulls. And there are going to be things that are done that the American people may never know about' (Press Gaggle by Ari Fleischer, 24 October 2002).

[338] See Article 50 GC IV, and generally Chapter 8 on Guantanamo Bay.

[339] See Chapter 8 on the procedural rights denied to persons who, like the Yemen targets, fall into the US 'enemy combatant' category.

assassinations, long rejected by the US,[340] was de facto reintroduced, of which the Yemen attack provides the clearest example.[341] The serious implications for the right to life are not isolated, but mirrored by other rights potentially adversely affected by a sloppy discourse on war replacing the language of law enforcement, some of which are discussed in Chapter 8 in relation to the rights of detainees.[342]

7B.3 Derogation and emergency post 9/11

Among the most controversial of the measures adopted post 9/11 are those that relate to the rights to liberty and fair trial. Prolonged or indefinite detention of persons perceived by government as dangerous and the limitation or denial of judicial guarantees has become widespread, including through adoption of new – or resort to existing – terrorism laws and 'creative' use of immigration laws. Examples of increasingly liberal resort to arrest and detention powers are plentiful, as highlighted in relation to 'Indefinite Detention' below and in the following chapter dedicated to the situation in Guantanamo Bay, Cuba.[343] As illustrated in that

---

[340] The ban, originally contained in an Executive Order adopted by President Ford in 1975, is now in force as Executive Order No. 12,333 (Exec. Order No. 12,333, 3 C.F.R. § 200 (1982), reprinted in 50 USC § 401 (1982)), though it has been noted that there are 'so many options . . . to get around the ban that the Order should not be viewed as a practical ban, but instead as a preventive measure to stop unilateral actions by officials within the government and a guarantee that the authority to order assassinations lies with the President alone'; N. Canestaro, 'American Law and Policy on Assassinations of Foreign Leaders: The Practicality of Maintaining the *Status Quo*', 26 (2003) *Boston College International and Comparative Law Review* 1 at 24. For a detailed discussion of the practice of the United States regarding 'assassination' and an analysis of the relevant national legislation, see M.N. Schmitt, 'State Sponsored Assassination', at 616 ff.

[341] Whilst denying that the US administration was about to formally rescind the executive order banning assassinations, the White House Press Secretary stated in relation to war in Iraq: '[T]he President has not made any decisions about military action or what military option he might pursue . . . I can only say that the cost of a one-way ticket is substantially less than that. The cost of one bullet . . . is substantially less than that . . . Regime change is the policy, in whatever form it takes'; Press Briefing by Ari Fleischer, 1 October 2002, available at http://www.whitehouse.gov/news/releases/2002/10/20021001-4.html#3.

[342] On the different rules applying to detention see Chapter 8 on Guantanamo Bay: the lawful bases for detention differ between IHL and IHRL and a more limited right of judicial oversight exists under the former.

[343] See para 7B.6, below. In addition to the examples below, see, e.g., Concluding observations of the Human Rights Committee: Yemen, UN Doc. CCPR/CO/75/YEM (2002), para. 18: 'while it understands the security requirements connected with the events of 11 September 2001, the Committee expresses its concern about the effects of this campaign on the human rights situation in Yemen, in relation to both nationals and foreigners. It is concerned, in

chapter, certain core aspects of the rights to liberty and fair trial cannot be derogated from in any circumstances.[344] However, much of the content of these rights can be restricted, provided there is a public emergency, the treaty provisions have been duly derogated and certain conditions are met. The following questions are among those to arise in relation to the legal requirements for derogation post 9/11, upon which the legitimacy of many measures, including those restricting liberty and security of the person, depend.

7B.3.1 An emergency threatening the life of the nation?

States are afforded broad, but not unlimited, discretion to assess their own security situations and whether there is in fact an emergency threatening the life of the nation.[345] Thus, had a derogation clause been invoked by the United States in the immediate aftermath of September 11, this issue would almost certainly not have been subject to dispute. The appropriateness of derogation did, however, give rise to controversy – and was the subject of legal challenge[346] – in the context of the United Kingdom, which derogated from its obligations despite the fact that it had not, and still has not, itself been the subject of any related terrorist attack in the UK; the threat to that country was, at the time of derogation, broadly perceived as speculative.[347] The fact that other European states failed to see the need for derogation (post 9/11 or indeed in the context of other 'terrorist' threats) compounded doubts as to the reality of the emergency and the necessity of derogation.

---

    this regard, at the attitude of the security forces, including Political Security, proceeding to arrest and detain anyone suspected of links with terrorism, in violation of the guarantees set out in the Covenant (Article 9).'

[344] Those aspects – such as the right to *habeas corpus* and the right to access counsel – are discussed in relation to the application of the legal framework to the Guantanamo detainees, in Chapter 8.

[345] The first question upon which valid derogation depends is whether there is in fact an emergency threatening the life of the nation. On the state's discretion in the context of the ECHR, see, e.g., *Brannigan and McBride* v. *the United Kingdom* (App 1453/89 and 1454/89), Judgment, 26 May 1993, *Series A*, No. 258, para. 43–7; *Ireland* v. *the United Kingdom*, Judgment, 18 January 1978, ECtHR, *Series A, No. 25*, pp. 78–9, para. 207.

[346] A challenge to the lawfulness of the UK's derogation to the ECHR was denied by the Court of Appeal in *A and others* v. *Secretary of State for the Home Department; X and another* v. *Secretary of State for the Home Department* [2002] EWCA Civ. 1502; [2004] QB 335. Leave to appeal to the House of Lords has been granted.

[347] D. Pannick, 'Opinion on the derogation from Article 5(1) of the European Convention on Human Rights to allow for detention without trial', on file with author.

This is not a new phenomenon – with several states having been under state of emergency for decades with no meaningful oversight of the legitimacy of that classification.[348] This casts shadows back to the insidious notion of the 'war without end'.[349] If, as has been suggested, the struggle against terrorism post 9/11 is a war the duration of which 'is measured by the persistence of fear that the enemy retains the capacity to fight',[350] there is a real risk of a perception of 'permanent emergency' whereby the exception becomes the norm.[351] This only serves to highlight the importance of clarity in the international sphere as to what constitutes an 'emergency' for these purposes and, as discussed below, the need for oversight of determinations by the state in this respect.

7B.3.2 A valid process of derogation?

As the framework in the preceding chapter notes, a valid process of derogation involves two elements. First, the state declares the emergency and engages in the process of derogating, which itself ensures a degree of transparency and accountability in the opaque world of counter-terrorism and national security. Second, despite great deference afforded to a state's assessment of its security situation, ultimately the body charged with oversight of the treaty in question determines whether the derogation is

---

[348] See generally the 'List of States which have proclaimed or continued a state of emergency' contained in the paper on 'The Administration of Justice and Human Rights: Question of Human Rights and States of Emergency' prepared by the Sub-Commission on Prevention of Discrimination and Protection of Minorities, 5 July 1999, UN Doc. E/CN.4/Sub.2/1999/31. An example is the state of emergency declared by Israel in 1948 which remained in force unexamined until 1996, when the Knesset replaced it with the Basic Law. Since then, the Knesset has routinely extended the state of emergency without seriously considering whether Israel's situation warrants such an extension (see Consideration of reports submitted by States parties under Article 40 of the Covenant: Israel, UN Doc. CCPR/C/ISR/2001/2 (2001); Concluding observations of the Human Rights Committee: Israel, UN Doc. CCPR/C/79/Add.93 (1998), para. 11). See other examples, notably from the Middle East, set out in the Framework section.

[349] See Chapter 6, para. 6B.1.2.3.

[350] Fitzpatrick, 'Speaking Law to Power', at 251.

[351] See Human Rights Committee, General Comment No. 29: Derogations during a state of emergency (Article 4) [2001], UN Doc. HRI/GEN/1/Rev.6 (2003) at 186, in particular at para. 2: 'Measures derogating from the provisions of the Covenant must be of an *exceptional and temporary nature*' and para. 4: '[A] fundamental requirement for any measures derogating from the Covenant . . . is that such measures are limited to the extent strictly required by the exigencies of the situation. This requirement relates to the duration, geographical coverage and material scope of the state of emergency and any measures of derogation resorted to because of the emergency.'

valid or not, thereby safeguarding the integrity of the treaty rights and derogation process.

Following the September 11 attacks, the UK derogated from its obligations under the ECHR and the ICCPR.[352] By contrast, the United States has not formally sought to derogate from its obligations under the ICCPR.[353] In law, the US would appear to be either accepting that the full range of human rights apply, or disregarding its obligations in respect of the operation of the human rights procedures. In practice, that the US administration considers itself in a situation of emergency is plain (as reflected in the internally declared state of emergency)[354] and the failure to notify derogation is difficult to interpret as anything other than contempt for international legal process.

The events of 9/11 and differing approaches to derogation in their aftermath may highlight the need – and provide the opportunity – to clarify whether derogation notification is a genuine prerequisite to be taken seriously or a formality of little real import. Ambiguity surrounding the concept of war and emergency post 9/11, and allegations as to their overuse and abuse, may in turn highlight the need for a more rigorous approach on the part of treaty bodies to overseeing the validity of the assertion of a state of 'emergency'.[355]

7B.3.3 Linkage between measures taken and the emergency?

Post 9/11, questions have arisen as to whether measures taken are necessary and proportionate to the emergency justifying derogation. In the UK context, for example, one of the most controversial questions was whether, assuming there was an emergency, the measures taken could be justified pursuant to it. In this respect, certain legal experts opined that the breadth of scope of the anti-terrorist law, covering, for example,

---

[352] Note Verbale from the Permanent Representation of the United Kingdom, dated 18 December 2001, registered by the Secretariat General on 18 December 2001: the text of the note is available at http://conventions.coe.int (last visited 30 January 2004).

[353] Immediately after the attacks of 9/11, the US President declared a state of national emergency (see Proclamation No. 7453, Declaration of a National Emergency by Reason of Certain Terrorist Attacks, 14 September 2001, 66 Fed. Reg. 48, available at http://www.whitehouse.gov/news/releases/2001/09/print/20010914-4.html). However, the US has never notified the state of emergency to the competent organs of the human rights conventions to which it is a party.

[354] See US Declaration of National Emergency, above.

[355] See Fitzpatrick, 'Speaking Law to Power', at 252, on the human rights bodies' 'generally deferential approach to states' claims of the existence of an emergency'.

persons suspected of having 'links' with a terrorist organisation (including organisations not involved in 9/11 and that posed no threat to the United Kingdom but rather to other states), meant that individuals fell within its scope that were in no way linked to the events of September 11 or the 'emergency' that was deemed to arise in its wake. It was therefore questioned to what extent these legislative measures could be said to be responsive to, still less 'strictly required' by, the particular emergency in the United Kingdom.[356]

Examples of measures affecting detention and fair trial rights post 9/11 that raise doubts as to the requirements of necessity and proportionality include the limitation on or denial of access to lawyers, or interference with lawyer–client confidentiality.[357] Broader questions have been raised repeatedly as to whether a rights restrictive counter-terrorism strategy is predictably counterproductive,[358] raising questions as to the satisfaction of the necessity and proportionality tests, as a strategy that cannot reasonably be considered effective to achieve the stated aim, logically cannot be necessary or proportionate to it.

7B.4 'Terrorism' and the legality principle

In the wake of 9/11, the Security Council called on states to take wide-ranging 'counter-terrorist' measures, including to '[e]nsure that any person who participates in the financing, planning, preparation or perpetration of terrorist acts or in supporting terrorist acts is brought to justice'.[359] Yet, as discussed in Chapter 2, there was not – and still is not, despite

---

[356] D. Anderson and J. Statford, 'Joint Opinion on Proposed Derogation from Article 5 of the European Convention on Human Rights; Anti-Terrorism, Crime and Security Bill, Clauses 21–32', on file with author.

[357] See International Bar Association's Task Force on International Terrorism, 'International Terrorism: Challenges and Responses' (2003) (hereinafter 'IBA Task Force Report 2003'), pp. 132–3.

[358] This risk has been underlined, *inter alia*, by the UN Secretary-General: 'By their very nature, terrorist acts are grave violations of human rights. Therefore, to pursue security at the expense of human rights is short-sighted, self-contradictory, and, in the long run, self-defeating. In places where human rights and democratic values are lacking, disaffected groups are more likely to opt for a path of violence, or to sympathize with those who do.' (Secretary-General's statement to the Security Council at Meeting to Commemorate the One-Year Anniversary of the Committee on Counter-Terrorism, 4 October 2002, UN Doc. SC/7523).

[359] SC Res. 1373 (2001), 28 September 2001, UN Doc. S/RES/1373 (2001), Article 2(e) and generally, at www.un.org/Docs/scres/2001/sc2001.htm.

efforts post 9/11 – an accepted definition of what constitutes terrorism under general international law.

The result has been a proliferation of specific anti-terrorism laws. While definitions differ dramatically, as the country reports of the Human Rights Committee post 9/11 illustrate, commonly they have been couched in broad-reaching and ambiguous language. The Committee has criticised numerous states for the 'exceedingly broad scope of . . . proposed legislation', and specifically for the adoption of 'broad and vague definition[s] of acts of terrorism',[360] which draw a broad range of conduct under their rubric, encompassing serious and less serious offences.[361] Yet the terrorist label is often invoked precisely to connote a degree of gravity, thereby purportedly to justify measures not otherwise considered acceptable.

At times the problem relates not only to the amorphous nature of 'terrorism' itself, but to a lax approach to those deemed to be associated with terrorism, or supportive of terrorist organisations, who are brought within the reach of the wide-ranging counter-terrorist measures. The United Kingdom Anti-terrorism, Crime and Security Act 2001,[362] for example, like the United States Military Order of 13 November 2001,[363] extends to persons considered to have undefined 'links' with organisations deemed to constitute a 'terrorist' threat.[364] The EU Common Position adopted post 9/11, which includes 'participating in the activities of a terrorist group', illustrates the manifestation of the problem on the international plane.[365]

---

[360] Concluding Observations of the Human Rights Committee: Philippines, UN Doc. CCPR/CO/79/PHL (2003), para. 9. See also, e.g., Concluding observations of the Human Rights Committee: Egypt, UN Doc. CCPR/CO/76/EGY (2002), para. 9; Concluding observations of the Human Rights Committee: New Zealand, UN Doc. CCPR/CO/75/NZL (2002), para. 11.

[361] See, e.g., Concluding Observations of the Human Rights Committee: Egypt, UN Doc. CCPR/C/79/Add.23 (1993), para. 8.

[362] See www.hmso.gov.uk/acts/acts2001/20010024.htm.

[363] Military Order relating to 'Detention, treatment, and trial of certain non-citizens in the war against terrorism', issued 13 November 2001 by the President of the United States.

[364] Both go beyond persons associated with the particular al-Qaeda terrorist organisation suspected of responsibility for the September 11 attacks. See also, e.g., the concern expressed by the Human Rights Committee in relation to the broad definition of terrorism and of 'belonging to a terrorist group' in Estonia's penal code: see Observations finales du Comité des droits de l'homme: Estonia (15/04/2003), UN Doc. CCPR/CO/77/EST, para. 8.

[365] See European Council, Common Position 2001/931/CFSP on the application of specific measures to combat terrorism, 27 December 2001, OJ L 344, 28 December 2001, p. 93, Article 2(3)(k): 'participating in the activities of a terrorist group, including by supplying information or material resources, or by funding its activities in any way, with knowledge of the fact that such participation will contribute to the criminal activities of the group'. See

Despite the lack of clarity as to its meaning, the terrorism label has been applied with grave effect post 9/11 to justify a range of measures, some of which are highlighted below, including expulsion, 'preventive' detention, criminal prosecution, including trial by special 'anti-terrorist' tribunals and the application of onerous penalties, interference with privacy, freedom of religion and free expression. The equally ambiguous mantra of 'counter-terrorism' has been relied on to grant impunity to those that violate human rights, as exemplified by the Russian law criticised in 2003 for exempting law enforcement and military personnel from liability for harm caused during counter-terrorist operations, thereby violating the rights of victims of abuses to justice and reparation.[366]

Obvious tension arises in respect of the principle of legality, a requirement for any restriction of rights, even in time of emergency.[367] Specific issues that relate to the particularly stringent requirements of legality and certainty in criminal law are addressed below.[368]

7B.4.1 Terrorism, criminal responsibility and nullum crimen sine lege

The obligations of the state in respect of the legality principle (*nullum crimen sine lege*), requiring clarity and precision in criminal law, are non-derogable and generally unaffected by national security concerns, or states of emergency. To the extent that laws enshrining vague and imprecise definitions of terrorism or related offences purport to criminalise conduct, concerns clearly arise regarding compatibility with Article 15

---

also the European Council Framework Decision on Combating Terrorism, 13 June 2002 (2002/475/JHA), OJ L 164/3 of 22 June 2002, which includes various forms of association with terrorists and other links with such groups (for a discussion of definition of terrorism contained in the Framework Decision, see Chapter 2, para. 2.1.5.1). To take effect these provisions should be translated into clear domestic criminal law.

[366] Concluding observations of the Human Rights Committee: Russian Federation, UN Doc. CCPR/CO/79/RUS (2003), para. 13: '[T]he Committee is concerned about the provision in the Federal Law 'On Combating Terrorism' which exempts law enforcement and military personnel from liability for harm caused during counter-terrorist operations.'

[367] See 'Study on the Principles Governing the Application of the European Convention on Human Rights during Armed Conflict and Internal Disturbances and Tensions', prepared by J. McBride, consultant to the Steering Committee for the Development of Human Rights of the Council of Europe, Doc. DH-DEV(2003)001, 19 September 2003, para. 6. See also J. Fitzpatrick, *Human Rights in Crisis. The International System for Protecting Rights During States of Emergency* (Washington, 1994), pp. 46–7.

[368] Some of the other human rights issues emerging from or related to the definitional ambiguity and the 'doubts and the opportunity for abuse of power' (*Castillo Petruzzi and others* v. *Peru*, Merits, Judgment of 30 May 1999, IACtHR, *Series C*, No. 52, para. 121) created thereby are highlighted later in this section.

of the ICCPR. Numerous criticisms have been levelled at states by human rights bodies in this respect since 9/11.[369] The Security Council does not escape criticism for its role in fomenting such violations, by 'opening the hunting season on terrorism', including calling for its criminalisation, absent guidelines as to its definition, meaning or scope.[370] On the other hand, international and regional definitions that have been advanced have themselves been criticised as falling short of the legality requirements.[371]

As noted above, vague definitions of terrorism are compounded by vague definitions of association with or membership of 'terrorist organisations', with serious effect. An illustration lies in Sudanese penal legislation, reported to the Security Council post 9/11,[372] where a very broad definition of terrorism, which involves threats aimed at 'striking terror or awe upon the people',[373] is matched by a definition of terrorist organisation which includes anyone who 'abets, attempts, participates or facilitates, by word of mouth, deed or publication the operation of an organised and planned network for the commission of any terrorist offence'.[374] The law stipulates that any person deemed to fall into this extremely elastic group will be prosecuted by an *ad hoc* combating terrorism court and if convicted 'shall be punished with death or life imprisonment'.[375]

As national laws come to be implemented over time, consistency with other aspects of Article 15 will deserve attention, such as the prohibition of retroactive application of criminal law or the extension of criminal law by analogy. A facet of the issue was highlighted by the Indonesian constitutional court which struck down new anti-terror legislation based on

---

[369] See Concluding observations of the Human Rights Committee: Estonia (above), para. 8.

[370] See SC Res. 1373, above, note 359, passed under Chapter VII of the UN Charter (thereby imposing a legal obligation on member states of the UN), which specifically required states to ensure that 'terrorist acts' are criminalised in domestic law.

[371] International or regional definitions of terrorism, proposed or adopted post 9/11, have been subject to criticism, e.g., for their extreme breadth and lack of specificity. See Chapter 2.

[372] This legislation, the Terrorism (Combating) Act 2000, was reported to the Security Council after 9/11 in support of Sudan's claim to have met its international obligations; see Sudan's Report to the Counter-Terrorism Committee Pursuant to Paragraph 6 of Resolution 1373, UN Doc. S/2001/1317, available at http://www.un.org/Docs/sc/committees/1373/submission_list.html.

[373] Terrorism includes threats 'aimed at striking terror or awe upon the people by, inter alia, hurting them or exposing their lives or security to danger . . . or exposing one of the native or or national strategic resources to danger', *ibid.*, Sn. 2.

[374] *Ibid.*, Sn. 6. The definition requires also that the act 'may constitute a danger to persons or property or public tranquillity'.

[375] *Ibid.*

retroactive effect.[376] As Article 15(2) acknowledges, the legality principle does not prevent prosecution for serious crimes established as such under international law – such as crimes against humanity for example, of the type committed on 9/11. It may however preclude prosecution for other acts that do not amount to such crimes, unless penalised in domestic law at the time committed: as discussed above, prosecution for 'terrorism' on the basis of its status as a crime under international law would be controversial, given definitional dilemmas, while inchoate offences such as membership of or support for terrorist organisations lays still less claim to international criminal status.[377]

7B.4.2 Terrorism, penalties and nulla poena sine lege

Post 9/11 the terrorist label has been invoked to justify exceptional measures, including exceptional penalties of greater severity than those that would attach to the conduct if differently classified. So far as greater penalties are imposed retroactively, a violation of the 'nulla poena sine lege' principle may arise.[378] Issues also arise regarding the proportionality of the penalties attaching to 'terrorist' offences which, given the potential scope of vague definitions, in reality may not be as grave as the terrorist epithet suggests.

Notably, one of the effects of burgeoning terrorism laws post 9/11 has been to 'increase the number of offences attracting the death

---

[376] Law No. 16 of 2004 was relied upon in the convictions in respect of the 'Bali bombings'. See, e.g., Bali terrorism conviction violates constitution, Indonesian court rules, 23 July 2004, at   http://www.cnews.canoe.ca/CNEWS/World/WarOnTerrorism/2004/07/23/553317-ap.html.

[377] Depending on the treaty in question, certain forms of support may constitute 'treaty crimes': see, e.g., the Convention for the Suppression of the Financing of Terrorism, New York, 9 December 1999, UN Doc. A/Res/54/109 (1999), which criminalises financial support for the activities of terrorist groups and requires parties to the Convention to cooperate in investigations and prosecutions of such financing.

[378] The principle of nulla poena sine lege is recognised in the Universal Declaration of Human Rights, Article 11(2): 'Nor shall a heavier penalty be imposed than the one that was applicable at the time the penal offence was committed', as in Article 7(1) ECHR, Article 9(2) ACHR, Article 7(2) African Charter and Article 23 (Nulla poena sine lege) of the ICC Statute. Note that the principle of legality is recognised also by the main instruments of IHL: see Article 99(1) GC III; Article 75(4)(c) AP I; Article 6(2)(d) AP II. The provision expressly does not preclude prosecution for acts which, at the time, were 'criminal according to the general principles of law recognised by the community of nations', such as crimes against humanity, despite the fact that no penalties are specified in international law. It would, however, apply to other acts labelled 'terrorist' but which are not established crimes under international law.

penalty'.[379] While the lack of general prohibition on capital punishment in international law has been noted above, as the Human Rights Committee has recalled post 9/11 an expansion of the penalty 'runs counter to the sense of article 6, paragraph 2, of the Covenant'.[380] Moreover, to the extent that the death penalty is being imposed in circumstances that do not meet the highest standards of justice – which must include clarity and precision in the definition of the crime as well as respect for fair trial rights – there is a real risk of violation of the right to life itself.[381]

7B.5 Torture and inhuman treatment: Abu Ghraib and beyond

Images of tortures inflicted on prisoners in Iraq have provided perhaps the most graphic and disturbing evidence of violations of human rights committed in the course of the 'war on terror'. Since those images were released, the US administration is increasingly accused of adopting a permissive policy towards torture,[382] of which Abu Ghraib was but one manifestation, with similar allegations regarding abuses emerging from elsewhere.[383] It has also transpired that significantly before the Abu Ghraib scandal became public, the ICRC had alerted Coalition Forces to serious concerns regarding 'brutality' and the 'excessive and disproportionate use of force', resulting in several cases in fatalities among detainees.[384] In respect

---

[379] Concluding observations of the Human Rights Committee: Egypt, UN Doc. CCPR/C/79/Add.23 (1993), para. 16.

[380] *Ibid.* Note also that the expansion of the death penalty is a direct violation of other treaty obligations, notably the ACHR, Article 4(2).

[381] See generally Chapter 7, under 'Specific Rights Protected', 'Life'.

[382] See 12 October memorandum from Lt Gen. Ricardo S. Sanchez, US commander of the combined joint task force in Iraq, calling for interrogators at Abu Ghraib to work with military police guards to 'manipulate an internee's emotions and weaknesses' and to assume control over the 'lighting, heating . . . food, clothing, and shelter' of those being questioned. Murphy, *ibid.*, p. 594, n. 15.

[383] For other allegations of abuse in Iraq and elsewhere, see Chapter 6, 6B.2.3, 'Humanitarian Protection of Prisoners: Executions, Torture and Inhumane Treatment'. See, e.g., S. Goldenberg, 'CIA Accused of Torture at Bagram Base', *The Guardian*, 27 December 2002 and S. Goldenberg, 'Guantanamo Record Contradicts Claims that Prisoner Abuse Was Isolated', *The Guardian*, 19 May 2004, reporting that 'the abuse at Abu Ghraib was systematic, part of a policy instituted at US military detention centres from Guantanamo and Afghanistan to Iraq'.

[384] 'Report of the International Committee of the Red Cross (ICRC) on the Treatment by the Coalition Forces of Prisoners of War and Other Protected Persons by the Geneva Conventions in Iraq during Arrest, Internment and Interrogation', February 2004, available at www.globalsecurity.org/military/library/report/2004/icrc_report_iraq_feb2004.htm. The report refers to several earlier occasions during 2003 when the issue of ill treatment was brought to the Coalition Forces' attention (para. 34). For an example of death resulting from ill-treatment (and issues concerning the apparent falsification of the death

of detainees 'deemed to have an intelligence value' the ICRC noted that ill-treatment potentially amounting to torture appeared to be 'systematic' and in certain cases 'part of the standard operating procedures by military intelligence personnel to obtain confessions and extract evidence.[385]

Concerns about the practice of torture and degrading treatment have been compounded by what is broadly perceived as official attempts to 'justify' it, exemplified by statements that torture might be 'justified by the executive branch's constitutional authority to protect the nation from attack'.[386] Likewise, suggestions that the possibility of resorting to torture in the context of interrogations is a matter of 'executive privilege', to be determined under 'the President's ultimate authority' and that criminal courts prosecuting torturers might be held to be interfering unlawfully with this power of the US President, are perplexing when considered alongside human rights law.[387] Torture, properly understood, is prohibited absolutely, and states are obliged, *inter alia*, to prosecute those responsible.

Apparent attempts to undermine the protection against torture can also be seen from an excessively restrictive approach to what constitutes 'torture' and the sort of interrogation techniques that might fall within the definition. This is evident for example in a leaked memo from the US Assistant Attorney General that advised, for example, that the severity threshold for torture required 'injury so severe that death, organ failure or permanent damage resulting in a loss of significant bodily function will likely result'.[388]

As regards the duty to hold to account those responsible for torture, while allegations of torture in Abu Ghraib have thus far provoked undertakings by the US authorities that they will be investigated thoroughly, the

---

certificate) see para. 16, and of several detainees fatally shot involving unnecessary or disproportionate use of force, see para. 45.

[385] *Ibid.*, para. 24. The report specifically highlighted Abu Ghraib as an example of such a case.

[386] Memorandum for Alberto R. Gonzales, Counsel to the President from Jay S. Bybee, Assistant Attorney General, on 'Standards of Conduct for Interrogation under 18 U.S.C. Sns. 2340–2340A,' 1 August 2002, p. 46.

[387] Memorandum on 'Standards of Conduct for Interrogation,' *ibid.*: 'Enforcement of the [torture] Statute would represent an unconstitutional infringement of the President's authority to conduct war,' p. 2. See also pp. 36–8.

[388] *Ibid.*, p. 13. Other qualifications included noting that death threats would not suffice unless the death was threatened 'imminently', and that the mental element for torture would not be satisfied unless the defendant acted with the 'express purpose to disobey the law' (p. 3), that knowledge that the severe physical or mental harm would result from his or her actions would not suffice if this was not ultimately his 'objective,' but instead he was committing the acts of torture in 'good faith' (pp. 4 and 8).

scope of those investigations – as to whether they will cover other alleged abuses and whether they will go beyond the immediate authors to the highest levels of responsibility – remains to be seen.[389]

Finally, it flows from the absolute prohibition on torture (as well as the right to a fair trial) that evidence obtained through torture should not be admitted in evidence in any proceedings, as reflected explicitly in Article 15 of the Convention against Torture.[390] As criminal prosecutions unfold, it may be that the mistreatment of prisoners will ultimately impact on the viability of prosecutions for 'terrorist' offences.[391] However, the recent approach adopted in the UK to allow evidence obtained through torture to be taken into consideration in deciding whether to detain persons, potentially indefinitely, albeit while affording that evidence less weight, may suggest a troublingly 'flexible' approach to this human rights protection.[392]

Torture and the debate that has unfolded around it provide chilling illustration of the extent to which legal standards that were once taken for granted have been questioned and rendered vulnerable since September 11.

7B.6 Indefinite detention

Broad-reaching indefinite detention of persons has become practice in many countries since 9/11. The most notorious case, of detentions at the military base in Guantanamo Bay, Cuba has provoked strident criticism and is discussed separately in the following chapter. That situation is, however, far from being the only case alleging arbitrary detention, even by the US, as noted by the 'many communications' received by the

---

[389] As of May 2004, seven military police officers had been charged; see Sean D. Murphy, Contemporary Practice of the United States Relating to International Law: International Criminal Law: U.S. Abuse of Iraqi Detainees at Abu Ghraib Prison', 98 AJIL 591 July, 2004. See para. 12, 'Accountability', below.

[390] Article 15 UN Convention against Torture.

[391] See Chapter 4, section B. The practice of torture also has implications for cooperation, given the prohibition on extraditing (and arguably providing other forms of cooperation) where there is a substantial risk of torture or inhuman or degrading treatment resulting in the state. See para. 7B.8 in this chapter.

[392] See A. Gillan, 'Torture Testimony "Acceptable" ', *The Guardian*, 22 July 2003 and 'Evidence Gathered by Torture', Story from *BBC News*, 31 July 2003, at http://news.bbc.co.uk/go/pr/ fr/-/1/ hi/programmes/ newsnight/3112905.stm. See also Amnesty International's criticism of the practice of the British Special Immigration Appeals Commission (SIAC): 'Justice Perverted under the Anti-terrorism, Crime and Security Act 2001', 11 December 2003, AI Index: EUR 45/029/2003.

Working Group on Arbitrary Detention since September 11.[393] 'Creative' use of existing immigration laws,[394] and the new USA Patriot Act[395] have provided the basis for prolonged detention absent normal procedural safeguards.[396] Cases of indefinite detention of US citizens deemed 'enemy combatants' on US territory have proceeded to, and been criticised in strident terms by, the US Supreme Court.[397] Outside the US, allegations abound as to detentions of non-nationals, by or at the behest of the US, in several countries around the world and on international waters.[398]

The US is also far from being the only state adopting such measures. In the UK for example, the Anti-Terrorism, Crime and Security Act permits long-term detention under immigration laws of persons the Home Secretary suspects of being terrorists, members of a terrorist organisation or otherwise linked to terrorism, where there is neither evidence to prosecute nor the possibility of deportation.[399] Although the UK scheme may benefit from comparison to that of its US partner in Guantanamo Bay, in that there is at least some limited judicial review, that process has itself given rise to serious due process concerns.[400]

In many other states indefinite detention is nothing new, but September 11 and international response thereto provides a pretext for hitherto unacceptable practice. An example may be found in Sri Lanka, where the

---

[393] Report of the Working Group on Arbitrary Detention, 16 December 2002, UN Doc. E/CN.4/2003/8, para. 61.

[394] See Human Rights First, *In Liberty's Shadow – U.S. Detention of Asylum Seekers in the Era of Homeland Security* (New York, 2004), in particular at pp. 7–16.

[395] *Uniting and Strengthening America By Providing Appropriate Tools Required to Intercept and Obstruct Terrorism Act*, Pub. L. 107–56, 115 Stat. 272 (26 October 2001) (hereinafter 'USA PATRIOT Act'). On the impact of the USA PATRIOT Act on civil liberties and on the specific issue of indefinite detention of certain aliens authorised by the Act, see W.A. Aceeves, 'Arbitrary Detention in the United States and the United Kingdom. Some post-9/11 Developments', in P. Hoffman (ed.), *ACLU International Civil Liberties Report 2003*, available at http://sdshh.com/ICLR/ICLR_2003/ICLR2003.html, ch. 3, at pp. 4–6.

[396] Minor immigration irregularities have often been relied upon in the US: see, e.g., 'Muslim Cleric Held in US', *The Guardian*, 15 January 2004, concerning 'a senior Muslim cleric . . . arrested . . . for allegedly making false statements when applying for American citizenship more than ten years ago'.

[397] See, e.g., *Hamdi v. Donald Rumsfeld*, US Court of Appeals for the Fourth Circuit, 8 January 2003, 316 F.3d 450 and Working Group on Arbitrary Detention, *ibid.*

[398] See Chapter 6, section B on detentions in Afghanistan and elsewhere. See also R. Brody, 'What about the Other Secret U.S. Prisons?' *International Herald Tribune*, 4 May 2004.

[399] See www.hmso.gov.uk/acts/acts2001/20010024.htm, Sn 21.

[400] For example, a somewhat anomalous situation arises whereby the detainee's lawyer of choice has very limited access to the 'evidence', and the security cleared 'special advocate', who can see the evidence, then has limited access to the client. See, e.g., 'Anti-terrorism Legislation in the UK', a publication of Liberty, at www.liberty.org.

Prevention of Terrorism Act – long criticised for permitting prolonged incommunicado detention[401] – was suspended prior to September 11, but proposals were floated by the government to effectively reintroduce it post September 11, representing a potentially serious setback for rights protection in that country.[402]

7B.7 Asylum and refugee exclusion

Some of the most potentially serious consequences of the application of the 'terrorist label' relate to asylum-seekers and refugees. Although none of those directly involved in the September 11 attacks were refugees or asylum seekers,[403] unjustifiable linkages with the threat of terrorism have provided a pretext for broad-reaching new measures providing for the detention, and ultimately removal, of asylum seekers.[404]

Security Council Resolution 1373 (2001) required states to refuse refugee status to those who have participated in or planned terrorist acts,[405] as did subsequent measures such as Resolution 2003/37 of the UN Human Rights Commission[406] and EU Common Position 2001/930,

---

[401] Detention is for up to an initial period of 72 hours without being brought before a judge, and thereafter for up to 18 months on the basis of an administrative order issued by the Minister of Defence. These features, and the denial of the right to be informed of the reasons for arrest or to judicial challenge, were criticised by the Human Rights Committee in 2002: see Concluding Observations of the Human Rights Committee: Sri Lanka, UN Doc. CCPR/CO/79/LKA (2003), para. 13. See also the decision of the Committee in *Sarma* v. *Sri Lanka* (Comm. No. 950/2000), Views of 31 July 2003, UN Doc. CCPR/C/78/D/950/2000.

[402] See Concluding Observations of the Human Rights Committee: Sri Lanka, above, para. 13. Despite a government undertaking not to apply the law, representing an important advance, the Human Rights Committee noted retrograde proposals to reintroduce the law through the Prevention of Organized Crimes Bill 2003.

[403] Fitzpatrick, 'Speaking Law to Power', at 258–60.

[404] The use of immigration laws to detain persons considered potentially dangerous has been a common feature of the human rights landscape post 9/11. For a detailed survey of the current situation in the US, see Human Rights First, *In Liberty's Shadow*.

[405] SC Res. 1373 (2001), above, note 359, para. 3(f).

[406] Human Rights Commission, Resolution 2003/37 on 'Human Rights and Terrorism,' 23 April 2003, UN Doc. E/CN.4/2003/L.11/Add.4. Para. 8 of the Resolution '[c]alls upon States to take appropriate measures in conformity with the relevant provisions of national and international law, including international human rights standards, before granting refugee status, with the purpose of ensuring that the asylum-seeker has not planned, facilitated or participated in the commission of terrorist acts, and to ensure, in conformity with international law, that refugee status is not abused by the perpetrators, organizers or facilitators of terrorist acts and that claims of political motivation are not recognized as grounds for refusing requests for the extradition of alleged terrorists'.

binding on EU member states.[407] As noted above, given the amorphous concept of terrorism, and a gung-ho approach to it that is particularly apparent post 9/11, the label can encompass serious crimes under international law as well as offences of lesser gravity, and potentially conduct otherwise not criminal at all. This may mean that refugees are in effect excluded from protection in circumstances that go far beyond the serious crimes that may justify exclusion under the Refugee Convention.[408]

The risk resulting from this 'flexible' approach to excluded categories is compounded by 'truncated status determination processes',[409] leading to concern 'that persons might be excluded without reliable proof of their personal involvement in genuine exclusionary conduct'.[410] Moreover, concerns arise as to asylum seekers being returned to their country of origin in circumstances where their rights in respect of non-refoulement are not adequately protected, as discussed below.[411]

7B.8 Cooperation in criminal matters and human rights post 9/11

Various regional and international developments with a view to enhancing cooperation in the global campaign against terrorism post September 11 have been described at Chapter 4, section B. To a large extent these developments are aimed at facilitating an end to impunity in respect of acts of 'terrorism' and as such contribute to the framework for human rights protection. However the focus of measures adopted in the aftermath of September 11 has been, perhaps unsurprisingly, on strengthening the obligations of states to extradite suspected terrorists. The question arises as to the impact of these measures on human rights, in particular the

---

[407] EU Common position 2001/930 of 27 December 2001 provides that the claims of asylum seekers who planned, facilitated or participated in the commission of a terrorist act are to be rejected before the merit of their case is considered. See S. Kapferer, 'Ends and Means in Politics', at 124–5.

[408] See Article 1F of the Convention on the Status of Refugees, which excludes from refugee protection: '[A]ny person with respect to whom there are serious reasons for considering that: (a) He has committed a crime against peace, a war crime, or a crime against humanity, as defined in the international instruments drawn up to make provision in respect of such crimes; (b) He has committed a serious non-political crime outside the country of refuge prior to his admission to that country as a refugee; (c) He has been guilty of acts contrary to the purposes and principles of the United Nations.'

[409] Fitzpatrick, 'Speaking Law to Power', at 259.   [410] Ibid.

[411] While human rights obligations in respect of non-refoulement apply to all persons, a common feature of concern in post 9/11 Human Rights Committee country reports has been the refoulement of asylum seekers. See below.

principle of 'non-refoulement' that protects individuals (whatever they may have done) from extradition or expulsion to countries where they are at risk of serious human rights violations.[412]

As has been noted, in Resolution 1373 the Security Council exercised its mandatory Chapter VII powers to call on states to, *inter alia*, cooperate, but failed to specify the obligation to do so consistently with human rights obligations. While potentially providing a pretext for disregarding those obligations, subsequent clarifications from the Security Council Committee, General Assembly and regional organisations others have clarified the importance of consistency with other areas of international law, including human rights and humanitarian law.[413] In some cases, bodies have specifically noted obligations in respect of cooperation and non-refoulement, and supported this with the issuance of Guidelines for states in combating terrorism consistent with those obligations.[414] Indirectly then, the Council's early foible led to a positive reassertion of the principle of non-refoulement.

However, beyond broad agreement in principle, a degree of confusion and inconsistency has attended legal standards advanced in the post 9/11

---

[412] While this section focuses on non-refoulement, note that other concerns have arisen from cooperation measures relating, e.g., to access to information and the exchange of personal data has also raised concerns regarding privacy and data protection: see, e.g., European Commission agreement of 16 December 2003 to the transfer of data from all airlines flying to the US to US authorities despite unresolved concerns over the privacy and data protections offered by the US. (Article 25(6) of the 1995 EC Data Protection Directive (95/46/EC)).

[413] For a European example, see, e.g., Council of Europe, Guidelines on Human Rights and Terrorism, which reaffirm 'States' obligation to respect, in their fight against terrorism, the international instruments for the protection of human rights and, for the member states in particular, the Convention for the Protection of Human Rights and Fundamental Freedoms and the case-law of the European Court of Human Rights' (preamble, para. (i)); Resolution 1271 (2002), 'Combating Terrorism and Respect for Human Rights', adopted by the Parliamentary Assembly of the Council of Europe on 24 January 2002). See also OSCE Charter on Terrorism, para. 7, providing that the OSCE participating states '[u]ndertake to implement effective and resolute measures against terrorism and to conduct all counter-terrorism measures and co-operation in accordance with the rule of law, the United Nations Charter and the relevant provisions of international law, international standards of human rights and, where applicable, international humanitarian law'.

[414] See para. 7, Council of Europe Resolution 1271 (2002), which recommends that, prior to the extradition of suspected terrorists to countries that still apply the death penalty, assurances must be obtained that this penalty will not be sought. Para. 8 confirms that member states should under no circumstances extradite persons who risk being subjected to ill-treatment in violation of Article 3 of the European Convention on Human Rights or being subjected to a trial which does not respect the fundamental principles. See also Council of Europe, Guidelines on Human Rights and Terrorism, Article XII ('Asylum, return ('refoulement') and expulsion) and Article XIII ('Extradition').

context regarding the circumstances in which states should not extradite.[415] This has raised doubts regarding consistency with human rights obligations, as well as the coherence of developing law in this field.[416]

An example is the Protocol to the European Convention against Terrorism adopted by the Council of Europe.[417] Upon its entry into force, the Protocol will amend, *inter alia*, Article 5 of the Convention, which already excludes the obligation to extradite where there are substantial grounds for believing that the request for extradition 'has been made for the purposes of discriminatory proceedings'.[418] The Protocol excludes the obligation to extradite terrorist suspects in cases where there are substantial grounds for believing that the person will be subjected to torture or the death penalty or (where the law of the requested State does not allow for life imprisonment) to life imprisonment without the possibility of parole.[419] By omitting reference to inhuman and degrading treatment or respect for fundamental principles of justice, the exceptions do not however cover the full range of rights in respect of which the European Court of Human Rights has determined that states party to the ECHR must refuse to extradite where there is a real risk of the rights being violated.[420] Arguably, the failure to cover enforced disappearance or extrajudicial execution is, in turn, at odds with the UN Declaration and Principles, respectively, dedicated to those particular violations.[421] Indeed, the

---

[415] Inconsistencies are not new, reflecting the piecemeal development of the law. However the concerted focus on these issues post 9/11 provided an opportunity to introduce greater coherence in the approach to standard setting; as indicated in the European example that opportunity may have been missed: see Chapter 4, section B.

[416] As noted above, an *ad hoc* approach is not new, as jurisprudence developed *ad hoc.* However, the adoption of legislative measures represents an opportunity to treat this question in a more comprehensive way.

[417] Protocol amending the European Convention on the Suppression of Terrorism, Strasbourg, 15 May 2003, ETS, No. 190 (not yet in force), Article 5(1) (hereinafter 'Protocol amending the European Convention against Terrorism)'. For another example of selectivity see also Council of Europe Resolution 1271 (2002), para. 8.

[418] It excludes extradition where the requested state has substantial grounds for believing that the request for extradition 'has been made for the purpose of prosecuting or punishing a person on account of his race, religion, nationality or political opinion, or that that person's position may be prejudiced for any of these reasons'.

[419] Article 4(2) and (3), Protocol amending the European Convention against Terrorism.

[420] See this chapter, section A.

[421] See Article 8 GA Resolution 47/133, 'Declaration on the Protection of All Persons from Enforced Disappearance', 18 December 1992, UN Doc. A/RES/47/133 (1992); and Principle 5 of the 'Principles on the Effective Prevention and Investigation of Extra-legal, Arbitrary and Summary Executions', Recommended by ECOSOC Res. 1989/65 of 24 May 1989, U.N. Doc. E/1989/89. Note, however, that neither the UN model treaty on

Protocol falls short of the Council of Europe's own guidelines passed only months before.[422]

However, despite this reticence to address the range of human rights concerns which may prevent extradition directly, the Council of Europe has subsequently sought to remove any apparent inconsistencies between the Protocol and generally recognised human rights standards. A draft Explanatory Report clarifies that 'Article 5 ensures that the Convention complies with the requirements of the protection of human rights and fundamental freedoms [and it] is intended to make this clear by reference to certain existing grounds on which extradition may be refused. The article is not, however, intended to be exhaustive as to the possible grounds for refusal.'[423] While it may be that, ultimately, the net result is an endorsement of the duty of non-refoulement, the selective and piecemeal approach to the treatment of this interrelationship in the elaboration of international and regional standards since September 11 may have generated uncertainty and undermined human rights protections.[424]

Extradition nor the Commonwealth Scheme include grounds of refusal relating to these particular issues.

[422] The Council of Europe 'Guidelines on Human Rights and the Fight against Terrorism' adopted by the Committee of Ministers on 11 July 2002, ('Council of Europe Guidelines on Human Rights and Terrorism') do not cover the full range of Convention rights either, but go beyond the Terrorism Convention and Protocol in covering for example the right to fair trial. The Guidelines make clear the *prohibition* on extradition in cases where: (1) there is 'a risk of being sentenced to the death penalty' (absent necessary guarantees), (2) there is 'serious reason to believe' that the person whose extradition has been requested will be subjected to torture or to inhuman or degrading treatment or punishment, or 'that the extradition request has been made for the purpose of prosecuting or punishing a person on account of his/her race, religion, nationality or political opinions, or that that person's position risks being prejudiced for any of these reasons'. The Guidelines further specify that there is *no obligation* to extradite in certain circumstances, namely, '[w]hen the person whose extradition has been requested makes out an arguable case that he/she has suffered or risks suffering a flagrant denial of justice in the requesting State, the requested State must consider the well-foundedness of that argument before deciding whether to grant extradition'.

[423] Para. 32, Draft Explanatory Report on the European Convention on Terrorism as it will be revised by the Protocol amending the Convention upon its entry into force, adopted on 13 February 2003 (text available at http://conventions.coe.int/Treaty/en/Reports/Html/090-rev.htm). Para. 69, with respect to Article 5(2) of the revised Convention, notes that 'in paragraph 2, only the risk of torture is mentioned. However, as stated above, this article is not intended to be exhaustive with regard to the circumstances in which extradition may be refused.'

[424] Note also that the draft UN Comprehensive Convention Against Terrorism itself raises questions as to compliance with the non-refoulement principle (see, in particular, draft Article 15). See the comment by Koufa in 'An Update on International Anti-Terrorist Activities and Initiatives', addendum to the Additional Progress Report by Ms Kalliopi

As regards the limited inter-state practice that has unfolded in the field of criminal cooperation since September 11, described in Chapter 4, section B, early indications are again of an uneven landscape in terms of respect for the principle of non-refoulement.

The transfer of persons in violation of their basic rights, indicating apparent disregard for non-refoulement obligations in the push towards anti-terrorism cooperation has been a constant source of concern for human rights monitoring bodies.[425] Reports suggest that in the US legislation is proposed to enshrine this dubious practice in law.[426] On the other hand, however, there are indications that at least certain states may be holding firmly to their responsibilities in this respect, despite the obstacle to cooperation – including with the United States – that this represents. Examples include the requirement of assurances that the death penalty will not be applied, reflecting long established practice in European–US cooperation.[427] More significant perhaps are statements by European state representatives regarding their inability to extradite (or provide other forms of cooperation) in light of dubious fair trial standards.[428]

Koufa, Special Rapporteur on terrorism and human rights, 8 August 2003, UN Doc. E/CN.4/Sub.2/2003/WP.1/Add. 1, para. 11 and F. A. Guzman, *Terrorism and Human Rights No. 1* (International Commission of Jurists, Geneva, 2002), pp. 208–9.

[425] Concluding Observations of the Human Rights Committee: Sweden, UN Doc. CCPR/CO/74/SWE (2002), para. 12: 'The Committee is concerned at cases of expulsion of asylum-seekers suspected of terrorism to their countries of origin'; Concluding Observations of the Human Rights Committee: New Zealand, UN Doc. CCPR/CO/75/NZL (2002), para. 11: 'The Committee is concerned about possible negative effects of the new legislation and practices on asylum-seekers, including by "removing the immigration risk offshore" and in the absence of monitoring mechanisms with regard to the expulsion of those suspected of terrorism'; Concluding Observations of the Human Rights Committee: Portugal, UN Doc. CCPR/CO/78/PRT (2003), para. 12: 'The Committee takes note that asylum-seekers whose applications are deemed inadmissible (e.g., on the basis of the exclusion clauses of article 1 F of the 1951 Convention relating to the Status of Refugees or because they have missed the eight-day deadline for submitting their applications) are not deported to countries where there is armed conflict or systematic violations of human rights. However, it remains concerned that applicable domestic law does not provide effective remedies against forcible return in violation of the State party's obligation under article 7'; Concluding observations on Egypt (UN Doc. CCPR/CO/76/EGY (2002), para. 16): 'The Committee notes furthermore that Egyptian nationals suspected or convicted of terrorism abroad and expelled to Egypt have not benefited in detention from the safeguards required to ensure that they are not ill-treated, having notably been held incommunicado for periods of over one month (Articles 7 and 9 of the Covenant).'

[426] D. Priest and Babington, 'Plan Would Let US Deport Suspects to Nations that Might Torture Them', *Washington Post*, 30 September 2004.

[427] See reference to state practice, including requests for assurances by France and Germany, in Chapter 4, para. 4B.2.3.2.

[428] See reference to state practice, including statements by a spokesman for Spain's Foreign Ministry as to fair trial prerequisites to cooperation, in Chapter 4, para. 4B.2.3.2.

This represents a progressive approach to human rights obligations, so far as it conditions extradition guarantees not only of trial by a fair and impartial tribunal and not trial by military commission, but also of a range of specific fair trial guarantees, such as public trial and the right to confront one's accuser.[429] It remains uncertain to what extent this approach will be adopted by other states and, significantly for the development of legal standards, to which rights it will be deemed to apply.[430] It also remains to be seen whether, and how effectively, states will monitor assurances obtained.[431]

There is also some indication that the principles underlying non-refoulement, precluding extradition, have been applied more broadly since September 11 to preclude other forms of cooperation that may lead to or facilitate human rights violations in third states. Notable examples relate to German and French insistence that information or documents be passed to the US authorities to assist with enquiries only on the condition that they are not used to obtain a conviction carrying a death penalty.[432] As noted in the first section of this chapter, human rights law is less clear on the obligations of non-cooperation in the context of mutual assistance than it is on extradition (although mutual assistance instruments reflect the right to refuse to cooperate on human rights grounds).[433] It

---

[429] J. Yoldi, 'España advierte a EEUU de que no extraditará a miembros de al-Qaeda,' *el Pais*, 23 November 2001.

[430] While the obligations of European states may be clear in respect of torture, death penalty and denial of justice, it remains unclear whether the same principle extends to other serious violations of rights, as noted in para. 7A.4.3.8.

[431] See Chapter 4A.2.1.2 on the requirement of human rights law regarding monitoring. The Human Rights Committee has noted that in order to legitimately rely on assurances, states must make 'serious efforts to monitor the implementation of those guarantees' and 'institute credible mechanisms for ensuring compliance of the receiving State with these assurances from the moment of expulsion'. Concluding observations of the Human Rights Committee: Sweden, UN Doc. CCPR/CO/74/SWE (2002), para. 12. See also Concluding observations of the Human Rights Committee: New Zealand, Un Doc. CCPR/CO/75/NZL (2002), para. 11.

[432] See Marylise Lebranchu, then French Minister of Justice: '[A]ny document should only be passed on to the Americans to help them with their enquiries on condition that such document [is] not used to get a conviction carrying a death penalty', at www.ahram.org.eg/weekly/2002/597/in4.htm. See also Germany's Justice Minister, Herta Daeubler-Gmelin's statement that documents would be provided only on condition that they 'may not be used for a death sentence or an execution', *Associated Press*, 1 September 2002. On the application of the principle of non-refoulement in extradition to non-cooperation to mutual assistance, see discussion in Chapter 4, para. 4A.2 and para. 7A.4.3.8 above.

[433] See, e.g., Article 4 of the UN Model Treaty on Extradition, which includes the death penalty and unfair measures to compel testimony as justifying refusal to assist, but not other aspects of the right to a fair trial.

may be that the attention dedicated to this issue in the years following 9/11 will serve to illuminate the nature and scope of states' human rights obligations in this respect and may serve to strengthen the argument that mutual assistance cooperation, like extradition, should be understood as subject to the human rights obligations of the state under the ECHR or other human rights treaties.[434]

The feature of international practice in 'cooperation' post September 11 that gives rise to greatest concern must be the frequent resort to extra-legal rendition of persons outwith the legal process. This has resulted from executive interference with pending legal process, or by-passing those legal procedures entirely, circumventing oversight of obligations in respect of non-refoulement.[435] NGOs such as Amnesty International report frequent US recourse to 'rendition' and the circumvention of formal extradition proceedings as a means to avoid assurances regarding the death penalty.[436] Since September 11, the Human Rights Committee has expressed its concern at the practice of expelling foreign persons suspected of terrorism without legal process, as a violation of the principle of legality, and exposing them to the risk of other grave violations, such as torture or ill-treatment.[437]

7B.9 'Proscribing dissent' – expression, association, assembly

Questions arise as to whether post September 11 legislative measures conferring wide-ranging powers on the executive to control information, effectively proscribe dissent, with serious implications for the rights to

---

[434] As Section A foreshadows, denying mutual assistance cooperation on human rights grounds may not be strictly required by human rights treaties, given their scope as applicable to persons within the state's 'jurisdiction,' but it is consistent with a purposive approach to those treaties, based on the principles of the ECHR and its Protocols.

[435] See Chapter 4 and para. 7B.11 in this chapter, which refer to widespread reports of 'informal' or extra-legal rendition.

[436] Amnesty International 'No Return to Execution – The US Death Penalty as a Barrier to Extradition', AI Report, 21 November 2001, AI Index: AMR 51/171/2001: 'Amnesty International is concerned by instances in which US agents have circumvented formal extradition procedures, thereby avoiding having to give assurances against the death penalty.' See also Human Rights Watch, *World Report 2003*, Introduction.

[437] Concluding Observations of the Human Rights Committee: Yemen, UN Doc. CCPR/CO/75/YEM (2002), para. 18: 'The Committee also expresses its concern about cases of expulsion of foreigners suspected of terrorism without an opportunity for them to legally challenge such measures. Such expulsions would, furthermore, be decided without taking into account the risks to the physical integrity and lives of the persons concerned in the country of destination' (Articles 6 and 7).

free expression, association, assembly and political participation,[438] and the role of human rights defenders around the world.[439]

While the principal source of the threat to these rights may be broad-reaching 'terrorism' and 'security' laws, another is found in the entrenchment of the notion of 'patriotism' and 'national unity'. Examples include the United States Patriot Act of 2001,[440] which affords the US Secretary of State broad discretion to declare persons seeking entry to the United States 'inadmissible' on the basis that they have undertaken advocacy undermining US anti-terrorist efforts.[441] In Uganda, the Anti-Terrorism Act of 2002 provides for the death penalty for journalists found guilty of publishing information deemed to promote terrorism.[442] Other examples suggest that the post September 11 climate is being taken advantage of to repress free speech and ideas with little or no apparent linkage to even broad notions of 'terrorism', such as a Jordanian decree proscribing the publication of 'information that can undermine national unity or the country's reputation' or 'undermine the king's dignity'.[443]

As the framework above indicates, human rights provisions relating to the rights to free expression or association explicitly allow for the rights to be restricted for the protection of certain aims, such as national security or public order; unlike derogation, this inherent flexibility does not depend

---

[438] In addition to the examples below, see, e.g., Concluding Observations of the Human Rights Committee: Russian Federation, UN Doc. CCPR/CO/79/RUS (2003), para. 19: 'The Committee is concerned that the proposed amendments to the law "On Mass Media" and the law "On Combating Terrorism", adopted by the State Duma in 2001 in the aftermath of September 11, are incompatible with article 19 of the Covenant.' As regards the impact of international definitions of terrorism on these rights, see, in general, 'Specific Human Rights Issues: New Priorities, in Particular Terrorism', Additional Progress Report prepared by Ms Kalliopi K. Koufa, Special Rapporteur on terrorism and human rights, 8 August 2003, UN Doc. E/CN.4/Sub.2/2003/WP.1, and F. A. Guzman, *Terrorism and Human Rights No. 2* (International Commission of Jurists, Geneva, 2003), pp. 62–3, who notes that the Algiers Convention, which includes 'disturbances at public utilities' within the definition of terrorism, may be relied upon to restrict legitimate trade union activity.

[439] Koufa, Report 2003, Addendum 1, para. 22.

[440] See www.epic.org/privacy/terrorism/hr3162.html.

[441] T. Mendel, 'Consequences for Freedom of Statement of the Terrorist Attacks of September 11', paper presented at the Symposium on Terrorism and Human Rights, Cairo, 26–28 January 2002, available at www.cihrs.org.

[442] D.O. Balikowa, 'The Anti-Terrorism Act 2002: the Media and Free Speech', 8.1 (2003) *The Defender*, 6.

[443] The law grants the government sweeping powers to close down publishing houses that contravene the ban. See amendment to the Jordanian Penal Code and Press Law, issued October 2001, reported in J. Stork, 'The Human Rights Crisis in the Middle East in the Aftermath of 11 September', paper presented at the Symposium on Terrorism and Human Rights, Cairo, 26–28 January 2002, available at www.cihrs.org.

on the existence of a national emergency. It does however depend on the restriction being provided for in clear and accessible law, and on it being necessary and proportionate to the particular 'legitimate aim' that it purports to serve. In respect of both examples given, and countless others, doubts may emerge as to the clarity and scope of the prohibitions and the legitimacy of their objectives. In particular, however, it is doubts as to the necessity (and proportionality) of these measures as a vehicle to address the genuine security concerns that may underpin them that is often determinative of lawfulness.[444]

Based on positions adopted in the past, it is likely that human rights bodies will look particularly unfavourably on the necessity of restricting the manifestation of opinions of a political nature, broadly understood, however offensive they may be to the state or indeed to the majority of the population therein.[445] The difficult question is how much of what has been deemed unpatriotic, or even perhaps demonstrative of terrorist sympathies or apology for terrorism, if seen through the prism of human rights, may in fact amount to protected political speech.[446]

7B.10 Profiling, protecting and anti-discrimination

The increasingly widespread practice of 'profiling' individuals as inherently suspicious[447] raises questions as to compatibility with the 'absolute

---

[444] Necessity has often been the key question in determining that terrorism measures fall foul of the human rights framework in respect of freedom of expression or political participation: see, e.g., the decisions of the Human Rights Committee in *Landinelli Silva et al.* v. *Uruguay* (Comm. No. 34/1978), Views of 8 April 1981, UN Doc. CCPR/C/12/D/34/1978, para. 8.4; *Keun-Tae Kim* v. *Republic of Korea* (Comm. No. 574/1994), Views of 4 January 1999, UN Doc. CCPR/C/64/D/574/1994, para. 12.4 and *Tae Hoon Park* v. *Republic of Korea* (Comm. No. 628/1995), Views of 3 November 1998, UN Doc. CCPR/C/64/D/628/1995, para. 10.3.

[445] See section A, this chapter, on political speech. Note, e.g., US law may be interpreted as covering political opposition to the US counter-terrorism strategy.

[446] For the insidious impact on religious freedom, not discussed here specifically, see, e.g., reported cases of prosecution for 'anti-state activity', 'attempted subversion of the constitutional order', or 'religious extremism' in 2003 in Uzbekistan; see Human Rights Watch, 'In the Name of Counter-Terrorism: Human Rights Abuses Worldwide', Briefing Paper for the 59th Session of the United Nations Commission on Human Rights, 25 March 2003, available at http://hrw.org/un/chr59/counter-terrorism-bck.htm.

[447] See extensive resort by US authorities after 9/11 to the practice of investigating individuals on the sole basis of their national origin or religious beliefs, as reported in S. Ellmann, 'Racial Profiling and Terrorism', 46 (2002–03) *New York Law School Law Review* 675; P. L. Hoffman, 'Civil Liberties in the United States after September 11', available at http://www.frontlinedefenders.com/en/papersweb/p3en.doc, p. 11, reporting the questioning of 5,000 young male non-citizens by FBI agents in November 2001.

prohibition on discrimination'.[448] It has been noted that certain distinctions – for example identifying membership of organisations as relevant criteria for further investigation – are an expected part of an investigative strategy. However, such distinctions must have an objective justification and measures taken must be proportionate to it. Thus it has been suggested that reliance on race, religion or nationality alone as a basis of suspicion cannot be justified as objectively justifiable. By contrast, while support for a particular ideology may in certain exceptional circumstances constitute a rational basis for identifying persons as worthy of further investigation, taking particular measures against such persons, such as detention for example, is likely to fall foul of the proportionality rule.[449]

The application of the non-discrimination rule in practice is not always straightforward. These issues are arising on a widespread basis post 9/11 as is apparent from the work of the monitoring bodies, in particular the committee on racial discrimination.[450] It may be that the application of the law to the real challenges presented by investigative and other counter terrorist strategies post 9/11 will lead to clarification, or strengthening, of the state's obligations in respect of 'profiling' and other potentially discriminatory practices.

The environment of discrimination and racial tension that erupted in many parts of the world post September 11 served to highlight the positive obligations of states in respect of countering intolerance and discrimination by private actors.[451] The steps that states might be expected to take

---

[448] See Koufa, Report 2003, Addendum 1, para. 23; Report of the Committee on the Elimination of Racial Discrimination, GAOR Fifty-seventh session, Supp. 18 (UN Doc. A/57/18), paras. 429 and 338.

[449] See IBA Task Force Report 2003, pp. 114–15, para. 4.4.2.

[450] Human rights monitoring bodies, and in particular the Committee on the Elimination of Racial Discrimination, have unambiguously condemned specific practices of racial profiling justified as means to combat international terrorism. See, e.g., Concluding Observations of the Committee on the Elimination of Racial Discrimination: Moldova, UN Doc. CERD/C/60/Misc.29.Rev.3 (2002), para. 15, where the Committee expressed concern that inquiries into potential terrorist activities of students of Arabic origins might raise 'suspicion of an attempt at racial profiling'. See also Concluding Observations of the Committee on the Elimination of Racial Discrimination: Canada, UN Doc. CERD/C/61/CO/3 (2002), para. 24; Concluding Observations of the Committee on the Elimination of Racial Discrimination: Russian Federation, UN Doc. CERD/C/62/CO/7 (2003), para. 24.

[451] The obligation to adopt positive measures to eliminate discrimination by private actors is set forth, e.g., by the Convention on the Elimination of All Forms of Racial Discrimination (CERD), New York, 21 December 1965, 660 UNTS 195, Article 2(1)(d) and by the Convention on the Elimination of All Forms of Discrimination Against Women (CEDAW), New York, 18 December 1979, 1249 UNTS 13, Article 2(e). See, in general, Human Rights Committee, General Comment No. 18: Non-discrimination [1989], UN Doc. HRI/GEN/1/Rev.6 (2003) at 146.

in this respect, as identified by the Human Rights Committee, include for example 'an educational campaign through the media to protect persons of foreign extraction, in particular Arabs and Muslims, from stereotypes associating them with terrorism, extremism and fanaticism'.[452]

7B.11   The role of the judiciary as guardian of human rights post 9/11?

A recurrent theme running through many of the measures giving rise to human rights concern post 9/11 is the apparent undermining of the role of the judiciary as the guardian of human rights. The most notorious may be the attempt by the US to entirely divest detainees held at Guantanamo Bay of access to justice as discussed in Chapter 8. But other examples abound, where the executive has assumed powers through legislation to act without judicial scrutiny or interfere with the judicial function in the name of national security.[453] In other cases interference in the judicial role is not legislatively sanctioned but adopted as a matter of practice. Some examples of the diverse manifestations of this phenomenon are highlighted below.

7B.11.1   'Listing' proscribed organisations

Questions arise regarding the increased resort on the international and national level to the practice of 'listing' proscribed organisations, and individuals considered associated with them, on the basis of which assets are frozen or, in some states, penal consequences can ensue. Among the concerns are those relating to transparency in the maintenance of such lists (generally prepared by the executive) and the lack of judicial oversight thereof.[454] Specific doubts arise as to the compatibility of such measures with the right to challenge before a court measures that restrict one's human rights.

The tone was set by Security Council Resolution 1267, adopted before the events of 9/11. The resolution established the so-called 1267 Committee, charged with, *inter alia*, designating the 'undertaking[s] owned

---

[452] Human Rights Committee, Concluding observations: Sweden, UN Doc. CCPR/CO/74/ SWE (2002), para. 12.

[453] See R. Weich, 'Upsetting Checks and Balances: Congressional Hostility Towards the Courts in Times of Crisis', in 'Report of the American Civil Liberties Union', November 2001, available at http://www.aclu.org.

[454] As noted in relation to principles of criminal law in Chapter 4, particular human rights issues also arise from attempts to criminalise membership of or association with listed groups or organisations. Criminal responsibility must be individual, not collective or objective.

or controlled' by the Taleban with a view of allowing the Member States to freeze the assets of those organisations.[455] Resolution 1390 makes the sanctions committee responsible for 'updating' the 'list' of banned individuals and groups tied to bin Laden, al-Qaeda, and the Taleban though it is unclear to what extent the sanctions committee promulgates the list based on national submissions, as opposed to independently examining the evidence.[456] The problems associated with this practice were, to some extent, subsequently recognised by the Council which introduced a 'de-listing' procedure.[457] At least one challenge has been launched under this procedure, notably a Swedish challenge that led to the removal of two individuals who had been included on the list despite no apparent evidence of terrorist links.[458] This case serves to highlight the dangers for the majority of organisations or persons, who cannot count on state willingness to represent them,[459] and who are denied the right of judicial oversight.

---

[455] SC Res. 1267 (1999), 15 October 1999, UN Doc. S/RES/1267 (1999), paras. 4(a), 4(b) and 6. The sanctions regime has successively been extended to cover 'individual and entities associated with [Osama bin Laden], including those in the al-Qaida organisation'. See SC Res. 1333 (2000), 19 December 2000, UN Doc. S/RES/1333 (2000), para. 8.

[456] See SC Res. 1390 (2002), 16 January 2002, UN Doc. S/RES/1390 (2002), which modifies the sanctions regime originally imposed in SC Resolutions 1267 (1999).

[457] See Resolution 1333 (2000), allowing for a 'de-listing' of the organisations designated by the 1267 Committee (para. 3). See also Security Council Committee Established Pursuant to Resolution 1267 (1999), Guidelines of the Committee for the Conduct of its Work (adopted on 7 November 2002 and amended on 10 April 2003), available at http://www.un.org/Docs/ sc/committees/1267/1267_guidelines.pdf (hereinafter, '1267 Committee, Guidelines').

[458] Sweden contested the US designation of three Swedish citizens of Somali origin as terrorist accomplices whose financial business must be suppressed. Reportedly, the US was reluctant to provide the Swedish authorities with evidence and when it did the evidence was scant. Sweden objected and two of the men were removed from the UN list in August 2002. Swedish concerns, expressed to the Human Rights Committee, included that there should be 'concrete evidence of the connection between an individual and an entity that had committed acts of terrorism, and that an underlying legal mechanism should establish the existence of such a connection' and that 'the accused should be able to make objections, so that the sanctions committees could review their decisions'. See 'Human Rights Committee Takes Up Sweden's Fifth Report on Compliance with International Covenant On Civil, Political Rights,' HR/CT/616 21 March 2002. Cases have also been lodged before the European Court of Justice concerning EU lists: see Case T-315/01, *Yassin Abdullah Khadi v. Council and Commission*, 5656/02, 21 February 2002; Case T-306/01, *Abdirisak Aden and Others v. Council and Commission*, 16 February 2002, OJ C 44, pp 27–8; Case T-318/01, *Omar Mohammed Othman v. Council and Commission*, 6763/02, 27 February 2002.

[459] In a climate where states are warned that 'either you are with us, or you are with the terrorists', states may be particularly reticent to take up such causes. See State of the Union Speech by the United States' President, 20 September 2001, in Chapter 5, section B.

7B.11.2 International 'cooperation': undermining the judicial function

Numerous examples of the erosion of the judicial function can be found in relation to developments in the field of international cooperation post 9/11, discussed in Chapter 4, section B. First, certain developments, purportedly designed to enhance international cooperation in the fight against terrorism, limit the judicial function in respect of extradition. For example, by undermining the 'double criminality' principle[460] or lowering normal requirements regarding exchange of evidence in extradition proceedings,[461] measures such as the European arrest warrant and new US–UK treaty have drawn criticism.[462] These moves to 'streamline' the extradition procedure – towards a more summary, or some would say perfunctory, procedure – risk undermining the essential judicial safeguard against violation of human rights and jeopardising the principle of non-refoulement.

Secondly, in practice, the role and independence of the judiciary has been eviscerated through the increased interference by the executive and/or the military in the legal process for surrendering persons between states discussed above.[463] Transfer of persons since September 11 has often been extra-legal, either by-passing the legitimate legal process for transfer of persons from one state to another entirely, or interfering to effect rendition despite extradition proceedings being pending or having been dismissed.[464] Thus judicial scrutiny and the legal protections inherent therein have been circumvented.

7B.11.3 Independence and impartiality impaired: 'special' courts

The judicial process has been further compromised post 9/11 by the introduction in several states of 'special' or military courts to judge terrorist

---

[460] The European Council Framework Decision on the European Arrest Warrant and the Surrender Procedure between Member States, 13 June 2002 (2002/584/JHA), OJ L 190/5, 18 July 2002 (hereinafter 'European Arrest Warrant') has drawn particular criticism in this respect, see Chapter 4, section B.

[461] See Article 8 'European Arrest Warrant' and Article 8(3)(c) US–UK Extradition Treaty between the Government of the UK and Northern Ireland and the Government of the USA (Washington, 31 March 2003). See Lofti Raissi case at Chapter 4 Section B.2.

[462] See Chapter 4, section B.

[463] See, e.g., in this chapter, para. 7B.8 and Chapter 4, para. 4B.2.

[464] See cases concerning cooperation between Bosnia and the US and Malawi and the US, where despite extradition cases having been dismissed and pending (respectively), the executive reportedly interfered to transfer the individuals in question to the US, discussed in Chapter 4, para. 4B.2.3.3.

related offences.[465] The introduction of military tribunals to try non-US nationals suspected of terrorism is discussed in the Chapter 8 case study on Guantanamo Bay. In this respect, as in others, US practice has been invoked as justification for dubious practice by other states, as illustrated by President Mubarak of Egypt's claim that resort to military tribunals in the US 'prove[s] that we were right from the beginning in using all means, including military tribunals' to curb terrorism.[466]

Notably, however, the resort to military tribunals in the US and beyond has met with critical response. In December 2001 the Inter-American Commission on Human Rights acted promptly to flag that the prospect of resorting to such commissions to try civilians in their hemisphere would be unacceptable.[467] The Human Rights Committee's rejection of the use of such courts post 9/11 was also unequivocal, with it expressing:

> alarm that military courts and State security courts have jurisdiction to try civilians accused of terrorism although there are no guarantees of those courts' independence and their decisions are not subject to appeal before a higher court (Article 14 of the Covenant).[468]

7B.12 Accountability

The importance of accountability as a human rights obligation in itself, and as a safeguard for other human rights, gives rise to numerous questions post 9/11. Some relate to the apparent neglect of criminal process as a response to 9/11 itself, discussed in Chapter 4, section B. The emphasis on military force rather than criminal law is evident also in the context

---

[465] See Human Rights Watch, 'In the Name of Counter-Terrorism'.

[466] See Stork, 'Human Rights Crisis in the Middle East'. Prime Minister Atef Abeid of Egypt commented that '[a]fter these horrible crimes committed in New York and Virginia, maybe western countries should begin to think of Egypt's own fight and terror as their new model', and Colin Powell noted that the Americans had 'much to learn' from Egypt's anti-terrorist tactics.

[467] See Inter-American Commission on Human Rights, *Resolution on Terrorism and Human Rights*, 12 December 2001: 'According to the doctrine of the IACHR, military courts may not try civilians, except when no civilian courts exist or where trial by such courts is materially impossible. Even under such circumstances, the IACHR has pointed out that the trial must respect the minimum guarantees established under international law, which include non-discrimination between citizens and others who find themselves under the jurisdiction of a State, an impartial judge, the right to be assisted by freely-chosen counsel, and access by defendants to evidence brought against them together with the opportunity to contest it.'

[468] Concluding Observations of the Human Rights Committee: Egypt, UN Doc. CCPR/CO/ 76/EGY (2002), para. 16.

of Iraq, where the possibility of ousting Saddam Hussein and prosecuting him 'in the style of the Milosović trial before the ICTY' was given little apparent credence in the run-up to the military intervention.[469]

Other questions relate to the as yet undetermined extent and scope of investigations into crimes committed in the course of the war on terror. It remains uncertain which crimes will be the focus of investigation, and as against which perpetrators, at which level of the chain of command? While some internal investigations have been conducted,[470] the refusal to conduct official investigations in certain cases, for example by UK authorities in respect of alleged killings of Iraqi civilians, has generated controversy and legal challenge.[471]

As discussed in Chapter 4, impediments to effective prosecution, including immunity from prosecution or the application of defences that afford impunity to those responsible, are impermissible. Despite this, a US executive branch report of 2003 suggests, for example, that 'the defense of superior orders will generally be available for U.S. Armed Forces personnel engaged in exceptional interrogations except where the conduct goes so far as to be patently unlawful'.[472] Likewise, the grant of wide 'immunities' to foreign personnel – including private contractors – in Afghanistan and in particular Iraq, which potentially protect from legal action even those responsible for serious rights violations, provides another source of concern.[473] Questions of immunity may well become critical if attempts to ensure accountability at the highest levels gather momentum.

---

[469] Harold Hongju Koh, 'Memorial Lecture Transnational Legal Process After September 11th', 22 Berkeley J. Int'l L. 337 2004.

[470] As of May 2004, seven military police officers had been charged in relation to Abu Ghraib; see Sean D. Murphy, 'Contemporary Practice of the United States Relating to International Law: International Criminal Law: U.S. Abuse of Iraqi Detainees at Abu Ghraib Prison', 98 AJIL 591 July, 2004.

[471] See, e.g., 'High Court Challenge over Iraqi Civilian Deaths', *The Guardian*, 28 July 2004, available at http://www.guardian.co.uk/Iraq/Story/0,2763,1270930,00.html reporting the case brought by the families of Iraqi civilians allegedly killed by British troops, challenging the UK Government's refusal to order independent inquiries into the deaths.

[472] See Working Group Report on Detainee Interrogations in the Global War on Terrorism: Assessment of Legal, Historical, Policy, and Operational Considerations (4 April 2003), at http://www.washingtonpost.com/wp-srv/nation/documents/040403.pdf in Sean D. Murphy, *ibid.*, p. 33.

[473] See the June 2003 Order of the Coalition Provisional Authority, in, e.g., http://www.cnn.com/2004/LAW/06/17/mariner.contractors/. See also Marie Woolf, 'Legality of Iraq Occupation "Flawed"', *Independent*, 5 May 2004, citing former senior UK civil servant Elizabeth Wilmshurst's criticism of the unprecedented breadth of immunities granted to US and British civilians by the occupying powers.

7B.13 Conclusion

The plethora of specific questions regarding compliance with human rights obligations, of which the foregoing is a small selection, have led to questions of a more general nature relating to human rights law post 9/11. Have the events of September 11, as Egypt's President Mubarak suggested, 'created a new concept of democracy that differs from the concept that western states defended before these events, especially in regard to the freedom of the individual?'[474] Are human rights marginalised, or just plain out of date? Have we witnessed a subordination of human rights law to security imperatives?

The extent to which rights appear to have been violated or jeopardised, as set out above, may tempt us to such a conclusion. In the immediate aftermath of 9/11, the focus on security and counter-terrorism, absent reference to human rights, most notably by the Security Council in Resolution 1373 which, unlike earlier resolutions addressing terrorism, omitted any reference to human rights, may have suggested a troubling marginalisation of that area of law by an authoritative body. Assertions made, *inter alia* by state officials, as to the inevitability of human rights violations in the face of state of emergency sought to juxtapose human rights and security as irreconcileable alternatives.[475] Questions asked as to whether certain acts such as torture can be 'justified' are not really a debate as to the lawfulness of particular acts in particular situations (as the unqualified prohibition on torture is legally incontrovertible at this stage), but as to whether the rule of law should be applied at all.[476]

However, despite these countless troubling developments, other emergent responses cast a more positive light on the perceived relevance of human rights law, and its future potential to provide much needed legal constraint in the unfolding 'war on terror'. Institutional developments may illustrate the point.

The apparent blindness of the Security Council to the role of human rights law in the fight against terrorism, manifest through Resolution

---

[474] Statement by President Mubarak of Egypt reported by Stork, 'Human Rights Crisis in the Middle East'.

[475] Such an approach is illustrated by the notorious declaration of a CIA agent, questioned on the allegations of ill-treatment of terrorist suspects by US officials: 'If you don't violate someone's human rights some of the time, you probably aren't doing your job'. See Priest and Gellman, 'U.S. Decries Abuse but Defends Interrogations'.

[476] 'Is Torture Ever Justified?', *The Economist*, 11–17 January 2003, Vol. 366. As a matter of law, the prohibition on such mistreatment is clear and incontrovertible, and permits of no excuse.

1373 (2001) and the work of the Counter-Terrorism Committee (CTC) in 2001[477] was subject to stern criticism. That position evolved, to some degree, in the course of the following year,[478] and in early 2003 the Council adopted a declaration which, in contradistinction to Resolution 1373, reaffirmed that terrorism can only be defeated in accordance with the UN Charter and international law, including human rights, refugee and humanitarian law.[479] Statements during Security Council debate at that time also revealed a far greater emphasis by states on the human rights agenda than previously.[480]

Other UN bodies for their part were somewhat speedier to step into the breach left by Resolution 1373.[481] In 2002 the General Assembly emphasised the requirement of combating terrorism consistently with international law, including human rights law, in its first resolution specifically dedicated to terrorism and human rights.[482] The Secretary-General in turn has used his position to underscore repeatedly the necessity of

---

[477] See above and Chapter 2, para. 2.2.2. The scarce concern for human rights issues initially demonstrated by the Security Council and by the Committee has been implicitly criticised also by the UN Secretary General: 'We should all be clear that there is no trade-off between effective action against terrorism and the protection of human rights . . . Of course, the protection of human rights is not primarily the responsibility of this Council – it belongs to other United Nations bodies, whose work you do not need to duplicate. But there is a need to take into account the expertise of those bodies, and make sure that the measures you adopt do not unduly curtail human rights, or give others a pretext to do so' (Security Council, Summary Record of the 4453rd meeting, 18 January 2002, UN Doc. S/PV.4453).

[478] Although in January 2002 the CTC stated that it would not address human rights, it developed a relationship with the Office of the High Commissioner for Human Rights, and, since June 2002, the CTC has been in dialogue with the Office of the High Commissioner for Human Rights. See Guzman, *Terrorism and Human Rights No. 2*, pp. 31–2.

[479] SC Res. 1456 (2003), 20 January 2003, UN Doc S/RES/1456 (2003), Preamble and para. 6.

[480] See Koufa, Report 2003, Addendum 1, para. 7.

[481] In addition to the role of the General Assembly and Secretariat, highlighted below, the Human Rights Committee stepped into the void created by SC Res. 1373 (2001) (28 September 2001, UN Doc. S/RES/1373 (2001)) by emphasising in its country reports since 9/11 that, e.g., states parties to the ICCPR are 'under an obligation to ensure that counter-terrorism measures taken under SC Res. 1373 (2001) are in full conformity with the Covenant'; Concluding Observations of the Human Rights Committee: Moldova, UN Doc. CCPR/CO/75/MDA (2003), para. 8. See, likewise, the Concluding observation adopted by the Committee in 2002 on Yemen (UN Doc. CCPR/CO/75/YEM, para. 18), New Zealand (UN Doc. CCPR/CO/75/NZL, para. 11), and in 2003 on Estonia (UN Doc. CCPR/CO/77/EST, para. 8). The Committee has also on occasion requested that states report back on measures taken in this respect: see, e.g., Concluding Observations on Moldova, above, para. 22.

[482] GA Res. 57/27, 'Measures to Eliminate International Terrorism', 19 November 2002, UN Doc. A/RES/57/27 (2002) and GA Res. 57/219, 'Protecting Human Rights and Fundamental Freedoms while Countering Terrorism', 18 December 2002, UN Doc. A/RES/57/219 (2002). See Koufa, Report 2003, Addendum 1, paras. 8 and 9.

ensuring respect for human rights in the international campaign to eliminate terrorism and the dual role of the United Nations in peace and security and the promotion of human rights for all.[483]

One manifestation of the apparent marginalisation of human rights law on the international stage in the immediate aftermath of 9/11 was the marginalisation of the authority and perceived relevance of human rights bodies. Mexican endeavours during the 2002 session of the UN Human Rights Commission to advance a resolution which would, *inter alia*, have urged a role for human rights institutions in the work of the UN Counter-Terrorism Committee, were blocked and ultimately withdrawn, giving rise to heightened concerns.[484] Notably, however, when the matter was revisited in 2003, the Commission was able 'without particular difficulty'[485] to adopt resolutions which reiterate the need to combat terrorism consistently with human rights and, while not establishing the specific mechanism as some had hoped,[486] promote the role of human rights bodies, and the High Commissioner for Human Rights in particular, in ensuring compliance with those obligations and interacting with the CTC.[487] Again, this shift of tone, emphasis and content from one

---

[483] See, e.g., 'Report of the Secretary-General submitted pursuant to General Assembly Resolution 57/219', UN Doc.E/CN.4/2003/120; 'Report of the Secretary-General submitted pursuant to Security Council Resolution 1456 (2003)', UN Doc. S/2003/191. For similar statements by the UN Secretary-General, see http://www.un.org/terrorism.

[484] See Guzman, *Terrorism and Human Rights No. 2*, p. 31.

[485] Koufa, Report 2003, Addendum 1, para. 16, referring to Resolution 2003/37 on 'Human Rights and Terrorism'.

[486] See Guzman, *Terrorism and Human Rights No. 2*, at p. 30. Instead, Resolution 2003/68 (below) calls on the UN High Commissioner for Human Rights to 'mak[e] use of existing mechanisms'.

[487] Human Rights Commission, Resolution 2003/37 on 'Human Rights and Terrorism', above, adopted by a recorded vote of 30 votes to 12, with 11 abstentions, affirms that measures to combat terrorism must comply with obligations under international law. But Resolution 2003/68, UN Doc. E/CN.4/2003/L.11/Add.7, adopted without a vote on 25 April 2003, went further. While affirming the consistency point (para. 3), it also: invites the United Nations High Commissioner for Human Rights and the Human Rights Committee to continue dialogue with the Security Council and further their mutual cooperation (para. 4); requests all relevant special procedures and mechanisms of the Commission on Human Rights and United Nations human rights treaty bodies, to consider, within their mandates, the protection of human rights and fundamental freedoms in the context of measures to combat terrorism (para. 5); encourages states to take into account relevant United Nations resolutions, decisions and recommendations (para. 6); requests the High Commissioner for Human Rights to assume an active role, including making general recommendations concerning the obligation of states and to provide assistance and advice to states, upon their request, on the protection of human rights and fundamental freedoms while countering terrorism, as well as to relevant United Nations bodies and to report on the implementation of the present resolution to the General Assembly at its fifty-eighth session and to the Commission at its sixtieth session (para. 7).

year to the next[488] may reflect a climatic shift towards greater recognition of the importance and centrality of the human rights dimension, as well as reflecting 'growing awareness and concern' regarding regressive anti-terrorist measures adopted since 9/11.[489]

The increasing engagement of international and regional human rights bodies has taken various forms. The issuance of statements and guidelines relating to their regional or thematic area of competence has, at times, represented a strong reassertion of international standards and, at a minimum, has underlined the centrality of human rights law in the 'war on terror'.[490] The role of such bodies in monitoring situations and assessing the lawfulness of specific counter-terrorism measures, which is critical post 9/11, is increasingly visible through, for example, country-specific reports and, with time, human rights courts and bodies will address specific cases. Their willingness and ability to tackle some of the difficult issues highlighted above (among them the application of human rights law extra-territorially and the relationship with IHL, for example), will be critical to their credibility as well as to the extent to which the 'war on terror' may serve to clarify, and perhaps ultimately to strengthen, human rights law in a positive enduring way. In turn, of course, the response of affected states to decisions by these bodies will ultimately determine their impact and authority.[491]

---

[488] Human Rights Commission, Resolution 2002/35, 22 April 2002, UN Doc. E/2002/23-E/CN.4/2002/200, for example, emphasised the responsibility of terrorist groups for human rights violations and the role of the human rights bodies and mechanisms in addressing this role. For a discussion of whether terrorist organisations can be responsible for human rights violations, see Chapter 3. Resolutions such as 2002/35 may foreshadow this as an area for legal development.

[489] See Koufa, Report 2003, Addendum 1, para. 16.

[490] See Commission on Human Rights, Resolution 2003/37 on 'Human Rights and Terrorism'; Committee on the Elimination of Racial Discrimination, Statement on Racial Discrimination and Measures to Combat Terrorism, adopted 8 March 2002, UN Doc. A/57/18; Statement of the UN Committee against Torture, 22 November 2001, UN Doc. CAT/C/VII/Misc.7. For a detailed analysis of the activities of the UN human rights monitoring bodies, see 'Terrorism and Human Rights', Second Progress Report prepared by Ms Kalliopi Koufa, Special Rapporteur on human rights and terrorism, UN Doc. E/CN.4/Sub.2/2002/35, and Koufa, Report 2003, Addendum 1, paras. 16–20. For initiatives at the regional level see, e.g., OAS General Assembly, Resolution 1906 (XII-O/02), 'Human Rights and Terrorism', 4 June 2002 and the thorough *Report on Terrorism and Human Rights* of the Inter-American Commission on Human Rights, above; Council of Europe, Guidelines on Human Rights and Terrorism, above. In the autumn of 2004 the African Commission indicated for the first time its willingness to consider its role in this respect (Agenda of the 36th ordinary session of the African Commission on Human and Peoples Rights, Dakar, November–December 2004).

[491] In this respect, the United States response in relation to the Inter-American Commission decision in respect of the Guantanamo Bay prisoners provides an unfortunate point of

On the national level also, excesses have not gone unchallenged, but have led, gradually, to litigation in various fora, some of which has already borne fruit. Examples of courts' willingness to take tough decisions for the protection of human rights include the historic Supreme Court decisions in the United States on detention rights,[492] the German appeal court's rejection of the first (and only) 9/11 conviction on fair trial grounds[493] and the decision of Indonesian courts that the *nullum crimen sine lege* principle was violated in respect of the definition of terrorism in domestic law.[494] Despite the undermining of the role of the judge post 9/11, outlined above, there are therefore also optimistic signs of the judiciary reasserting its essential role as a bulwark against human rights abuse in the name of counter-terrorism.

In conclusion, that 9/11 and its aftermath present an enormous challenge to human rights law and institutions is self-apparent. It is probably too early to reach even tentative conclusions as to the long-term impact on standards of respect for human rights. Comfort can however be drawn from the fact that muted concerns voiced post 9/11 have given way to an increasingly robust approach by states, organisations and others charged with the guardianship of human rights. The apparent marginalisation of human rights law in the immediate aftermath of 9/11 has given way to increasing emphasis, as time unfolds, on the requirement that counter-terrorist measures be executed consistent with human rights obligations. Rejection of the dichotomy between human rights and security, in favour of the complementarity of respect for human rights and an effective counter-terrorism strategy, is now commonplace. It is thus questionable whether 9/11 will have led to a lasting sea change

departure; see United States Government, *Response of the United States to Request for Precautionary Measures – Detainees in Guantanamo Bay, Cuba* (15 April 15), 41 (2002) ILM 1015.

[492] *Rasul* v. *Bush, Al Odah* v. *United States* (Cases 03-334 and 03-343), Supreme Court Certiorari to the United States Court of Appeals for the District of Columbia, 28 June 2004, p.1. See Chapter 8.

[493] The conviction in the case against Motassadeq was quashed on 3 March 2004 by the German Federal Supreme Court on the basis, essentially, that potentially exculpatory evidence had been withheld by US authorities. See decision of the Federal Supreme Court of Germany, 3 March 2004 reported in BGH, Strafberteitiger, StV 4/2004, also discussed at Chapter 4, para 4B.1.1, 'Paucity of Prosecutions'.

[494] On 23 July 2004, Indonesia's Constitutional Court ruled that the use of new anti-terrorism legislation, Law No. 16 of 2004, to convict those accused of the 2002 Bali bombings violated the non-retroactivity principle in the constitution and annulled the law. See, e.g., Bali terrorism conviction violates constitution, Indonesian court rules, 23 July 2004, at http://www.cnews.canoe.ca/CNEWS/World/WarOnTerrorism/2004/07/23/553317-ap. html.

in attitude to the application of human rights law on the international sphere.

As regards legal development, while the content of law is likely to be clarified through the application of the framework to the 'war on terror', it is unlikely that, viewed with some distance from the events of 9/11, there can be said to have been substantive changes in international human rights law.[495] As regards *de facto* respect for that law, much remains to be seen as the 'war on terror' continues to unfold. The danger is that some of the flagrant violations, even if not themselves accepted or endorsed by others, create a space in which 'lesser' violations are tolerated or even assume relative respectability. Or that unacceptable practices duplicate as states find comfort of the company of others, in particular those that have in the past laid claim to a role as human rights standard setters. One legacy very likely to endure is an undermining of the authority of such states to call others to account without attracting the charge of hypocrisy and double standards.[496]

The excesses of the 'war on terror', and the readiness with which human rights standards were set aside in the name of security, may however highlight the importance of holding more tenaciously to legal standards in time of crisis, and perhaps in some respects to strengthening those standards. But the key challenge, even more apparent after 9/11 than before, lies in enforcement rather than standard setting. The important role of institutions has been highlighted, and the critical role of third states in respect of violations unfolding outside their territory is one of the issues raised in the next chapter, in relation to the most striking of the human rights 'innovations' post 9/11 – the off-shore detention of prisoners in Guantanamo Bay.

---

[495] The principal source of human rights obligations is treaty law, based on widely ratified human rights conventions, which does not change with state practice in the way that customary law may, although its content is clarified through interpretation and application. Moreover it should be recalled that many norms protecting fundamental human rights are generally considered to be *jus cogens* norms, which can only be replaced by other *jus cogens* norms and are therefore extremely resistant to change.

[496] Apparent double standards can be seen from the annual reports of the US State Department on the human rights records of other countries, which have constantly criticised practices similar to the ones adopted by the United States since 9/11. See Annual Country Reports on Human Rights Practices Released by the Bureau of Democracy, Human Rights, and Labor of the Department of State, available at http://www.state.gov. While perhaps to a lesser degree, questions arise also as to EU measures: although it has assumed moral leadership as the US's role is in this respect diminished (see Fitzpatrick, 'Speaking Law to Power', at 161), it too is to some degree impeded in its role as promoter of human rights by questionable human rights practices by member states.

Case study – Guantanamo Bay detentions under international human rights and humanitarian law

Following the commencement of the military campaign in Afghanistan on 7 October 2001, the United States, assisted by its allies, began detaining persons in Afghanistan and elsewhere 'for reasons related to the conflict'. Since early January 2002, hundreds of people, including nationals of some forty states, have been transferred to and held in detention facilities on the United States Naval Base in Guantanamo Bay, Cuba ('Guantanamo Bay').[1]

The location of the detention centre on Guantanamo Bay, which the United States authorities claim is beyond US sovereign territory, is an apparent attempt to circumvent the application of human rights protections in the United States constitution and access to United States courts. The detainees are referred to as 'enemy combatants', which is then relied upon in turn to justify the non-application of the protections of international humanitarian law. They have been held in what has correspondingly been described as a 'legal black hole'[2] or 'legal limbo'.[3]

This chapter will analyse the application of the framework of international human rights and humanitarian law, set out at Chapters 6 and 7,

---

[1] Letter from the President to the Speaker of the House of Representatives and the President Pro of the Senate, 20 September 2002, referring to the 550 detainees in Guantanamo Bay at that time (available at www.whitehouse.gov/news/releases). See also 'US flies terror suspects home', *The Guardian*, 29 October 2002, reporting that '[a]bout 625 people are detained at the base'. See also 'Lelyveld J. in Guantanamo', *New York Review of Books*, 7 November 2002: 'By now more than forty names out of 598 have come into the public domain, despite the obsessive secretiveness that marks the whole operation. It is now understood by those who try to keep abreast of what is happening at Guantanamo that [there are] thirty-four or forty-three nations from whom the detainees are drawn – the varying estimates may be explained by dual nationalities in some cases'.

[2] In *R (Abbasi and another)* v. *Secretary of State for Foreign and Commonwealth Affairs* [2002] EWCA Civ. 159 (hereinafter '*Abbasi*'), the UK Court of Appeal stated that the Guantanamo detainees are 'arbitrarily detained in a legal black-hole' (para. 64).

[3] Dembart, 'For Afghans in Cuba, Untested Legal Limbo: Old Laws Hard to Apply to Modern Terrorism', *International Herald Tribune*, 25 January 2002.

to the Guantanamo detainees. The 'plight' of the Guantanamo detainees raises multiple human rights concerns,[4] but this chapter focuses specifically on the procedural rights of the Guantanamo detainees. In particular, it addresses the right to have the basis of their detention, and status as detainees, determined, if appropriate, by a competent tribunal; to be informed of the reasons for detention; to judicial review of detention; and, so far as the reason for their detention relates to their possible implication in criminal offences, to basic due process guarantees, including access to legal counsel and the right of appeal. While other issues, such as whether the detainees are being treated humanely, might be subject to dispute, the fact that the procedural rights that would normally be afforded to persons in detention have been denied to the Guantanamo detainees has either been publicly acknowledged by the United States or established by law.[5]

The chapter is structured in three sections. The first is an overview of basic facts, which highlights facts regarding Guantanamo Bay, the treatment of detainees, their quest for justice to date and the legal 'procedures' applicable to them. The second section is the legal framework of obligations binding on the detaining power, which addresses applicable humanitarian and human rights law, describes the categories of prisoner under IHL and explores specific rights to which each category is entitled and the extent to which they are being respected in the situation at hand. The third section explores the rights and duties of third states to respond, the reaction of the international community thus far and the potential implications and repercussions of the Guantanamo Bay situation for the US, for other states, and for the rule of law more generally.

8A Guantanamo Bay and its detainees: the basic facts

Guantanamo Bay was let to the United States by the Republic of Cuba in 1903 under an agreement that provides in relevant part:

---

[4] These include the absolute prohibition on cruel or inhuman treatment or punishment, the rights to private and family life or freedom of expression and religion.

[5] See discussion below regarding the Presidential Military Order relating to 'Detention, treatment, and trial of certain non-citizens in the war against terrorism', issued on 13 November 2001 (below, note 45), and the Rules of Procedure on Military Commissions set forth by Military Commission Order No. 1, issued by the US Department of Defense on 21 March 2002 (hereinafter 'Rules of Procedure').

While on the one hand the United States recognises the continuance of the ultimate sovereignty of the Republic of Cuba over [Guantanamo Bay], on the other hand the Republic of Cuba consents that during the period of occupation by the United States of said areas under the terms of this agreement the United States shall exercise complete jurisdiction and control over and within said areas with the right to acquire . . . for the public purposes of the United States any land or other property therein by purchase or by exercise of eminent domain with full compensation to the owners thereof.[6]

Guantanamo Bay has been described – by Legal Counsel of the Justice Department[7] and the United States Navy,[8] respectively – as 'under the exclusive or concurrent jurisdiction' of the United States, and as 'a Naval reservation, which, for all practical purposes, is American territory.' A US court in 1992 described it as 'a military installation that is subject to the exclusive control and jurisdiction of the United States'.[9] It occupies a substantial area of more than 45 square miles and is 'entirely self sufficient, with its own water plant, schools, transportation, and entertainment facilities'.[10] Despite this the United States government asserts, controversially, that the Bay lies beyond its sovereign territory, and beyond the jurisdictional purview of US courts.[11] Paradoxically, however, US officials have

---

[6] Article III, Agreement between the United States and Cuba for the Lease of Lands for Coaling and Naval Stations, 16–23 February 1903, T.S. No. 418. The lease was continued by a subsequent treaty in 1934, and the United States has indicated its intention to continue that lease indefinitely.

[7] Legal Counsel of the Justice Department has described the Guantanamo Base as constituting land 'acquired for the use of the United States, and under the exclusive or concurrent jurisdiction thereof', Opinion of Assistant Attorney General Olsen, 29 March 1982, in 6 (1982) *Opinions of the Office of Legal Counsel of the Department of Justice*, 236 at 242.

[8] The United States Navy website describes Guantanamo Bay as 'a Naval reservation, which, for all practical purposes, is American territory. Under the [Lease] agreements, the United States has for approximately [ninety] years exercised the essential elements of sovereignty over this territory, without actually owning it.' See *The History of Guantanamo Bay: An Online Edition* (1964), available at http://www.nsgtmo.navy.mil/history.htm.

[9] *Haitian Centers Council, Inc.* v. *McNary*, 969 F2d 1326 (2nd Circuit 1992), 1342.

[10] G.L. Neuman, 'Surveying Law and Borders: Anomalous Zones', 48 (1996) *Stanford Law Review* 1197, n. 5 (1996).

[11] This argument, and the counter argument that as a matter of US law the area does fall within US sovereign territory, were presented in the context of litigation in US courts, including in *Al Odah* v. *United States* before the Court of Appeals for the District of Columbia (see, below, note 46). The US Government cites the Lease Agreement between Cuba and the US, which states that 'the United States recognises the continuance of the ultimate sovereignty of the Republic of Cuba' over the land, as definitive. The Plaintiffs' brief, supported in this respect by two *amicus curiae* briefs (one by a group of legal scholars and human rights groups and another by INTERIGHTS), argues that the question of the

also argued that it is within US jurisdiction for the purposes of excluding the application of the Torture Victim Protection Act[12] which gives US courts jurisdiction over torture committed in foreign jurisdictions.

8A.1.1 Treatment of detainees in Guantanamo Bay

The President of the United States stated that 'to the extent appropriate and consistent with military necessity' the detainees would be treated 'in a manner consistent with the principles of the Geneva Conventions of 1949'.[13] Upon arrival at Guantanamo Bay, the detainees were initially shackled, and photographs of them were published widely around the globe.[14] The ICRC was initially denied, but later allowed, access to the detainees.[15] Early reports by human rights groups and the press signalled cramped conditions, excessive heat, poor sanitation, measures in contravention of the prisoners' religious beliefs, such as forcibly shaving prisoners' beards.[16] Reports consistently questioned whether conditions at the camp met acceptable international standards of detention.[17] Reports

---

necessary jurisdictional link – forged by the relationship of control between the individuals and the detaining State – is distinct from the question of sovereignty.

[12] See the confidential report prepared by a Working Group of executive branch lawyers for the US Secretary of Defense, assessing legal constraints on the interrogation of persons detained by the US in the 'war on terrorism': Report on Detainee Interrogations in the Global War on Terrorism: Assessment of Legal, Historical, Policy, and Operational Considerations, 4 April 2003, available at http://www.washingtonpost.com/wp-srv/nation/documents/040403.pdf.

[13] Letter from the US President to the Speaker of the House of Representatives and the President Pro of the Senate, 20 September 2002, note 1, above.

[14] E.g., see *BBC World News*, 20 January 2002, 'Prison camp pictures spark protests' at http://news.bbc.co.uk/1/hi/world/americas/1771687.stm. The ICRC criticised the dissemination of these photos as themselves violations of the duty under Article 13 of the Third Geneva Convention not to subject prisoners of war to public curiosity.

[15] 'What are the conditions at Guantanamo?', *The Guardian*, 22 January 2002.

[16] See, Amnesty International, 'Memorandum to the US Government on the rights of people in US custody in Afghanistan and Guantanamo Bay', AI Index: AMR 51/053/2002 15/04/2002, http://web.amnesty.org/ai.nsf/recent/AMR510532002?OpenDocument; 'What are the conditions at Guantanamo?', *The Guardian*, 22 January 2002; 'Lelyveld J. In Guantanamo', *New York Review of Books*, 7 November 2002; 'A Letter from Guantanamo: How a lovesick homeopath found himself imprisoned as a terrorist', *Time Magazine*, 29 October 2002.

[17] Amnesty International has reiterated its concern about conditions in violation of minimum standards: see, e.g., 'USA: Detainees from Afghan Conflict Should Be Released or Tried' (AI Index: AMR 51/164/2002, 1 November 2002). See also 'Memorandum to the US Government on the Rights of People in US Custody in Afghanistan and Guantanamo Bay', AI Index: AMR 51/053/2002, 15 April 2002; T. Conover, 'Inside Camp Delta', *The Observer*, 13 July 2003, 19, although the latter, for example, indicated an improvement

of detention of children,[18] to whom special obligations are owed under international law,[19] give cause for particular concern. With very few exceptions, detainees continue to be denied access to their families, as have their families been denied information concerning them.[20] Upon the release of a small group of detainees in 2003, serious allegations of torture and ill-treatment began to emerge.[21]

From the outset, particular controversy and confusion has surrounded the reason for the arrest of detainees, their status (in particular whether they are entitled to be treated as prisoners of war (POWs)), and the rights, if any, to which they are entitled.[22] Despite the US authorities having

in this respect by the middle of 2002. See also 'Rights Flouted at Guantanamo Bay', *The Guardian*, 9 September 2002: 'Camp Delta is smarter and better built than its improvised predecessor, Camp X-Ray, which was made-up of cages in a heat-trap valley, with no ventilation.'

[18] See Amnesty International, 'Children detained at Guantanamo should be released', *AI News Release*, 23 April 2003, available at http://news.amnesty.org/mav/index/ENGAMR512404033; Amnesty International, 'USA: Children among those held in Guantánamo Bay', *AI News Release*, 20 November 2003, available at http://news.amnesty.org/mav/index/ENGAMR512011032003. As noted by Amnesty International, '[t]he detention and interrogation of unrepresented children in Guantanamo, as well as contravening international law and standards that apply to both adults and children, violate principles reflecting a broad international consensus that the vulnerability of under-18-year-olds require special protection'. Although the 'younger' juveniles detained in Guantanamo (i.e. those aged between 13 and 15 years) have been recently released (see 'Transfer of Juvenile Detainees Completed', *DoD News Release No. 57/04*, 29 January 2004, available at http://www.defenselink.mil/releases/2004/nr20040129-0934.html), reports by NGOs and by the ICRC denounce that people under the age of 18 are still detained in the US Military Base in Cuba: see I. James, 'Group: Teens Still Held at Guantanamo', *Washington Post*, 30 January 2004.

[19] See, e.g., the special guarantees provided for juvenile defendants and detainees by Articles 10(2)(b) and 10(3) and Article 14(4) of the ICCPR and the obligation to demobilise and rehabilitate former child soldiers provided for by the 'Convention on the Rights of the Child: Optional Protocol on the Involvement of Children in Armed Conflict' (GA Res. 54/263, 25 May 2000, UN Doc. A/RES/54/263 (2000)). The US has ratified the Optional Protocol on 23 December 2002 (source: UNICEF, at http://www.unicef.org/crc/crc.htm).

[20] The response to families of detainees requesting information was that 'we are not in a position to address the particular circumstances of any of the individuals detained at Guantanamo Bay'. See letter from the US Embassy in London in the *Abbasi* case, note 25, below. According to Louise Christian, lawyer for some of the UK national detainees, in some cases the UK families were informed of the detentions by journalists.

[21] See 'Guantanamo abuse same as Abu Ghraib, say Britons', *The Guardian*, 14 May 2004 and Chapter 7, section B, above. Reports note also that Major General Geoffrey Miller, the official in charge of US military's prisons in Iraq, including the notorious Abu Ghraib prison, had previously served as commander of Guantanamo Bay detention camp. See, e.g., S. Goldenberg, 'Guantanamo Record Contradicts Claims that Prisoner Abuse was Isolated', *The Guardian*, 19 May 2004.

[22] See para. 8B.3 in this chapter.

originally stated that there was going to be 'a case-by-case determination of each and every one of these individuals to see if they qualify under the Geneva Convention as prisoners of war',[23] the position shifted shortly thereafter to one of generalised denial of POW status to all Guantanamo detainees.[24] While the detainees have consistently been referred to as dangerous 'enemy combatants',[25] they have also been referred to as unlawful and illegal combatants, although at least one US official appeared to suggest publicly that among the detainees were some who were 'victims of circumstance' and probably innocent.[26] Despite the US President's continued emphasis on the circumstances of detention being justified by the fact that 'these are bad people',[27] some detainees have since been released, just as they were held, at the discretion of the US government.[28]

For the vast majority remaining in detention, no information has been made available as to the reason for their capture, or continued detention, or the anticipated duration of their detention, and indeed whether they will, eventually, be released. With the exception of the few who have been identified as subject to trial by military commission,[29] the detainees do not know whether the authorities intend to bring charges against them before a military tribunal or a court. Until February 2004, when two Guantanamo detainees were indicted,[30] no formal charges had been lodged, despite periods of detention that in some cases ran to several

[23] 'Press Briefing by Ari Fleischer', 9 January 2002, available at http://www.whitehouse.gov/news/releases/2002/01/20020109-5.html.

[24] For discussion, see 'Entitlement to POW Status' below.

[25] See *Abbasi*, para. 9, citing a letter from the First Secretary at the US Embassy in London to solicitors acting for the claimants in the *Abbasi* case which states that 'The United States Government believes that individuals detained at Guantanamo are enemy combatants', 2 July 2002, in 'Skeleton Argument of the Claimants', para. 6, on file with author. The term was defined in 2004: see 'Categories of Detainees' below.

[26] 'A Nation Challenged: Captives; an Uneasy Routine at Cuba Prison Camp', *New York Times*, 16 March 2002, quoting the deputy camp commander, Lt Col Bill Cline.

[27] Press Conference of President Bush and British Prime Minister Tony Blair, 17 July 2003, at http://www.whitehouse.gov/news/releases/2003/07/20030717-10.html.

[28] The Department of Defense reports that, as at 8 September 2004, 150 detainees had been released. ('Combatant Status Tribunal Implementation Guidance Issued', DoD News Release, 30 July 2004, available at http://www.defenselink.mil/releases/2004/nr20040730-1072.html). 'US releases 20 held at Cuban base', *The Guardian*, 25 November 2003, reporting that, to that date, 84 detainees had been returned to their countries of origin, and four had been transferred to Saudi prisons. Note, however, that the same article denounces the fact that new detainees continue to be transferred to Guantanamo Bay from 'undisclosed locations'.

[29] See para. 8A.1.4 this chapter.

[30] The detainees, of Yemeni and Sudanese nationality, were reportedly charged with 'violat[ing] the laws of war and engag[ing] in terrorism'. See N.A. Lewis, 'Qaeda suspects

years. Various attempts to seek judicial oversight have thus far failed. In the summer of 2004, some movement occurred in a situation that has held most of the detainees without procedural protection for over two years. As discussed below, this involved a judgment of the US Supreme Court, issued in June 2004, holding that the detainees are entitled to judicial review by civilian courts of the lawfulness of their detention. Various military procedures, involving a 'Status Review Tribunal' and 'Administrative Review Board', were then adopted by the Department of Defense in response to – or arguably in an attempt to circumvent – that Supreme Court decision.[31]

8A.1.2 Seeking justice in US and other courts

Several legal actions have been brought before US courts, by or on behalf of Guantanamo detainees, seeking access to families, to a lawyer or to a court of law. Among them cases were brought during 2002 on behalf of British and Australian detainees,[32] and another on behalf of twelve Kuwaiti detainees.[33] The government moved to dismiss these actions for want of jurisdiction, given the location of the detention facilities outside United States sovereign territory, and the fact that the detainees are not US citizens. In decisions that attracted strong criticism,[34] the court of first instance ruled that it had no jurisdiction to entertain claims from aliens

---

face first military trials', *New York Times*, 25 February 2004. See also para. 8A.1.4, this chapter, 'Trial by Military Commission' below.

[31] The nature of these procedures is highlighted at para. 8A.1.3, and the extent to which they meet the obligations of the state is discussed in relation to 'Specific Rights of Detainees under IHRL and IHL', para. 8B.4 below.

[32] *Rasul et al.* v. *George Walker Bush et al.*, No. 02–5288 2002, petition for a writ of *habeas corpus* filed before the District Court for the District of Columbia by the families of an Australian and two British citizens held by US forces in Guantanamo Bay.

[33] *Al Odah* v. *United States*, No. 02–5251 2002, action brought by relatives of twelve Kuwaiti nationals detained at Camp X-Ray in Guantanamo Bay. The plaintiffs sought a declaratory judgment and injunction ordering that they be informed of any charges against them and requiring that they be permitted to consult with counsel and meet with their families. The complaint was consolidated with *Rasul* v. *Bush* and treated by the court as an application for *habeas corpus*.

[34] See, e.g., 'US Court decision on Guantanamo detainees has serious implications for the rule of law', Press release of the UN High Commissioner for Human Rights, 12 March 2003, reporting the comment of Param Cumaraswamy, Special Rapporteur on the independence of judges and lawyers, on the decision of the US Court of Appeals for the District of Columbia Circuit in *Al Odah*. See also the unusually strong criticism expressed by the judges of the UK High Court in *Abassi*, above.

held outside the sovereign territory of the United States[35] and the appeal court upheld this decision.[36]

However, during 2003 the prospect of a different approach emerged. Another first instance court, hearing a similar case, found that:

> we simply cannot accept the government's position that the Executive Branch possesses the unchecked authority to imprison indefinitely any persons, foreign citizens including, on territory under the sole jurisdiction and control of the United States without permitting such prisoners recourse of any kind to any judicial forum, or even access to counsel, regardless of the length or manner of their confinement.[37]

The various decisions of US courts were then brought, together, before the United States Supreme Court. The Supreme Court was asked to determine the 'narrow but important question whether the United States courts lack jurisdiction to consider challenges to the legality of the detention of foreign nationals captured abroad in connection with hostilities and incarcerated at the Guantanamo Bay Naval Base, Cuba'.[38]

In a historic judgment supported by six of nine judges of the Supreme Court bench, the Court found that 'federal courts have jurisdiction to determine the legality of the Executive's potentially indefinite detention of individuals who claim to be totally innocent of wrong doing'. While the Supreme Court did not and could not itself consider the merits of the detainees' claims or itself provide remedy for them, its decision to remand the case to the district court to consider the merits provides at least the prospect that the detainees may, at some point, have the opportunity to determine the validity of their detention that has thus far been denied them. The Supreme Court judgment prompted the introduction of several irregular procedures, highlighted in the next section.

It should be noted that attempts to seek redress for the detainees in other countries have also failed. In a case brought before the English courts by family members of one of the seven UK nationals detained at Guantanamo Bay, the court noted its 'deep concern that, in apparent contravention of fundamental principles of law, Mr Abbasi may be subject to indefinite

---

[35] *Rasul* v. *Bush*, 215 F.Supp. 2d 55 (DC Dist. 2002), hereinafter '*Rasul*'.

[36] An appeal against the decision in *Rasul* was dismissed by the Court of Appeals for the District of Columbia on 11 March 2003 (*Al Odah et al.* v. *United States*, 321 F.3d 1134 (DC Cir. 2003), hereinafter '*Al Odah*').

[37] *Gherebi* v. *Bush*, No. 03–55785, 2003 *WL* 22971053, at 8 (9th Cir., 2003).

[38] *Rasul* v. *Bush*, *Al Odah* v. *United States* (Cases 03–334 and 03–343), Supreme Court Certiorari to the United States Court of Appeals for the District of Columbia, 28 June 2004, p. 1. On grant of *certiorari*: *Rasul* v. *Bush*, *Al Odah* v. *United States* (Cases 03–334 and 03–343), 10 November 2003, 72 USLW 3327.

detention in territory over which the United States has exclusive control with no opportunity to challenge the legitimacy of his detention before any court or tribunal'.[39] The English courts did not, however, have jurisdiction to provide a remedy directly to persons held by another state on the sole basis of their nationality. Nor, contrary to the applicant's submissions, was there any duty incumbent on the Secretary of State to make diplomatic representations on behalf of Mr Abbasi that could have been subject to judicial review in the English courts.

8A.1.3 Overview of military procedures governing detention

Following the Supreme Court decision in the summer of 2004, two sets of procedures were put in place by the US military in Guantanamo Bay. The first was the introduction of 'Combatant Status Review Tribunals',[40] composed of three officers of the US armed forces, charged with determining whether particular detainees meet the US's definition of 'enemy combatant'.[41] Although the Department of Defense has stated that the process 'will provide an expeditious opportunity for non-citizens detainees to receive notice and an opportunity to be heard', the substantive scope of this hearing is limited; it will not consider, for example, whether the detainee ought, as a matter of law, to be classified as a POW rather than an 'enemy combatant' or whether he is being afforded the rights to which he is entitled under international law. The detainee will have a 'personal representative' before these tribunals, but not a lawyer, and detainee–representative communications will not be confidential.[42] This review is conducted once only.

[39] *Abbasi*, para. 107. At paras. 66–7 the court noted that the treatment of detainees was 'objectionable', and had given rise to 'serious concerns internationally'.

[40] The procedure was established by an Order of the Deputy Secretary of Defense of 7 July 2004 (available at http://www.defenselink.mil/news/Jul2004/d20040707review.pdf). The procedure is detailed in the 'Implementation guidance for the Combatant Status Review Tribunal Procedures for enemy combatants at Guantanamo Bay, Cuba', issued on 29 July 2004 (available at http://www.defenselink.mil/news/Jul2004/d20040730comb.pdf).

[41] The definition of enemy combatant that is cited in all the documents relating to the Status Review Tribunals is that given by the Order of the Deputy Secretary of Defense of 7 July 2004 establishing the tribunals: 'An enemy combatant . . . shall mean an individual who was part of or supporting Taliban or al Qaeda forces, or associated forces that are engaged in hostilities against the United States or its coalition partners. This includes any person who has committed a belligerent act or has directly supported hostilities in aid of enemy armed forces.' See 'Categories of Detainees', para. 8B.3 below.

[42] See 'Security Detainees/Enemy Combatants', Human Rights First, available at http://www. humanrightsfirst.org/us_law/detainees/militarytribunals.htm Security Detainees/Enemy Combatants (visited September 2004).

The second procedure, introduced this time in anticipation of the Supreme Court decision, is an annual 'Administrative Review' procedure, whereby a board of military officers assesses whether the 'enemy combatant' poses a threat to the United States, or its allies, or whether there are other factors bearing on the need for continued detention, such as the 'intelligence value' of the detainee.[43] Based on that assessment, it may recommend release, transfer or continued detention. As at September 2004, 55 of the 594 detainees had undergone the review procedure and one had been released.[44]

8A.1.4 Trial by military commission

On 13 November 2001 a Military Order was issued by the President of the United States, relating to 'Detention, treatment, and trial of certain non-citizens in the war against terrorism.'[45] It provides, *inter alia*, that the trial of any individual subject to it will be by a military commission. Persons subject to the Order are those with respect to whom the President determines that there is reason to believe (1) that s/he is a member of al-Qaeda or (2) that s/he was engaged in international terrorism, or (3) that it is in the interests of the United States that s/he should be subject to the Order. The Order specifically excludes from the jurisdiction of the Commissions citizens of the United States.

The Rules of Procedure of the Commissions were first published in March 2002, but have been amended several times since then.[46] They have provoked widespread criticism on the basis that, while certain of the due process guarantees normally associated with criminal prosecution have

---

[43] The Procedure was created immediately prior to the Supreme Court decisions but was implemented shortly thereafter. See 'Final Administrative Review Procedures for Guantanamo Detainees', DoD News, 18 May 2004, available at http://www.defenselink.mil/transcripts/2004/tr20040518-0784.html) and the rules of procedure in 'Administrative review implementation directive' issued by the Department of Defense in September 2004 (available at http://www.defenselink.mil/news/Sep2004/d20040914adminreview.pdf). 'Combatant Status Tribunal Implementation Guidance Issued', DoD News Release, 30 July 2004, available at http://www.defenselink.mil/releases/2004/nr20040730-1072.html.

[44] *Ibid.*

[45] Presidential Military Order on Detention, Treatment, and Trial of Certain Non-Citizens in the War Against Terrorism, issued by President Bush, 13 November 2001, 66 FED. REG. 57833 (2001) (hereinafter 'Presidential Military Order').

[46] See above, note 5. The rules set forth in the DoD Military Commission Order No. 1 have subsequently been detailed by the Military Commission Instructions Nos. 1–8, issued by the Department of Defense on 30 April 2003 (hereinafter 'DoD Military Commission Instructions'), available at http://www.defenselink.mil.

been reflected, others are either limited or discarded entirely, as discussed below.[47]

In July 2003 President Bush designated six alleged al-Qaeda members detained at Guantanamo Bay as eligible for trial before the Military Commissions.[48] This was followed one year later by the designation of another twenty persons[49] as subject to the military order, although none of them had yet been charged with any particular offence. Although the Chief Prosecutor for the military commission had announced in October 2003 that the beginning of trials before the Commission was 'imminent',[50] the preliminary hearings in the first four military commissions began on 24 August 2004.[51]

---

[47] See 'Military Commission and the Right to Fair Trial by an Independent and Impartial Tribunal', para. 8B.4.5.1 in this chapter. For a discussion of the legality of the Military Commission under IHRL and IHL, see, *inter alia*, H.H. Koh, 'The Case Against Military Commissions', 96 (2002) AJIL 337; R. Wedgwood, 'Al Quaeda, Terrorism and Military Commissions', 96 (2002) AJIL 328; J. Paust, 'Antiterrorism Military Commissions: Courting Illegality', 23 (2002) *Michigan Journal of International Law* 1; J. Paust, 'Antiterrorism Military Commissions: The Ad Hoc DOD Rules of Procedure', 23 (2002) *Michigan Journal of International Law* 677; For a helpful analysis of the Commission's procedures see 'Trials Under Military Order: a Guide to the Final Rules for Military Commissions,' Human Rights First, updated August 2004, available at www.humanrightsfirst.org.

[48] Two members of the group are British citizens, and a third is Australian. The identities and nationalities of the other three have not been made public. 'President Determines Enemy Combatants Subject to His Military Order', DoD News Release, 3 July 2003 (available at http://www.defenselink.mil/releases/2003/nr20030703-0173.html).

[49] In July nine persons were designated subject to the order: 'Presidential Military Order Applied to Nine More Combatants', DoD News Release, 7 July 2004, available at http://www.defenselink.mil/releases/2004/nr20040707-0987.html. In August 2004 a further eleven were so designated: 'Fourth Military Commission Concludes Week of Trials', DoD News Release, 27 August 2004, available at http://www.defenselink.mil/releases/2004/nr20040827-1180.html.

[50] See J. Mintz, 'First Trial By Tribunal "Imminent," Official Says – 6 Al Qaeda Suspects Chosen as Eligible', *Washington Post*, 31 October 2003.

[51] See 'First Military Commission Convened at Guantanamo Bay, Cuba', DoD News Release, 24 August 2004, available at http://www.defenselink.mil/releases/2004/nr20040824-1164.html reporting on 'the first U.S. military commission in more than 50 years being convened [in Guantanamo Bay] today in the case of *U.S. vs. Salim Achmed Hamdan* who is accused of conspiracy to commit violations of the law of war'. The second of four military commissions was convened in the case of David Hicks, an Australian citizen, accused of conspiracy, attempted murder by an unprivileged belligerent, and aiding the enemy. (See 'Australian Citizen is the Second Commissions Case', DoD News Release, 25 August 2004, available at http://www.defenselink.mil/releases/2004/nr20040825-1169.html). See also 'Third Military Commission Interrupted by Yemeni Detainee Request', DoD News Release, 26 August 2004, available at http://www.defenselink.mil/releases/2004/nr20040826-1174.html and 'Fourth Military Commission Concludes Week of Trials', DoD News Release, 27 August 2004, available at http://www.defenselink.mil/releases/2004/nr20040827-1180.html.

8B Application of humanitarian and human rights law to detainees in Guantanamo Bay

So far as the prisoners are detained by the United States in the context of or in relation to an armed conflict, they are subject to the legal framework set out in international humanitarian law.[52] The United States is bound by IHL as a party to the armed conflict in Afghanistan.[53] In addition, it remains bound, in the context of armed conflict, by international human rights law. To the extent that at least some detainees are held, not pursuant to the armed conflict in Afghanistan but to a broader 'war on terror' which, as discussed at Chapter 6, section B, does not constitute an armed conflict in any legal sense,[54] or if they are detained on suspicion of involvement in crimes committed before the conflict or unrelated to it, then IHL does not apply.[55] In this case, the situation is subject only to applicable rules of IHRL.[56]

While not always clear or consistent, the US authorities have on occasion asserted that those held at Guantanamo Bay were detained pursuant to the conflict in Afghanistan and this chapter therefore outlines applicable rules of IHL as well as IHRL.[57]

---

[52] For a definition of armed conflict, see Chapter 6, para. 6A.1, 'Where and When IHL Applies'.

[53] The questions when that conflict started and whether it continues to exist are addressed at Chapter 6, para. 6B.1.2, 'The Afghan Conflict, its Nature, Beginning and End'. What is beyond dispute is that, whether it arose with the attacks of 11 September 2001 or with the military response thereto on 7 October, and whether it continues, there was clearly an armed conflict at a certain point. The date of the detentions of most if not all detainees was during this conflict. The US has stated that the detentions were related to that conflict.

[54] See Chapter 6, para. 6B.1.1, 'Armed Conflict and "Terrorist Groups of Global Reach"'.

[55] On the breadth of charges that have thus far been brought against four accused, see para. 8A.1.4, 'Trial by Military Commission', above.

[56] Note that detention for reasons related to the conflict is not incompatible with criminal investigation of persons so held. Although held as combatants, IHL allows that individuals may still be prosecuted for crimes arising before and during detention, and at the end of the conflict such ongoing proceedings may justify continued detention. However, if persons, such as, e.g., aliens in United States territory suspected of support for terrorist organisations (who may also be held under the Presidential Military Order) were detained, the reason for detention would most likely not be directly related to the conflict in Afghanistan, and their detention would be pursuant to a criminal law enforcement operation. While it may be pursuant to the 'war on terror' it would not relate to an armed conflict in any legal sense and IHL would not govern those detentions.

[57] Government response in *Al Odah*, n. 8, on file with author. See the Memo from the President of the United States, 'Humane Treatment of al Qaeda and Taliban detainees', 7 February 2002, on file with author, which concludes that: there are 'armed conflicts' with

8B.2.1 The framework: international humanitarian law

For present purposes, key provisions of IHL are those relative to the treatment of persons detained during an international armed conflict, embodied in the four Geneva Conventions of 1949 and in the First Additional Protocol to the Geneva Conventions of 1977.[58] The United States, like Afghanistan, is party to the four Geneva Conventions, which are therefore binding as treaty law.[59] Treaties to which the United States is not party remain relevant so far as they reflect customary law, and the bulk of the provisions of AP I are generally recognised, by the United States and others, as so doing.[60] Specifically, Article 75 of AP I – which is an elaboration of the principles set forth in Common Article 3 of the Geneva Conventions, which have been described by the International Court of Justice as 'beyond doubt' customary in nature,[61] – has itself been

al Qaeda and the Taliban, but that IHL 'does not apply to our conflict with al Queda' and that it does apply to the conflict with the Taliban but does not protect them as POWs (discussed below). See, by contrast, the Department of Defense reference to 'detainees held at Guantanamo Bay as enemy combatants in the war on terror' ('Fourth Military Commission Concludes Week of Trials', DoD News Release, 27 August 2004, available at http://www.defenselink.mil/releases/2004/nr20040827-1180. html).

[58] Note that, as discussed in Chapter 6, section B, as of June 2003 the Afghan conflict is most likely 'non-international'. The aspects of the framework relative to IHL in international armed conflict apply to the bulk of the individuals detained, captured before that date. Many of the same provisions apply in any event also in non-international armed conflict: by contrast to the finding of the President of the US that Common Article 3 does not apply to al Qaeda or Taliban prisoners as they are involved in 'international' conflicts (see Presidential Memo, 7 February 2002, *ibid.*), it is well recognised that Common Article 3, for example, embodies principles applicable in all conflicts. However, certain other provisions (notably those relating specifically to POWs) do not. See Chapter 6, para. 6A.1.1.

[59] The Geneva Conventions have been ratified by the US and by Afghanistan on 2 August 1955 and 26 September 1956, respectively (source: International Committee of the Red Cross, www.icrc.org).

[60] The United States has not ratified AP I, but it signed it on 12 December 1977. On AP I as customary law, see T. Meron, *Human Rights and Humanitarian Norms as Customary Law* (Oxford, 1991), p. 67, suggesting that the US has accepted the bulk of AP I as customary law. The ICTY has noted that 'it is not controversial that major parts of both Protocols reflect customary law' (*Prosecutor v. Kordic and Cerkez*, Case No. IT-95-14/2-PT, Decision on the Joint Defence Motion to Dismiss the Amended Indictment, 2 March 1999, para. 30).

[61] According to the International Court of Justice, Common Article 3 reflects customary international law applicable in all situations of conflict. See *Military and Paramilitary Activities in and against Nicaragua (Nicaragua v. United States of America), Merits, ICJ Reports 1986*, pp. 14 ff., para. 218.

recognised as customary law in a report prepared for the US Chiefs of Staff.[62]

8B.2.1.1 Beyond US sovereign territory: scope of obligations under IHL

As described in Chapter 6, international humanitarian law does not apply merely on the zone of battle, nor within a state's own borders.[63] Specifically regarding prisoners of war, the ICTY has noted that 'with respect to prisoners of war, the convention applies to combatants in the power of the enemy; it makes no difference whether they are kept in the vicinity of hostilities'.[64] The key question then is whether persons fall under the power or control of one of the parties to the conflict – in this case whether the Guantanamo detainees are under US control, which is clearly the case.[65]

Provided the detainees are held pursuant to an armed conflict, it does not matter to the application of IHL whether such persons are held in the territory of the United States, in Afghanistan, or elsewhere. The issues in dispute regarding the territorial or sovereign status of Guantanamo Bay are therefore irrelevant to IHL obligations.

8B.2.2 *The framework: international human rights law*

Although neglected in much of the official discourse, the United States is also bound to observe both human rights treaties to which it is party and international customary human rights law. As a State Party to the International Covenant on Civil and Political Rights,[66] this treaty provides the clearest source of human rights obligations binding upon the United States, which is bound also by the American Declaration on the Rights and Duties of Man.[67] It has signed (but not ratified) the American Convention

---

[62] Meron, *Human Rights and Humanitarian Norms*, p. 65, refers to a study of IHL prepared for the Joint Chiefs of Staff which states that Article 75 is one of the provisions of IHL that is 'already part of customary law.' See also Remarks of M. J. Matheson (Deputy Legal Adviser, US Department of State) at a panel on 'The United States Position on the Relation of Customary International Law to 1977 Protocols Additional to the 1949 Geneva Conventions' at the Sixth Annual American Red Cross–Washington College of Law Conference on International Humanitarian Law, 2 (1987) *American University Journal of International Law and Policy* 415 at 425–6.

[63] *Tadic*, Jurisdiction Decision, para. 70.   [64] *Ibid.*, para. 68.

[65] See ICRC Commentary to AP I, para. 2910.

[66] The ICCPR was ratified by the US on 8 September 1992 (source: UN High Commissioner for Human Rights, *Status of Ratification of the Principal International Human Rights Treaties*, available at www.unhchr.ch).

[67] American Declaration of the Rights and Duties of Man, OAS Res. XXX, adopted in 1948 by the Ninth International Conference of American States. It is also bound by the Convention

on Human Rights,[68] thereby expressing its willingness to act consistently with its provisions.[69]

States can derogate from certain treaty obligations, including under the ICCPR, on the basis that they face a 'public emergency threatening the life of [the] nation'. However, this is subject to certain conditions, as explained in Chapter 7, in respect of which the following points should be noted in relation to the situation at hand.[70]

First, there is a procedure for derogation that must be followed.[71] The United States has not chosen to avail itself of this procedure and the ICCPR therefore remains binding in its entirety.

Second, even in case of a valid derogation, there can be no suspension of the core of 'non-derogable' human rights. As discussed in more detail in relation to each of the rights below, many of the procedural rights in question in the present situation cannot be set aside even in time of emergency.[72]

Third, any measures that restrict rights on the basis of an emergency justifying derogation must be 'strictly required by the exigencies of the situation and proportionate to it'.[73] Thus, the legitimacy of denying a right, such as the right of access to counsel, for example, depends on a showing that the security risk would be increased as a result of allowing such access. Similarly, if alternative measures or safeguards are reasonably available to meet or minimise the security concerns, such as informing detainees of the reasons for detention while limiting the provision of sensitive information,[74] for example, the denial of the right is not strictly necessary and cannot be justified. As constantly underlined by the monitoring bodies of the main human rights conventions, the final assessment of the

---

Against Torture and Other Cruel, Inhuman or Degrading Treatment or Punishment, New York, 10 December 1984, 23 ILM 1027, but this is not developed, given the focus of the chapter.

[68] The United States signed the ACHR on 1 June 1977 (source: Organization of American States).

[69] Article 18, VCLT 1969 provides for the obligation of signatory states not to defeat the object and purpose of the treaty.

[70] See Human Rights Committee, General Comment No. 29: 'Derogations during a state of emergency' (Article 4) [2001], UN Doc. HRI/GEN/1/Rev.6 (2003) at 186, para. 7.

[71] See, e.g., Article 4 ICCPR; Article 27 ACHR and Article 15 ECHR.

[72] While an emergency will impact upon the rights to liberty and to fair trial, as discussed below it does not set them aside.

[73] E.g., Article 4 ICCPR.

[74] This is set forth in the *Paris Minimum Standards of Human Rights Norms in a State of Emergency* applicable to situations of emergency; see R. B. Lillich, 'Current Development: The Paris Minimum Standards of Human Rights Norms in a State of Emergency', 79 (1985) AJIL 1072 at 1073.

legitimacy of derogatory measures adopted to face a state of emergency must rest with the judiciary.[75]

Fourth, restrictive measures must be consistent with other international obligations. Notably, derogation from human rights treaties does not affect the obligations enshrined in IHL, which do not permit of any derogation.[76] As noted below, many of the rights in question are protected by IHL as well as IHRL. Thus no attempt to derogate from, for example, fair trial rights under human rights law could limit the fair trial rights to which detainees in armed conflict are entitled under IHL.

Fifth, measures of derogation must not be discriminatory. US citizens arrested under similar circumstances to the Guantanamo detainees are not held on Guantanamo Bay, and are subject to a different legal regime – that allows for example for access to a court – and are specifically excluded from being subject to trial by military commission contained in the Presidential Order.[77] The onus is on the state to demonstrate

---

[75] See, e.g., *Habeas Corpus in Emergency Situations (Arts. 27(2) and 7(6) of the American Convention on Human Rights)*, Advisory Opinion OC-8/87 of 30 January 1987, IACtHR, *Series A*, No. 8 (1987), para. 27: 'since not all . . . rights and freedoms may be suspended even temporarily, it is imperative that "the judicial guarantees essential for (their) protection" remain in force. Article 27(2) does not link these judicial guarantees to any specific provision of the Convention, which indicates that what is important is that these judicial remedies have the character of being essential to ensure the protection of those rights.' See also decision of the ECtHR in *Al-Nashif* v. *Bulgaria* (Appl. No. 50963/99), Judgment, 20 June 2002, paras. 123–4: 'Even where national security is at stake, the concepts of lawfulness and the rule of law in a democratic society require that measures affecting fundamental human rights must be subject to some form of adversarial proceedings before an independent body competent to review the reasons for the decision and relevant evidence . . . Failing such safeguards, the police or other State authorities would be able to encroach arbitrarily on rights protected by the Convention.' The necessity of a judicial review of the measures adopted by the executive during a state of emergency has been repeatedly underlined also by the Human Rights Committee: see, e.g., Concluding observations of the Human Rights Committee: Israel, UN Doc. CCPR/C/79/Add.93 (1998), para. 21: 'The Committee takes due note that [the State party] has derogated from Article 9 of the Covenant. The Committee stresses, however, that a State party may not depart from the requirement of effective judicial review of detention. The Committee recommends that the application of detention be brought within the strict requirements of the Covenant and that effective judicial review be made mandatory.'

[76] See General Comment No. 29, note 70 above.

[77] See *Hamdi* v. *Donald Rumsfeld*, US Court of Appeals for the Fourth Circuit, 8 January 2003, 316 F3d 450, concerning a national of Saudi Arabia, born in the US who claims US citizenship. Although captured in Afghanistan and held initially in Guantanamo Bay, he was transferred to custody in Norfolk, Virginia. The government rejected the claim for *habeas corpus* presented by his father in the District Court for the Eastern District of Virginia, Norfolk Division, but has not contested the jurisdiction of US courts, as it has in relation to the Guantanamo detainees. In September 2004 the US announced that Hamdi would be released: see E. Lichtblau, 'US to Free "Enemy Combatant" Bowing to Supreme Court Ruling', *New York Times*, 23 September 2004. On the differential treatment of other

that these measures imposed on non-US citizens are objectively justifiable.[78]

In these circumstances, the United States cannot be considered to have derogated from its treaty obligations. Nevertheless, in assessing basic applicable rights and obligations to the Guantanamo situation, this chapter will address only the minimal core of human rights applicable in all situations.

In addition to its treaty obligations, the United States is also bound by customary human rights law and many issues that arise in relation to Guantanamo Bay relate to customary law rules. Moreover, certain of the norms addressed, notably the prohibition of prolonged arbitrary detention, are generally recognised as *jus cogens* norms of international law.[79] No circumstances (and of course no derogation), could ever justify violating rights and obligations that have attained this status.[80] Regard may also be had to relevant non-binding international instruments – including the Helsinki Declaration of Minimum Humanitarian Standards,[81] the Paris Minimum Standards of Human Rights Norms in an Emergency ('Paris Standards')[82] and the UN Body of Principles for the Protection of All Persons under Any Form of Detention or Imprisonment[83] – that may give more detailed expression to treaty provisions and reflect customary law.

---

states nationals, notably as between the Australian detainee Hicks and nationals of other states, see para. 8C.7, 'The International Response to the Guantanamo Detentions', below. On non-discrimination, see CERD, Article 5 (ratified by the US in 1994). See also Principle 5, Body of Principles for the Protection of Persons under any form of Imprisonment; Principle 6(1) Standard Minimum Rules on the Treatment of Prisoners. All three cover discrimination based on nationality.

[78] Such objective justification would be found, for example, by reference to IHL. In certain circumstances the nationality (or allegiance) of an individual may determine the status of the detainee and the legal framework applicable to his or her situation under IHL. See the definition of 'civilian' entitled to the protection of the GC IV, for example, in Categories of Detainees/Civilians, below. However, as will be seen, detainees are protected in all cases, irrespective of nationality or status, by one or other aspect of the legal framework.

[79] See Chapter 1, above, and Chapter 7.

[80] The nature of the obligations varies in time of conflict: what amounts to arbitrary detention in international law is different in armed conflict than in time of peace, as discussed below.

[81] The Helsinki Declaration on Minimum Humanitarian Standards, adopted in December 1990, sets forth the core human rights that must be preserved in every situation and at all times. See T. Meron and A. Rosas, 'Current Developments: A Declaration of Minimum Humanitarian Standards', 85 (1991) AJIL 375 at 375–7.

[82] Paris Minimum Standards of Human Rights Norms in a State of Emergency, approved by consensus during the 61st Conference of the International Law Association, Paris, 26 August – 1 September 1984 (reprinted in 79 (1985) AJIL 1072).

[83] GA Res. 43/173, 'Body of Principles for the Protection of All Persons under Any Form of Detention or Imprisonment', 9 December 1988, UN Doc. A/RES/43/173 (1988).

8B.2.2.1 Beyond US sovereign territory: scope of obligations under IHRL

Human rights obligations apply in respect of all persons in a state's territory or subject to its jurisdiction, which may extend beyond the borders of the state where it exercises its authority or *de facto* control abroad.[84] The degree of controversy attending the precise test to be applied to the scope of a state's extra-territorial human rights obligations was discussed in Chapter 7.[85] In respect of the Guantanamo detainees, however, any of the standards (for example whether requiring effective control of territory on which individuals are present, or simply control over the individuals themselves) would be satisfied, as Guantanamo Bay and its detainees are within the exclusive *de facto* control of the United States. The location of the detention centres on land that may not be United States 'sovereign' territory is therefore of no significance for IHRL.

Confirming this, the Inter-American Commission on Human Rights, in a recent request to the government of the United States to take certain 'precautionary measures' to protect the detainees, noted that:

> [t]he determination of a state's responsibility for violations of the international human rights of a particular individual turns not on that individual's nationality or presence within a particular geographic area, but rather on whether, under the specific circumstances, that person fell within the state's authority and control.[86]

As the Inter-American Commission indicates, the fact that detainees of various nationalities are held at Guantanamo Bay does not affect the rights due to them under IHRL, though it may raise questions of unlawful discrimination. For human rights law, based on the principle of universality, the key question is whether persons fall within the control of the state, not the allegiance owed by such persons to the state.

8B.3 Categories of detainees

The US authorities categorise the detainees, collectively, as enemy combatants:

---

[84] See Chapter 7, para. 7A.2.1. The apprehension of suspects constitutes exercising such authority abroad: see *Reinette* v. *France* (1989) 63 DR 189.

[85] Chapter 7, *ibid.*

[86] Inter-American Commission on Human Rights, *Precautionary Measures in Guantanamo Bay*, Cuba, 13 March 2002.

> The United States Government believes that individuals detained at Guantanamo are enemy combatants, captured in connection with an on-going armed conflict. They are held in that capacity under the control of US military authorities. Enemy combatants pose a serious threat to the United States and its coalition partners.[87]

Although the term has been used since the beginning of detentions at Guantanamo Bay it was defined by the US Department of Defense in an order in July 2004:

> An enemy combatant . . . shall mean an individual who was part of or supporting Taliban or al Qaeda forces, or associated forces that are engaged in hostilities against the United States or its coalition partners. This includes any person who has committed a belligerent act or has directly supported hostilities in aid of enemy armed forces.[88]

As a matter of international law, this 'enemy combatant' classification does not, however, denote the legal status of prisoners.[89] In armed conflict, the particular status of persons captured by a party to the conflict, and the corresponding rights to which they are entitled, is determined by IHL.[90] Detainees are either wounded, sick or shipwrecked armed forces (protected by the First or Second Geneva Conventions), prisoners of war (protected by the Third Geneva Convention) or civilians (protected by the Fourth Geneva Convention). All persons subject to detention have some status under IHL. This general principle is embodied in all four Geneva Conventions, described by the authoritative ICRC Commentary on the Fourth Geneva Convention thus:

> Every person in enemy hands must have some status under international law: he is either a prisoner of war and, as such, covered by the Third Convention, a civilian covered by the Fourth Convention, or again, a member of the medical personnel of the armed forces who is covered by the First Convention. There is no intermediate status; nobody in enemy hands can be outside the law.[91]

---

[87] Letter from the First Secretary at the US Embassy in London to solicitors acting for the claimants in the *Abbasi* case, 2 July 2002, in Skeleton Argument of the Claimants, para. 6, on file with author.

[88] Combatant Status Review Tribunals Order of the Deputy Secretary of Defense of 7 July 2004 (available at http://www.defenselink.mil/news/Jul2004/d20040707review.pdf).

[89] 'Enemy combatants' may cover privileged combatants, entitled to POW status, or other fighters who have the legal status of civilians, as discussed below.

[90] See also rights under IHRL, as explained above.

[91] ICRC Commentary to GC IV, p. 51.

Moreover, as will be seen, residual provisions of IHL also ensure by way of safeguard that any person not afforded greater protection – under provisions applicable to the above categories of detainees – remains subject to basic minimal protections under IHL.[92]

The detainees have also been described, on many occasions, as 'unlawful combatants'. While this term is not an international legal one either, and does not denote the status of persons under IHL as described above, it has some legal significance which is better captured by the alternative term 'unprivileged combatant'. Under IHL, certain persons enjoy what is known as 'combatant's privilege' which entitles them to engage in hostilities and protects them from prosecution for the mere fact of participation. As opposed to these 'legal' combatants who enjoy immunity from prosecution for mere participation in hostilities, other persons who take a direct part in hostilities may be criminally prosecuted for doing so.[93] Once captured, however, such persons remain entitled to the protection of IHL as 'civilians', or at a minimum to the above-mentioned residual protection under IHL, as discussed further below.

8B.3.1 Entitlement to POW status

Under IHL, 'combatant's privilege', mentioned above, entails three important consequences.[94] First, the privileged combatant is allowed to conduct hostilities and as such cannot be prosecuted for bearing arms or attacking enemy targets, unless the conduct amounts to a war crime.[95] Second, he or she is a legitimate target to the opposing forces. Third, in the event of capture, such combatants are afforded POW status.

The group of persons entitled to combatant's privilege, and in the event of capture to prisoner of war status, is defined in GC III, Article 4(A). These include members of the armed forces of another party, as well

---

[92] This may arise because they fail to satisfy the nationality requirements of GC IV. See para. 8B.3.2 on civilians, below.

[93] See 'POWs', para. 8B.3.1, below. While IHL does not expressly prohibit persons from taking part in hostilities, they do not have the 'privilege' of not being prosecuted for doing so.

[94] The distinction between privileged and unprivileged combatants is reflected in the US Supreme Court's distinction between lawful and unlawful combatants in the decision *ex parte Quirin* (1942) 317 US 1 at 30–1.

[95] Privileged or lawful combatants are subject to capture and detention as prisoners of war, and can be prosecuted only for serious crimes such as war crimes or crimes against humanity, whereas unprivileged or unlawful combatants can, in addition, be subject to trial and punishment 'by military tribunals for acts which render their belligerency unlawful'. Letter from the US Embassy in London in the *Abbasi* case, above, note 109.

as irregulars such as members of militia or volunteer corps that fight alongside a party to the conflict, provided they satisfy four conditions: being 'commanded by a person responsible for his subordinates; having a fixed distinctive sign recognisable at a distance; carrying arms openly; and conducting operations in accordance with the laws and customs of war.'

POW status is therefore automatically due to persons who fought in the armed forces of a state – in this case as members of the Taleban armed forces. The fact that the government was not the recognised representative of the State is not relevant for present purposes, as the Taleban undoubt-edly were the *de facto* government and the *de facto* armed forces of the state of Afghanistan.[96] Some of the individuals designated 'enemy combatants' by the US, which includes the Taleban, may therefore be POWs.

Although the US recognised that the Third Geneva Convention could, in principle, apply to the members of the Taleban army,[97] it justified the continued denial of POW status across all detainees on the basis that 'Taleban combatants have not effectively distinguished themselves from the civilian population of Afghanistan' and that they are 'allied' with a terrorist group.[98] However, the criteria set forth by Article 4 of the Third Geneva Convention only apply to irregulars that fight alongside a party to the conflict and not to the armed forces of a party to the conflict itself. The fact that armed forces may, for example, have been 'armed militants that oppressed and terrorized the people of Afghanistan', or that they did

---

[96] No party to the conflict denies that the Taleban were the *de facto* government of Afghanistan given that they controlled 90 per cent of the State's territory prior to the conflict.

[97] See 'Statement by the Press Secretary on the Geneva Convention', 7 May 2003: 'Afghanistan is a party to the Geneva Convention. Although the United States does not recognize the Taliban as a legitimate Afghani government, the President determined that the Taliban members are covered under the treaty because Afghanistan is a party to the Convention' (transcript available at http://www.whitehouse.gov/news/releases/2003/05/20030507-18. html).

[98] In his statement on the Geneva Convention, the White House Press Secretary, after having recognised the potential applicability of GC III to members of the Taleban, continued: 'Under Article 4 of the Geneva Convention, however, Taliban detainees are not entitled to POW status. To qualify as POWs under Article 4, . . . Taliban detainees would have to have satisfied four conditions: They would have to be part of a military hierarchy; they would have to have worn uniforms or other distinctive signs visible at a distance; they would have to have carried arms openly; and they would have to have conducted their military operations in accordance with the laws and customs of war. The Taliban have not effectively distinguished themselves from the civilian population of Afghanistan. Moreover, they have not conducted their operations in accordance with the laws and customs of war. Instead, they have knowingly adopted and provided support to the unlawful terrorist objectives of the al Qaeda.'

not conduct operations in accordance with the laws of war does not affect their entitlement to POW status.[99]

The position is different as regards other 'irregulars', including al-Qaeda fighters, whose entitlement to POW status depends on their meeting the four-part test in Article 4(A). With respect to members of al-Qaeda, US authorities justify the decision not to recognise them as POWs on the basis that, since 'al Qaeda is an international terrorist group and cannot be considered a state party to the Geneva Convention . . . , its members . . . are not covered by the Geneva Convention'.[100] It is a question of fact, but must be doubted, whether those detainees who were members of al-Qaeda and not Taleban forces would meet the four-part test, by being distinguishable from the civilian population,[101] and being capable of conducting military operations in accordance with IHL (as distinct from the question whether they have committed violations).[102]

In the event of doubt as to entitlement to such status, the matter must then be determined by a 'competent tribunal'. The prisoners must be presumed POWs pending such determination.[103] Moreover the onus is on a detaining power to demonstrate that detainees, purportedly captured for their role in the conduct of hostilities, do not deserve POW status.[104] This significant burden corresponds to the serious consequences for the

---

[99] The US position in respect of the Taleban may conflate and confuse the treatment of the armed forces of a party to the conflict and the fourfold criteria applicable to determine the entitlement to POW status of irregulars that fight alongside it. See the memorandum from the White House Counsel to the US President on 'Decision re application of the Geneva Convention on Prisoners of War to the conflict with Al Qaeda and the Taleban', 25 January 2002, p. 3 (available at http://pegc.no-ip.info/archive/White_House/gonzales_ memo_20020125.pdf). See, in similar terms, the Memorandum from the President of the United States, 'Humane Treatment of al Qaeda and Taliban detainees', 7 February 2002, on file with author.

[100] Ibid.

[101] See A. Neier, 'The Military Tribunals on Trial', New York Review of Books, at http://www. nybooks.com/articles/15122 who argues that '[i]n Afghanistan, neither Taleban fighters nor members of the Northern Alliance have worn uniforms. Therefore the requirement of a "fixed distinctive sign" can't be met literally; but since most of these combatants were not attempting to disguise themselves as civilians pretending to be other than what they were, the lack of uniforms should not prevent those captured in combat from being recognised as prisoners of war.'

[102] It is insufficient for the detaining power to note that violations of the laws and customs of war have occurred – an allegation routinely made by one side against the other in the context of conflict.

[103] See Article 5(2) GC III on the independent tribunal that must be established in case of doubt.

[104] The presumption of POW status is reflected in Article 45(1) and (2) AP I, and can only be displaced by a tribunal.

combatants in question, including penal consequences[105] and loss of their entitlement to the enhanced rights protections due to POWs under GC III which in some respects go beyond those guaranteed by IHRL. These include the right to be 'protected, particularly against acts of violence or intimidation and against insults and public curiosity',[106] to 'complete latitude in the exercise of their religious duties, including attendance at the service of their faith',[107] to be treated with due respect for rank and age, to be allowed to send and receive communications, and to keep personal property and effects.[108]

8B.3.2 'Civilian' detainees

If not treated as POWs, the detainees must be protected as civilians, 'who, at a given moment and in any given manner whatsoever, find themselves in case of conflict or occupation, in the hands of a Party to the conflict . . . of which they are not nationals'.[109] Such persons are protected by the Fourth Geneva Convention. Following the position adopted by the authoritative ICRC Commentary to the Fourth Geneva Convention,[110] the ICTY has noted:

> there is no gap between the Third and Fourth Geneva Conventions. If an individual is not entitled to the protection of the Third Convention as a prisoner of war or of the First or Second Convention, he or she necessarily falls within the ambit of [the Fourth Convention], provided that its Article 4 requirements are satisfied.[111]

The question arises whether persons who have taken up arms and fought with the opposing party, as unprivileged or unlawful combatants, should still be entitled to civilian status upon capture. Such persons certainly lose their status as protected civilians for the purpose of conduct of hostilities law and can legitimately be targeted for as long as they take up

---

[105] They may be prosecuted for mere participation as opposed to only for crimes under international law.

[106] Article 13 GC III.

[107] Article 34 GC III.   [108] Article 18 GC III.   [109] Article 4 GC IV.

[110] See ICRC Commentary to GC IV, p. 51: 'Every person in enemy hands must have some status under international law: he is either a prisoner of war and, as such, covered by the Third Convention, a civilian covered by the Fourth Convention, or again, a member of the medical personnel of the armed forces who is covered by the First Convention. There is no intermediate status; nobody in enemy hands can be outside the law.'

[111] *Prosecutor* v. *Delalic et al.*, Case IT-96-21-T, Judgment (Trial Chamber), 16 November 1998, para. 271.

arms.[112] However, once captured, they have 'civilian' status, and are entitled to the protections afforded to that category of detainees. The ICRC Commentary thus explicitly notes that resistance fighters, for example, who do not fall within the GC III, Article 4 criteria required for POW status, are entitled to be treated as civilians under GC IV: 'If members of a resistance movement . . . do not fulfil the conditions [for POW status], they must be considered to be protected persons within the meaning of the present convention.'[113] Other commentators likewise note that unprivileged combatants are entitled to be treated as civilians upon capture, and afforded the procedural and substantive protections of GC IV.[114]

Unlike POWs, who were privileged combatants entitled to fight, those who took up arms without meeting the criteria for privileged combatant can be prosecuted for their belligerent acts.[115] They must, however, in this respect as in others, be afforded the protections of GC IV which include due process rights, discussed below. As the ICRC Commentary notes, the fact that persons may be entitled to protection as civilians 'does not mean that they cannot be punished for their acts, but the trial and sentence must take place in accordance with the provisions [on due process] of Article 64 and those that follow it.'[116]

Certain limited categories of persons may, however, be excluded by GC IV, which is principally directed towards the protection of civilians associated with the adversary against whom the state is engaged in conflict. The Convention appears on its face to exclude 'nationals' of co-belligerent states and neutral states,[117] although, as recent determinations of the ICTY indicate, this exclusion should be treated restrictively. In the *Tadic* case, the ICTY Appeals Chamber held that, rather than imposing a strict nationality test, GC IV should be understood to protect persons with a perceived 'allegiance' to the adversary[118] and 'who do not have the nationality of

---

[112] Chapter 6, para. 6A.3.1, 'Targeting: the Principle of Distinction and Proportionality'.

[113] ICRC Commentary to GC IV, pp. 50 ff.

[114] W.T. Mallison and S.V. Mallison, 'The Juridical Status of Combatants Under the Geneva Protocol of 1977 Concerning International Conflicts', 42 (1978) *Law and Contemporary Problems* 4 at 5.

[115] Some commentators note the duty to prosecute such persons. See for example L. Vierucci, 'What judicial treatment for the Guantanamo detainees', 3 (2002) *German Law Review*, available at http://www.germanlawjournal.com/article.php?id = 190.

[116] ICRC Commentary to GC IV, p. 50, and Article 126 GC IV.   [117] Article 4 GC IV.

[118] *Prosecutor* v. *Dusko Tadic*, Case No. IT-94-1-A, Judgment (Appeals Chamber), 15 July 1999 (hereinafter '*Tadic* Appeal Judgment'), para. 165: 'already in 1949 the legal bond of nationality was not regarded as crucial . . . the lack of allegiance to a State . . . was

the belligerent in whose hands they find themselves'.[119] In the *Delalic* case, the ICTY added that GC IV:

> if interpreted in light of its object and purpose, is directed to the protection of civilians to the maximum extent possible. It therefore does not make its applicability dependent on formal bonds and purely legal relations.[120]

To the extent that persons held at Guantanamo were arrested for their allegiance, or perceived allegiance, to 'enemy' forces, and are not US nationals, they fall into the group that GC IV was intended to protect.

8B.3.3 Persons not covered by GC III or GC IV?

If any of the detainees are for any reason deemed excluded from both categories protected by GC III and GC IV,[121] they are nonetheless protected by customary law, binding on the United States. As noted, Common Article 3 to the Geneva Conventions and Article 75 of the First Additional Protocol to the Four Geneva Conventions, 1977 (AP I) are binding in this context as customary law and provide a minimal level of protection for all persons falling into the hands of a party to the conflict.[122]

Common Article 3, which protects persons taking no part in hostilities (including persons who once did but who are *hors de combat*, or have otherwise laid down their arms), articulates the core principles that are elaborated upon throughout the Geneva Conventions, and as such has been described as a 'convention in miniature'.[123] It provides a 'compulsory minimum' and an 'invitation to exceed the minimum',[124] and has been referred to by the Appeals Chamber of ICTY as the 'quintessence of

---

regarded as more important than the formal link of nationality'. The tribunal's caution that 'an approach, hinging on substantial relations more than on formal bonds, becomes all the more important in present-day international armed conflicts' (*ibid.*, para. 166) has resonance in the current context. See also ICTY Appeals Chamber, *Prosecutor* v. *Delalic et al.*, Case No. IT-96-21-A, Judgment, 20 February 2001, para. 73.

[119] See *ibid.*, para. 56, citing *Tadic* Appeal Judgment, para. 164.

[120] *Prosecutor* v. *Delalic et al.*, Case No. IT-96-21-A, Judgment (Appeals Chamber), 20 February 2001, para. 57, citing *Tadic* Appeal Judgment, para. 168.

[121] If, e.g., the nationality/allegiance requirements of GC IV were considered not met, an individual unprivileged combatant may be deemed not to fall under either GC III or GC IV. See, however, 'Civilian Detainees' above.

[122] On Common Article 3 as custom, see above, note 61. On the generally recognised customary character of some of the provisions of AP I, see above, note 62.

[123] See, e.g., ICRC Commentary to CG IV, Commentary to Common Article 3, p. 48.

[124] *Ibid.*, p. 52.

the humanitarian rules found in the Geneva Conventions as a whole'.[125] It protects against, *inter alia*, 'the carrying out of sentences without previous judgment pronounced by a regularly constituted court, affording all the judicial guarantees which are recognised as indispensable by civilised peoples'.

Article 75 of Additional Protocol I, entitled 'Fundamental Guarantees', applies to persons 'who do not benefit from any greater protections'. It is applicable to persons 'who are arrested, detained or interned for reasons related to the armed conflict . . . until their final release, repatriation or re-establishment, even after the end of the armed conflict'.[126] This provision represents the most basic level of protection under IHL due to any human being detained for any reason related to the conflict.

As the authoritative ICRC Commentary to Additional Protocol I notes: 'there can be no doubt that Article 75 represents a *minimum* standard which does not allow for any exceptions'.[127] Article 75 includes a number of safeguards specifically directed towards ensuring that detention is governed by a framework of legality, and maintaining basic due process rights, as discussed below in relation to each of the specific rights in question.

8B.4 Specific rights of detainees under IHL and IHRL

The following section explores particular procedural rights, owed to the detainees under applicable IHL and IHRL. It will consider the rights that correspond to particular categories of prisoners under IHL, as well as the minimal rules of IHL applicable to all prisoners held in relation to the conflict and IHRL applicable to all prisoners, and the extent to which these rights have been respected in relation to the Guantanamo detainees (as highlighted at the end of each section).

8B.4.1 *Existence of a lawful basis for detention*

In accordance with the rule of law, the liberty of individuals cannot be restricted other than in accordance with clear and accessible law. This 'principle of legality' is explicitly provided for in human rights law,[128] but

---

[125] *Prosecutor* v. *Delalic et al.*, Case No. IT-96-21-A, Judgment, 20 February 2001, para. 143.
[126] See Article 75(1) and (6), reinforced by Article 45 AP I.
[127] ICRC Commentary on AP I, para. 3032 (emphasis added).
[128] See, e.g., Article 9(1) ICCPR and Article V, American Declaration of the Rights and Duties of Man.

it is a fundamental principle that underpins any system of law, national or international.

This principle of legality applies no less in time of armed conflict than in time of peace, although the legal justifications for detention differ. During conflict, IHL permits, for example, the detention of combatants to preclude further participation in hostilities and, in extreme circumstances, the detention of civilians where imperative reasons of security so demand. By contrast, outside armed conflict where IHRL is the primary source of applicable law, 'preventive' or 'administrative' detention is justifiable only very exceptionally and where appropriate safeguards are secured.[129] In time of conflict or of peace, detentions may also be justified where persons are accused of having committed a crime for which they may be punished,[130] or in exceptional circumstances where there is reasonable suspicion that the individual involved has committed an offence[131] and necessary safeguards are applied.[132] While 'reasonable suspicion' has been interpreted quite broadly in relation to terrorist offences, it is unquestionable that the suspicion must be specific and relate directly to the individual subject to the arrest, and not to every individual belonging to a particular 'suspect' group.[133]

The lawful basis for detention may thus be found in IHL or in IHRL. If however, at the outset of detention, or at any point in the course thereof, there is no clear legal basis for the detention of any individual,[134]

---

[129] See Chapter 7, para. 7A.4.3, 'Specific Rights Protected: Liberty and Security' and para. 7B.6, 'Indefinite Detention – Repatriation', above.

[130] As noted above, unprivileged combatants can be prosecuted for involvement in hostilities whereas privileged combatants can be prosecuted only for war crimes.

[131] See, e.g., the decision of the ECtHR in *Fox, Campbell and Hartley* v. *the United Kingdom* (App. Nos. 12244/86; 12245/86; 12383/86), Judgment of 30 August 1990, Series A, No. 182, para. 32: 'The "reasonableness" of the suspicion on which an arrest must be based forms an essential part of the safeguard against arbitrary arrest and detention which is laid down in Article 5(1)(c). [H]aving a "reasonable suspicion" presupposes the existence of facts or information which would satisfy an objective observer that the person concerned may have committed the offence.'

[132] Preventive detention is permissible under IHRL only exceptionally and for a limited duration, and where the safeguards such as judicial oversight are respected. See para. 8B.5.2, 'Indefinite Detention – Repatriation', below.

[133] *Ibid.*: 'the exigencies of dealing with terrorist crime cannot justify stretching the notion of 'reasonableness' to the point where the essence of the safeguard secured by Article 5(1)(c) is impaired.

[134] As noted in Chapter 6, section B, if persons are detained pursuant to an international armed conflict and that conflict then ceases, or becomes a non-international conflict, the original lawful basis for detention may no longer exist. Persons must be released unless there is another lawful basis for continued detention.

then that detention is not governed by the principle of legality and is arbitrary.[135]

Confusion has surrounded the question which law, if any, purports to underpin the detention of the Guantanamo detainees. They have been collectively referred to as dangerous 'enemy combatants', but as noted above this is not a legal classification established in national or international law and cannot therefore provide a legal basis for detention.[136]

The annual review board procedure, which can recommend release, assesses whether detainees are 'dangerous' or whether other 'factors', such as intelligence value, justify detention. To the extent that the criteria purport to represent the justification for detention, it is noted that a massive policy of (prolonged) detention on broad grounds related to possible preventive effect, the potential utility in solving other crimes, or other (unspecified) factors, cannot be reconciled with the constraints of the international legal framework highlighted above, including its emphasis on clear grounds for detention proscribed in law.

There may well have been a lawful basis for detaining at least some of the Guantanamo prisoners on the bases set out above as regular combatants (Taleban) detained during a real armed conflict in Afghanistan (as opposed to the metaphorical 'war on terror'), as unlawful combatants charged with unlawful conduct of hostilities or as persons detained on reasonable suspicion of having committed a crime, properly understood

---

[135] As noted above, arbitrary detention is not only a violation of a treaty obligation incumbent on the US and others, it is also conduct prohibited by customary law and is often qualified as a *jus cogens* rule, *i.e.* as a rule belonging to that very restricted set of norms from which no derogation is ever admitted under international law. See, e.g., L. Hannikainen, *Peremptory Norms (Jus Cogens) in International Law: Historical Development, Criteria, Present Status* (Helsinki, 1988), pp. 425 ff., T. Meron, 'On a Hierarchy of International Human Rights', 80 (1986) AJIL 1. It is interesting to note that the extremely authoritative *Restatement (Third) of the Foreign Relations Law of the United States* is one among the many authorities that support the qualification of the prohibition of arbitrary detention as a *jus cogens* rule (see *ibid.*, Section 702 Comment N, Reporters' Note 11). See the *amicus curiae* brief on arbitrary detention in international law presented to the US Court of Appeals in the case of *Rasul et al. v. George Walker Bush et al.*, No. 02–5288 2002 United States District Court for the District of Columbia. On file with author.

[136] 'Administrative Review Implementation Directive Issued', DoD News Release, 15 September 2004, available at http://www.defenselink.mil/releases/2004/nr20040915-1253.html. The directive implementing the ARB suggests that the Board will consider whether continued detention may be justified on the basis that 'there is continued reason to believe that the enemy combatant poses a threat to the United States or its allies, or . . . there are other factors bearing upon the need for continued detention, including the enemy combatant's intelligence value in the Global War on Terror'. These criteria cannot themselves represent lawful bases of detention.

as such according to criminal law applicable at the relevant time, including war crimes or crimes against humanity. However, the lack of clarity as to the law pursuant to which they are held and its application to any individual, coupled with the lack of procedural oversight (discussed below), is an anathema to the fundamental principle that detention can be justified only when pursuant to clear and accessible law.

8B.4.2 Status determinations

As discussed above, all persons in the hands of the adversary have a status under IHL, and the particular legal protections that apply to them as civilians, POWs or other, depend on this status. As such, determining the status of the detainees is a procedure upon which the application of the correct framework of legal protection of rights depends. Other rights, such as the rights to be informed of the reasons for arrest or detention or to challenge the legitimacy of detention, logically depend on this first step – the establishment of the reasons for detention. Moreover the foregoing question as to lawfulness of detention are to some degree intertwined with questions as to status, as the grounds justifying detention of civilians differ from those relating to the detention of combatants.

In respect of status determinations, several points are worthy of emphasis in this context. First, the status of prisoners (and the corresponding rights to be afforded to them) are *legal* questions to be determined according to the rules of international law. The decision to afford particular status to prisoners is not itself a matter for executive, or military, discretion. There can, of course, be no discretion to go beyond or discard the law.[137]

Second, the determination of the status of individuals (and closely related to it, the lawfulness of detention) must be made on an *individual* case by case basis. If persons have been detained *en masse*, absent any individual assessment at any stage as to the reasons for detention of particular individuals, this detention necessarily falls foul of the principle of legality and is arbitrary.

The third and critical point relates to process. The Inter-American Commission on Human Rights[138] emphasised, in a letter to the

---

[137] See above for a statement by the US President that 'to the extent appropriate and consistent with military necessity' the detainees would be treated 'in a manner consistent with the principles of the Geneva Conventions of 1949'. Letter to the Speaker of the House of Representatives and the President Pro of the Senate, 20 September 2002.

[138] The Inter-American Commission on Human Rights is an organ of the Organisation of American States, of which the United States is a member.

United States government concerning the Guantanamo detainees that:

> the importance of ensuring the availability of *effective and fair mechanisms* for determining the status of individuals falling under the authority and control of a state, as it is upon the determination of this status that the rights and protections under domestic and international law to which those persons may be entitled depend.

The Commission therefore requested that the United States:

> take the urgent measures necessary to have the legal status of the detainees at Guantanamo Bay determined by a competent Tribunal.

This requirement of 'fair and effective mechanisms' to determine fundamental questions that affect individual rights is reflected throughout human rights law.[139] It is also manifest in IHL, including in Article 5 GC III, which provides that in case of doubt as to whether detainees might be entitled to be treated as POWs, the matter must be determined by a 'competent tribunal'. This customary principle of international law[140] has been long recognised by United States officials,[141] as well as in United States military regulations[142] and practice.[143]

Serious doubts as to whether the denial of POW status to some of those persons defined as 'enemy combatants' (including members of the Taleban) is consistent with GC III have been expressed above.[144] The US authorities have, however, denied that any 'doubt' exists as to the status of detainees or the question whether any of them have been wrongfully denied POW status. Somewhat paradoxically, it supports this proposition

---

[139] The Commission referred to 'numerous international instruments, including Article XVIII of the American Declaration' by which the United States is bound. See judicial oversight, below.

[140] Most of the provisions of GC III are considered to be reflective of customary international law. See ICJ, Advisory Opinion on *Nuclear Weapons*, paras. 79, 82. See also R. Baxter, 'Multilateral Treaties as Evidence of Customary International Law', 41 (1965–66) BYIL 275, at p. 286.

[141] Matheson, 'United States Position on the Relation of Customary International Law'.

[142] Joint Service Regulation on Enemy Prisoners of War, Retained Personnel, Civilian Internees and Other Detainees (1 October 1997), Chapters 1–6 (a) and (b), in *Department of the Army, the Navy, the Air Force and the Marine Corps*, Washington DC (1997) at p. 2.

[143] See Directive Number 20–5 of 15 March 1968, 'Inspections and Investigations of War – Determination of Eligibility', in C. Bevans (Assistant Legal Adviser, Department of State) and Sibler J (Office of the General Counsel, Department of Defense), *Contemporary Practice of the United States Relating to International Law*, 62 (1968) AJIL 754 at 768.

[144] See 'Entitlement to POW status', above.

on the basis that 'the President's determination that Taleban detainees do not qualify as POWs is conclusive . . . and removes any doubt that would trigger the application of the Convention's tribunal requirement'.[145] As with any legal standard, the existence of doubt must be assessed with a degree of objectivity and not according to the exclusive determination of the power potentially affected by it. The widespread debate and speculation around status, and conflicting views even from within the US administration itself as to POW entitlement,[146] leaves little room for debate that there exists at least 'doubt' as to the correct status of certain detainees in question, which should be resolved in accordance with the procedure set out in the Third Geneva Convention.[147]

IHL is not prescriptive as to the precise process to be followed in determining status. The executive and military hence enjoy certain discretion to decide on how best to make this determination. However, the principle of supervision by a 'tribunal' in the event of doubt enshrined in Article 5 provides a basic safeguard of objective impartial determination of the question. The ICRC Commentaries make clear that a unilateral executive or military determination of status is insufficient.[148] The official US view that the question of status is an 'eminently military one', thus not susceptible to external oversight, is therefore inconsistent with this basic requirement. As one US spokesperson reportedly noted in relation to the dispute regarding status: 'This has to go to a court because it is a legal decision not a political one.'[149] Moreover, the Supreme Court has rejected the notion that matters which are essentially 'military' are therefore beyond supervision: 'the allowable limits of military discretion and whether or not they have been overstepped in a particular case are judicial questions'.[150]

While Article 5 relates only to determinations regarding prisoner of war status, it may be seen, not as a provision in a vacuum, but as a

---

[145] Argument of the United States government before the Supreme Court in *Hamdi* v. *Rumsfeld* (Case 03–6696), Supreme Court Certiorari to the United States Court of Appeals for the Fourth Circuit, 28 June 2004, referred to in the partially dissenting opinion of Souter J and Ginsburg J p. 12.

[146] See, e.g., 'Memorandum for the President', note 99 above.

[147] The Inter-American Commission has referred to 'well-known . . . doubts . . . as to the legal status of the detainees' in its *Request for Precautionary Measures in Guantanamo Bay, Cuba*, addressed to the Government of the United States of America on 13 March 2002.

[148] ICRC Commentary on AP I, Part III, Section II: Combatant and prisoner-of-war status, paras. 1745–6.

[149] Richard Waddington, 'Guantanamo inmates are POWs Despite Bush View', ICRC, Reuters, 9 February 2002 cited in *Rasul* brief, p. 52.

[150] *Hamdi* v. *Rumsfeld*, above, note 145, Supreme Court Judgment, p. 28.

manifestation of a general principle that fair mechanisms are essential if the rights contained in IHL are to be given meaningful practical effect.[151] The principle of fair process is also reflected in Article 78 GC IV relating to the detention of civilians, which specifically establishes periodic review and the right of appeal.[152] In accordance with the request from the Inter-American Commission, it may be that objective mechanisms should be invoked where any dispute as to status arises that impacts on the rights to be afforded to the persons, as has been the case with the Guantanamo detainees.[153] Moreover, it may be that experience since 9/11 illustrates the need to address how to make existing mechanisms more effective, for example safeguarding the application of the Article 5 tribunal requirement, perhaps – for example – by expanding it to include an international component.[154]

The US failure to meet the requirement of Article 5 continued beyond the establishment of the so-called 'Combatant Status Review Tribunals' in July 2004. Despite its name, as noted above, this procedure provides

[151] Given the criteria for establishing POW status, it may be that this issue was thought to be the one most likely to give rise to dispute that may require resolution by a suitably qualified and objective body, as well as one of the issues most likely to impact on the rights afforded to the person in captivity, given the enhanced rights due to POWs over other categories of prisoners. If, however, other issues, such as whether persons are entitled to civilian status, were to arise in a manner that significantly impacted on the rights to be afforded, the same principle that underlies Article 5 may be argued to apply.

[152] See Articles 43 and 78 GC IV (which are similar, with the latter applying to detentions during occupation): decisions to detain civilians for imperative security reasons must be 'made according to a regular procedure'. Such procedure 'shall include the right of appeal for the parties concerned' and 'Appeals shall be decided with the least possible delay.' Moreover, in the event of the decision on 'detention' being upheld, such decision shall be subject to periodical review, if possible every six months, by a competent body set up by the detaining power. The services of the ICRC must also be accepted (Article 143(5)). On these standards see H.-P. Gasser, 'Protection of the Civilian Population', in D. Fleck, *The Handbook of Humanitarian Law in Armed Conflicts* (Oxford, 1995), p. 209, especially at pp. 288–9.

[153] The right to be heard by a competent impartial tribunal where one's rights are at stake is part of international human rights law – see Article 14, ICCPR, Article 8 American Declaration on the Rights and Duties of Man, Article 8 American Convention on Human Rights and Article 6 ECHR.

[154] See H. Duffy, 'Report of the Working Group on Detention', paper presented at the 27th Round Table on Current Problems of International Humanitarian Law, 'International Humanitarian Law and other Legal Regimes: Interplay in Situations of Violence', Sanremo, 4–6 September 2003 (hereinafter '2003 Sanremo Round Table on IHL'), reporting on a presentation by Hans Peter Gasser. The proceedings of the Round Table will be published in G. L. Beruto and G. Ravasi (eds.), *27th Round Table on Current Problems of International Humanitarian Law; Sanremo, 4–6 September 2003; 'International Humanitarian and other legal regimes: interplay in situations of violence'* (Milan, forthcoming).

individuals with a limited opportunity to challenge whether they fall within the 'enemy combatant' category, not to determine their correct status under international law, such as entitlement to POW status. This question has been 'pre-determined' by the US president. As the 'enemy combatant' label potentially embraces within its reach a range of persons, some entitled to POW status and others civilians, including some who may have committed crimes for which they should lawfully be detained and prosecuted, the process is of little legal significance.

8B.4.3 Information on reasons for arrest and detention

It follows from the requirement that there be clear reasons for an arrest, provided in law, and from the duty to determine the prisoners' status, that information concerning these matters should be conveyed to the prisoners themselves. Only once this has happened can they assert the precise rights that correspond to them under international law. The right to such information is enshrined as one of the minimal standards of protection due to persons in the hands of the enemy under IHL and in human rights law.[155]

Article 75(3) of AP I provides that:

> Any person arrested, detained or interned for actions related to the armed conflict shall *be informed promptly, in a language he understands, of the reasons why these measures have been taken.* Except in cases of arrest or detention for penal offences, such persons shall be released with the minimum delay possible and in any event as soon as the circumstances justifying the arrest, detention or internment have ceased to exist.[156]

The right to be informed promptly of the reasons for detention under IHL thus applies to persons detained for any reason related to the conflict – it does not depend on the person being suspected of a criminal offence.

There is no precise time frame associated with the requirement of 'promptness', as account must be taken of all the circumstances including (for as long as relevant) military considerations arising out of the detention of persons in the zone of battle.[157] However, as the ICRC Commentary to the Additional Protocol itself makes clear, 'even in time of armed conflict, detaining a person for longer than, say, ten days, without

---

[155] Article 9(2) ICCPR.   [156] Emphasis added.
[157] This requirement should be interpreted in the light of human rights law. See the approach taken to promptness of judicial review of detention, below.

informing the detainee of the reasons for his detention would be contrary to this paragraph' (Article 75(3)).

Under IHRL also, detainees must be informed promptly of the reasons for their arrest and detention, as set forth in Article 9(2) of the ICCPR. As with the IHL protection in Article 75(3), this applies to all detainees, not only those held pursuant to the suspected commission of a criminal offence.[158] The Paris Standards, for example, include the right to know the reasons for the detention within seven days as a 'minimum right' of the detainee. Provided that the essence of the right is respected, the Paris Standards note that:

> disclosure of such facts in support of the grounds as the detaining authority considers to be prejudicial to the public interest need not be made to the detainee, without prejudice to the power of the reviewing authority in its discretion to examine *in camera* such facts if it considers it necessary in the interests of justice.[159]

The detainees therefore have a right to be informed of the reasons for their arrest under the minimum rules of IHL protection applicable to all persons and under human rights law.

Following their detention, neither individual detainees nor their families were informed of the reasons for their detention, beyond a general statement that the detainees are enemy combatants and dangerous to the national security of the United States or its allies. Enquiries seeking further information met with little response.[160] The nascent Combatant Status Review Tribunals, described by the Department of Defense as providing the detainee with 'an opportunity to review unclassified information relating to the basis for his detention', may represent a step forward in this respect. It remains to be seen whether they will operate in a way that ensures detainees reasonable access to information. This procedure may prove to be too little to safeguard this right, and it is indisputably too late; almost three years after the Guantanamo detentions began, the

---

[158] For example, the Human Rights Committee has noted that 'if so-called preventive detention is used, for reasons of public security, it must be controlled by these same provisions [of Article 9], i.e. it must not be arbitrary, and must be based on grounds and procedures established by law (para. 1), *information of the reasons must be given* (para. 2), and *court control* of the detention must be available (para. 4)'. See Human Rights Committee, General Comment No. 8: Right to liberty and security of the person (Article 9) [1982], UN Doc. HRI/GEN/1/Rev.6 (2003) at 130, para. 4.

[159] The UN Body of Principles similarly includes this right, as one guaranteed to persons under any form of detention (Principle 10).

[160] See, e.g., the letter from the United States embassy in London to solicitors acting for Abbasi, above, note 25.

obligations to provide prompt and timely information concerning reasons for detention have not been met, on even the most flexible approach to these standards.

8B.4.4 Judicial oversight of detention

IHRL enshrines the rights to be brought promptly before a court upon arrest[161] and to challenge the lawfulness of arrest and continued detention.[162] Under that body of law, judicial review of all forms of detention by a judicial body is guaranteed as a fundamental right in itself and a safeguard against violation of other rights. The Human Rights Committee has noted accordingly that procedural guarantees, including 'judicial guarantees'[163] and the right to 'a remedy' in respect of violations[164] remain effective notwithstanding serious security concerns or the existence of a national emergency.[165]

The jurisprudence of the European Court of Human Rights is instructive in this respect, given its considerable experience in considering the compatibility of counter-terrorist measures with fundamental human rights standards under the European Convention on Human Rights (which for present purposes is substantively the same as the ICCPR). On several occasions it has acknowledged that 'the investigation of terrorist offences undoubtedly presents the authorities with special problems'.[166]

With regard to promptness of judicial supervision, the European Court of Human Rights has shown some flexibility in allowing longer lapses of time in extreme security situations than would otherwise be permissible. There is no precise formula for the length of time envisaged by the requirement of promptness, as all the circumstances must be taken into account. In this respect battlefield logistics and the need to transfer detainees from one location to another[167] may be compelling factors contributing to delay

---

[161] See, e.g., Article 9(3) ICCPR; Article 7(5) ACHR; Article 5(3) ECHR; Article 59(2) ICC Statute.

[162] See, e.g., Article 9(4) ICCPR; Article 25 American Declaration of the Rights and Duties of Man; Article 7(6) ACHR; Article 5(4) ECHR.

[163] General Comment No. 29, paras. 11, 13 and 15.

[164] Article 2(3) ICCPR.   [165] General Comment No. 29, para. 14.

[166] *Aksoy* v. *Turkey* (Appl. No. 21987/93), Judgment of 18 December 1996, ECtHR, *Reports* 1996-VI, para. 78.

[167] In *Koster* v. *The Netherlands* (Appl. No. 12843/87), Judgment of 28 November 1991, ECtHR, *Series A*, No. 221, the claim that military maneuvers prevented the detainee from being brought before a military court for five days was rejected. It was noted, however, that some allowance should be made for the military context, although in that case the military court could have sat sooner, if necessary on Saturday or Sunday (para. 25). See also McBride, 'Study on Principles', above, note 80, para. 45.

immediately following arrest, but presumably not to the on-going denial of judicial supervision several thousand miles away and several years later.

However, this flexibility is subject to limits and premised on the satisfaction of certain conditions. First, the state has to demonstrate valid reasons as to why it cannot 'process' suspects any earlier. Second, the permissibility of extended periods without judicial oversight a) depends on the existence of other attendant safeguards absent in the present case, and b) has never been deemed permissible for such prolonged (still less indefinite) periods of detention as are involved in the present situation.[168] Detention without judicial supervision for twelve to fourteen days[169] and for four days and six hours[170] have been deemed excessive, while in one case (concerning the United Kingdom which was found to have validly derogated on account of a state of emergency) seven days was found permissible.[171] However, this was on the basis of the other attendant safeguards for the detainee, including the essential right to access counsel, discussed below.

With regard to the right to challenge the lawfulness of arrest, or the right of *habeas corpus*, human rights jurisprudence from national and international courts and bodies confirms straightforwardly that this is a fundamental right that must be respected at all times. As the English Court of Appeals noted in relation to the Guantanamo detainees, 'the recognition of this basic protection in both English and American law long pre-dates the adoption of the same principle as a fundamental part of international human rights law'.[172] The UN Human Rights Committee has clarified that 'the principles of legality and the rule of law require that . . . in order to protect non-derogable rights, the right to take proceedings before a court to enable the court to decide without delay on the

---

[168] See, e.g., *Chahal* v. *United Kingdom* (Appl. No. 22414/93), Judgment of 15 November 1996, ECtHR, *Reports* 1996-V, paras. 131, 132: 'the Court considers that neither the proceedings for habeas corpus and for judicial review of the decision to detain Mr Chahal before the domestic courts, nor the advisory panel procedure, satisfied the requirements of Article 5(4) . . . This shortcoming is all the more significant given that Mr Chahal has undoubtedly been deprived of his liberty for a length of time [more than three years] which is bound to give rise to serious concern.'

[169] *Aksoy* v. *Turkey*, para. 78. See also *Sakik and Others* v. *Turkey* (App. Nos. 23878/94–23883/94), Judgment of 26 November 1997, ECtHR, *Reports* 1997-VIII.

[170] *Brogan* v. *United Kingdom* (Appl. No. 11209/84), Judgment of 29 November 1988, ECtHR, *Series A*, No. 145. There was no derogation in force in respect of this case.

[171] *Brannigan and McBride* v. *United Kingdom* (App. Nos. 14553/89; 14554/89), Judgment of 25 May 1993, ECtHR, *Series A*, No. 258. The Court found that there was a valid derogation in force.

[172] *Abbasi*, para. 63.

lawfulness of the detention must not be diminished by a State party's decision to derogate from the Covenant'.[173] As the Committee noted, it is precisely in such exceptional emergency situations that judicial supervision assumes greatest importance.[174] The Inter-American Court on Human Rights has recognised that *habeas corpus* is one of 'the judicial guarantees essential for the protection of [non-derogable] rights', and as such is itself non-derogable.[175]

The fact that IHL also recognises the principle of independent oversight of essential questions concerning rights protection in conflict was discussed above, in the context of the right to have one's status determined by a competent tribunal and review of administrative detention.[176] Were there to be any such proceedings, depending on their nature (if for example they involved bringing the person before a court[177] and the opportunity to present arguments as to the lawfulness of the arrest), they may satisfy the various requirements of judicial oversight of the lawfulness of detention under IHRL.[178] The majority decision of the Supreme Court, in a case concerning a US citizen denied *habeas corpus* in respect of his detention in the US, referred to the 'possibility' that the convening of 'an appropriately authorised and properly constituted' Article 5 tribunal could meet the standards required of *habeas* proceedings, although a dissenting opinion cautions against the idea that 'an opportunity to litigate before a military tribunal might obviate or truncate enquiry by a court on habeas'.[179]

The Guantanamo detainees have been subject to no judicial process, in many cases years after their transfer to the US naval base. The Presidential Military Order authorising their detention specifically excludes the right

---

[173] General Comment No. 29, para. 16.

[174] General Comment No. 29, above, note 70, para. 12.

[175] IACtHR, *Habeas Corpus in Emergency Situations*, paras. 35–6.

[176] See Article 5 GC III and Articles 42 and 78 GC IV. While the 'regular procedure' for handling decisions on administrative detention involves a right to be heard, this is not necessarily by a judicial body. However the duty of periodic review and the right to appeal must be to a court or independent administrative body; see Gasser, 'Protection of the Civilian Population', p. 289.

[177] Note that the ECtHR stated that it was not enough to have access to a judicial authority since 'the judge or judicial officer must actually hear the detained person and take the appropriate decision'. See *Duinhof and Duijf* v. *The Netherlands* (Appl. No: 9626/81, 9736/82), Judgment of 4 May 1984, ECtHR, *Series A*, No. 79, para. 36.

[178] The requirement of promptness for example has been violated in respect of those prisoners already held for several months. A court or tribunal could, however, in the future be established in a way that would charge it with considering the status of prisoners, and the lawfulness of their arrest.

[179] *Hamdi* v. *Rumsfeld*, above, note 145.

to judicial challenge, declaring that 'the individual shall not be privileged to seek any remedy or maintain any proceeding, directly or indirectly, or to have any such remedy or proceeding sought on the individual's behalf, in (i) any court of the United States, or any State thereof, (ii) any court of any foreign nation, or (iii) any international tribunal'.[180] While the US Supreme Court judgment provides some hope, the fact remains that attempts to secure judicial supervision and to challenge the lawfulness of detention have thus far failed.

Moreover, the procedures that have been introduced, belatedly, following the Supreme Court decision, are insufficient to satisfy these rights. They do not allow an opportunity to challenge the lawfulness of detention. The status review tribunal, for example, is not competent to determine whether detentions are lawful, but only the much more limited question whether detainees meet the 'enemy combatant' definition set forth by the Department of Defense.[181] The annual review board addresses whether certain other criteria are met, although as described above, even if they are, these criteria cannot justify lawful detention and the review board does not appear to be competent to decide the broader question of the lawfulness of detention.

The 'military procedures' are, in any event, non-judicial and their rules of procedure deny access to counsel and limit access to information. It is therefore doubtful whether, in these respects also, the procedures would be sufficient to satisfy the requirements of either international law or the Supreme Court judgments in terms of providing 'meaningful' opportunity to challenge the lawfulness of detention.[182] Whatever their intended

---

[180] Presidential Military Order, Section 7(b)(i).

[181] See the Department of Defense Combatant Status Review Tribunals Order, 7 July 2004 (available at http://www.defenselink.mil/news/Jul2004/d20040707review.pdf). Even within the limited scope of the tribunal, it is noted that the procedure offers little meaningful opportunity to challenge even one's designation as an 'enemy combatant', given factors such as the lack of a right to counsel and limited access to relevant information.

[182] Although not a case concerning the Guantanamo detainees, in the *Hamdi* v. *Rumsfeld* case, above note 177, concerning the right of the US citizen to challenge lawfulness in a court of law, the Supreme Court sets down minimum requirements that must be met for judicial oversight: these involve the detainee having 'a meaningful opportunity to contest the factual basis for that detention before a neutral decisionmaker', p.1; the detainee having notice of the grounds for his detention and an opportunity to be heard at a 'meaningful time and in a meaningful manner', p. 26; and the detainee 'unquestionably' having 'the right to access to counsel', p. 32. For analysis of compatibility, see Human Rights First, Security Detainees/Enemy Combatants, note 56 above.

purpose, they cannot impede or preclude the access to civilian courts mandated by the US Supreme Court.

Several years after their detention, none of the detainees have had any judicial review of their detention, providing the clearest manifestation of the arbitrariness of their detention, described by the English Court of Appeals in the following terms:

> in apparent contravention of fundamental principles recognised by both [US and English] jurisdictions and by international law, Mr Abbasi is at present arbitrarily detained in a 'legal black-hole' . . . What appears to us to be objectionable is that Mr Abbasi should be subject to indefinite detention in territory over which the United States has exclusive control with no opportunity to challenge the legitimacy of his detention before any court or tribunal.[183]

8B.4.5 Prosecution – fair trial rights

In respect of each potential category of prisoner, this section summarises who can be prosecuted for which crimes, then explores the fair trial rights to which they are entitled and compares briefly these standards and the military commission procedures in operation in Guantanamo Bay.

As noted above, the legal status of a prisoner impacts on the legitimacy of prosecuting that detainee for certain crimes related to the conflict. Specifically, if detainees were formerly privileged combatants (entitled to be treated as POWs), they may not be prosecuted for acts of war, while those unprivileged combatants, who fought absent the right to do so, may. All categories of prisoner, however, may equally be prosecuted for the commission of international crimes such as war crimes or crimes against humanity.[184]

GC III provides that any POW subject to judicial proceedings is entitled to a fair trial.[185] So seriously are these rights taken that 'wilfully depriving a prisoner of war of the rights of fair and regular trial prescribed in this Convention' is a grave breach, which states parties are obliged to prosecute.[186] For civilians who are subject to penal sanction, GC IV requires respect for the basic 'judicial guarantees generally recognised as indispensable'[187]

---

[183] *Abbasi*, para. 64. The decisions to which the Court referred are subject to appeal. The judgment therefore noted that '[i]t is important to record that the position may change when the appellate courts in the United States consider the matter'.

[184] Indeed international law recognises the obligation on states to prosecute for such egregious crimes. See Chapter 4.

[185] See Articles 82–8 and 99–107 GC III.

[186] Article 130 GC IV.   [187] Article 72 GC IV.

and notes that 'the trial and sentence must take place in accordance with the provisions [on due process] of Article 64 and those that follow it'.[188] By way of minimum standard for any person not falling into the above categories, Article 75(4) AP I provides:

> (a) ... for an accused to be informed without delay of the particulars of the offence alleged against him and shall afford the accused before and during his trial all necessary rights and means of defence.[189]

Basic due process rights are therefore provided for under IHL for all categories of detainee. The interpretation of certain of these rights, such as the content to be associated with the right to 'all necessary rights and means of defence' should be interpreted in the light of human rights law, which provides, in greater detail, the fair trial rights to be afforded to any person who may be subject to criminal proceedings.

Under IHRL, the right to a fair trial contained in the Universal Declaration of Human Rights[190] was fleshed out in notable detail by Article 14 of the International Covenant on Civil and Political Rights. Certain aspects of the right – for example the right to a 'public' trial – are explicitly subject to restriction to the extent that genuine reasons of public security or protection of witnesses so require.[191] Others – such as the right to trial without 'undue delay' – enshrine an inherent flexibility that has regard to all circumstances, including peculiarities of armed conflict.[192] However, basic fair trial rights apply in all circumstances. As the Human Rights Committee has noted, the 'principles of legality and the rule of law require that *fundamental requirements of fair trial* must be respected

---

[188] ICRC Commentary on GC IV, p. 50, and Article 126.

[189] Common Article 3 further provides that persons taking no part in hostilities (including persons who once did but who are *hors de combat*, or have otherwise laid down their arms), are 'entitled to certain judicial guarantees generally recognised as indispensable'.

[190] Article 10 provides that '[e]veryone is entitled in full equality to a fair and public hearing by an independent and impartial tribunal, in the determination of ... any criminal charge against him'.

[191] The ECtHR has found that security considerations do not justify a failure to hold a trial in public, particularly as measures can be taken to accommodate security concerns, such as preventing the identity of witnesses becoming known to the public. See, e.g., *Doorson* v. *Netherlands*, ECtHR judgment of 26 March 1996 and *Van Mechelen* v. *Netherlands*, ECtHR judgment of 23 April 1997.

[192] 'The difficulty in bringing someone to trial because of conflict and disturbance would be a legitimate consideration in assessing the reasonableness of the length of any pre-trial detention but there would still be a need to demonstrate that continued efforts were being made to hold the proceedings.' Council of Europe Expert Study, para. 45. However (as discussed above), the relevance of factors such as battlefield logistics have diminished, if not vanished, years and miles from the original zone of battle.

during a state of emergency'.[193] Likewise, the Inter-American court has included 'minimum due process rights' as guarantees applicable in states of emergency.[194] A Council of Europe study notes that:

> [w]hile the ordinary system of criminal justice is subject to considerable strain during situations of conflict . . . there is no scope for compromise in the need to provide a fair procedure.[195]

A plethora of issues arise regarding the compatibility of the military commissions with the requirements of IHRL. For example, consistent with the principle of legality, persons can only be prosecuted for acts that constituted, at the time of their commission, crimes clearly defined in law. The substantive jurisdiction of the military commissions, by contrast, has been criticised for its breadth and uncertainty: 'war crimes', for example, are prosecuted despite serious doubts as to the 'armed conflict' threshold having been met.[196] Among the most fundamental human rights is the presumption of innocence, reflected in human rights bodies[197] and IHL.[198] In this respect, the fact that the President of the United States has on numerous occasions said of the detainees, collectively, that '[t]hese are killers – these are terrorists', exemplifies the concerns arising.[199] Respect for the basic right to defend oneself in a meaningful way is also subject to

---

[193] General Comment No. 29, para. 16.

[194] *Judicial Guarantees in States of Emergency (Arts. 27(2), 25 and 8 of the American Convention on Human Rights)*, Advisory Opinion OC-9/87 of 6 October 1987, IACtHR, *Series A*, No. 9 (1987).

[195] McBride, 'Study on Principles', above, note 77, para. 40.

[196] See, e.g., charges brought against the four persons whose trials by military commission began in August 2004, available at http://www.defenselink.mil/news/Feb2004 and http://www.defenselink.mil/news/Jul2004. Charges include e.g., 'war crimes', without a clear link to an armed conflict situation: they cover not only crimes committed in the armed conflict in Afghanistan but apparently also action in other states over a period of, in some cases, several years, presumably pursuant to the broader war allegedly waged against al-Qaeda (see Chapter 6, para. 6B.1.1, 'Armed Conflict and "Terrorist Groups of Global Reach"'). The Commission's jurisdiction has been criticised as 'overbroad' and as lowering the threshold of armed conflict to cover isolated incidents: see 'Trials Under Military Order: a Guide to the Final Rules for Military Commissions', Human Rights First, updated August 2004, available at www.humanrightsfirst.org, p.2. Note also potential scope of crimes such as 'aiding the enemy', charged in the case of Australian David Hicks; see http://www.defenselink.mil/news/Feb2004 and Human Rights First, *ibid.*, p.13.

[197] General Comment No. 29, above, note 63, para. 11.   [198] Article 75(3)(d) AP I.

[199] Statement of President Bush, 20 March 2002, reported in Amnesty International, 'Memorandum to the US Government on the rights of people in US custody in Afghanistan and Guantánamo Bay', 15 April 2002, AI Index 51/053/2002. See also the statement of President Bush reported above, note 27. See also the role of the President under the Military Order, para. 8B.4.5.1 below.

question in light of certain characteristics of these commissions, including limited access to information and evidence, and indeed limitations on the right to be present at parts of the accused's own trial.[200] It is doubtful also whether certain rules of evidence inherent in the essence of the right to a fair trial, precluding, for example, reliance on confessions or other evidence obtained in circumstances where rights were seriously compromised, will be respected.[201]

Moreover, the imposition of the death penalty other than pursuant to a process that meets the fair trial requirements of IHRL has been recognised as an arbitrary deprivation of the right to life. If the death penalty is invoked, as provided for in the Military Order, a violation of fair trial rights may also give rise to other violations, notably the right to life.[202]

Three additional specific issues which have caused particular concern are addressed in more detail below, namely the right to trial by an 'independent and impartial' tribunal, access to counsel and the right of appeal.

8B.4.5.1 Military commissions and the right to trial before an independent and impartial tribunal

Resort to military commissions to prosecute the Guantanamo detainees has, in and of itself, raised considerable controversy, on account of apparent inconsistency with various aspects of applicable IHL and IHRL. First, a particular issue arises under IHL in respect of the rules governing

---

[200] Secret evidence can be employed, during which time the accused cannot attend his trial, though his military lawyer may do so. The accused will not have access to 'protected information' (which is broadly defined and may go beyond 'classified' information), and while the military lawyer must see all incriminating evidence, there is no obligation to disclose to the accused or his counsel all exculpatory evidence if national security might be implicated. See Military Commission Order No. 1, Section 7 (B).

[201] Evidence obtained through torture or inhuman treatment should be inadmissible, whereas, e.g., evidence obtained in breach of the right to respect for private life under Article 8 may still be used in a prosecution so long as, in all the circumstances, this would not make the trial unfair. The latter is likely to be so where there are doubts about the voluntariness of any admission (see *Allan* v. *United Kingdom* (Appl. No. 48539/99), Judgment of 5 November 2002, Reports 2002-IX) or there are reasons to doubt the authenticity of the evidence concerned (*Khan* v. *United Kingdom* (Appl. No. 35394/97), Judgment of 12 May 2000, Reports 2000-V). See also *Singharasa* v. *Sri Lanka*, Communication No. 1033/2001, Human Rights Committee, Views of 23/08/2004, UN Doc. CCPR/C/81/D/1033/2001.

[202] Article 6(1) ICCPR prohibits the arbitrary deprivation of life and Article 6(2) explicitly requires that any imposition of the death penalty is subject to certain requirements, *inter alia*, that it is imposed by a competent court in a manner that is 'not contrary to the provisions of the present Covenant'. See Chapter 7. It may also amount to inhuman or degrading treatment: see *Öcalan* v. *Turkey* (Appl. No. 46221/99), Merits, Judgment of 12 March 2003, unreported.

prisoners of war. According to GC III, POWs 'can be validly sentenced only if the sentence has been pronounced by the same courts according to the same procedure as in the case of members of the armed forces of the Detaining Power, and if, further more, the provisions of this present chapter have been applied'. The Military Order explicitly excludes US citizens from the jurisdictional reach of the Military Commissions, and US armed forces would be subject to the Uniform Code of Military Justice, which provides in some detail for the protection of rights denied to the detainees in the current situation.[203] As controversy surrounds the status of at least certain detainees, and they are entitled as a matter of law to be presumed POWs until their status has been determined by the requisite competent tribunal,[204] it would appear that recourse to such tribunals is a violation of the GC III obligations.

Beyond the question of disparities in treatment between POWs and others, a question of more broad-reaching effect is whether the Commissions are 'competent independent and impartial tribunal[s] established by law',[205] that meet the fair trial guarantees to which all prisoners are entitled. In other contexts the US itself has criticised the use of military courts on the basis that 'they do not ensure civilian defendants due process before an independent tribunal'.[206] Human rights bodies have consistently

---

[203] See, for instance, Articles 66 and 67 of the US Uniform Code of Military Justice, that provide for two levels of appellate review, the second to the US Court of Appeals for the Armed Force, which is composed of civilian judges. The accused may then seek review by the US Supreme Court through a petition for a writ of *certiorari*. For a comparison of the procedural guarantees set forth by the US Uniform Code of Military Justice and by the Rules for Courts-Martials with those afforded to the defendants before the Military Commission established after 9/11, see Human Rights Watch, 'Due Process Protections Afforded Defendants: A Comparison between the Proposed U.S. Military Commissions and U.S. General Courts-Martial', 17 December 2001, available at http://www.hrw.org/press/2001/12/miltribchart1217.htm.

[204] Article 5(2) GC III.

[205] See R. Goldman and D. Orentlicher, 'When Justice goes to War, Prosecuting Persons before Military Commissions', 25 *Harvard Journal of Law and Public Policy* 653 at 659, noting, *inter alia*, that so far as the Commissions allow for trial of civilians they are 'utterly inconsistent' with 'human rights instruments' and that 'Human rights instruments binding on the United States mandate that criminal defendants, whatever their offenses, be tried by independent and impartial courts that afford generally recognised due process guarantees.' The authors conclude that '[b]y their very nature, military commissions do not satisfy this basic test', at 659–60. See also A. Neier, 'Unjust, Unwise, Unamerican', *The Economist*, 12 July 2003, p. 9.

[206] See, e.g., the criticism of the use of military tribunals contained in the report of the State Department on the human rights record of Peru (US Department of State, Bureau of Democracy, Human Rights, and Labor, *1999 Country Reports on Human Rights Practices*, 25 February 2000).

found the use of military courts to try civilians in Guatemala,[207] Peru,[208] Chile,[209] Uruguay[210] and elsewhere to violate fundamental due process rights.[211] The Working Group on Arbitrary Detention has expressed concern that 'virtually none of them respects the guarantees of a fair trial'.[212]

In the context of the Guantanamo detainees, various independent intergovernmental bodies and NGOs have expressed concern that use of military commissions jeopardises essential fair trial rights under human rights law.[213] The Special Rapporteur on the independence of judges and lawyers for example, expressed concerns in relation to the Military Order and the intended use of military tribunals.[214] Concern stems in large part from the lack of independence of such commissions from the executive branch and from the military.[215] In the words of British law lord, Lord Steyn: 'The

---

[207] See Inter-American Commission on Human Rights, *Report on the Situation of Human Rights in the Republic of Guatemala* (1983), OEA/Ser.L./V/II. 61, Doc. 47, at 96.

[208] Inter-American Commission on Human Rights, *Second Report on the Situation of Human Rights in Peru* (2000), OEA/Ser.L/V/II.106, Doc. 59 rev; see also *Castillo Petruzzi and others* v. *Peru*, Merits, Judgment of 30 May 1999, IACtHR, *Series C*, No. 52.

[209] See Comision Inter-Americana de Derechos Humanos; *Segundo Informe sobre la Situacion de los Derechos Humanos en Chile* (1976), OEA/Ser.L./V/II.37, Doc. 19.

[210] See Inter-American Commission on Human Rights, *Report on the Situation of Human Rights in Uruguay* (1978), OEA/Ser.L./V/II.43, Doc. 19; see also Human Rights Committee, *Moriana Hernandez Valentini de Bazzano* v. *Uruguay* (Comm. No. 5/1977), Views of 15 August 1979, UN Doc. CCPR/C/7/D/5/1977.

[211] See generally Chapter 7 and F.A. Guzman, *Fuero Militar y Derecho Internacional* (International Commission of Jurists, Bogotá, 2003).

[212] UN Doc. E/N.4/1996/40, p. 107.

[213] See, e.g., Amnesty International, 'USA: Military Commissions Bypass Fundamental Principles of Justice', AI Press Release, 20 March 2002: Human Rights Watch, 'U.S.: New Military Commissions Threaten Rights, Credibility', News Release, 15 November 2001 and 'U.S.: Commission Rules Meet Some, Not All, Rights Concerns', News Release, 21 March 2002.

[214] Letter dated 16 November 2001 to the United States, available at http://www.unog.ch/unog01/files/002_media/f2_cmq.html.

[215] *Ibid.* Human rights monitoring bodies have constantly expressed deep concern about the use of special tribunals or commissions: as noted by the Inter-American Court of Human Rights: 'A basic principle of the independence of the judiciary is that every person has the right to be heard by regular courts, following procedures previously established by law.' States are not to create '[t]ribunals that do not use the duly established procedures of the legal process . . . to displace the jurisdiction belonging to the ordinary courts or judicial tribunals' (*Castillo Petruzzi and others* v. *Peru*, above, paras. 130–1); see also the decision of the ECtHR in *Öcalan* v. *Turkey*, Merits (note 202, above), para. 114. Also the practice of having civilians tried by military tribunals and courts has been the object of strong criticism, as has the trial of certain serious human rights related offences. See, e.g., Concluding Observations of the Human Rights Committee: Uzbekistan, UN Doc. CCPR/CO/71/UZB (2001), para. 15; Concluding observations of the Human Rights Committee: Lebanon, UN Doc. CCPR/C/79/Add.78 (1997), para. 14; Concluding observations of the Human Rights Committee, Slovakia, UN Doc. CCPR/C/79/Add.79 (1997).

military will act as interrogators, prosecutors, defence counsel, judges, and when death sentences are imposed, as executioners', a situation he described as a 'monstrous failure of justice'.[216]

However, concerns relate also to specific aspects of the Commissions that fail to satisfy the requirement of due process, contained in IHL and IHRL. Among the most problematic issues, discussed below, are the limited right to access counsel and the absence of the right to appeal as such.

8B.4.5.2 Access to counsel

The assistance of a defence lawyer is a primary means of ensuring the protection of the fundamental rights of people suspected or accused of criminal offences, protected both under IHL and IHRL.

IHL provides, explicitly and implicitly, for access to counsel for persons suspected of having committed a criminal offence, irrespective of their status as POWs, civilians or persons entitled to the basic minima of human rights protection. The detailed rights afforded to POWs under GC III include the right to legal representation.[217] Likewise, among the due process rights afforded to civilians protected by GC IV is the right 'to be *assisted by a qualified advocate or counsel* of their own choice, who shall be able to visit them freely and shall enjoy the necessary facilities for preparing the defence'.[218]

The minimal standard set out in Article 75(4) provides simply for an accused: '(a) . . . to be informed without delay of the particulars of the offence alleged against him and shall afford the accused before and during his trial all necessary rights and means of defence'. The ICRC Commentary to AP I notes that 'all necessary means of defence' must be interpreted to include the right to communicate with a 'qualified defence lawyer'.[219] The right to 'all necessary rights and means of defence' provision explicitly applies 'before and during . . . trial', and should be interpreted in the light of human rights law which, as explained below, includes access to counsel from the early stages of detention as one of the core protections against abuse and arbitrariness.[220]

---

[216] Lord Steyn, 'Guantanamo Bay: The Legal Black Hole', Twenty-Seventh F. A. Mann Lecture, 25 November 2003.

[217] Article 84 GC III.   [218] Article 72 GC IV.

[219] ICRC Commentary on AP I, para. 3096: 'he must be able to understand the assistance given by a qualified defence lawyer. If these conditions were not fulfilled, the defendant would not have the benefit of all necessary rights of defence.'

[220] See para. 8.5.1, 'Rights Regarding Interrogation', below.

The right to consult counsel is explicit in the fair trial provisions of Article 14(d) ICCPR. The Human Rights Committee has noted that it operates from the earliest stages of detention and is a particularly important right at the time when individuals are to be subject to interrogation.[221] It is insufficient that counsel be afforded only at the trial, or immediate pre-trial stage.[222]

Likewise, paramount among the safeguards that the European Court of Human Rights has emphasised must be in place from the earliest stage of detention is the right to access a lawyer. In *Brannigan and McBride* the right to consult a lawyer within the first days of detention was an essential element in the decision that detention for one week without judicial review could, in exceptional circumstances, be justified. This was so notwithstanding the declared state of emergency in that case.[223]

The *Paris Standards*[224] include 'the right to communicate with, and consult, a lawyer of his own choice, at any time after detention' as a core right. The *UN Body of Principles* provides for the detainee's 'right to defend himself or to be assisted by counsel as prescribed by law', adding that 'communication of the detained or imprisoned person with the outside world, and in particular his family or counsel, shall not be denied for more than a matter of days'.[225]

The right under human rights law, reflected in some of the IHL provisions, is to counsel of choice,[226] safeguarding the essential relationship of trust between lawyer and client. There is, however, no objection in principle to the requirement of security clearance for lawyers providing advice and representation, provided their independence is not compromised and the right to a lawyer of choice is not entirely undermined, for example by exclusive use of lawyers from the armed forces.[227]

In Guantanamo Bay, detainees have been held and interrogated for prolonged periods without access to counsel. There is no right to consult

---

[221] See para. 8.5.1, below.

[222] The Human Rights Committee has stated that 'all persons who are arrested must immediately have access to counsel'. See Concluding observations of the Human Rights Committee: Georgia, UN Doc. CCPR/C/79/Add.74 (1997), para. 28.

[223] *Brannigan and McBride* v. *United Kingdom*, note 171 above, paras. 62 and 64.

[224] See Article 5.   [225] Principle 11.

[226] Article 14(3)(d) ICCPR. See also Principle 1 of the Basic Principles on the Role of Lawyers; Article 8(2)(d) of the ACHR; Article 6(3)(c) of the ECHR; Article 7(1)(c) of the ACHPR, Article 21(4)(d) of the ICTY Statute; Article 20(4)(d) of the ICTR Statute, Article 67(1)(d) of the ICC Statute. Under IHL, the right to choose one's defence lawyer is guaranteed by Article 105 GC III.

[227] See *Chahal* v. *United Kingdom*, above, note 168.

or be represented by a lawyer as part of either the Combatant Status Review Tribunals or Administrative Review Board procedures. Only the few detainees designated as subject to trial by military commission have any right to a lawyer at all, in apparent disregard of the safeguard requiring access to counsel from the earliest stages of detention, including during interrogation.

In the context of trial by military commission, Department of Defense rules of procedure provide for the right to be assisted by defence counsel.[228] However, it appears that the right of the accused to legal assistance of choice will not be sufficiently guaranteed by the rules of procedure. Those rules require that military lawyers approved by the US Department of Defense are appointed; while a civilian lawyer of choice may be added, his or her access to documents and participation in proceedings is limited.[229] The fact that the rules of procedure state that the defendants before the Military Commissions 'must be represented at all relevant times' by the military counsel, implies that defendants who have chosen to be represented by civilian lawyers will however be forced to retain military co-counsel against their wishes.[230]

The effective implementation of the right to consult counsel requires that counsel can 'communicate with the accused in conditions giving full respect for the confidentiality of their communications'.[231] Confidential consultation with his or her defence lawyers is as an essential aspect of the right of every defendant to prepare his or her defence.[232] By contrast, Military Order No. 3 of 5 February 2004 provides explicitly for the regulation and monitoring of lawyer–client communications.[233] Moreover, by implying that defendants who have chosen to be represented by civilian lawyers may be forced to also have military co-counsel present at all times, the procedure appears likely, as a matter of fact, to

---

[228] The rules of procedure provide that every accused shall be assigned a defense counsel, chosen by the Chief Defense Officer among the Judges Advocate of the United States Armed Forces (see Instruction No. 4, Section 3).

[229] See Instruction No. 4, Section 3.

[230] On this basis the Special Rapporteur on the independence of judges and lawyers has expressed concern regarding the absence in the Military Order establishing the Military Commissions of the right to legal representation and advice while in detention.

[231] Human Rights Committee, General Comment 13, para. 9.

[232] See, e.g., Article 8(2)(d) ACHR, Article 67(1)(b) of the ICC Statute; Principles 22 and 8 of the Basic Principles on the Role of Lawyers, Principle 18 of the Body of Principles for the Protection of All Persons under Any Form of Detention or Imprisonment.

[233] Department of Defense, Military Order No. 3, 5 February 2004, on 'Special Administrative Measures for Certain Communications Subject to Monitoring', available at http/www.defenselink.mil/news/Feb2004.

impede confidential communications between a detainee and his lawyer of choice.

8B.4.5.3 The right of appeal

The right to an appeal is inherent in the right to a fair trial.[234] This right is detailed in Article 14(5) ICCPR – which provides that 'everyone convicted of a crime shall have the right to his conviction and sentence being reviewed by a higher tribunal according to law' – and in other human rights and international criminal law instruments.[235]

The right ensures that each case will be subject to two levels of judicial inquiry. Review of a decision undertaken by the original trial judge will not discharge the obligation of Article 14(5).[236] Likewise, an executive – as opposed to judicial – review, will not satisfy the right to appeal which necessarily involves judicial oversight. The review by a higher independent and impartial tribunal must consider questions of both fact and law. The Human Rights Committee has underscored that judicial review without a hearing and on matters of law only falls short of the requirements of Article 14(5) to provide for a full evaluation of the evidence and conduct of the trial and, consequently, found a violation of the Article in this case.[237] The UN Special Rapporteur on extra-judicial, arbitrary and summary executions has also noted concern at the use of appeals procedures which only allow for an examination of the law and not the facts.[238]

---

[234] *Melin* v. *France* (Appl. No.12914/87), Judgment of 22 June 1993, ECtHR, *Series A*, No. 261. See also Human Rights Committee, *Mansaraj et al.*; *Gborie et al.*; and *Sesay et al.* v. *Sierra Leone* (Comm. Nos. 839, 840 and 841/1998), decision of 4 November 1998, UN Doc. CCPR/C/64/D/839, 840 and 841/1998 at paras. 2.1, 2.2, 5.6, 6.1 and 6.3.

[235] The right of a convicted person to have the conviction and sentence reviewed by a higher tribunal is present in regional human rights guarantees: Article 8(2)(h) of the American Convention, Article 2 of Protocol 7 to the European Convention, and Article 7(a) of the African Charter. This right is also articulated in the Statutes establishing the three major international criminal tribunals: Article 24 of the ICTY Statute, Article 23 of the ICTR Statute, Article 81(b) of the ICC Statute.

[236] *Salgar de Montejo* v. *Colombia* (Comm. No. 64/1979), views of 24 March 1982, UN Doc. CCPR/C/15/D/64/1979.

[237] See Human Rights Committee, *Domukovsky, Tsiklauri, Gelbekniani and Dokvadze* v. *Georgia* (Comm. Nos. 623, 624, 626 and 627/1995), Views adopted on 29 May 1998, UN Doc. CCPR/C/62/D/623/1995, at para. 18.11. See also *Gómez Vázquez* v. *Spain* (Comm. No. 701/1996), Views of 11 August 2000, UN Doc. CCPR/C/69/D/701/1996, where the Human Rights Committee found a violation of Article 14(5) where there was no right to review the factual account of a case as determined by a judge (paras. 3.1, 11.1 and 13).

[238] Report of the UN Special Rapporteur on extra-judicial, summary or arbitrary executions, 7 December 1993, UN Doc: E/CN.4/1994/7, at paras. 113 and 404.

The Military Commission's Rules provide that the verdicts of the Military Commissions will be submitted to automatic 'review' by a three-member 'Review Panel', consisting of three military officers appointed by the Secretary of Defense.[239] The panel will review trial findings and either provide a recommendation to the Secretary of Defense or return the case for further proceedings. The final review of every decision, however, lies with either the Secretary of Defense or the President.[240]

The review panel is not therefore a civilian court of appeal, by contrast to that provided for example in courts martial under the US Uniform Code of Military Justice.[241] Indeed section 7(b) of the Military Order precludes resort to such courts.[242] Moreover, the rules of procedure foreshadow what may transpire to be a summary procedure, by providing that the review panel is not obliged to review submissions by the defence, or the prosecution, and it has discretion whether to allow oral argument.[243]

In assessing the compatibility of the Military Order with this right, the terminology used – review as opposed to appeal – is not the critical question: the HRC has noted that there is no substantive difference between the terms 'appeal' and 'review'.[244] What matters is whether the action meets the Covenant's requirements by providing for a full review, by an independent and impartial judicial body, of the facts and law that gave rise to conviction and sentence.[245] Despite the 'review' process by those at the apex of the military chain of command, there is no substantive right to appeal from the military commissions. In this respect, the proceedings before the Military Commissions appear to violate, among other rights, the right of appeal under internationally accepted fair trial standards.[246]

---

[239] Section 6.H(4), DoD Military Commission Order, above.

[240] Under section 4(C)(8) of the Military Order the Secretary of Defense reviews the record of the proceedings for each case and delivers the final decision, without prejudice to the President's power to grant pardons or reprieves (section 7(a)(2)). According to the Presidential Military Order, the Military Commission Order expressly reserves the 'final review' of every decision to the US President or to the Secretary of Defense. See Section 4.C(8), Presidential Order; section 6.H(5) and (6) DoD Military Commission Order.

[241] On the right of Appeal to the Court of Appeals for the Armed Forces, staffed by a civilian panel outside the chain of command, see 10 USC Sections 867 and 942, in Human Rights First, 'Trials under Military Order', p. 4.

[242] Section 7(b)(i).

[243] Section 4(C)(3) and 4(C)(4)(b), DOD Military Commission Order.

[244] *Domukovsky, Tsiklauri, Gelbekniani and Dokvadze* v. *Georgia*, above, note 237.

[245] *Ibid.*

[246] It appears to also seek to preclude the right to a remedy, protected at all times under IHRL.

8B.5   Standards of protection compared: implications of POW status?

The foregoing demonstrates that basic rights relating to detention and fair trial apply to the Guantanamo detainees whether they are to be considered POWs, civilians or unlawful combatants not entitled to any greater protection under IHL. POW status, while undoubtedly significant in terms of the added protections that GC III affords to individuals, is not therefore essential to the protection of the basic rights in question, such as the right to know the reasons for one's arrest, to access counsel at an early stage of detention, to have recourse to judicial oversight of the detention and ultimately the right to a fair trial. It is perhaps then surprising that the debate on affording POW status to the majority of the detainees was considered so significant, and from a US administration point of view so potentially problematic in light of the broader objectives of the war against terror.

Two particular issues entered into the fray as reasons why affording POW status would bring with it protections apparently incompatible with policy objectives, namely the rules governing interrogation of POWs and the duty to repatriate POWs. While, of course, no security issue or other policy concern can justify denying detainees the status to which they are entitled as a matter of law, it is worth considering these issues with a view to asking whether, on these as on other issues, the protections afforded to POWs in fact differ fundamentally from those afforded to other detainees under international law.

8B.5.1   Rights regarding interrogation

IHL provides special rules that govern, and strictly limit, the information that POWs must provide to a detaining power. According to GC III, POWs need only provide their name, date of birth, rank and serial number. Furthermore, no 'form of coercion may be inflicted on prisoners of war to secure from them information of any kind whatsoever' (Article 17). Thus, it was suggested that affording POW status may be prejudicial to the security of the United States and others, which may depend upon information obtained during interrogation.

This view may reflect an oversight of several points. There is no prohibition on questioning POWs *per se* or seeking to secure information from them. The prohibition is on coercing a response, and IHRL (and IHL) contain an array of protections for persons during questioning which, if respected, effectively preclude the sort of coercive interventions envisaged in any event. Freedom from physical or psychological mistreatment is guaranteed by the right to humane treatment that appears as a core minimum in IHL, including common Article 3 and Article 75 AP I, and in IHRL. Moreover, the right against self-incrimination, the right to remain silent, and the right to be assisted by counsel before being questioned and to have counsel present during questioning are recognised as international standards applicable to persons that appear before international criminal courts and tribunals accused of war crimes, crimes against humanity or genocide.[247] If the detainees are not treated as POWs but as other categories of prisoner detained under IHL, or pursuant to a criminal investigation, other provisions of human rights and humanitarian law may well provide at least as great protection to these other categories of prisoner.

In this respect, as in others, the emphasis that has been put on the denial of POW status may be misplaced. There is no prohibition on detailed questioning of any prisoner, including POWs. What is prohibited, for all categories of prisoner, is the infliction of unlawful coercion or the questioning of persons who are potential suspects absent respect for their basic due process rights.

8B.5.2 Indefinite detention – repatriation

Another purported reason why affording POW status appears to have been considered so significant relates to the rules on repatriation.[248] Article 118 of GC III provides that 'POWs shall be released and repatriated without delay after the cessation of active hostilities'.

However, this right does not apply to persons who have been charged with a criminal offence where proceedings are pending, or where the detainee has been convicted and is serving a sentence, in which case Article 119 provides an explicit exception to the duty to repatriate. There is therefore nothing to prevent the US or other states from conducting criminal proceedings against persons responsible for criminal conduct.

The problem that the duty to repatriate was perceived to represent may be encapsulated by the words of one commentator who noted that 'if the captives are POWs, they must eventually be returned . . . the Taleban

---

[247] Human rights treaties recognise the right against self-incrimination. The ICC Statute and the Statutes of the ICTY and ICTR, provide, in greater detail, for the rights of the accused. The ICC Statute in particular, negotiated by 160 states over several years, might be considered to give expression to internationally accepted standards. See Articles 55 and 67 ICC Statute.

[248] The English Court of Appeal in the *Abbasi* cases described this assumption as follows: 'Furthermore, whereas in a conventional war prisoners of war have to be released at the end of hostilities, there is the possibility that, by denying the detainees captured during the war against terrorism the status of prisoners of war, their detention may be indefinite.'

fighters may be too dangerous ever to be released . . . which . . . commits the US to detaining them indefinitely'.[249] Concern about affording POW status may reveal an insidious assumption that if GC III does not apply there is no legal framework to limit the power to detain indefinitely.

Whether or not GC III applies, at a certain point hostilities will cease and reasons 'related to the conflict' that may justify detention under IHL, will also cease to exist. The remaining question will then be whether there is any other basis justifying detention, in accordance with IHRL. In most cases, such justification arises where a person is suspected of, and charged with, a criminal offence.

Preventive detention may also be allowed, although under IHRL this can be only in very limited circumstances, where provided for in clear accessible law and subject to strict safeguards, and could certainly never be justified indefinitely. As the Human Rights Committee has noted: 'if so-called preventive detention is used, for reasons of public security, it must be controlled by these same provisions [of Article 9, ICCPR], i.e., it must not be arbitrary, and must be based on grounds and procedures established by law (para. 1), *information of the reasons must be given* (para. 2), and *court control* of the detention must be available (para. 4)'.[250]

Whether or not they are POWs, the legal framework and the principle of legality itself preclude prolonged or indefinite detention of the Guantanamo detainees on the basis that, although they cannot be accused of having committed any crime, they are nonetheless perceived by US authorities to be dangerous.[251]

8C Responding to Guantanamo

8C.6 The obligations of third states

This chapter has focused on the obligations of the United States, as the detaining power, under IHL and IHRL. It is pertinent to reflect however

---

[249] M. Dorf, 'What is an "unlawful" combatant and why does it matter?' FindLaw Forum, 23 January 2002 (at http://www.cnn.com/2002/LAW/01/columns/fl.dorf.combatants.01.23/).

[250] Human Rights Committee, General Comment No. 8: Right to liberty and security of the person (Article 9) [1982], UN Doc. HRI/GEN/1/Rev.6 (2003) at 130, para. 4.

[251] While this study focuses on non-derogable rights such as those related to arbitrary detention, those guarantees that can be suspended in time of emergency would come back into play when the emergency threatening the life of the nation subsides.

on the obligations incumbent on third states to respond in the face of flagrant violations as in the situation at hand.

As we have seen in Chapter 6, under IHL, states parties to the Geneva Conventions have positive obligations to *ensure* respect for the Conventions, described as meaning that they should 'do everything in their power' to ensure that they are respected universally.[252] Several points are worthy of emphasis in the context of the on-going Guantanamo experience. First, states are not simply *entitled*, but are *obliged*, to take measures to respond to violations of IHL, and as authoritative commentators have noted, the proper working of the system under the Geneva Conventions demands that they do so.[253] Secondly, the obligation is both a negative and a positive one.[254] It requires states to refrain from committing violations, facilitating violations or cooperating with an offending state, for example by arresting and transferring detainees to a power that is believed to be violating the rights of those prisoners under IHL.[255] It also involves positive measures of prevention, without prescribing what measures the state may deem necessary or effective.[256]

The action that states should take is not prescribed, and available options may include invoking the under-utilised inter-state judicial mechanisms that exist,[257] or, at a minimum, it may be expected that states would make meaningful diplomatic representations that the violations should stop. As 'observance of humanitarian law transcends the sphere of interest of any individual state',[258] representations should not be limited to the

---

[252] Noted at Chapters 3 and 6. Article 1(1) of AP I paraphrases this positive obligation set forth in Article 1 of the 1949 Conventions.

[253] ICRC Commentary GC I, p. 18.

[254] In this respect it reflects human rights law, but its scope is more limited, as discussed below.

[255] Questions arise for those states that directly assist in arrest and transfer of suspects after a point at which they should reasonably have known of those serious issues as regards respect for IHL.

[256] See Chapter 6, IHL, references to Common Article 1 of the Geneva Conventions; D. Fleck, 'Non-International Armed Conflict: Legal Qualifications and Parties to the Conflict', and Sassòli, 'Non-International Armed Conflict: Qualification of the Conflict and Its Parties', background papers presented at the 2003 Sanremo Round Table on IHL; see also *Nicaragua*, paras. 220 and 255 and Articles 40 and 41 of the ILC's Articles on State Responsibility.

[257] Recourse to the ICJ is available between states, and although rarely utilised in practice, human rights bodies such as the Human Rights Committee under the ICCPR are available and could be invoked by one state against another.

[258] H.P. Gasser, 'International Humanitarian Law, an Introduction', in H. Haug (ed.), *Humanity for All: the International Red Cross and Red Crescent Movement* (ICRC, Geneva, Haupt 1993), p. 22.

protection of nationals of the state but reflect the role of states parties to the Geneva Convention system as guardians of the protections contained therein.

Finally, a specific positive obligation under IHL is the obligation, in the event of grave breaches of the Conventions – such as wilfully depriving prisoners of war of the rights of defence – to seek out and prosecute those individuals responsible.[259] The mechanism of individual accountability referred to above (and the rights of individuals to redress)[260] thus coincides with states' obligations under IHL.

The obligations of states under human rights law are cast differently, and while there is a duty to 'ensure' that the right of those within the state's control are respected, there is no general duty to ensure that *other* states refrain from violations. However, as discussed in Chapter 7, where the state itself exercises its authority or control abroad, IHRL is invoked. Moreover, under IHRL states may not transfer persons within their jurisdiction to another state where there is a significant risk of rights violations in the other state, such as torture or inhuman treatment,[261] or a 'flagrant denial of justice',[262] which may be implicated if states were asked to extradite or transfer persons to Guantanamo Bay for detention and/or prosecution.[263] Finally, the basic obligations to give effect to the object and purpose of a treaty to which a state is party, in good faith, presumably generally precludes facilitating or encouraging other states to commit violations of it. In this respect, questions arise as to whether other forms of state cooperation with the process of Guantanamo detentions or the trials by military commission, such as through intelligence

---

[259] See 'Grave Breaches', Chapter 6, p.xxx.   [260] See Chapters 4 and 7.

[261] Note that the imposition of the death penalty or life imprisonment without any possibility of early release may fall foul of Article 3 of the Convention; see, e.g., the ECtHR's admissibility decision in the *Einhorn v. France* case (Appl. No. 71555/01), 16 October 2001, para. 27 and *Öcalan v. Turkey* (Appl. No. 46221/99), Merits, Judgment of 12 March 2003, Chapter 7.

[262] See, e.g., *Drozd and Janusek v. France and Spain*, 26 June 1992, para. 110, discussed at Chapters 4 and 7.

[263] It is interesting to note further in the current context that the *Inter-American Convention to Prevent and Punish Torture* includes among the situations where extradition will not be granted, the existence of 'grounds to believe' that, among other things, the person 'will be tried by special or *ad hoc* courts in the requesting state'. Article 13, Inter-American Convention to Prevent and Punish Torture, Cartagena de Indias, 9 December 1985, in force 28 February 1987, *OAS Treaty Series* No. 67. See Chapter 7 A.4.3.8.

sharing or evidence gathering,[264] would breach the spirit, if not the letter, of IHRL.

Developments in relation to state responsibility are also relevant to this assessment of the interests and obligations of third states in face of the sort of basic violations of human rights and IHL that Guantanamo Bay epitomises.[265] Arbitrary detention and denial of basic fair trial guarantees have been authoritatively described as peremptory norms of international law, by virtue of which the obligations are owed to the community as a whole.[266] As the International Law Commission has indicated, where such obligations are breached, any state has an interest in acting to invoke the responsibility of the offending state, stopping the violation and ensuring that the wrong is put right.[267] Moreover, where a state is responsible for a gross or systematic breach of such a norm,[268] the ILC shifts from permissive to mandatory language, requiring that states 'shall' cooperate to end the breach.[269]

In short, the obligations to ensure respect for IHL, the more contained obligations of IHRL and developments in relation to state responsibility in international law together reflect an important principle that certain egregious violations are not matters for the state itself, but for the international community as a whole. The legal imperative for states to take action to address the Guantanamo situation is plain, even if they are left considerable scope to decide how best to do so. They should not take steps, whether in military or criminal matters, that directly or indirectly

---

[264] While jurisprudence has not yet provided any clear indication as to such an obligation of non-cooperation, beyond in cases of extradition, it may be that unfolding practice in this current context will pave the way for obligations to be interpreted and given broader effect: see Chapters 4 and 7.

[265] See Chapters 3 and 7.

[266] See Chapter 7. The HRC includes 'collective punishments, through arbitrary deprivations of liberty or by deviating from fundamental principles of fair trial' on its illustrative list while the International Law Commission, in its Commentary to the 2001 Articles on Responsibility of States for Internationally Wrongful Acts, lists the prohibitions of aggression, genocide, slavery and racial discrimination, crimes against humanity, torture, apartheid, the basic rules of humanitarian law in armed conflict and the right to self determination. See, respectively, General Comment 29, para. 11 and ILC Commentaries to Articles on State Responsibility, Introductory Commentary to Part Two, Chapter 3. Commentators include human rights, from the non-derogable rights common to the 'three major human rights treaties' to longer lists: see Chapter 7, para. 7A.1., 'International Human Rights Law', Framework.

[267] Article 48, ILC's Articles on State Responsibility; see Chapter 7, IHRL Framework.

[268] Article 40, *ibid.* [269] Article 41, *ibid.*

facilitate or contribute to the violation and they should invoke effective means, through diplomatic or other channels, to end the violations of rights of all detainees and restore the rule of law.

8C.7 The international response to the Guantanamo detentions

The situation of the Guantanamo detainees has provoked the condemnation of the international community like few incidents in recent years. Serious concerns expressed by international human rights mechanisms and non-governmental organisations were perhaps predictable.[270] But opponents have been vociferous, coordinated and diverse, illustrated by an unusually vocal statement of concern from the ICRC[271] and strident criticism being levelled from quarters not usually associated with international human rights advocacy.[272] Examples from the UK alone, the US's foremost ally in the 'war on terror', may illustrate the point. The UK Court of Appeal took the unusual step of commenting on what it viewed as the 'objectionable' lack of oversight by another country's courts.[273] Breaking with the convention that Law Lords do not speak out on politically sensitive issues, still less criticise another state's government, a distinguished English Law Lord condemned publicly the 'monstrous failure of justice',

---

[270] International organisations having criticised the situation include the Working Group on Arbitrary Detention (see Report of the Working Group E/CN.4/2003/8PARAS 61–64) and the Inter-American Commission on Human Rights, see *Precautionary Measures in Guantanamo Bay*. Although the US is reported as having twice ignored letters from the Working Group requesting a visit to Guantanamo, it has responded to both the reports, challenging the conclusions and questioning the jurisdiction of the mechanisms to address issues of IHL.

[271] See, e.g., 'Guantanamo Bay: Overview of the ICRC's work for Detainees', available at www.icrc.org.

[272] This section focuses on interventions from sources not predictably vocal on such issues to demonstrate the unusual nature of the situation and response thereto. Human rights groups have been predictably preoccupied by the issue; in addition, special interest groups, campaigns and websites have been formed. International bodies have expressed concern: see the Report of the Working Group on Arbitrary Detention and the decision of the Inter-American Commission mentioned above. See also statement by the United Nations High Commissioner for Human Rights, 16 January 2002 at www.unhchr.ch/huricane/huricane.nsf, where the High Commissioner stated that '[a]ll persons detained in this context are entitled to the protection of international human rights law and humanitarian law, in particular the relevant provisions of the International Covenant on Civil and Political Rights (ICCPR) and the Geneva Conventions of 1949. The legal status of the detainees, and their entitlement to prisoner-of-war (POW) status, if disputed, must be determined by a competent tribunal, in accordance with the provisions of Article 5 of the Third Geneva Convention.'

[273] See *Abassi*, above.

describing the military commissions as 'kangaroo courts' which 'convey the idea of a pre-ordained arbitrary rush to judgment by an irregular tribunal which makes a mockery of justice'.[274] A total of 175 members of both houses of the UK parliament, crossing party lines, took the unprecedented step of lodging an amicus brief with the US Supreme Court, adding to the many other briefs submitted to the Court.[275] The media have been similarly critical, including those otherwise sympathetic to controversial aspects of the 'war on terror'.[276]

Official inter-state reactions, for their part, are generally less transparent and more difficult to measure meaningfully. Protracted negotiations between the US and certain governments (notably the UK and Australia) were widely reported, but apparently focused on the situation in respect of their own nationals detained in Guantanamo.[277] Presumably as a result of these negotiations, a few of the detainees were returned to their country of origin, while in respect of others special arrangements were made for the application of better standards than those applicable to detainees of other nations, including undertakings that the death penalty would not be applied.[278] This is exemplified by the case against David Hicks, the Australian national who is one of the first four detainees to be tried by military commission, but on the basis of different arrangements than apply to the other accused of Yemeni and Sudanese nationality.[279]

---

[274] Lord Steyn, 'Guantanamo Bay: The Legal Black Hole', Twenty-Seventh F. A. Mann Lecture, 25 November 2003. Lord Steyn declared also that the trials before the military commissions would be 'a stain on United States justice' (*ibid.*).

[275] Many other briefs were filed from jurists and organisations around the world. They can be found at www.ccr-ny.org.

[276] See, e.g., 'Unjust, Unwise, Unamerican: America's plans to set up military commissions for the trials of terrorist suspects is a big mistake', *The Economist*, 12 July 2003, which notes the support offered by that publication to military action in Iraq and Afghanistan, while condemning the proposed military commissions as 'illiberal, unjust and likely to be counter-productive'.

[277] 'Guantanamo deal for Australia duo', *BBC on-line*, 26 November 2003, reporting that Australia has reached a deal with the United States for the trial of two Australians held at Guantanamo Bay, whereby the men will not face the death penalty, but they could face a military tribunal (http://news.bbc.co.uk/1/hi/world/asia-pacific/3238302.stm). Similar reports of a British policy of negotiating a separate agreement with the Pentagon so that British prisoners would not receive the death penalty have been criticised. See, e.g., Lord Steyn, 'Guantanamo Bay, The Legal Black Hole': 'This gives a new dimension to the concept of 'most-favoured nation' treatment in international law. How could it be morally defensible to discriminate in this way?'

[278] *Ibid.*

[279] See 'Guantanamo Detainee Charged', DoD News Release, 10 June 2004, available at http://www.defenselink.mil/releases/2004/nr20040610-0893.html. The department of defense press release notes that 'based on the specific facts and circumstances of Hicks'

As regards UK nationals remaining in Guantanamo, the UK Foreign Secretary stated that 'our position remains that the detainees should either be tried in accordance with international standards or they should be returned to the UK'.[280] In this context, the UK Attorney General took the unusual step of publicly criticising the proposed military commissions as 'not meeting acceptable fair trial standards.'[281] Ultimately, their return to Britain was formally requested by the government on this basis.[282]

Less clear, however, has been the willingness of states to intervene beyond the protection of their own nationals. There is some limited indication of such representations having been made by the German government.[283] As discussed in Chapter 4, section B, indications have also been given by states as to their unwillingness (or inability, given the constraints of IHRL) to cooperate with the US in respect of a military commission process that may lead to the death penalty, unfair trial, or other

case: if convicted, the prosecution will not seek the death penalty; the security and intelligence circumstances of Hicks' case are such that it would not warrant monitoring of conversations between him and his counsel; Hicks has access to an Australian lawyer with appropriate security clearance as a foreign attorney consultant; subject to any necessary security restrictions, two appropriately cleared family members of Hicks will be able to attend the trial, as well as representatives of the Australian government; if Hicks is convicted, the Australian government, as well as the defense team, may make submissions to the review panel on appeal; and the U.S. and Australian government will continue to work towards putting arrangements in place to transfer Hicks, if convicted, to Australia to serve any penal sentence in accordance with Australian and U.S. law.'

[280] 'Foreign Secretary statement on return of British detainees', 19 February 2004, available at http://www.pm.gov.uk/output/page5381.asp.

[281] At a speech to the International Criminal Law Association annual conference, 'Terrorism and the rule of law' in London on 25 June 2004, Lord Goldsmith stated: 'While we must be flexible and be prepared to countenance some limitation of fundamental rights if properly justified and proportionate, there are certain principles on which there can be no compromise. Fair trial is one of those – which is the reason we in the UK have been unable to accept that the US military tribunals proposed for those detained at Guantanamo Bay offer sufficient guarantees of a fair trial in accordance with international standards.' See M. Tempest, '"No compromise" on Guantánamo trials', *The Guardian*, 25 June 2004.

[282] See J. Lovell, 'Blair asks Bush to return Guantanamo detainees', *Reuters AlertNet*, 26 June 2004, at http://www.alertnet.org/thenews/newsdesk/L26579540.htm.

[283] According to Louise Christian, lawyer for some of the UK Guantanamo detainees, the German government made representations despite no German nationals being detained there. Presentation at London School of Economics, 13 February 2003. The German government has been openly critical of the Guantanamo detentions as contrary to the rule of law. See, e.g., interview with Interior Minister Otto Shilly. *Süddeutschen Zeitung*, March 2004, at www.sueddeutsche.de/deutschland/artikel/764/28736/. On criticism of the government for its reticence to intervene on behalf of German residents: see Martin Kreickenbaum, 'The case of Murat Kurnaz', 28 May 2004, at www.cageprisoners.com/articles.php?aid=1787.

serious violations of human rights.[284] It remains unclear whether states such as the UK, which has condemned that process, will be willing to follow through and seek to ensure the basic rights of all detainees, who are entitled, equally, to the protection of the international standards found to be lacking at Guantanamo Bay.

Thus, criticism has been voiced by states, representations have been made and non-cooperation has been threatened. Although practice remains limited, and may develop as the military tribunal process unfolds, the focus of concerted state action has to date been on the protection of the state's own nationals. While defence of a state's nationals is wholly appropriate, by so limiting interventions the approach has been to rely on different rather than equal treatment in respect of the protection of universally applicable human rights standards. This falls considerably short of the requirements of international law referred to in the previous section.

8C.8 Guantanamo Bay: implications and potential repercussions?

The implications for detainees held without legal protection, and for their families, are as immediate as they are apparent. Less so perhaps are the broader implications of this situation for the state primarily responsible, for third states and for the application of international law in the future.

For the state directly responsible, it is the reaction of other states towards the violations, preventing repetition – and whether those states meet *their* obligations, activated in the face of serious violations, as set out above – that is likely to have the critical impact on the offending state, potentially ending violations, preventing repetition and reasserting the rule of law. As noted, states or groups of states can exercise this influence to end breaches and protect the rule of law in many ways, including appropriate representations through diplomatic channels supported by conditioning cooperation in a range of contexts, military or law enforcement, upon compliance, and have done so to date to some, albeit quite limited, degree.

Legal mechanisms also exist whereby this unlawfulness may be challenged. Some of these rely on inter-state action, and therefore depend on the rare willingness of states to stand up for international law (and most

---

[284] See Chapter 4, section B. Practice is not transparent and therefore difficult to measure assuredly. Some states have voiced public concern, while others, allegedly, continue to offer various forms of support.

critically in this context to stand up to the US).[285] Other mechanisms, under IHRL, enable victims of those violations to vindicate their rights directly,[286] but these ultimately depend on political will to ensure their impact and effectiveness. Indeed, in response to a petition concerning the Guantanamo situation, the Inter-American Commission on Human Rights requested that the US take precautionary measures to protect the detainees' fundamental rights.[287] While the decision spoke well of the Commission's willingness to grapple with the politically unenviable, the US response was predictably dismissive, and little apparent weight was attributed to the decision thereafter. In this respect, one of the lessons of Guantanamo may be the importance of strengthening mechanisms enshrined in IHRL[288] and IHL[289] and the international community's commitment to them.

It may be, however, that international law 'enforcement' will be given meaningful effect only in relation to Guantanamo when responsibility is attributed not only to the state but also to the appropriate individuals; to paraphrase the Nuremberg judgment, when the individuals who ordered and gave effect to these violations, and not only the abstract state entities through which they act, are held to account.[290] Accountability of individuals may arise in respect of Guantanamo Bay from allegations of torture or inhuman treatment, wilfully depriving prisoners of war of fair

---

[285] See discussion of the obligations of, and options available to, other states, below. See, e.g., the role of the International Court of Justice, in Chapter 5, para. 5A.1, 'The Obligation to Resolve International Disputes by Peaceful Means'.

[286] The US has not ratified the ICCPR Optional Protocol, however, on which the right of individual petition to the Human Rights Committee depends. However, the Inter-American Commission on Human Rights has jurisdiction under the American Declaration on the Rights and Duties of Man, see below. Although there is no dedicated mechanism to address violations of IHL, human rights bodies can and do also adjudicate issues of IHL that impact on the protection of human rights in conflict situations. On the relationship between IHRL and IHL, see 'Harmony in Conflict?', Chapter 7, para. 7A.3.4, above.

[287] See Inter-American Commission on Human Rights, *Precautionary Measures in Guantanamo Bay*, above. While the potential impact was undermined by the refusal of the US to do as requested by the Commission, it remains significant as a reassertion of the role of international law in this context.

[288] Many other mechanisms exist not referred to here: for human rights mechanisms, see Chapter 7, above.

[289] The role of the ICRC may be worthy of note as telling a more positive story on Guantanamo: initial refusal of access was rescinded and the ICRC have monitored compliance and have taken a relatively outspoken approach which was important, given their role in underscoring the continued application of appropriate IHL standards.

[290] Judgment of the International Military Tribunal, in *The Trial of German Major War Criminals: Proceedings of the International Military Tribunal sitting at Nuremberg, Germany*, Part 22 (London, 1950), p. 447.

trial rights, or subjecting them to arbitrary prolonged detention.[291] While legally possible on the international level, the more conceivable prospect is of individual accountability enforced nationally, if not in the state of territory, in the courts of another state exercising universal jurisdiction or passive personality jurisdiction.[292] It remains to be seen whether there will be, in the fullness of time, any meaningful individual or state accountability in respect of the Guantanamo situation.

Questions also arise as to the broader implications of the Guantanamo situation for the legal framework and the rule of law. As at a certain point the tolerance or acquiescence of third states may contribute to a shift in customary law, state reactions may be relevant not only to the enforcement of law, but to the maintenance of international standards. However, even if the particular norms were susceptible to change,[293] international opposition to – and refusal to confer legitimacy on – the Guantanamo regime and the considerable concern expressed, as highlighted above, seriously undermine any risk that the law will itself be directly affected in this way.

It is also doubtful to what degree Guantanamo demonstrates a compelling need for such development of legal standards. It may, of course, highlight areas where the law could be clarified or developed, for example to better serve the humanitarian purpose of IHL and guard against abuse of this sort in the future.[294]

---

[291] See Chapter 4. Wilfully depriving a prisoner of war of fair trial rights is a grave breach of the Geneva Conventions. Arbitrary detention was not included, e.g., in the ICC Statute, though it may amount to a crime against humanity.

[292] See Chapter 4. On the national level, states may exercise, e.g., universal jurisdiction or passive personality jurisdiction for those states with such bases of jurisdiction in their domestic systems. As noted, the conferral of jurisdiction (unlike criminal responsibility) can be *ex post facto*. ICC jurisdiction is unlikely as most detentions were before its entry into force and, in any event, it would only have jurisdiction if a national of a state party to the ICC Statute (not an American) was responsible, or the offences arose on the territory of a state party, or a state decided to accept jurisdiction over the offences retroactively. An *ad hoc* tribunal could be set up, but the Security Council route would be vetoed leaving the Nuremberg model of several states collectively establishing a body. While this may be legally possible, it is hardly conceivable politically, at least at this stage.

[293] Note the resistance to change of *jus cogens* norms; see Introduction and Chapter 7.

[294] ICRC has identified areas for further discussion in its 'Challenges' paper, among them, 'elaboration of the precise meaning of "direct participation in hostilities"' and the consequence thereof. A further specific suggestion for possible improvement that has been advanced is that the competent tribunal procedure under Article 5 GC III be extended to status determinations not only of POWs in international armed conflict, but also other categories of detainees, or that procedure accommodate an international element to safeguard and reinforce its critical role. It would then better approximate an independent as well as competent arbiter of these status determinations. See Gasser p. XXX.

Most likely, however, the situation represents not a shift in the law, or a gap in the law, but a striking violation of it, with uncertain repercussions. One critical question is the impact of the Guantanamo experiment on the international protection of rights, beyond the United States. Will it give credence to the insidious notion of legal limbo – that certain persons fall entirely outside the framework of international legal protection? Will it contribute to the view that in practice human rights are the first casualty of terrorism and conflict, to be discarded in security-sensitive situations? Will other states seek to circumvent basic legal obligations by crude manipulation of the principle of territoriality, by unilateral decisions regarding detainees' status or by applying the law only 'to the extent appropriate'?[295]

Evidence already exists of other states, many of whom are not new to human rights repression, relying on the same principles as the US – security over rights, exclusion of certain persons from the protection of law, and military commissions to try civilians – justifying their actions explicitly or implicitly by reference to the Guantanamo situation.[296] Unsurprisingly, an additional by-product of this role for the US is that its credibility to act as the restraining force it once was on human rights issues is seriously undermined,[297] with its condemnation of, for example, military commissions and arbitrary detentions[298] resonating between absurd and hypocritical when juxtaposed alongside the notoriety of Guantanamo Bay.

---

[295] US policy declared in a statement of the Office of the Press Secretary, 7 February 2002: 'The United States is treating and will continue to treat all of the individuals detained at Guantanamo Bay humanely, and to the extent appropriate and consistent with military necessity, in a manner consistent with the principles of the Third Geneva Convention.' See also letter from the US President to the Speaker of the House of Representatives and the President Pro of the Senate, 20 September 2002, note 1, above.

[296] See, e.g., statement by President Mubarak of Egypt that resort to military commissions 'prove[s] that we were right from the beginning in using all means, including military tribunals' to curb terrorism, in J. Stork, 'The Human Rights Crisis in the Middle East in the Aftermath of 11 September', paper presented at the Symposium on Terrorism and Human Rights, Cairo, 26–28 January 2002, on file with author and available at www.cihrs.org.

[297] Guantanamo does not stand in isolation, but is the most serious of several acts of exceptionalism on human rights issues – including the establishment of an ICC, banning of child soldiers, creation of mechanims for individual redress for torture – and in other fields, such as environmental protection, that had already diminished the moral standing of the US internationally.

[298] See 'Annual Country Reports on Human Rights Practices Released by the Bureau of Democracy, Human Rights, and Labor of the Department of State', available at http://www.state.gov.

8C.9 Conclusion

The anomalous situation in which the Guantanamo detainees are held, without basic legal protections, is not a casualty of any 'legal limbo' or 'black hole' in international law. The Guantanamo detainees are entitled, under international human rights and humanitarian law, to certain core human rights protections irrespective of where they are detained, or their nationality. While the applicability of particular provisions of humanitarian law depends upon the status of the detainees (and, in accordance with the principle of legality, status determinations must undoubtedly be made in a fair and effective way), the basic rights protections at issue are contained in all potentially applicable provisions of IHL. The denial of POW status does not therefore carry the implications that some have suggested – of rendering the captives devoid of the protection of the framework of international law. The core rights in question remain protected under international law irrespective of status.

The apparent denial of the specific rights to which the detainees are entitled represents a rejection of the fundamental principle that state action – whether military, law enforcement or both – must at all times be governed by law and subject to the procedural fairness that is inherent in it. While that law itself must, and does, take account of and adapt to security concerns, it is not subordinate to such concerns. If the law is to have any compelling effect, it cannot be open to applying it selectively or only 'to the extent appropriate', as adjudged by the state itself.[299]

The following has recently been said of Guantanamo Bay:

> At present we are not meant to know what is happening at Guantanamo Bay. But history will not be neutered. What takes place there today in the name of the United States will assuredly, in due course, be judged at the bar of informed international opinion.[300]

The US may well be judged harshly. But it will not be judged alone. Other states, and the international community more broadly, stand to be judged for their determination, or their failure, to protect not only the Guantanamo detainees but the rule of law.

The Guantanamo situation is on-going and much remains to be seen. The nature of the judgment history renders and the long-term impact of Guantanamo will depend on unfolding national and international

---

[299] See notes 1 and 296 above.
[300] Lord Steyn, 'Guantanamo Bay: The Legal Black Hole'.

reactions. Positive indicators on the national level include the US Supreme
Court's decision on Guantanamo detainees, which begins to redeem the
reputation of US justice by reasserting the independence of the judiciary
and its role as an essential check on executive excess even – or especially – in
time of strain. The Supreme Court's caution in the context of the parallel
decision concerning US citizen 'enemy combatants' detained in the US,
that 'a state of war is not a blank check for the President',[301] demonstrates
the power of judicial independence and the critical ballast it represents
in face of exorbitant claims to executive discretion as epitomised by the
Guantanamo situation.

On the international level other states, and the international community, may stand by and watch the systematic undermining of human rights
and humanitarian law and the attack on the rule of law unfold, or, they may
rise to meet the international responsibilities that rest with them. States
which have negotiated the release of (or special deals for) their nationals
may back off, reducing the pressure on the US and leaving many without
protection, or they may turn their attention, individually or collectively,
to a more principled approach in line with respect for international law.
States from whom military and law enforcement support and cooperation is sought, including once the military tribunals are operational,
may provide such support to the US or deny it unequivocally, on the
basis of their own responsibilities in the face of egregious violations. In
this respect, early indications of resistance to cooperation on the basis of
human rights concerns are encouraging.[302]

If tolerated, Guantanamo may be not only a 'stain on American justice',[303] but a stain on the rule of law, and licence to disregard human rights
protection in the name of security. If the momentum behind the condemnation of Guantanamo Bay consolidates, and is coupled with long-term
consequences for the offending state, the situation may ultimately serve
to underscore the rule of law and its relevance to all states, for the protection of all persons, at all times, including in conflict and crisis when the
safeguards it affords are most critical.

---

[301] *Hamdi* v. *Rumsfeld*, above, note 145, Supreme Court Judgment, p. 28. This case, decided
alongside the Guantanamo detainees case, concerned a US citizen and the court in that
case stated that: '[A] state of war is not a blank check for the President when it comes
to the rights of citizens.' Although perhaps somewhat less robustly, it reached the same
conclusion in respect of non-citizens at Guantanamo Bay in the *Rasul* case, note 38, above.

[302] See Chapter 4, para. 4B.2.3, 'Inter-state Cooperation in Practice post 9/11'.

[303] Lord Steyn, 'Guantanamo Bay: The Legal Black Hole'.

Conclusion

It is of course acknowledged that international law is not an exact science, but it surely does not have to appear as bizarre as some of its practitioners have made it appear in recent months?

> Baroness Ramsay of Cartvale (Parliamentary Debates,
> Hansard, 17 March 2003)

Any sacrifice of freedom or the rule of law within States – or any generation of new tensions between States in the name of anti-terrorism – is to hand the terrorists a victory that no act of theirs alone could possibly bring.

> Secretary-General Kofi Annan (Statement to the Security
> Council ministerial meeting on terrorism, 20 January 2003)

9.1 September 11 as opportunity and the 'war on terror' response

September 11 was an international tragedy. It was a crime under international law and, as the Security Council promptly determined, a threat to international peace and security. It was followed by widespread, perhaps unprecedented, expressions of international solidarity with the United States. The Security Council expressed its willingness to act. States and institutions committed their shared determination to cooperating more effectively to combat terrorism and to hold to account those responsible.

It is tempting to speculate that September 11 represented a moment of unique opportunity: international law could have been reasserted over the international chaos and anarchy that the attacks represented; accountability norms and mechanisms could have been consolidated, bolstered with improved multilateral enforcement; the lagging system of international cooperation in criminal justice could have been enhanced and strengthened; the established collective security system could have been invoked to uphold international law and protect international peace and security improving the credibility and effectiveness of that system.

The 'war on terror', however, unfolded differently. Its emphasis has, as the epithet suggests, been overwhelmingly military. That military response was essentially unilateral, and multilateral to the extent that 'coalitions of the willing' supported the US military campaign(s). Despite a manifestly sympathetic Security Council, no attempt was made to engage it to take the action considered necessary in Afghanistan to defend the US and maintain international peace and security more generally. Questions as to the marginalisation of the UN collective security system therefore arose before the notorious divisions that characterised the advent and aftermath of military intervention in Iraq.

An expansive interpretation of the law of self defence was promoted in support of intervention in Afghanistan, by contemplating self defence against terrorist organisations – allowing for bombardment of states not themselves legally responsible for the attack being defended against – and promoting 'regime change' as a legitimate objective of self defence. This was followed by a broader approach to self defence in the doctrine of pre-emption advanced in support of the Iraq intervention and published as US policy for the future in the United States National Security Strategy. However, the principal justification for resort to force in Iraq was that Security Council authorisation to use force was 'implicit' in old UN resolutions passed in other contexts – an argument advanced once when explicit authorisation proved impossible to achieve given the depth of division within the Council.

The enormity of the September 11 crimes appears not to have been matched by an enormous criminal law enforcement initiative. The prospect of international justice was sidelined shortly after 9/11, yet national prosecutions have hardly borne fruit, frustrated it seems by the emphasis on the military execution of the 'war' and a failure of international cooperation, including as a result of US refusal to share intelligence with foreign courts. In many other instances, the post 9/11 practice of international 'cooperation' has been an extra-legal enterprise, with persons being transferred between states entirely outwith the legal framework and the protection of law.

Following September 11 a flurry of proclamations condemned terrorism and committed states to cooperate to combat it, most significant among them Security Council Resolution 1373, which mandated a host of measures aimed at, for example, preventing terrorism, criminalising it, cutting off funds to terrorists and denying them refugee status. This firmness of action was not, however, coupled by any firmer understanding of the conduct to which such action was to be directed. Insistence on the use of undefined and malleable terms such as 'terrorist' and states that 'harbour or support' them as the basis for wide-ranging prescriptions, coupled with the rhetoric of 'war', exacerbated the vulnerability of human rights post 9/11.

In the states driving the 'war on terror' and beyond, new practices emerged, and old practices continued with a renewed sense of legitimacy, many of which fell foul of or jeopardised international standards of protection under human rights and humanitarian law. Images of torture in Iraq or arbitrary detention in Guantanamo Bay illustrate the extent to which basic standards have been jettisoned pursuant to a 'war on terror' in which 'softer' forms of indefinite detention, inhuman treatment, denial of basic fair trial rights or the quashing of political dissent, for example, threaten to become commonplace. It is perhaps the ultimate paradox of the 'war on terror' that the horrendous acts of lawlessness witnessed on 11 September 2001 have been relied upon to justify repeated violations and further disregard for the international rule of law.

9.2 The legal framework

This book has focused on the international law that provided the framework for lawful responses to the events of 9/11 and against which the lawfulness of measures taken fall to be assessed.

The framework of international law applicable to the September 11 attacks and the responses thereto contains no gaping holes. It is not excessively complex, nor inaccessible, still less irrational. It is not blind to, but responds to accommodate, in various ways, security challenges of the type epitomised by 9/11. It provides norms and mechanisms to act against those who commit egregious crimes or threaten international peace and security. It protects states from unlawful interference by others and individuals from arbitrary interference by the state, while permitting the restriction of certain rights – subject to limits and insofar as genuinely necessary – in situations of emergency or to protect national security and public order. While there are areas for legitimate disagreement, and others where the law may indeed change as a result of 9/11 or its aftermath, what 9/11 exposed – and the 'war on terror' confirmed – was not so much the inadequacy of law but the fragility of respect for it, and the pressing challenge of enforcement.

The 'war on terror' raises issues from across the spectrum of international law. As Kofi Annan told the Security Council on 4 October 2002, 'Terrorism affects every aspect of the UN agenda – from development to peace to human rights to the rule of law.' The foregoing chapters have sought to sketch out the framework of some of the key areas of law implicated in the 'war on terror'. These areas are inherently interconnected and cannot be understood in isolation, but by reference to one another and to the underlying principles of the international legal system from which they derive. An atomised approach to the law – a feature not uncommon in international legal discourse since 9/11 – risks presenting a fragmented and misleading portrait of the normative framework, suggesting gaps, anomalies and inconsistencies where there may in fact be none.

Examples of the 'interconnectedness' of the framework are apparent throughout preceding chapters. The rules regarding 'terrorism' for example (Chapter 2) must be understood not only by reference to the much cited absent definition, but also by reference to those existing norms in the criminal law field that provide individual accountability for serious crimes under international law (Chapter 4), to IHL where a specific form of terrorism in armed conflict exists (Chapter 6), to norms governing whether a state can be held responsible for terrorism (Chapter 3), to the obligations on states to protect the life and security of persons within their jurisdiction, which mandates state action against terrorism (Chapter 7) and to the law on the use of force and friendly relations between states (Chapter 5) that imposes obligations on states to prevent the use of their territory by terrorists and provides for (and limits) the possibility of resort to force to address the terrorist threat.

The permissibility of the use of force in self defence, as a last resort where all peaceful means are exhausted, implies at least some consideration of the possibility that criminal law enforcement, backed up if necessary by collective coercive enforcement, might constitute an effective defence against terrorism. The legitimacy of that criminal law framework depends, however, on its implementation in accordance with human rights law (or, in armed conflict, also with IHL), with the rights of victims providing one of the imperatives behind an effective criminal process, and the rights of suspects and accused persons limiting the way in which that process is carried out. Certain serious breaches of international law, relating to the use of force, human rights law or IHL for example, may in turn invoke the right and responsibility of other states in accordance with the rules on state responsibility to act, to stop the breach, restore the rule of law and secure accountability, but always within the framework of law.

During armed conflict applicable law must be understood by reference both to IHL and IHRL, which are intrinsically intertwined. Perceptions as to the inadequacy of the international framework – including for example the myth that certain persons lie entirely outwith the protection of the law, propagated in the context of Guantanamo Bay – stem at least in large part from a fragmented approach to the legal framework and a failure to appreciate or recognise the diverse sources of legal protection applicable in any one situation.

9.3 The 'war on terror' and international legality: some essential characteristics

Certain features emerge from the landscape of the 'war on terror', sketched out in previous chapters, and its relationship with international law. Highlighted in turn below, these relate to the exercise of unstructured discretion and undermining the role of objective mechanisms to determine and apply the law, selectivity in the approach to and application of international law, and confusion as to its content and relevance. Each are manifestations of an overarching characteristic which is the erosion of the principle of legality itself.

Quite different manifestations of the promotion of unfettered executive discretion in matters of security emerge from across the spectrum of responses to 9/11. The exclusion, or marginalisation, of the role of judicial oversight of the lawfulness of measures adopted in the name of security, and judicial protection of human rights, is a common feature of the post 9/11 landscape discussed in relation to human rights and international criminal law. The removal of judicial review of detention, limitations on the role of the judge through summary extradition procedures, replacement of regular impartial and independent courts with *ad hoc* tribunals and restrictions on fair trial guarantees that make the judicial process meaningful, exemplify the phenomenon. The suggestion that matters such as the status of detainees and lawfulness of detention are exclusively 'military' matters not susceptible to judicial determination (rejected by the US Supreme Court) and the refusal to meet the obligation under IHL to have a competent tribunal determine detainees' status, provide other illustrations from the laws of war.

A rather different manifestation of the unstructured exercise of broad-reaching powers without objective safeguards is seen in the essential unilateralism that has characterised the use of military force since 9/11. The interventions in Afghanistan and Iraq, and most graphically the National Security Strategy advanced by the US, may reflect the refusal of certain militarily powerful states to be beholden to a collective security system that they do not control.

Second, selectivity – in respect of which law applies, to whom and for whose protection – emerges as a recurrent feature of the relationship between the 'war on terror' and international law. Selectivity is the antithesis of universality, and is itself a slight on the legality principle. First, it is most obviously manifest in the increasingly blatant resistance to the role and relevance of international law as a constraint on *all* states. The sort of approach that has led to allegations of exceptionalism and double standards by the US administration is best illustrated by the US National Security Strategy: international law is mentioned only once, as a vehicle by which rogue states are defined, yet is entirely absent from the lengthy exposition of the US policy of pre-emption, which is broadly considered to be of, at best, dubious legality. Other examples are found in US State Department reports condemning unequivocally the unlawfulness of arbitrary detention, torture or inhuman treatment by particular states, which juxtapose starkly alongside the travesties of the 'war on terror'. Likewise, US public insistence on Iraqi respect for American POW rights, while legitimate, gave rise to cries of double standards in the light of their own persistent denial of the basic rights of detainees to have their status determined and the rights that flow therefrom respected. The message appears to be that while international law is important for other states, it cannot constrain the exercise of the United States' unique power.

In this respect it is noteworthy that since September 11 states have not infrequently invoked international law as a pretext for taking action to 'enforce' legal standards. The notion of states using 'force to enforce' international law was floated in several contexts on both sides of the Atlantic, by reference for example to unfulfilled obligations under Security Council resolutions on Iraq or in relation to the surrender of bin Laden by Afghanistan, but also, to some degree, to human rights violations committed by the Taleban or Saddam Hussein regimes. The states 'enforcing', however, rather than the Security Council or other collective mechanism, are charged with determining who are the 'rogues' and who the 'enforcers'. Ironically, the 'enforcement missions' have then often themselves violated the international standards in whose name they purported to act.

Another form of selectivity arises in the 'pick and choose' approach to which particular areas of law, or particular rules therein, are acknowledged as applicable, in accordance with the policy agenda of the moment. An example explored in this book relates to targeted killing of suspected al-Qaeda operatives, where IHL standards are invoked to justify targeting which would be unlawful outside armed conflict, but not accepted as applicable to protect similarly situated persons in the event that they are detained. The fact that detainees are 'criminals' is invoked to question the appropriateness of affording them the protection of IHL and their status as 'combatants' to justify the non-application of criminal law and human rights guarantees.

A selective approach to international law is apparent, finally, in the scope of persons protected by law. While rightly advancing the duty to protect the 'innocent' from attack, the suggestion is that some states or persons are so 'evil' or dangerous that they are rendered beyond the protection of law. In short, a perception emerges of international law that protects 'us' but not 'them', and constrains 'them' but not 'us'.

A third characteristic that emerges from the treatment of international law in the 'war on terror' is confusion and obfuscation. By implying an intense degree of uncertainty around 'technical' legal rules, and without due regard to underlying legal principles, the authority of law has been undermined. The debate on the status of prisoners is one example, focusing on particular provisions concerning classification, while largely ignoring the fundamental principle that there are basic rights to which any person is entitled irrespective of status. Areas of legal controversy appear at times to be manipulated to obscure the law that does govern and has, sometimes quite straightforwardly, been violated. In turn, as regards those areas of law that are unsettled or were perhaps unclear at the time of the September 11 attacks, such as those relating to the law on terrorism and responsibility for it, it is questionable how much weight has been lent to clarifying the law, as opposed to favouring ambiguity – whether perceived or real – and the greater 'flexibility' it affords.

9.4 Early reactions and key challenges: is the pendulum swinging and where might it stop?

It is difficult to see the treatment of international law in the 'war on terror' as other than an opportunity squandered and a serious setback for the international rule of law. While the past few years have been bleak ones for international law, the situation remains very much in flux. Tentative signs may be emerging, from the international practice highlighted in preceding chapters, of an international reaction to the 'war on terror' as currently characterised, albeit belated and, as yet, insufficient.

Strident and vocal international opposition to the Iraq war, described at Chapter 5, section B, contrasts starkly with the passive reaction, and virtual absence of serious debate as to lawfulness or longer term implications, that attended military intervention in Afghanistan in the wake of 9/11. The staunch unilateralism coupled with the doctrine of pre-emption raised in the context of Iraq and set forth in the US National Security Strategy, provoked reaction and reassertions by world leaders of the importance of multilateralism and the collective security system.

There are also indications of egregious violations of human rights and humanitarian law prompting an increasingly robust reaction from the international community. As discussed in Chapter 8, at least in the extreme case of Guantanamo Bay, condemnation from states, international bodies and other sources not normally known for human rights advocacy is widespread and growing. A number of states have backed up their condemnation with indications of unwillingness to cooperate with US trials if human rights practices continue to fall short of international standards, as noted in Chapters 4, section B and 7, section B. The apparent blindness of certain states and of the Security Council to human rights concerns post 9/11 in favour of security imperatives has given way to frequent recognition of the complementarity of an effective counter terrorist strategy with respect for the rule of law, human rights and international humanitarian law as highlighted in Chapter 7. International institutions are actively engaged in monitoring and assessing the compatibility of counter-terrorist measures with human rights standards, and to some degree with those of IHL. Unhelpful confusion on IHL has generated a more helpful debate, led by the ICRC, on the potential development, and critically more effective implementation, of IHL in light of the experience since September 11, discussed in Chapter 6.

The shift in the approach of domestic courts highlighted in Chapter 7, is illustrated by the landmark decisions of the US Supreme Court upholding the basic rights of detainees to access a court and reasserting the role of the judge in time of conflict, which may serve to inspire judicial independence beyond US shores.

It is certainly too early to offer a view as to the likely long-term impact of the 'war on terror' on standards of protection and the international rule of law. Violations committed during the 'war on terror' may be allowed to stand – with few implications for wrong-doing nations and without individual accountability – and to lead, with time, to an erosion of law's essential legitimacy and that of those that purport to enforce it. Or, if the developments highlighted above are an indication, it may be that the excesses of that 'war', and the alacrity with which legal standards and basic human rights standards were jettisoned in the name of security, have served as an alarming reminder of the dangers of a 'fast and 'loose' approach to international law. Much depends on how the international community addresses the fundamental challenges that terrorism and counter-terrorism currently pose.

The key challenge to be faced in the road ahead is plainly to ensure that the scourge of terrorism be addressed, and that this is done effectively. Images of the events of 9/11 and the proliferation of attacks since then, whether in Bali, Istanbul, Baghdad, or Madrid, pay chilling testament to the need to meet this challenge, as well as serving to foment debate on the effectiveness of the strategy pursued to date.

The related challenge, neglected in much state practice to date, is to ensure that this is done within the framework of international law, in a way that restores, rather than further undermines, the rule of law. Promoting respect for international law is essential to ensuring that the 'war on terror' does not score a devastating own goal by eroding permanently the rule of law and the international standards that protect us all. Otherwise, as the Secretary General's quote cited at the outset of the chapter noted, 'we deliver a victory to terrorists that no act of theirs could achieve'. Ultimately, the principle of legality – the clarity and coherence of law, its universality and the principle of due process inherent therein – must be reasserted, and the challenge of effective international enforcement met.

First, confidence must be restored in the capacity, relevance and credibility of international law, as providing an essential legal framework which, while imperfect, is equipped to address the normative consequences of 9/11 and its aftermath. The perception of the 'bizarre' nature of international law must be countered. In some areas where the law may indeed be unclear, the challenge lies in clarifying the normative framework, or strengthening mechanisms to give effect to it. Proposals for normative change, which in any vibrant system of law will inevitably follow a challenge such as 9/11, should therefore be encouraged. They must however be distinguished from the erroneous view that there is currently no effective system of law, or from attempts to excuse violations by reference to unfavoured aspects of the current system of law.

Second, essential to reasserting the principle of legality is underlining the universality of law, demonstrating that international law applies to all states, for the ultimate protection of all persons. The continued recovery of the central role of international human rights law, and clarification of its universal application, *whenever* (including in times of crisis or conflict), *wherever* (whether at home or abroad) and in relation to *whomsoever* the state exercises its authority or control will contribute to this process.

The universality and objectivity of the law is safeguarded by its application according to procedural principles. The importance of the role of courts and legal mechanisms, national and international, is clear. As regards collective security mechanisms, there is plainly a new imperative around the old debate on reform of the Security Council. While it is debatable whether a new model of collective security could overcome the shortcomings that have dogged the current system, better command international respect and more effectively enforce the rule of law, what is essential is to regain international confidence in collective mechanisms, capable of being effective while ensuring essential restraint on the otherwise unfettered exercise of power of any one state.

The perceived universality, and hence legitimacy, of the international system depends on the law applying to, and purporting to constrain, the more powerful as well as the less. The willingness and ability of the international community to hold 'to account' states, and individuals, who violate fundamental international norms, whether through 'terrorism' or in the name of counter terrorism, is therefore a crucial aspect of the challenge ahead. The role and responsibilities of third states in the face of serious violations of international law, and the positive obligations to act individually or in 'community' to repress serious breaches and ensure that those responsible are brought to justice, are therefore of potentially critical importance. As seen from the legal framework highlighted in various chapters, such responsibility is not only moral or political but reflected in established and developing law and practice on state responsibility, human rights, humanitarian law and international criminal law. It will be the extent of the international community's commitment, to clarify and strengthen international law, not only by reiterating standards but by ensuring that they are respected, that will define where the pendulum stops and the ultimate impact of the 'war on terror' on the international rule of law.

BIBLIOGRAPHY

Abromovich, V. and Guembe, M.J., 'Challenging Amnesty Law in Argentina', 14.1 (2002) *INTERIGHTS Bulletin* 7

Akehurst, M., 'Custom as a Source of International Law', 47 (1974–75) BYIL 1

Aldrich, G., 'The Laws of War on Land', 94 (2000) AJIL 42

Alvarez, J.E., 'Judging the Security Council', 90 (1996) AJIL 1

Ambos, K., 'Article 25. Individual Criminal Responsibility', in O. Triffterer (ed.), *Commentary on the Rome Statute of the International Criminal Court* (Baden-Baden, 1999), p. 475

Amnesty International, 'Universal Jurisdiction: The Duty of States to Enact and Implement Legislation', AI Index: IOR 53/002/2001

Anderson, D. and Statford, J., 'Joint Opinion on Proposed Derogation from Article 5 of the European Convention on Human Rights; Anti-Terrorism, Crime and Security Bill, Clauses 21–32', on file with author

Arend, A.C. and Beck, R.J., *International Law and the Use of Force* (New York, 2001)

Balikowa, D.O., 'The Anti-Terrorism Act 2002: The Media and Free Speech', 8.1 (2003) *The Defender* 6

Bantekas, I., Nash, M. and Mackarel, S., *International Criminal Law* (London, 2001)

Bassiouni, M.C., 'Crimes Against Humanity', in Bassiouni, *International Criminal Law*, vol. I, 2nd ed. (New York, 1999), pp. 522 ff.

Bassiouni, M.C., 'International Terrorism', in Bassiouni (ed.), *International Criminal Law*, vol. I, 2nd ed. (New York, 1999), p. 765

Bassiouni, M.C. (ed.), *International Criminal Law*, vol. I, 2nd ed. (New York, 1999)

Baxter, R., 'Multilateral Treaties as Evidence of Customary International Law', 41 (1965–66) BYIL 275

Beck, R.J. and Arend, A.C., 'Don't Tread on Us: International Law and Forcible State Responses to Terrorism', 12 (1994) *Wisconsin International Law Journal* 153

Ben-Naftali, O. and Michaeli, K.R., '"We Must Not Make a Scarecrow of the Law": A Legal Analysis of the Israeli Policy of Targeted Killings', 36 (2003) *Cornell International Law Journal* 233

Bennoune, K., '"Sovereignty vs. Suffering"? Re-Examining Sovereignty and Human Rights through the Lens of Iraq', 13 (2002) EJIL 243

Beruto, G.L. and Ravasi, G. (eds.), *27th Round Table on Current Problems of International Humanitarian Law (Sanremo, 4–6 September 2003): International Humanitarian and other Legal Regimes: Interplay in Situations of Violence* (Milan, forthcoming)

Boelaert-Suominen, S., 'Repression of War Crimes through International Tribunals', International Institute of Humanitarian Law, 77th Military Course (1999) (on file with author)

Boelaert-Suominen, S., 'The Yugoslavia Tribunal and the Common Core of International Humanitarian Law applicable to All Armed Conflict', 13 (2000) LJIL 619

Borelli, S., 'The Treatment of Terrorist Suspects Captured Abroad: Human Rights and Humanitarian Law', in A. Bianchi (ed.), *Enforcing International Law Norms Against Terrorism*, Oxford (2004)

Bothe, M., 'Terrorism and the Legality of Preemptive Force', 14 (2003) EJIL 227

Bovino, A., 'The Victim before the Inter-American Court of Human Rights, 14.1 (2002) *INTERIGHTS Bulletin* 40

Bowett, D.W., 'Reprisals Involving Recourse to Armed Force', 66 (1972) AJIL 1

Bowett, D.W., *Self Defence in International Law* (New York, 1958)

Brody, R. and Duffy, H., 'Prosecuting Torture Internationally: Hisséne Habré, Africa's Pinochet?', in H. Fischer, C. Kreß and S.R. Lüder, *International and National Prosecution of Crimes Under International Law* (Berlin, 2001), pp. 817 ff.

Brownlie, I., *International Law and the Use of Force by States* (Oxford, 1981)

Brownlie, I., *Principles of Public International Law*, 6th ed. (Oxford, 2003)

Byers, M., 'Terrorism, the Use of Force and International Law after September 11', 51 (2002) ICLQ 401

Byers, M., 'The Shifting Foundations of International Law: A Decade of Forceful Measures Against Iraq', 13 (2002) EJIL 21

Campbell, L.M., 'Defending Against Terrorism: A Legal Analysis of the Decision to Strike Sudan and Afghanistan', 74 (2000) *Tulane Law Review* 1067

Canestaro, N., 'American Law and Policy on Assassinations of Foreign Leaders: The Practicality of Maintaining the *Status Quo*', 26 (2003) *Boston College International and Comparative Law Review* 1

Cassese, A., *International Criminal Law* (Oxford, 2003)

Cassese, A., *International Law* (Oxford, 2001)

Cassese, A., 'On the Current Trend towards Criminal Prosecution and Punishment of Breaches of International Humanitarian Law', 9 (1998) EJIL 2

Cassese, A., 'The International Community's "Legal" Response to Terrorism', 38 (1989) ICLQ 589

Cassese, A., Gaeta, P. and Jones, J. (eds.), *The Rome Statute of the International Criminal Court: A Commentary*, 3 vols. (Oxford, 2002)

Charlesworth, H. and Chinkin, C., *The Boundaries of International Law: A Feminist Analysis* (Manchester, 2000)

Charney, J., 'Universal International Law', 87 (1993) AJIL 529

Clapham, A., 'Human Rights, Sovereignty and Immunity in the Recent Work of the International Court of Justice', 14.1 (2002) *INTERIGHTS Bulletin* 29

Clapham, A., 'Peace, the Security Council and Human Rights', in Y. Danieli, E. Stamatopoulou and C.J. Dias (eds.), *The Universal Declaration of Human Rights: Fifty Years and Beyond* (New York, 1998), pp. 375 ff.

Combacau, J. and Alland, D., '"Primary" and "Secondary" Rules in the Law of State Responsibility: Categorizing International Obligations', 16 (1985) NYIL 81

Conetta, C., 'Strange Victory: A Critical Appraisal of Operation Enduring Freedom and the Afghanistan War', Project on Defense Alternatives, Research Monograph No. 6, 30 January 2002, available at http://www.comw.org/pda

Cortright, D. and Lopez, G.A., *The Sanctions Decade: Assessing UN Strategies in the 1990s* (London, 2000)

Cottier, M., 'Did NATO Forces Commit War Crimes during the Kosovo Conflict? Reflections on the Prosecutor's Report of 13 June 2000', in H. Fischer, C. Kreß and S.R. Lüder (eds.), *International and National Prosecution of Crimes under International Law: Current Developments* (Berlin, 2001), p. 505

Cottier, M., 'What Relationship Between the Exercise of Universal and Territorial Jurisdiction? The Decision of 13 December 2000 of the Spanish National Court Shelving the Proceedings Against Guatemalan Nationals Accused of Genocide', in H. Fischer, C. Kreß and S. R. Lüder, *International and National Prosecution of Crimes Under International Law: Current Developments* (Berlin, 2001), pp. 843 ff.

Craven, M., 'Humanitarianism and the Quest for Smarter Sanctions', 13 (2002) EJIL 43

Crawford, J., 'Democracy and International Law', 44 (1993) BYIL 113

Crawford, J., *The International Law Commission's Articles on State Responsibility: Introduction, Text and Commentaries* (Cambridge, 2002)

Crawford, J., Sands, P. and Wilde, R., 'Joint Legal Opinion on bilateral agreements sought by the United States under 98(2) of the ICC Statute' at http://www.iccnow.org/documents/otherissuesimpunityagreem.html.

David, E., *Eléments de droit pénal international – Titre II, le contenu des infractions internationales*, 8th ed. (Brussels 1999)

Dennis, M.J., 'Current Developments: The Fifty-Seventh Session of the UN Commission on Human Rights', 96 (2002) AJIL 181

Dinstein, Y., *War, Aggression and Self Defence* (Oxford, 2000)

Dixon, R., 'Article 7. Crimes Against Humanity', in O. Triffterer (ed.), *Commentary on the Rome Statute of the International Criminal Court* (Baden-Baden, 1999), pp. 121 ff.

Doswald-Beck, L., 'The Value of the 1977 Geneva Protocols for the Protection of Civilians', in M.A. Meyer (ed.), *Armed Conflict and the New Law. Aspects of the 1977 Geneva Protocols and the 1981 Weapons Convention* (London, 1989), pp. 137 ff.

Drumbl, M.A., 'Judging the September 11 Terrorist Attack', 24 (2002) HRQ 323

Duffy, H., 'National Constitutional Compatibility and the International Criminal Court', 11 (2001) *Duke Journal of Comparative and International Law* 5

Duffy, H., 'Report of the Working Group on Detention', paper presented at the 27th Round Table on Current Problems of International Humanitarian Law (Sanremo, 4–6 September 2003), proceedings to be published in G.L. Beruto and G. Ravasi (eds.), *27th Round Table on Current Problems of International Humanitarian Law: International Humanitarian and other Legal Regimes: Interplay in Situations of Violence* (Milan, forthcoming)

Dugard, J., 'Criminal Responsibility of States', in Bassiouni (ed.), *International Criminal Law*, vol. I, 2nd ed. (New York, 1999), pp. 239 ff.

Dugard, J., 'The Problem of the Definition of Terrorism in International Law', conference paper, Sussex University, 21 March 2003 (on file with author)

Dugard, J. and Van den Wyngaert, C., 'Reconciling Extradition with Human Rights', 92 (1998) AJIL 188

Dumitriu, E., 'The EU's Definition of Terrorism: the Council Framework Decision on Combating Terrorism', 5 *German Law Journal* 587

Dupuy, P.-M., 'Due Diligence in the International Law of State Responsibility', in *Legal Aspects of Transfrontier Pollution* (Paris, 1977), pp. 369 ff.

Ellmann, S., 'Racial Profiling and Terrorism', 46 (2002–2003) *New York Law School Law Review* 675

Erickson, R.J., *Legitimate Use of Military Force Against State-Sponsored International Terrorism* (Maxwell Air Force Base, 1989)

Fenrick, W.J., 'A First Attempt to Adjudicate Conduct of Hostilities Offences: Comments on Aspects of the ICTY Trial Decision in the *Prosecutor v. Tihomir Blaskic*', 13 (2000) LJIL 931

Fenrick, W.J., 'Article 8. War Crimes', in O. Triffterer (ed.), *Commentary on the Rome Statute of the International Criminal Court* (Baden-Baden, 1999), pp. 173 ff

Fenrick, W.J., 'Attacking the Enemy Civilian as a Punishable Offence', 7 (1997) *Duke Journal of Comparative and International Law* 539

Fischer, H., 'Protection of Prisoners of War', in D. Fleck (ed.), *The Handbook of Humanitarian Law in Armed Conflicts* (Oxford, 1995), pp. 321 ff

Fischer, H., Kreß, C. and Lüder, S.R. (eds.), *International and National Prosecution of Crimes under International Law: Current Developments* (Berlin, 2001)

Fitzpatrick, J., *Human Rights in Crisis. The International System for Protecting Rights During States of Emergency* (Washington, 1994)

Fitzpatrick, J., 'Speaking Law to Power: The War Against Terrorism and Human Rights', 14 (2003) EJIL 241

Fleck, D., 'Non-International Armed Conflict: Legal Qualifications and Parties to the Conflict', paper presented at the 27th Round Table on Current Problems of International Humanitarian Law (Sanremo, 4–6 September 2003), proceedings to be published in G.L. Beruto and G. Ravasi (eds.), *27th Round Table on Current Problems of International Humanitarian Law: International Humanitarian and other Legal Regimes: Interplay in Situations of Violence* (Milan, forthcoming)

Fleck, D. (ed.), *The Handbook of Humanitarian Law in Armed Conflicts* (Oxford, 1995)

Fletcher, G.P., *Rethinking Criminal Law* (Oxford, 2000)

Franck, T.M., *Recourse to Force. State Action Against Threats and Armed Attacks* (Cambridge, 2002)

Franck, T.M. 'When, If Ever, May States Deploy Military Force without Prior Security Council Authorization?' 5 (2001) *Washington University Journal of Law and Policy* 51

Gardam, J., 'Proportionality and Force in International Law', 87 (1993) AJIL 391

Gasser, H.-P., 'International Humanitarian Law: An Introduction', in H. Haug, *Humanity for All* (Berne, 1993), pp. 22 ff.

Gasser, H.-P., 'Protection of the Civilian Population', in D. Fleck (ed.), *The Handbook of Humanitarian Law in Armed Conflicts* (Oxford, 1995), pp. 209 ff.

Gilbert, G., *Aspects of Extradition Law* (Dordrecht, 1991)

Gray, C., 'From Unity to Polarisation: International Law and Use of Force against Iraq', 13 (2001) EJIL 1.

Gray, C., *International Law and the Use of Force* (Oxford, 2000)

Gray, C., *Judicial Remedies in International Law* (Oxford, 1987)

Gray, C., 'The US National Security Strategy and the New 'Bush Doctrine' on Preemptive Self Defense', 2 (2002) *Chinese Journal of International Law* 440

Greenwood, C., 'International Law and the Pre-emptive Use of Force: Afghanistan, Al-Qaida, and Iraq', 4 (2003) *San Diego International Law Journal* 7

Greenwood, C., 'International Law and the "War against Terrorism"', 78 (2002) *International Affairs* 301

Greenwood, C., 'Scope of Application of Humanitarian Law', in D. Fleck (ed.), *The Handbook of Humanitarian Law in Armed Conflicts* (Oxford, 1995), pp. 39 ff.

Gross, E., 'Thwarting Terrorist Attacks by Attacking the Perpetrators or Their Commanders as an Act of Self Defence: Human Rights Versus the State's Duty to Protect its Citizens', 15 (2001) *Temple International and Comparative Law Journal* 195.

Guariglia, F., 'The Rules of Procedure and Evidence for the International Criminal Court: A New Development in International Adjudication of Individual

Criminal Responsibility', in A. Cassese, P. Gaeta and J. Jones (eds.), *The Rome Statute of the International Criminal Court: A Commentary* (Oxford, 2002), pp. 1111 ff.

Guzman, F.A., *Fuero Militar y Derecho Internacional* (International Commission of Jurists, Bogotá, 2003)

Guzman, F.A., *Terrorism and Human Rights No. 1* (International Commission of Jurists, Geneva, 2002)

Guzman, F.A., *Terrorism and Human Rights No. 2* (International Commission of Jurists, Geneva, 2003)

Hall, C.K., 'Universal Jurisdiction: Challenges to Implementation since Pinochet I', 14.1 (2002) *INTERIGHTS Bulletin* 3

Hannikainen, L., *Peremptory Norms (Jus Cogens) in International Law: Historical Development, Criteria, Present Status* (Helsinki, 1988)

Harris, D.J., *Cases and Materials on International Law*, 5th ed. (London, 1998)

Haug, H. (ed.), *Humanity for All: the International Red Cross and Red Crescent Movement* (ICRC, Geneva, 1993)

Henckaerts, J.-M., 'Binding Armed Opposition Groups through Humanitarian Treaty Law and Customary Law', 27 (2003) *Collegium* 123, available at http://www.coleurop.be/collegium/Collegium27.pdf.)

Henkin, L., 'The Universal Declaration at 50 and the Challenge of Global Markets', 25 (1999) *Brooklyn Journal of International Law*, 25

Henkin, L., 'Use of Force: Law and US Policy', in Henkin *et al.*, *Right v. Might: International Law and the Use of Force* (New York, 1991), pp. 37 ff.

Herold, M., 'A Dossier on Civilian Victims of United States' Aerial Bombing of Afghanistan: A Comprehensive Accounting', most recent edition available at http://pubpages.unh.edu/%7Emwherold

Higgins, R., 'Derogations under Human Rights Treaties', 48 (1976–77) BYIL 281

Higgins, R., 'International Law in a Changing International System', 58 (1999) *Cambridge Law Journal* 78

Higgins, R., *Problems and Process: International Law and How We Use It* (Oxford, 1994)

Higgins, R., 'The General International Law of Terrorism', in R. Higgins and M. Flory, *International Law and Terrorism* (London, 1997)

Hirai-Braun, N., 'Country Report on Japan', Conference on 'Terrorism as a Challenge for National and International Law', Max Planck Institute for Comparative Public Law and International Law, Heidelberg, 24–25 January 2003, at www.edoc.mpil.de/conference-on-terrorism/country.cfm

Hoffman, P., 'Civil Liberties in the United States after September 11', available at http://www.frontlinedefenders.com/en/papersweb/p3en.doc

Hoffman, P. (ed.), *ACLU International Civil Liberties Report 2003*, available at http://sdshh.com/ICLR/ICLR_2003/ICLR2003.html

ICRC, Report on 'International Humanitarian Law and the Challenges of Contemporary Armed Conflict' (Geneva, 2003)

Jennings, R.Y. and Watts, A. (eds.), *Oppenheim's International Law*, vol. I, 9th ed. (London, 1992)

Jinks, D., 'September 11 and the Laws of War', 28 (2003) *Yale Journal of International Law* 1

Jinks, D., 'State Responsibility for Acts of Private Armed Groups', 4 (2003) *Chicago Journal of International Law* 83

Kapferer, S., 'Ends and Means in Politics: International Law as Framework for Political Decision-Making', 15 (2002) *Revue québéquoise de droit international* 101

Kreß, C. and Lattanzi, F. (eds.), *The Rome Statute and Domestic Legal Orders: Volume 1* (Baden-Baden, 2000)

Kreß, C., 'Witnesses in Proceedings Before the International Criminal Court', in H. Fischer, C. Kreß and S.R. Lüder (eds.), *International and National Prosecution of Crimes under International Law: Current Developments* (Berlin, 2001), pp. 375 ff.

Krisch, N., 'The Rise and Fall of Collective Security: Terrorism, US Hegemony and the Plight of the Security Council', in Walter *et al.* (eds.), *Terrorism as a Challenge for National and International Law: Security versus Liberty?* (Berlin–Heidelberg, 2003)

Lamb, S., 'Legal Limits to UN Security Council Powers', in G. Goodwin-Gill and S. Talmon (eds.), *The Reality of International Law: Essays in Honour of Ian Brownlie* (Oxford, 1999), pp. 361 ff.

Lattanzi, F., 'Crimes against Humanity in the Jurisprudence of the International Criminal Tribunals for the Former Yugoslavia and Rwanda', in H. Fischer, C. Kreß and S.R. Lüder (eds.), *International and National Prosecution of Crimes under International Law: Current Developments* (Berlin, 2001), pp. 480 ff.

Levitt, G., 'Is 'Terrorism' Worth Defining?' 13 (1986) *Ohio Northern University Law Review* 97

Lietzau, W.K., 'Combating Terrorism: Law Enforcement or War?', in M.N. Schmitt and G.L. Beruto (eds.), *Terrorism and International Law, Challenges and Responses* (Sanremo, 2003), pp. 75 ff.

Lieven, A., 'The Roots of Terrorism, and a Strategy Against It', 68 (2001) *Prospect Magazine* 13

Lillich, R.B., 'Civil Rights', in T. Meron (ed.), *Human Rights in International Law. Legal and Policy Issues* (Oxford, 1984), pp. 116 ff.

Lillich, R.B., 'Current Development: The Paris Minimum Standards of Human Rights Norms in a State of Emergency', 79 (1985) AJIL 1072

Lillich, R.B., *Humanitarian Intervention and the United Nations* (Charlottesville, 1973)

Lowe, V., 'The Iraq Crisis: What Now?', 52 (2003) ICLQ 859

Lutz, E. and Sikkink, K., 'International Human Rights Law in Practice. The Justice Cascade: The Evolution and Impact of Foreign Human Rights Trials in Latin America', 2 (2001) *Chicago Journal of International Law* 1

McCoubrey, H., *The Regulation of Armed Conflict* (Dartmouth, 1990)

Maier, J.B.J., *Derecho Procesal Penal. Tomo I* (Buenos Aires, 1996)

Mallison, W.T. and Mallison, S.V., 'The Juridical Status of Combatants Under the Geneva Protocol of 1977 Concerning International Conflicts', 42 (1978) *Law and Contemporary Problems* 4

Martin, F., 'Using International Human Rights Law for Establishing a Unified Use of Force Rule in the Law of Armed Conflict', 64 (2001) *Saskatchewan Law Review* 347

Matheson, M.J., 'Remarks at panel on the United States Position on the Relation of Customary International Law to 1977 Protocols Additional to the 1949 Geneva Conventions', at the Sixth Annual American Red Cross–Washington College of Law Conference on International Humanitarian Law, 2 (1987) *American University Journal of International Law and Policy* 415

Mendel, T., 'Consequences for Freedom of Statement of the Terrorist Attacks of September 11', paper presented at the Symposium on Terrorism and Human Rights, Cairo, 26–28 January 2002, available at www.cihhr.org

Meron, T., 'Classification of Armed Conflict in the Former Yugoslavia: Nicaragua's Fallout', 92 (1998) AJIL 236

Meron, T., *Human Rights and Humanitarian Law as International Customary Norms* (Oxford, 1991)

Meron, T., *Human Rights in Internal Strife: Their Protection* (Cambridge, 1987)

Meron, T., 'On a Hierarchy of International Human Rights', 80 (1986) AJIL 1

Meron, T., 'The Geneva Conventions as Customary Law', 81 (1987) AJIL 348

Meron, T., 'The Humanization of Humanitarian Law', 94 (2000) AJIL 239

Meron, T. (ed.), *Human Rights in International Law* (Oxford, 1988)

Meron, T. and Rosas, A., 'Current Developments: A Declaration of Minimum Humanitarian Standards', 85 (1991) AJIL 375

Mundis, D.A., 'Agora: Military Commissions: The Use of Military Commissions to Prosecute Individuals Accused of Terrorist Acts', 96 (2002) AJIL 320

Murphy, J., 'International Law and the War on Terrorism: The Road Ahead', 32 (2002) *Israel Yearbook on Human Rights* 117

Murphy, S., 'Legal Regulation of the Use of Force', 93 (1999) AJIL 628

Murphy, S.D. (ed.), 'Contemporary Practice of the United States Relating to International Law Contemporary Practice', 96 (2002) AJIL 237

Myjer, E.P.J. and White, N.D., 'The Twin Towers Attack: An Unlimited Right to Self-Defence?', 7 (2002) *Journal of Conflict and Security Law* 5

Neier, N., 'Unjust, Unwise, Unamerican', *The Economist*, 12 July 2003

Neuman, G.L., 'Humanitarian Law and Counterterrorist Force', 14 (2003) EJIL 283

Neuman, G.L., 'Surveying Law and Borders: Anomalous Zones', 48 (1996) *Stanford Law Review* 1197

Nicholls, P.B., Montgomery, C. and Knowles, J., *The Law of Extradition and Mutual Assistance. International Criminal Law: Practice and Procedure* (London, 2002)

Nowak, M., *UN Covenant on Civil and Political Rights: CCPR Commentary* (Kehl am Rhein, 1993)

O'Connell, M.E., 'Debating the Law of Sanctions', 13 (2002) EJIL 63

Obote-Odora, A., 'Defining International Terrorism', 6.1 (1999) *E Law – Murdoch University Electronic Journal of Law*, available at http://pandora.nla.gov.au/parchive/2001/Z2001-Feb-26/www.murdoch.edu.au/elaw/issues/v6n1/obote-odora61.html.

Oellers-Frahm, K., 'Country Report on Italy', Conference on 'Terrorism as a Challenge for National and International Law', Max Planck Institute for Comparative Public Law and International Law, Heidelberg, 24–25 January 2003, at www.edoc.mpil.de/conference-on-terrorism/country.cfm

Oeter, S., 'Methods and Means of Combat', in D. Fleck (ed.), *The Handbook of Humanitarian Law in Armed Conflicts* (Oxford, 1995), pp. 105 ff.

Orentlicher, D., 'Settling Accounts: The Duty to Prosecute Human Rights Violations of a Prior Regime', 100 (1991) *Yale Law Journal* 2537

Parks, W.H., 'Air War and the Law of War', 32 (1990) *Air Force Law Review* 1

Paust, J., 'Addendum: Prosecution of Mr. bin Laden *et al.* for Violations of International Law and Civil Lawsuits by Various Victims', *ASIL Insights* No. 77, 21 September 2001, at www.asil.org

Paust, J., 'Antiterrorism Military Commissions: Courting Illegality', 23 (2002) *Michigan Journal of International Law* 1

Paust, J., 'Antiterrorism Military Commissions: The Ad Hoc DOD Rules of Procedure', 23 (2002) *Michigan Journal of International Law* 677

Paust, J., 'Legal Responses to International Terrorism', 22 (1999) *Houston Journal of International Law* 17

Paust, J., 'There is No Need to Revise the Laws of War in Light of September 11th', November 2001, available at http://www.asil.org/taskforce/paust.pdf

Paust, J., 'Use of Armed Force against Terrorists in Afghanistan, Iraq and Beyond', 35 (2002) *Cornell International Law Journal* 533

Pisillo Mazzeschi, R., 'The "Due Diligence Rule" and the Nature of International Responsibility of States', 35 (1992) GYIL 9

Plachta, M., '(Non-) Extradition of Nationals: A Neverending Story?', 13 (1999) *Emory International Law Review* 77

Pronto, A.N., 'Terrorist Attacks on the World Trade Center and the Pentagon. Comment', *ASIL Insights* No. 77, 21 September 2001, available at www.asil.org

Randelzhofer, A., 'Article 2(4)', in B. Simma *et al.* (eds.), *The Charter of the United Nations. A Commentary*, 2nd ed. (Oxford, 2002)

Ratner, S.R. and Abrams, J.S., *Accountability for Human Rights Atrocities in International Law: Beyond the Nuremberg Legacy* (Oxford, 1998)

Reisman, W.M., 'Coercion and Self Determination: Construing Charter Article 2(4)', 78 (1984) AJIL 64

Reisman, W.M., 'International Legal Responses to Terrorism', 22 (1999) *Houston Journal of International Law* 3

Reydams, L., 'Prosecuting Crimes Under International Law on the Basis of Universal Jurisdiction: The Experience of Belgium', in H. Fischer, C. Kreß and S.R. Lüder (eds.), *International and National Prosecution of Crimes under International Law: Current Developments* (Berlin, 2001), p. 799

Robinson, D., 'Developments in International Criminal Law: Defining "Crimes against Humanity" at the Rome Conference', 93 (1999) AJIL 43

Rogers, A.P.V., 'Terrorism and the Laws of War: September 11 and its Aftermath', 21 September 2001, available at http://www.crimesofwar.org/expert/attack-apv.html

Sadat, L., 'Terrorism and the Rule of Law', 3 (2004) *Washington University Global Studies Law Review* 135

Sandoz, Y., 'Mechanisms of Implementation under International Humanitarian Law, International Human Rights Law and Refugee Law', paper presented at the 27th Round Table on Current Problems of International Humanitarian Law (Sanremo, 4–6 September 2003), proceedings to be published in G.L. Beruto and G. Ravasi (eds.), *27th Round Table on Current Problems of International Humanitarian Law: International Humanitarian and other Legal Regimes: Interplay in Situations of Violence* (Milan, forthcoming)

Sandoz, Y., *The International Committee of the Red Cross as Guardian of International Humanitarian Law* (Geneva, 1998)

Sassòli, M., 'Non-International Armed Conflict: Qualification of the Conflict and Its Parties', paper presented at the 27th Round Table on Current Problems of International Humanitarian Law (Sanremo, 4–6 September 2003), proceedings to be published in G.L. Beruto and G. Ravasi (eds.), *27th Round Table on Current Problems of International Humanitarian Law: International Humanitarian and other Legal Regimes: Interplay in Situations of Violence* (Milan, forthcoming)

Sassòli, M., 'State Responsibility for Violations of International Humanitarian Law', 84 (2002) IRRC 401

Schabas, W.A., 'Punishment of Non-State Actors in Non-International Armed Conflict', 26 (2003) *Fordham International Law Journal* 907

Schachter, O., *International Law in Theory and Practice* (Dordrecht, 1991)

Schachter, O., 'The Lawful Use of Force by a State Against Terrorists in Another Country', reprinted in H. H. Han (ed.), *Terrorism and Political Violence: Limits and Possibilities of Legal Control* (New York, 1993)

Schachter, O., 'The Right of States to Use Armed Force', 82 (1984) *Michigan Law Review* 1620

Scharf, M., 'Application of Treaty Based Universal Jurisdiction to Nationals of Non-Party States', 35 (2001) *New England Law Review* 363

Schense, J. and Flattau, I., 'Implementation of the Rome Statute', 14.1 (2002) *INTERIGHTS Bulletin* 34

Schiedeman, S., 'Standards of Proof in Forcible Responses to Terrorism', 50 (2000) *Syracuse Law Review* 249

Schindler, D., 'The Different Types of Armed Conflicts according to the Geneva Conventions and Protocols', 163 (1979-II) RdC 117

Schmitt, M.N., 'State Sponsored Assassination in International and Domestic Law', 17 (1992) *Yale Journal of International Law* 609

Schmitt, M.N. and Beruto, G.L. (eds.), *Terrorism and International Law, Challenges and Responses* (Sanremo, 2003)

Shearer, I. A. (ed.), *Starke's International Law*, 11th ed. (Sydney, 1994)

Shelton, D., 'Private Violence, Public Wrongs, and the Responsibility of States', 13 (1990) *Fordham International Law Journal* 1

Sluiter, G.K., 'Cooperation with the International Criminal Tribunal for the Former Yugoslavia', in H. Fischer, C. Kreß and S.R. Lüder (eds.), *International and National Prosecution of Crimes under International Law: Current Developments* (Berlin, 2001), p. 681

Stanbrook, I. and Stanbrook, C., *Extradition: Law and Practice* (Oxford, 2000)

Stork, J., 'The Human Rights Crisis in the Middle East in the Aftermath of 11 September', paper presented at the Symposium on Terrorism and Human Rights, Cairo, 26–28 January 2002

Taft IV, W.H. and Buchenwald, T., 'Agora: Future Implications of the Iraq Conflict: Preemption, Iraq, and International Law', 97 (2003) AJIL 557

Tejan-Cole, A., 'The Special Court for Sierra Leone', 14.1 (2002) *INTERIGHTS Bulletin* 37

Teson, F., *Humanitarian Intervention: An Inquiry into Law and Morality*, 2nd ed. (New York, 1997)

Travalio, G.M., 'Terrorism, International Law and the Use of Military Force', 18 (2000) *Wisconsin International Law Journal* 145

Triffterer, O. (ed.), *Commentary on the Rome Statute of the International Criminal Court* (Baden-Baden, 1999)

Vierucci, L., 'What Judicial Treatment for the Guantanamo Detainees', 3 (2002) *German Law Review*, available at http://www.germanlawjournal.com/article. php?id=190

von Glahn, G., *Law Among Nations*, 6th ed. (New York, 1986)

Waldock, C., 'The Regulation of the Use of Force by Individual States in International Law', 81 (1952) RdC 455

Wedgwood, R., 'Responding to Terrorism: The Strikes against Bin Laden', 24 (1999) *Yale Journal of International Law* 559

Weich, R., 'Upsetting Checks and Balances: Congressional Hostility Towards the Courts in Times of Crisis', in *Report of the American Civil Liberties Union*, November 2001, available at http://www.aclu.org

Yoo, J., 'Agora: Future Implications of the Iraq Conflict: International Law and the War in Iraq', 97 (2003) AJIL 563

Zimmerman, A., 'Crimes within the Jurisdiction of the Court', in O. Triffterer (ed.), *Commentary on the Rome Statute of the International Criminal Court* (Baden-Baden, 1999), p. 98

INDEX